CO-AJQ-601

CONTENTS

PREFACE

INTRODUCTION

PART I CONCEPTUAL FOUNDATIONS OF STRATEGY & PLANNING: AN OVERVIEW

1 ENVIRONMENTAL IMPERATIVES   **5**

Strategic Development; The Environment; Case: Southeastern Shipyards, Inc.

2 ORGANIZATIONAL IMPERATIVES AND OBJECTIVES   **29**

Organizational Objectives; Gap Analysis; Case: Cottage Gardens, Inc. (A)

PART II ANALYTICAL CONSIDERATIONS IN STRATEGY & PLANNING

3 COMPETITION FOR MARKETS   **65**

The Nature of Competition; Analysis of Competition; Share of Market; Marketing Strategies; Strategy Policy Formulation; Case: Smithson Plastics, Inc.

4 COMPETITION FOR RESOURCES 95

Introduction; Competition for Capital and Finances;
Competition for Manpower and Skills; The Personnel
Planning System; Competition for Materials; Problems of
Source Selection; Buying Locally vs. Buying Internationally

PART III THE STRATEGIC PLANNING PROCESS

5 THE ASSESSMENT OF PRESENT CAPABILITIES 131

Determination of the stage in the Corporate Life Cycle;
Present Situation Assessment; Expectations of Owners
and Public; Case: Mount Carmel Mercy Hospital
& Medical Center

6 THE ASSESSMENT OF FUTURE REQUIREMENTS 179

Innovative Developments and Predictions; Prediction and
Effect of Intervening Contingencies; Assessment Analysis;
Case: Wall Drug

7 STRATEGIC ANALYSIS 217

Strategic Search; Selection of Alternatives; Case:
International Business Machines, Inc.

PART IV THE IMPLEMENTATION OF STRATEGY & PLANNING

8 THE PRACTICAL APPLICATION OF ALTERNATIVE ANALYSIS 249

Interpretive Planning Process Design; Planning Models;
Alternative Generation; Case: Triangle Construction
Company

9 STRATEGY IMPLEMENTATION AND CONTROL 279

Strategy Implementation; Feedback and Control of the
Strategic; Planning Process; Case: Independence Federal
Savings & Loan Association

APPENDIX THE THEORETICAL ANALYSIS OF ALTERNATIVE STRATEGIES 313

CORPORATE STRATEGY & PLANNING

GRID SERIES IN MANAGEMENT

Consulting Editor
STEVEN KERR, University of Southern California

Adams & Ponthieu, *Administrative Policy and Strategy: A Casebook,* Second Edition
Anthony & Nicholson, *Management of Human Resources: A Systems Approach to Personnel Management*
Clover & Balsley, *Business Research Methods,* Second Edition
Chung, *Motivational Theories and Practices*
Deitzer, Shilliff & Jucius, *Contemporary Management Concepts*
Deitzer & Shilliff, *Contemporary Management Incidents*
Kerr, ed., *Organizational Behavior*
Knapper, *Cases in Personnel Management*
Lewis, *Organizational Communications: The Essence of Effective Management,* Second Edition
Lewis & Williams, *Readings in Organizational Communications*
Lundgren, Engel & Cecil, *Supervision*
Murdick, Eckhouse, Moor & Zimmerer, *Business Policy: A Framework for Analysis,* Third Edition
Ritti & Funkhouser, *The Ropes to Skip and The Ropes to Know: Studies in Organizational Behavior*
Rogers, *Corporate Strategy and Planning*

OTHER BOOKS IN THE GRID SERIES IN MANAGEMENT

Balsley, *Basic Statistics*
Klatt & Urban, *Kubsim: A Simulation in Collective Bargaining*
Nykodym & Simonetti, *Business and Organizational Communication: An Experiential Skill Building Approach*
Roman, *Science, Technology and Innovation: A Systems Approach*
Sandver & Blaine, *Teachneg: A Collective Bargaining Simulation in Public Education*
Steinhoff, Deitzer & Shilliff, *Small Business Management: Cases and Essays*
Tersine, Altimus & Davidson, *Problems and Models in Operations Management,* Second Edition

CORPORATE STRATEGY & PLANNING

by

Rolf E. Rogers

California Polytechnic State University—
San Luis Obispo

Grid Publishing, Inc., Columbus, Ohio

198976

658.401
R 728

© COPYRIGHT 1981, GRID PUBLISHING, INC.
  4666 Indianola Avenue
  Columbus, Ohio 43214

ALL RIGHTS RESERVED. No part of this publication may be reproduced, stored in a retrieval system, or transmitted, in any form or by any means, electronic, mechanical, photocopying, recording or otherwise, without prior written permission of the copyright holder.

Printed in the United States

1 2 3 4 5 6 ☒ 3 2 1

Library of Congress Cataloging in Publication Data

Rogers, Rolf E.
    Corporate strategy and planning.

    (Grid series in management)
    1. Corporate planning.   2. Management.   I. Title.
HD30.28.R644   658.4'01   79-19772
ISBN 0-88244-205-8

PART V SELECTED INTEGRATED CASES IN CORPORATE STRATEGY AND PLANNING

1. Fredonia State Bank
2. Quality Supermarket, Inc.
3. United Products, Inc.
4. Carter Distribution Corp. (A)
5. Carter Distribution Corp. (B)
6. Carter Distribution Corp. (C)
7. Hartz Mills (A)
8. Hartz Mills (B)
9. Hartz Mills (C)
10. Carson/Burger/Weekly, Inc.
11. Queen of Hartz

INDEX   **437**

*TO NANCY, CAREY
AND ROB*

PREFACE

The teaching of strategy, policy, planning, decision-making, and related subjects has experienced substantial change in recent years. A major reason for this is undoubtedly the result of changes in the objectives and priorities of organizations that were precipitated by technological innovation, societal modulations, value modifications, and the awareness of international competition. In addition, the emergence of the not-for-profit sector as a major organizational and management phenomenon has emphasized the necessity to re-evaluate traditional approaches to corporate strategy and planning.

In this book, we have deviated from the traditional "functional" approach and emphasized an "analytical framework" approach. Thus, we are presenting a sequence of evaluative concepts to develop a systematic analysis of the factors involved in strategic development and planning. In this context, our purpose was to provide a configurational construct within which the strategic process would take place systematically, regardless of the degree of relevance of any one particular assessment factor. To provide an application of the material, we have included a case evaluation at the end of each chapter. These cases represent a cross-section of different types of organizations to demonstrate the application of strategic analysis and planning to different objectives, organization designs, products, and services.

This book is designed for courses in strategy, planning, decision-making, and business policy. In the latter case, it may be used as a supplement to traditional case books or as a primary text if the instructor emphasizes strategy analysis and planning in his course. As noted, we have included a selected case at the end of each chapter with a suggested evaluation. Our objective was not to provide solutions or answers but rather to demonstrate a proposed, consistent approach to the analysis of complex situations. We have also added several integrative cases at the end of the book. These cases are not evaluated and, thus, permit the student to apply the concepts of strategic analysis and planning in a "real world" simulation.

Obviously, a book such as this cannot be written without the help and suggestions of many colleagues, students, and associates. Space does not permit the recognition of all who were instrumental in this effort. However, I wish to specially thank the authors and publishers of the cases and copyrighted material who gave permission to use their work. My special appreciation goes to Professor Paul Zivkovich of the California Polytechnic State University, San Luis Obispo for his helpful suggestions during the writing of the manuscript.

R.E.R.

INTRODUCTION

Today's contemporary organizations are experiencing a seemingly endless diversification in technology, products, markets, and services. Competition for resources, a relatively rare phenomenon just a few years ago, has become a primary consideration in planning for organizational growth and survival. Changes in values of consumers, clients, and customers have further added to the complexity of the managerial decision-making process. Finally, the impact of rapid fluctuations in the environment, not only domestic but international, resulted in a renewed emphasis on organizational strategy formulation, analysis, and planning.

Strategic analysis and planning is essentially an art. It is a primary ingredient of the executive management function and therefore, subject to the same psychological and organizational complexities as "leadership." It is true that we have today many scientifically based planning programs, constructs, models, and techniques; however, in the final analysis, the ultimate selection of the "optimum strategy" is still controlled by intuitive considerations. This is not to say that we cannot develop analytical constructs to minimize the intuitive aspects of the process, it simply means that total reliance on a given construct is no more realistic than total reliance on intuition would be. The answer obviously is an integration of the two, using a consistent strategic framework appropriate for the particular organization along with the application of "intuitive reality."

Strategy development is a continuous sequential analysis. It consists of the development of objectives; an environmental assessment; the reevaluation and modification (if required) of the original objectives, based on the environmental analysis; the development of strategic alternatives; the selection of the plan or plans; and the implementation (translation) of the plan into tactical or operational plans. Figure 1 depicts this general sequence in graphic form. Strategic plans are usually long-range, spanning different periods of time (3 or 5 years, for example) depending upon the organization and industry. Tactical or operational plans are usually one year organizational unit implementations of the strategic plan.

In this book we have attempted to approach the development of strategy and planning within the configuration of this framework and to provide a discussion of and elaboration of each major step in the analytical se-

1

quence. (See Figure 2). Our purpose was to provide students, managers, and planners with a systematic approach to strategy formulation, analysis, and planning. Our major consideration, however was to emphasize the importance of strategy and planning in the management process. If we have succeeded in this, our objectives will have been achieved.

A FRAMEWORK FOR STRATEGY ANALYSIS
AND PLANNING
Figure 1

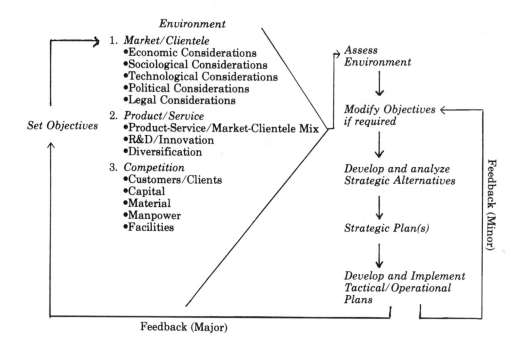

FIGURE 2

	Strategic Analysis Framework	Discussed in Chapter
Step 1 -	Set Objectives	1, 2
Step 2 -	Environmental Assessment	
	1. Market/Clintele	3
	2. Product/Service	3,4
	3. Competition	4
Step 3 -	Modify Objectives	5
Step 4 -	Develop and Analyze Strategic Alternatives	5, 6, 7
Step 5 -	Select/Optimize Plan(s)	7, 8
Step 6 -	Implement Plans	8, 9
Step 7 -	Feedback/Control	9

PART I
Conceptual Foundations of Strategy & Planning – An Overview

Environmental Imperatives

STRATEGIC DEVELOPMENT

An examination of current business literature reveals a great deal of attention being devoted to corporate strategy. The first question that requires an answer is: What is corporate strategy? Andrews offers the following interpretation which appears to relate a consensus of opinion in the literature:

> The pattern of major objectives, purposes, or goals and essential policies and plans for achieving those goals stated in such a way as to define what business the company is in or is to be in and the kind of company it is or is to be.[1]

The essential nature of the strategic planning process is to shape the future of the business enterprise. While a strategic decision can be made at any given point in time, its influence serves to determine the characteristics of the firm well into the future. In this manner, strategy is concerned with long term implications for the organization.

Ansoff[2] views the strategic decision process as the formulation of decision rules which determine the choice of product markets. The firm is related to its environment and must therefore have a means of responding to environmental changes. It is the decision rule process of strategy which permits the response to the environment. An environmental change occurs and the strategic planning process tells the firm what its response is to be. The ongoing nature of the strategic process is shown by the evaluative aspect. Once the decision is made, results are evaluated and become an input into the strategic process. In this regard, strategic planning is never "completed." Once a specific decision is made, it is integrated into the overall view and the process continues.

The determination of strategy is the prerogative of top corporate management. It is only at this organizational level that the overall view of the organization may be obtained. This does not mean that the process is carried out without reference to the lower levels. It is of vital importance that the lower levels provide some input into the strategy of the firm, for it is at the sub-unit level that implementation will take place. Organizational sub-units have an expert understanding of their particular aspects of an organization's operation. This understanding cannot be neglected. However, it must be noted that what is desirable for an organizational sub-unit may not be desirable for the overall organization. It is from this point of view that strategic planning is handled by the topmost managerial levels.

Strategic planning attempts to organize and provide a direction for the organization as a whole. The process itself must also be organized. The diverse aspects of planning make it impossible for top corporate executives to address themselves to each individual aspect. This gives rise to a planning staff. This group aids top management in strategic planning, relieving the corporate executive of the detail. It, however, remains the responsibility of top management to provide a framework in which strategic planning is carried out.

Three different types of responses to environmental changes may be observed by examining business organizations.[3] The enterprise can react to an environmental factor. This method is undesirable for such a stance involves management in the capacity of continually "putting out fires." A second behavior noted is the anticipation of environmental problems. This level of planning is most frequently observed in present day business organizations. The third type of behavior noted is planning for, not only problems which may develop, but also planning with respect to opportunities which present themselves. This is what we will define as strategic planning.

THE IMPORTANCE OF STRATEGIC PLANNING

The environment in which today's corporation operates is uncertain. Strategic planning does not eliminate risk or uncertainty but allows the corporation to deal with uncertainty. In addition to the complicated environment in which the firm operates, the firm itself is an entity composed of many facets. It is through the strategic planning process, that the firm is able to integrate the various aspects of the organization with a view that relates to the environment. Strategic planning searches out alternatives which permit the organization to exist in a rapidly changing environment.

The importance of strategic planning may be seen by examining which companies are employing this technique. Large organizations are characterized by having a high degree of diversity to their operations. In a study conducted by Rue,[4] it was found that only a small percentage of such organizations do not employ a long term planning function. The importance of this aspect of organizational activity is therefore being recognized in that most companies are involved to a greater or lesser extent with planning. The article further indicates that this is a relatively new phenomenon. Nearly one half of the companies considered in the study had adopted formal long-range planning in the five year period prior to the study (1973).

The emphasis on the long range planning activity is established with the creation of a formal planning department as an aid to top management. Outside consultants are also often employed in the planning process. In these two ways, planning is becoming formalized, which implies that a methodology is being developed. No longer is planning simply a guiding principle formulated in the managerial mind. It is becoming systematically developed.

A possible link may be seen between success in the business process and the use of strategic planning. Problems facing the organization and opportunities available to the organization become apparent to the managers through strategic development. In this manner, the organization is managed more efficiently and success in its operations is more likely to be achieved. Success may also be viewed as developing an approach which gives a competitive advantage to the firm in question. It is precisely this advantage which the strategic process determines in its evolution.

STRATEGIC AND TACTICAL PLANNING

A useful distinction to be made at this point, involves that between strategic planning and tactical planning. In broad terms, strategic planning directs itself to overall corporate considerations while tactical planning is chiefly concerned with the functional implementation of the strategic plan. Resource deployment in respect to the strategic plan may be seen as operating at the macro-organizational level while resource deployment under tactical planning is concerned with the deployment of resources in the micro-units.

Strategic planning determines policies for the organization while tactical planning results in specific courses of action which are the results of policies specified at the strategic level. Ackoff suggests a continuum of planning results.[5] Policies are found at the highest level of generality whereas courses of action are confined to a particular act at a given time and situation.

HIERARCHY OF PLANNING

Where does the strategic plan fit into the hierarchy of planning? Figure 1 indicates the strategic plan as the top-most planning level in the organization. Within this context, long term plans are developed in three areas; long term resource deployment, long term operating plans, and long term product-market development. Each of these areas is further segmented to arrive at the short term, day-to-day, plans.

The strategic plan incorporates the objectives of the firm, its strategies and the resource allocation for the firm *as a whole*. Targets or goals are the translation of the organizational objectives into measurable terms. This process results in the strategic budget which considers resource allocations within a specific time span.

For the long term, resource deployment, operating and product market development plans are developed. Each of these areas is considered within the

HIERARCHY OF PLANNING
Figure 1

Source: H. I. Ansoff, Corporate Strategy (New York: McGraw Hill, 1965) p. 221, adopted in modified form. Used with permission of McGraw-Hill Book Company.

context of the strategic plan. An estimate of the firm's current position gives rise to a budget which is used in the same manner as the strategic estimate and budget.

The lowest level in the planning hierarchy involves the short term, day-to-day plans. Each of the three long term plans is broken down into these specifications. An example would be the operating plan. Included in this area are the specific short term decisions made concerning marketing, distribution, purchasing and manufacturing.

The Strategic Plan is the key document which gives guidance and allocates resources among the major activities of the firm.[6]

Detailed long term plans are developed with respect to resource deployment, operations and product-market development. Short terms plans are embedded in the long term plan structure.

CHARACTERISTICS OF STRATEGIC PLANNING

The development of strategy is not to be confused with forecasting. Forecasting is but one input into the strategic process. The concern of strategy is "*not* making future decisions but making current decisions in light of their futurity."[7] Risk is not eliminated but is minimized through an understanding of the components of risk. In the strategic analysis all aspects of the firm are considered. The comprehensive nature of the process requires that it be flexible. A feedback mechanism provides information on the results of the planning. This is necessary in order that the process may be monitored to determine its effectiveness. The opportunistic character of the firm's strategy allows the firm to use environmental changes to its best advantage. Strategic planning considers opportunities in a manner in which specifics may be unknown at the time the plan is developed. Should the opportunity present itself at a later date, they are recognized and the necessary steps are taken in order to obtain the advantages.

THE ENVIRONMENT

The environment of the business enterprise may be viewed as being composed of two systems: The internal and external environment. The environment imposes certain constraints on a firm in relation to its operations. These constraints determine the degree of flexibility or the amount of control a firm has over its operations. The environment also acts to determine what opportunities are available to the firm. Therefore, it can be seen that an analysis of the environment serves these two purposes.

There are several factors related to both environmental systems (external and internal). These are the economic, the social, the legal, the technological and the ecological environment factors. There is a considerable amount of interdependency among these components. For example, advances in technology, such as the development of the automobile have had an impact on each of the other factors. The following diagram shows the interdependence among any three of the environmental factors.

The interdependency among the environmental factors exists in both systems, the internal and the external. The systems themselves also overlap. This may be shown in the following diagram.

However a firm needs only to address itself to a subset of the overall external environment because there are only some particular aspects of the environment which pertain to a given industry. This can best be shown by the following diagram.

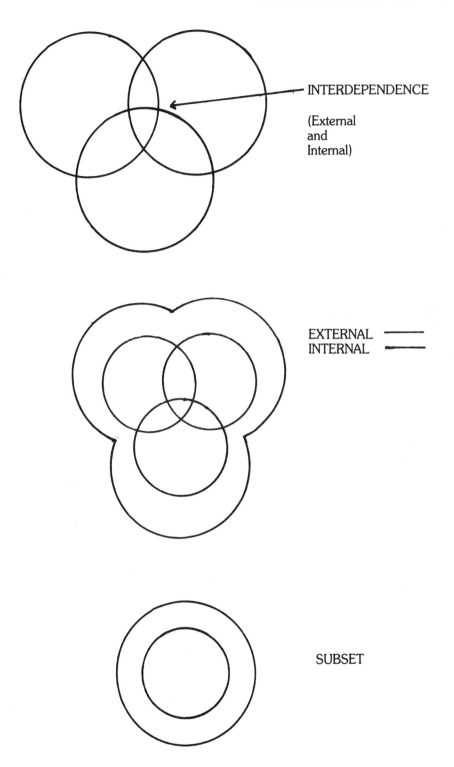

INTERDEPENDENCE

(External
and
Internal)

EXTERNAL ——
INTERNAL ——

SUBSET

From this discussion, it is apparent that the interaction is very complex. It would be impossible to deal with all the interdependencies among the two systems of factors; therefore, for purposes of discussion, the two systems are analyzed separately in the following section.

THE EXTERNAL ENVIRONMENT

1. Social

This environmental component directs itself to the values and norms of the society in which the firm exists. Western society views profit-seeking as a legitimate goal. However, the firm is not free to pursue this goal in an irresponsible manner. Limitations are prescribed delineating what the firm may or may not do. If the firm conducts its business under a different set of cultural values, then it may act only within the prescribed limits. The social environment not only differs across national borders but can be very different within the same country.

The business enterprise must therefore act in a manner which is deemed socially responsible. If the firm does not perform in this manner, society will react through its legislative arm to prescribe the desired behavior. Examples of this action may be seen in regulations concerning pollution control and advertising. Such legislation ensures that the corporate citizen behaves in a responsible manner.

2. Technological

Advances in technology are common, every-day occurrences in the present business world. Today's innovation may be rendered obsolete tomorrow. It is important to view technology not only as a threat to the firm, but also as providing opportunities for the organization to utilize its resources in a more efficient manner. The development of the airplane was responsible for a decline in the railroad passenger business but gave birth to the airline industry.

Consideration of technology is vital in the area of competition. It is the firm that can best use new technology that is able to establish a competitive advantage. In order to employ technology in the firm's undertakings it is necessary that the technological environment be monitored to become aware of advances.

3. Legal

The legal component of the environment manifests itself in laws which concern: 1) the establishment of the organization; 2) how the firm may conduct its business; and 3) a framework delineating what may or may not be done in the case of expansion, merger or acquisition. Corporate management must therefore be aware of the legal implications of their actions or proposed actions.

The corporation may be subject to a number of different legal jurisdictions. This is obvious in the case of the multinational companies. Within the legal environment there are a number of different levels. The city or municipal level prescribes zoning and planning regulations. State legislation covers areas such as labor relations. At the federal level, there are the provisions of the anti-trust laws. These laws prohibit activity which has the effect of reducing competition.

The complicated nature of the external legal environment makes the assessment of this factor difficult. An effective method of incorporating this aspect into the planning process is to have a member of the corporate legal staff involved in strategic planning.

4. Economic

Examination of the various environmental factors has shown that the business organization must concern itself with a number of aspects. The firm, however, is primarily concerned with the allocation of resources. Resources become available through the economic environment. The examination of the economic environment is of central concern for the business enterprise.

The general state of the economic environment serves to determine the availability of resources. In periods of economic upswing, resources are more readily available than in periods of downswing. The state of the economic environment may be determined through price indices, growth of the G. N. P. or an examination of unemployment rates. The state of the economy exerts its influence by determining the availability of financial capital and the demand for a firm's products. Taxation and money supply, determined by the authorities, exert their influence upon the activities of the firm.

5. Ecological

The ecological factor of the external environment is becoming an important consideration for the firm. A large number of the natural resources used by industry are non-renewable. Industrial pollution is widespread. If these trends continue, the very existence of humanity is threatened. Responsible use of technology is required in order to support the world's basic system, the eco-system.

THE INTERNAL ENVIRONMENT

1. Social-Psychological

It is possible to view the business organization as a society in itself. The members of this "society" develop their own set of norms and values. Corporate management brings their own set of values into the organization. In the case where management is dominated by a strong individual, the values of this individual tend to become those of the company. In the "team approach" to management, a consensus regarding goals and objectives is reached among the members of the management team involving a degree of "give and take" between the team members.

The personnel or industrial relations departments play an important role in the internal social environment. The type of individual hired and the type and degree of satisfaction obtained from the job will play an important role in determining the overall effectiveness of the organization. A sense of dissatisfaction within the organizational ranks can prove to be dysfunctional for the company and result in poor communication within the organization.

2. Economic

The internal economic environment relates the firm to its direct economic concerns. A specific market is generally found within a specific industry. The total industry provides a basis upon which the firm's market share is calculated. If changes occur within the industry, their impact will also be felt by the firm. The availability of the raw material requirements are an important concern of the industry for the resources. Competition also exists in the final product market.

The nature of the business is a component of its economic environment. Capital is required in order to support the organization in its various activities. If funds are readily available from the firm's operations, commitments are easily met. In the case where the firm is relatively new, funds are in short supply since efforts are focused upon the survival of the enterprise.

3. Technological

The internal technological environment is the techniques employed by the organization in its resource conversion process. Technology which is directly applicable to the organization, includes methods used to increase production through a more efficient utilization of its resources. This may be manifested through labor-saving devices (automation), more efficient uses of energy or the employment of the computer as an aid in conducting the business of the firm.

The employment of obsolete technology can put the firm at a serious competitive disadvantage in a dynamic industry. This is especially true of the large firm. This type of organization utilizes many different technologies throughout the scope of its operations. It is important that the firm is not only aware of technological developments, but that it participates in the development process. These two functions are fulfilled by its research and development departments.

4. Ecological

All firms may be viewed as having an internal ecological environment. Participation in this environment is determined by the nature of the undertakings of the firm. If the industry is based upon natural resources such as the fishing industry, for example, the ecological component of its environment is of prime consideration. Wastes produced by manufacturing industries must be disposed. These wastes include non-usable by-products of the manufacturing process. Disposal must be carried out in a manner which does not inflict injury upon the eco-system. The interdependent nature of the environmental systems becomes apparent. If the firm is found to be acting in an irresponsible manner in respect to the ecological component of its environment, sanctions may be invoked through the legal system.

FORECASTING

There has been a tendency to equate the planning process with forecasting. Planning uses forecasting as a part of the input to be considered. It is the goal of the planning process not only to forecast, but also to determine the causal links or an explanation as to why events occur. Forecasting also tends to limit itself to economic factors. The previous section has indicated that economic factors are *not* the sole determinant of the firm's environment. Other factors, such as the social and legal factors, may have an important impact upon the firm. The role of forecasting in the strategic planning process should therefore concern itself with the prediction of the firm's total environment.

Cohen and Cyert[8] point out a basic problem with forecasting. The prediction of the environment is relatively straightforward under stable conditions. In simplified terms, the prediction of what will occur tomorrow is simply what has happened today. In a period of constant change (which is characteristic of the business environment) prediction is more difficult. It is under conditions of change that the planner has the greatest need for forecasting and it is this same time when forecasting is most difficult to accomplish.

Forecasts are subject to a degree of error. The error generally increases as the time horizon expands. Strategic planning directs itself to concerns which may require projections well into the future. Because of a large possible error in the forecast, it would appear that predictions far into the future would be of little value. The forecast need not provide a single value estimate of a future state. Probabilities may be assigned to different possible outcomes. In this manner several estimates are obtained and these may be used in the planning process.

1. Economic Forecasting

It has been indicated earlier that the external environment of the firm was viewed as being primarily the economic environment. We have shown that this is not the only environmental factor which should be considered; however, forecasting methodology has tended to focus upon the economic environment and is better developed in this area.

Economic forecasting should start with predictions in respect to general economic conditions, such as GNP projections. The scope of these predictions may be world-wide in the case of the multi-national corporation or the firm may restrict itself to the national level. The extent of the organization's operations will determine which is the appropriate level.

The general level of economic activity provides some of the input necessary for the next step. This is the estimate of the total industry market for a given product. The estimate of the industry depends to a greater or lesser extent upon the general economic conditions. The nature of the industry will determine to what extent industry demand may be correlated with general economic condition indicators. Industry demand is also associated with demand in other industries. An example of this may be seen in the automobile industry. Demand for automobiles influences the demand for steel.

Once an estimate of the industry demand is complete, the firm proceeds to the forecast of its own sales in the industry or an estimation of its market share. Sales forecasts may be determined in a variety of ways. These methods include the judgment of the manager, the estimation of sales by the salesmen in the field and various quantitative techniques. Quantitative techniques may also include the use of computer simulation. Steiner points out that "even where the most sophisticated tools of forecasting are used, managerial judgment is exercised throughout the process."[9] The sales forecast provides a basis upon which the resource requirements for production are determined.

2. Forecasting and Causal Links

The discussion on economic forecasting had as its starting point some measure of the overall economic condition such as the G.N.P. It did not attempt to indicate what factors influence the level of the G.N.P. Other methods of forecasting, especially the quantitative methods, make forecasts based upon past data. The assumption of such methods is that what has occurred in the past will continue to occur in the future. If there is a change in the environment, these forecasts may not be reliable predictors of future events. Forecasting should therefore be accompanied by an attempt to understand the factors which may affect a trend. If these factors are identified and monitored, forecasting becomes a valuable tool for management.

SUMMARY

We have seen that the assessment of the environmental imperatives is a complex process. Gathering and co-ordinating the necessary information may pose a problem for the firm. This process can be aided by the organizational structure. Departments and divisions are in a position to provide input into the environmental examination. Whether or not the information from the various sub-units reaches the corporate management level is dependent upon the adequacy of the company's information gathering, processing, communication and integrative systems. If these functions are not explicitly built into the organizational structure, the process will be performed without the specific insights available at the lower organizational levels.

14

ENDNOTES

1. K. Andrews, *The Concept of Corporate Strategy* (Chicago: Dow-Jones-Irwin, 1971), p. 28.
2. H. Igor Ansoff, *Corporate Strategy* (New York: McGraw-Hill, 1965), p. 8.
3. *Ibid.,* p. 208.
4. Leslie W. Rues, "The How and Who of Long Range Planning," *Business Horizons,* XVI (December, 1973), 23-30.
5. Russell L. Ackoff, *A Concept of Corporate Planning* (New York: Wiley Interscience, 1970), p. 42.
6. Ansoff, *op. cit.,* p. 221.
7. George A. Steiner, *Top Management Planning* (London: Macmillan 1969) p. 18.
8. Kalman J. Cohen and Richard H. Cyert, "Strategy: Formulation, Implementation and Monitoring," *The Journal of Business,* SKVI (July, 1973), 354.
9. Steiner, *op. cit.,* p. 229.

CASE

SOUTHEASTERN SHIPYARDS, INC.

THE BACKGROUND

The history of Southeastern Shipyards, Inc. dates back to 1875, when the Mercury Drydock Company was formed on the northside of the St. Johns River in downtown Jacksonville. It began operations in the construction and repair of small- to medium-size ocean-going vessels, and enjoyed moderate success. In 1911 the Gables Corporation was formed on the opposite side of the St. Johns and operated primarily as a builder of medium to large ships. Both of these companies operated successfully through World War II, although neither enjoyed substantial growth or had significant profits. During the war both companies assisted in the effort with the construction of victory ships and repair work for the U.S. Navy as the navy required. They returned to normal operations at the conclusion of the War and no significant developments took place until 1955, at which time the Gables Corporation went through reorganization, necessitated by mismanagement rather than economic conditions. Mr. Gables died in 1951 and the resulting management team, headed by his son, was unable to properly direct operations. At this time, Aero General Inc. obtained control during the reorganization and attempted to put the Gables shipyard on the southside of the river back on its feet during the next two years. Meanwhile the Mercury Drydock Company across the river had been sold to a Jacksonville financier, G.R. Harrell in 1959, who gained 100 per cent control by 1965. During this period under Harrell's control, the name was changed to Southeastern Shipyard Inc., and the shipyard became very profitable with earnings in the $1 million range each year. At the same time the shipyard on the opposite side of the river was floundering under Aero's control and in early 1965 Harrell expanded his operations by acquiring the entire southside yard from Aero General. From 1965 to 1969 this consolidated shipyard in downtown Jacksonville was known as Southeastern Shipyards, Inc. and enjoyed profitable though not spectacular success.

This case was prepared by James V. Knutzen in cooperation with Associate Professor William H. Tomlinson and Associate Professor M. Reza Vaghefi of the University of North Florida's College of Business Administration, as a basis for classroom discussion and not to illustrate either effective or ineffective handling of an administrative situation.
Distributed by the Intercollegiate Case Clearing House. Soldiers Field, Boston, Mass. 02163. All rights reserved to the contributors. Printed in the U.S.A. Used with permission.

During this period in the late 1960's a large number of international companies were diversifying and expanding, and conglomerates and holding companies were becoming fashionable. Consequently, Harrell decided that it may be a good time to put his ownership of the shipyards on the open market and realize a substantial capital gain. This is exactly what transpired, and in 1969 the Frankfurt Company, primarily a manufacturer of truck trailers in Detroit, Michigan, purchased 100 percent of the outstanding stock of Southeastern Shipyards from Harrell. Operations were not disrupted, and the only change Frankfurt made in the management was to bring in Mr. D.L. McFarland from Maryland Shipyards, Inc. (another subsidiary of Frankfurt) as president. Under Frankfurt policy, Mr. McFarland was given substantially a free hand in his running of the shipyards, and was able to obtain huge company loans for purposes he felt were critical to the shipyard's growth. McFarland stated that"...most of the equipment in the shipyards was of World War II vintage when we purchased it in 1969, and it repairs more tankers than any other yard in the United States." Consequently, he embarked on an ambitious expansion program, and subsequently stated in 1971 that "...Southeastern Shipyards, Inc. is now one of the best equipped yards in the country." The basis for this statement was the fact that during those two years the shipyards were thoroughly modernized with the addition of two large new dry docks, each capable of handling ships up to 13,000 tons. In addition mobile cranes were purchased, and a 27,000-square-foot building was constructed to house the metal trades at the yards. As a result of these and other improvements "...business was expected to increase by some 50 per cent by 1973 to $58 million,..." stated McFarland in 1972.

As the year 1972 came to a close, the financial statements revealed that it was a record year both in terms of revenues and earnings, although the growth was not as spectacular as McFarland has projected. Following is a table of pertinent financial highlights for the period 1965 through 1972:

| | (In Thousands) | | | |
	1965	1968	1970	1972
Quick assets	$ 8,222	$ 8,010	$12,593	$ 8,350
Current assets	$ 9,418	$10,624	$14,202	$ 9,846
Total assets	$15,029	$16,299	$20,406	$28,979
Current liabilities	$10,566	$ 8,126	$ 3,917	$ 4,513
Non-current liabilities	$ 2,735	$ 1,508	$ 654	$ 206
Equity and parent company loans	$ 1,728	$ 6,613	$15,835	$24,260
Revenues	$28,601	$35,856	$36,722	$38,344
Earnings before taxes	$ 2,221	$ 2,900	$ 2,565	$ 2,832
Taxes	1,175	1,571	1,261	1,392
Earnings	$ 1,042	$ 1,329	$ 1,304	$ 1,440

Frankfurt was satisfied with the performance of McFarland and the shipyard since 1969 and continued to give McFarland a free hand as 1973 approached. At this point Southeastern Shipyards, Inc. was one of the largest employers in the city of Jacksonville, employing almost 3,000 men. Four separate yards were in operation, three along the northern bank of the St. Johns and one across the river. The primary source of revenue was repair and maintenance work on medium- to large-size ships, and to perform this the shipyards had six dry docks in use, four on the northside and two across the river. Late in 1972 McFarland had been successful in acquiring some waterfront property adjacent to the docks on the northside yard, and decided to consolidate operations by closing the southside yard and moving those two drydocks to some of the waterfront space obtained by the acquisition. This move was expected to result in the sale of all real estate on the southside, which would realize several million dollars.

In order to better understand the operations and use of dry docks by Southeastern Shipyards, Inc., a short discussion of dry-docking factors reveals that dry docking is a technique which is used to remove a ship from the water so that the underwater portion can be inspected, repaired, maintained, or altered. The three primary reasons for dry docking are: (1) to remove marine growths which cause fouling, (2) to prevent hull erosion, and (3) to make repairs or alterations. Fouling is caused by barnacles, mussels, and other marine organisms attaching themselves to the ship. This fouling seriously impedes the ship's speed, thereby increasing the cost of operations. Corrosion of the underwater hulls of ships is caused by electrochemical reactions. Paint or other cover materials applied periodically to the hull will protect the steel as long as the material remains intact. Periodic and casualty repairs to the underwater hulls of ships are required for propellers, shafting, rudders, and sea connections. Alterations are sometimes made to obtain more speed, use less horsepower to obtain the same speed, or to improve maneuverability.

The frequency that a ship requires dry docking is governed by the five following factors: (1) preservation of the hull of the ship, (2) accidents necessitating repairs to the hull, (3) regulations of the U.S. Coast Guard for all American ships, (4) regulations of classifications, such as the American Bureau of Shipping, Lloyd's Register of Shipping, and Bureau Veritas, for ships which are inspected and classed by them, and (5) the trade in which the ship operates. Most owners dry dock their ships yearly for inspection, cleaning, painting, and routine repairs. Some owners find it economical to do this semi-annually.

Dry docks can be of four different types: marine railway, floating, graving, and mechanical lift. Floating dry docks have become more popular in recent years because they can be constructed in sections, and accommodate larger ships. Southeastern Shipyard facilities presently include six of these floating-type dry docks, as mentioned earlier. To operate this kind of dry dock, the dock is first submerged to provide the required depth of water over the keel blocks, by partially filling the tanks with water. The tanks of the dock are then rapidly pumped out; as soon as the ship is positioned by powerful pumps located within the dock walls, the ship is lifted out of the water. The water within the cell of the dry dock spills out of the opening of the dock as the dock rises out of the water. The floating dock has several advantages such as lower initial cost, greater mobility, and greater size since they can be constructed in sections and hinged together. The six floating dry docks that the shipyards were operating at the end of 1972 were all in sound working order and could be expected to provide several more years of service with proper maintenance.

The management of the shipyards was a finely structured hierarchy with Mr. McFarland at the top. He was highly qualified for this position, having been the president of Maryland Shipyards, Inc., for several years prior to his coming to Jacksonville. The following organization chart reveals the other people in key positions. Substantially all of these individuals were long-standing employees who had worked their way up the ladder, which is the normal method of filling positions at the shipyard. All key personnel are compensated solely by a yearly fixed salary with the exception of McFarland and Shapiro who received bonuses determined by the profitability of the yard. Salaries were substantial and the motivation and morale of management appeared to be high. One unique fringe benefit of the shipyard was a special dining room/bar called the "Blue Room" where twenty designated key employees could gather for drinks and lunch. This was considered to be a motivating factor for those intent on reaching management positions. The only employee other than those shown on the top management line was the controller, Bob Jayson. The Blue Room was also used extensively to entertain potential customers, port and city officials, and others during the week. Substantially all employees other than management and office personnel were represented by an industrial union which negotiated a contract with the company every three years. The average hourly rate for these semiskilled and skilled workers was $4.25 per hour. As a result of heavy work loads a large portion of the men worked significant amounts of overtime at time and a half and the salaries are considered high in the community. Consequently the company has never had any serious labor problems and expected negotiations in 1973 to run smoothly when the three-year contract expired. However, the shipyard constantly had trouble obtaining and retaining highly skilled workers in the machine trades.

Due to the nature of the ship repair industry, Southeastern Shipyards did not require intricate sales and marketing staffs as do most businesses. Competition for repair work was such that the few facilities in existence in the United States had all the work that they could handle, and the shipyard had no active sales force to speak of. Rather, future business and sales depended on maintaining strong customer relations, and on being fair in price negotiation and in giving excellent and prompt service. The normal way in which an individual job proceeds is for a ship representative and a shipyard "estimator" to sit down and determine the extent and scope of work, and the scheduling. Then at the completion of the work, the same two people sit down and negotiate a settlement based on direct labor, materials, overhead and a normal profit margin. These negotiations are conducted in a firm but flexible manner, since both parties are dependent on each other.

The projected sale of real estate on the southside of the river, as was mentioned earlier, was expected to realize several million dollars for potential use by the shipyard. Mr. McFarland was already given the verbal go-ahead by Frankfurt to examine investment opportunities for the expected available cash. The planning function at the shipyards was not highly structured, although a planning department, headed by R.M. Cocker, did exist. Various ideas were sought out by Mr. McFarland from management for areas in which to expand or diversify in late 1972, and three projects were finally decided on as definite possibilities for expansion based on preliminary studies. These three projects were: (1) Purchase a giant floating dry dock at a cost of approximately $15 million which would facilitate super tankers, (2) Purchase a shipbuilding company in Jacksonville at a cost of approximately $3 million, and (3) Purchase an engineering firm in Houston, Texas for approximately $2 million. It was not decided whether one, two or all of these projects should be undertaken, and detailed feasibility studies were made of all three. The first form of expansion would require a tremendous investment and its success was depen-

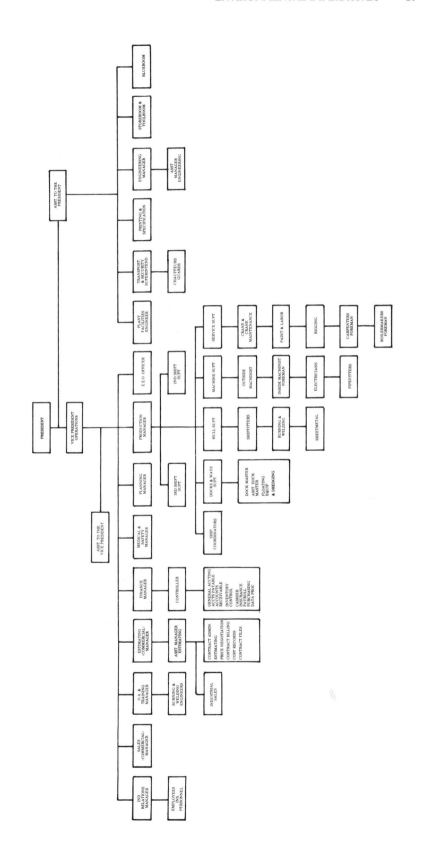

SOUTHEASTERN SHIPYARDS INC.
ORGANIZATION CHART

dent on many factors such as (1) Jacksonville harbor and port facilities, (2) Jacksonville resources and economy, (3) sales and market potential, (4) and the availability of skilled workers and harbor space.

The other two projects were much smaller in magnitude, and were different types of expansion. Purchase of a shipbuilding company was one form of vertical acquisition, since Southeastern Shipyards repaired ships. The other, purchase of an engineering firm, was another form of vertical integration, since this acquisition was expected to replace the substantial sandblasting work performed at the shipyard and being subcontracted. The results of the company's research on these three projects is highlighted in the following paragraphs.

PURCHASE OF GIANT DRYDOCK

The shipyards felt four areas, as mentioned in the preceding paragraph, would be critical in making a final decision as to this purchase. The company's research in these four areas is revealed as follows.

Harbor and Port Facilities. Jacksonville is sometimes referred to as the "gateway to the Southeast". The Jacksonville Port Authority has a progressive attitude toward expansion of the harbor facilities, and the port is in the process of becoming truly a deep water ocean port.

Since the creation of the Jacksonville Port Authority in 1963, the primary wharves and docks at Tallyrand have experienced a complete transformation. These facilities now include 3,964 linear feet of marginal wharf, 611,000 square feet of covered storage, and extensive support and maintenance equipment. The Port Authority also is proud of its facilities at Blount Island, which is strategically located in the St. Johns River, halfway between Jacksonville and the Atlantic Ocean. The island facilities house space, and with the completion of a 45-ton, twin-light container crane in 1972, the Blount Island container terminal has become the most modern in the southeast. This improvement and expansion program is continuing as 1973 begins, and the Port Authority is presently financing construction of a new steel and concrete bridge from Heckscher Drive to Blount Island, to help move cargo from the rapidly expanding complex.

The port of Jacksonville, Florida, lies along the lower 24.5-mile stretch of the St. Johns River, 145 nautical miles south of Savannah, Georgia, and 345 nautical miles north of Miami, Florida. The deep-water entrance and channel leads West from the river's mouth to the Florida East Coast Railway Bridge (24.5 miles above mouth) in downtown Jacksonville. As a result of the various River and Harbor Acts of Congress since 1880, the entrance and channel have been maintained in a manner to accommodate ocean going vessels. The River and Harbor Act of October 17, 1965, provided for a deepening of the present channel from 34 feet to 38 feet to accommodate the large super-cargo-type vessels. This project is now in progress and is a vital necessity if Southeastern Shipyards, Inc., is to capture its portion of the repair and maintenance work on these large ships. At the end of 1972, the 38-foot channel reached the halfway point, and bids for extending the improvement already have been received by the Army Corps of Engineers.

It is apparent that the Jacksonville Port Authority has every intention of making Jacksonville a modern and truly deep-water port which is essential for Southeastern Shipyards, Inc., in the years ahead.

Jacksonville's Resources and Economy. The resources of Jacksonville, including the availability of skilled workers, growth of the economy, and inland transportation facilities, will play a vital role in determining the advisability of Southeastern Shipyards, Inc., making this acquisition. The proposed dry dock would require in excess of 400 skilled workers, for operation, which the labor market in the Jacksonville area would have to absorb. The continued growth of Jacksonville, both in terms of economic output and transportation facilities, is a necessity for the years ahead also.

The population of Jacksonville has increased from 455,400 in 1960 to now almost 600,000. This trend is expected to continue in the future, with a projection of over 700,000 by 1980, and over 1,000,000 by the year 2000. Over 60 percent of the people in this area earn a living by wages or salaries, as opposed to proprietor's income, property income, or transfer payments. From the expected trend in population and the evidence of a large and stable work force in Jacksonville, it appears that an available supply of workers would be available in this area.

The year 1972 can be considered possibly the most important year in the history of Jacksonville's economic growth as a result of the decision of Westinghouse-Tenneco to locate their joint venture, Offshore Power Systems (OPS), on Blount Island. This development is expected to provide massive economic stimulus to the area for many years ahead. An impact of the growth that has also been taking place can be seen by comparing general cargo imports in 1966 to 1971. In this relatively short period of five years, the total tonnage handled increased from 638,729 tons to 1,307,759 tons or roughly doubled.

Inland transportaion represents a significant part of total operating cost for industry and is of primary concern to shippers. The cost of moving freight throughout the Southeast is related to affluence and population concentrations, as well as the geographic distances between communities. In comparing Jacksonville to cities in the industrial crescent, it was determined that a shipper serving the Southeast could cut his transportation costs by more than 50 per cent originating his shipments in Jacksonville. In addition, this location has been improving with time because the growth (both population and income) in the Southeast is taking place in Florida.

All these statistics and studies on the resources of Jacksonville reach the same conclusion: the city is a dynamic and growing area, and is on the verge of becoming the major seaport of the region.

Sales and Market Potential. Southeastern Shipyards, Inc. presently has six floating dry docks in use. The largest of these has a lifting capacity of 18,000 tons, is 622 feet long, and has a width of 93 feet. The proposed new dry dock would have a lifting capacity of 40,000 tons, a length of 827 feet and a width of 144 feet. In other words, the proposed "super dry dock" would accommodate ships over twice as big as those now being handled. To determine the number of ships presently in operation which are too large for the 18,000-ton class dry dock, the company obtained a list from Lloyd's Register of Shipping, from world fleet totals. This list, as of February 1972, is as follows:

Tankers	1,210
Ore and bulk carriers	760
General cargo and passenger	80
	2,050

A determination was made by the company that approximately 500 of these vessels trade on the East Coast of the United States at one time or another. According to the sales department, on numerous occasions during 1972 the company has been approached from both domestic and foreign ship owners and operators, offering ships that could not be dry-docked with present facilities. During January and February 1972, alone, twelve vessels were refused service at Jacksonville because of size.

An estimate by the company that sales can be increased by $10,000,000 a year can be substantiated by analyzing present company sales. In 1971, the largest dry dock at Southeastern Shipyards, Inc., realized sales of $5,500,000. The dry dock was occupied 239 days during the year, which means that the average daily sales was approximately $23,000. Since the proposed new dry dock is expected to handle ships over twice as large as those presently docked, the proposed dry dock will anticipate fees of $50,000 a day. Assuming a minimum of 200 days of utilization a year, this would produce an increase in sales to the company of at least $10,000,000 per year.

Most of the large flag ships now trading on the East Coast are now being repaired in foreign countries because of the lack of facilities in the United States. At the present time only two dry docks exist on the Eastern Seaboard which are of the large variety required, and neither of these is handling the tanker and cargo ship repair business. Sun Shipbuilding on the Delaware River cannot compete with the climate, location and lower billing rates of foreign ports and the other, in Newport News, Virginia, is restricted because of the heavy Navy activity. In addition, both of these yards are used primarily for shipbuilding, rather than repair work.

Overall, the shipping and market potential for repair work on the large ships appears to be plentiful and on the increase on the East Coast of the United States.

Availability of Skilled Workers & Harbor Space. An equally important consideration is whether resources can be provided in the Jacksonville area to accommodate this type of expansion.

As pointed out, over four hundred workers will be required to operate the proposed dry dock, most of these skilled. The shipyard is having trouble at the present time even finding and keeping qualified people for present positions and has resorted to company training programs to create new skills in workers.

The port and harbor facilities of Jacksonville have been expanded and updated significantly, as was brought out earlier. The importance of the continued development of the port, and the deepening of the channel to 38 feet is critical to the long range future of the company, according to Jackson. However, he feels that present facilities are more than adequate to insure that the large super-tankers would be accessible to the company. He pointed out that the bulk of the shipping trade in these ships takes place between the oil fields and refineries of Texas and Louisiana and the commercial markets in the northeastern United States. The ships must pass Jacksonville on their return voyages to the oil refineries. Since the vessels are empty at this time, Jackson indicated that the present channel of 34 feet would be satisfactory.

PURCHASE OF SHIP BUILDING COMPANY

The ship-building company that Southeastern Shipyards was considering acquiring was a long-standing firm in the Jacksonville area and consisted of a single location on the intracoastal waterway at Atlantic Boulevard. The facilities permitted construction of only one to three small to medium-sized ships at a time, which took twelve to eighteen months each. Ferries and ocean going research vessels were typical of the ships produced.

The company usually realized a profit on these contracts of ten to twenty percent, which averaged out to approximately $200,000 a year before taxes for the years 1965 to 1972. Following is a copy of the company's balance sheet at December 31, 1972:

ASSETS

CURRENT ASSETS:

Cash	$ 194,460
Accounts receivable, less allowance for doubtful accounts of $2,980	205,604
Costs and estimated earnings in excess of collections on progress billings on uncompleted contracts	190,941
Inventory of materials and supplies	66,143
Other	1,412
Total Current Assets	658,560
PROPERTY, PLANT AND EQUIPMENT	1,365,150
	$2,023,710

LIABILITIES AND STOCKHOLDERS' EQUITY

CURRENT LIABILITIES:

Notes payable, bank	$ 430,000
Accounts payable and accrued expenses	313,470
Accrued payroll and amounts withheld from employees	70,595
Amounts due an affiliated company	5,560
Current portion of long-term debt	24,996
Total Current Liabilities	844,621
LONG-TERM DEBT	33,813
STOCKHOLDERS' EQUITY:	
Common stock, $1 par value; authorized, issued and outstanding, 10,000 shares	10,000
Retained earnings	1,135,276
	145,176
	$2,023,710

Southeastern Shipyards felt that this acquisition would enable them to enter a related field in which they had know-how and job related experience.

PURCHASE OF AN ENGINEERING FIRM

The third possibility for expansion being considered by Southeastern Shipyards was the acquisition of Key Houston, Inc., in Houston, Texas. The company was in the business of developing, constructing and marketing abrasive blasting and recovery equipment used extensively in the shipbuilding and ship repair industry. They had a reputation in the ship-repair industry of marketing a superior product and had done extensive business with Jacksonville Shipyards over the years. This business consisted primarily of selling sand-blast equipment, which Southeastern Shipyards used extensively to clean the hulls of ships of barnacles, mussels and other marine organisms, prior to the painting of the hulls. Key Houston had been a leader in its industry for years and had enjoyed financial success, realizing after tax profits in the $150,000 range for the four years prior to 1973. Following is a balance sheet of Key Houston at August 31, 1972, which reveals their strong financial position.

ASSETS

CURRENT ASSETS:

Cash		$ 31,874
Accounts receivable, less allowance for doubtful accounts of $2,300		151,002
Inventories:		
Raw materials		$171,191
Work in process and finished goods	49,600	225,791
Deferred Federal taxes on income		28,000
Prepaid expenses		621
TOTAL CURRENT ASSETS		437,288
OTHER ASSETS:		
Patents (Note A)	10,266	
Investment in Key Europe, Ltd.	4,162	14,428
PROPERTY AND EQUIPMENT:		
Land	$350,000	
Buildings	450,000	
Equipment on rental	93,000	
Automobiles	20,496	
Furniture and equipment	19,544	
	933,040	
	134,289	$ 798,751
		$1,250,467

LIABILITIES AND STOCKHOLDER'S EQUITY

CURRENT LIABILITIES:

Accounts payable - trade		$ 63,298
Accounts payable - stockholder and officers		79,922
Accrued expenses		8,960
Deferred income		47,099
Federal income taxes payable		109,600
Payments due within one year on long-term debt		16,802
TOTAL CURRENT LIABILITIES		325,681
LONG-TERM NOTE PAYABLE, less portion due within one year under original repayment plan, included in current liabilities		77,036
STOCKHOLDER'S EQUITY:		
Common stock, par value $1 a share; authorized, 100,000 shares; issued and outstanding, 10,000 shares	$ 10,000	
Retained earnings	837,750	847,750
		$1,250,467

Southeastern Shipyards president D.L. McFarland stated that . . . "Key Houston would be a good vehicle with which to enter a field directly related to the company's activities, and would afford the opportunity to lead in a phase of shipyard work which has been troublesome and costly to every shipyard, domestic and foreign."

EVALUATION OF THE SOUTHEASTERN SHIPYARDS CASE

SUMMARY

This case deals with the issues involved when an organization has to adjust to dynamic changes in its organization structure and design and in the environment in which it operates. The firm is a rapidly growing subsidiary of a large Northern Transportation Manufacturing organization and is involved in shipbuilding and ship repairing in the Southeastern United States.

KEY ISSUES

1. What are the planning strategies of the organization?
2. What are the objectives and goals of the organization?
3. Has money and capital been invested properly?
4. Should the company expand or diversify? If so, which proposal or proposals is best, given the resources and economy of Jacksonville, sales and market potential, harbor and port facilities, and the objectives of this company?

DISCUSSION

1. Planning Strategies

Southeastern Shipyards, Inc., dates back to 1975, when it used to be in the business of construction and repair of small-to-medium-size ocean-going vessels. As time passed, the small business expanded into a huge conglomerate of other shipyards. As the organization grew into a huge company, little or no attention was given to strategic planning. The company did not specify what kind of work or processes it would prefer to specialize in. Also, guidelines were not established for the types of ships and vessels to be handled by the company. The organization is now in a favorable position and has money to invest, but, because strategic planning has not been performed in the past, there is a lack of direction to follow.

2. Objectives and Goals

The objectives and goals of the organization have not been clearly defined. If the goals had been defined, the alternative proposals of investment could be selected on the merits of objective related priorities. As a result, the company has limited ability to determine which investment alternative would be the most benficial.

3. Profitability and Capital Investment

The company has realized profits of over $1 million for the past four years. This would, at first glance, seem to indicate that the organization was operating successfully. However, this profit might be lower than it could be when considering the profits made by competing companies in the same industry. Other investments may have resulted in higher profits than what was actually realized. A "good investment" in this company is hard to define because no basis exists by which to measure success. In the past, the company has invested in equipment to the point that Southeastern Shipyards Inc., is one of the best equipped yards in the country. However, it is questionable whether this approach optimizes profitability. The purpose of the heavy investment in equipment is not clear. Also, according to Mr. McFarland, by acquiring Key Houston, the company would be a leader in equipment used extensively to clean hulls of ships. The 1972 financial statements indicate that the growth of the company was not as great as anticipated. If growth was one of the major objectives, then investment should be planned in a manner that would achieve this objective the best. On the other hand, if profit is one of the major objectives, then the company would probably have to select a different investment choice.

4. Expansion Diversification

Southeastern Shipyards Inc., currently has a revenue level of over $38 million, with almost 3,000 employees. The first proposal for expansion, building a giant drydock, would require a substantial investment and its success would depend on many factors, such as (1) sales and market potential, (2) Jacksonville harbor and port facilities, (3) Jacksonville resources and economy, and (4) the availability of skilled workers and harbor space.

Sales and Market Potential. The proposed giant drydock would accommodate ships over twice as big as those now being handled. According to the sales department, on numerous occasions during 1972 the company has been approached by domestic and foreign ship owners and operators, offering ships that could not be drydocked with present facilities. An estimate by the company stating that sales can be increased by $10 million a year can be substantiated by analyzing present company sales. Most of the large flag ships now trading on the East Coast are now being repaired in foreign countries because of the lack of facilities in the United States. At the present time, only two drydocks exist on the Eastern Seaboard that are large enough for this purpose, and neither of these is handling tanker and cargo ship repairs.

Overall, the shipping and market potential for repair work on large ships appears to be plentiful and on the increase on the East Coast of the United States.

Harbor and Port Facilities. Since the creation of the Jacksonville Port Authority in 1973, the primary wharves and docks have experienced a complete transformation. The Jacksonville Port Authority has a progressive attitude toward expansion of the harbor facilities. The entrance and channel have been maintained in a manner to accommodate ocean going vessels as a result of various Harbor Acts of Congress since 1880. The River and Harbor Act of 1965 provided for a deepening of the present channel to accommodate the large super-cargo-type vessels. This project is a vital necessity if Southeastern Shipyards, Inc., is to capture its portion of the repair and maintenance work on these large ships.

Jacksonville's Resources and Economy. The resources of Jacksonville, growth of the economy, and the inland transportation facilities, will play a vital role in determining whether Southeastern Shipyards, Inc., should make this acquisition. The proposed drydock would require over 400 skilled workers which the labor market in the Jacksonville area would have to provide. The continued growth of Jacksonville, both in terms of economic output and transportation facilities, is a necessity for the years ahead also. From the expected trend in population and the evidence of a large and stable work force in Jacksonville, it appears that a valuable supply of workers would be available in the area.

The decision of Westinghouse-Tenneco to locate their joint venture, Offshore Power Systems, on Blount Island will provide massive economic stimulus to the area for many future years.

In comparing Jacksonville to other cities in the industrial areas, it would seem that a shipper serving the Southeast could cut his transportation cost by more than 50% by originating his shipments in Jacksonville.

Availability of Skilled Workers and Harbor Space. Over 400 workers will be required to operate the proposed drydock, most of these skilled. The shipyard is having difficulty at the present time finding and keeping qualified people for present positions. Company training programs have been established to create new skills. The importance of the continued development of the port, and the deepening of the channel to 38 feet is critical to the long range future of the company.

The second form of expansion would involve the purchase of a ship building company. The ship-building company is a longstanding firm in the Jacksonville area and consists of a single location in the intracoastal waterway at Atlantic Boulevard. One to three small to medium-sized ships can be built at the same time, at a construction period of twelve to eighteen months each. The company usually made a profit on these contracts of between ten to twenty percent, an average of approximately $200,000 per year before taxes. This acquisition would enable Southeastern Shipyards to enter a related field in which they have expertise and job related experience.

The third possibility for expansion that is being considered is the acquisition of Key Houston, Inc., in Houston, Texas. This company has a reputation in the ship-repair industry of marketing a superior product. Also, they have become known by the shipyards over the years. Key Houston has been a leader in its industry for years and has enjoyed financial success, realizing after tax profits in the $150,000 range for the four years prior to 1973.

According to president D.L. McFarland, Key Houston would be a good way to enter a field directly related to the company's activities, and would afford the opportunity to lead in a phase of shipyard work which had been troublesome and costly to the shipyard.

ALTERNATIVE CONSIDERATIONS

The following represent selected alternatives which should be considered by Southeastern Shipyards in formulating their future strategy:

1. The company can continue to operate as is (status quo) with no reorganization or new investments (expansion).

    Advantages: No new risks would be involved.

    Disadvantages: Goals and objectives remain undefined; strategic planning is not implemented; competitors would probably continue to expand their facilities and eventually get most of the business; profit opportunities are lost.

2. The company can expand by purchasing the giant dry dock.

    Advantages: Revenues could possibly double; the company would capture a share of the large vessel market; more jobs would be provided.

    Disadvantages: The channel will have to be deepened because of the high investment in dry dock facilities; high capital investment requirements with extensive borrowing; increased risk because of investment in one base industry; availability of skilled workers is limited;

high dependence on Jacksonville resources and economy; dependence on Jacksonville Port Authority's progressive attitude; competition with the same industry in foreign markets.

3. The company can purchase the ship building firm.

Advantages: Entry into a related field in which the company has experience and expertise; expansion of the company, increased profits.

Disadvantages: Increase in current liabilities; added complexity and possible sub-optimization because organization has not defined objectives; higher risk of failure.

4. The company can purchase the engineering firm.

Advantages: Allows company to enter a field directly related to its activities; possible leadership in this phase of shipyard work; stronger financial position; diversification.

Disadvantages: Geographically distant from other company operations to easily integrate into present activities; lack of sales and marketing force or knowledge to operate this type of firm; higher risk of failure.

As noted, one of the basic problems in this case is that Southeastern Shipyards Inc., has not performed any strategic planning or defined corporate objectives. There are presently conflicting objectives which is evidenced by past investment decisions. In order for this company to decide on appropriate alternatives it must establish organizational objectives, develop a corporate strategic plan, and then choose the investment alternatives that will maximize these objectives the best.

2

ORGANIZATIONAL IMPERATIVES AND OBJECTIVES

ORGANIZATIONAL OBJECTIVES

Objectives may be defined as the implicit formulations or the explicit statements which establish the fundamental direction or the purpose of the organization. Targets or goals state in quantitative terms the degree to which the objectives of the organization are to be attained during some defined time period.

Two broad categories of objectives may be seen to exist within the business firm. These are "stylistic" and "functional" objectives.[1] The objectives of the firm are states or outcomes that are desired by top management. Stylistic objectives are an expression of the "tastes" of the corporate management and may not be ultimately quantifiable. Functional objectives, on the other hand, are ultimately quantifiable and address themselves to the performance of the resource conversion mechanism. Functional or performance objectives are typically the focus of the planning process. Stylistic objectives obviously impart some direction to the business organization and, therefore, deserve mention in an examination of objectives.

Goals and targets are often used synonymously and represent quantified objectives. For example, one of the firm's objectives may be expressed as: "to increase the firm's rate of return on investment to ten percent by 1982." The objective, therefore, addresses itself to a particular attribute. A "yardstick" or a scale of measure is developed and the desired value on the scale is determined. This "desired value" becomes the goal.[2] Figure 1 illustrates the process sequence of converting qualitative objectives into goals.

Before discussing the elements of Figure 1, the question might be asked: Why set objectives and goals for the organization? The typical firm includes decision-makers on various levels of the organization hierarchy. Objectives and goals are necessary because if they are absent, it is possible that subunits of the organization may substitute their own objectives and goals for

FIGURE 1

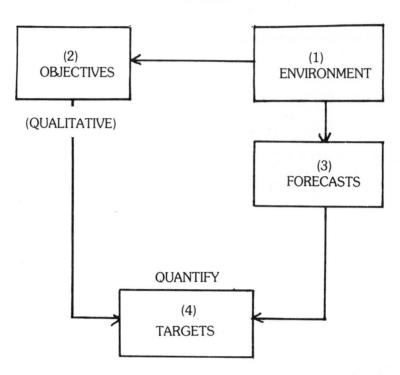

those of the organizaion. This may result in a conflict between the objectives of the firm as a whole and the goals of the sub-units. While the definition and communication of corporate objectives and goals does not guarantee that harmony will occur, it does provide a direction for the decision-process on all levels. The examination and definition of corporate objectives and goals also serves the purpose of defining broadly what business the company is in. Often, the lack of such a definition gives rise to the pursuit of different objectives which prove to be dysfunctional for the organization.

Environment and Objectives

The first element in Figure 1 is the firm's environment. This includes both the firm's external and internal environments which have been discussed previously. The environment provides two inputs to the objectives of the firm. The first input determines the flexibility the organization has in the determination of its objectives. A large number of environmental constraints will allow less latitude to the firm in the setting of its objectives. Also, if one environmental factor is of primary importance to the company, its objectives must address themselves to this environmental factor. In the case where the firm has few environmental constraints, objectives may be considerably more flexible.

The second input to the firm's objectives provided by the environment is the determination of the various objectives of the organization. There is one underlying reason for the existence of the business organization, namely, to provide a profit to the firm's owners. Now the profit of the firm is constrained by the environment in which it functions. This gives rise to a number of objectives which the firm can pursue. For example, the profit a firm is able to pursue is constrained by social factors. The organization is a member of the society in which it exists. It also forms a micro-society made up of the members of the organization. The firm must be perceived as acting in a responsible manner by the society in which it exists. The satisfaction of the members of the organization may also become an objective for the enterprise. This will result in personnel policies designed to increase the efficiency of the undertakings of the organization. Similarly, other objectives are defined through the firm's other environmental factors. We have indicated that environmental factors are interdependent. In a similar fashion, the various objectives of the organization become interdependent. It is difficult to disassociate the different objectives of the firm because each is related to the others to a greater or lesser degree.

Objectives-Determination and Constraints

A great deal has been written on the subject of the objectives of the business organization. The economic view of the business enterprise sees the organizational objective as profit-seeking. The objective is further expanded in that the firm exists to make a maximum profit. The economic point of view is not, however, the only aspect of the firm's environment which has an effect upon the organization. We have seen that other environmental constraints enter into the picture.

Argenti[3] defines the objective of the firm in the following manner. "A company has one and only one permanent unalterable *raison d'être,* namely to make a profit." He further defines means and constraints:

> *Means* are those actions which a company will take if it believes that they will improve profits.
> *Constraints* are those actions which a company will take *whether or not* they improve profits.[4]

Ansoff,[5] on the other hand, views the maximization of the rate of return of the organization as a "central theoretical objective" of the organization. It becomes necessary to translate this "theoretical" objective into one which is practical for the firm. This gives rise to a system of objectives which have an effect on the rate of return and are meaningful for the company. The problem would appear to be one of definition of level. Profit or rate of return tends to be a concept which is difficult to measure. Accountants can provide a large number of ways to determine the profitability of a firm. Similarly, the rate of return on investments is subject to different interpretations. Clearly, there is a need for other measures along with the economic measures of the firm's activities. It is in this sense that the firm has a number of objectives.

1. The Nature of the Firm

The objectives of a given business firm are generally dependent upon the nature of the firm. Companies differ on the basis of their product-markets. The firm in the steel industry probably has a different set of objectives than those of the food distribution industry. Not only will objectives differ across industry lines, but also they will differ because of the number of product-markets involved. The organization involved in a single product market will have a smaller, less comprehensive set of objectives than a large firm with many different activities. Objectives also change with time. The objectives of the company in the past are continually being revised and evolve over a period of time. A company may be seen as being in one stage or another of its life cycle. The new firm seeking to establish itself within a competitive product market will probably focus upon aspects which maximize its current profitability. The well established company, which has a relatively secure position within the product market, may tend to direct its attention toward long term growth opportunities.

The financial structure of the firm exerts an influence upon the objectives it will follow. The company may have access to large amounts of capital which then may be invested in opportunities which require a large, fixed investment. This will limit the future opportunities available to the firm. If the company is highly liquid, a large number of new product markets may be examined. When the financial resources of the firm are committed, opportunities available are restricted. In the former situation objectives will focus upon expansion, while in the latter case the objectives are directed toward the internal aspects of the firm.

The nature of the firm with respect to its defensive-aggressive position is manifested in the company's objectives. For example, a defensive company may endeavor to have a diversity of customers in different market segments and employ different technologies in its processes. This is a "risk-averter" type of approach.

2. Sophistication of the Planning Process

Ackoff indicates that there are three levels of sophistication in the planning process. These are "satisfying," "optimizing" and "adaptivizing."[6] At the lowest level, objectives are simple and not related between themselves. There is no provision for mediation of conflict between objectives. The second type of planning, "optimizing," gives rise to objectives which permit the firm to do as well as possible under a given set of circumstances. Objectives formulated at the "adaptivizing" level of planning consider the environmental impact upon objectives. Alternate courses of action are developed which permit the attainment of objectives under a variety of conditions.

3. The Determination of Objectives

The specification of corporate objectives in the strategic planning process is made by the topmost level of management. In the case where management is dominated by one individual it may be that the corporate objectives incorporate the values of the individual. In most circumstances, however, the corporate objectives are determined by a management team. Personal values of individual members of the management team are not normally imposed into the organizational objectives, but aspects of management's personal values may be seen within organizational objectives. It is necessary that a consensus be reached among the individuals involved in the objective setting process. This requires a compromise between the personal values of the management team which is manifested in the corporate objectives.

4. Classification of Objectives

Corporate objectives are determined at the upper management level. Realization of the corporate objectives is carried out in the functional levels of the organization. Therefore, corporate objectives must eventually be defined in functional terms. Functional objectives are more explicit than those defined at the corporate level. The purpose of the definition of functional objectives is to ensure that they are not in conflict with corporate objectives.

Objectives at the corporate level fall into two categories. The first category is the proximate term objectives. Proximate objectives direct themselves to current (short-term) concerns. These include current sales and current product markets. Long run objectives direct themselves to the future profitability of the company and are expressed in terms of new product markets, the acquisition of future resources or diversification.

5. Objectives

The definition of profit-seeking as the objective of the business organization is one which essentially defines the firm only in its economic context. The modification of this overall objective by the environment gives rise to the system of objectives which are particular to a given company. Economic objectives normally retain an important position in the resultant set of objectives. The "theoretical" or profit objective may be viewed in the following equation:

$$\text{ROI or profit} = f \text{ (economic factors, non-economic factors)}$$

Economic factors give rise to objectives such as sales quotas within the firm's product markets. Non-economic objectives are expressed in relation to the other factors within the environment. These objectives address themselves to the social responsibilities of the organization and any other factor which could have an impact upon the profitability of the firm. The number of constraints acting upon the organization will determine the extent of flexibility the firm has in determining its objectives.

FORECASTING

The third component indicated in Figure 1 is the forecast. The forecast provides the link between the environment and the targets which are the quantified objectives. Forecasting involves three steps. In the first step an analysis is undertaken to determine what is to be forecasted and the detail of the forecast which is necessary. Secondly, past *trends* are then extrapolated into the future. The third step involves an identification of those factors which have contributed to the profitability of the firm in the past. Finally, possible components of the firm's future profit picture are determined. In this manner, it is determined how the future will be different from the past.

Forecasts are used as predictions of future profits given that the firm does nothing different from what it is doing presently. When the forecasts are compared with the established target, then the firm's management is able to determine what must be done. The profit gap is the difference between the profit target and the profit forecast. This difference represents the extra effort required of the organization and the size of the task facing the firm's management.

Forecasts are not definitive predictions of future conditions. Forecasts are made under uncertainty and the error of a forecast increases the farther one projects into the future. It is therefore necessary that the probabilistic accuracy of the forecast be expressed. This permits the evaluation of alternative plans under the conditions which are believed most likely to occur. The combination of the firm's overall objectives stated in qualitative terms, and the forecasts of future conditions permits the organization to express goals or targets in quantitative terms. This stage is represented by the fourth element in Figure 1.

Targets or Goals

Now that the objectives of the company have been determined, it is necessary to decide upon targets which are the quantification of the company's objectives. We have indicated that the overall objective of the firm is to make a profit. Constraints imposed by the environment translate the overall objectives of the firm into a vector or set of objectives. Each component of the profit function will hopefully contribute to the overall profitability of the firm. Targets are determined for the major activities within the scope of the company's operations. An example of a target could be the company's sales volume target. In this case, a ten percent increase in sales could be the goal. Goals which involve a level of attainment must also be expressed in terms of a target date. In the present example, the complete specification of the goal would be a ten percent increase in sales by 1982. It may, however, be impossible to specify an exact value for a goal. In this case, a range of values is defined as being acceptable. The goal threshold is defined as the value below which the

34

goal is not accomplished. Above the threshold value, the goal is considered reached by the organization. This concept may be illustrated by the following diagram (Figure 2):

FIGURE 2

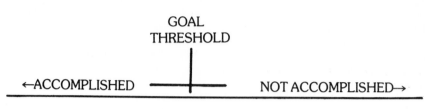

GOAL
THRESHOLD

←ACCOMPLISHED   ————————————   NOT ACCOMPLISHED→

RANGE OF VALUES

1. Goal Rank Ordering

The various goals established by the organization may be viewed as a rank ordering of goals. In accordance with the basic objectives established by the organization some goals are of greater importance to the company than other goals. In the case of less important goals, it may be that the company will not be in a position to attain the goal. Goals which are high on the goal hierarchy are by definition important to the organization. If it becomes impossible to attain these goals or a downward revision of the goal is indicated, a re-examination of the environment is called for. It is through the environment that causal links may be determined.

FIGURE 3

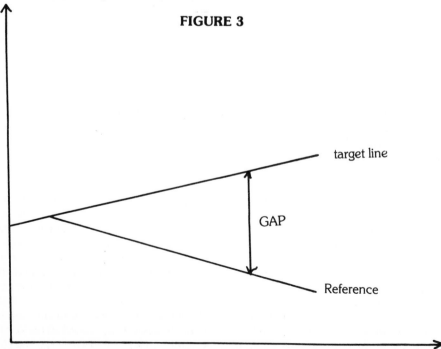

target line

GAP

Reference

Source: H.I. Ansoff, *Corporate Strategy* (New York: McGraw-Hill, 1965), pp. 148, modified adaptation.
Used with permission of McGraw-Hill Book Company.

The preceding diagram (Figure 3) illustrates the relationship between the various concepts which have been discussed in this section. The target line represents the quantification of the firm's objectives.

The reference projection line may be viewed as a possible result if the firm does no planning. Incorporated into this line is the concept of the firm's product-market life cycle. The product market cycle is viewed as having two stages. The first stage is an increasing level of production. In the second stage production decreases after passing the maximum level. This is illustrated in the diagram where the target and reference projection lines coincide with each other. The firm's position in its production life cycle may enable it to attain its target for a period of time. Ansoff[7] does not allow for this period where the two lines may coincide. He views the two lines as diverging throughout the period of the planning horizon.

The "gap" is defined as the difference between the reference projection and the target lines. The gap represents the magnitude of the task faced by the corporate planner. Analysis of this gap is the subject of discussion in the next section of this chapter.

GAP ANALYSIS

In previous section we have seen how the qualitative objectives of the organization are expressed in goals or targets of a quantitative nature. The target line was developed and a reference projection was established on the basis of the forecast under the assumption that management does not intervene with planning. The two lines are seen to diverge giving rise to the gap. The analysis of this gap is the subject of our following discussion.

Purpose of Gap Analysis

Gap analysis may be viewed as determining the magnitude of the task facing the firm's management. Expressed in equation form the gap is defined as follows.

Magnitude of GAP	=	PROJECTED TARGET	−	CURRENT PROJECTION	(if nothing is done)

The magnitude of the gap could also provide some indication of the extent to which strategic planning has been used in the past. If the gap is large, it could indicate that little strategic planning has been effectively implemented in the past. The gap also provides a measure of the planning which will be required in the future. Again, a large gap will indicate that a great deal of attention will have to be devoted to the planning process. If the gap is small, it could indicate that planning has been effective in the past, and the task facing the organization with respect to the planning process is not as great. These considerations are of a general nature and do not show what must be done to close the gap.

The gap analysis narrows down the strategic search for alternatives. An investigation is carried out to determine whether the gap can be closed by the full utilization of the firm's current internal resources. If it is determined that the gap cannot be closed through internal analysis, then external sources of resources will be required.

By conducting an investigation of this nature, the magnitude of the resource requirements is determined. Resources may be obtained either within the present organization or from sources which are outside the organization. This information enables management to restrict the search for alternatives to fill the gap.

Examples are given in Figure 4 which illustrate how the search is narrowed.[8] The first diagram illustrates the possibility that the defined target equals the current projection. In this case, the gap is zero and no strategic search is required.

The second diagram is a representation of filling the gap through the use of internal resources. If it is discovered that internal resources are adequate to fill the gap, then a search is required only of internal alternatives.

FIGURE 4

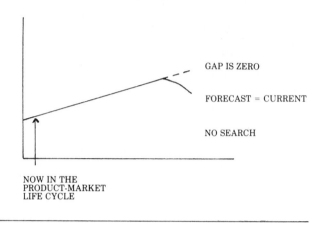

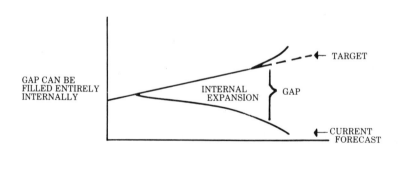

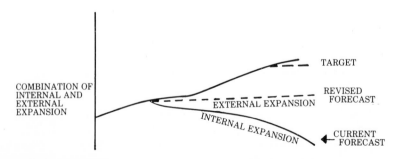

*Interpretation of Diagram by H.I. Ansoff, *Corporate Strategy* (New York: McGraw-Hill, 1965) pp. 148. Used with permission of McGraw-Hill Book Company.

In the case where internal resources are inadequate to fill the gap, then alternatives outside the business organization will be considered. This is the situation represented in the third diagram. Alternatives outside the company are limited only to those alternatives comparable to the magnitude of the external resource required. In this manner, the search is narrowed down.

It is apparent that the strategic search may be reduced considerably by an analysis of this nature. The first step in the strategic search is to conduct an internal appraisal of the gap. As we have indicated previously, the internal search is all that may be required to close the gap. The procedure for this internal appraisal will be referred to as the "micro-process."

Internal Gap Analysis-The Micro-Process

The internal gap analysis is an examination of the strengths and weaknesses of the organization. The analysis directs itself to the resources of the company. Included in the firm's resources are financial resources, personnel resources (both management specialists and operating personnel), facilities, raw material, and equipment. The strengths and weaknesses of the organization are then evaluated in terms of the overall corporate objectives and goals. The method used to evaluate the strengths and weaknesses of the organization is called the microprocess. It is a "micro" view of the firm because the units examined are the various operating units which make up the organization. We have seen in the previous section that the setting of objectives and targets is performed at the "macro" level of the organization. The plans which are formulated at the macro level with respect to the internal aspects of the company must eventually be implemented by the various operating units of the organization. For this reason, corporate management consults the lower management levels for their input into the planning process. The input of the lower levels of management consists of each major subunit of the organization formulating its own plan over the relevant time horizon which has been defined according to the nature of the enterprise.

Before the plans of the sub-units are formulated, it is necessary that corporate management provide guidelines for the lower management levels. Included in this framework is the necessity of the operating units to consider the long-run implications of their recommendations. It is common to find the operating units concerned only with the short term, day-to-day problems of their particular unit. The long-term considerations become secondary and the overall perspective is lost. The goals which are relevant to the sub-unit are explicitly stated to lower management by the corporate managers. This explicit determination is necessary to avoid any ambiguity. Finally, each operating unit is provided with the broad environmental considerations in terms of forecasts and predictions. The framework for the planning process at the sub-unit level is now complete and the individual managers may now proceed with the formulation of their own particular plans.

The micro-process provides corporate management with valuable data on the organization. The large firm encompasses a large number of activities and and is extremely complex. Information which is obtained through the micro-process would not be available otherwise to corporate management. The involvement of the sub-units in the planning process permits the input of lower management giving them a sense of purpose and the opportunity to express ideas which may prove to be valuable for the overall corporate performance. Since decisions made at the corporate level must ultimately be implemented in the sub-units, the participation in the decision making process by the sub-units can serve to ensure that the decisions are carried out in an efficient manner.

The sub-unit which is the appropriate level for the micro-process to take place, is defined as the product division or the operating unit. Results obtained through the micro-process permit top management to be aware of the opportunities and the limitations present in each of the major sub-units. The formulation of plans at the micro level provides an approximation of how closely the unit can reach the goals assigned over the long run. Now that the information is available to corporate management, the next step is to process the information in the context of the overall organizational perspective.

Aggregation and Evaluation

Plans developed at the level of each sub-unit are now available to the corporate planning group. It is now necessary for the planning group to evaluate the plans which have been produced at the lower levels. Caution must be exercised in the acceptance of such plans. There may be a tendency for the division or sub-unit manager to overestimate the performance capabilities of his particular unit. Therefore, the plans submitted by the division should be carefully examined to ensure the picture presented is a realistic one. Conflicts may become apparent between the plans submitted by the different sub-units. In this case, corporate management must make a decision with respect to the acceptance of plans of one sub-unit and the rejection of those submitted by another sub-unit. The decision is made on the basis of which set of plans is in the best interest of the overall or corporate viewpoint. The upward aggregation and integration of the plans developed by the sub-units is a difficult but necessary step of the strategic planning process.

Once divisional plans and forecasts are appraised and evaluated, they are integrated to arrive at the overall current and future corporate picture. A competence profile of the organization is developed which shows the overall strengths and weaknesses of the organization. The individual plans are also used to indicate areas of industry growth potential. In the section of this chapter devoted to the environmental examination we indicated that the environment can provide the firm with opportunities. These opportunities may be seen as being the growth potential of the industry. The potential can be determined by examining aspects of the industry such as its product market structure, life cycle stage and marketing methods. Forecasts are used to determine the pattern of industry trends with respect to market demand, technology and the product market structure. In this manner the industry growth potential is incorporated into the plans and forecasts produced by the organizational sub-units. The revised or internal expansion forecast results from the incorporation of the two factors.

The revised forecast may be illustrated with the aid of the following equation:

REVISED FORECAST	=	Current forecast	+	Analysis of strengths and weaknesses and the determination of potential growth within the firm
(internal expansion forecast)				

The purpose of the revised forecast is to show how much of the gap can be filled by internal expansion. It may be possible that the gap is closed by internal expansion. In this case, the search for alternatives is terminated. If the gap is not closed through internal expansion, external analysis in the form of diversification alternatives will be necessary.

FIGURE 5

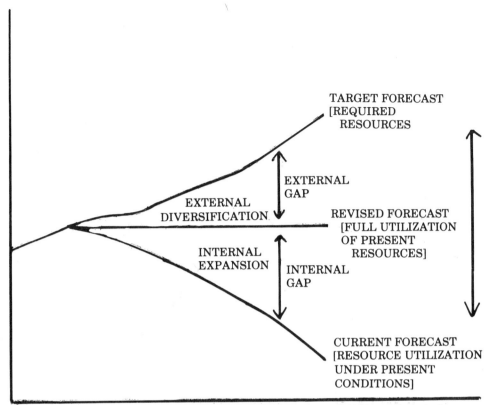

*Interpretation of Diagram by H.I. Ansoff, *Corporate Strategy* (New York: McGraw-Hill, 1965) pp 148. Used with permission of McGraw-Hill Book Company.

External Gap Analysis

An analysis of Figure 5 shows internal expansion partially closing the gap between the current forecast line and the target forecast line. Internal gap analysis is essential in order to determine whether external gap analysis is required. If the revised forecast equals the target, no further examination is necessary. However if this is not the case, then the revised forecast line serves as a basis for determining the magnitude of the external gap or total resources required for diversification.

Resource requirements are illustrated through the following relationship:

TOTAL RESOURCE REQUIREMENTS FOR DIVERSIFICATION (EXTERNAL GAP)	=	TOTAL RESOURCE REQUIREMENTS (TARGET FORECAST)	−	TOTAL RESOURCE REQUIREMENTS FOR INTERNAL EXPANSION (REVISED FORECAST)

The external gap, therefore, shows the shortage of resources which must be overcome to achieve the target within the present resource confines of the organization. Total resources limit both expansion and diversification resources:

TOTAL RESOURCES	=	TOTAL EXPANSION RESOURCES	+	TOTAL DIVERSIFICATION RESOURCES
(TOTAL GAP)		(INTERNAL GAP)		(EXTERNAL GAP)

The decision to pursue some degree of diversification can be related to the question of control of the organization. If additional resources are required, they may be obtainable only at the expense of dilution of control. The degree of dilution of control may be approximated by the magnitude of the external gap. In the case where the gap is small, diversification may be effected with a minimal loss of control. Under the circumstances of a large external gap, the question of control concerns not only the corporate management, but also the owners of the firm, the stockholders.

Gap analysis is employed to narrow the limits in which the strategic (external) search will be conducted. In this manner, gap analysis may be viewed as the preliminary phase to the strategic search. The next step is to decide what can be done about the "gap." This is the strategic search process, which will be discussed in a subsequent chapter.

SUMMARY

Strategic planning may be separated into three stages; development, implementation, and control and appraisal. The developmental stage begins with an examination of the internal and external environment of the organization. This assessment is necessary in order to determine the framework in which the firm can specify its objectives. Forecasting of environmental factors permits the organization to translate its set of objectives into realistic goals or targets which are quantitative and ultimately measurable as indicators of performance. A difference will normally exist between the specification of the target and the performance of the firm if it remains in a status quo position. Specific action must be taken if the target is to be achieved. The firm must seek out means of closing the "gap" between its target and its "if no action taken" projection. This begins the strategic search. The search starts with an examination of what can be done internally to close the gap. The various divisional or product-market sub-units of the organization provide their input into the firm's strategy at this point. The input is then aggregated and evaluated at the corporate level in order to determine what can be done within the context of the present organization to close the gap. The internal analysis of alternatives is now complete. If the target still cannot be reached, the analysis continues with an examination of alternatives outside the limits of the present organization. In this manner, external alternatives are added to the list of means available to the firm to close the gap.

ENDNOTES

1. R.L. Ackoff, *A Concept of Corporate Planning* (New York: Wiley Interscience, 1970) p.24.
2. H.I. Ansoff, *Corporate Strategy* (New York: McGraw-Hill, 1965) p.40.
3. John Argenti, *Corporate Planning* (London: I. Nelson & Sons, 1974), p32.
4. *Ibid.,* p33.
5. Ansoff, *op. cit.,* p.43.
6. Ackoff, *op. cit.,* p.6-20.
7. Ansoff, *op. cit.,* p.148.
8. *Loc. Cit.,* The diagrams have been adapted and modified.

CASE

COTTAGE GARDENS, INC. (A)

The Cottage Gardens, Inc. is a wholesale grower and distributor of shade trees, evergreens, and shrubs. Located in Lansing, Michigan, it serves an area roughly defined as the Midwest. In 1971, it showed a net profit of $14,503 on sales of $1,330,688. For five years, 1967-71, profit as a percent of sales ranged from 0.24 to 1.05. William Hicks, son of the President and currently Shipping and Office Manager, summarized his feelings about the future of the company when he said in June 1972, "I know many things that need to be done, but I don't know where to start."

Company History

The Cottage Gardens nursery was founded in 1923 by Mr. Nick I.W. Kriek, a former Dutch-bulb broker, who took over a neglected nursery and developed it into a viable business. At first he operated as a landscape nurseryman but gradually constructed propagation houses and sold liners as well as landscape material. As the firm grew, valuable expertise was gained in the propagation of trees and evergreens, and by the 1940's the company had developed a reputation for quality plant material. It was among the first (if not the first) to introduce yews into Michigan landscapes. Its 1930 catalogue listed: "New to trade; 'Hicks Yews' 1½ foot plants at $8.00 each." Nick Kriek's basic policy was: "If you can make a profit on an item, sell. Don't hold it for a possible higher price. You may not get it."

In 1946, Mr. Harold Hicks, Nick Kriek's son-in-law, joined the firm. Under the influence of Harold Hicks, who was heavily sales-and volume-oriented, the firm gradually changed from a landscape business to a wholesale grower, or production-agency nursery. It grew in Michigan only those species that could be produced economically there. Most of the plant material was in containers and was "jobbed" to large retail outlets. The company supplied other landscape garden centers with its own plant material or that bought and shipped from other areas of the country.

Compiled and written by Bruce P. Coleman, Graduate School of Business Administration, Michigan State University. This case was prepared as a basis for classroom discussion and not to illustrate either effective or ineffective handling of an administrative situation. All rights reserved by the author.
Distributed by the Intercollegiate Case Clearing House, Soldiers Field, Boston, Mass. 02163. All rights reserved to the contributors. Printed in the U.S.A. Used with permission.

The company continued to expand in that general direction and in 1972 was one of the largest growers and buyers of shade trees in the United States and among the larger growers and distributors of evergreens. In 1969 it added rhododendrons and azaleas to its line. Cottage Gardens serviced its customers by providing "the right plants, at the right time, in the right quantities, and at the right price."

Product and Production

The product line of Cottage Gardens consisted of liners and general nursery stock-shade and ornamental trees, evergreens, and shrubs. The 1972 Fall Wholesale Price List contained 135 different types and varieties of plants. The shade and ornamental trees consisted of maple, birch, crabapple, ash, cork, cherry, oak, and mountain ash. Evergreens and shrubs included juniper, yew, azalea, burning bush, and rhododendron.

Plant material was both grown and purchased by Cottage Gardens. The following table summarizes the estimated percentages of material grown and purchased in 1972.

Type of Plant Material	Percent Grown	Percent Purchased
Shade trees	60	40
Evergreens (including) azaleas, rhododendrons)	90	10
Shrubs	30	70
Liners	0	100

The company was moving toward growing all of the shade trees it sold. It had no tree propagation of its own, but did propagate its evergreens.

In 1972 the company leased 580 acres of land from the owners.[1] Half of the land was under cultivation. The following table summarizes the location and cultivation of the leased farm land.

Location	Acres Leased	Acres Cultivated	Percent Cultivated
Lansing, Michigan	80	80	100
Kemos, Michigan	120	60	50
Copemish, Michigan	240	20	8
Perry, Ohio	140	130	93
Total	580	290	50

Shade trees were grown on the Michigan farms and evergreens on the Ohio farm.

In addition, three companies grew exclusively for Cottage Gardens. Pertinent data are summarized in the table below.

Owner's Name	Location	Size of Farm (Acres)	Acres Cultivated
Milarch	Copemish, Michigan	100	60
Petruska	Perry, Ohio	40	40
Youdath	Perry, Ohio	30	30

As with the leased land, shade trees were grown in Michigan and evergreens in Ohio. These latter farms accounted for about 30 percent of sales. Prices for material grown were set by Cottage Gardens.

---

[1] The land in Ohio was owned by Harold and William Hicks, Jim Sabo, and his assistant. The Michigan land was owned by both Hicks, Ted Myers, and the field supervisor. (See organization chart, Exhibit 1.)

The amount of material planted was based on estimates of demand. These estimates included not only the type of plant material to be grown, but also the number of each for different size requirements. Thus the lead time for planting was one to seven or more years—a short time for evergreens and shrubs, longer for various sizes of trees.

Production operations consisted of planting, growing, and harvesting. The growing season lasts from April to October. Plants were harvested from late March to December, although harvesting could continue through to January. Plants, when harvested, were shipped in one of three forms—potted, bare root, or balled and burlapped. They were then shipped by truck, often in truck load lots.

Weed and insect problems were well controlled through new technology. Two other problems associated with production operations persisted. The first was personnel requirements. These fluctuated from 20 workers in the winter to 150 in spring, 50 in summer, and 150 in fall. The peak demand for personnel occurred during harvesting. The second problem was weather and its effect on harvesting. If there was too much snow, rain, or cold in the spring, harvesting was difficult or impossible. Summer might come too quickly; some plants could not be dug after buds began to sprout leaves.

Sales and Advertising

Although sales growth had been 30 percent during the past five years, and 1971 showed a 10 percent increase in sales over 1970, the growth had now been steady. While 1971 sales were at a record high, the previous two years had shown a decline. (See Exhibit 3.)

Approximately 80 percent of total sales volume was in Michigan, with 10 percent in Ohio, 5 percent in Iowa, and the remainder in Indiana and Illinois and other locations throughout the United States. The three major types of customers were: 1) landscapers, constituting 35 percent of total sales, mainly trees; 2) garden centers (including chain stores), 40 percent of sales, mainly evergreens and shrubs; and 3) municipalities, 25 percent of sales, all shade trees.

Cottage Gardens had about 500 customers (700, if individual stores of chains are counted separately as they were billed). Among its major customers were Frank's Nursery Sales, Inc. (Detroit), Richter's Gardens, Inc. (Lansing), K Mart (Lansing), and Anderson's (Maumee, Ohio). The cities of Chicago and St. Paul were accounts.

The company had three salesmen, five distributors, and four local representatives. Salesmen were paid on a commission basis. They took orders in five midwestern states but concentrated on Michigan. The three sales territories consisted of: Metropolitan Detroit; half of Michigan, and Iowa; and half of Michigan, Illinois, Indiana, and Ohio. The distributors were wholesalers who bought the company's plants for discount (equal to salesmen's commissions) and held the plants for distribution in their respective areas. They also handled non-competing lines of plant material. The local representatives were nurseries in the areas of Detroit, Flint, Saginaw-Bay City, Michigan and Indianapolis. In addition, there were five house accounts.

The company also had a distribution function in Lansing. This consisted of a cash-and-carry arrangement for small orders--over the minimum order size of $300 but too small for shipment. Plants were kept on hand (in inventory) for local landscapers.

Cottage Gardens served as the Michigan representative for several other nurseries. They included Monrovia Nursery Company of Mazusa, California for container-grown plants; Bork Nurseries of Illinois for peatballed plants; and Rhode Island Nursery for yews (18' − 24 + "); and small specialized nurseries. As the representative, Cottage Gardens received a 10 percent commission; half was given to the salesman and half retained by the company.

Prices were set by adding to the current year's prices whatever increase was believed needed to cover projected expenses and still be supported by the market. Cottage Gardens kept a close watch over competitors' prices. Prices were quoted FOB Lansing, but savings were provided the customer for material ordered direct from sources. Quantity discounts were provided. Municipal sales were made on a bid basis. In February 1972, a $50,000 shade tree order for Chicago was won.

Very little advertising was undertaken. Mailing fliers and advertisements in trade magazines constituted the total effort. A very small ad was placed in each issue of *American Nurserymen.* The ad contained the name of the company, address and telephone number, owner's names, and the words, "Shade and Ornamental Trees-Evergreens-Shrubs." A quarter-page ad in the *1972 Michigan Association of Nurserymen Year Book* contained most of the items which appear in the smaller ad but also cited their 49 years of experience, the names of salesmen to contact and the words, "Shade and Ornamental Trees-Evergreens-Rhododendrons-Azaleas-Shrubs." All advertisements contained the logo of a Dutch girl picking tulips.

Organization and Management

The 1972 organization of the Cottage Gardens, Inc. is illustrated in Exhibit 1.

Nick Kriek was Chairman of the Board. Though mostly retired, he signed checks occasionally and took part in such major decisions as the acquisition of land.

The President was Harold Hicks who was primarily responsible for the growth of the company during the last 15 years. William said of his father:

> His philosophy has been to make a profit and keep up with the competition. Most of the time he has succeeded at both. But the problem is he has done this all himself. He has objectives, but they are only in his mind, not explicitly written down. He has just now started to delegate some of his work and responsibilities to his subordinates. He very much enjoys what he is doing but at the same time doesn't get carried away, so he has lots of time to enjoy his family. I think it is fair to say the same of every executive or supervisor working in the company.

The Sales Manager, Gene Ryan, had been working for the company for ten years. He had risen through the ranks to his present position and only recently had started getting the true responsibilities of sales manager delegated to him.

The Shade Tree Manager, Ted Meyers, and the Evergreen Manager, Jim Sabo, had been working for the company for seven years. William stated: "Both have done a good job of building the quantity and quality of products sold in an economical way." Jim Sabo, Ohio Evergreen Manager, was reputed to be one of the best evergreen propagation experts in the nation. He had developed new methods of propagation, new and hardier strains of evergreens, and new methods for growing and protecting plants.

William N. Hicks had the title of Shipping and Office Manager. He received his B.S. degree in Business Administration from Michigan State University in 1972. William had grown up in the company beginning in the field pulling weeds at age 6. He worked during weekends and vacations throughout his schooling and obtained a wide variety of experience in the operations of the firm. He also gained knowledge of the business by going on sales trips, attending association meetings, and visiting competitors. William said: "Even though I have yet to prove myself under year-round, everyday operations, I have done sufficiently well during the Spring rush to be accepted as a fellow executive and future boss. I think the cooperation and coordination among the other executives and myself is very good and we all have a feeling of team effort to bring the company along."

There were about 25 full-time employees which increased to 150 in harvest and shipping times of spring and fall. About half of these reported to Dick Hart, the Ohio Field Supervisor, and half to Tony Pulido, the Michigan Field Supervisor.

Accounting and Finance

A local CPA firm drew up financial statements for the company for income tax purposes. Exhibits 2 and 3 contain consolidated financial statements for the years 1967 through 1971 based upon a year-end date of March 31. Exhibits 4, 5, and 6 contain financial data for the period April 1, 1971 through January 31, 1972 to reflect the change of accounting year-end date in 1972.

Purchases included material that was bought and planted for future sales and material that was bought for resale during the same season. Of the total, about 75 percent was for resale.

Cottage Gardens was classified as an agricultural business. Accounting statements conformed to reporting requirements for firms so classified. While the agricultural classification had certain tax benefits for the company, it placed restrictions upon operations. One such requirement was that the company grow at least fifty percent of what it sold.

EXHIBIT 1

THE COTTAGE GARDENS, INC.

Organization Chart, 1972

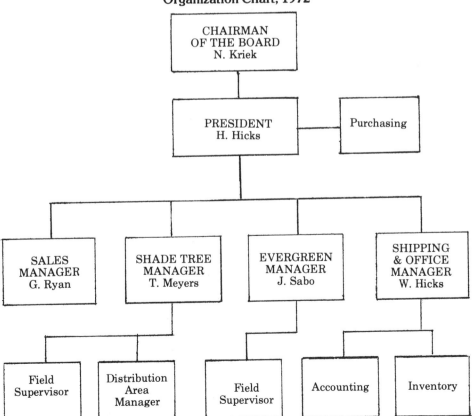

The company did not keep an inventory of nursery stock on hand, either growing or in the warehouses ready for delivery. Those items were considered as a cost of sale or purchased at the time acquired or as a sale when delivered. The result of this practice was that the inventory was not included in any annual balance sheets. The physical inventory of all nursery stock, at wholesale prices, taken by the management, was $1,212,290 as of March 31, 1971, and $1,928,728 as of January 31, 1972. This included saleable and non-saleable stock at all farms.

Exhibits 7-11 are excerpts from an Operating Cost Study conducted by the Horticulture Research Institute. Exhibits 7-9 provide data for all 51 reporting wholesale nurseries. Of those companies, ten had sales of under $200,000; 19 had sales of $200,000 to $499,999; and 22 had sales of over $500,000. Exhibits 10 and 11 provide operating cost data reported by the larger firms. In exhibits 10-11 the "lower, median, and higher cost" percentages are not averages; they are actual costs of a particular company in an array of the total. They define quartiles. One fourth of the companies had costs below the lower cost figure, one fourth had costs above the higher cost figure, etc. Furthermore, in utilizing the data for comparative analysis, costs must be compared on a line-by-line basis. Not every firm in the study reported all costs; thus each item was treated separately. Adding columns will not equal the total shown except by coincidence.

Ownership of the corporation in 1972 was held by three individuals: Harold Hicks (79 percent), Nick Kriek (20 percent), and Eugene Ryan (1 percent).

Association Activities

The company maintained memberships in the American Association of Nurserymen (AAN) and the Michigan Association of Nurserymen (MAN). The AAN is very active in lobbying, conducting research, sponsoring management seminars, monitoring legislation and other activities related to nursery operation, and in disseminating information through pamphlets, research reports, and its bi-monthly publication, *American Nurseryman.* This latter publication contains a wealth of information related to association activities, research, marketing, advertising, pricing, and production.

Company personnel had been or were active in the MAN. For example, Nick Kriek was Secretary-Treasurer in 1932-33 and Harold Hicks was President in 1959. In 1972, Gene Ryan and Harold Hicks were on several MAN Committees, Gene Ryan was a representative to the MAN Board of Directors, and Ted Meyers was Secretary-Treasurer of the Central Michigan Landscape & Nurseryman Association. The stated purpose of MAN was:

> To unite the Nurserymen of the State of Michigan for mutual benefit, protection, and improvement in their business.
>
> To encourage among the members a closer personal acquaintance and a friendly spirit of cooperation.
>
> To gather, receive and disseminate such information, with respect to the nursery and allied business, as may seem helpful to the members.
>
> To forward and promote the general welfare and prosperity of the members, and to attain and maintain a high standard of business ethics in all dealings with the public.
>
> To cooperate with all governmental agencies, both legislative and administrative, and to assist in the furtherance of all commendable horticultural developments.

Competition

Competition in the nursery business was characterized by many small firms in a region and by a few large ones. William Hicks made this observation:

> We have four or five major competitors in the Midwest and thousands of minor competitors who raise plants for their local area. The competition is very keen among the major competitors and this keenness of competition has led to no cooperation among companies. There are no figures on total sales in the U.S. or any other figures to help the individual companies see where they stand.

Principal competitors identified by William are listed in the following table. Also provided are the location and product lines of each company. Sales information is not available.

Name	Location	Product Line
Horton Nurseries	Madison, Ohio	Evergreens, shrubs
Cole Nurseries	Circleville, Ohio	Shade trees
Manbeck Nurseries	Dayton, Ohio	Shade trees
Wandell's Nurseries	Urbana, Illinois	Shade trees
Northland Evergreen Co.	Monroe, Michigan	Evergreens, shrubs
Zelenka Nursery Co.	Grand Haven, Michigan	Evergreens, shrubs

Industry Trends

A number of trends in the American nursery industry were identified in issues of the *American Nurseryman* throughout 1971. Summarized they were:

1. Because of the rising income level, the landscaping business will continue to boom.
2. Specialized landscaping will evolve because of the increase in townhouses, apartments, mobile homes, etc. in such forms as roof gardens and container planted balconies.
3. The continued concern for the beautification of the environment will transfer the nursery industry's products from the luxury category to that of a basic commodity.
4. More and more cities are passing "landscape ordinances," i.e., public housing such as townhouses and apartments as well as business offices must be landscaped.
5. Chain and department stores that sell plants and garden supplies only in the Spring for promotion will, in the future, either discontinue those sales altogether or elevate the status of the garden department to a year-round operation.
6. The chain-garden center, e.g., Franks, will become the major marketing vehicle for nursery products.
7. The historical mail-order type nursery is on the decline.
8. Assembly-line landscaping will be the mode of production in the future. Small growers will grow their specialities up to a certain size and ship them to regional interim growers who will assemble the entire range of plants suitable for an area. The interim growers will then grow the plants to a larger size and be geared to efficient distribution and installation.

The Future

William Hicks commented on several problems which he saw in the operations of the company.

> The present bookkeeping system puts out a statement for the entire company and leaves it at that. We have no idea which divi-

sion is doing best or worst. We have an idea that the distribution area is losing money but we have no way of knowing for sure. Therefore, a new accounting system (I hope to have it underway in a year or two) is needed that will break down the accounts according to divisions to give us much of the basic information we need to guide the company. The costs, sales, and contributions to profits of each division would aid us greatly in making decisions. Along with the accounting system, some advice on our financing is badly needed. Not being a financing expert, I don't know what we could do, but I do know that we borrow several hundred thousand dollars each year from the bank. There is a good possibility of either cutting this sum down through good financial planning or obtaining loans somewhere else. This part of the business has never been touched upon because there are many other problems closer to the day-to-day operations that need attention.

A cost analysis system is needed to support a pricing policy. At present, price is obtained by adjusting our price to the prices in the general market. We make a small attempt to include costs but the real costs are so unknown that nothing that even approaches accuracy can be obtained. For this reason I have stressed getting a cost analysis system in use that is simple yet elaborate enough to give us some costs that are at least close to the real cost of the plant. A true cost would be very hard to obtain because of the thousands of variables that are in play when a plant takes 5 to 10 years to grow. But I'm sure that some usable figures could be arrived at through careful and consistent analysis. These figures could then be applied toward a pricing policy that would be much more realistic in covering costs. It has been shown through simple cost analysis that large volumes of plants have been sold at a loss while it was believed a profit was being made.

A third area that needs investigating is sales. We presently sell to anyone who has good credit (or cash) and who wants to buy our products. I think an analysis of our customers should be made. We need to investigate the potential of each customer especially the larger ones to see if we can capitalize more on our opportunities. Also, we need to drop several small customers that cost us more than they are worth (or at least we should set up a special system or better-operated division for them). I think a crucial decision must be reached in the near future on whether we are going to try to service the large retail chain stores or the landscapers and cities, or expand enough to supply both. The latter is what we are trying to do now, but we will have to grow at a much faster pace if we intend to keep up.

In commenting on the basic direction of the company, William made these observations.

To start with we need to sit down and study where our competitive advantages lie. We have started in that direction by specializing in shade trees and evergreens, but a little more in-depth study may show a few surprises.

Once we have decided where our emphasis will be, we must set some definite objectives—objectives that can and will be reviewed each year. These objectives should be things like a 10 percent increase in profits, or a 10 percent decrease in costs, and other attainable goals.

Strategies need to be set. Questions should be asked like: Are we going to meet our competition head on or should we take up the slack they leave? I think in our case we can beat them at head-on-head competition, so now we must decide how to do it. Our strategy or plan of attack should be mapped out very carefully with every step and implementation of steps carefully thought out. Since nothing like this has ever been done before, I think our strategies should be built with extreme care yet must remain very flexible so that they can be changed to fit our needs. I don't want to get very specific about the strategies we should take because I think this is something we must all consider and meet about several times.

Finally, in reflecting on the organization and his future in the company, he had this to say:

The organization structure has just recently been changed to accommodate me and the new responsibilities that have been given to the other managers. I also expect it will keep changing rapidly in the future for two reasons. One is that, because the company is so small, it is easy to change the structure without really affecting the variables involved too much. The other is to accommodate my (hopefully) rapid advancement up through the company. At first I thought my advancement would create many personnel conflicts and problems throughout the company, but so far this advancement has been expected by all. Two of my co-executives seem to be supporting me very strongly. They say they are very happy with their positions and the opportunities they see for themselves. I would like to think that they are encouraging me because I have proven myself with my present accomplishments, but this seems unbelievable to me. So while they are encouraging my rapid advancement, I am trying to slow things down so that I don't extend myself and my experience. It becomes very confusing at times.

Exhibit 2
THE COTTAGE GARDENS, INC.

Consolidated Balance Sheets, 1968-71, Years Ending March 31

ASSETS	1971	1970	1969	1968
Current Assets				
Imprest Cash	$ 700	$ 700	$ 700	$ 700
Cash in Bank	7,223	7,864	12,448	782
Accounts Receivable	203,983	163,109	207,040	169,816
Notes Receivable	3,150			
Less Allowance for				
Doubtful Accounts	1,510	1,179	2,117	3,431
Employee Advances	918			421
Bid Deposits	6,901	3,971	3,601	2,626
Inventory-Supplies	6,920	3,513	4,557	9,451
Total Current Assets	$228,285	$177,978	$226,229	$180,365
Fixed Assets				
Machinery and Equipment	110,999	100,224	90,545	93,943
Furniture and Fixtures	3,819	3,125	3,012	2,405
Autos and Trucks	36,934	35,770	30,940	20,480
Yard Improvements	473	473	473	473
Less: Allowance for				
Depreciation	103,785	92,795	76,283	67,206
Total Fixed Assets	$ 48,440	$ 46,797	$ 48,688	$ 50,095
Other Assets				
Lake Geneva Lot (At Cost)	1,888	1,823	1,823	1,823
Total Assets	$278,612	$226,598	$276,740	$232,283
LIABILITIES AND STOCKHOLDERS EQUITY				
Current Liabilities				
Accounts Payable	$ 74,437	$ 13,781	$ 36,205	$ 63,846
Accounts Receivable-				
Credit Balance			21,062	
Notes Payable	147,450	147,181	161,681	112,885
Employee Advances		67	40	
Employee Savings	4,553	13,736	6,513	5,816
Employer Insurance				
Deductions	38	358	189	36
Accrued Social Security				
Taxes	1,400	1,014	1,049	
Accrued Interest Payable	734	460		
Total Current Liabilities	$228,612	$176,597	$226,740	$182,583
Stockholders Equity				
Common Stock-Par Value $10 per Share				
Authorized and Issued				
5,000 Shares	50,000	50,000	50,000	50,000
Total Liabilities				
and Equity	$278,612	$226,598	$276,740	$232,583

Source: Company Annual Reports, 1968-1971

Exhibit 3
THE COTTAGE GARDENS, INC.

Income Statements 1967-1971, Years Ending March 31

	1971 Dollars	%	1970 Dollars	%	1969 Dollars	%	1968 Dollars	%	1967 Dollars	%
Sales of Nursery Stock										
In Michigan	$ 988,524	74.3	$ 941,077	78.0	956,800	76.1	$1,045,869	79.5	$ 848,426	83.5
Outside Michigan	343,694	25.8	274,536	22.7	310,507	24.7	278,449	21.2	178,448	17.6
Total Sales	$1,332,218	100.1	$1,215,613	100.7	$1,267,307	100.8	$1,324,318	100.7	$1,026,874	101.1
Less Discounts Allowed	1,530	.1	8,939	.7	9,977	.8	9,316	.7	10,812	1.1
Net Sales	$1,330,688	100.0	$1,206,674	100.0	$1,257,330	100.0	$1,315,002	100.0	$1,016,062	100.0
Expenses										
Purchases (Net)	$ 717,336	53.9	$ 644,420	53.4	$ 697,051	55.4	$ 585,348	44.5	$ 466,653	46.0
Salaries-Administration	39,987	3.0	39,785	3.3	41,230	3.3	39,973	3.0	37,287	3.6
Salaries-Office	26,925	2.0	27,591	2.3	26,980	2.1	25,641	1.9	18,296	1.8
Salaries & Wages-Operations	253,800	19.1	241,305	20.0	260,089	20.7	329,981	25.2	224,475	22.0
Commissions	29,691	2.2	29,729	2.5	17,491	1.4	24,752	1.9	11,720	1.2
Advertising	5,165	.4	6,915	.6	4,941	.4	3,375	.3	4,395	.4
Bad Debts	1,775	.1	976	.1	0	-	1,361	.1	417	-
Depreciation	13,129	1.0	16,512	1.4	14,014	1.1	16,626	1.3	11,563	1.2
Donations	1,605	.1	280	-	371	-	84	-	52	-
Dues & Subscriptions	1,678	.1	1,619	.1	1,570	.1	1,661	.1	1,410	.1
Electricity & Water	2,237	.2	1,767	.1	1,577	.1	1,826	.1	1,256	.1
Freight In	57,041	4.3	50,167	4.2	52,216	4.1	69,134	5.4	62,306	6.1
Freight Out	9,121	.7	10,866	.9	(3,998)	(.3)	26,654	2.0	23,851	2.4
Fuel Heat	1,823	.1	1,479	.1	1,412	.1	740		2,071	.2
Insurance	4,920	.4	8,063	.7	9,562	.8	14,795	1.1	10,434	1.0
Insurance-Employee Benefits	1,353	.1	1,285	.1	1,249	.1	1,346	.1	1,161	.1
Interest	6,745	.5	4,103	.3	6,218	.5	1,641	.1	2,693	.3
Legal and Audit	2,468	.2	2,277	.2	2,467	.2	1,305	.1	1,105	.1
Rents	31,758	2.4	9,880	.8	20,245	1.6	18,395	1.4	14,303	1.4
Maintenance & Repair	34,223	2.7	36,213	2.9	40,282	3.3	63,349	4.8	41,238	4.1
Mileage and Auto	5,007	.4	4,992	.4	5,774	.5	4,454	.3	3,048	.3
Supplies-Office	3,572	.3	2,699	.2	3,373	.3	2,950	.2	3,102	.3
Supplies-Operations	57,200	4.3	52,097	4.3	47,039	3.8	56,835	4.3	56,004	5.6
Small Tools	1,330	.1	1,064	.1	1,442	.1	1,888	.1	1,551	.1
Taxes	25,958	1.9	25,654	2.1	25,679	2.1	25,646	1.9	20,421	2.0
Telephone & Telegraph	7,805	.6	8,252	.7	7,155	.6	6,523	.6	5,093	.5
Travel	5,970	.4	6,017	.5	6,541	.5	5,717	.4	4,443	.4
Miscellaneous	1,848	.1	2,964	.2	2,406	.2	11,712	1.0	2,651	.3
Customer Relations	3,021	.2	3,374	.3	3,080	.2	1,901	.1	1,861	.2
Collection Costs	732	.1	149	-	710	-	0	-	-	-
Labor Not on Payroll	11,536	.9	1,587	.1	-	-	-	-	-	-
Employees' Retirement Plan	7,801	.6	8,374	.7	-	-	-	-	-	-
Total Expenses	$1,375,565	103.4	$1,250,458	103.6	$1,298,449	103.3	$1,345,618	102.3	$1,035,862	102.0
Excess of Net Sales over Expenses	$ (44,877)	(3.4)	$ (43,784)	(3.6)	$ (41,119)	(3.3)	$ (30,616)	(2.3)	$ (19,800)	(2.0)
Other Income										
Interest Income	5,445	.4	4,155	.3	2,500	.2	2,803	.2	4,112	.4
Miscellaneous	106	-	110	-	729	-	413	-	96	-
Over and Short	(70)	-	(5)	-	-	-	10	-	2	-
Sales Commissions	53,290	4.0	50,218	4.2	40,418	3.3	36,638	2.8	15,895	1.6
Rent Received	600	.1	610	-	430	-	190	-	0	-
Total Other Income	$ 59,381	4.5	$ 55,088	4.5	$ 44,077	3.5	$ 40,054	3.0	$ 30,605	3.1
Net Income	$ 14,504	1.1	$ 11,304	.9	$ 2,958	.2	$ 9,438	.7	$ 10,805	1.1

*Add: Damages-State Highway Dept.-$10,500.
Source: Company Annual Reports, 1967-71.

Exhibit 4
THE COTTAGE GARDENS, INC.

Balance Sheet
January 31, 1972

ASSETS

CURRENT ASSETS			
Imprest Cash			$ 700.00
Cash in Bank			11,408.68
Accounts Receivable-Customer	$ 76,977.96		
Accounts Receivable-Employees	1,638.74		
Notes Receivable	2,650.00	$81,266.70	
LESS Allowance for Doubtful Accounts		815.97	80,450.73
Land Contract Receivable			
(Due Within One Year)			144.00
Bid Deposits			3,383.50
Inventory-Supplies			8,102.75
Prepayments			20,846.19
TOTAL CURRENT ASSETS			$125,035.85

FIXED ASSETS	COST	ACCUM. DEPREC.	COST LESS DEPREC.	
Machinery & Equipment	$110,715.22	$ 77,382.90	$33,332.32	
Furniture & Fixtures	3,818.65	2,369.24	1,449.41	
Autos & Trucks	36,794.28	28,279.14	8,515.14	
Yard Improvements	473.50	188.72	284.78	
	$151,801.65	$108,220.00		43,581.65

OTHER ASSETS		
Land Contract Receivable		
(Due After One Year)		2,211.62
		$170,829.12

LIABILITIES

CURRENT LIABILITIES		
Accounts Payable		$ 16,224.99
Notes Payable:		
Michigan National Bank	$55,938.28	
N.I.W. Kriek	2,900.78	
H.E. Hicks	30,329.23	89,168.29
Employee Savings		2,285.06
Accrued Social Security Tax		875.46
Accrued Interest		400.13
Employee Insurance		504.37
TOTAL CURRENT LIABILITIES		$109,458.30

STOCKHOLDERS' EQUITY		
Common Stock-Par Value $10.00 Per Share		
Authorized & Issued 5,000 Shares	$50,000.00	
Shareholders' Undistributed		
Taxable Income	11,370.82	61,370.82
		$170,829.12

Source: Company records.

Exhibit 5
THE COTTAGE GARDENS, INC.

Statement of Income
April 1, 1971 to January 31, 1972

	MICHIGAN	OHIO	TOTAL	% OF SALES
SALES				
In Michigan	$657,580.64	$260,653.90	$ 918,234.54	80.9
Outside of Michigan	217,320.65		217,320.65	19.2
Inter-Department	37,722.50	37,722.50	-0-	
TOTAL SALES	$837,178.79	$298,376.40	$1,135,555.19	100.1
LESS Discounts Allowed	1,031.14	-0-	1,031.14	.1
NET SALES	$836,147.65	$298,376.40	$1,134,524.05	100.0
COST OF SALES (See Schedule)	757,037.50	272,106.02	1,029,143.52	90.7
GROSS PROFIT ON SALES	$ 79,110.15	$ 26,270.38	$ 105,380.53	9.3
COMMISSIONS ON DIRECT SHIPMENTS	47,994.53	-0-	47,994.53	4.2
GROSS INCOME	$127,104.68	$ 26,270.38	$ 153,375.06	13.5
2 GENERAL EXPENSES				
Salaries-Administrative	$ 24,062.98	$ 7,187.64*	$ 31,250.62	2.8
Salaries-Office	21,890.87	6,538.83*	28,429.70	2.5
Commissions	26,995.72	8,063.66*	35,059.38	3.2
Advertising	2,602.12	777.26*	3,379.38	.3
Bad Debts	2,358.47		2,358.47	.2
Depreciation	656.81		656.81	.1
Donations	1,291.85		1,291.85	.1
Dues & Subscriptions	1,507.00	20.00	1,527.00	.1
Electricity & Water	148.24	41.74	189.98	-
Fuel	279.58	57.38	336.96	-
Insurance	538.79		538.79	-
Insurance-Employee Benefits	197.52	24.48	222.00	-
Interest	5,592.63	1,670.53*	7,263.16	.6
Legal & Auditing	2,280.00		2,280.00	.2
Employee Retirement Plan	3,185.45	68.19	3,253.64	.3
Rent	3,240.00		3,240.00	.3
Mileage & Auto Expense	2,191.48		2,191.48	.2
Office Supplies	2,936.51		2,936.51	.3
Taxes	5,599.37		5,614.89	.5
Telephone	5,168.79	627.76	5,796.55	.5
Travel Expenses	2,808.93	196.93	3,005.91	.3
Miscellaneous Expense	1,297.38	624.78	1,922.16	.2
Cash Over & Short	2,380.26	66.30	2,446.56	.2
Collection Expense	254.98		254.98	-
TOTAL GENERAL EXPENSES	$119,482.92	$ 25,980.98	$ 145,463.90	12.8
NET OPERATING INCOME	$ 7,621.76	$ 289.40	$ 7,911.16	.7
OTHER INCOME				
Interest	$ 1,449.65		$ 1,449.65	.1
Miscellaneous	1,410.01		1,410.01	.1
Rent	600.00		600.00	.1
	$ 3,459.66		$ 3,459.66	.3
NET INCOME FOR THE PERIOD	$ 11,081.42	$ 289.40	$ 11,370.82	1.0

* Expense allocated to Ohio on a sales ratio (23 percent).

Source: Company records.

Exhibit 6
THE COTTAGE GARDENS, INC.

Schedule of Cost of Sales
April 1, 1971 to January 31, 1972

	MICHIGAN	OHIO	TOTAL	% OF SALES
PURCHASES	$503,584.15	$ 89,186.72	$ 592,770.87	52.2
DIRECT EXPENSES				
Salaries & Wages-Administrative	-0-	16,140.00	16,140.00	1.4
Salaries & Wages	149,058.67	86,150.43	235,209.10	20.8
Contract Work	478.15	1,290.00	1,768.15	.2
Depreciation	7,265.21	3,579.58	10,844.79	1.0
Electricity & Water	1,334.15	375.63	1,709.78	.2
Freight In	17,143.20	4,194.10	21,337.30	1.9
Freight Out	1,841.43		1,841.43	.2
Fuel		516.40	516.40	-
Insurance	4,849.15	1,373.78	6,222.93	.5
Insurance-Employee Benefits	790.08	97.92	888.00	.1
Employer Retirement Plan	351.89	57.30	409.19	-
Rent	3,960.00	2,760.00	6,720.00	.6
Maintenance & Repairs-Bldg. & Grounds	608.27	1,695.84	2,304.11	.2
Maintenance & Repairs-Machinery & Equipment	30,130.09	4,853.21	34,983.30	3.1
Maintenance & Repairs-Trucks	8,301.94	2,015.20	10,317.14	.9
Mileage & Auto Expense	2,604.16		2,604.16	.2
Small Tools	420.57	972.70	1,393.27	.1
Supplies-Operations	16,618.54	49,192.24	65,810.78	5.8
Taxes-Social Security	6,560.67	5,167.39	11,728.06	1.0
Travel Expenses	1,137.18		1,137.18	.1
Taxes-Property		2,487.58	2,487.58	.2
TOTAL COST OF SALES	$757,037.50	$272,106.02	$1,029,143.52	90.1

Source: Company records.

Exhibit 7
THE COTTAGE GARDENS, INC.

Annual Trends-Wholesale Nurseries*
(All Data Shown Are Medium Figures)

I. PERCENTAGE OF ANNUAL SALES BY MONTH

	JAN	FEB	MAR	APR	MAY	JUN	JUL	AUG	SEP	OCT	NOV	DEC
1968	3.4	6.4	16.0	26.3	13.9	5.2	3.7	4.1	5.7	6.2	6.0	3.1
1969	5.3	6.7	12.8	24.8	14.5	4.7	3.6	4.2	6.0	6.2	6.8	4.4
1970	4.4	6.6	17.0	23.4	13.0	5.1	3.4	3.8	5.4	7.1	6.6	4.2
1971	3.9	6.0	14.9	26.0	13.0	5.4	3.0	3.7	6.3	6.4	7.2	4.2

II. OPERATING COST HIGHLIGHTS

	1967	1968	1969	1970	1971
Total Cost of Goods Sold	67.0%	64.7%	59.3%	67.5%	67.7%
Storage, Maintenance, Packaging & Shipping Costs	8.4%	7.8%	11.2%	7.8%	8.4%
Selling Expenses	3.7%	3.9%	3.4%	2.8%	3.7%
Administrative Expenses	14.2%	13.4%	13.0%	12.3%	14.3%
Net Profit Before Taxes	7.1%	7.1%	6.5%	3.8%	3.2%

III. COMPARATIVE HIGHLIGHTS

	1967	1968	1969	1970	1971
Bad Debt Losses	.6%	.6%	.7%	.1%	1.0%
Pension & Benefit Costs	1.7%	2.0%	1.7%	2.0%	1.9%
Full Time Employees	22	18	18	20	21
Sales Per Acre	$1,287	$2,059	$1,450	$1,691	$1,735
Sales Per Full Time Employee	$16,001	$19,554	$20,842	$18,276	$21,265
Net Profit To Total Net Worth	10.0%	10.7%	12.3%	17.4%	12.6%
Net Profit To Net Working Capital	21.4%	14.0%	21.0%	23.7%	15.4%

IV. NET PROFIT BEFORE TAXES-By Volume

	1967	1968	1969	1970	1971
All Companies	7.1%	7.1%	6.5%	3.8%	3.2%
Under $200,000	8.7%	7.2%	7.7%	1.2%	5.0%
$200,000 to $499,999	7.2%	6.0%	12.4%	2.6%	2.8%
Over $500,000	4.6%	7.2%	6.2%	8.3%	4.9%

* Based on a study of 51 companies.

Source: Horticultural Research Institute, Inc., *Research Summary: Operating Cost Study*. Washington, DC, 1972, p. 5. Used with permission.

Exhibit 8
THE COTTAGE GARDENS, INC.

1971 Operating Cost Date-Wholesale-All Companies

	PERCENT OF TOTAL SALES		
	Lower Cost	Median Cost	Higher Cost
1. *SALES*			
1a Plant Materials Produced	85.4	98.0	100.0
1b Plant Materials Purchased & Resold	2.3	14.0	27.0
1c Hard Goods	.2	.7	1.0
1d Other	1.4	3.0	6.2
2. *DIRECT COSTS*			
2a Direct Production Labor	24.1	32.1	39.8
2b Nursery Stock	5.7	8.5	12.0
2c Fertilizers, Herbicides, etc.	1.3	1.9	3.5
2d Production Equipment & Supplies	6.1	9.4	13.0
2e Production Facilities	4.4	6.5	11.2
2f Research & Breeding	.2	.5	.9
2g Total Cost of Materials Produced	49.6	58.5	70.8
2h Cost of Plant Material Purchased For Resale	2.0	12.0	27.7
2i Cost of Hard Goods	.2	.5	.9
2j Cost of Other Sales	1.5	2.3	3.2
2k TOTAL COST OF GOODS SOLD	55.8	67.7	75.6
3. *GROSS PROFITS ON SALES*			
3a From Plant Materials Produced	40.0	30.4	21.2
3b From Plants Purchased & Resold	9.6	4.0	.6
3c From Hard Goods	.3	.2	.2
3d From Other	4.0	1.4	.5
3e TOTAL GROSS PROFIT ON SALES	44.2	31.7	24.3
4. *STORAGE, MAINTENANCE, PACKAGING, SHIPPING*			
4a Direct Labor-Storing & Maintaining	.7	2.6	5.8
4b Direct Labor-Packaging & Shipping	1.9	5.5	9.2
4c Total Direct Labor	3.3	6.0	15.4
4d Packaging & Shipping Supplies	.8	2.1	4.0
4e Other Costs	1.3	2.4	5.6
4f TOTAL STORAGE, MAINTENANCE, PACKAGING, SHIPPING	3.5	8.4	17.5
5. *SELLING EXPENSES*			
5a Salesmen Compensation & Expenses	.9	2.5	4.6
5b Direct Mail	.3	.4	1.1
5c Space Advertising	.2	.5	1.2
5d Promotion	.3	.5	1.2
5e Other	.4	.8	1.6
5f TOTAL SELLING EXPENSES	1.5	3.7	5.7
6. *ADMINISTRATIVE EXPENSES*			
6a Managerial	86.2	8.3	12.2
6b Office & Administrative	1.9	3.8	5.7
6cGeneral	.7	1.4	4.8
6d TOTAL ADMINISTRATIVE EXPENSES	10.2	14.3	18.4
7. *TOTAL STORAGE, MAINTENANCE, PACKAGING, SHIPPING, SELLING & ADMINISTRATIVE*	15.9	28.5	36.2
8. *NET PROFIT ON WHOLESALE OPERATIONS*	9.7	3.8	(- .9)
9. *OTHER WHOLESALE INCOME*	2.3	.7	.4
10.*OTHER WHOLESALE EXPENSE*	1.1	2.4	3.5
11.*NET PROFIT BEFORE TAXES*	8.9	3.2	(-1.2)

Source: Horticultural Research Institute, Inc., Research Summary: *Operating Cost Study.* Washington, D.C., 1972, p. 6. Used with permission.

Exhibit 9
THE COTTAGE GARDENS, INC.

1971 Operating Cost Data-Wholesale-All Companies

	Lower Cost	Median Cost	Higher Cost
A. BAD DEBT LOSSES	.2%	1.0%	1.0%
B. ALLOWANCES FOR DEPRECIATION	1.8%	3.5%	4.6%
C. PENSION & BENEFIT COSTS	.7%	1.9%	5.0%
D. FULL TIME EMPLOYEES	7	21	42
E. PART-TIME EMPLOYEES	1	6	17
F. SEASONAL EMPLOYEES	11	30	70
G. SALES PER FULL TIME EMPLOYEE	$32,138	$21,265	$12,700
H. SALES PER ACRE	$ 4,943	$ 1,735	$ 1,137
I. NET PROFIT BEFORE TAXES TO TOTAL NET WORTH	34.9%	12.6%	4.3%
J. NET SALES TO NET WORTH	321.6 Times	80.0 Times	14.5 Times
K. NET PROFIT BEFORE TAXES TO NET WORKING CAPITAL	57.5%	15.4%	5.0%
L. CURRENT RATIO	125.2 to 1	38.6 to 1	2.0 to 1

Source: Horticultural Research Institute, Inc., *Research Summary: Operating Cost Study*. Washington, DC, 1972, p. 7. Used with permission.

Exhibit 10
THE COTTAGE GARDENS, INC.

1971 Operating Cost Data-Wholesale Companies-
Sales Over $500,000

	PERCENT OF TOTAL SALES		
	Lower Cost	Median Cost	Higher Cost
1. SALES			
1a Plant Materials Produced	95.3	99.3	100.0
1b Plant Materials Purchased & Resold	.6	2.0	27.0
1c Hard Goods	*	.5	*
1d Other	*	*	*
2. DIRECT COSTS			
2a Direct Production Labor	22.7	31.7	39.8
2b Nursery Stock	1.7	3.2	8.3
2c Fertilizers, Herbicides, etc.	1.5	2.3	3.5
2d Production Equipment & Supplies	4.8	8.9	11.5
2e Production Facilities	3.7	5.5	10.8
2f Research & Breeding	*	*	*
2g Total Cost of Materials Produced	44.6	56.2	67.7
2h Cost of Plant Material Purchased For Resale	.5	1.7	17.6
2i Cost of Hard Goods	*	.5	*
2j Cost of Other Sales	*	*	*
2k TOTAL COST OF GOODS SOLD	49.4	62.6	73.0
3. GROSS PROFITS ON SALES			
3a From Plant Materials Produced	49.6	35.1	23.4
3b From Plants Purchased & Resold	5.3	.8	.5
3c From Hard Goods	*	*	*
3d From Other	*	*	*
3e TOTAL GROSS PROFIT ON SALES	50.6	37.4	27.0
4. STORAGE, MAINTENANCE, PACKAGING, SHIPPING			
4a Direct Labor-Storing & Maintaining	1.4	2.7	4.6
4b Direct Labor-Packaging & Shipping	1.2	4.6	14.5
4c Total Direct Labor	2.2	6.8	16.8
4d Packaging & Shipping Supplies	.6	1.7	2.8
4e Other Costs	.4	2.4	6.8
4f TOTAL STORAGE, MAINTENANCE, PACKAGING, SHIPPING	3.3	14.4	22.2
5. SELLING EXPENSES			
5a Salesmen Compensation & Expenses	.8	3.4	5.4
5b Direct Mail	.2	.3	.8
5c Space Advertising	.2	.4	.9
5d Promotion	.2	.6	.9
5e Other	.3	.8	1.8
5f TOTAL SELLING EXPENSES	1.0	4.9	6.6
6. ADMINISTRATIVE EXPENSES			
6a Managerial	5.0	6.5	10.4
6b Office & Administrative	2.1	3.8	5.5
6c General	.6	1.2	5.9
7. TOTAL STORAGE, MAINTENANCE, PACKAGING, SHIPPING, SELLING & ADMINISTRATIVE EXPENSES	20.7	28.5	38.0
8. NET PROFIT ON WHOLESALE OPERATIONS	12.3	5.1	.2
9. OTHER WHOLESALE INCOME	4.8	1.3	.6
10. OTHER WHOLESALE EXPENSE	.6	2.6	4.8
11. NET PROFIT BEFORE TAXES	9.7	4.9	.2

* Insufficent data.

Source: Horticultural Research Institute, Inc., *Research Summary: Operating Cost Study*. Washington, DC, 1972, p. 12. Used with permission.

Exhibit 11
THE COTTAGE GARDENS, INC.

1971 Operating Cost Data-Wholesale Companies-
Sales Over $500,000

	Lower Cost	Median Cost	Higher Cost
A. BAD DEBT LOSSES	.2%	.8%	1.1%
B. ALLOWANCES FOR DEPRECIATION	1.4%	3.0%	3.9%
C. PENSION & BENEFIT COSTS	.9%	1.8%	4.1%
D. FULL TIME EMPLOYEES	28	46	70
E. PART-TIME EMPLOYEES	2	8	25
F. SEASONAL EMPLOYEES	50	67	100
G. SALES PER FULL TIME EMPLOYEE	$31,255	$18,230	$12,804
H. SALES PER ACRE	$ 2,804	$ 1,632	$ 1,137
I. NET PROFIT BEFORE TAXES TO TOTAL NET WORTH	23.9%	9.5%	1.8%
J. NET SALES TO NET WORTH	100.0 Times	56.0 Times	16.5 Times
K. NET PROFIT BEFORE TAXES TO NET WORKING CAPITAL	17.6%	8.5%	3.0%
L. CURRENT RATIO	68.5% To 1	19.3 To 1	2.5 To 1

M. PERCENTAGE OF ANNUAL SALES:

JAN	FEB	MAR	APR	MAY	JUN	JUL	AUG	SEP	OCT	NOV	DEC
4.2%	6.3%	15.5%	26.1%	13.4%	5.2%	2.9%	3.8%	6.3%	6.2%	6.4%	3.7%

Source: Horticultural Research Institute, Inc., *Research Summary: Operating Cost Study.* Washington, DC, 1972, p. 13. Used with permission.

Evaluation of the COTTAGE GARDENS (A) Case

SUMMARY

This case deals with a wholesale grower and distributor of shade trees, evergreens, and shrubs, in the Midwest. The company has grown to be one of the largest growers and buyers of shade trees in the United States. About one half of company owned land is under cultivation. Three outside companies grow exclusively for Cottage Gardens. For a number of years, however, the company has shown a very low profit as a percent of sales.

KEY ISSUES

1. Are goals and objectives adequately defined?
2. Are profits a goal of the owners/managers?
3. Are there methods to assure goal congruency, motivation, and incentive throughout the organization?
4. Is there a need for a tighter control and information feedback system to determine how much each division and subgroup is doing?
5. Are price-setting methods optimal?
6. Are accounting procedures adequate and consistent? Should most bookkeeping and financial reporting be handled internally?
7. Should unprofitable aspects of the operation be dropped?

DISCUSSION

1. Goals and Objectives

The first prerequisite of a successful organization is the establishment of measureable and achievable goals and objectives. It is stated that the objectives are only in the mind of one man, the president. It is impossible to achieve goal congruency if the goals are not even known to others in the organization. Goals must be defined and should be in writing. Then strategies can be developed to meet these objectives.

2. Profitability, Goal Congruency, and Control

There exist no cost or profit-centers. It is impossible to determine where problem areas are. In this type of business, a fair degree of decentralization can occur; responsibility/accountability and the corresponding authority can be delegated to the areas where the most relevant information exists for decision-making. Since the organization is assumed to be permanent, there should be written directives. This would assure that the temporary or permanent loss of one or several key people will not seriously disrupt the operation of the organization.

3. Pricing

Price setting is almost completely intuitive. Some effort should be made to maximize revenue when prices are set. Setting prices at "what the market will bear" could be detrimental to total revenue as it is possible that demand could substantially increase with a small drop in price.

4. Accounting

The accounting group needs some sort of standard cost reporting system. Standards could be set, budgets formulated, and a basis for judging performance established.

5. Financial Analysis

The financial statements shown are difficult to interpret. In 1972 the format was changed and the income statement is for the period April 1 to January 31. It appears from earlier statements that the company loses on all except "other income." However, as the 1972 statement shows more clearly, it is difficult to separate the expenses that would be present if the firm were to become only a distributor and receive a sales commission. The company, in fact has a rather high return-on-investment ($14,504/$50,000=29%) in 1971. Furthermore many of the expenses are less than industry standards (averages). For example, bad debts are only .1% of sales.

ALTERNATIVE CONSIDERATIONS

The following represent selected alternatives which should be considered by Cottage Gardens in formulating their future strategy:

1. Move the accounting function to a staff position.

   Advantages: Frees this function from line control; allows unbiased accounting and information/budget systems.
   Disadvantages: Possible temporary dysfunction while reorganizing.

2. Owners/management define company goals and objectives.

    Advantages: Provides basis for performance evaluation of individuals, sub-groups, groups, divisions and the company; increases the possibility of goal congruence because the goals are known.

    Disadvantages: Possible reluctance of key people to spend time to do so.

3. Hire a competent comptroller.

    Advantages: Financial statements could be prepared internally; set up information feedback systems to measure performance.

    Disadvantages: Added cost.

4. Develop Profit Center Accounting System.

    Advantages: This would show which areas and divisions are profitable and which are not. It will expose aspects of the operation which need special attention.

    Disadvantages: Costs of such a system. Possible misuse of budget system to "place blame" rather than as a constructive tool.

5. Initiate a more sophisticated pricing system.

    Advantages: Higher probability of maximizing revenues and therefore profits.

    Disadvantages: Unknowns and uncertainties are still present; cost of system.

6. Set up inventory system for control purposes.

    Advantages: More realistic presentation of assets on financial statements; more information for management decision-making.

    Disadvantages: Difficulty of inventory control; costs of keeping records on large volumes of growing items which turnover constantly.

7. Drop the nursery part of the business and become a wholesaler/distributor.

    Advantages: Could possibly eliminate the least profitable part of the business; minimizes problems of weather and varying requirements for personnel.

    Disadvantages: Without cost/profit studies, it cannot presently be determined which part of the business is profitable; possible loss of tax advantage; present success and goodwill may be largely based on expertise in the nursery and tree propagation field.

8. Decentralize organization; delegate authority and accountability; train to insure any job could be handled by one of several people.

Advantages: It is too risky to have the company rely on a few highly skilled people; the company should be able to continue functioning smoothly with the loss of any one person.

Disadvantages: Some loss of control at the top; added costs in training, and possibly additional personnel.

As noted above, company goals and objectives should be established and defined. This will provide a basis for evaluating performance at all levels throughout the organization.

The level of activity of sales requires that a competent comptroller be obtained and placed in a staff position in the organization. He would be required to establish an information feedback system, such as a Profit Center Accounting System. This type of system, properly administered, will provide information as to which parts of the organization are functioning profitably and which require attention.

Consideration should also be given to product pricing. The recommended accounting system can provide information concerning costs. Rather than seeing what the market will bear, consideration should be given to the possibility of a rather elastic demand curve, that is, a small drop in price might induce a relatively large increase in quantity demanded, thus increasing revenue.

PART II

Analytical Considerations in Strategy & Planning

3

Competition for Markets

INTRODUCTION

This chapter deals with that area of corporate strategy which describes the enterprise's posture (or position) and plan with respect to the disposition of its end products. The central objective of our discussion is to tie the effects of the strategic plan to the potential markets and customers for the firm's products. The effects of the plan are viewed as being determined by the reigning force in the marketplace -- competition.

An enterprise's success has in the past and will in the future continue to be dictated by its knowledge and understanding of the many facets of competition. This chapter discusses the environment within which the competitive forces exist. Strategic planning is then related to the elements of competitive structure and some of the tactics employed. Competitive structure and behavior are described in detail and the possible consequences are discussed and summarized. A variety of strategic dimensions are discussed in the competitive context and a few major decision models are outlined. We conclude with a composite picture of the future plan with its major competitive implications.

THE BUSINESS ENVIRONMENT

The basic concept of a business is that of a match between a given product group and a given market. In this context, defining a business involves three elements: a definition of the product, a definition of the market, and an explicit determination of the connection between the two. Each business consists of a specific product group sold to a particular market segment. And, while the definition of the product is important, the definition of the match between the product and some specific market is even more important.

Business strength comes from the ability to serve a market, and this requires more than just a good product. To survive and prosper, every business must provide wanted products (or services), delivered at a price the customer is willing to pay, at the time and place they are wanted. Science and technology, which make possible the ever-increasing range of products and services, do not tell the businessmen which of these to produce. So he must mediate between the evolving wants of society and the evolving abilities for solving these wants. This task is performed within the competitive market system.

In a free enterprise society, no business can survive unless it maintains some kind of an advantage over its competitors. That advantage may be only a convenient location relative to certain customer groups (e.g., the neighborhood grocery or drugstore). It may only be preferential personal relationship with certain friends or relatives (e.g., some types of brokers or salesmen). It may be only the temporary availability of products in short supply (e.g., a marginal producer). But without some advantage, some distinctive competence, no company can induce a customer to do business with it rather than with its competition.

In controlled economics (such as the Soviet Union, for example), businesses frequently have the advantage of being the only available suppliers. Thus customers are obliged to patronize the company or do without the particular service or product. Such businesses survive and prosper as long as they are protected (by tariffs, laws, customs and traditions, cartels and agreements) from more efficient or responsive competitors, but they are extremely vulnerable whenever the old artificial protection breaks down. The lack of a genuine market - based competitive advantage is what currently concerns many European firms, who foresee future inroads by companies from other countries as economic alliances, such as the E.E.C. and G.A.T.T., become more workable. What these articially protected firms must realize is that competition, properly pursued, can produce far more consistent profits than any conspiracy. Executive thinking must change from the old idea that the only way to protect profits is through keeping prices up, to the modern conception that they must be truly competitive in every sense of the word, not only through pricing policies. They must strive for an understanding of the positive forces of competition, such as getting into new products and new markets.

THE FUNCTION OF MARKETING

One of the primary functions of marketing is communication. Marketing effort is directed at providing the right information to the right person at the right time so that it will influence the buyer, or help him make up his mind. The elements of the marketing mix such as advertising and selling are obviously intended to provide the buyer with information. Even price communicates some important but varied information. When a buyer is not well informed about the brand, price may tell him what the product is in the sense of what product class it belongs in; here it can be an identifier. When he is not only poorly informed but also has no other ready source of information, it may tell him something about how good the brand is; it can be an evaluator. Most commonly, price tells him how much he will have to give up of other things (foregone opportunities) if he buys the brand; here it is a constraint. Buyers need information; they are psychologically uncomfortable if they are forced to buy when information is inadequate. Thus, the communication of needed information to the buyer is one of the marketer's major functions. Other functions include: availability, physical distribution to required locations, and so on.

THE NATURE OF COMPETITION

A competitor is one who sells a product that in the view of the buyer is substitutable for some other product or brand. A buyer has a set of needs or motives. He perceives a certain set of product categories as meeting these needs. The array of brands in a product category can be conceptualized as a product class. The seller of one of the brands in the product class must share his sales with competitors. Competitive structure gives an objective view of the process by which this sharing is accomplished.

First, there is the market-positioning view of competition, which considers the position of one brand in relation to other brands in the product class along various product dimensions. To the extent that brands are "close" to one another (buyer's judgment of brand differences) they are substitutable, and competition can be thought of as intense. The marketer attempts to determine what overall position the buyers would like best and thus tries to obtain the ideal market-position by changing the product and using marketing efforts to communicate that change to buyers.

The second level of competition arises because buyers typically do not consider all possible brands in a product class when they contemplate buying a brand. They know enough about a few brands to be able to compare them on other dimensions and to let price be the relevant choice criterion. Price competition is likely to be intense among these particular brands because the buyer is not motivated to search for a better brand when his aspiration level has been met.

The marketing system can be perceived as emcompassing four distinct levels or planes of a product distribution path, namely: manufacturer, wholesaler, retailer and consumer. Manufacturers compete with manufacturers on the same plane, wholesalers with wholesalers, retailers with retailers and buyers with buyers. Typically, the most important rivalry occurs on the same plane, but rivalry between different levels does happen, and it is sometimes enough to make a great difference. The wholesalers strives to buy from the manufacturer as cheaply as he can and sell to the retailer as profitably as he can. In several industries, the wholesaler has increasingly been caught in the middle between strong manufacturers and large retailing chains.

In order to plan effectively, the marketer is required to anticipate the actions of his competitors, and as far as possible, prevent them from anticipating his actions. He can accomplish this by keeping his own plans confidential and in some cases even using outright deception. The actions of a company depend upon what it expects its competitors to do. The necessity of acting upon such expectations leads to the state of mutually recognized interdependence. As transportation and communication have improved historically, more companies have come to serve the "national" market, interdependence has increased.

Competitive interdependence is more prevalent than it usually appears as a result of a series of geographically linked markets. Distance and the consequent freight costs may tend to seal some markets off from one competitor; but a certain amount of overlapping generally exists. Extensive brand-switching may occur in overlapping markets as a result of the intensity of competitive rivalry. If in the past the marketer has observed a fairly constant market share, he has probably been unaware of a great amount of hidden switching activity.

Within each of his product lines, the marketer has to decide which particular groups of customers are going to represent the focus of his strategy. He cannot really expect to have an equal chance in appealing to all kinds of customers. He has to select that customer group or groups from which he offers some specific appeal, and then design a combination of tactics which will give him a competitive edge in those well-defined markets. The selection of a particular customer group, and the design of a particular combination of tactics, are important strategic choices. They will influence the company's performance at least as much as anything else that company personnel can do.

The decision as to what the product really is, is another significant strategic choice. The product is rarely just the physical material itself. The automobile industry long ago discovered that what people bought was not just a car—they were equally concerned with more abstract concepts such as status appeal, reliability, and service. The same is true to varying degrees of all other products.

COMPETITIVE TACTICS

The area of competitive tactics is a very broad one, since a company has a very wide range of choice in selecting what mix of activities it will emphasize in its attempt to reach its market objectives. It may choose advertising impact, service reliability and field training, prestige appeal, door-to-door selling, or many other approaches or combinations of approaches.

In general, competitive stance refers not so much to a single tactic, but to a whole broad range of policies. These may range from research policy through labor relations to facilities planning and market mix.

It should be emphasized that there are two different kinds of tactical objectives. One is superior performance with respect to those companies already in a particular market segment. The other is persuading companies not yet in a particular market segment not to enter.

Innovation is frequently the most successful competitive tactic because it offers the potential of radically changing competitive relationships. It can do this either by creating new product concepts which set the company apart, or by creating a new market or marketing concept which has the same effect. The opportunities for innovation with respect to markets, are no less than with respect to products.

Many successful growth companies illustrate the principle that growth is obtained by concentrating one's strength in markets where a competitive advantage can be obtained by doing just that.

Markets are dynamic. As they are always changing, there is a payoff to the company that can understand the market's dynamics well enough to identify the time when the change occurs and prepare effectively for probable future trends. An accurate analysis of a company's strengths and weaknesses provides the necessary insight to adapt to unforeseen developments. Since no one can precisely predict the future, every company must be reasonably sure that it has the required ability to exploit unforeseen opportunities or respond to unanticipated threats. In some companies, reliance is placed on the R & D function, which is counted on to come through with the new products required to either counteract a competitive development or exploit a suddenly changing market. In other companies, the marketing group is the foundation on which adaptive capability is built; and in still others, it may be the ability of the production people to move rapidly with high quality and low cost. However, a company may have as its basic superior capability a skill that has not been formally recognized—for example, its willingness to move rapidly into new areas of opportunity or to experiment objectively with important parts of its business. Whatever the skill that is relied on as a competitive base, the continuing assessment of its current validity is a constant management challenge.

A major determinant of corporate profitability is the supply-demand relationship in the industry. A period of excess demand provides opportunities for high profit, while a period of excess supply puts pressure on profit margins; both cases are caused largely by factors beyond the scope of the enterprise itself. Consequently, to estimate its future profitability, a company must pay careful attention to its own investment plans, its competitors' investment plans, and projected variations in demand.

In some industries, demand is relatively stable, but there are major fluctuations in supply. This is especially true where additional capacity tends to produce very large increments, but it may also come about when individual companies in an industry act without reference to competitor's actions. In addition, where the market size is limited relative to companies who may enter, being first with additional capacity may be a prime strategic advantage.

Supply-demand relationships are so important a factor in performance that they should be made explicit. This can be done by identifying the factors which influence demand and supply in a given business, and then estimating how much they are likely to change over a given time period. Making these assumptions explicit is an important responsibility of management.

Where the technology in an industry is dynamic, the characteristic pattern of product evolution is an important backdrop to strategy determination. However, even in industries where technology has traditionally evolved slowly, a firm must beware of sudden technological revolution: e.g., the watchmaking industry.

A characteristic cycle for many products can be discussed in terms of an introduction phase, a take-off phase, and a maturity phase. In the introduction phase, the major requirement for competitive success is R & D capability. At this point in the cycle, the total demand is low, the price and margins high, and the rate of new technological development very rapid. As the product moves into the take-off stage, volume increases very sharply, and the rate of technological development slows somewhat. Frequently, demand far outruns supply, and the essential competitive skill is the production know-how which permits reliability to be achieved and new capacity to be brought on stream quickly. As the product reaches maturity, the rate of technological development slows even further and the basis for competitive success becomes marketing. At this point, the essential factors are: having broad distribution capability, indentifying significant market segments and matching design to them, and engineering to carefully determined price ranges.

This pattern of evolution poses major issues of strategic choice to any .company wishing to participate in such an industry. A company must determine whether or not to play the game at all with respect to a particular product.

An industry can be described as a system of competitors, in the sense of a group of companies which have an impact on each other's performance. From this point of view, the nature of the competitive problem changes substantially as the geographic boundaries of the system are changed. For many industries today, the world has become the only valid perspective for considering competitive stance. As logistic and political barriers to international commerce have rapidly dwindled, sources abroad, overseas investment, foreign competitors, and third country markets have become increasingly significant aspects of strategy.

Economy of scale is so basic an economic concept as to hardly need emphasis. In a number of industries, the economic size of incremental capacity is increasing. This has significant implications for concentration in the industry. Larger units generally mean concentration in the production of commodity grades, because only the bigger companies can afford the big units. The smaller companies must either sell out or retreat to the lower volume specialties.

The impact of the learning curve is similar to that of economies of scale: costs tend to decrease as volume increases because of the greater skill of the more experienced organization. Consequently, the learning curve gives a competitive advantage to the company that first increases its volume, even against other companies with installed capacity of equal magnitude. This effect can be used by leading producers in some industries to maintain a significant and continued discrepancy between its own profit margins and those of its competitors. By lowering prices as it benefits from the effect of the learning curve, the leading producer can squeeze those having smaller volume.

One of the significant shifts taking place in a number of industries is the extent to which companies have broadened the degree of their deployment so as to encompass a greater number of processing stages. The single-stage company in an industry where integration is increasing, faces a continuing strategic problem. Competition comes not only from others offering the same service, but also from the possibility that its own success may induce downstream companies to move back a notch, or upstream companies to move forward. This company is especially vulnerable to price swings in its materials and product markets, while its integrated competitors may be able to absorb these in their overall operations.

In many industries, all of the effects mentioned here occur simultaneously. As a result, the determination of competitive posture for a company requires that these effects be considered, both individually and in relation to each other, before stating the company's competitive position.

ANALYSIS OF COMPETITION

Competition leads to certain kinds of competitive behavior and to certain consequences: structure causes behavior and behavior causes consequences. An analysis of competition raises several different kinds of questions. The first is concerned with the structure of competition. Why do the companies in an industry exhibit a particular type of rivalry? The strategic planner must have an understanding of the cause of this behavior in order to gain insights into the competitive behavior in his industry that will aid him in predicting future competitive behavior. All of the major factors that determine an industry's competitive behavior, taken together, are called the structure of competition.

The second deals with competitive behavior. How do the companies constituting an industry behave in relation to one another, for example, with respect to price? Do they tend to use price rivalry, or do they follow a "live and let live" policy of very limited price rivalry while perhaps competing on other dimensions? What are the consequences of any given type of behavior? Often called "performance", the issue here is the effect of a particular kind of competitive behavior upon company objectives such as profit and growth.

COMPETITIVE BEHAVIOR

In the typical market, companies have conflicting attitudes. In the first place, each company would like the industry to be as profitable as possible; the greater the industry profits become, the greater will be the absolute value of a company's share of industry profits, other things being equal. Thus, the notion not to compete on price is encouraged, because with the price higher than it otherwise would be, industry profits can be much greater. On the other hand, rivalry is also encouraged, because each company wants the largest possible share of the total market, and price cutting can be an effective temporary device for increasing a company's share. An examination of competitive behavior is essentially an analysis of these two types of conflicting pressures and the pattern of behavior that emerges from their resolution.

Five patterns of competitive behavior can be distinguished:

1. perfect collusion
2. effective collusion
3. limited collusion
4. price leadership
5. chaotic competition

Perfect collusion among competitors involves complete coordination on all competitive fronts, not only price. It necessitates the establishment of a mutually satisfactory sales quota (expected market share) for each company. Although such arrangements have been made, they are unusual because of the inability of the participating companies to agree on the value of such an arrangement, and the possible violation of antitrust statutes.

Effective collusion exists when companies set identical prices and divide the market among them but do not agree on other, nonprice competitive dimensions such as industrial research, advertising, salesmen, etc. Effective collusion has been fairly common in Great Britain in the past, and examples of it have been discovered by the antitrust agencies in the United States. Except in areas where the federal antitrust laws do not apply, effective collusion is probably uncommon.

Limited collusion implies the type of intermittent behavior that first involves price agreement and then price rivalry that occurs when fuller collusion is weakened by internal dissension within a group of companies and by secret price shading. Its key characteristic is the absence of market' sharing arrangements. As the files of the antitrust agencies readily reveal, this type of behavior is often found in American industry.

Price coordination among competitors — often called tacit collusion — may take place in the complete absence of any overt collusion. Price modifications arising out of cost variations or shifts in demand usually take place through price leadership. One company becomes the accepted leader, and no one changes price until the leader changes; then all companies follow. Price leadership is often necessary to avoid market instability when price changes are made. There are essentially two kind of price leaders in an industry: the dominant-firm variety and the barometric variety. A dominant-firm price leader is a company that has a dominant share of the market; in the extreme case, the industry is made up of this one large company with a competitive fringe of many small companies. The competitors can sell all they wish at the price set by the leader, so there is no reason for them to cut prices below those of this company. Alternatively, if the small companies set a higher price, they will lose sales to the leader. In this situation, the leader estimates its most profitable combination of price and sales volume, using its known costs of production and subtracting from industry demand the volume its estimates its competitors will offer at its proposed price. Then it proceeds to set this price.

The barometric price leader, on the other hand, derives its name and position from the fact that its actions in setting prices are believed by the rest of the industry to be a good barometer for them to follow. The other members realize that the price set by the leader is a satisfactory one and that it acts with tolerable promptness when a change in market conditions suggest the need for a different price.

Price leadership covers a great variety of behaviors and a large proportion of American manufacturing industry. Consequently, it is useful to think of three levels of price leadership analogous to the three levels of collusion: perfect, effective, and limited. A large market share encourages perfect price leadership: the rest of the industry follows without exception. Effective leadership is more common, however; the competitors follow most of the time. Limited leadership, where they follow occasionally, is probably the most common.

Chaotic competition is another type of behavior often found in a market. An identifying characteristic of chaotic competition frequently is that after the price leader has cut his price, the follower will cut below the lowered price instead of merely meeting it. This behavior arises under one of the following conditions:

1. when interdependence is not mutually recognized, and one or more companies do not know that there is strong interdependence bet-

ween their actions and the behavior of competitors;

2. when, especially in situations where mutual interdependence is recognized, wrong predictions are made as to how competitors will react;

3. when there are significant differences among the companies as to the belief each holds about which price will best serve the interest of the industry;

4. when a company feels fairly sure that it has strength enough to win the battle.

The more extreme form of chaotic competition, sometimes called a "price war", is not likely to occur for a long period because losses will force a truce. A truce will be brought about in a way which depends upon structural conditions.

Different industries will exhibit different types of competitive behavior, and even within a given industry, behavior may vary from time to time. It is essential for the strategic planner to understand the competitive behavior in his industry.

COMPETITIVE STRUCTURE

The competitive behavior found in an industry does not spring so much from the personalities of the executives in that industry as from the structure of competition within which the industry operates.

There are several dimensions of competitive structure. As indicated above, the effects of these dimensions upon competitive behavior is a function of their influence upon the degree of mutually recognized interdependence among the actions of different companies in a given market. The dimensions from traditional economic analysis are: number of firms, and degree to which the product is somewhat different among the firms. From these two dimensions economists deduce five market structures:

1. Monopoly - Single seller of a product class.

2. Pure Oligopoly - Few sellers selling an identical product, where "few" is defined in terms of whether mutual interdependence is recognized and "identical product" means that all buyers' motives are alike. This implies that the aggregate response function for the firm has the same slope as for the product class and that buyers are perfectly informed.

3. Differential Oligopoly - A few sellers each with a somewhat different product. This means that the buyers of the different brands can have varying motives.

4. Monopolistic competition - Many sellers with a somewhat different product.

5. Pure competition - Many sellers with an identical product.

The number and size distribution of the companies constitute one of the most important structural dimensions. The fewer the sellers in a product class, the greater the likelihood that interdependence will exist among the companies and price will be avoided as a competitive tool, as far as possible. Multiproduct competition is more common, however, and it can be more complex than the single product competition implied above. Assume a company A has a very large share of product X and an average share of product Y, while B has a small market share of X and an average share of Y. If so, B can be price aggressive in X because it knows that for A to meet its price for X, A will have to spend a lot of money (either in advertising or lowered price) and thus will have less to spend on Y. This will make A vulnerable in Y to B's effort. Assuming single-product competition, the more an industry is characterized by one large firm and several small ones in product class, the easier it will be for the large company to act as a price leader, since it can enforce its leadership more effectively. This leadership is likely to prevent periods of "price fighting" when prices must be changed as a consequence of changed cost and demand conditions.

Price leadership (usually of a noncollusive nature) becomes even more common where a few companies - oligopolists - make up the entire industry. Most economists believe that as a consequence profits are higher.

A common situation is for two essentially antagonistic groups of companies to exist within an industry: a few large companies and several small ones. The bloc made up of the smaller firms resorts heavily to price competition. There is some clear evidence of this in the British economy, for example, where in the past collusive arrangements have been legal, but not in the sense of being legally enforceable. Since trade associations are the vehicle through which collusion is usually carried out in Britain, there are sometimes two separate trade associations.

The degree of difference between each brand and competing brands is important. These brand differences, as it is often put, dull the sharp edge of competition. This implies that the objective is to make it more difficult for the buyer to discriminate among the brands and so to confuse him.

Just as on the selling side of the market, the number of participants on the buying side makes a difference. If there are many buyers, the loss of one to a seller is typically not tragic, and so he does not readily lower price in order to hold or acquire a customer. The size of the buyer also matters. If it is large — an oligopsonist or even monopsonist—the seller is more likely to cut price and so trigger serious competitive behavior to hold or acquire the company as a customer.

The buyer has two characteristics other than size that particularly influence competition: level of information and motive content. The more a buyer is capable of making intercompany product-quality comparisons, the more likely he is to turn his attention with confidence to other features of the purchase, such as price, and to select products accordingly. When buyers become price conscious, pressure is put on selling companies to use price as a competitive tool. The lowering of price by one or more selling companies usually means that competitors will follow.

The greater the length of the marketing channel in terms of the number of middlemen to which each manufacturer sells (eg., wholesaler, retailer, and contractor), the greater the chances for price rivalry. When manufacturing companies in the same industry use different marketing channels, the problem of coordinating prices among themselves becomes even greater.

It is possible for a company to be almost isolated from the influence of its competitors because of prohibitive shipping costs due to weight, bulk or perishability of the product. This isolation is seldom complete, however. The other extreme is represented by companies located adjacent to each other and selling to buyers located in the immediate area. The spatial pattern of the market exerts a strong influence on the degree of interdependence among the competitive actions of the companies involved.

Historically, the antitrust laws have had as their objective the enforcement of price rivalry. They undoubtedly serve to discourage formal price agreements. It would be naive, however, to assume that formal agreements are, in fact, completely eliminated, and it would be even more naive to assume that coordinated behavior is prevented.

In the short term the nature of the competing organizations also shapes the nature of competition. A company that has a goal to grow faster than the industry and that effectively transmits that goal down through the corporate hierarchy to the pricing decision can cause great instability, especially if the competing companies have good information as to their respective shares of the market. Thus a central problem, especially in oligopolistic markets, is to prevent miscalculation of a competitor's intent.

Movements in industry demand over time are a critical influence upon competitive behavior. Some economists argue that the effect of price on total industry sale for some product, especially capital goods, varies directly with the business cycle — buyers respond more to price cuts during prosperous periods than in periods of depression. If so, for such products as capital goods, price is less effective as a tool for expanding industry sales in periods of depression.

The long term aspect of demand as a dimension of the competitive structure determining competitive behavior is also important. A long term decline in demand occurs when either technological change or a shift in consumer motives causes buyers to discontinue certain purchases. The effects are similar to those of a cyclical nature, except that because secular declines are more or less permanent, some of the companies making up the affected industry must eventually go out of business.

The competitive structure of costs exerts a significant influence on competitive behavior. The stability of costs dictates the frequency of necessary price changes. In order to compensate for the fluctuating costs, the price must often be changed in order to maintain satisfactory profit margins. Fixed costs are those incurred irrespective of the levels of production and sales. In the short term, a company will ordinarily continue to produce and sell as long as the price is high enough to yield a revenue that covers current operating costs, even though little or nothing is contributed to overhead or fixed costs. If price wars break out, price can be driven down until the companies with higher current operating costs stop producing. Thus, in industries where fixed costs are high relative to current operating costs, companies must be exceptionally careful to avoid price as a means of obtaining sales.

It is for reasons such as these that the old principles of executive thinking must yield to the more modern and comprehensive conceptions of true competition in every sense, not only through pricing policies.

COMPETITIVE CONSEQUENCES

The consequences of the above mentioned dimensions of competitive structure and behavior can be summarized in the following general observations. The fewer the number of companies, for example, the greater the tacit collusion or coordination on competitive dimensions. Even with a very few companies, however, miscalculation can lead to serious rivalry, especially if supported by other dimensions such as declining industry demand or large buyers.

Direct selling (no middlemen), high fixed cost, and spatial scattering of competition, all discourage rivalry.

Public policy is typically intended to encourage rivalry, but in some cases it may have the opposite effect.

In general, the effects of rivalry are to erode profits; yet it may bring growth because the lowered prices tap new demands that did not exist for the higher prices.

Several possible courses of action in intensely competitive situations are implied in the analysis of the competitive structure. Rapid, well informed pricing is one possible response. By responding quickly, the company avoids losing customers and indicates to price-cutting competitors that their gains will be short-lived, thus discouraging price-cutting behavior in the future. If well informed about costs, the company will not cut prices lower than necessary and will avoid misleading competitors so that they do not engage in dangerous miscalculations. Effort devoted to identifying market segments in which the company has a particular advantage can be highly useful. Minor product improvements such as a modification of the package to better serve a segment can give some, but often temporary, protection from rivalry. Advertising skill in discovering and developing new dramatic appeals to the relevant segment can also help.

The courses of action can be taken at the managerial level. It is also important to note that they have strategic implications — doing things today which make a more favorable market for tomorrow. Much of the efforts of the strategic planner and the chief executive are devoted to changing the company's competitive position, ideally in such a way as to create a favorable future environment for the company's products. The competitive position is changed largely via product development, typically of a completely new product but in a product class familiar to the buyer that will truly better fit the motives of the buyer. This is a very effective way of gaining protection, and since World War II, it has become the common course of action in the American market. A new distribution system which lowers cost or improves availability and service can also be effective. Price agreements among competitors are also possible at this level. They are illegal, however, and unless joined with market sharing, are not greatly effective.

The chief executive has even greater options for changing the structure of competition itself. Mergers which reduce the number of competitors and increase relative size are one way. Federal antitrust agencies follow this activity carefully, especially among the larger companies, and impose severe legal limits. This course of action, however, should not be confused with the merger movement of the past decade, which was much more of a conglomerate nature. Expansion was in new-product classes instead of in market share of existing product classes. By directing the construction of new plants the company can also affect the level of cost and even the fixed/variable cost ratio. It can locate the new plant so as to be more favorably situated to serve customers. It can work through trade associations to bring about favorable changes in public policy. Finally, it can completely change the company organization, such as by using a brand manager type of organization that will unify the marketing of company brands.

ASSUMPTION OF COMPETITION

The competitive argument of economic liberalism is that if there are many companies competing in the same product class, whether they like to or not the "unseen hand of the market" will force them to serve the consumer's interest. Adequacy of options protects the consumer.

Public policy criteria include profits, but from an opposite point of view to that of the company's criteria for growth and profits. If profits are too high, this could indicate that prices are too high, but neither should they be too low because such a company cannot long survive to meet the consumer's needs. Another criterion is efficiency: Are the companies producing as cheaply as they might? High profits discourage efficiency. Progressiveness is still another: Do the companies develop new and better products to the extent they should, or do they go so far as to suppress useful inventions to protect an existing market? There is also the criterion of suitability of product: Do the products conform closely to consumer's needs? Finally, there is promotion: Are advertising, selling, and other expenses higher than they need be, and is the price consequently higher because it must cover these costs?

When these criteria are applied to an industry with a competitive structure of four firms or less, some conclude that the criteria are seriously violated and action ought to be taken. It is alleged, for example, that four firms or less in an industry is the critical dividing line between competitive and higher-than-competitive pricing, as in the cereal industry in the United States.[1] The argument runs as follows: In a concentrated industry, where a few companies share the market, the companies tacitly collude and so obtain higher than competitive prices. There is also some evidence that profits may be higher when there are a few firms.[2] But whether the higher prices are caused by the "fewness" and, if so, whether four is the crucial dividing line, are less clear.

Further, this protection from competitive forces is alleged to cause companies to compete on such undesirable dimensions as "high volumes of advertising", and "a proliferation of surface variations in the basic product, particularly in matters of style and design."[3] This high level of advertising encourages further concentration by differentiating brands. It also serves as a barrier to market entry because of advertising economies of scale: Only large firms can afford to use advertising, since it is costly and the outcome uncertain. This barrier is supposedly because the larger the share of market, the more profitable advertising is, since the sales resulting from it are shared with fewer competitors. Why this should be so is not clear. The implication is that advertising contributes nothing to the customer. This conclusion follows because where the problem of economies of scale in factory size are discussed, no serious consideration is given to the benefits of advertising to the customer.

Finally, it is alleged that firms in a concentrated industry do not compete on "technological progress", which should be interpreted as meaning "socially desirable product development". Why they do not, while competing on advertising and "surface variations" of product, is not clear either, but the proposition seems to be accepted as resting on empirical fact. Some evidence indicates that large firms have no greater advantage than middle-size firms, but middle-size firms do have technology-creating advantages over small firms.[4]

Whenever a great company gets away from market factors and starts talking about its need, such talk constitutes an open invitation to government to start applying the fair-return concepts by which public utilities are regulated. The results could be a quasi-public utility — i.e., forced to announce price rises in advance and justify them in public hearings. When a company is regulated by a competitive market, government price interventions are unnecessary and disruptive. Certainly price decisions should be free from government harassments under the pretext of antitrust and tax investigations. But market "regulation" also requires of the price leader keener insight, better public relations, and sounder commercial judgment.

SHARE OF MARKET

So far we have discussed three ways of viewing competition: the performance of an industry or company, the competitive behavior of that industry, and the structure of competition. In this third method of viewing competition, one of the key dimensions is the size distribution of the competing companies, which can be measured by share of market.

Share of market is often accepted by the antitrust enforcement agencies as evidence of monopolistic power, since the antitrust statutes prohibit the attempt to monopolize or the act of monopolizing if it can be shown to be detrimental. After determining that "monopoly" exists (based on excessive market share), the agencies will then proceed to prohibit certain practices — practices that would have been acceptable if the share of the market had not been excessive. Breaking up the company — divestiture — is an alternative course of action.

Usually the share-of-market criterion is applied to the single large company. The criterion may also be applied to a collusive arrangement.

An "acceptable" share has never been definitely established but has varied from case to case. However, a company which approaches a significant market share is a likely candidate for investigation.

Some companies wishing to expand have been motivated by the fear of antitrust prosecution to diversify rather than increase the sales of their existing products. Probably much more important, however, is that some marketing practices that would ordinarily be interpreted as acceptable are viewed as suspect when carried out by a company with a large market share. "Refusal to sell," for example, might then be interpreted as a device to monopolize the market. In general, the larger the share, the more susceptible the company is to criticism from the antitrust agencies.

MARKET SEGMENTATION

All customers of a product class are not alike. Differences in customers are, in principle, differences in consumption needs. There are obvious geographic differences (some people live in the South and others in the North), demographic differences (some are young and some are older), and psychographic differences (some have one set of needs and others have other needs). If these measurable differences happen to also indicate differences in the supply/demand response curves, they offer opportunities for the company to market differently and more profitably than if the differences are ignored and all buyers are treated alike. This can be more profitable because it can offer a market protected from competition and the erosive effect of competition upon profit margins.

Companies follow the practice of segmenting much less than they would like to, for three reasons. First, segmenting obviously adds to cost. Second, the differences in response curves among the segments may not be sufficient to justify the cost. Third, companies follow the segmenting practice less than they would like because they don't know what the segments are.

Segmentation also considers the ideas of target markets and market positioning as essential concepts of marketing psychology. An alternative strategy to segmenting the given market is to expand the product class and thus enlarge the market.

ADVERTISING

In sales and service oriented companies, great emphasis is often placed upon strategy formulation in the advertising area. The ower of a well-thought-out strategy as a communication instrument can be the major component of competitive advantage in the market place. The need for strategy arises in part from communication requirements. Because of the great difficulty in evaluating advertising, and therefore, in evaluating the quality of an advertising decision after the fact, emphasis is placed instead upon the quality of the logic that leads to the decision in the first place.

In practice, at least among more progressive companies and agencies, the logic is clear. One attempts to segment the market and so identify target markets. One can analyze the competition and pick out the best among the possible competitive positions. Positioning can be the most important decision in advertising. Motivating these judgments are, typically, the goals of growth and profit.

MARKETING STRATEGIES

Marketing strategies are related to the competitive structure by a number of concepts. First, segmentation is used to identify markets in which the company has a particular advantage so that in serving them it can enjoy protection from the sharpest head-on competition. Second, these markets become its target market. The characteristics of the customers in the target market are examined carefully to determine the attributes of the product brand that will best suit their needs. If, for example, the target market is people over 50 years of age and in the higher income brackets, the brand attributes for a food could be mild in flavor and non-fattening.

Third, with this information the marketing manager examines the competitive situation in terms of the possible market positioning of his brand. Using a two dimensional type of analysis with mildness as one dimension and non-fattening as another, he might find that company A is already serving that market segment, and he knows that company A is a very tough competitor with marketing skill and good cash reserves. If this is the case, he would reconsider this segment as his target market. On the other hand, if he found a competitive "hole," a vacancy, at this segment, he would proceed.

Fourth, the target market characteristics and the corresponding competitive situation become the foundation in formulating a strategy. Thus, the general range of relevant brand characteristics is defined, as is the general range of marketing mix elements. Fifth, considerations of profit and growth lead to the selection of the specific elements of the marketing mix. Sixth, these marketing mix elements become the foundation of the marketing plan. Finally, the strategy not only serves as a guide in selecting the future plan, but when the strategy is agreed upon with the president, the strategy becomes a standard of performance by which future performance is evaluated.

The analytic concepts associated with competitive structure and related to the idea of brand positioning and target markets are central ideas in strategy formulation. The basic theory underlying the preceding discussion is that competitive structure determines competitive behavior, which in turn determines how sales in the product class are shared. This has obvious consequences for the achievement of individual company goals.

The competitive structure sets a broad framework in which a variety of forces that impinge upon strategy decisions can be organized. It brings together demand, cost, competition, and organization in one central focus. The structure is especially useful when combined with the various levels of decision in the organization hierarchy. By means of it we can see that much of the decision activity at higher levels is actually directed toward the profit possibilities in the future for the lower levels. Specifically, the chief executive's decisions can improve future opportunities for the company's products. The strategy is directed at improving the environment for the operating activity. We also see here, however, why the brand manager searches avidly for favorable market segments. Segmentation is a way of relieving sharp competitive pressures.

FORMULATION OF COMPETITIVE STRATEGY

James Brian Quinn defines a strategy as a plan that determines how the organization can best achieve its desired ends in light of the opposing pressures exerted by competition and by its own limited resources.[5] He suggests that the essence of strategic planning is the marshalling of an organization's resources so that its strengths are emphasized and the competitors' strengths minimized. One could carry this point further by observing that the choice of a niche in the market is the key to planning a strategy that will give the firm some kind of competitive advantage. Management needs a plan based on the characteristics of the market, the resources of the firm, and the conditions of the economic environment.

In developing a competitive strategy aimed at securing markets and customers for the enterprise, the planner must ask a series of questions. The resulting answers will form the guidelines of the future plan. The central question in this area is concerned with how the firm should pursue the objectives specified in the economic mission or goal statement in each field of its endeavor. Logic answers flow from one level of examination to the next providing strategy constraints much the same as in a logic flow chart.

At the initial point the question to be answered is: What are the possible product-market opportunities for each field of endeavor in the economic mission of the firm? Product-market opportunities (characterized by the significant features that are expected to influence their outcome) are specific combinations of product-market-sales approaches which define possible ways of exploiting a field of endeavor. What is the potential market for each product-market opportunity? What has been the performance of potential competitors in each product-market opportunity? What are the capabilities and resources of potential competitors in each product-market opportunity?

The second level of examination would answer: What modifications are required in the firm's functional capability profile in order to exploit each product-market opportunity? Based on the information developed in the initial examination, an analysis may be made of the firm's functional capabilities with respect to research and development, marketing, production, finance and management. Changes required for successful implementation of each alternative product-market opportunity may be defined as product-market plans. Relevant questions to be answered would be: How do the product-market opportunities compare with respect to resource requirements? How do the product-market opportunities compare with respect to performance potential?

The next level of examination concerns itself with alternatives to the optimal strategy. What are the alternative possible strategies for the firm? Combining plans for the more attractive product-market opportunities with one another, or with existing plans in fields of endeavor in which the company is already operating, will serve to develop alternative strategies for the firm as a whole. The relevant questions would then be: What synergy effect would be generated in the functional areas through adoption of each alternative strategy? What synergy effect would be generated with respect to performance objectives through adoption of each alternative strategy?

The alternatives to be considered will be affected by the market share-growth condition that the organization or division finds itself in. Important examples of how corporate strategies are changed and reformulated under various conditions can be derived using the matrix below, checking the Strategic Mix (see Figure 1).

STRATEGY POLICY FORMATION

Many new firms start out in the upper righthand quadrant (I). They start initially with a new product (or service) in a new or growing industry (a single-product policy). As such their market share is low, but the growth potential is high. Their main objective for change is to move over to the upper left quadrant (II). Here, they have penetrated to become a dominant factor in a high growth industry. Eventually, if the product follows the typical maturation process, the firm will drop into the lower left quadrant (III). At this point the firm should consider restructuring its corporate strategy to accomodate a changed environment.[6]

Finally, the logic flow directs the planner to choose his strategy. What should the competitive strategy be? This decision defines the directions in which the company will move toward its objectives in each environment included in the economic mission. The particular ways in which performance objectives will be pursued in each field of endeavor, together with the functional goals necessary for their accomplishment, are specified, thus providing the framework for development of a program of action.

FIGURE 1

MARKET SHARE

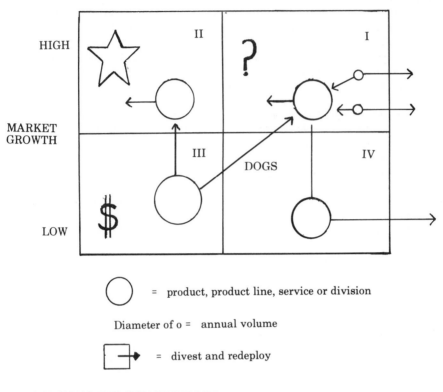

CHECKING THE STRATEGIC MIX

By: the Boston Consulting Group

Source: From Paine, F.T., and Naumes, W. *Organization Strategy and Policy,* p. 157, (c) 1974, by the
W.B. Saunders Company, Philadelphia, PA. Used by permission.

Unfortunately, many companies have tried to tackle the problem of managing their future evolution by going directly to the development of long-range plans without first constructing meaningful competitive strategies. As a result, many executives view planning as merely an extension of the budgetary process, rather than as a careful delineation of basic strategic decisions.

This approach misplaces the emphasis among factors influencing future performance. The primary consideration in budgeting is how much money can be obtained from the total corporate budget against the competition of other divisions and projects. The primary consideration in strategy is how much money can be obtained from customers against the claims of competing companies and products. The customer is by far the most significant source of future funds, and the key to the customer is strategy.

SUMMARY

The changing physical realities of the marketplace and the intangible element of changing the consumer values are posing new challenges to the firm. The enterprise of the future is faced with the challenge of heeding the new demands of the marketplace and adapting accordingly. A society that has placed the free-enterprise system at the very center of society is now endeavoring to revise the values and public philosophy that support it. The public is criticizing the apparent depersonalization and lack of concern displayed by the large companies and institutions. This climate can offer creative opportunities for firms to be overtly responsive to consumer mistrust by mechanisms that clearly demonstrate business commitment to the public. In the future, as in the past, competition will continue to be the dominant force that determines the allocation of customers and markets. But just as technology will dictate the pace of progress, so the understanding of the positive forces of competition will dictate which companies develop the new products and capture the new markets.

Competitive strengths should be exploited as far as possible. They will provide the basis for the future strategic plans. Thus, it makes sense that the basic strategy for all companies should be to concentrate resources where the company presently has, or can readily develop, a meaningful advantage. The narrowest possible product/market scope should be selected for each unit consistent with unit resources and with market requirements.

The implications of the competition for markets and customers are of major importance to enterprises both large and small. For the large company, it is essential that management keep its eye on the relative concentrations and proportions of its various activities. It should not try to get the last dollar of profit out of an item or the last percentage point of market share. These increments are always more costly than capturing larger shares of other market segments. The large company should be content to dominate the principal product lines and to service the most important customers, leaving the peripheral business to smaller competitors, who can service the small-volume segments more efficiently.

The small company, competing against very large ones, must exhibit a more opportunistic behavior. It should capitalize on the initiatives developed on a relatively short time horizon, counting on superior knowledge of the market and customers which will enable the firm to respond more quickly, more creatively, and more effectively than its larger and better financed opponent. The small company should not attempt any form of direct competition until it has developed some special advantage over the giant. It should select only those markets in which the products, outlets, locations, and services can be so segmented that the small company can choose a unique basis on which to compete. The definition of scope for a small company should be based upon the identification of market niches where competition is either absent or has little or no strength. The small firm must be more responsive than its large competitors to changes in demand within a chosen market segment if it is to continue to satisfy the market. It must be continually alert to additional product-service opportunities which arise within that market, so that new competitors are discouraged from entry. An important concern will be to maintain some reserves and preserve key strength against retaliation. If a major confrontation takes place, the small firm will be able to choose among a large number of alternatives, because it will still have uncommitted resources. Also, if the market segment can be captured without calling attention to the company's success, the likelihood of retaliation is reduced. Thus, the small company should deploy its limited resources in ways which do not invite direct counterdeployment by competitors with vastly larger resources.

The overriding implication of the competitive marketplace for all companies is that planning is crucial. Without planned direction, managers tend to allocate their time and resources according to which activities occur most frequently or are most troublesome, rather than those which are most productive.

ENDNOTES

1. Statements of the *Antitrust Law and Economics Review,* submitted to the subcommittee for Consumers of the Committee on Interstate and Foreign Commerce, U.S. Senate, August 4, 1970.
2. Joe S. Bain, *Barriers to New Competition* (Cambridge, Mass.: Harvard University Press, 1956).
3. *Antitrust Law and Economics Review, op. cit.*
4. R.R. Nelson, M.J. Peck, and E.D. Kalachek, *Technology, Economic Growth and Public Policy* (Washington, D.C.: The Brookings Institution, 1966).
5. J.B. Quinn, *Technological Planning at the Corporate Level* (Harvard Business School, Division of Research, 1962).
6. F. Paine and W. Naumes, *Organization Strategy and Policy Formation* (Philadelphia: W.B. Saunders, 1974).

CASE

SMITHSON PLASTICS, INC.

Smithson Plastics is a small but growing company engaged in the design and production of thermoformed plastic parts and products. These parts and products are extremely varied with respect to shape, color, surface texture, and materials used. Sizes range from a few inches to more than six feet in length. Containers, machine housings, food and tote trays, display domes, and a wide assortment of custom fabricated items are among the company's products.

MARKETING

The customers of Smithson Plastics include a number of the leading firms in American industry. Because much of the work they contract to firms such as Smithson is of a developmental nature, they are highly interested in reliability and quality of service. Smithson has earned a good reputation in this regard and is interested in enhancing its reputation in order to obtain profitable repeat business. Repeat business presently accounts for about 10 percent of the company's output.

The thermoforming industry is quite competitive and pricing as well as quality is important. Smithson bases its prices on anticipated costs of materials, direct labor (plus a 200 percent burden rate), tooling, and setup, with a 15 percent target profit and a commission of 7 to 10 percent on the total value, exclusive of tooling. Smithson has recently been sucessful on about two-fifths of its quotes but it has been less successful in landing the larger-volume orders. It has considered modifying its pricing formula for large orders but its accountants have advised against this.

Initially, the company's major sales effort was conducted by Roger Smith, the principal owner and its chief technical and production expert, together with one full-time salesman. Mr. Smith is still deeply involved in sales because many sales cannot be completed without considerable engineering of the product to the needs and desires of the customer, a process that often requires much technical skill and ingenuity.

This case was prepared by Professors Sidney J. Claunch and Gordon K.C. Chen of the University of Massachusetts/Amherst as a basis for class discussion rather than to illustrate either effective or ineffective handling of an administrative situation. Presented at the Case Workshop of Dartmouth and Intercollegiate Case Clearing House, October, 1974. Distributed by the Intercollegiate Case Clearing House, Soldiers Field, Boston, Mass. 02163. All rights reserved to the contributors Printed in the U.S.A. Used with permission.

About a year ago, Smithson began to increase its marketing impact by selling through sales representatives, organizations that offer their customers a full line of industrial services by representing a number of different types of producing firms. The function of a sales representative is essentially to open the door for a company sales engineer who then visits the customer, discusses his requirements, and completes the sale. It is anticipated by Smithson, however, that the sales representatives will ultimately gain enough experience and expertise to play a larger role in the completion of sales. Smithson's order rate has doubled since the addition of the new sales representatives.

PRODUCTION

The basic method of manfacture used by Smithson is vacuum forming, a process using as its raw material sheet plastic in a wide range of types and thicknesses and utilizing a single-surface mold constructed of wood, epoxy, or cast aluminum. Because the tooling is of relatively low cost, the process is especially well suited to low-volume production runs, for example, from several dozen to several thousand.

The vacuum forming machines used by Smithson are basically frameworks of arms and levers that can be adjusted to hold the mold and the plastic blank and bring them into contact. The principal molding pressure of 14.9 pounds per square inch (the pressure of the atmosphere) is transmitted directly from a vacuum pump to the mold by flexible hoses. Although this vacuum pressure is sometimes supplemented by from five to eight pounds of pressure created by compressed air, the structure of the machine is required to exert little more force than that necessary to carry the weight of the tooling. For this reason, vacuum molding machines weigh only a few thousand pounds and are correspondingly inexpensive. A large machine presently on order by Smithson—it will take blanks up to 60×96 inches—was priced at $36,000.

Other types of molding processes, such as injection and compression molding, require clamping pressures on the mold of several tons per square inch and these pressures must be created and contained within the structure of the machine. These machines are therefore quite heavy and relatively expensive. For example, one small injection molding machine—one which can inject a maximum of 9 oz. of plastic into the mold—has a clamping pressure of 100 tons, a floor weight of 4½ tons, and a price of $31,000. Larger machines may weigh 100 tons or more and cost hundreds of thousands of dollars. The matched metal molds required by these processes are also very expensive, many times the cost of the single-surface molds required for vacuum forming. These processes, however, are much more automatic and operate at higher speeds. They are therefore more economical for high-volume production runs than the vacuum forming process used by Smithson.

Much of Smithson's business is prototype work, the development and initial production of parts and products that will later be transferred to a higher-volume process. Some of the company's business is, in fact, referred to it by injection molding companies that expect to participate in the later production.

Whether by such a referral or by the efforts of its sales representatives, after an initial customer contact has been made and product specifications received, Smithson estimates its cost and submits a quotation. At the same time, a delivery date is estimated and a route sheet prepared that may be used later in the scheduling of production. If the quote is accepted, a contract is signed and the production process begins.

Smithson designs the molds and dies and any other special tooling needs. The construction of most of this tooling is subcontracted to firms that specialize in this kind of work but an increasing amount is being done in the company's own shop. All special tooling is billed to and becomes the property of the customer.

The required type and thickness of plastic material (usually between one-eighth and one-quarter inch) is obtained from one of a number of suppliers who either distribute plastics of many kinds or produce the required type from the basic ingredients. Because the sheet plastic comes in standard sizes (4 × 8 feet, for example) the first production operation is usually one of cutting the purchased sheets into smaller "blanks" of perhaps 2 × 2 feet to match the size of the mold being used. The mold may be designed to produce one or a number of units in a single forming operation, depending on the size of the item and the capacity of the machine.

Setup for the forming operation involves mounting the mold and its associated hardware in the forming machine and running the process through a number of cycles to test different heating and vacuum times and other variables associated with the operation. If the plastic is insufficiently heated, it will not be drawn fully into conformity with the mold while if it is heated for too long (or if the vacuum period is too short) it it will refuse to retain the desired shape when the vacuum is removed. The required heating time is affected by the type of material, its color, and its thickness. From one-half to one second is required per mil of thickness. Setup requires about two hours and is usually done by the machine operator.

After the setup has been completed, the forming operation can proceed at a fairly constant and predictable rate. The operator first locks a plastic blank into a metal frame mounted in the machine. Then, on the operation of a series of switches, the frame is moved into the oven at the rear of the machine, held for the predetermined heating time, and returned to a position above the mold. The mold is then brought into contact with the frame, forming a seal, and a vacuum is applied. The plastic immediately takes the shape of the mold. After a few seconds, the vacuum is removed and the plastic and frame are cooled with a fine air and water spray. The blank is then removed from the frame and the process repeated with a new blank. Production rates vary between eight and twelve blanks per hour. Although the operator is quite busy during certain parts of the operation, the cycle time is largely determined by the heating and cooling requirements of the plastic.

Following the forming operation, the parts are separated from the blanks by one of a number of cutting operations and sent ahead to any other operations required (such as deburring and the attachment of metal parts). The scrap portions of the blanks are salvaged and sold for reprocessing.

Smithson has recently employed between fifteen and thirty production workers, depending on the volume of business. These workers are supervised by the Production Manager and by two supervisors who also work on tooling and function as machine operators. Direct labor, which is responsible for about one-third of the direct costs and for about two-thirds of the cost of all production labor, is paid an average rate of $3.00 per hour. Labor turnover of approximately fifty percent per year is experienced.

Smithson's day-to-day production scheduling is under the control of the Production Manager. He is concerned with due dates, changes, breakdowns, the many rush jobs, and with keeping his people busy. At any one time, he has from eight to twelve jobs in the shop. Although the complexity of these jobs varies greatly, they average about ten operations per job. Because jobs and operations differ as to the skills (or level of skill) required, the assignment of workers is an important function of the Production Manager. Ultimately, he would like to give each employee the training and experience to handle any job in the shop.

General administration involves, in addition to Mr. Smith himself, the Treasurer (who performs estimating and other functions in addition to his financial duties) and an Office Manager with a staff of two.

In a weekly meeting, the management group reviews the jobs completed and in process to determine progress toward completion and to compare actual with estimated costs.

FORECASTING AND PLANNING FOR PLANT AND EQUIPMENT

Because Smithson is a job shop (producing to customer orders) and because it uses a wide assortment of materials, it orders materials only as they are needed and does not stock them in anticipation of need. Most suppliers are conveniently located and deliveries are dependable, requiring from four to six weeks.

Forecasting (again because Smithson is a job shop) can be done only in a very general way. Some forecasting is necessary, however, to provide for equipment and space needs.

The company is presently considering its space needs for the future. Its past growth was accommodated by leasing increasing amounts of adjoining space in its present location on the third floor of an old factory building. It is now occupying 32,000 sq. ft. and there is no more space available. Any further expansion will require a move to a new location or the addition of a second shift. The company has recently been forced to resort to a second shift on several occasions.

Mr. Smith has been studying the question of a new building. He feels that a new single-story building built to Smithson's specifications would offer a number of advantages. First, the larger bays of the new building—40 feet as contrasted with 16 feet in the present building—would permit more flexible and efficient layout and would actually provide the same production capacity in about two-thirds the space. Second, the improved layout and the elimination of elevators could save about ten percent of the time of approximately fifteen production workers and make it possible for one man to deal with the materials-handling function that requires the equivalent of three men at present—two full time and several others during shipping and receiving activities. Third, such a building would remove equipment constraints imposed by the limited floor-loading capacity of the present building. Fourth, the added space and single-story layout would permit Smithson to take on the distributorship of a line of plastics, an opportunity that is available to the company but impractical in the present location. Fifth, a modern building would offer a sales advantage by making a better first impression on visiting customer representatives. Finally, such a building would be a positive morale factor to the employees who work in it. The value of the last two considerations is necessarily subjective, but Mr. Smith considers them to be quite important.

Mr. Smith estimates that a building of 25,000 sq. ft. could be constructed on five acres of land in an industrial park for a total cost of $350,000 to $400,000. Mortgage money on a twenty-year basis should be available at 10-12 percent. The annual cost of heating, maintenance, taxes, and insurance for the new building should be about $20,000. These costs can be compared with a rent of $48,000 for 32,000 sq. ft. in the old building.

The company would plan to use 20,000 of the 25,000 sq. ft. in the new building for production activities and the remaining 5,000 for distributorship functions, that is, for warehousing and for the cutting of panels to customer orders. This new activity would require the employment of one man at about $8,000 annually and an investment of $15,000 in capital equipment. Mr. Smith estimates an annual margin of about $20,000 on this operation between the cost of the materials and the sales revenue.

The new building is only in the conjectural stage. It might affect the company's breakeven point and it would certainly involve a long-term commitment. In spite of the many advantages, the return on the investment and the associated risks are difficult to calculate.

ACCOUNTING AND FINANCE

The financial statements of Smithson Plastics are prepared by public accountants. The following information (rounded) was taken from recent income statements:

	1970	1971	1972	1973	(Unaudited) 1974
Net Sales	273,000	312,000	231,000	355,000	516,000
Gross Profit	127,000	109,000	58,000	86,000	197,000
Net Income or (Loss)	10,000	29,000	(36,000)	(4,000)	47,000

The equity capital of the corporation was contributed by Roger Smith and his family. Additional long-term financing has been obtained through loans from banks and the Small Business Administration.

Recent conditions affecting the financial markets and supplies of raw materials have. resulted in suppliers demanding payment within 30 days rather than the 90 days previously required and this has created a cash drain for Smithson. The company has responded by increasing its efforts to reduce the average term of its accounts receivable. It has also obtained the agreement of some of its customers to bill them for raw materials at the time of procurement rather than waiting until the final product is delivered.

As the company prepares to close its books on 1974, its sixth year of operations, its managers are optimistic about the future of the plastics industry and confident of sharing its growth. They feel that in their first few years of operation they have developed the capabilities necessary for success in this competitive industry.

SMITHSON PLASTICS, INC.
BALANCE SHEET as of
DECEMBER 31, 1973

ASSETS

CURRENT ASSETS:		
Cash	2,924	
Accounts Receivable	46,976	
Deposits	3,018	
Inventories	23,457	
Prepaid Items	3,940	
Total Current Assets		80,315
FIXED ASSETS:		
Shop Equipment	50,484	
Office Equipment	5,891	
Leasehold Improvements	2,017	
Tools and Dies	26,308	
Autos	6,329	
Total	91,029	
Less: Accumulated Depreciation	56,327	
Total Fixed Assets		34,702
TOTAL ASSETS		115,017

LIABILITIES and CAPITAL

CURRENT LIABILITIES:
Accounts Payable	54,666	
Note Payable - Bank - Current Portion	8,236	
Note Payable - Auto - Current	1,070	
Note Payable - Insurance - Current	2,406	
Note Payable - Officers	10,275	
Accrued Items	3,816	
Total Current Liabilities		80,469

LONG-TERM LIABILITIES:
Note Payable - Bank - Non Current	36,537	
Note Payable - Auto - Non Current	1,998	
Note Payable - Insurance - Non Current	1,146	
		39,681

CAPITAL:
Capital Stock	10,000	
Retained Earnings	(15,133)	
Total Capital		(5,133)

TOTAL LIABILITIES AND CAPITAL		115,017

SMITHSON PLASTICS, INC.
STATEMENT of INCOME and RETAINED EARNINGS
FOR the YEAR ENDED DECEMBER 31, 1973

Sales - Production	300,529	
Sales - Prototype	5,430	
Sales - Tooling	45,735	
Other Income	4,781	
Total Sales		356,475
Less: Discounts		979
Net Sales		355,496
Less: Cost of Goods Manufactured and Sold		269,456
Gross Profit		86,040
Less: General and Administrative Expenses		90,139
Net Income or (Loss) from Operations		(4,099)
Retained Earnings - January 1, 1973	(10,393)	
Adjustments	(641)	(11,034)
Retained Earnings - December 31, 1973 - Deficit		(15,133)

TERMS AND CONDITIONS OF SALE

1. PRICES: Prices are F.O.B. our plant unless otherwise stated.
2. TERMS OF PAYMENTS: Net 10 days from invoice date.
3. PRICE INCREASES: Prices on undelivered portion of order are subject to increases by amount of additional proportionate and allowable costs of Smithson Plastics, Inc., due to new Federal and State Legislation, higher cost of molding compounds, and higher basic labor rates, together with the prevailing applicable overhead. Any dispute concerning this provision shall be settled by arbitration under the provision of the State Arbitration Law.
4. CREDIT: Smithson Plastics, Inc. may, at any time alter or suspend credit, refuse shipment, or cancel unfilled orders, when in our opinion, the financial conditions of Purchaser; or the status of the account, warrants any such action, or when delivery is delayed by fault of Purchaser, or when Purchaser is delinquent on any payment.

5. LIEN: Smithson Plastics, Inc., shall have a lien upon all molds, dies, tools or parts of Purchaser in our possession for any unpaid balances due us for any molds, dies, tools or parts and for any orders shipped, in process or fulfilled; it being the understanding that such lien shall continue until all the provisions of any contract or contracts between the parties are completed and all payments are made.

6. CANCELLATION: This order is not subject to cancellation, change reduction in amount, or suspension by Purchaser except with written consent by us and upon terms indemnifying us, against loss or extra costs resulting therefrom.

7. MOLDS AND DIES: Purchaser shall pay the cost of molds and dies as quoted upon customer acceptance of proto parts, and Purchaser shall also pay the cost for all changes in molds and dies, made necessary by changes in specifications accepted in writing by us, and shall assume all risk of resultant damage. In consideration of the engineering services necessary in the designing of molds and dies, such molds and dies, not coupled with a substantial order for parts, shall remain in our possession for at least one year. Thereafter the purchaser desiring delivery of such molds and dies shall pay an engineering surcharge of twenty-five percent of the original price of such molds and dies. Smithson Plastics, Inc. shall maintain (in good condition) at our expense, all molds and dies for a period not exceeding one year after the completion of the most recent production order, reasonable wear and tear excepted. A mold or die, for which no production order has been received for eighteen months, shall be considered obsolete, and we shall be under no responsibility for its continued existence or availability after such period of inaction whether or not written notification of the expiration date had been furnished to Purchaser. We do not insure customer's molds and dies in our possession.

8. TOLERANCES: When dimensions and tolerances are not otherwise specified and agreed upon, molds and dies will be constructed to produce vacuum formed or press molded fibre glass goods within the standard tolerance specifications of plus or minus .060 inches. We will not be responsible for color or thickness variation in vacuum formed sheets from which fabrications are made, nor, for other material variation beyond our control.

9. QUANTITIES: Delivery of ten percent more or less than the quantity specified shall constitute fulfillment of this order and any excess not exceeding ten percent shall be accepted and paid for by customer.

10. GENERAL CONTINGENCIES: Manufacturer shall be under no responsibility or liability for any loss or damage occurring by reason of delay or inability to deliver caused by fires, machinery breakdowns, accidents, strikes, lockout, embargoes, car shortages, delays of carriers, insurrections, riots, act of civil or military, or from any other cause beyond our control, and, if delay from any such cause occurs, the delivery time shall be correspondingly extended.

11. CLAIMS AND RETURNS: Claims for shortage or rejection for defects must be made in writing by Purchaser within ten days after receipt of parts. Returns must be made only with prior written authorization by us. No credit will be given on any parts returned which have been altered or defaced in any way or upon which an additional operation has been performed.

12. INFRINGEMENT: Purchaser hereby agrees to indemnify and hold us harmless against any loss resulting from infringement of patents or trade marks, or from claims of such infringements arising from Purchaser's orders.
13. DELIVERIES: Parts will be shipped and billed as they are produced.
14. ARBITRATION: All disputes arising under this contract shall be settled by arbitration under the Laws of the State, the cost thereof to be borne by the party demanding arbitration.

EVALUATION OF THE SMITHSON PLASTICS CASE

SUMMARY

This case centers around growth and competition. The company is relatively young, and after two years of losses in net income it hopes this year to increase its net income to $47,000. Smithson is a competitive business, and pricing (based on quotes) and quality is very important. The company has earned a good reputation for their reliability and quality of services and is interested in enhancing this reputation to obtain profitable repeat business.

Smithson uses a low volume production molding process called vacuum forming, as compared to the injection and compression methods which are used for higher production runs. Much of the company's business is prototype work, that is, the development and initial production of parts and products. Much of this work is referred to Smithson by injection molding companies. Recently, Mr. Smith, President of Smithson Plastics, has been considering the possibility of purchasing a new building. It is his belief that this new building would offer many advantages to his company - both economically and psychologically. The company has also had recent cash drains because of supplier's shortages of materials and their demand for payment within 30 days instead of the previous 90 days.

KEY ISSUES

1. Has Smithson Plastics, been effective and competitive in going after available business opportunities? Is their sales effort effective and efficient?
2. Have production operations been handled efficiently?
3. What is the strategic plan(s) for Smithson Plastics?
4. Are Smithson's accounting procedures effective? Is there a need for improving "quote" procedures?
5. Are Smithson's "terms and conditions of sale" to their benefit?

DISCUSSION

1. Growth and Marketing

Smithson Plastics, Inc., is a small but growing company which hopes to increase its reputation to obtain profitable repeat business. Repeat business is currently only 10% of total volume. Most repeat orders are obtained after prototype work has been completed and usually involves high volume production runs. Smithson is well-known for its quality work and design in prototypes but lacks the proper machinery and equipment to capture the high production sales and, therefore, loses out to competitors.

Smithson's sales revenue has increased 45% since the initial idea of sales representatives to improve company sales was implemented. With this increase in sales, a substantial increase in selling and administrative costs has also occurred (about 66%). Much of the increase in costs can be attributed to salesmen's salaries (the outside sales representative and the Smithson Company sales engineer).

2. Production Operations

The company uses the vacuum forming molding process for low volume production. Tooling costs are low and the machinery is relatively inexpensive. However, vacuum forming is not efficient for high volume runs because of the added costs of direct labor and operations. The company is unable to bid low for any type of high volume production because of the high costs of operations. Workers are hired according to the volume of business and recently, double shifts had to be used to handle increased volume. Production salaries are low, morale appears to be low, and there is a 50% turnover in experienced labor. Much of the company's business is in prototype work which requires substantial time and labor, but produces little revenue in return. There seems to be no effective way to evaluate job performance and control procedures in the production department.

3. Strategic Planning

Smithson seems to have little, if any, strategic planning. The company has lost money for two years; however, the company is considering to buy a new building and becoming a distributor for plastics. Materials are only ordered when needed and there is no warehouse to store inventory and materials. The firm wants to develop its repeat business but has no apparent plan for getting it.

4. Financial Management

Smithson's accounting procedures do not provide required management information. The company's current ratio and working capital is low causing it to be a poor credit risk. It would probably be difficult for Smithson to obtain a loan at the present time. The accountants have advised Smithson not to modify its prices for large orders. It would seem that large orders could reduce fixed costs, however, it is also possible that the labor and other costs required for large orders are too high to allow for any modification in pricing. The present accounting system does not appear to provide data for planning, control, or performance measurement.

The quotes used have been successful on approximately two-fifths of the small orders but there has been little success in obtaining repeat business. Estimating is an important aspect of this business and must be accurate to maximize profitability.

5. Sales Contracts

After a quote has been accepted, a contract is signed and the production process begins. The present contract of sales does not seem to maximize benefits for the company and does not result in efficient operations. The company needs to collect its accounts receivable faster and to obtain cash for liquidity purposes. The "Terms of Payment" of 10 days seems to be too short and may discourage sales. Under "Mold and Dies," Smithson agrees to pay expenses up to one year for any molds or dies in their possession that belong to the purchaser. Under "Quantities," Smithson seems to charge for materials not ordered by the purchaser and amount wanted by the purchases is not always delivered.

ALTERNATIVE CONSIDERATIONS

The following are some alternatives which should be considered by Smithson Plastics, Inc. in developing a viable strategy for future operations:

1. Acquire injection molding equipment for high volume production.

   Advantages: Ability to obtain high volume business.
   Increase revenues.
   Obtain repeat business.

   Disadvantages: There is no guarantee of obtaining the high volume business.
   Company has limited funds to buy new equipment.
   Expense of conversion.

2. Eliminate sales representatives and hire company salesman.

   Advantages: Possible reduction in selling and administrative expenses.
   More efficient control of sales.
   Company salesman have technical expertise.

   Disadvantages: Company salesman may not be able to obtain the same level of sales.
   Sales training costs.

3. Drop prototype work completely.

   Advantages: Decrease in production costs.
   Prototype work is not profitable.
   Concentrate in other areas which are more profitable.

   Disadvantages: Prototype is present basis for repeat business.
   Loss of current expertise and reputation.

4. Increase salaries of work force.

   Advantages: Reduce turnover, therefore, possibly, increase efficiency.
   Reduce costs of training.
   May increase morale.

   Disadvantages: Increase payroll costs.
   Does not guarantee increase in efficiency.

5. Review and define objectives, establish strategic planning.

   Advantages: Establish goals to be achieved.
   Establish measurement for performance evaluation.
   Establish basis for controlling future of organization.

   Disadvantages: There are no apparent disadvantages other than the usual anxiety associated with any major type of change in policy and operation.

This company would benefit by the development of a strategy in all areas of operation; objectives, profitability, products, marketing, manufacturing, financial, management, etc. This case represents an example of the small firm that has grown without simultaneously establishing the objectives, controls, and performance measurements necessary for its operations. Many of the problems in this case are symptomatic of companies in highly competitive markets with specialized products or services.

4

Competition for Resources

INTRODUCTION

The first half of the 1970's has presented the North American economy with problems that could prove devastating for the economies and the enterprises within them if new approaches and solutions are not found to cope with the challenges created by shortages of critical materials, explosive inflationary trends and a breakdown of financial markets, at a time when industry is desperate for new capital.

Several years ago, when forecasts of the forces shaping the seventies were made, the issues were vigorous economic growth, rising real incomes, increasingly stiff competition in world markets, heavy demands on the capital markets, etc. all in all the indicators of a turbulent decade.[1] However, the magnitude of the forces at work were apparently not foreseen. Firms in the United States are operating in an environment where the rate of inflation has been running in the teens per year, and a worldwide production boom and increasing demand in many industries has strained supplies of most of the vital input factors, such as metal, timber, feed, and above all energy fuel. The scale of costs to industry of increasing government intervention in the areas of consumer protection, product safety and quality and environmental protection is enormous and increasing; interest rates have been increasing at a record breaking rate, while the financial markets almost totally collapsed when the demand for capital was at an all-time high due to a combination of capital needs created by expansion, modernization and compliance with government regulations.

One of the most important trends has been toward the development of a truly international, world wide economy, from which no single nation can isolate itself and where forces generated by excess demand or supply in one part translates itself into reciprocal price and/or production problems in another part. Also, political changes around the world have brought on profound changes in the ownership of key resources and often the less developed countries, now finding themselves in control of huge reserves of various resources, can and do create, as we have seen happening with the O P E C countries, abrupt shortages and price jumps with respect to resources vital to the survival of our economies and industries.

It is within this new economic and political context that the firm's strategic planner is placed; it is a time when even tactical planning appears difficult and where strategic planning appears nearly impossible; however, for the organization's survival and growth no other activity is now more vital.

This chapter will address three major competitive components of strategy more specifically, the competition for resources: Finances, Manpower and Skills, and Materials.

COMPETITION FOR CAPITAL AND FINANCES

INTRODUCTION

In our economy, where investment needs are increasing rapidly because of increased production efforts and modernization demands as well as a large variety of other externally generated factors, the need for long-range financial planning is becoming increasingly obvious to ensure enterprise survival. Optimally, long range financial planning can and does play a major part in steering a company toward the best financial course of action in terms of its long range objectives and its commitment to product and growth planning, i.e. it must be a fully integrated component of overall enterprise strategic planning.

The financial planning objective can be stated as:

a) the attainment of the best possible current yield level as measured by both dividends and growth;
b) increasing the expected future yield level;
c) optimizing the level of risk and uncertainty under the specific enterprise circumstance, with respect to a) and b).

Long range financial planning enables the enterprise to, for example, start negotiations with financial sources, once found, before the need for the funds arises and thereby gain time to negotiate and weigh alternatives without urgency. Unfortunately, exact forecasts for future capital needs are usually difficult to make and a stable series of steps to be followed from A to Z over a long period of years cannot be derived. The firm's financial planner must consider a wide range of possible options and plans and their probable occurrence. Where does the company plan to be in five or ten years in terms of sales and earnings? How will this growth be financed? How will this financing carry the company forward to meet new, evolving objectives? A long range financial plan should afford flexibility. It should consider probable combinations of events, such as: if sales of product X and Y grow to the point where a new plant is required in five years from now and the market for common shares is poor, what will the company do? What are the main alternatives? If interest rates should fall, will it be possible to refund or repay a high rate debt?

Successful execution of financial planning therefore requires the ability to forecast the financial position of the enterprise under a wide variety of assumptions about policies and environmental conditions.

FINANCIAL MODELS

The traditional financial model of the firm utilized for planning is the enterprise's accounting system. However, this system has not in the past few decades lent itself to the accurate, rapid and easy manipulation required for planning purposes. One attempt to improve the system's usefulness for financial planning purposes has been the suggested adoption for both internal and external usage, of statements prepared via Price Level Accounting. The key distinction of Price Level Accounting is the indication of non-monetary assets, i.e. those subject to misrepresentation on the financial statements because of inflation at amounts restated to current dollars. This can improve the system's usefulness by ensuring that revenues and investment dollars are expressed in the same dollars and thereby reflect a more accurate picture of profits. This is a serious problem when we consider the general overstatement of corporate earnings due to the seventies level of inflation. When assets and materials used by the firm are stated in "old dollars", a misleading financial situation is expressed when it will take a considerably greater number of today's dollars to replace those assets.

Another approach to improving the accounting system's value as a financial model is the adoption of Current Value Accounting, i.e. costs are restated to reflect the price at which an individual asset could be sold or the new cost to replace it.

The financial model should be used to predict the amounts and types of funds available in the future and thereby enable the enterprise to plan the generation and/or acquisition of finances when and if required.

The main issue discussed in this section of the chapter revolves around the competition for financial resources within the external environment, based upon predetermined company requirements. If a shortage of internally generated funds is expected to arise at some time in the future, the firm should consider all available alternatives at that point in time; i.e. stock issues, debt funding, leaseback arrangements, etc. and through systematic evaluation achieve an optimizing, competitively feasible financial plan.

SOURCES OF FUNDS

Generally, the enterprise will plan to obtain external funds in order to supplement internally generated capital. Undoubtedly, the firm would prefer to finance internally, in order to avoid the "cost" of interest payments. Other factors influencing the use of retained earnings are that "they are within full control of management and available without delay, uncertainty, negotiation, interference, publicity and explanation."[2]

When retained earnings are utilized to finance company growth, the common stockholder foregoes some percentage of his current return on investment in anticipation of increased future earnings. Also, generally, as the enterprise retains earnings, and applies them to, for example, new facilities, its asset base increases and so does the stock price, which is to the shareholder's benefit. The use of retained earnings does have an implied opportunity cost, however.[3] The firm must also realize that if internally generated funds are to be used exclusively, the sum of after-tax net profits sets a maximum growth rate for development and expansion.

The current dynamic business environment, for the vast majority of firms, offers and demands much more rapid growth, which would necessitate an examination and choice of sources with respect to external fund opportunities, if the enterprise is to grow.

DEBT VS. EQUITY FINANCING

Usually, corporations will strive for a suitable combination between debt and equity financing. The actual ratio is usually defined as the ratio of total debt to tangible net worth.[4] The type of financing is determined by management decision as much as by external factors applicable at the time the financing decision plan is activated.

EQUITY FINANCING

Generally, when a firm considers raising capital by selling common shares to the public it should consider the following factors:

a) When the corporation has already in the past obtained large sums through debt financing, equity financing may be needed before further debt issues can be economically considered.

b) If the firm's debt/equity ratio is considerd satisfactory at present, equity financing now can maintain a "borrowing reserve" for the future.

c) If the firm is presently enjoying market popularity, equity financing could be considered to cash in on a possibly high price/earnings ratio.

d) If the firm wishes to show a fairly stable net profit, equity financing could be preferable, i.e. the higher the percentage of equity capital, because of the leverage principle, the more stable published earnings can be.

e) Stock may be sold without significant loss of control by the present owners, and without becoming subject to the usual restrictive covenants necessary in debt issues.

At the present time the American financial system is strained, the capital markets are "flat on their backs". The degeneration of the stock market brought on by high interest rates — generated by a tight check on the money supply and inflationary expectations — has made it practically impossible for companies to sell equity issues. "The market today is dominated by institutional investors — the trusts and pension funds and their holdings appear concentrated on a few favorite stocks; as a consequence the free "auction" market is virtually non-existent at this time."[5]

Present equity market conditions indicate the importance of financial planning to an enterprise; hopefully problem situations existing today, can be accommodated within the planning process and thereby avoid the firms' absolute dependency on the external factors mentioned.

DEBT FINANCING

Management, when evaluating the decision as to whether to finance with debt or equity must evaluate the cost, risk and availability of funds, as well as the personal attitudes with respect to enterprise control of the present owners.

Assuming the firm already has some common stock, financial leverage - up to a point - is advantageous in terms of

a) maximizing the market value of common stock

b) mimimizing the average cost of capital — beyond that "optimal debt ratio" additional debt raises the cost of capital and lowers the value of the firm.[6]

The interest payment on debt is a tax deductible item and as such debt is a cheaper source of funds than equity; i.e. a 5% interest charge could cost a company approximately 2.5% in after tax profits, whereas a 5% stock dividend costs the full 5%.

As G. Donaldson points out:

"With ultimate performance being judged largely in terms of the market price of the common stock and earnings per share, the disadvantages of financing by means of an increase in the number of shares are apparent. Within the normal range of profitability, interest rates, and price earnings ratios, an E.P.S. comparison will show debt to be clearly the better alternative. The use of debt relieves the current market of the direct threat of dilution due to more shares being traded. Even on a cash flow comparison and after allowing for sinking fund payments, debt may not show up too unfavorably, since management must make allowance for added cash dividends on the new common stock - a payment that is likely to be at a higher rate per dollar of invested funds and that does not have a tax shield."[7]

For debt funds, whether they are loans, mortgages, bonds or funded debt, the company agrees to pay a fixed rate of interest and to repay the debt according to a prescribed schedule.

The equity owners merely share in the enterprise's profits, i.e. they may oscillate between high returns in profitable years to none at all in poor.

Often, well secured debt funds have a comparatively low cost and offer good opportunities to the firm showing good earnings potential; i.e. if a company can borrow at 10% and earn 15% on its use, the extra 5% is available to the stockholder for distribution or further company expansion. The advantage in terms of borrowed capital earnings power depends on the state of the economy and lending conditions of course; also, the use of a high percentage of debt financing widens the firm's potential swings between gains and losses for ownership shares.

The ability of the company to obtain debt capital will depend upon such factors as the stability of its earnings, the industry to which the firm belongs, its capital structure at the time of request, etc. Risk can be a big deterrent to debt borrowing; i.e. if a possibility exists that the firm may not be able to meet its obligation by having sufficient earnings for interest payments, default can lead to bankruptcy.

PUBLIC DEBT FINANCING

One of the principal methods of financing corporate growth is through the sale of bonds to the general public. A public sale broadens the company's base of investors and usually assures that fairly substantial sums of money can be raised. The appeal of the bonds issued by the corporation, will depend upon interest rates, methods of payment, redeemability, conversion rights, risk attitudes of the purchasers, etc.

Different classes of investors favor different types of securities and to minimize the corporation's cost of capital the financial planner should "package" the securities to appeal to a potential investment sector. The most frequently issued forms of long term financing are as follows:

MORTGAGE BONDS

With this type of bond, the corporation pledges certain real assets and conveys the property held to a trustee for the benefit of the bondholders in the event of default of interest or principal. This type of bond affords the investor a great degree of risk protection, and as such companies may find it possible to obtain lower rates of interest payments. If the enterprise has a weak credit rating this may be the only way of raising debt capital, in addition, institutional investors who are frequently prohibited by law from investing in unsecured issues, may be attracted by the corporate mortgage bond offering. The disadvantages associated with mortgage financing are the cumbersome handling problems of mortgaged assets and the difficulties that can arise if a merger is contemplated.

DEBENTURES

These are long term debt issues that rest solely on the company's credit standing, and therefore ultimately depend on its earning capacity. Because of the risk attached to this type of security, interest rates are usually higher than on mortgage bonds and to make them more attractive to the potential investor, warrants may be attached or they may have a convertible feature.

From the point of view of the issuing enterprise, a debenture eliminates the necessity of pledging property to secure the issue, which may aid in contemplated mergers and/or consolidations. Depending on the corporate time frame and on the ease with which the firm expects to be able to repay the debt, the usually shorter life span of a debenture compared to a mortgage bond may be either an asset or a liability. The following disadvantages should be considered by an enterprise before issuing debentures:

1. They may carry provisions limiting additional debt (holders of debentures may prefer the corporation not to issue further debt which could have a prior claim on assets in the event of default);
2. they may require a heavier sinking fund and be more expensive than mortgage bonds;
3. they could affect the corporation's financial rating materially and thereby decrease the possibility of future debt issues;
4. they may require the corporation to maintain a specific working capital ratio and therefore reduce financial flexibility.

INCOME BONDS

These are usually the least investor-attractive of debt issues and are based strictly on the corporation's credit standing. Most frequently issued in corporate reorganizations they may be secured or unsecured, cumulative or not, and like preferred stock dividends, it is the prerogative of the board of directors to declare interest payments only when corporate earnings appear to justify it. From the corporation's viewpoint, the issue of income bonds is advantageous because interest is tax deductible, however, these types of bonds often carry quite burdensome provisions with respect to additional debt issues and the controls put on other financial actions of the firm.

If a company desires to sell its debt through a public offering, two alternate methods are available, each of which will substantially affect the price of the bond:

1. **The Negotiated Sale**

   Under this approach, the issuing corporation selects the investment banker and together they negotiate bond provisions which are acceptable to the firm and will enable the banker to sell the securities under the then prevailing market conditions.
2. **Competitive Bidding**

   The issuing corporation accepts sealed bids from various investment banking houses with respect to its publicly offered issue. This has up to the present time not been common for industrial issues, but is widely used by government regulated utilities.[8]

PRIVATE PLACEMENT OF CORPORATE DEBT

The selection of the type of market in which the corporation will offer its debt issues is of primary importance to its total financial picture. Both the public and private market have certain advantages and disadvantages that may make one more appropriate than the other at certain points in time.

ADVANTAGES OF THE PRIVATE SALE

Of utmost importance to the corporation issuing the securities is their cost. According to an S.E.C. report[9] the direct cost of a private placement is often lower than that of a public offering; there is no underwriter's spread because the risk he has to bear is considerably smaller, i.e. he is essentially paid for "services rendered" and not risk since he only locates the purchasers to whom the company will sell the issue directly. Financing expenses are generally materially lower and therefore the corporate proceeds are greater in a private placement because:

1. there is no prospectus to prepare
2. accounting and legal fees may be reduced
3. there is less engraving of certificates

(The above savings decrease as the size of the issue increases -comparatively.) A further advantage of the private sale is that it can be arranged more quickly than a public sale, since no registration statements, prospectus and waiting period between filing and offering is involved. Timing and covenant changes are also more flexible and necessary delays or postponement can be accomplished with greater ease than with a public offering, especially once registration is under way. For many companies involved in complicated financing or types of production that are difficult to explain in a prospectus, or where trade secrets are involved, it is easier to deal with a small group of sophisticated investors on a confidential basis.

Where a close relationship is developed between the lender and borrower in a private sale situation, the company may also save itself from the "unloading" that occasionally takes place when a difficult market situation develops.

DISADVANTAGES OF THE PRIVATE SALE

The private sale is not considered advantageous for every firm. If widespread ownership of its securities is a corporate objective, possibly in the hope of increasing sales or developing markets for a second issue, private placement is of course not the answer. One main disadvantage of the private sale is the difficulty of redeeming the issue once placed; it may be repaid more rapidly then originally agreed to, at a premium, but not redeemed in total. The degree of disadvantage is of course dependent upon market interest rates.

The coupon rate, price and other terms of private placement are determined by lender demands and borrower strength, it should be remembered that private placement may strip a company of its bargaining power and weaken its position to determine interest rates and price.

The private placement market for corporate debt, which usually provides funds ranging into the multi-billion dollars has become almost inaccessible to corporations warranting a BAA rating or lower; the big institutional lenders, i.e. pension funds, insurance companies and foundations, have had their portfolios seriously eroded and coupled with the increasing cost of doing business, appear to have run short of lending funds. This could and likely is seriously affecting corporate financial planning, since traditionally corporations have turned to this private market because of its flexibility. In the past, the institutional lenders, relying on their own research and strict debt covenants, have been able to lend to corporations with a lower quality credit rating. But because of changing circumstances, even A rated firms have difficulties obtaining funds and for those corporations with less than A rating, the dollars even at higher interest are just no longer available.

Under these conditions "financial planning" may dictate that the corporation use short terms with their banks, rather than locking the company into high interest costs on long term money. However, that implies curtailment of investment activity if the pressure does not ease. As can be seen from the above comments, adequate financial planning becomes highly complex under today's market conditions.

BANK BORROWING

Another prime source of company funds is bank borrowing and the vast majority of companies will resort to bank loans at one time or another.

Bank loans can be considered as the most orthodox form of external financial aid available. Typically they are short term loans, requiring repayment within one year at an interest cost that shifts according to demand and prime lending rates. The rate charged in specific instances also depends on the size of the loan, and the collateral and freedom from risk the borrower brings to the transaction.

For both banks and firms, a well established relationship is advantageous. It makes major financial planning easier and less erratic when an assured short-term line of credit is available as needed and the bank can better forecast its own future need for loan funds and the maximum amount it will lend under these types of arrangements.

THE VENTURE CAPITAL COMPANY DOLLAR

A firm is a prime candidate for venture capital if it has a substantially developed product line or service; a ready market with products that have basic appeal either nationally or industry-wide or where a new raw material has been found or a method that performs tasks better, and where management is competent and able to operate efficiently.[10]

Venture capital companies provide a valuable source of funds, often into the millions of dollars, to growing firms fitting within the above framework. Where profit possibilities exist, but where firms are short of capital and unable as yet to obtain equity financing or are unable to obtain loans, venture capital companies will assist in a type of partnership arrangement. Firms wishing to secure this type of financing must recognize that by way of offering an attractive enough investment to realize a substantial profit in the future (approximately 25% or more per year), the firm will likely either be merged with or sold to another company in the future or will have to be sufficiently attractive to other investors to enable the issue of public stock within a relatively short time frame, i.e. five to ten years. This type of financing has the advantages of:

1. attracting equity capital without going public at the time of financing;
2. immediate placement costs are usually less than either debt or equity financing;
3. increasing firm contracts and receipt of professional advice and counsel;
4. generally improving the firms debt/equity ratio and increasing its borrowing potential;

However, venture capital financing also eventually can result in sharing or loss of the company ownership through public sale, merger or acquisition and will likely involve the interference in management by outside interests.

SUMMARY

Strategic financial planning in our present volatile capital markets presents a great challenge that must be met if the enterprise is to survive and grow. This section has discussed the various methods and their advantages and disadvantages, available to the firms in their fund raising efforts, i.e.

a) The financial model of the firm
b) Retained Earnings as a source of funds
c) Debt vs. Equity Financing; and the alternate types of debt markets in which it can be raised
d) The importance of bank borrowing
e) The Venture Capital Company Dollar

Corporations are now desperately searching for more capital to finance growth as well as continued production of goods and services. Yet this capital is getting harder and harder to come by, forcing corporations into the new poorly functioning money market. Because of high rates of inflation, which increase a company's cost of maintaining productive capacity, the enterprise's ability to finance net new additions to plant, equipment and inventory from internal funds has dropped by 20% in six years, according to one study.[11] In this inflationary environment companies can no longer count on tax sheltered depreciation funds for replacement monies, but have to increasingly utilize retained earnings for growth and, of course, shareholders are becoming more aware of that fact, since of necessity dividends fall when this strategy is followed.

All of this means that corporations are now turning to more and more outside sources for expansion - especially debt financing; with debt/equity ratios changing from a 1 to 3 ratio in the 1960's, to a 3 to 1 ratio now, which imposes heavy debt loads, often for the long term, on the borrowing corporation. Even though most corporations would like to raise more equity capital, that is exceedingly difficult now, with low price/earnings ratios and a hesitant stock market.

The usual alternative to equity financing is the long term bond market, but high interest rates have turned corporations to short term bank loans as an alternative. The banking systems have been under severe capital pressures of their own and sources of funds are drying up.

The overall competition for funds has continued to mount and because of this, large corporations like Ford, Kaiser Aluminum and other giants have concluded that the only feasible contingency plan is to slow their growth rate drastically, even in the face of increasing demand.

All of the above suggest a need for government action on tax legislation, and the acceptance of new accounting reporting procedures. Also, companies, with new and imaginative approaches to the financial growth planning problem, should determine more efficient and effective solutions to the difficulties associated with capital markets and related problems in planning for financial resources.

COMPETITION FOR MANPOWER AND SKILLS

INTRODUCTION

Manpower planning has been a much discussed concept over the past few years. External factors such as the increasing educational level, mobility and self-actualization demands of the labor force, as well as government regulations, general attitude changes and economic conditions have brought about the realization that enterprise growth and success depends as much on effective, operational personnel planning as it does on capital and resources. Corporate attitudes are changing and because of increasing competition, especially for high talent manpower, firms are beginning to recognize the necessity of treating manpower as an economic resource, rather than as a nuisance cost factor of production.

The implication of this increasing competition by industry, government and educational institutions alike, for the available and future supply of capable manpower, is that a necessity for strategic manpower planning arises. Companies must assure that they have sufficient manpower, both quantitatively and qualitatively, to satisfy future needs. This section of the chapter will therefore examine management's responsibility to:

1. relate human resource needs to the overall activities of the enterprise;
2. make long-range estimates of the enterprise's specific and general manpower needs;
3. determine a plan of action to meet those needs.

OVERVIEW

Human resource accounting research is at present developing a methodology that enables the firm to estimate the dollar investment made in building its human organization, as well as estimating the present discounted productive value of that human organization. The importance and financial value to the firm of its manpower resources can be adequately implied by the demonstration that in dollar terms, the worth of the human organization to an enterprise can approximate as much as 15 times earnings.[12] This indicates the strategic and competitive advantage to recruiting, retaining and deploying the right personnel, qualitatively speaking, as well as the potential dollar loss of under or misutilization of manpower.

Manpower planning then must be a systematic process which ensures that an organization has:

1. the right types or kinds of skills
2. of the right level or degree of skill
3. in the needed amount
4. at the right place
5. at the right time
6. performing activities necessary to the vitality of the organization.

The basis for manpower planning is a detailed analysis, indicating where the organization is currently, i.e. an inventory of skills and a census of available manpower capabilities, as well as obtaining adequate information with respect to the dynamic forces that affect the manpower resource; i.e. continuous monitoring of attrition, evaluation of promotion and advancement criteria and trends, assessment of new hiring standards and performance and an evaluation of skills and their upgrading through training and manpower development. These factors are vital to effective manpower management. Manpower planning also entails some degree of forecasting. This involves projecting the dynamic resource and skills inventory or census of current resources to obtain estimates of future availability of manpower. The forecasting and planning process entails comparing these projected future resources with broader objectives of the company and using this information as the basis for the development of manpower management policies and programs.

The organization must analyze the components which together constitute company manpower resources; and whose interplay determines the magnitude of corporate manpower resources:

1. The number of employees and the personnel structure; which is influenced by hirings, transfers, promotions, etc.

2. The working hours, which are usually regulated by either law, policy or collective agreements, but the total productive hours available vary within that framework through such factors as absences, vacations, shift work, etc.

These two factors, contributing to determine the total size of company manpower resources, are relatively easily measured and controlled. The third factor involved, i.e. the sum of individual contributions, is difficult to measure and the forces influencing it are not known with any degree of certainty.

The time horizon involved in strategic manpower planning is generally long term and it must therefore be co-ordinated with overall company strategy with respect to investments, production, and marketing, etc. as well as with plans relating to company organizational development, based on the previously mentioned factors.

THE PERSONNEL PLANNING SYSTEM
QUANTITY

Manpower planning for the short term can be expressed as a personnel budget, vs. the long term manpower forecast. The personnel budget consists mainly of an indication of the number of positions of various types which corporate management has set as a directive to different units; these budgets should be prepared by the heads of the departments involved. Once the budgets are centrally co-ordinated, the company as a whole should be able to derive a cost and quantity acceptable planning forecast to accommodate short term manpower requirements.

Long term manpower planning, or the manpower strategy, which constitutes this section's main emphasis, is based on the same principles as personnel budgeting. The manpower plan must first determine a quantitative plan, which relates expected long term company changes to the personnel requirements with respect to the units, levels and occupational categories involved.

In determining the quantitative aspects of manpower planning, it has to be realized that frequently organizational goals are set before personnel requirements are finally determined and therefore they may not receive adequate consideration in formulating those goals. Generally, the enterprise wishes to maximize some function of profit and to further this objective, the company should attempt to minimize total personnel costs for the level of income desired, through better utilization and planning of its manpower function.

One method of minimizing either the number or cost of personnel if a relatively large number of individuals are involved in the same task, for example, is the usage of a personnel response function, which usually takes the shape shown in Figure 1.[13]

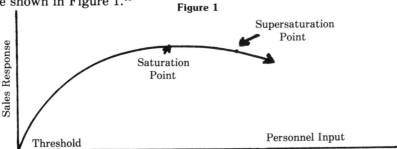

Figure 1

Source: R.L. Ackoff, Corporate Planning (Wiley-Interscience, 1970) p. 71. Used with permission.

A marketing function can be used for illustrative purposes. A certain amount of marketing effort is required before an account begins to respond, for example, a call by one salesman once a year will not likely yield many sales. The point at which the response "takes off" is called the threshold. In general, the response then increases approximately in proportion to the amount of effort until the customer is "saturated." Additional effort beyond this point has little positive effect, and at the supersaturation point a "negative" effect can be expected.

If a similar curve could be determined for a set of specific outputs, or for classes of activities with similar response functions, the organization could determine that amount of personnel that can be expected to maximize profit or some other function of income and expense.

Unfortunately, most planners, because of the time and cost involved in developing personnel response functions, utilize a linear response function, obtained by fitting a straight line to a set of points representing personnel inputs with certain related outputs. The main disadvantage of this type of function is its general failure to predict a correct relationship beyond the saturation point and presents only an assurance of the continuation of previously attained efficiency levels, rather than offering a chance for improvement.

Some problems arise where the planner has to determine desired quantities of personnel with respect to the many types of tasks within an organization that collectively involve many individuals on an interrelated basis, but where the tasks are relatively unique and specialized. This is becoming increasingly frequent, especially among high technology firms. Centralized planning may be very difficult under this type of circumstance and a more "implicit", judgmental response function has to be developed, mainly incorporating a high degree of flexibility with respect to the qualitative aspects of the personnel involved. This is also referred to as the possibility of cross-training.

Practically, organizations have to incorporate those restraining factors that are relevant to the specific environment within which the firm operates, i.e. minority personnel planning up to a certain proportional representation objective; union contract clauses relating to total manpower to be employed per function; etc. The third factor, acknowledged previously as partially determing the magnitude of a company's manpower component, is the quality of the individual employee, i.e. his individual contribution. This contribution is obviously affected by factors such as aptitude or suitability for the work, the training and education of the individual and his degree of motivation.

INTERNAL SOURCES OF MANPOWER

It should be considered highly desirable from both the viewpoint of the organization and of the individual employee, to ensure that the company's internal source of manpower be utilized as effectively and efficiently as possible. Up to the present time, because of cost factors, it has been mostly within the large organizations that the individual was given formal training with the objective of improving "his or her quality"; however, it is becoming more and more imperative that all organizations utilize the internal reservoir of manpower to the fullest extent.First, because many positions require knowledge pertaining to the specific company, its organization and processes and, second, outside recruitment of qualified personnel is becoming more difficult and expensive.

Generally, the organizational training and development process encompasses the determination of specific training and developmental needs, employee orientation, skill training, appraisal interviews, coaching and counseling. In addition to normal experience and enterprise supported educational opportunities away from the job, a wide variety of in-organization training can be arranged to upgrade the individual's skills and knowledge. For optimum effectiveness and validity of the development process, systematic attention should be given to motivating employees, assessing the value of different training and developmental methods and to creating an environment conducive to intellectual and emotional growth.

The above human resource policy can be expected to increase the intracompany supply of scarce talent, as well as giving some assurance that the internal wage relationships under the job evaluation system are not distorted by outside labor market prices. This should be an effective tool to ensuring that the company can "compete" for labor services within its own organization. This includes the planning of a wage and benefit system appropriate to the above policy that will reflect the relationship of changing characteristics of the job mix and the manpower related to it, to the realities of the external labor market for individual occupations and knowledge. Employees can be secured internally by:

- upgrading the employee now holding a position;
- promoting from a lower ranked job;
- transferring the employee from a similar position elsewhere in the organization.

Increasing skill requirements in various areas, affecting the semiskilled production laborer as well as the middle and upper manager, can result in a situation where the individual can no longer perform his job effectively because the educational or skill demands have increased beyond his present level of capacity. Any organization, to remain competitively viable, has to ensure that its personnel remains effective in terms of their skills and therefore through manpower planning should ensure a systematic training and development process, that maintains that internal source of manpower.

Promotion can be defined as the movement of the employee to a "higher" position in which responsibilities are increased and where a greater amount of money, status or prestige may be involved for the individual. Promotions should theoretically be based on merit because of the desirable incentive effect, however, in particular where unions are involved, it is often based on the seniority principle. Regardless of the method used in granting promotions, there are several important advantages of promotion as a source of manpower. Every time an employee is promoted to a higher position, the firm's value of investment in him increases; also management can observe the employee's actions in a subordinate position and thereby better forecast his probable future success. Also, qualitatively speaking, the employee whose behavior, interpersonal relationships with others, aspirations and initiative are known, can likely be more effectively fitted to a position of greatest suitability, from the point of view of the organization as well as the individual.

Long term transferring should be used where the individual's capabilities will be better utilized and the organization's objectives furthered, by the change. Short-term transfers should not *generally* be considered as an effective planning device, because of the anxiety and problems caused for the individual with respect to his social and work routine interruptions.

EXTERNAL MANPOWER SOURCES

Ultimately, positions must be filled from outside the organization, unless the enterprise is reducing its work force. The basic need for external hiring is precipitated by a lack of skills within the organization to fill available or forecasted positions, and as such every enterprise is dependent upon the quality and quantity of human resources external to it. Changing demands for skills and educational backgrounds within the labor market have a direct bearing on manpower planning. The rapid obsolescence of products, equipment and work methods, because of technological and process innovations in particular, can create shortages or surpluses of skills over a relatively short period of time. This may suggest the need to develop specialized internal training or to encourage educational institutions to expand programs in certain skill areas.

Changes in general economic conditions or cutbacks in government spending can have an abrupt and extensive effect on manpower availability. For example, in the late sixties a decrease in defense and space programs spending produced massive layoffs of engineers and scientists. Attitudes and legislation in the community with respect to race, national origin, religion, age, sex and handicaps also have an important bearing on manpower planning; for example, in some organizations attitudes may tend to minimize employing individuals of certain races or religions in certain jobs and this not only reflects a serious possible underutilization of capable manpower, but also contravene the law. Since sentiments against discrimination are increasingly being reflected in legislation, the corporate manpower planner must adjust accordingly. The changes in legislation are mainly designed to protect qualified individuals against unrealistic job specifications.

The traditional assumptions about working women are being refuted, and this group constitutes a vast and increasingly better trained pool of manpower resources. It has been estimated that in the U.S., over 1/3 of the working women were the sole wage earners in the household; also it has been suggested that women are just as concerned about opportunities for self-actualization and promotion as men.

Attitudes, such as managers insisting that applicants for technical sales positions have engineering degrees where jobs may not warrant it, or insisting on hiring "top of class graduates" only, have a negative impact on manpower planning, and must be recognized realistically.

Union-management relations also affect manpower planning to the extent that the labor contract has provisions regulating transfers, demotions, discharges, bidding on jobs and subcontracting work. These provisions must be considered when planning the manpower component.

A necessary prerequisite for collecting data is the intelligent planning of the questions to be answered by the data; and these questions will determine the system to be used; such as — what jobs in the plan require chemical engineering degrees? How many newly graduated specialists will we need over the next five years considering our planned expansion program, etc.

The specific external source of manpower that the planning process has to evaluate will vary with the type of employee desired. Some of the possible sources merit further discussion:

1. Personal applications

Firms usually receive unsolicited applications through the mail or in person from individuals seeking employment. This source should be used with care, because it requires more screening than other sources.

2. Competing enterprises

These are often the preferred source of manpower supply, in particular where scarce technical or administrative manpower is concerned, or where a high wage firm can attract employees with desired skills from the low wage firm. This is the case because often the individual is a "known" quantity whose reputation can be evaluated. This is particularly true with professional people.

3. Labor organizations

These are also often valuable sources (and in some instances the only permitted source) of supply for skilled tradesmen. In manpower planning, it has to be recognized that some unions control the total supply of some labor through such methods as apprenticeship programs, special registration procedures, etc. Whenever this method of obtaining labor provides the firm with capable employees the arrangement must be recognized.

4. Employee agencies

Firms specializing in the recruitment of certain skill categories are becoming more and more available. Their utilization, in particular with respect to locating top-level technical and administrative staff, is increasing and efficient, if they are reputable.

5. Educational institutions

Generally speaking, the higher the skill level and knowledge required of a position, the higher the level of the educational institution from which the employee is recruited. However, in particular with inexperienced college recruits, special care should be taken to match their personal abilities and personality with the requirements of the position.

6. Leased manpower

Many firms are presently utilizing this alternate source of manpower to supplement organizational manpower on a temporary basis, for example, clerical and maintenance workers. The benefits to the company include reduced hiring and salary expenses, minimized record keeping and fringe benefit cost and possibly better use of highly paid enterprise employees by decreasing the clerical content of their positions. This also enables the corporation to avoid fluctuating hiring practices and thus stablizing their work force.

In determining sources of personnel, the organization should make an intensive study of the relevant labor market in which it operates. For example, companies operating in remote areas, such as oil exploration, mining, etc., have found it necessary to provide planned communities to attract workers, above average salaries to retain them and extensive advertising to recruit them initially. In fact, without having a planned "phasing in" of production, based to a large extent upon personnel availability, these projects cannot become operational. The more necessary it becomes to base the manpower planning decision on the same information that company management uses in their more general assessment of the company's future in a changing environment, such as, educational trends, demands for skills and occupations based on technological and scientific innovations, the more important systematic strategic manpower planning will become.

SUMMARY

For manpower planning to be effective, it must be integrated with overall company strategy and objectives and be systematic in evaluating all relevant factors affecting the manpower resource of the organization; from an analysis of skill levels within the organization and their continuous monitoring and upgrading to an evaluation of external sources of manpower and changing trends affecting the total relevant availability of labor.

With the increasing scarcity of skilled manpower, resource planning is becoming more and more vital for corporate survival and growth, and must therefore represent a standard aspect of total corporate strategy.

COMPETITION FOR MATERIALS

INTRODUCTION

The most striking characteristic of the world economy today is its inflationary bias — in total as well as within each of its component parts. The industrialized nations of the world are seeking to achieve both full employment and maximum production and this pooled demand for commodities and energy is putting an increasingly dangerous and escalating strain on available materials and supplies.

Changes in resource ownership brought about by the end of colonialism (both political and economic) around the world, have created enormous threats to the economic continuity of the supply of vital resources to nations, which now have no longer control of the raw material resource. The "energy crisis" brought on by the Middle East oil embargo is a case in point.

The interdependence of the national economies, the free flow of money between them, and the breaking down of the pre-1971 rigidly maintained fixed U.S. dollar exchange rate vs. the gold standard, has in several instances caused sudden surges of demand for products in countries where a devaluation had taken place. This has resulted in inflationary price explosions which play havoc with rational corporate strategic planning.[14] Within the context of this volatile economic and political environment, corporate strategic planners are finding the competition for materials an increasingly vital and complex concern.

This section of the chapter will analyze those key factors necessary to ensure proper strategic planning with respect to the material necessary for corporate survival and growth.

WORLD ECONOMIC AND POLITICAL CONSIDERATIONS

Economies throughout the world have been hit with shortages in a wide variety of commodities, cotton and steel, oil, lumber, paper, cement, and others, as well as a wide variety of manufactured component parts. These sudden shortages have stirred a heated debate as to the causal factors involved.

One commonly cited reason - that the world is running out of basic material - may be of questionable validity. As geologists point out, the planet itself is made of minerals, and "a single cubic kilometre of the earth's crust contains an average of approximately 200 million tons of aluminum, 110 million tons of iron, 800,000 tons of zinc and 200,000 tons of copper, all of which are not irretrievably lost through usage, as is the case with fuels, but can be recovered from scrap."[15] The real question pertains of course not to these resources in total, but to those mineral reserves which can be exploited with present technology and at "currently acceptable" prices. In the past, and it is believed that we can extrapolate to the near future at least, known mineral reserves have been increasing constantly, in line with consumption. This has come about mainly because of price increases and improved technological advances enabling improved exploration methods. Since the inherent shortage reason cannot therefore be validated, we must examine the conglomeration of short-term and long-term factors that, combined, cause the supply shortages we are experiencing at the present time.

CAPACITY

Many materials and processing industries found themselves in an overcapacity situation in 1969 and 1970. These declining profit years caused a failure to expand capacity in the early seventies, when demand had drastically increased. Another contributing factor was increasing environmental controls, which for example, prevented site acquisitions for new plants and forced large capital outlays to ensure continued operations at present capacity. Also, in particular in the United States, foreign companies were able to gain inroads into markets such as steel and textiles because of an overvalued dollar and strikes, which caused domestic producers to curtail expansion plans.

DEMAND

During 1973, many of the major industrial nations expanded in unison, thereby causing a huge demand for raw materials, with implicit world wide shortages occurring. This demand was recognized by industrial consumers and speculators alike; they invested heavily in the commodities markets to hedge against expected currency shifts and inflation. In the United States, price controls further short-circuited the balancing of supply and demand via the free market price mechanism. The energy crisis, caused by a simultaneous shortage of fuel, petrochemical feedstocks and rising costs, compounded the problem, especially in the U.S. and the European economies.

Basically, the coincidence of all the above factors caused a shortage impact beyond the actual physically caused dimensions, a "snowballing" effect; that is, consumers sought substitutes for unavailable goods and thereby caused shortages in other product areas. The scarcity of critical materials and sub-component parts created manufacturing bottlenecks that, for example, restricted the supply of goods needed to expand the production of the item originally in short supply.

In recent years, raw material prices have been rising significantly thereby dampening demand, as well as creating an incentive for large scale expansion. These factors could minimize many of the crisis proportion material shortages. Some indication of this can already be noticed with such commodities as wool, cotton, lumber, rubber and nonferrous metals such as copper, zinc and lead.

FUTURE MATERIAL PLANNING: STRATEGY CONSIDERATIONS

The critical question appears to be whether material shortages will continue and intensify in the future; this creates a difficult problem, since it involves speculation with respect to future demand trends and industry responses, as well as the world wide political atmosphere.

The synchronous movement of the major industrial economies in the early 1970's is one of the phenomena that produced intense demand pressures. This could happen again, since both the growing interdependencies of national economies and the increasing tendency of governments to accede to political pressures, suggest that they will stimulate their economies despite high inflation. This creates a tendency for large and rapid shifts in demand pressures, and therefore alternate scarcity and surplus of supplies as well as fluctuating commodity prices can be expected.

Industry technological factors also have to be considered. Some of the shortages that plagued industries such as chemicals, oil and some metals and paper producers, have long lead times for the construction of new facilities and in many industries this is so close to maximum that any sudden increase in demand could cause serious shortages. Also, because of the spiraling cost of new construction and capital, and a fear of recession and therefore softening demand, many companies are expected to be hesitant about expanding capacity. This could result in a capacity gap if growth demand should materialize in the future.

Economic nationalism is a potential source of material shortages because of the uncertain political climate that has been erupting in many of the developing primary raw material producing nations. Many of these countries have expressed grievances over the alleged "exploitation" of their natural resources by the industrialized nations. There is an increasing trend toward expropriation of "foreign-owned" operations by local governments. For example, exporters of copper, bauxite, iron ore and mercury during 1973 openly discussed setting up a cartel arrangement; Morocco unilaterally tripled its price for phosphate rock while Jamaica boosted its tax and royalties on bauxites. These actions have been made possible through the control that a relatively few countries hold over the world export of some essential minerals.[16] There is some doubt that this economic "blackmail" of supply restrictions would be effective enough for these nations to succeed in the creation of devastating shortages (oil was an exception case). First, demand with respect to non-ferrous metals is relatively elastic and rapidly increasing prices spur substitution within a few months or years. Also, world reserves of many minerals are found in countries of such diverse political and trade loyalties and economic levels that full co-operation at a producer cartel level appears unlikely. In short, the materials supply outlook for the future is highly unstable for most industries, and it appears obvious, that these "external" factors must strongly influence the type of competition for materials and the appropriate corporate strategic plan to ensure the best use of scarce and high cost materials.

PRINCIPLES OF CORPORATE STRATEGIC PLANNING FOR MATERIALS

To examine the complex industrial material planning system requires a framework for the analysis of the major phases of the process involved.

To facilitate this analysis, we can view the strategic planning process for materials as a set of analytically distinguishable factors which are in constant interaction with each other and within the total organizational framework, and through the latter with other external systems surrounding the enterprise. As will be demonstrated, the main strategic factors with respect to the material planning process, i.e. Quality, Time, Source, and Price, interact as an open system with organizational objectives and the importance of and emphasis on each factor varies in some proportion to this framework as well as the broad external environment. (See Figure 2)

Quality

With reference to materials, quality is related to suitability and ultimate cost (not purchase price) and the best quality is that which can be purchased at the lowest total cost to satisfy the intended function for which the material is purchased. Quality is determined by balancing two major considerations:

1. The technical consideration of suitability
2. The economic consideration of price and availability with due reference to 1.

Significant elements of quality for materials and components that relate to goods, both for manufacturing and other types of processing, include:[17]

> analysis and dimension; physical, chemical and dielectric properties; workability; uniformity and analysis and dimension, to ensure the desired and end product result with minimum spoilage or machine readjustment; special characteristics tending to increase the salability or usefulness of the product to the purchaser.

When dealing with maintenance and operating supplies, significant properties would include utility, ease of application or use, efficiency and economy of use

Figure 2

Relevant
World
Framework

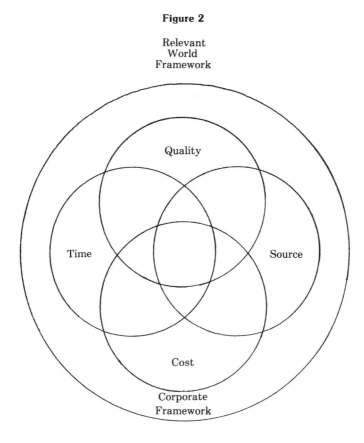

and durability. When dealing with machinery and equipment, the properties to be considered include productivity, versatility, dependability, economy of operation and maintenance and time and labor saving features. In terms of planning for materials within the competitive external context, the firm has to ensure that the above factors are given due consideration when processes are considered that produce the desired materials. For example, are they "in control", providing products within predictable specification ranges; or if specifications are difficult to develop, a policy of brand name purchasing may be the best course of action.

The practical requirement of availability must be considered, i.e. the requirement that an item be readily and economically obtainable in sufficient quantity to serve continuing needs, within a reasonable lead time, and preferably from alternate sources. Where such conditions are not present, existing quality specifications may have to be questioned and careful planning is indicated if material specifications cannot be varied. Substitute materials from either existing or newly developed processes can at times ensure the desired "quality" of materials. Here future forecasts and monitoring of technological developments are of major importance.

The cost aspect of materials as related to the quality factor should influence both technological and economic considerations. Unfortunately, technological suitability is seldom accorded the same thorough analyses given to economic considerations. For example, value analysis is probably the greatest cost-saving technique used in industry. This analysis focuses on the cost side of the quality problem and seeks to achieve the proper relationship among cost, price and value received by better integrating the technical and economic factors of quality.

SOURCES

The success or failure of planned supplier development is of great significance and can be ruinous if not done properly. Planning with respect to sources of supply should include the establishment of the desired goals considering material specifications, legal terms, the selection of the supplier, and an evaluation of the benefits that will result for both parties from this process.

Every enterprise has two primary sources of supply: the company itself and outside suppliers. Management creates the internal source by capital investment in men, machines, materials and management. It usually purchases the products and services of the external source as a supplement to its own internal capacities. Both sources are vital to a company's success. The important "make or buy" decision will not be considered in any detail here because of our primary emphasis on the competition for material resources, that is, the external emphasis.

For any enterprise, supplier goodwill is an important asset, and the development of a mutually profitable relationship is a primary concern. Regardless of planning and skill in production and sales, forecasting problems may develop and only a co-operative supply source will assist the firms. For example, sudden demand surges, unforeseeable production breakdowns or contract cancellations can occur. In our present day volatile supply market, reliable and cooperative suppliers of materials are of prime importance. The planning process for materials must first determine the type and enterprise characteristics of desirable suppliers and then locate them and attempt to establish a relationship considered desirable by both parties. The preferred source of information on suppliers is the firm's own past experience with the supplier. Other sources that can be utilized are supplier catalogs, trade registers and directories, trade journals, salesmen, trade fairs and exhibitions. In evaluating the supplier, it would be difficult to improve upon the following definition:

A good supplier is one who is at all times honest and fair in his dealings with the customers, his own employees and himself; who has adequate plant facilities and know-how so as to be able to provide materials which meet the purchaser's specifications, in the quantities required, and at the time promised; whose financial position is sound; whose prices are reasonable both to the buyer and to himself; whose management policies are progressive; who is alert to the need for continued improvement in both his products, and his manufacturing processes and who realizes that in the last analysis, his own interests are best served when he best serves his customers.[18]

PROBLEMS OF SOURCE SELECTION

SINGLE VS. MULTIPLE SOURCES

The advantages of purchasing all requirements from a single source are:

1. it usually makes maximum use of the corporation's purchasing power, resulting in, for example, quantity discounts, special price concessions, etc.
2. the administrative work of the buyer organization is decreased.
3. in times of shortages, the supplier may be more predisposed to allocate the usual order quantity to a large purchaser.

The disadvantages are the increased risk of a complete production stoppage at the buyer because of circumstances originating with the supplier, such as, fires, strikes, etc. Another problem may relate to the size of the supplying enterprise; for example, if the buyer purchases a high percentage of the supplier's output, the latter may develop a dependency to the extent that his own survival is at stake, and may possibly curtail the desired flexibility of the buying enterprise.

The advantages of multiple sources are the lessened risk of supply interruption because of supplier problems. Active competition and therefore better price and service can be stimulated, if supply contracts are given out on a, for example, 70% - 30% basis, and if the buyer establishes new supply relationships with previously unknown supply sources.

BUYING LOCALLY VS. BUYING INTERNATIONALLY

LOCAL BUYING

In some situations, public relations dictate that maximum use be made of local (national, state, municipal) sources. This type of policy is frequently desirable solely on an economic basis, and appears to have the following advantages:

1. Closer co-operation between buyer and seller is possible due to close physical proximity.
2. Delivery problems due to transportation factors are less likely to occur, and also usually require less lead time.
3. Overall lower cost because of proximity.
4. In many instances where the desired input is a raw material or energy, the production enterprise must of necessity locate at the source of that input because of overall cost considerations.

BUYING INTERNATIONALLY

This is a post World War II phenomenon as far as the material purchasing planner is concerned. International buying involves many complex problems, such as:

1. Communication difficulties caused by language barriers.
2. Differences in purchasing laws and the implied need for increased care in contract negotiations.
3. Foreign currency problems.
4. Lack of familiarity with foreign quality standards.
5. Possibly unreliable delivery schedules.
6. Long procurement lead times.
7. High transportation costs.
8. Political uncertainties.

Despite these problems, buying by American firms is rapidly increasing. This is caused mainly by the lack of economic local supplies, the unavailability of raw materials from any other source, or the increasing specialization of production processes. Other reasons may include the desire to break a domestic supply monopoly, lower costs of purchasing, etc.

OTHER CONSIDERATIONS

Any continuing buyer-seller relationship based on mutual confidence and satisfaction must imply a policy of loyalty to suppliers, i.e. the antithesis of constant buying "opportunism." The latter could sacrifice assurance of supply and would make every procurement a problem and planning for material sources a literal impossibility. Also, the progressive buyer must realize that a healthy, successful supplier is necessary and beneficial for both enterprises to prosper. Suppliers should be involved in enterprise planning in two important ways. One, they can provide significant forecasts concerning market conditions, and second, provide input to plans for expansion or retrenchment in the industries. They can in many instances help with material acquisition planning, for example, in periods of shortage, suppliers may follow a custom of allocating their products on the basis of what share of production customers received in the past. Another important and complex planning decision with respect to the supply of materials, relates to the cost-benefit analysis of a merger or acquisition to acquire sources of material.

TIME AND PRICE

Planning usually proceeds from the general to the very specific immediate need. Enterprise must consider long range forecasts of probable supply, delivery and price when planning for materials. Competitive pressure may be so great, however, that many companies are forced into producing new products faster than they anticipated.

Time, therefore, is a very important element and planning time horizons are contracting. One planning technique that appears well suited to these problems is network analysis. This method provides the scientific scheduling of a complex chain of events and activities which is aimed at a specific end result. It can spell out a planned program of material procurement and thereby provide the right material at the right time. Generally speaking, the importance of timing varies with the type of materials purchased and the type of market in which materials are purchased.

In terms of planning, markets in which the factors of supply and price are relatively stable over time, present few problems, except to the extent that they become unstable because of demand and supply factors. Instability being equated with a market where supply and prices fluctuate substantially.

Timing becomes an important factor under unstable market conditions, since usually the purchaser cannot influence the market price, but can plan to achieve some control of the price he pays. Under highly competitive conditions, the result of timing can significantly affect both the competitive position and profitability of the enterprise. When planning to acquire materials, two policies should be considered:

1. purchase according to current requirements and largely disregard market action (which is too conservative to be commendable)
2. purchase according to market conditions.

Characteristically the latter has two types of buying behavior:

Speculative Purchasing involves the purchase of material in excess of foreseen requirements, in anticipation that a need for the material will arise and the firm will profit from a current purchase. To successfully utilize this method, prices must advance with steepness or rapidity, the enterprise must be able to recognize abnormally low price levels and there must exist the possibility of utilizing the materials relatively promptly. If this policy is to be used, strategic planning requires that certain special facilities are available, such as requisite storage space for extra quantities of materials over a protracted period and sufficient working capital funds.

Forward Buying is a "toned-down" version of the above plan, that is, materials are not bought beyond actual foreseeable requirements. The advantages accruing here may be the acquisition at favorable prices which possibly permits quantity purchases at volume transportation rates. In unstable markets this involves some knowledge of material costs. This is especially important where contract prices are being adhered to by the buyer and the resale of manufactured products is involved. The main advantage can be a decrease in risk because of inadequate deliveries caused by pending material shortages, unreliable deliveries, or transportation difficulties. Both of the above methods must adhere to some general final dollar controls set by the organization.

The price of materials only becomes an important planning feature where a large number of sources of the appropriate quality and reliability are available. Planning can achieve improvements in the average price of materials under various forecasting conditions and future price movements. One of the approaches, for example, that can be considered a good planning tool was suggested by P.G. Carlson and J. Corrigan, who noted that for commodities with a cyclical price pattern the average price per unit over a time period, the price per time unit and average carrying costs are plotted on a scale, comparing price per unit to time units and an optimum time to purchase is derived therefrom (utilizing constant consumption and reorder cost assumptions).[19]

For commodities with non-periodic price characteristics, i.e., whose price fluctuates randomly, an economic order quantity variation approach can be used. This approach provides a measure of how high or how low a material price is, and therefore total inventory can be based on the level of price indication. When these data are combined with records of performance, some economic guide for the acquisition of raw materials exists.

There are, of course, other types of decision models that can provide some frame of reference to the material acquisition function. It should be remembered, however, that planning in this area must incorporate the system's capacity for decision making flexibility according to each unique situation.

SUMMARY

The sudden development of world wide shortages in key materials is forcing management to reassess its priorities and planning issues. Today's "executive is likely to be less concerned about selling his own product, than about buying the products necessary to make it."[20]

The unavailability of raw materials is affecting corporate planning to the extent that the emphasis of where to build plants may be shifting from the areas where the markets are to those where raw materials exist.

The question is no longer only a decision as to where the product will be produced, but whether it will be produced at all. For many large projects, the commitment of supply availability to manufacture the product is of first importance; prices appear of little consequence in a world of shortage. Companies are buying more abroad, some are even hedge-buying supplies for their suppliers; plans for expansion are carefully reappraised; and Research and Development departments of large corporations such as Kaiser Aluminum, are spending as much as 75% of their time studying supply issues.[21]

Long range supply considerations are making planning with respect to backward integration or investing in new products with more reliable supply sources than the old ones, a matter of survival. The shortages experienced at the present are not only those of material supplies but also of equipment and plants to produce materials.

More and more companies will have to live with the planning possibilities of continuing supply shortages and adjust accordingly.

ENDNOTES

1. "The 1970's A Second Look" *Business Week*, September 14, 1974.
2. Donaldson, G. *Corporate Debt Capacity* (Graduate School of Business Administration, Harvard University, Boston, 1961) p. 70.
3. In the absence of taxation, the minimum cost of retained earnings is the cost of equity capital, based upon the current market price of the stock.
4. Tangible Net Worth = the sum of all outstanding preferred or preference stocks and outstanding common stock, surplus and undivided profits less any intangible items in the assets i.e. goodwill, trademarks, patents, copyrights, leaseholds, mailing lists, treasury stock, organization expenses and underwriting discounts and expenses.
5. op. cit., *Business Week*, September 14, 1974, p. 53.
6. F. Weston and Brigham, *Managerial Finance* (Holt, Rinehart, Winston, 1972) Chapter 11.
7. Donaldson, *op. cit.*, pp. 70-71.
8. K. White, *Financing Company Expansion* (AMA Research Study 64) p. 71.
9. op. cit., *AMA Research Study 64*, p. 77.
10. op. cit., *AMA Research Study 64, p. 43.*
11. *op. cit., Business Week, September 14, 1974.*
12. R. Likert and D. Bowers, "Organizational Theory and Human Resource Accounting" *American Psychologist* Vol. 24, No. 6, June 1969, pp. 585-592.
13. R. Ackoff, *Corporate Planning* (Wiley-Interscience, 1970) p. 71.
14. op. cit., *Business Week*, September 14, 1974. .
15. ibid.
16. ibid.
17. S. Heinritz, *Purchasing, Principles and Applications* (Prentice-Hall, 1971) p. 122.
18. L. Lee and D. Dobler, *Purchasing and Materials Management* (McGraw-Hill, 1965) p. 79.
19. P.G. Carlson and J. Corrigan, *Guides to More Effective Purchasing* (AMA Report 68) 1962, pp. 25-35.
20. op. cit., *Business Week*, September 14, 1974.
21. ibid.

CASE

BARNES LUMBER COMPANY

Raw Material, Equipment, and Financing Problems
of a Small Lumber Company

INTRODUCTION

Jack Barnes, at age 55, was one of three owners of the closely held
Barnes Lumber Company. Jack had originally formed the company, and
watched it grow from a small sawmill, producing five thousand board feet of
lumber per day in 1950 to its present capacity of sixty thousand board feet per
day. In order for him to expand to that level, however, he took in two partners,
Harold Thompson and Jim Lewis, to provide expertise in forest management
and engineering, and office management and sales. Jim Lewis graduated from
a forestry school in the Pacific Northwest with a degree in forest engineering.
He supervised the raw materials side of the company and was responsible for
acquisition, harvest, and transportation of all raw materials. Harold Thompson had attended a business school and had primary responsibility for the office procedures as well as sales management. His job included everything from
preparing the balance sheet to closing orders for lumber in distant markets.
The company went public in 1946. Jack Barnes owned most of the stock, so he
maintained general vigilance over all company operations except those of running the mill, for which he alone made the decisions affecting mill operations.

BACKGROUND

The company mill was located in Gladewater, a town of about two hundred people on the east slopes of the Coast Range in Oregon. The primary
species used in manufacture was Douglas-fir, which accounted for 95% of the

This case was made possible by the cooperation of a business firm which remains anonymous. It was prepared by
Graduate Assistant Bill Blankenship, under the supervision of Professor Stuart U. Rich, Director of the Forest Industries
Management Center, University of Oregon. The case was designed for class discussion rather than to illustrate either effec-
tive or ineffective handling of an administrative situation.

Copyright, 1974, by Professor Stuart U. Rich

Distributed by the Intercollegiate Case Clearing House, Soldiers Field, Boston, Mass. 02163. All rights reserved to
the contributors. Printed in the U.S.A. This case is produced with the permission of its author, Dr. Stuart U. Rich, Professor
of Marketing, and Director Forest Industries Management Center, College of Business Administration, University of Oregon,
Eugene, Oregon.

mill volume produced annually. The Western Hemlock, White Fir, Incense Cedar, and Western Redcedar which the company obtained in its timber sales were primarily sold as logs to other mills. Barnes Lumber Company produced a wide range of lumber products in its mill, most of which required old-growth, clear Douglas-fir logs as primary raw materials. Jim Lewis had developed a "trade" policy with other mills whereby he traded the logs of the species other than Douglas-fir to these mills for high-quality, old-growth Douglas-fir.

The mill produced lumber ranging from 1" × 3" boards to 10" × 12' mine timbers. The mill also produced a wide variety of specialty products including stadium seats, lumber for boats, and truck body stock. These specialty items accounted for 6% of present production. Additionally, 10% of dimension lumber production was exported to Holland and Germany. The export market required rough, very clear lumber because the lumber was remanufactured in Europe.This export market paid a premium over domestic markets and was free of many of the export restrictions which plagued the export of logs (as contrasted with lumber). The other lumber produced by the company was sold primarily in Northwest markets, except for a small amount of Utility grade which was shipped to Southern California. All lumber sales were f.o.b. at the mill.

The company owned three thousand acres of old-growth Douglas-fir with a total volume of approximately ten million board feet. Company policy dictated holding this timber in reserve, and purchasing all timber from government and private timber sales. The company was surrounded by BLM (Bureau of Land Management) land. In the past, Jim Lewis had been able to purchase most of the required timber from the BLM sales, which were generally sold in May and June. Sometime he purchased logs on the open market in addition to trading for them.

The company did all its own logging, hauling, and road building. Jim Lewis felt that as long as the company could log and haul as cheaply as it could subcontract, the company would continue to do its own logging and hauling. The company had never purchased a timber sale farther than forty-nine miles from the mill and did not plan to do so in the immediate future.

The company's logging equipment consisted of a recently purchased reconditioned, 1966 M-2 Berger tower and yarder, a 1961 M-3 Marion heel-boom log loader, a 1966 C-6 Euclid crawler with U-shaped blade, and a 1968 D-6c Caterpillar crawler with straight blade. The C-6 Euclid was used primarily for road building and the D-6c was used to log timber sales which were on relatively flat ground and did not require the use of tower and yarder. The company owned three logging trucks; a 1961 Peterbilt, and two recently purchased 1972 Peterbilts. Originally, the 1961 Peterbilt had been kept as a spare truck when the other Peterbilts were traded for the new 1972 trucks. They also owned two late-model International dump trucks which were used for road-building. One of the trucks was also fitted with a water tank for use as a fire truck during the summer.

The mill contained a seven-foot headrig. Recent investments in the mill had improved efficiency to the point where a 35% overrun was realized. Jack Barnes was upset, however, at the requirements the ecology movement had placed on him. Oregon had passed a law outlawing wigwam burners and small mills like Jack's were among the hardest hit by this legislation. In order to continue operations, Jack had been forced to install a $50,000 machine for converting the bark waste to hog fuel, since he could no longer burn it. The hog fuel netted no return; he simply gave it away to the fuel companies in the local area. He figured he was better off than some companies, who had to pay the fuel companies to truck the bark away. Additionally, he was forced to install a hopper to hold the shavings made by the planer. These shavings were sold to companies for use in manufacturing flakeboard, and the mill's sawdust was sold to a pulp mill for use in manufacturing tissue paper. His net return from these by-products, however, did not pay for the operating costs and initial investment of the equipment he purchased to convert the waste materials. He figured he was losing $5,000 per year converting the waste, instead of burning it.

COMPETITION AND SOUCES OF TIMBER

Since the Barnes Lumber Company was surrounded by BLM land containing fine-quality old-growth timber the firm had experienced increasing competition in bidding for the timber sales near their mill. United States Papers bordered the company to the north, and Lebanon Lumber Company bordered them to the south. Jack Barnes felt that he deserved consideration from the other companies in keeping the stumpage bid within his grasp because he had built his mill and established his area of raw material supply before the other two companies became competitors. U.S. Papers was a very large, international company that could have been extremely competitive because they could have used much of the timber presently being logged by Barnes. However, their chief forester was a good friend of Jim Lewis, and they managed to carry this friendship forward in timber bidding. Lebanon Lumber Company was a cutthroat operation. It was a regional multi-product company, which bought much of the old-growth Barnes sought, logged the sales, and sold the logs to many of the plywood companies in the local area. The plywood peeler logs characteristically sold for more than Barnes could afford to pay for them. Lebanon required 15.75 million board feet of logs per year, of which it usually sought 15% from Barnes' area. Lebanon had lost an export lumber contract to Barnes and intended to get revenge in future timber sales. (See Exhibit 1). Lebanon needed 30% hemlock in its annual production. Lebanon management knew they could probably bid Jim Lewis up on sales to maximum bid, then subsequently buy the hemlock, white fir, and cedar from him for the appraised price because Barnes had little use for these species. Also, Lebanon management knew they could trade clear Douglas-Fir logs for Barnes' hemlock at an even better exchange rate. Jim Lewis knew he would need to calculate an exact price he could afford to bid for each upcoming sale. He would also have to bid on every upcoming sale in order to secure his supply of old-growth logs, even though some sales did not contain as much Douglas fir as he would like. And he knew that he would have to sell or trade most of the unusable species to Lebanon. (See Exhibit 2)

Recently the BLM was starting to place more thinning sales on the market. In addition, many small private land owners, interested because of the high stumpage prices presently being paid, approached Jim Lewis and asked him to buy their timber. Jim had turned these sales down in the past because (1) he needed old-growth timber to manufacture his current products, and (2) the present mill could not saw a log smaller than 14" in diameter. Logs smaller than 14" in diameter which Barnes had obtained on timber sales in the past were either sorted at the mill and sold to other mill operators, sold at the landing, or left in the woods. These logs accounted for 20% of present logged volume. Jim was wondering if the addition of a small mill to handle logs down to 5" in diameter would be a worthwhile investment. He talked to mill-equipment salesmen and determined that a mill which would produce 32 M b.f. of lumber (mostly Utility grade) per shift would require an investment of $750,000, including the purchase of a log stacker to move the logs around from the cold deck to the feed ramp of the mill. The small mill, according to the salesmen, should produce a 50% overrun on small logs. Jim believed he could obtain 4.5 million board feet of these small logs per year with no difficulty, and these logs probably would not cost more than $150 per M b.f. Milling costs on the old mill were $29.50 per M b.f. log scale, and would be $17.50 per M b.f. log scale in the new mill.

Jim knew that if his company did not add the new mill, they would have to change their method of scaling these small logs which they sold. The logs were presently sold on a lump sum basis; that is, a prospective buyer would offer of total price for a deck of logs. Jim was sure the company lost 35% of the scale volume of these logs by selling them in this fashion. The reason for this 35% loss was that the scaler did not have time to properly scale the many small logs in these decks. The scaler who presently worked for them was swamped with work. Adding a new scaler would mean a cost of $17,500 a year, including industrial safety insurance and employer taxes. Other options included weight scaling of the trucks, but this required an investment of $17,500 in scales and required an additional man to operate the scales and maintain the scales and area around them. Jim estimated this man would cost the company $11,500 per year. An electronic log scaler would cost $75,000 and would require the logs to be run through one at a time, which meant many handling problems, so Jim dropped the electronic scaler from consideration.

EQUIPMENT CONSIDERATIONS

Some of the company's logging equipment was rapidly becoming a maintenance headache. Jim thought the purchase of the new tower and yarder would solve many of the company's logging shutdown problems, but recently the loader was causing as many delays as the old yarder caused. The 1956 model loader was in need of extensive maintenance. Normally, Jim could rely on logging 160 days of the year, but a look at 1972 trucking days showed that only 151 days of logging occurred. All but one of the extra down days was caused by the loader. Jim had talked with some of the equipment dealers and found that he liked the new Link-Belt loaders best of all, but he felt the company was not in a financial position to buy a new one. He compared specifications of two new loaders with two used models and found the following relationship to exist:

Brand	Model Year	Purchase Price	Annual Sched. Maintenance Cost[1]	Annual Allow. for Unscheduled Maint.[2]	Useful Life	Salvage Value
Link-Belt	1973	$121,740	1.458%	$4,500	10 Yrs	$5,500
Lorain	1973	$127,100	1.65%	$4,300	10 Yrs	$6,000
Link-Belt	1968	$ 66,500	3.1%	$4,900	6 Yrs	$5,600
Bucyrus-Erie	1967	$ 51,200	4.7%	$6,100	5 Yrs	$5,400

[1] Annual scheduled maintenance cost is a percentage of purchase price. These figures were supplied by the equipment dealers.
[2] Both new machines carry two-year warranties covering *all* unscheduled maintenance not caused by operator negligence or abuse. These figures were obtained from owners of similar loaders.

The decision of which loader to buy was an important one, because he did not want to be shut down for maintenance due to the old loader this year. The winter had been an unusually dry one, so he expected an unusually dry summer with more logging days shut down for lower humidity than normal. All dealers offered him $6,000 trade-in allowance for his old loader. Another alternative was that of leasing the loader at 4% of the purchase price per month with no maintenance expenses by the Barnes Lumber Company.

Compounding the equipment issue was that of the truck issue. Jim Lewis had been reluctant to keep the 1961 Peterbilt truck when the other two Peterbilts were traded in last year on the two new trucks. Although he had originally planned to use one truck as a spare, he found that the 1961 Peterbilt was being used every day, because the logging operation required three trucks to keep up with the new tower and yarder. Jim figured hauling costs averaged $7.25 per thousand board feet on his average haul of 25 miles. Unscheduled maintenance on the 1961 Peterbilt had pushed this rate to $7.50 for the last six months. Jim used the $7.25 rate for devising his timber-bidding strategy and was convinced keeping the old truck would change his hauling rate to $7.50. He knew the trucks averaged four loads of logs per day, and figured 25 miles was the average length of haul. After a good deal of debate with Jack Barnes and Harold Thompson over the investment in a new truck, Jim had obtained the following facts on which truck to purchase, if the company decided to purchase (All trucks listed are new):

Brand	Purchase Price	1961 Peterbilt Trade-in Allow.	Useful Life	Salvage Value
Peterbilt	$31,089	$5,500	12 Yrs	$5,500
Diamond Reo	$26,564	$4,100	10 Yrs	$3,500
Mack	$36,500	$5,500	12 Yrs	$5,950
Kenworth	$31,197	$5,000	12 Yrs	$5,700

Jim did not compare prices of the lighter trucks, such as Ford, Chevrolet, and International because he preferred the ruggedness of the trucks listed above. He preferred Peterbilts because of the dependability the company had experienced with these trucks in the past. The Mack dealer pointed out, however, that his truck, coupled with the Mack engine, offered the following advantages over the other trucks in his field of considerations:

1. Only six forward gear speeds, instead of a twenty as in other trucks. This resulted in 30% to 40% less gearshifting, or an estimated 10% to 15% less maintenance than his current Peterbilts.
2. 10% better fuel economy.
3. 10% higher trade-in value.
4. Only Mack trucks currently meet 1975 emission standards, so no modifications would be necessary in the next two years to meet emission standards. Jim estimated that all trucks, except the Mack, would get five miles per gallon fuel mileage, and diesel fuel would cost 25¢ per gallon. Maintenance and upkeep averaged $2100 per year on the Peterbilts, so he decided to use this base for computing maintenance costs.

Jim was also considering leasing the trucks through a leasing agency. The agency would supply any one of the trucks he desired, at a rate of 1.8% of the purchase price per month. These payments would be paid only during the months the trucks would be in use, so that no payments would be due from November through February when the trucks were inoperative. The leasing agency would perform all maintenance and upkeep. Barnes Lumber Company would just supply the fuel and driver. At any rate, the truck decision would need to be made in the very near future because the drivers had just informed him that the old Peterbilt needed an engine overhaul.

Jim looked to a new loader as a means of reducing logging costs from the present $28 per thousand board feet to about $26 per thousand board feet. He believed a new truck could effectively reduce average hauling costs to $7.00 per thousand board feet. But he was not sure what to buy and if the company could afford to buy this equipment.

OTHER CONSIDERATIONS

One of the mill workers had pointed out the fact that the headsaw had to saw cants into smaller pieces before they went to the resaw. This resulted in a 30% loss of production at the headrig. Jack Barnes toyed with the idea of installing a "pony" headrig in the main sawmill in order to relieve the load on the headrig. The pony headrig would cost $41,000 to install, have a twenty-year useful life, and cost $1,000 annually to maintain. Jack was aware that the remainder of the present mill was not able to handle the entire output of the headsaw, if the headsaw did not saw up the cants. Bottlenecks in the manufacturing process would allow only 67% of the increase in production to pass through the mill without stopping the headrig, if the pony headrig were installed. The installation of the pony headrig would also require the hiring of another sawyer. The union wage for sawyers was currently $6.26 per hour.

Mr. Thompson, the office manager, had been reluctant to change any of the financing policy the company had been following. His logic was that since the operation was relatively small, they could not afford to go heavily into debt and rely on monthly payments to creditors. Several times in the past, a large company had produced an excess of one of Barnes' main products. The company subsequently dumped these products on the market at a very low price, causing Barnes to stockpile its products until the price went up. Sometimes this waiting period consumed three to four months. Barnes would not have been able to meet its monthly payments if it had had a large number of investments. Barnes therefore acquired financing on three-year contracts with one-third down, and the balance due in three years on all investments greater than $10,000 and less than $50,000. The company used a three-year payback criterion for all small investments. All single investments greater than $150,000 used appropriate long-term financing. The penalty for following this procedure was that interest rates on the three-year contracts averaged 9.5%. The Gladewater bank informed Jack Barnes that they would provide interest rates of 8.25% on these same contracts, if paid back in monthly installments. Currently, the company had $75,000 financed in three-year borrowings, and any purchases of new equipment would raise this figure radically. Mr. Thompson continued to point out that the corporation paid income taxes on $28,000 worth of earnings last year and the higher interest rate gave them a good tax break. Jack Barnes did not know whether to believe him or not.

Other companies in the local area had been forming so-called export companies, and Jack Barnes had considered doing likewise. The company did not export any logs because it harvested its timber from federal lands which had an export quota, and the company felt the amount of timber allowed for export from any one sale was generally too small to worry about. The 10% profit (after harvesting costs and hauling costs to the port) obtained from exporting logs was less than the return to be made on manufacturing and selling the lumber. The company nonetheless did export lumber. The advantage of forming an export company is that one can leave one-half of the year's profits as retained earnings in the export company and not pay income tax on those earnings until the earnings are taken out. Thus the company can hold money until a less profitable year before taking the money out. Costs of forming the company would amount to $5,000. Jack was not sure he wanted to invest that money, even if the tax break was good.

CONCLUSION

The spring of 1973 left Barnes Lumber Company with many issues to be resolved. Jack Barnes wondered if the installation of the small mill was a worthwhile venture and if he should install a pony headrig in the main mill. Jim Lewis knew that he would have to buy some of the upcoming timber sales, but he had not calculated how much he could afford to pay for the timber. He wanted to replace the old equipment, but did not know which of each to buy. Financial considerations plagued the company. More important, all three owners were worried that they could not afford to pay the high prices for raw materials in the future that some of their competitors were already paying.

Once a sale was purchased, the company would have to wait a year before it could harvest the sale since it had a backlog of previously purchased sales to log. Thus management was afraid the price of lumber would drop drastically at any time, leaving them holding much high-priced stumpage.

EXHIBIT 1
UPCOMING TIMBER SALES
MAY 24, 1973
BUREAU OF LAND MANAGEMENT

Parcel #	Species	Estimated Volume	Appraised Price/Mb.f.	Estimated Volume Times App. Price
14	Douglas-fir	3,599	$160.35	$577,099.65
	Hemlock	724	82.55	59,766.20
	Western Redcedar	179	83.55	14,955.45
	Total	4,502		$651,821.30
	Log export volume allowed: 360 Mb.f.			
16	Douglas-fir	908	144.50	$131,206.00
	White fir	3	86.00	258.00
	Hemlock	46	81.35	3,742.10
	Western Redcedar	53	77.20	4,091.60
	Total	1,010		$139,297.70
	No logs shall be exported			
17	Douglas-fir	885	146.75	$129,873.75
	White fir	15	85.55	1,283.25
	Hemlock	10	83.85	838.50
	Incense Cedar	103	74.05	7,627.15
	Western Redcedar	37	74.35	2,750.95
	Total	1,050		$142,373.60
	No logs shall be exported			
18	Douglas-fir	3,697	145.25	$536,989.25
	White fir	22	91.00	2,002.00
	Incense Cedar	33	80.85	2,668.05
	Total	3,752		$541,659.30
	Log export volume allowed: 300 Mb.f.			
19	Douglas-fir	2,742	137.30	$376,476.60
	Hemlock	36	75.00	2,700.00
	Western Redcedar	209	65.00	13,585.00
	Total	2,987		$392,761.60
	Log export volume allowed: 239 Mb.f.			

EXHIBIT 2
SELLING PRICE AND ANTICIPATED SALES, 1973

Product	% of Company Sales	Avg. Price 1972	Anticipated Price 1973
Export Clear Lumber (European Markets)	10%	$397/Mb.f.	$489/Mb.f.
Crossarms & Mine Timbers	18%	$257/Mb.f.	$389/Mb.f.
Large Planks	29%	$227/Mb.f.	$327/Mb.f.
Timbers	12%	$314/Mb.f.	$425/Mb.f.
Utility	25%	$167/Mb.f.	$207/Mb.f.
Stadium Seats, other specialty products	6%	$460/Mb.f.	$555/Mb.f.

EVALUATION OF THE
BARNES LUMBER COMPANY CASE

SUMMARY

This case centers around the operations of the Barnes Lumber Company. The company is experiencing financial problems because of competitive increases in the price of lumber. Also, the company has lost valuable logging time caused by the breakdown of equipment. Barnes has been considering the purchase of new equipment to replace the old equipment and also the purchase of equipment to alleviate the backlog of previously purchased logs. Management is concerned that the price of lumber may drop drastically at any time, leaving them with a high-priced inventory of previously purchased lumber.

KEY ISSUES

1. Has Barnes Lumber Co. defined its goals and objectives?
2. Has a strategic plan been established?
3. Has the processing of logs been scheduled efficiently?
4. Do the owners of the company utilize the financial data available to them for making purchase decisions?
5. Should the company expand facilities?
6. If the company decides to purchase new equipment, how should the acquisition be financed?

DISCUSSION

1. Goals, Objectives, and Planning

Goals and objectives may be expressed in many different ways (capacity, net income, etc.) but they must be defined in measurable terms to provide a basis for performance evaluation. There is no evidence of any specific planning to meet future demand. Purchases of logs must be planned in advance to arrange the financing. Also, unplanned purchases create a backlog of logs to be processed since present facilities have a capacity limitation. Poor scheduling of the main mill facilities has left management with a large amount of expensive lumber to process. If the price of logs drops, the company may suffer substantial losses.

2. Financial Analysis

A large amount of financial information is available regarding the costs of purchasing new equipment. It appears, however, that analysis is not being performed to compare different alternatives.

The main mill at this time does not have the facilities to saw a log under 14" in diameter. These logs are either sold to other operators at a loss or left in the woods. The company can analyze their financial data to determine if the benefit of setting up a mill to handle the small logs, exceeds the cost of the new mill.

Barnes Lumber is presently in need of funds to bid on log sales and for the purchase of equipment. Also, financing will be needed if expansion is decided upon. There are several financing alternatives, including short term borrowing, long term borrowing, and issue of additional stock.

Alternative Considerations

There are always a number of alternatives that should be considered in evaluating the solution to any type of organizational problem. These alternatives include, but are not limited to, the following:

1. Status quo - continue to operate the company in the same manner.

    Advantages: No expenditures for new equipment and facilities.

    Disadvantages: Financial problems may continue to the point where the company will not be able to remain in operation.

2. Establish a scheduling system for purchases, facilities, and equipment use - the large backlog has put management in an unprofitable position. The backlog should be reduced.

    Advantages: Increased efficiency in the utilization of facilities and the establishment of "preventive maintenance" system for equipment to reduce breakdowns.

    Disadvantages: The schedule may not have the flexibility needed for the mill and equipment may be too "worn out" to receive any benefit from preventive maintenance.

3. Hire a financial consultant - have an expert evaluate different alternatives for purchasing new equipment.

    Advantages: Most efficient investment in new equipment, resulting in cost minimization.

    Disadvantages: The cost of the consultant.

4. Expand the present facilities to process logs less than 14" in diameter.

    Advantages: The increased production could increase profitability and reduces losses which resulted previously from selling small logs to other mills at a low price.

    Disadvantages: The cost of the new mill may exceed the benefits to be derived.

5. Define goals and objectives.

    Advantages: Establish a basis for performance measurement.

    Disadvantages: The fluctuations in the lumber industry may make it difficult to set measurable goals and objectives for a short term basis.

This company has several problems which must be addressed. First and foremost is the establishment of a long-range corporate strategy with measurable goals and objectives. As noted, in this particular industry, objectives are not easily defined; however, strategic planning is essential if growth and expansion are the basic goal of the organization. Additional problems which require immediate consideration include equipment and capacity utilization, production processes, financing of new equipment and facilities, and performance evaluation.

PART III

The Strategic Planning Process

5

The Assessment of Present Capabilities

IMPORTANCE OF ASSESSMENT PROCESS

Planning is based on assumptions or forecasts about what the planner expects to occur within the company's environment. In addition to isolating these external factors, company resources are studied to see what steps can be taken to meet the requirements of the environmental situation and to exploit company strengths.

All planning is done within the context of external premises which may be explicitly stated or implicitly understood. These external premises are based upon specific assumptions about economic, social, political, industry and market factors that will affect the firm's future profitability and/or inability.

The assessment process, with which the next two chapters are concerned, is the process of evaluating all environmental factors which affect the operations of the particular enterprise. The task of the strategic planner is to make an appropriate analysis of the relevant environment, to make recommendations with respect to that environment, to generate strategic alternatives, to obtain top managements' decisions on a particular alternative, and to express and communicate the resulting strategic decisions in an operational manner. As the following flow chart illustrates,[1] the assessment process of appraisal and analysis is a necessary and vital prerequisite which must necessarily precede the generation of strategic alternatives. No worthwhile strategic alternative can be determined without an explicit or implicit process of assessment of the enterprise's present and future capabilities, resources and an analysis of strengths and weaknessess. An organization would be foolish if it planned to compete in the market place in a field of endeavour in which it lacked any special advantage or capability. Only if all the opposition were of equal or greater incompetence could the enterprise be realistically expected to survive!

The strategic planning process requires the determination, at an early stage, of the assessment phase; what is the appropriate forecast period or time horizon for this particular industry and enterprise?

132

FIGURE 1
Strategic Planning: Simple Flowchart of Key Steps

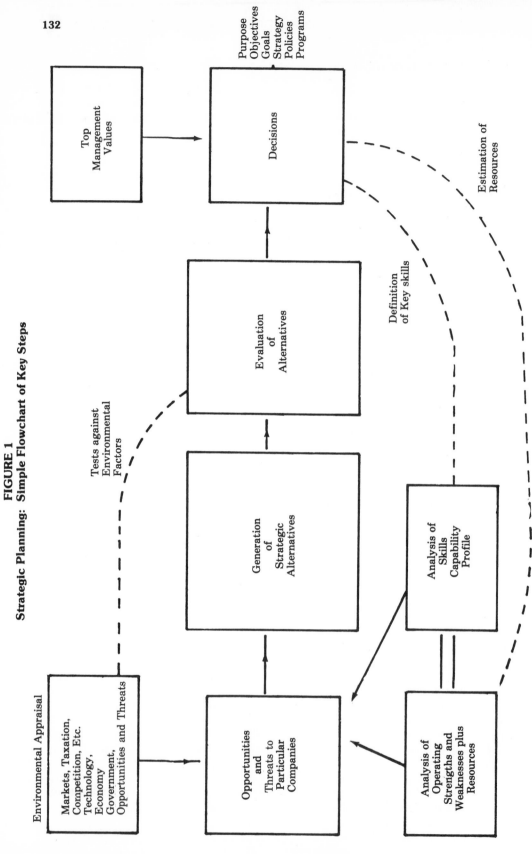

Source: B.W. Denning, Corporate Planning: Selected Concepts, p.8 Copyright (c) 1971, McGraw-Hill Book Co. (UK) Ltd. Reproduced by permission.

DETERMINATION OF APPROPRIATE PLANNING HORIZONS

The enterprise which seeks to assess future capabilities and innovative developments must take into account the fact that the appropriate planning horizon differs greatly from industry to industry. A major reason for this difference is the vastly differing rates of technological change, resource availability and substitutability, and the relative speed with which the industry infrastructure can be altered to meet new and unexpected challenges. An appropriate planning horizon for a ladies fashion clothing manufacturer most likely would be entirely inappropriate for a public utility firm, for example!

Different companies, therefore, find it necessary to plan according to different time horizons. There is a general tendency to choose five years as a reasonable compromise between the need for an adequate time perspective and the costs of planning in detail for time periods which, because of so many unknowns, would only yield an expensive and unrealistic exercise.

The selection of an appropriate time horizon for planning purposes is therefore necessarily one which requires sound judgment and cannot be derived from any formula. It is possible, however, to use the following guides as tools which the planner may find useful when faced with the problem of seeking to determine what is an appropriate time horizon for planning. The guides are:[2]

1. The planning cycle should be long enough to include the full time for bringing new large capital projects into existence, including the time required for negotiating the necessary outside finance.
2. The planning cycle should be longer than any cyclical patterns that may exist in the economy if the product sold is affected by cyclical swings.
3. The planning cycle should be long enough to allow reasoned consideration of major technological changes.
4. Special planning cycles and processes may be necessary to deal with projects of especial length, such as forest plantations, oil exploration and development, and any other enterprise which necessitates longer than average planning cycles.
5. Long-range planning should be a continuous process. This means that while three, five, or seven years may be selected as the time horizon over which planning takes place, the forward planning for this time period should be carried out every year. In other words, the concept of a rolling plan should be adopted in which the plan is reviewed annually and projected into the future one year further.

There are few companies of any considerable size that can afford not to indulge in systematic strategic planning over a time horizon of less than three years. Whenever a requirement exists for massive capital investment in facilities which have long payout periods and require long lead times, an appropriate time horizon for strategic planning may be 25 years or even longer. The forest products industries and the petroleum industry are two examples which readily come to mind of industries for which exceptionally long range planning is not only desirable, but crucial if these enterprises are to be capable of ensuring their long-range survival.

It should be apparent that the selection of the appropriate time horizon for planning purpose is a decision which cannot be taken lightly. Consideration should include a careful examination of such factors as foreseeability of environmental change, level of error in predictions which is tolerable, particular length of planning cycle required for capital investment, and the evaluation of any variable which is unique to that industry.

Because of the serious results which may result from the selection of an inappropriate time horizon such a decision should be made at the highest management level. The allocation of corporate planning responsibilities merits close examination in any organization which seeks to engage in strategic planning.

ALLOCATION OF CORPORATE PLANNING RESPONSIBILITIES

Planning is a primary responsibility of management at all levels in an organization. As the hierarchical ladder is ascended, however, the nature and scope of planning responsibilities will vary. At the highest corporate levels, management is responsible to establish the fundamental direction of the enterprise and to formulate overall strategies to achieve corporate objectives. At the lower management levels, planning efforts are generally short-range and deal with matters primarily under the jurisdiction of the respective manager. In between these extremes, the nature of planning duties changes with level, scope of managerial authority and company organization.

If the planning to be done is relatively narrow in scope, the organizing and staffing stages are relatively simple. An operating manager starting his planning may be faced only with organizing his own time or his own job, in order to leave time for planning. The complications grow as the size of the project grows. As a result, the corporate planner's job is quite different from that of the operating manager's planning job, even though the two levels of planning are interdependent and each planner makes use of the same overall planning process.

The corporate planner frequently becomes involved in formally organizing a department or corporate function. He also becomes enmeshed in the many political and personal management problems encountered in getting others to do planning and in setting a favorable climate for developing plans and carrying out plans at the operating level. The human problems are thus extremely important in planning, and to ignore them may spell disaster for any planning effort.

The trend among larger companies seems to be towards treating planning as a separate and distinct functional area comparable to production, finance, and marketing.

A recent survey of the allocation of corporate planning responsibilities showed that of all firms with formal planning organizations, planning was a separate and distinct function with its own full-time director for two-thirds of the firms surveyed. Only one-sixth organized the planning function within the existing finance and control group, and only one-sixth assigned planning functions to executives who also performed other duties. All companies assigned the planning responsibility to a higher echelon executive.[3]

In the majority of companies studied there is a fairly consistent division of planning responsibility. The division is between a corporate staff group of executive who develops overall strategic plans, coordinates planning, analyzes proposed new ventures, and the managers of staff and operating (or line) units who are responsible for developing short and long-range operating plans for their respective departments or divisions.

In many companies the corporate planner has a staff to assist him in performing his duties. One of the major jobs of this staff is to supply the operating managers with the environmental information needed to prepare plans. This information covers such areas as general economic forecasts, total product demand, the share of that demand the company can expect to sell, and projected potential company sales by product and by major market. The staff would also supply operating managers with strategic planning information (overall company objectives, policies, and other strategic factors limiting planning), as well as information on available resources. In addition, the corporate planning staff develops procedures for preparing plans.

Final approval for comprehensive plans usually rests with the chairman of the board, president, or executive vice-president. Overall comprehensive plans are, therefore, always reviewed by one of these executives or an executive committee appointed by them. Generally these reviews are made once a year, although they may be reviewed semi-annually or even quarterly. The majority of comprehensive plans are for five years, and so cover both long- and short-term plans.

Corporate planning is an inseparable part of the job of all chief operating executives; the future of their companies depends upon the plans generated by them. The only constant in the management of business organizations is change. The leadership in adapting corporate operations to the changing business world must come from the chief executive. Unless company presidents who have heretofore shunned the planner role give hard and fast attention to the future of their enterprises by personal involvement in planning, only the most fortuitous circumstances will enable their firms to avoid declines in sales, profits, and market positions.

After an appropriate planning horizon has been determined and an allocation of corporate planning responsibilities has been completed, the planner must next seek to select the following: what are the basic objectives which shape the character of the company?

BASIC OBJECTIVES WHICH SHAPE THE CHARACTER OF THE COMPANY

Every firm must make a series of basic decisions. It must decide what opportunities it wants to pursue and what risks it is willing to undergo. Decisions must be made regarding the scope of the business, and the proper balance between specialization, diversification, and integration. It must decide between spending time to build an organization and buying an established business such as by acquisition, joint venture, or merger. It must decide on an organization structure appropriate to its economic realities and its opportunities.

The net result of this series of policy decisions is to establish a corporate identity which is unique to that firm. These decisions proclaim to the world the type and kind of business in which the firm is engaged. The very character of the personnel is predetermined, because staffing activity is fitted to policy parameters.

According to W.H. Newman, the first decision to be made for any company is the industry in which it will operate.[4] Then the place a company seeks in its industry may be defined in terms of

1. major functions to be performed;
2. specialization versus diversification of activities;
3. quality or price level sought; and
4. size of operation.

The aim of a company regarding size, quality level, specialization versus diversification, and major economic functions will go a long way in defining one basic set of objectives for a company. The planner must recognize that the place a company seeks in its industry will have a marked effect on the company character.

A firm's disposition toward change is another area which has a profound influence on its character. This facet of character can be considered in terms of:

1. progressiveness - the seeking of better ways;
2. aggressiveness - drive in making changes;
3. willingness to take risks; and
4. willingness to share ownership control.

A third set of basic objectives which shape the character of a company deal with its social philosophy: its

1. community relations;
2. government and economic responsibilities;
3. customer service;
4. supplier relationships;
5. stockholder relations;
6. competitor relationships; and
7. employee relationships.

There is also a fourth type of objective which also has a profound influence upon the character of the company. This is concerned with the management philosophy which is reflected in

1. centralization versus decentralization of decision-making;
2. quality of key personnel;
3. extent of advance planning and research going into such plans; and
4. manner of supervision or strictness of control.

Every business firm develops a character, an individuality of its own. A sensing of this character is necessary for a member of the company or an outsider to really understand the enterprise as a dynamic entity. The planner who seeks to engage in the process of assessing a firm's resources and capabilities must keep in mind the constraints imposed upon him by the basic company character. The planner should, therefore, endeavour to aim for things the company is qualified to do in terms of technical skill, temperament and resources attainable; and strive for internal compatibility among its objectives.

After determining the company character, it is necessary to determine what relevant factors need to be measured in order to proceed to the assessment phase of the strategic planning process.

DETERMINATION AND MEASUREMENT OF RELEVANT FACTORS

The firm must be analyzed both internally and externally to determine the firm's special competencies and weaknesses so that the next step, that of developing alternative plans, will be based on shoring up the firm's difficult areas and leading from strength on the firm's competitive advantages.

If the external environment influences a firm and the strategy it pursues, then it must necessarily follow that the planner needs to examine the external influences or potential influences on it. The environmental factors that need to be examined can be classified into four general categories: social, political, technological, and economic. These factors do not exist by themselves in isolation, they are interrelated.

1. Social Influences

A number of factors change the social environment and will affect the firm. Such factors as demographic shifts, urbanization, changing levels of education and changes in the membership of the labor force (i.e., more working women) all are important social changes which need to be examined by the planner.

2. Political Influences

Political organizations and their actions will have immediate and/or long-range influence on the firm. Government agencies can exercise three types of influence on a firm:

1. direct competition with the firm,
2. protecting and/or stimulating its growth, and
3. regulate (i.e. limit) it or its industry.

The amount and extent of government regulations varies widely, of course. The finance industry is closely regulated (banks, insurance, stock market) and so is the utility industry. Other industries are strongly influenced such as public broadcasting, drugs, food, and air transport. Some industries are little affected, such as clothing and some personal services. The planner, therefore, needs to carefully analyze the present and potential impact of government policy on the industry and the company in question.

3. Technological Influences

To a greater or lesser extent, technological change has an impact on all firms. The greater the potential impact, the more likely a firm needs to have extensive research and development facilities to survive. If the company makes transistors, for example, technology will have had far greater impact on the firm during the past 20 years than if it makes men's shoes.

Technology will frequently affect production methods and/or the products or services offered by the firm. New materials have been developed that may affect the firm's products - for example, plastics replacing glass or wood, synthetic fibers replacing cotton and wool. New machinery, of which the computer is a good example, may have a tremendous impact on the operations of a business.

4. Economic Influences

Economic and market factors which influence the success of the firm include: the nature of competition in the industry, including ease of entry, size of investment required to enter, liquidity or convertibility of assets needed or used in the industry. Additional factors include the impact of suppliers and labor on the firm, the nature of the channels in the market the firm sells to, and the volatility of the product/service life cycle in which the firm is currently involved. Obviously, the present demand and supply of products and services, and general economic consideration, such as, the phase of the business cycle the economy is in are very important to this assessment process.

5. Assessment of the Firm's Internal Strengths and Weaknesses

After searching the environment and assessing it, it is time to look inward to see how the company is performing when measured against its environment and against standards of good business practice. Internal appraisal of the firm means appraisal of how well it is performing its business functions (for example, marketing, engineering, finance, accounting, personnel-labor relations, and production). An important aspect of this analysis is to face up to the problems, that is, to look at all the data and see where the firm's strengths and weaknesses are.

A detailed assessment of the firm's performance of its internal operations provides input data for the development of alternative plans for future corporate strategy. After a close look at the firm, the planner should now be aware of its capabilities. If its capital structure is strained and the external environment calls for innovation, the planner should realize that certain strategies such as growth through merger are not possible, unless new sources of funds can be developed.

At this point in the assessment process, the unique special capabilities and strengths the firm has should also be known. These factors will be inputs for development of future strategy.

Before the corporate planner can actually begin utilizing the assessment process for determining a firm's present capabilities and its strengths and weaknesses, he must have determined:

1. what planning horizon is appropriate,
2. what is the allocation of corporate planning responsibilities,
3. what basic objectives shape the character of the company and
4. what relevant factors are going to be measured in his assessment of the firms environment?

Only then can the planner properly proceed to the phase of assessing present capabilities in detail.

IMPORTANCE OF ASSESSING PRESENT CAPABILITIES IN RELATION TO CORPORATE OBJECTIVES

The primary objective in conducting an overall assessment is to identify problems, threats, and opportunities in the organization's environment and structure and to devise plans that include practical responses to the environmental and structural situation. The second objective of the overall assessment process is to evaluate the operation of specific strategies and specific managers for corrective action by the organization where necessary.

Describing the enterprise's present scope and deployments enables us to identify the actual present strategy. Comparing the organization's performance characteristics (specifications) with those of competitors, with the values assigned to each parameter by the owners or managers (objectives), and with the characteristics of other industries or activities to which the company's resources and competence could be applied, provides a basis for evaluating past performance and future prospects.

In evaluating an enterprise's performance, we should not apply some arbitrary, external standard which may or may not be applicable in the specific situation. Of first importance is the objective or objectives that the company's top management wants to achieve. To the degree that these objectives can be translated into operational targets and articulated to the organization, they provide the fundamental standards against which actual performance should be measured.

A company deliberately kept small by its management so that they can maintain close personal control over operations should not be evaluated poorly on the parameter of size and rate of growth since such a parameter was not a corporate objective anyway. Similarly, a company whose management deliberately chooses to keep the full complement of workers employed during a sales downturn should not be faulted for the consequent effect upon current profits. Rather, company performance should be assessed in terms of how well these stated targets were achieved.

Most companies have annual budgets which define at least some kind of size objective and profitability target. Comparing actual performance against these targets, if they are carefully and realistically constructed, provides a general measure of company "success." Use of arbitrary budget figures or mere historical extrapolations of the past may prove more of an indictment of management's way of thinking than a measure of company performance. Thus, the more specific and realistic top management can be in setting performance specifications, the better the opportunity for evaluating that performance effectively.

The planner who seeks to assess the past and present performance of an enterprise must also determine what stage of corporate development exists in that particular enterprise at this point in time. This determination of the stage of corporate development will facilitate the environmental audit which will follow.

DETERMINATION OF THE STAGE IN THE CORPORATE DEVELOPMENT LIFE CYCLE

The stage of corporate development, when determined by the planner, will facilitate the assessment of resources, capabilities, strengths and weaknesses, and the competency profile of the enterprise. The stage of corporate development is itself a significant environmental factor which can be a major constraint for the planner. Many alternative plans for future strategy may not be compatible with the particular stage of corporate organization. The planner may in fact be faced with the requirement for advocating a shift in corporate organizational form before other plans can be considered.

According to D.H. Thain, the stages of corporate development can be briefly described as follows:[5]

As companies that are relatively successful grow larger in size and scope, they experience a number of fairly obvious changes. This evolution occurs as:

1. Sales, expenditure, gross profits and investments increase
2. The number of employees increase
3. Resources increase
4. Activities and functions increase in size, scope and number
5. Operating and management problems increase in size, complexity and risk
6. Operating and managerial specialization increases
7. Product lines increase either vertically (diversification in the same industry) or horizontally (diversification into different industries)
8. The number and specialization of organizational subunits increase

This evolution of companies from small and simple to large and complex tends to be marked by three main stages of development as shown in Tables 1 and 2.[6]

TABLE 1

MAIN STAGES OF CORPORATE DEVELOPMENT

Small and Simple Stage I	Transitional Stage II	Large and Complex Stage III
One Unit: "One Man Show"	One Unit: Functionally Specialized Group	Multiunit: General Office and Decentralized Divisions

Although all companies can be classified on this spectrum as to their stage of corporate development, not all are "pure" examples of any one of the stages, that is, many are in a phase of transition from Stage I to II or from II to III.

TABLE 2

- Typical organization charts of corporate development of Stage I, Stage II, and Stage III companies.

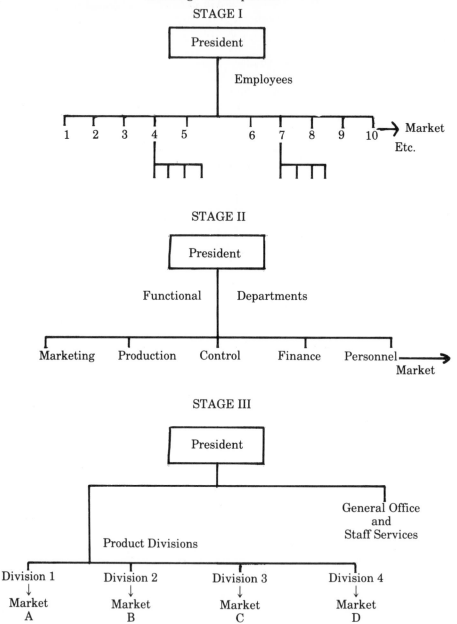

1. Stage I

The vast majority of all firms began operations in Stage I. The major characteristic of the Stage I company is that it is primarily a "one man show." With the exception of perhaps a few shares doled out to directors, relatives, or long-time key employees, the company manager maintains absolute ownership and control. The company's strengths, vulnerabilities and resources are closely correlated with his personality, ability, style of management, and personal financial situation. He makes all the important decisions, relying on sales, production and office supervisors only to the extent necessary to see that his unilateral decisions are carried out.

Because of its tightly limited resources and lack of back-up managers and staff, the Stage I owner-manager tends to be a notoriously authoritarian, short-term operator. It is therefore no accident that nearly all business bankruptcies occur in Stage I companies. Although the flexibility for decision making and organizational change may be great, the constraints resulting from lack of resources and narrow vistas impose severe limitations on the owner-manager's scope for action.[7]

2. Stage II

The distinguishing characteristic of Stage II is that it is a one-unit enterprise run by a team of managers with functionally specialized responsibilities. In a small, simple, newly developed Stage II company the functional team might be limited — perhaps only the president, a sales manager, and a production manager. In a large, highly developed, complex Stage II company the group might include marketing, production, engineering, quality control, finance, personnel, industrial relations, public relations, and long-range planning. In addition each of these functional units might be further subdivided: for example, marketing might include departments for sales, advertising, brand management, and marketing research. In other firms the traditional functional groupings might be subunits that more effectively relate to the particular operating problems of the business. In a large integrated oil company, for example, the functional specialization might be exploration, drilling, pipelines, transportation, refining, and marketing.[8]

3. Stage III

The hallmark of the Stage III company is a headquarters or general office with ultimate control over multiple operating divisions, each similar to a Stage II company. Although the general offices may vary widely in size, organization, power and operating control, their control functions are investment trusteeship; supervision, control and evaluation of division managers and operations; staff advice, and further diversification. As investment trustees, managing a "portfolio" of enterprises, they carry out the process of capital budgeting for the corporation as a whole. The cash flows from the divisions are remitted to the general office for reinvestment in the most necessary or highest payoff projects to be found within the corporation or outside the enterprise. If a division cannot produce a profit above the required minimum rate of return, it is sold, liquidated, or otherwise disposed of.

The successful Stage III company has many strengths that can make it a formidable international economic unit. Its ownership is almost always public and its resources are tremendous. Large cash flows, management depth, functional specialization and market diversification make its vulnerability to bankruptcy very low. It has great powers to regroup and survive even in the event of such a serious crisis as the complete failure of an entire product or division (e.g., Ford's Edsel).

Perhaps the most significant weakness of the gigantic Stage III company is that its organization is so large and complex that it tends to become relatively inflexible. Organizational restraints are necessarily great, defense of the "status quo" becomes built in, and a time-consuming, bureaucratic approach complete with formal and informal administration by "due process" becomes institutionalized. So many checks and balances become operative that significant change may be beyond the power or control of any one man or small group.

In order to avoid this type of dysfunctional consequences a number of major corporations such as IBM, XEROX, LITTON, and TEXTRON have adopted a FREE-FORM type of organization. This organization form allows each unit to plan its own strategic posture but the final strategic plan for each unit is evaluated and revised in light of total enterprise commitments and objectives. All resources are viewed as if in a common pot, and they are redistributed frequently to achieve desired emphasis and priorities.[9]

Assessment of Strategies for Corporate Development

The most straightforward strategic problems in regard to corporate development are those of the Stage I manager. The immediate strategic problem is to increase sales and generate sufficient cash flows to carry the overhead cost of supporting a management, even if it is only two or three members. The manager must then switch from player to coach, delegating operating responsibility and developing, challenging, encouraging, measuring and rewarding and punishing his top management group. As growth permits, added management specialists can be added to the team.

Corporate development for the Stage II company can in general take one or both of two routes:

1. expansion through the present product line, or
2. diversification by adding new product divisions.

Therefore, depending on prospects for the company's basic product-market niche, resources, distinctive competences, management ability, and motivation and perceived market opportunities, the Stage II president can plan:

a) to increase growth and penetration in present product markets, or
b) to enter new business.

Strategy (a) is based on moves to compete more effectively so that the company can increase present shares in static or declining markets to hold present shares in growing markets and/or moving to integrate backward or forward into closely related products and activities.

Strategy (b) requires that the company exercise the make or buy option and get into new, nonrelated products via the internal route—research and development, new product development and marketing—or the external route—acquisition of product-market niches that can be more favorably purchased than developed.

The options for growth in a Stage III company are to expand through present product divisions or to develop and/or acquire new product divisions. In most respects such decisions are similar to those confronting the Stage II company, except that the Stage III company should be much more experienced and skilled in approaching and solving the many problems involved.

BLOCKS TO CORPORATE DEVELOPMENT

Some of the major internal and external blocks to development are briefly summarized below in outline form.[10]

1. Internal blocks to development
   a) Stages I to II
      1. Lack of ambition and drive
      2. Personal reasons of owner-manager for avoiding change in status quo
      3. Lack of operating efficiency

    4. Lack of quantity and quality of operating personnel
    5. Lack of resources such as borrowing power, plant, and equipment, salesmen, etc.
    6. Product problems and weaknesses
    7. Lack of planning and organizational ability

b) Stage II to III
    1. Unwillingness to take the risks involved
    2. Management resistance to change for a variety of reasons including old age, aversion to risk taking, desire to protect personal empires, etc.
    3. Personal reasons among managers for defending the status quo.
    4. Lack of control system related to appraisal of investment of decentralized operations
    5. Lack of budgetary control ability
    6. Organizational inflexibility
    7. Lack of management vision to see opportunities for expansion.
    8. Lack of management development, i.e. not enough managers to handle expansion
    9. Management turnover and loss of promising young managers
    10. Lack of ability to formulate and implement strategy that makes company relevant to changing conditions
    11. Refusal to delegate power and authority for diversification

2. External blocks to development
a) Stages I to II
    1. Unfavorable economic conditions
    2. Lack of market growth
    3. Tight money or lack of an underwriter who will assist the company "to go public"
    4. Labor shortages in quality and quantity
    5. Technological obsolescence of product

b) Stages II to III
    1. Unfavorable economic, political, technological and social conditions, and/or trends
    2. Lack of access to financial or management resources
    3. Overly conservative accountants, lawyers, investment bankers, etc.
    4. Lack of domestic markets of size necessary to support large diversified corporations
    5. Content with the status quo, lack of desire to grow and develop.

The planner, having completed a careful and detailed examination of the enterprise's stage in the corporate development life cycle, will now be prepared to undertake a thorough assessment of the firm's external and internal environment.

PRESENT SITUATION ASSESSMENT

External Environment-Situation Audit

Changes in technology, legislation or social demands may affect entire industries and result in dramatic changes. Pressures from some citizen groups concerned with safety and pollution problems represent a potent factor in corporate and governmental planning. A lack of perceptive managers who can recognize such environmental changes may be disastrous. The astute planner must therefore focus his attention on those areas that will have a significant impact on the survival of the organization. The range of possibilities is very broad, but can be classified into four general categories: social, political, technological, and economic.

Social Considerations

The composition and thinking of society as a whole plays a significant part in the process of generating policies. The values or demands of society are used as inputs when corporate strategy is reformulated or reviewed and updated.

Many organizations have been forced to alter their corporate strategies, or cease operations altogether, because of changing social factors. The corporate planner must be constantly alert to indicators of shifts in the values and norms of the society in which his firm plans to conduct operations. Attitudes toward the importance of work and the desirability or need for goods and services have changed, and attitudes toward behavior at work also have changed. Moreover, increasing education and the all-pervasive influence of powerful media, especially television, have accelerated the speed and impact of these changes.

Each firm must assess to what extent these broad social changes have had and are likely to have an impact on their products and/or services and employees. Are the firm's products likely to become obsolete because of these changes (e.g. cigarettes, certain farm and small-town products, services, retail outlets, etc.)? Because of environmental problems and value changes, are products with great potential just taking off (e.g. mass-transit facilities, pollution-control devices, noise-control mechanisms, etc.)? These are some of the types of questions that the firm must ask itself when it attempts to assess the impact of social changes on its products and/or services and employees.

Political Considerations

Changes in government purchasing practices, subsidies, tariffs, export financing and R & D funding can all pose tremendous threats to the validity of a previous corporate plan. Industries which have been notoriously sensitive to shifts in government policy are mining and transportation. The aerospace industry is perhaps one of the best examples of an industry that must take into account political influences as being vital factors in both long and short-range planning.

A corporate planner working in the aerospace industry in the U.S. in the mid-60's would have been wise to notice social trends taking place which would eventually show up as political influences on all levels of government. The growing antiwar mood in the U.S. should have indicated a high probability of decreased defence spending in the forseeable future. Such did in fact occur with adverse effects on both aerospace and other defense industries. This is an example of the common situation where changes in society are soon reflected in the political field as well. Many environmental factors must therefore be regarded as being interactive and not existing in isolation.

Technological Considerations

The planner must have a clear understanding of the present state of technology affecting his products. A knowledge of the technological rate of change in the particular industry is an additional requirement. The greater the potential impact on the firm of rapid technological change the more critical this aspect of the situation assessment becomes. Many industries have found to their sorrow that what seemed at first as irrelevant unrelated technological changes in other industries proved to be the means which would ultimately threaten their very survival. Many textile firms were forced out of business because they could not see the effects that various, newly developed petroleum and chemical based derivatives would have on their products. Synthetic fibers gained a foothold in clothing and related markets, and many organizations that had not previously been a factor in the market became significant competitors or supply agents (e.g. Dupont).

The technological consideration is far more critical for some industries than for others. The cement and gypsum industries, for example, have not been affected by technological change at anywhere near the rate that the aerospace, electronics, or computer industries have been in the past two decades!

Economic Considerations

A significant factor in any compilation of environmental forces must of course include economic considerations. All too often the new enterprise or the diversification move taken by an enterprise fails because of changes in the economy. Many new enterprises are undercapitalized to begin with and thus are not equipped financially to cope with a general economic down-turn. Many of the managers of these new firms behave as if they thought the economy would keep on expanding forever! Their failure to develop strategic plans for reasonably foreseeable contingencies represents a severe indictment against the management concerned.

The planner must have a thorough understanding of the effects of the economy on the industry and on his particular firm. The firm which develops plans based upon the effects of economic considerations will have a distinct advantage over competitors who have not done so, and the advantage will be greatest when the severity of the economic turn-around is at its worst.

The planner must also be able to distinguish between long- and short-term economic factors. In the short-term the firm must recognize that "boom and bust" periods are of relatively short duration and that one will inevitably follow the other in the natural cycle of events. The failure of many small firms can be traced to the lack of consideration given to this most basic phenomenon. If the management of these firms who failed had taken into account the short term nature of the business cycle, many of these same firms might have survived.

However, if the other factors occurred which were longer lasting or even permanent, such as a major structural change in the economy, it is conceivable that nothing might have been able to save the firms. Liquidation would then be the only alternative to bankruptcy.

For some industries, such as the so-called countercyclical industries, a general economic down-turn increases demand for their products. The planner must therefore know or be capable of determining whether the industry in which his firm operates is cyclical, counter-cyclical or stable in relation to the business cycle. Any plans which err in this area will prove to be dangerous tools to place one's faith in.

After completing a thorough assessment of the external environment, the planner is now in a better position to assess the internal resources which the firm possesses.

INTERNAL ENVIRONMENT - RESOURCE AUDIT

After searching the environment and assessing it, it is time to look inward to see how the company is performing measured against its environment and against standards of good business practice. Internal appraisal of the firm means appraisal of how well it is performing its business functions (marketing, finance, accounting, personnel-labor relations, and operations).

Marketing

The marketing skills of the firm under review can be assessed by analyzing sales in terms of:

1. sales by customer category
2. sales by product category
3. sales by channel of distribution
4. sales by price/quality category

Sales by customer category should be grouped according to type, size, location, and other characteristics to determine the relevant concentration. The sales concentration is a valuable input to the identification and description of the present strategy. It can also reveal strengths or weaknesses which need to be examined for future planning.

Sales by product category are most typically classified by similarity in manufacturing process or similarity in raw materials or ingredients. It may be more useful to the planner however to categorize sales by usage, since this will be more significant for analysis and future planning.

Sales by channel of distribution is especially important where many channels of distribution are potentially available and their characteristics and requirements are very different.

Sales by price/category may reveal important characteristics about the customers and markets which would be hidden in a classification of sales by other categories.

Accurately documenting the scope of the firm's present operations is essential to understanding the company's situation, evaluating its performance, and planning for its future health and survival.

Finance

An analysis of the firms financial records should identify the main strengths and weaknesses of the firm: earnings ratios (to sales, to net worth, to working capital) earnings per share, debt ratios (current and acid tests, to inventory, to working capital, to net worth), capitalization structure. The trends in the basic financial facts should give indications as to the firm's prospects for growth in sales volume and rate of earnings.

The quality of the firm's financial management merits examination as well. The firm should know its cost of capital and have long-range financial plans for capital expenditures. The borrowing capacity of the firm should be known and the extent of any unused cash resources be determined. The pattern of existing cash flows can be a valuable item for the planner when assessing the total internal environment. Cash flows provide an indication of the current relative contribution of each unit to the total enterprise. A company cannot be described in a useful or meaningful way without identifying the sources of the cash which keep it alive and provide the basis for its future progress.

Operations

The quickening pace of technological change requires special attention to the ability of the engineering and manufacturing departments to cooperate effectively in bringing new products into production and in utilizing new processes. It requires special caution with respect to firms with heavy investments in inflexible capital equipment because such investments might be susceptible to almost overnight obsolescence.

The quality of the firm's production-scheduling, quality control and other industrial engineering methods needs to be closely assessed. The use of such techniques as "value engineering" should be assessed for its possible benefits which are the result of simplifying product designs and thus reducing costs.

The firm's operating and product costs should be compared with those of the competition in that industry. Any costs greater than industry average should be given a close and detailed examination to determine the reason why. Break-even points should be known and compared to the competition if at all possible.

The age and condition of the firm's plant and equipment should be assessed and compared to the rest of the industry. Perhaps the firm is in danger of obsolescence of much of its facilities which would necessitate a massive capital investment project in the near future to remain competitive.

Raw Material Supply Availability and Inventory

An internal environmental resource audit also needs to assess the firm's present capabilities in the area of raw material inventory and supply availability. Many manufacturing and process industries require tremendous volumes of raw materials for their continuous operation. Some of these raw materials are relatively stable in price and supply while others may fluctuate wildly in cost and availability. The firm faced with an uncertain supply of raw materials and low inventories is in a precarious position for continuing operations with any probability of success. The internal resource audit should therefore seek to determine the raw material supply/demand characteristics of the particular industry at the present time and then assess whether the firm's purchasing procedures are adequate to maintain sufficient inventories to ensure continuous operation.

Personnel

An additional factor which needs to be assessed is the personnel resources of the firm at the present time. Both the quantity available and the quality need to be determined in order to assess the present capability of the firm. A firm with a labor force composed of skilled, highly motivated, productive workers will possess a powerful competitive advantage over a firm who cannot fill vacancies, has high turnover and absenteeism, and has below average productivity per worker.

The assessment process should have revealed what resources the firm possesses. The planner may now progress to the next step, that of determining what are the particular strengths and weaknesses of the enterprise under review.

COMPETENCY PROFILE OF THE FIRM

In a free enterprise society, no business can expect to thrive unless it maintains some kind of an advantage over its competitors. That advantage may be only a convenient location relative to certain customer groups (e.g. the corner drug store or local service station). It may be only a preferential personal relationship with certain friends or relatives (e.g. some types of brokers or salesmen). It may be only the temporary availability of products in short supply (e.g. a marginal producer). But without some advantage, some distinctive competence, no company can induce a customer to do business with it rather than with its competition.

A viable competitive advantage is most frequently related to the excellence of outstanding personnel. As such, it is expressed in terms of one or more of the following factors:

1. Excellence in product design and/or performance (engineering ingenuity). Examples: Rolls-Royce and Ferrari.

2. Low-cost, high-efficiency operating skill in manufacturing and/or distribution, Examples: GM, Ford.)
3. Leadership in product innovation. Example: Polaroid, IBM.
4. Efficiency in customer service. Example: Sears.
5. Personal relationships with customers. Example: Co-operatives.
6. Efficiency in transportation and logistics. Example: Lufthansa, United.
7. Effectiveness in sales promotion. Example: Sony, G.E.
8. Merchandising efficiency - high turnover of inventories and/or of capital. Example: Safeway.
9. Skillful trading in volatile price movement commodities. Example: Mitsui.
10. Ability to influence legislation. Examples: ITT, Bell Telephone.

A competitive advantage may also stem from the company's resource base:

11. Highly efficient, low-cost facilities. Example: Alcan.
12. Ownership or control of low-cost or scarce raw materials. Example: U.S. Steel (owns iron-ore mines).
13. Control of intermediate distribution or processing units. Example: Standard Oil.
14. Massive availability of capital. Example: GM.
15. Widespread customer acceptance of company brand name (reputation). Example: KODAK.
16. Product availabilty, convenience. Example: Moore Business Forms.

This listing cannot pretend to be all-inclusive but it does indicate the kind of competitive edge which a company may hold over its competitors.

Table 3 summarizes many of the areas which merit inclusion in the competency profile of an enterprise. The use of a systematic format should reduce the possibility of missing one or more relevant areas, however, it must be recognized that each firm will not be concerned to the same degree with a particular capability.

After the planner has completed all phases of the assessment of present capabilities, an assessment should be made of the expectations of the owners (shareholders) and the public at large. These expectations will be constraints which the planner must recognize and which may severely limit the range of alternate plans which can be realistically generated.

EXPECTATIONS OF OWNERS AND PUBLIC

OWNERS' EXPECTATIONS

The owners' expectations may be assessed from three different viewpoints:

1. financial expectations,
2. social expectations, and
3. constraints upon the selection of alternative strategies.

1. Financial Expectations

The financial expectations of the owners of a firm must, of necessity, be considered when strategic planning is being done. Unless the shareholders are significantly fragmented and lack any influence upon the board of directors,

TABLE 3 - CHECKLIST FOR COMPETITIVE AND COMPETENCE PROFILES

	Facilities and Equipment	Personnel skills	Organizational Capabilities	Management Capabilities
General management and finance	Data processing equipment	Depth of general management Finance Industrial relations Legal Personnel recruitment and training Accounting Planning	Multidivisional structure Consumer financing Industrial financing Planning and control Automated business data processing	Investment management Centralized control Large-systems management Decentralized control R&E intensive business Capital equipment, intensive business Merchandising Intensive business Cyclical business Many customers Few customers

Research and development	Special lab equipment
	General lab equipment
	Test facilities
		Areas of specialization
		Advanced research
		Applied research
		Product design:
		    industrial
		    consumer
		    military specifications
		Systems design
		Industrial design:
		    consumer
		    industrial
			Systems development
			Products development
			    industrial
			    consumer
			    process
			    compliance
				Utilization of advanced state of the art
				Application of current state of the art
				Cost-performance optimization

Operations	General Machine shop Precision machinery Process equipment Automated production Large high-bay facilities Controlled environment	Machine operation Tool Making Assembly Precision machinery Close tolerance work Process operation Product planning	Mass production Continuous-flow process Batch process Job Shop Large complex product assembly Subsystems integration Complex product control Quality control Purchasing	Operation under cyclic demand Military specifications Tight cost control Tight scheduling
Marketing	Warehousing Retail outlets Sales offices Services offices Transportation equipment	Door-to-door selling Retail selling Wholesale selling Direct industry selling Department of Defense selling Cross-industry selling Applications enginering Sales promotion Servicing Contract administration Sales analysis	Direct sales Distributor chain Retail chain Consumer service organization Industrial service organization Department of Defense Inventory distribution and control	Industrial marketing Consumer merchandising Department of Defense marketing State and municipality marketing

Source: H.I. Ansoff, *Corporate Strategy* (New York: McGraw-Hill, 1965) pp. 98-99. Used with permission of McGraw-Hill Book Company (C).

their views will have a strong influence upon what objectives are acceptable.

A common measure of financial performance is the Return on Investment (R.O.I.). The shareholders of a blue chip company will obviously want the firm to maintain this status and thus the shareholders will expect that the firm continue to earn a ROI comparable to past years. Shareholders of "growth" companies will expect their firm to continue its growth record and a constantly rising rate of profitability may be demanded.

Management must therefore continually assess the advantages versus the disadvantages of acceding to the owners expectations. It is a well known fact that it is easily possible to create short term profits at the expense of profits over the long term. This is achieved by an extravagant use of company resources (for example, a failure to provide for plant renewal, R & D, or to train personnel in new skills). Conversely, heavy capital expenditure, buying of raw materials in quantities beyond those current required and increasing finished goods held in stock could conceivably lead to a marked improvement in long term profits at the expense of short term profitability. The firm's management engaged in planning must, of necessity, engage in "trading-off" long term versus short-term profits, profits versus competitive position in the market and cost reduction now versus costs necessary for long range profit improvement.[11]

2. Social Expectations

In those companies where the stockholders are also the key men in its management, there is, generally, no major problem of stockholder relations. When the active management has passed from the hands of the owners to professional executives, a different situation arises. Should the stockholders be treated as partners in the venture, or should they be regarded as distant relatives upon whom the executives occasionally bestow dividends in an effort to discourage visits to the family homestead?

This question becomes relevant to the assessment process when one is made aware of the fact that over 30 of the largest U.S. corporations—including AT&T, IBM, GULF OIL, GENERAL MOTORS, FORD, and CHRYSLER —have faced proxy challenges in the past decade from environmentalists, civil rights activitists, consumer advocates, and church groups.[12] It should be emphasized here that this is not pressure from the public at large, but by shareholders of the firm who are also members of the concerned activist groups.

The annual stockholders meeting has emerged as a new battleground in the struggle over the social responsibility of business. Organized corporate critics in growing numbers are pressing proxy votes and raising questions from the floor on issues like minority hiring, pollution, defense production and company operations in South Africa.

More and more foundations, universities and even mutual funds are carefully examining the social consequences of their investment policies. As an example, the Dreyfus Corp. recently started the $24 million Third Century Fund, which will invest only in firms that its directors consider socially responsible.

3. Constraints Upon Selection of Alternate Strategies

From the preceding illustration it should be apparent that many owners' expectations can present powerful constraints upon a firm's choice of business strategies. If a firm can expect rebellion and open confrontation from its past and present behavior, management may be influenced to drop such strategies in the future. It can be speculated that more and more firms will adopt strategies that make provision for environmental protection, occupational health and safety, consumer protection and equal employment opportunity. The planner will be faced with the problem of trading-off financial expectations versus social expectations of the owners. A great deal of skill will be required in order to satisfy the stockholders' moral indignation without unduly pinching their pocketbook because of lower earnings!

PUBLIC EXPECTATIONS

An assessment of the public expectations of corporate behavior can be categorized as:

1. responsibility toward environment,
2. responsibility toward customers and employees, and
3. constraints upon alternate corporate strategies.

1. Responsibility Toward Environment

The combination of the external environmental trends and internal behavioral influences can lead to decisions that often do not directly affect the productive capability of the organization. The concept of social responsibility within the firm involves one of these areas. Nevertheless, this issue must be squarely faced in a society where increasing emphasis is placed on the responsibility of the organization towards its environment.

A strictly rational corporate strategy would focus solely on the economic advancement of the firm. Such a policy, however, raises ethical, legal and economic problems which the firm cannot easily ignore. The corporation which refuses to protect the ecology of its region of operations may have short-term profits but may arouse so much animosity that its medium and long-term survival is placed in jeopardy. An additional point to consider is whether the short-term gain in earnings compensates for a perhaps permanent blot on the corporate image. A firm's reputation takes many years to develop but can be ruined very quickly by hasty or irresponsible behavior. Legally, the firm may face lawsuits and fines which may represent a considerable cost burden upon the firm's earnings.

The corporate planner is under a considerable obligation, therefore, to closely assess the firm's responsibility towards the environment in light of the public's expectation of corporate responsibility.

2. Responsibility Towards Customers and Employees

Depending on the type of business, customers may be other manufacturers, distributors, dealers, or ultimate consumers. An assessment of the firm's responsibility towards its customers as perceived by the public, may be obtained from the use of attitude surveys. Such surveys should reveal to what extent the firm's behavior in this area meets the public's expectations. A poor assessment in the area of customer relations should trigger immediate search techniques to determine causes. Failure to determine the reasons for a poor assessment in this area will mean possible sales losses, lowered earnings and a declining market share.

Significant indicators for assessing the public's expectations of corporate responsibility towards its employees might include: stability of employment, improvement in standard of living compared to industry or national averages, job opportunities (number of new hirings), and family security. These could be expressed in quantitative indexes prepared from statistical data on such factors as average number of hours worked per week, average number of employees and hourly wages in terms of what they will buy.

Completion of this phase of the assessment process will enable the planner to better determine what constraints upon alternate corporate strategies exist because of public expectations.

3. Constraints upon Alternate Strategies

The image of the firm is a crucial determinant of the success of the organization. Success of a particular action could enhance the image; failure could lower it. The necessity of presenting the firm in a favorable light to the investing public and institutions enhances the importance of favorable image and increases the consequences of decisions which will affect that image.

The assumption of a socially responsible doctrine will have a definite impact on the scope and direction of managerial attention. The attention of organizational managers, particularly those in the upper echelons, will increasingly be towards extra-organizational affairs. This occurrence has resulted, in part, from new profit opportunities that appear to be available by paying close attention to the external environment. In addition, new threats are being posed by this environment and this will necessitate both offensive and defensive strategic action by top level managers.

The political and economic sectors are posing new problems also. Increasingly, legislation is appearing which demands actions by businesses that once were thought to be at the organization's discretion. The new consumerism and a more expectant consuming public are creating additional pressure. There is an increased public awareness of what is going on in the world and what rights individuals have vis-a-vis business organizations. The consequence of this awareness has been increased sensitivity to the external and public implications of managerial decisions. Consumerism, environment, corporate accountability, urban decay are just some of the dominant external societal issues to which managers of today are now required to give their keen attention. With the increasing significance of the external environment more planning attention needs to be directed towards this new challenge.

There are two fundamental routes available for the firm: one, the organization can close its eyes, look the other way, and wait for government intervention; or two, it can take positive, affirmative action to cope with its changing environment. The latter course of action would seem to be the one which offers the greatest potential for the firm's long-term viability. The first solution reminds one of the fate of the dinosaurs; the most powerful animals that ever existed on the face of the earth, became extinct when they failed to adapt to a changing environment.

SUMMARY

No selection of alternative plans of action should be initiated until a thorough assessment is made of the past, present, and forecasted future capabilities of the firm and the environment in which it seeks to operate. Alternative plans, in order to have any value for strategic planning, must be realistic. Alternative plans can only be realistic if they are founded upon careful and detailed research and an assessment of all relevant factors.

A firm seeking to control the direction of its corporate development needs to know, at an early stage, what is an appropriate planning horizon for its particular industry. The selection of an inappropriate planning horizon could negate any potential benefits which could otherwise arise from strategic planning.

Strategic planning, in order to be effective, must be accepted by all those personnel who will ultimately be expected to implement, monitor and be held responsible for results of the plans. Strategic plans, which do not adequately recognize the character of the company, may prove to be incompatible with basic corporate objectives.

The primary objective in conducting an overall assessment of the firm is to identify problems, threats, and opportunities in the organization and its environment and to devise plans based upon a thorough assessment of the firm's past, present, and forecasted future capabilities. It is only through following such a systematic procedure, that plans can include practical responses to the changing organization and environmental situation.

An assessment of the firm's present internal and external environment, enables the planner to identify particular strengths and weaknesses of the firm. Weaknesses indicate specific areas which require correction, as soon as possible, but it is the company's strengths, which offer the potential for future profitability, through identification and exploration of areas of competitive advantage.

The management of any enterprise operating in the latter half of the twentieth century must consider the expectations of the owners and the public at large, which may prove to place severe constraints upon the generation of viable alternative strategies. A firm's success and profitability is frequently dependent upon a good corporate image in the market place. Such an image is often dependent upon compatability of corporate actions with the public's and owner's expectations.

ENDNOTES

1. B.W. Denning, *Corporate Planning: Selected Concepts,* McGraw-Hill Book Co. (UK) Ltd., 1971, p. 8.
2. Ibid., p. 57-58. Reproduced by permission.
3. R.J. Mockler, *Business Planning and Policy Formation,* New York: Appleton-Century-Crofts, 1972, p. 17-20.
4. W.H. Newman, "Basic Objectives Which Shape the Character of a Company" *Journal of Business,* Vol. 26. No. 4, 1953, pp. 211-223.
5. D.H. Thain, "Stages of Corporate Development" *Business Quarterly,* Winter, 1969, pp. 33-45. Used with permission.
6. Ibid., Tables 1 and 2, reproduced by permission.
7. Ibid.
8. Ibid.
9. Ibid.
10. Ibid., Based on presentation by D.H. Thain. Used with permission.
11. B.H. Walley, *How to Apply Strategy in Profit Planning,* London: Business Books Ltd., 1971, p. 34.
12. Rise of Portfolio Power, *TIME* (Canadian Edition) June 5, 1972, p. 64.

CASE

MOUNT CARMEL MERCY HOSPITAL AND MEDICAL CENTER

HISTORY OF MOUNT CARMEL MERCY HOSPITAL

Mount Carmel Mercy Hospital and Medical Center was established in 1939. It is owned and operated by the Sisters of Mercy of the Province of Detroit. When it opened in 1939, it had 325 beds with 125 bassinets. There were 208 employees. Through expansion programs over the years, the total size of the facility had increased to 557 beds.

As of July, 1972 Mount Carmel Mercy Hospital had 1,700 employees, a medical staff of 375 physicians and a house staff of 125 physicians. During the fiscal year 1971-1972 there were 19,098 admissions to the hospital, and 33,618 people were treated in the emergency room. Mount Carmel's operating income was 24.2 million dollars, and its asset size was 22.4 million dollars. Construction plans for the next fiscal year included a parking deck for 750 cars and a new three million dollar professional office building that would be erected on the Mount Carmel grounds. In terms of size, Mount Carmel is one of the largest hospitals in the United States. Of the 44 hospitals in Detroit, only three are larger.

Mount Carmel Mercy Hospital is a non-profit, non-governmental community hospital devoted to the objectives of

1. providing a wide range of quality patient care services to the community and
2. participating in the education of physicians and other health care professionals.

Relative to physician training, there are 125 interns and residents. As a teaching hospital, Mount Carmel has training programs in nursing service, pharmacy, dietary, medical records, radiology, anesthesia, respiratory care,

This case was prepared by Jonathon S. Rakich (Professor of Management and Director, Graduate Program in Business, The University of Akron). The writer wishes to thank Mount Carmel Mercy Hospital and Medical Center for its cooperation in the preparation of this case, particularly its adminstrator, Dr. Thomas R. O'Donovan. Any errors or oversights are those of the writer. Some of the data have been modified in minor ways for clarity of presentation. This case was prepared for instructional purposes and is not meant to illustrate either effective or ineffective handling of administrative situations. Copyright, © 1975 by Jonathon S. Rakich. Presented at a Case Workshop and distributed by the Intercollegiate Case Clearing House, Soldiers Field, Boston, Mass. 02163. All rights reserved to the contributors. Printed in the U.S.A. Used with permission.

pathology, physical medicine and rehabilitation, and a physician assistant program.

Committed to the purpose of providing quality care to all who seek it, regardless of race, creed, or ability to pay, Mount Carmel has continuously provided the community with a wide range of services. Among its medical service departments are:

1. Surgery,
2. Internal Medicine,
3. Obstetrics and Gynecology,
4. Pediatrics,
5. Laboratory,
6. Radiology,
7. General Practice and
8. Physical Medicine.

Exhibit 1 presents an organization chart of Mout Carmel. Exhibit 2 presents data pertaining to patients discharged, total patient days and average stay by type of service during the 1971 and 1972 fiscal years.

In terms of patient care, 104,000 people were treated on an in-patient and an out-patient basis (including the emergency room) in 1972. There were over 19,000 admissions in 1972. The average length of stay was 9.3 days. The hospital had an 86.6 percent occupancy rate with an average daily census of 483. Total income was 24.1 million dollars. Exhibits 3 and 4 present income statements and balance sheets for 1971 and 1972.

In August of 1972 Mount Carmel was faced with a major decision. The number of deliveries had declined from a high of 6,733 in 1958 to a current low of 2,610. As a result, the Obstetrical Department of 70 beds had an occupancy rate of only 46 percent. At issue was whether the Obstetrical Department should be closed and the service be provided by other facilities in the area or reduced in terms of bed size. Prior to a presentation of that issue, the subject of the growth of the nation's hospitals, changes in health care delivery since 1965, and the nature of the hospital industry will be presented.

GROWTH OF HOSPITALS IN THE UNITED STATES AND THEIR ROLE IN HEALTH CARE DELIVERY

Relative to the history of medicine, hospitals are a recent phenomenon. In 1873, a little over a hundred years ago, there were 296 hospitals in the United States. The data in Exhibit 5 indicate that by 1909, a period of thirty-six years, there were 4,359 facilities in the United States having a total of 421,000 beds or an average of 96 beds per facility. In 1924, the number of hospitals in the United States peaked at 7,370 with a total bed capacity of 813,000 beds. Although the number of hospitals declined since that time, the total number of beds increased. For example, in 1972 there were 7,061 hospitals of all types in the United States with a total of 1,549,000 beds. During that year 33 million people were admitted to these facilities resulting in an average occupancy rate of 78 percent. The average daily census was 1,208,000 people with an additional 219 million out-patient visits (including emergency room visits) being made.

In discussing the history of hospitals and their role in the delivery of health care, Thomas R. O'Donovan, Ph.D., Administrator of Mount Carmel, indicated that their growth was attributed to a number of factors:

The growth of hospitals in the United States was a post Civil War phenomenon. The major factors affecting hospital growth were

EXHIBIT 1
MOUNT CARMEL MERCY HOSPITAL
AND MEDICAL CENTER
ORGANIZATION CHART
1972

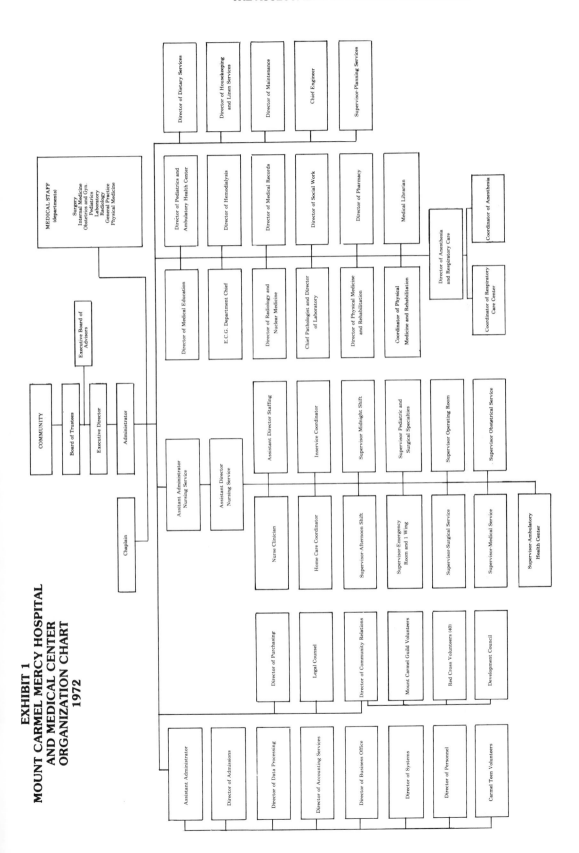

(1) changes in medicine, (2) a change in public attitude toward hospitals, (3) the hospital accreditation movement, and (4) the rise of hospitalization insurance. Today, the role of the hospital is that of being the hub or focal point of the health care delivery system. Only they are able to acquire and staff the sophisticated equipment so necessary for providing quality patient care.

EXHIBIT 2
MOUNT CARMEL MERCY HOSPITAL AND MEDICAL CENTER
Patients Discharged, Total Days and Average
Stay by Type of Service, Fiscal Years 1971 and 1972

	Patients Discharged		Total Days		Average Stay in Days	
	1971	1972	1971	1972	1971	1972
Department of Medicine	6,383	6,946	74,716	80,890	11.7	11.7
Surgery	9,940	9,330	90,239	83,668	9.1	9.0
OB and GYN	4,893	4,193	25,141	22,339	5.1	5.3
Pediatrics	2,984	3,012	13,791	15,024		
General Practice	666	661	6,723	8,556	10.1	12.9

Source: Mount Carmel Mercy Hospital and Medical Center - *1972 Annual Report.* Used with permission.

EXHIBIT 3
MOUNT CARMEL MERCY HOSPITAL AND MEDICAL CENTER

INCOME STATEMENT
(Year Ending June 30)

		1972		1971
PATIENT REVENUE		$24,141,531		$21,569,657
OTHER REVENUE (net)		59,609		81,213
		$24,201,140		$21,650,870
LESS EXPENSES				
Salaries and Wages	$14,829,442		$13,374,411	
Supplies	3,503,032		3,101,157	
Employee Benefits	1,446,984		1,283,950	
Repairs and Maintenance	1,143,350		1,055,927	
Depreciation	602,257		582,664	
All Others	1,922,926		1,608,053	
TOTAL EXPENSES		23,447,991		21,006,162
EXCESS OF INCOME OVER EXPENSE		$ 753,149		$ 644,708
REDUCTIONS FROM INCOME FOR MOUNT CARMEL'S CHARITABLE COMMUNITY SERVICES		376,137		334,953
NET EXCESS AVAILABLE FOR EXPANSION OF SERVICES		$ 377,012		$ 309,755

EXHIBIT 4
MOUNT CARMEL MERCY HOSPITAL AND MEDICAL CENTER

BALANCE SHEET
(Year Ending June 30)

	1972		1971
CURRENT ASSETS			
Cash	$ 133,255		$ 519,272
Patient Accounts Receivable			
(net)	3,347,804		3,519,272
Other Accounts Receivable	37,883		30,180
Inventories and Prepaid Expense	447,290		505,521
TOTAL CURRENT ASSETS	$ 3,966,232		$ 4,721,874
OTHER ASSETS			
Investment (at cost)	$ 489,283		$ -0-
Building Fund Savings Account	554,726		273,530
Unamortized Debt Expense	150,403		65,000
TOTAL OTHER ASSETS	1,194,412		338,530
FIXED ASSETS			
Land, Buildings and Equipment	$17,589,357		$15,479,818
Less Accumulated Depreciation	7,007,200		6,431,394
	$10,582,157		$ 9,048,424
Construction in Progress	6,655,962		1,186,810
TOTAL FIXED ASSETS	17,238,119		10,235,234
TOTAL	$22,398,763		$15,295,638
CURRENT LIABILITIES			
Accounts Payable	$ 1,052,448		$ 1,248,024
Accrued Salaries	501,822		371,857
Accrued Vacation/Sick Pay	791,112		719,892
Other Payables	770,028		107,152
Medicare and Blue Cross			
Advances	535,410		943,200
Mortgage Payable-Current	105,697		90,000
TOTAL CURRENT LIABILITIES	$ 3,756,617		$ 3,480,125
LONG—TERM LIABILITY			
Mortgage Payable	$ 920,000		$ 1,010,000
Notes Payable	4,836,085		500,000
TOTAL LONG-TERM LIABILITY	5,756,085		$ 1,510,000
CAPITAL			
Balance at June 30	12,886,161		10,305,513
TOTAL	$22,398,763		$15,295,638

EXHIBIT 5
MOUNT CARMEL MERCY HOSPITAL AND MEDICAL CENTER

Number of Hospitals (All Types) and Total
Number of Beds - United States -
for Selected Years

Year	Number of Hospitals	Total Number of Beds	Average Bed Size
1873	296	na	na
1909	4,359	421,000	96
1924	7,370	830,000	110
1937	6,128	1,124,000	183
1940	6,291	1,226,000	194
1951	6,637	1,529,000	230
1961	6,923	1,670,000	241
1971	7,097	1,556,000	219

Sources: *Hospital Care in the United States* (Commission on Hospital Care); *Historical Statistics of the United States - Colonial times to 1957* (U.S. Department of Commerce); and *Hospital Statistics,* 1972 (American Hospital Association). Used with permission.

STATUS OF MEDICINE

Prior to the turn of the century medicine was truly in its infancy stage. It wasn't until the 1870's that it was learned that microorganisms caused disease. During this period the importance of sterilization and aseptic surgery were recognized. As a result, death rates in hospitals decreased substantially. Other major diagnostic and treatment discoveries, such as the X-ray and blood-typing, were also made near the turn of the century.

In 1910 Abraham Flexner reported his findings on medical education in the United States. His study was commissioned by the Carnegie Foundation. Flexner's indictments were so severe that it forced the closing of a number of proprietary medical schools. As a result, the trend toward four years of medical education began, entrance requirements were upgraded and internships became common practice after World War I.

STIGMAS

Also contributing to the growth of hospitals was the fact that by 1900 the public's attitude toward them had begun to change. Prior to the turn of the century, they were crowded , unsanitary, and along with the rather crude level of medical knowledge of the day, they deterred people from entering them voluntarily. In addition, most hospitals at the time cared for charity patients and there was a public stigma associated with being admitted to a hospital.

Ignorance, prejudice, the low quality of service, the death-house stigma and the fact that admission was an indication of economic status were many of the deterrent factors which were slowly being overcome. Once these images were changed, the growth of hospitals exploded. Since then, their role in the delivery of health care has become increasingly important. Finally, some of the secondary factors that assisted the growth of hospitals were the rise of the nursing profession and the first World War.

ACCREDITATION MOVEMENT

The period 1920 through 1945 was one of consolidation for the nation's hospitals. By the end of the period more beds were in place in fewer facilities.

The consolidation of hospitals was, in a large degree, affected by the hospital accreditation movement initiated in 1913 by the American College of Surgeons. The College of Surgeons outlined a whole system of requirements related to

1. medical staff,
2. patient records and
3. diagnostic and therapeutic requirements which had to be met before a hospital would be placed on its approved list.

In 1918, the college reviewed 671 hospitals and only 80 of them were approved. Consequently, a number of substandard hospitals were closed. The college carried on these accreditation activities until 1951 when they were transferred to the Joint Commission on Accrediation of Hospitals.

HEALTH INSURANCE

Health insurance had a major impact on hospitals. The movement for some form of hospital health insurance began shortly after World War I. However, the earliest of the group hospitalization agreements occurred in 1929 between the Baylor University Hospital in Texas and a group of local teachers. The effect of the group hospitalization plans was substantial. First, they enabled the working class of America to mitigate the financial disaster of a major illness by spreading the risk over a larger enrolled population. Second, they enabled the fee-for-service health care delivery system to mature. To indicate the importance of this trend, it should be pointed out that in 1936 there were only seventeen non-profit hospital service plans covering 250,000 people. Today over eighty percent of the population has some form of hospital care insurance coverage.

Because of the advances in medicine, the removal of the "death-house" stigma, the accreditation movement and hospitalization insurance, hospitals grew substantially. Today they are the primary institution in the health care delivery system. Without them, the level of care currently provided to the nation would not be possible nor would it be as efficient as it is.

CHANGES IN HEALTH CARE DELIVERY SINCE 1965

In order to place the hospital in perspective, relative to the delivery of health care, Dr. O'Donovan made the point that in the last seven years the administrative flexibility afforded the hospital administrator has been constrained. Not only must he be cognizant of and responsible to political, social and economic pressures, he must also balance these pressures against the hospital's primary purpose - providing quality patient care. He elaborated by stating:

The changes that have taken place and are currently taking place in the delivery of health care since 1965 have had and will continue to have a significant impact on hospitals and the administration of them. These changes range in a spectrum from (1) increased demand for services, (2) to rising costs, (3) to greater administrative accountability, (4) to structural changes in delivery, and (5) to changing expectations of society relative to health care. Often these pressures are in conflict between the two measures of performance, that is, the quality of care and cost of care provided.

INCREASING DEMAND

Much of the increase in demand for hospital services can be attributed to three major factors. The first is the expansion of third party hospitalization coverage. Today, over eighty percent of the civilian population has some form of hospitalization benefit.

Second, the changing nature of medical technology, the ever increasing complexity of equipment and the specialization of services have resulted in the hospital being the central point of the delivery of health care. As a result, equipment expenditures have increased greatly.

Third, increasing affluence and changing demographic characteristics of our population have had an impact on hospital utilization. Increased disposable income has decreased the hesitancy of certain people to seek hospital care. In addition, the increased proportion of elderly among the population has heightened the demand for hospital services since this segment is often more susceptible to illness. Finally, the emergency room has become, in many instances, a substitute for the family physician and thereby, places a greater demand on hospitals.

RISING COSTS

For the patient, the most notable change since 1965 has been the rapid increase in the cost of hospital and medical care. For example, in fiscal year 1960 total health care expenditures were 25.8 billion dollars. In fiscal year 1965 total health care expenditures in the United States were 38.8 billion dollars which represents a 52 percent increase over 1960. Finally, in fiscal year 1972 expenditures increased by 115 percent over the 1965 period to a total of 84.7 billion dollars, of which 32.6 billion dollars were for hospital care. Exhibit 6 presents aggregate national health care expenditures for selected fiscal years from 1929 to 1972. Exhibit 7 presents those expenditures as a percent of Gross National Product and on a per capita basis.

The rising cost of health care has been caused by a number of factors. Among them are:

1. higher prices;
2. a greater number of people using facilities due in part to a larger proportion of the population being covered by third-party insurance (including Medicare and Medicaid),
3. the increased scope and range of services provided; and
4. technological developments which require highly sophisticated equipment along with skilled personnel needed to operate that equipment.

Since two-thirds of all hospitals expenditures are in the form of payroll, they can be called labor intensive organizations. One factor greatly affecting rising hospital costs is employee wages. Traditionally low, wages are now beginning to be competitive with other occupations. The rise of unionism, the requirement for more highly trained personnel and the shortage of certain types of professionals, such as nurses and medical technicians, have contributed to an increased wage bill for the nation's hospitals.

GREATER ACCOUNTABILITY

The rising trend in health care costs has led Congress and the public to cry "inefficiency". This movement has been translated into a demand for greater accountability on the part of institutional providers, hospitals and

EXHIBIT 6
MOUNT CARMEL MERCY HOSPITAL AND MEDICAL CENTER
Aggregate National Health Expenditures,
by Type, Selected Fiscal Years, 1928
through 1972

Type of Expenditure	1928-29	1934-35	1939-40	1949-50	1954-55	1959-60	1964-65	1965-66	1966-67	1967-68	1969-70	1970-71	1971-72
	Aggregate amount (in millions)												
Total	$3,589	$2,846	$3,863	$12,027	$17,330	$25,856	$38,892	$42,109	$47,860	$53,563	$68,083	$75,629	$84,710
Health Services and Supplies	3,382	2,788	3,729	11,181	16,392	24,162	35,664	38,661	44,324	49,599	63,067	70,175	78,649
Hospital care	651	731	969	3,698	5,689	8,499	13,152	14,245	16,921	19,384	25,895	29,300	21,691
Physicians' services	994	744	946	2,689	3,632	5,580	8,405	8,865	9,733	10,734	13,450	15,086	16,626
Dentists' services	476	298	402	940	1,457	1,944	2,728	2,866	3,158	3,498	4,233	4,637	5,048
Other professional services	248	150	173	384	552	848	989	1,140	1,139	1,210	1,386	1,516	1,598
Drugs and drug sundries	601	471	624	1,642	2,282	3,591	4,647	5,032	5,480	5,864	7,111	7,602	8,157
Eyeglasses and appliances	131	128	180	475	606	730	1,151	1,309	1,514	1,665	1,814	1,922	2,034
Nursing-home care	--	--	28	178	291	480	1,271	1,470	1,592	2,070	2,860	3,212	3,480
Expenses for prepayment and administration	101	91	161	290	605	807	1,234	1,446	1,820	1,935	2,105	2,383	3,156
Government public health activities	89	112	156	351	384	401	671	731	884	1,001	1,437	1,698	2,273
Other health services	90	63	92	534	896	1,262	1,416	1,620	1,978	2,238	2,776	2,819	3,586
Research and medical-facilities construction	207	58	134	847	938	1,694	3,228	3,448	3,536	3,964	5,015	5,455	6,001
Research	--	--	3	110	194	592	1,391	1,545	1,606	1,800	1,846	1,850	2,049
Construction	207	58	131	737	744	1,102	1,837	1,903	1,930	2,164	3,169	3,605	4,012

EXHIBIT 7
MOUNT CARMEL MERCY HOSPITAL AND MEDICAL CENTER

Aggregate and Per Capita National Expenditures
and Percent of Gross National Product for Selected
Fiscal years 1928-29 through 1971-72

Fiscal year	Gross national product (in billions)	Health expenditures		
		Total		
		Amount (in millions)	Per capita	Percent of GNP
1928-29	$ 101.0	$ 3,589	$ 29,.16	3.6
1934-35	68.7	2,846	22.04	4.1
1939-40	95.1	3,883	28.83	4.1
1949-50	283.4	12,023	78.33	4.6
1954-54	379.7	17,330	103.76	4.6
1959-60	495.6	23,883	141.63	5.2
1964-65	633.6	38,892	197.75	5.9
1965-66	718.3	42,109	211.56	5.9
1966-67	771.4	47,880	237.83	6.2
1967-68	827.0	53,583	263.38	6.3
1968-69	899.0	59.977	292.08	6.7
1969-70	954.8	68,083	328.17	7.1
1970-71	1,013.3	75,629	380.94	7.5
1971-72	1,100.6	84,710	400.36	7.7

Source: *Social Security Bulletin*, Vol. 37, No. 2 (February, 1974), p. 4. Used with permission.

long term care facilities, along with those responsible for managing them. In many instances, inter-facility competition, the reimbursement formulas based on cost and the necessity to offer a wide-range of services have placed the administrator in a position where he must balance patient care with costs. Greater accountability demands are being made on the administrator, yet, his freedom of operating flexibility is being reduced. The dilemma is how to be responsible and help retard the rise of costs, and still manage a facility which provides quality care.

STRUCTURAL CHANGES

Among the structural changes occurring since 1965 have been alternate delivery forms and the prospect of National Health Insurance. The implications of both are great.

Structural changes that have occurred range from the creation of prototype delivery systems such as Health Maintenance Organizations (HMO's) to the formation of group-physician practices and clinics. HMO's have the purpose of enrolling a designated population on a capitation basis, that is, providing all of the health care needs to its enrollees for a fixed annual fee.

The prospect of National Health Insurance is one with which hospitals must contend. Questions to be answered are, will it eventually result in hospitals being regulated like utilities? What effect will it have on the demand placed on hospitals? How will it be financed and what effect will it have?

Some insight can be derived from the Medicare and Medicaid programs which were enacted in 1965. Medicare is a federal program providing hospitalization and other medical care coverage for those people sixty-five and over. It is financed by the Federal Government under the Social Security Administration with enrollee premiums and some co-payments. Medicaid, on the other hand, is financed totally by the Federal and State Governments. Under Medicaid a wide range of hospital and other medical services are provided to certain categorically eligible people such as the blind, disabled and indigent.

Both programs provided the means by which large segments of the population became eligible for hospitalization and other medical care. Consequently, the demand for hospital services during the late 1960's increased dramatically. In addition, Federal guidelines, reimbursement formulas, reporting requirements and area-wide planning agencies, limited the operational freedom of the hospital administrator.

SOCIETY'S EXPECTATION

The final major change in health care delivery that has occurred since 1965 has been society's expectation of quality care. Today, health care is regarded as a right rather than a privilege of the affluent. The populous expects quality care.

THE HOSPITAL INDUSTRY

Hospitals in the United States are classified in various ways. The most common classification is by ownership:

1. federal,
2. state and local,
3. non-governmental non-profit (sometimes called community general or voluntary hospitals) and
4. non-governmental for-profit.

Others are by type of stay (long stay and short stay) and type of service (general, medical and surgical, psychiatric, tuberculosis, etc). In 1972, 6,046 of the nation's 8,061 hospitals were short stay, general hospitals. Fifty percent of the total consisted of non-governmental non-profit (community general) hospitals, and they accounted for 41 percent of the total beds. Exhibit 8 presents a breakdown of United States hospitals by type for 1972.

Another interesting characteristic of the nation's hospitals is the fact that most of them are relatively small. Of the total 7,061 in 1972, 639 hospitals or 9.0 percent were larger than five hundred beds; 267 or 3.7 percent were between 400 and 499 beds; 436 or 6.2 percent had a bed size of 300 to 399 beds; 734 or 10.4 percent had between 200 and 299 beds; and 1,433 or 20.1 percent were between 100 and 199 beds. The remaining 3,552 hospitals, or 50.3 percent, were less than 100 beds in size. Thus, in terms of size, over one-half of the nation's hospitals had fewer than one hundred beds and only nine percent were larger than five hundred beds.

In terms of activity, Exhibit 9 presents data pertaining to the hospital industry for the period 1962-1972. Specifically, included by year are the number of hospitals, total beds, admissions, occupancy rate, outpatient visits, number of personnel and payroll expenses.

Four major trends developed during that period. Admissions had increased from 26 million in 1962 to 33 million in 1972. The occupancy rate, the average number of beds being utilized, had declined while out-patient visits rose substantially to 218 million during 1972. In addition, the number of births declined by 18% from the high of 3.8 million in 1962. Finally, the number of hospital personnel per 100 census almost doubled to 221.

THE HOSPITAL QUADRANGLE

In 1968 four hospitals located in the northwest metropolitan section of Detroit formed the "Metropolitan Northwest Detroit Hospitals, Inc." Generally known as the "Quadrangle", the four members are:

1. Mount Carmel Mercy Hospital and Medical Center,
2. Grace Hospital, N.W.,
3. Sinai Hospital, and
4. Providence Hospital[1]

Exhibit 10 presents the bed size, occupancy rate, number of annual admissions, total expenses, payroll and number of personnel of each of the four Quadrangle members.

Exhibit 8
MOUNT CARMEL MERCY HOSPITAL AND MEDICAL CENTER
Classification of Hospitals by Type,
Total Beds (in Thousands), and
Percentage - 1972

Total		Federal		State/Local		Non-Governmental Non-Profit		Non-Governmental For-Profit	
Hospital	Beds	Hospitals	Beds	Hospitals	Beds	Hospitals	Beds	Hospitals	Beds
7061	1550	401	143	2300	699	3.515	639	845	65
100%	100%	5.6%	9.2%	32.6%	45.0%	50.0%	41.2%	12.0%	4.1%

Source: *Hospital Statistics, 1972* (American Hospital Association), pp. 20-21. Used with permission.

The objectives of the Quadrangle were to

1. seek means by which the quality of patient care provided by its members could be maintained and/or improved,
2. seek means by which the total cost of hospital care delivered in the northwest section of Detroit could be reduced and
3. provide a forum by which cooperative efforts of the four hospitals could be channeled in constructive directions.

With the trends of increased demand for adminstrative accountability by the public and government, rapidly rising level of hospital care cost and the trend toward structural changes in health care delivery, the four hospitals sought to find means by which they could positively respond. One consideration was the sharing of professional services.

---

1 Providence Hospital is located in the adjoining suburb of Southfield; however, all four hospitals are located within a four-mile distance of each other.

Exhibit 9

MOUNT CARMEL MERCY HOSPITAL AND MEDICAL CENTER

Data pertaining to United States Hospitals
for the Period 1962-1972

YEAR	HOSPITALS	BEDS (in thousands)	ADMISSIONS (in thousands)	AVERAGE DAILY CENSUS (in thousands)	ADJUSTED AVERAGE DAILY CENSUS (in thousands)	OCCUPANCY (per cent)	AVERAGE LENGTH OF STAY	OUTPATIENT VISITS (in thousands)	NEWBORNS Business	NEWBORNS Births	PERSONNEL Number (in thousands)	PERSONNEL Per 100 Census	PERSONNEL Per 1000 Adjusted Census	PAYROLL Amount (in millions)	PAYROLL Per Patient Day	PAYROLL Per Adjusted Patient Day	EXPENSES TOTAL Amount (in millions)	EXPENSES TOTAL Per Patient Day	EXPENSES TOTAL Per Adjusted Patient Day	ASSETS Plant (in millions)	ASSETS Total (in millions)
1962	7,028	1,689	26,531	1,407		83.3		99,382	104,101	3,857,626	1,763	125		6,735	13.12		10,129	19.73		16,460	19,980
1963	7,138	1,702	27,502	1,430		84.0		118,238	104,695	2,784,666	2,840	129		7,270	13.93		10,956	21.00		17,450	21,309
1954	7,127	1,696	28,266	1,421		83.8		125,123	103,350	2,729,282	1,887	133		7,975	15.38		12,031	23.20		18,937	23,275
1965	7,123	1,704	23,812	1,403		82.3		125,793	101,287	3,565,344	1,952	139		8,551	16.70		12,948	25.29		19,993	24,502
1966	7,160	1,679	29,151	1,390		83.3		142,201	100,555	3,385,113	2,106	151		9,286	18.27		14,198	27.94		20,824	26,336
1967	7,172	1,671	29,361	1,380		82.6		143,229	99,296	3,283,711	2,203	160		10,461	20.76		16,395	32.54		21,813	27,922
1968	7,137	1,663	29,766	1,378		82.9		156,139	97,319	3,268,431	2,309	168		11,997	23.78		19,061	37.78		23,113	31,019
1969	7,144	1,650	30,729	1,346		81.6		163,248	94,949	3,319,315	2,426	180		13,803	28.11		22,103	45.01		25,061	33,547
1970	7,123	1,616	31,759	1,298		80.3		181,370	97,128	3,537,000	2,537	196		15,706	33.16		25,556	53.95		26,575	36,159
1971	7,097	1,556	32,664	1,237		79.5		199,725	94,344	3,464,513	2,589	209		17,635	39.07		28,812	63.32		28,175	38,625
1972	7,061	1,550	33,265	1,209		78.0		219,182	92,960	3,231,875	2,671	221		19,530	44.17		32,667	73.89		31,048	43,157

Source: Hospital Statistics, 1972 (American Hospital Association), p. 19.

EXHIBIT 10
MOUNT CARMEL MERCY HOSPITAL AND MEDICAL CENTER

Detroit Quadrangle Hospitals
1971

	Number Of Beds	Annual Admissions	Average Daily Census	Average Occupancy Rate	Total Expenses (Dollars in Thousands)	Total Payroll (Dollars in Thousands)	Number of Personnel
Mount Carmel Mercy Hospital and Medical Center	557	19,846	495	88.9	21,037	11,804	1,527
Grace Hospital, N.W.	418	14,450	373	87.6	15,600	NA	1,250
Providence Hospital	400	15,270	358	89.5	16,057	9,288	1,090
Sinai Hospital	478	17,189	435	95.2	21,305	10,956	1,347

Source: Hospital Guide Issue, 1972 (American Hospital Association), p. 111 and 117. Used with permission.
Note: Data represents a twelve month period ending September 30, 1971.

A unique characteristic of non-governmental non-profit hospitals, versus industrial organizations is that charges and payments made by third-party payers, such as Blue Cross, the Federal government, and private insurance companies to hospital providers, are based on reasonable costs incurred. Consequently, for a specific facility there is little incentive for it to reduce costs and services so long as they are comparable to the costs of other facilities in the area.

In a geographic area where there is an excess of hospital beds, that is, facilities are being under-utilized, the fixed costs of empty beds are spread over those beds that are filled. Consequently, the costs for any individual facility may be in line with those in its area, however, the total cost of care provided to the community is higher.

As a result, the Quadrangle sought to examine potential service areas that could be consolidated. The impact would be the reduction of the total number of beds allocated to the specific service for all four facilities and the increased occupancy rate of the facility or facilities that would maintain the service. It was felt that the sharing and consolidation of some professional services would enable

1. better care to be provided and
2. the costs of hospital care for the community as a whole to be reduced.

The chairman of the steering committee of the Detroit Hospital Quadrangle was Thomas R. O'Donovan, Administrator of Mount Carmel Mercy Hospital and Medical Center. He described the Quadrangle's philosophy of sharing services as follows:

> by exploring the sharing of professional services, such as obstetrics and pediatrics, neighboring hospitals can better utilize their current available space. They may even save money by avoiding the construction of expensive facility additions for other high demand services by reclassifying the beds in the closed service. To make the sharing of services work requires team-work and cooperation. Historically, hospitals have been "stand alone" facilities with each offering a totality of services. Here-to-fore, there has been little need or incentive to work together to accomplish patient care objectives. The question is, can cooperation work or does institutional chauvinism prevail?

The Hospital Quadrangle was formed to explore these problems and attempt to instill a sense of inter-hospital cooperation.

ADMINISTRATIVE PHILOSOPHY

In elaborating on his administrative philosophy, Dr. O'Donovan stated:

> I am a firm believer in Management by Objectives and the development of capable staff to administer the day-to-day operations at Mount Carmel. I feel that Mount Carmel is an innovative hospital. I am quite aware of the fact that the Executive Director and I have the responsibility for managing an organization that will enable physicians to treat their patients. However, it is my hope that this hospital may serve as a model for others. We are a non-profit hospital dedicated to providing quality care and teaching. In that respect, our ultimate responsibility is to the community both in terms of offering a wide range of services and providing quality care at reasonable costs.

Some of the things we have attempted to do in the last seven years are (1) be cost effective, (2) be responsive to the needs of the community and (3) to maintain our tradition of a high level of care to all who seek it. As one of the largest hospitals in Detroit and the nation, for that matter, Mount Carmel must serve in the role of one of the institutional leaders. Among the internal changes we have introduced are (1) the development of a comprehensive wage and salary structure and (2) the overseeing of various expansion programs. Among the various external activities in which I have had a part are serving as the National Educational Director of the American Academy of Medical Administrators and actively participating in area committees formed for the purpose of initiating cooperative efforts among area hospitals. The Detroit Hospital Quadrangle is one example.

In the 1972 fiscal year, several specific service areas have required my attention. The first was the dramatic increase in the utilization of our emergency room. For example, the utilization frequency rose from 27,705 in 1969 to 39,151 in 1972. As a result, early this year construction to double the size of our emergency room was begun in order to accommodate this service area shift needed by the community.

However, we are experiencing another shift in service utilization, specifically, in Obstetrics and Gynecology (OB-GYN) where there has been a decline in the number of deliveries. During the 1971 fiscal year 2,610 babies were delivered while only 2,152 were deliverd in the 1972 fiscal year. That represents the lowest number of babies delivered since 1942 and a 68 percent decline from our peak number of deliveries of 6,733 in 1958. Exhibit 11 shows the number of deliveries at Mount Carmel for the fiscal years 1940-1971. Since our 70-bed Obstetrical Department now has an occupancy rate of 46 percent in the 1972 fiscal year, my immediate concern is whether to continue, modify (in terms of beds allocated) or discontinue this service.

SHARING OB

In keeping with the Quadrangle's objective of sharing services, the alternative of consolidating the Obstetrical Department within one or several of the other member hospitals was being considered. Three of the four hospitals had experienced a low occupancy rate during 1971. Exhibit 12 presents the number of OB beds, average daily census, percent of occupancy and length of stay for the four Quadrangle hospitals.

When evaluating the advisability of maintaining or phasing out the obstetrical service, Dr. O'Donovan made the following points:

We have to evaluate many factors in order to make a decision. Mt. Carmel, being a 557-bed hospital and having had an active Obstetrical Department since it was founded in 1939, has many reasons to continue this department. Even though many smaller hospitals with small OB units have closed throughout the country, never before in history has a unit as large as our (70 beds) been closed.

The OB service is one of the services we provide in order to fulfill our community responsibility. However, we also have another responsibility which consists of cooperating with area-wide planning agencies and the Quadrangle. Relative to the latter, the Quadrangle has the purpose of sharing services in order, (1) to avoid duplication of facilities and services, (2) to help decrease costs to the community as a whole, (3) to improve the quality of patient care.

EXHIBIT 11
MOUNT CARMEL MERCY HOSPITAL AND MEDICAL CENTER

Total Deliveries at Mount Carmel
Hospital 1940-1971

Fiscal Year	Deliveries	Fiscal Year	Deliveries
1940	234	1956	6418
1941	1581	1957	6615
1942	2558	1958	6733
1943	4296	1959	6106
1944	4270	1960	5790
1945	3610	1961	5123
1946	3665	1962	4505
1947	4501	1963	4190
1948	4726	1964	4019
1949	4565	1965	3966
1950	4773	1966	3620
1951	5485	1967	3480
1952	6113	1968	3036
1953	6463	1969	2884
1954	5865	1970	2766
1955	6299	1971	2610

Source: Internal Records

EXHIBIT 12
MOUNT CARMEL MERCY HOSPITAL AND MEDICAL CENTER

Quadrangle OB Data
Fiscal Year 1971

	MOUNT CARMEL	GRACE N.W.	SINAI	PROVIDENCE
No. of OB Beds Available for Delivered OB's	70	67	53	50
Average Daily Census OB's Delivered	39	38	46	35
Percent of Occupancy OB's Delivered	56	57	87	70
OB's Delivered	2,610	2,646	3,336	2,623
Inpatient Days OB's Delivered	14,145	13,971	16,796	12,880
Average Length of Stay, OB's Delivered	5.4	5.3	5.0	4.9
Total Births (including SB's)	2,640	2,671	3,384	2,656

Source: Mount Carmel Mercy Hospital and Medical Center - internal records.   Used with permission.

ADVANTAGES TO PHASING OUT OB

Dr. O' Donovan mentioned that the reasons favoring Mt. Carmel Mercy Hospital closing its Obstetrical Department are:

1. *Declining Occupancy.* The 70-bed unit at Mount Carmel Mercy Hospital has had a steadily declining census due to the declining birth rate. The birth rate data point toward a continued downward decline in the years ahead. At this time in 1972 the average occupancy of the obstetrical department was 46%. This means that over 38 of the 70 beds were vacant on any given day. Generally, when a hospital has an occupancy rate in obstetrics of less than 70%, this results in an unfavorable financial position for the hospital.

Mt. Carmel has lost over $350,000 per year in its Obstetrical Department in the last few years even though our room charges are $67 a day for a ward, $72 a day for a semi-private room, $48 a day for the nursery and $170 for use of the delivery room. Generally, many hospitals tend to suffer financial losses in their obstetrical department, regardless of their level of occupancy, because of the up-and-down nature of the level of occupancy. It is difficult to predict the peaks and valleys of births that will take place in any given hospital. It is not easy to temporarily layoff OB nurses when the census is down for a few days at a time.

Even with declining occupancy, one of our options would be to continue the service on a reduced scale, specifically, establishing a unit of perhaps 35 to 40 beds. This would result in a unit that would have a sufficient number of beds to maintain an 80% to 90% occupancy rate, unless, of course, the birthrate continued to slide in the years ahead.

It is also important to note that if the hospital gave up OB, the present 70 OB beds could be devoted immediately, without any remodeling necessary, to medical/surgical beds. This would increase the occupancy from the present 46% for the 70 beds, to over 90% since this has been the general level of occupancy in the medical/surgical area at Mt. Carmel in recent years. Demand for medical/surgical beds is expected to be high in the years ahead. In fact, there is a large waiting list, and the Urgent and Emergency List is quite extensive. Thus, reassignment of these OB beds to medical/surgical would tend to serve the community more by taking care of the patients that are waiting at home for beds, and of course, it would serve the internists, surgeons, and general practitioners of the hospital medical staff very well.

2. *Remodeling Required.* In order to continue its Obstetrical Department, a major program of remodeling would be necessary as required by the Michigan Department of Public Health. The architect's estimate for these changes is 1.3 million dollars. The hospital would face a major challenge in obtaining the 1.3 million dollars. A further issue here is that the Economic Stabilization Program of the Federal Government is in full swing and there is a question as to whether or not Mt. Carmel can increase its costs to the point of being able to obtain a price exception. On the other hand, the required funds could possibly be obtained by debt financing.

3. *A furtherance of the spirit of sharing services.* The prime purpose of the Quadrangle is to share services. Deletion of the obstetrical program of our hospital and merging it within the Quadrangle, would be an extremely important act of teamwork. For example, Providence Hospital had an occupancy rate of 70 percent in 1971 based on 50 beds and Grace Hospital, N.W. had an occupancy of 57% based on 67 beds. If the majority of our OB-GYN physicians delivered their patients at Providence or

Grace, this would increase their hospital's occupancy and also reduce their costs/bed. In addition, a larger concentration of patients and house staff would result in better patient care and improvements in their teaching programs.

4. *Decreased costs to the community.* The final advantage of phasing out Obstetrics Department would be the reduction of the number of OB beds in the area. Consequently, those members of the Quadrangle retaining OB beds would experience higher occupancy rates, and the total costs to the community would be decreased by reason of eliminating the costs associated with empty beds.

DISADVANTAGES OF PHASING OUT OB

Among the reasons for not phasing out the Obstetrical Department, Dr. O'Donovan mentioned the following:

1. *Disadvantaged Patients.* One of the major reasons for not phasing out the Obstetrical Department is the fact that over 700 of the births last year at Mount Carmel were made by low-income patients. We have a contract with the Detroit Maternal Infant Care Program. It is a federally financed program, administered by the state, in which low income mothers are given pre-natal care, the delivery, and post-natal care of the child.

The question is whether or not we can obtain community support for a phase-out decision. If these disadvantaged mothers were turned away because it was not possible for them to be delivered at Providence or at some other hospital with a reasonable level of convenience and without a reduction in the level of care, the community would certainly react negatively. Much thought has to be given to our community service responsibility in this area.

2. *Are There Sufficient Beds Available in the Area?* Another important consideration is whether the three other Quadrangle Hospitals could absorb our patient load. This matter has to be examined very carefully.

3. *Staff Privileges.* Provided that an adequate number of beds are available at Providence, Grace N.W. and Sinai Hospitals, it is extremely important that all Mount Carmel OB-GYN physicians be given additional staff privileges at some or all of those hospitals to take care of their OB patients. One consideration is that the vast majority of the OB-GYN doctors at Mt. Carmel be extended privileges at Grace and Providence Hospital. Most of the OB-GYN doctors at Mt. Carmel will probably accept this arrangement, although they would have preferred that the facilities at Mt. Carmel be continued. The reason for this is that they will have to make rounds at two hospitals, if they did their GYN at Mount Carmel and their OB at Providene and/or Grace.

4. *Present OB Personnel.* A major question is what to do with the 110 employees presently working in our OB-GYN department. They include nurses, LPN's, and nurse's aides. Some could be hired at Providence (perhaps about 10%), and the remaining number could be retrained through in-service programs and reassigned to medical/surgical, pediatrics, emergency, or the intensive care units.

5. *Image.* Another problem facing Mt. Carmel is that a major hospital with over 500 beds tends to retain a much better image if it has a well-rounded program. Retention of the Obstetrical Department would maintain this strong image.

6. *Potential Loss of GYN Surgery.* It is most important for a general hospital to retain a well-rounded program. Even if OB is lost, it is still important to retain GYN. There are many who would predict that a hospital that loses its OB service would tend to lose its GYN service within a few years because of the tendency of the OB-GYN doctors to want to do their OB and their GYN work at the same hospital.

If, in fact, a loss of GYN did occur at Mt. Carmel in the future, this would affect the teaching program of medical education. Not only would the house staff in other clinical areas not have the OB department for experience, but they would also lose the GYN surgery. This might make it quite likely for the residency review boards to discontinue approval of residencies in Radiology, Medicine, and General Surgery, if a sufficient range of clinical material were not available at the hospital.

Mt. Carmel could, of course, promote GYN surgery as much as possible by extending favorable boarding times and assigning beds to the GYN physicians who moved to Providence and/or to the other two Quadrangle hospitals. It is also important for a hospital to have GYN residents cover our GYN clinic on a rotation basis.

7. *Lack of Acceptance on the Part of the Medical Staff.* This has been alluded to before, but it is an important disadvantage for a hospital to lose its OB department when the physicians do not accept that decision of the Board of Trustees. There have been cases in the United States in which a hospital has given up an Obstetrical Department and the medical staff has sued the hospital to prevent this from happening. This creates all kinds of conflict, and it certainly points out the great importance to any hospital, that attempts to share services, that medical staff involvement at each and every step of the way is necessary.

Since the Michigan Department of Health has ordered that physical renovation of the Obstetrics Department begin by January 1, 1973. Dr. O'Donovan must
1. evaluate the alternatives available to Mount Carmel,
2. decide on a course of action and
3. develop the implementation plan within the next six months.

Evaluation of the
Mount Carmel Mercy Hospital Case

SUMMARY

The growth of hospitals in the United States was a post Civil War phenomenon. The major factors affecting growth included changes in medical technology, a change in public attitudes toward hospital, hospital accreditation requirements, and the rise of hospitalization insurance. The role of the hospital today is that of being the focal point of the health care delivery system.

The changes that have taken place and are currently taking place in the delivery of health care have had a great impact on hospitals and the administration of them. These changes range from increased demand for services, to rising costs, to greater administrative accountability, to structural changes in delivery, and to changing expectations of society relative to health care. Often these pressures are in conflict with the measurement of performance, that is, providing a wide variety of quality health services to the community and efficiency as related to the cost of the health care provided.

KEY ISSUES

1. What is the effect of declining trends in the birth rate in the United States?
2. How is health care productivity measured?
3. Can hospitals be evaluated the same way as industrial organizations?
4. What are the effects of the general health care industry?
5. How does society's perception of health care affect the administration of a hospital?

DISCUSSION

1. Effect of Declining Birth Rate

The 70-bed unit at Mount Carmel Mercy Hospital has had a steadily declining census caused by the declining birth rate. Birth rate forecasts point toward a continued downward decline in the years ahead. At the present time, the average occupancy of the Obstetrics Department is 46%. This means that over 38 of the 70 beds are vacant on any given day. Generally, when a hospital has an occupancy rate of less than 70%, the result is an unfavorable financial position for the hospital.

2. Productivity Measurement

The rising trend in health care costs has led Congress and the public to cry "inefficiency." There is now a demand for greater accountability on the part of institutional providers, hospitals and long term care facilities, along with those responsible for managing them. Inter-facility competition, the reimbursement formulas based on cost, and the necessity to offer a wide-range of services have placed the hospital administrator in a position where he must balance patient care with costs. He now faces greater accountability demands yet his freedom of operating flexibility is being reduced. When a hospital experiences under-utilization because of low occupancy rates, their costs might still be reasonable in relation to other hospitals in the area. However, the cost of hospital care provided to the total community may be much higher than it has to be. For example, if there was sharing of services between hospitals, costs could be reduced. Since community hospitals do not work on a profit basis, reimbursement by third-party payers on a basis of cost becomes an important issue.

3. Evaluation

Since Mount Carmel is considering eliminating Obstetrics, the analysis of the hospital could be approached in a similar fashion as the analysis of an industrial organization that is considering dropping a product line. Such an approach could include cost-benefit analysis or trade-off studies. For example, what would be the loss of market share because the service is not offered, or what would be the decrease in costs by discontinuing the service? Because this hospital does not operate on a profit basis, it is important to remember that performance is measured on reimbursement which is based on costs.

4. Growth of Health Care

The growth of the health care program has had a significant impact on hospitals and the administration of them. The changes that have taken place include increased demand for services, rising costs, greater administrative accountability, structural changes in delivery, and changing expectations of societal attitudes about health care. These pressures create conflict between two measures of performance, that is, the quality of care and the cost of care provided.

5. Societal Perceptions

Today, health care is regarded as a right rather than a privilege by many. The public expects quality health care. The implementation of a National Health Insurance program, for example, means that a large population would become eligible for hospitalization and other medical care. This would imply that Federal guidelines, reimbursement formulas, reporting requirements, and area-wide planning agencies could limit the operational freedom of the hospital administrator. This would probably also affect the financing and the demand for hospitals. Hospitals could become regulated like utilities.

ALTERNATIVE CONSIDERATIONS

The following include some alternative considerations which address the current issue of the Obstetrics Department. Other factors are obviously operative in this case and should be considered in future planning.

1. Reduce the size of the OB Department to 35-45 beds.

Advantages:	This would result in a sufficient number of beds to maintain an 80% to 90% occupancy rate; total costs would be decreased by eliminating the costs associated with empty beds.
Disadvantages:	In order to continue its Obstetrics Department, $1.3 million is required to bring the facility up to standard.

2. Leave the OB Department as is (status quo).

Advantages:	This would maintain the hospital's image as a well-rounded health care facility and fulfill its responsibility to the community.
Disadvantages:	The low occupancy rate; the under-utilization of facilities; the higher total cost to the community; the duplication of facilities and services; and the cost of remodeling.

3. Discontinue OB services.

Advantages:	The 70 OB beds could be converted to medical/surgical beds; increase in occupancy to over 90%; no remodeling required; reduction in the number of OB beds in the area; costs to community are decreased.
Disadvantages:	The community could react negatively because the service has been discontinued; can other hospitals absorb the additional patient load?; loss of possible GYN service and patients in the future; lack of acceptance by medical staff.

In keeping with the Quadrangle's objective of sharing services, the alternative of discontinuing the service and of consolidating the Obstetrics Department within one or several of the other member hospitals appears to be a viable alternative. The Quadrangle has the purpose of sharing services in order

1. to avoid duplication of facilities and services,
2. to help decrease costs to the community as a whole
3. to improve the quality of patient care.

The serious consideration of this alternative would seem to achieve these objectives in a realistic fashion.

6

The Assessment of Future Requirements

Having examined the process of assessing a firm's present capabilities and the expectations of its owners and the public, in the last chapter, our analysis now turns to an examination of the role of forecasting changes in the external enviornment of a firm.

INNOVATIVE DEVELOPMENTS AND PREDICTIONS

Planning and forecasting go so much hand in hand, that many businessmen confuse the two. Forecasting is the predicting, projecting or estimating of some future events or conditions of the organization's environment; matters mostly outside of management control. Planning on the other hand, is concerned with setting of objectives and goals and with developing alternative courses of action to reach them; matters generally within management control. In other words, the forecasting problem is to attempt to see probable events in the future and to evaluate probable conditions; while the planning problem is to innovate and to find the unique strategy with which to control, in a desired manner, the impact of the expected environmental changes on the organization. Thus, while forecasting is not planning, forecasting should be an indispensible, even automatic part of planning; a vital planning input, a management tool for deciding now what a business must do to realize in the future its desired profit and other goals.

The need for forecasting or predicting changes in the external environment and for assessing the impact of these environmental changes on the operations of the firm, increases as the firm's environment becomes more dynamic and complex. Given the rate of change in the technology, market structure, and other factors in the environment of firms in today's rapidly changing societies, we can see that the forecasting of these changes is very important to effective strategic planning.

Changes in the external environment can be segmented into two broad categories. The first category can be labelled "Innovative Developments," as these changes in the external environment result from the development and application of new innovative techniques in areas such as productive technology, distribution methods and resource utilization. The second category can be labelled "Intervening Contingencies," as these changes in the external environment result from changing expectations and requirements of governments and citizens (both national and international in scope), as well as from changes in resource availability (both natural and man-made shortages in resources required for the operation of the firm). Both of these categories of changes in the external environment of a firm will be examined in detail later in this chapter, but first it seems appropriate to briefly outline some of the common forecasting techniques used by business enterprises to predict changes in their particular environments. The commonly used forecasting techniques to be examined are:

1. Extrapolation of Historical Trends
2. Extrapolations Using Regression Analysis
3. Informed Judgment

FORECASTING TECHNIQUES

Extrapolation of Historical Trends

Extrapolation of Historical trends refers to the prediction of future trends or developments on the bases of past trends or developments. This forecasting technique usually takes the form of plotting past trends against time on a graph and simply extending or extrapolating the resulting line or curve beyond the present or known range, into the uncertain future.

Figure 1.

Declining Transportation Time
for Shipping Goods Between
Two Specified Points Over Time

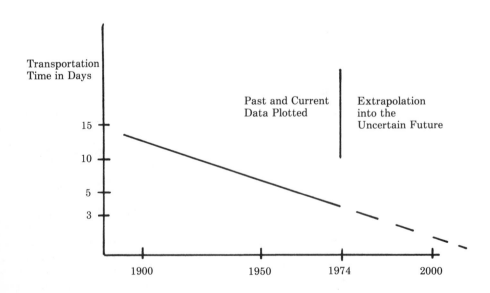

As shown in Figure 1, if transportation time is plotted against historical dates, the resulting line is downward sloping from left to right. This hypothetical example intends to approximate the decreasing transportation time for shipping goods between two points, that resulted from the increasing technology in producing speedier transport facilities, developed from the 1900's to 1974. In this example, the solid line represents this relationship as plotted on the basis of historical data, while the broken line represents an extrapolation of this past trend or relationship into the future. The problem with extrapolation of historical trends is that past trends may not extend similarly into the future. In other words, there may be no further advances in transportation technology after 1974, whereupon the line would become horizontal after 1974, or there may be tremendous advancement in transportation technology after 1974, whereupon the line would become almost vertical after 1974.

Extrapolations Using Regression Analysis

A second forecasting technique involves the use of linear or curvilinear multiple regression lines. This forecasting technique assumes that the specific variable to be predicted is a dependent variable which is a function of certain independent variables. This technique also assumes that the present relationship between the dependent and independent variables will continue to exist in the future. Regression analysis establishes how one variable is related to other variables. It provides an equation wherein the known value of one or more variables may be used to estimate the unknown value of another variable. The general regression equation is as follows:

$$Y = a + b_1 x_1 + b_2 x_2$$

where Y = unknown value of the dependent variable
   a = a constant which represents the value of Y, if all the independent variables (x's) are zero.
   b = regression coefficients which are constants that express the Net Change in Y for a one-unit change in the corresponding x.
   x = known value of the various independent variables.

Using available statistical correlation techniques, the constant (a and the b's) can be calculated and then by substituting the known values of the independent variables (x's) into the equation and performing the necessary multiplication and addition calculations, we obtain an estimate of the value of the dependent variable (Y), when the independent variables are at each particular level.

Predictions of the future values of the dependent variable (Y) can be obtained by estimating the future value of the independent variable (usually through extrapolation of historical data or trends), placing these estimated values into the regression equation, and calculating the corresponding value of the dependent variable.

One of the primary limitations in using the extrapolation of historical trends for predictions and in regression analysis is that the resultant forecast is dependent upon the observed past relationship between a dependent and independent variables. In a dynamic environment, these past relationships can shift suddenly and dramatically. However, to the extent that the observed relationships between dependent and independent variables are true relationships and to the extent that these relationships do not change over time, extrapolations and regression analysis can be used to effectively predict or forecast the future values of dependent variables. This is especially true in short term analyses.

Informed Judgment

In some cases, data do not exist to establish trends in technological, political or sociological developments, so forecasts or predictions must rest solely on the intuitive opinions of an expert or a group of experts. Examples would include forecasts of future scientific breakthroughs or future changes in the attitudes of government or the public towards any particular industry. Although this is a type of "educated guess" approach to forecasting techniques, it warrants mention, because the intuition of the best-informed individuals may in the last resort, turn out to be one of the least costly, as well as the most accurate and useful sources of forecasts. Also, this technique can be and often is used as supplementary information to more elaborate forecasting techniques.

Our analysis, having briefly examined some commonly used forecasting techniques, now turns to an examination of the types of changes in the external environment, that affect a firm's operations and that must be predicted for optimum efficiency of the strategic plan. As mentioned above, the changes in the external environment of a firm can be separated into two broad categories, the first being "innovative developments" and the second being "intervening contingencies." Both of these categories of changes in the external environment of a firm will be examined in some detail, beginning with "innovative developments" and followed by "intervening contingencies." The objective of this part of our analysis is to show how the various types of changes can affect the operations, profitability, and even survival of the firm. It is also intended to point out the importance to the firm of trying to forecast or anticipate these changes in its external environment and the importance of assessing the impact of these anticipated changes on the firm's operations. It is only through devoting some time and resources to forecasting future changes, that the affect of these changes upon the firm's operations can be assessed and the firm's strategic plan be expanded to provide alternative courses of action for the firm, if these predicted changes in its environment do occur at some time in the future.

PREDICTION AND EFFECT OF INNOVATIVE DEVELOPMENTS

In the context of our discussion, innovative developments refer to changes in a firm's environment resulting from the development and application by man, of new and more efficient techniques of carrying out business operations. This section will concentrate on the effect and prediction of innovative developments in the following three areas of business operations:

1. Technological Change
2. Change in Market Structure and Distribution Methods
3. Changes in Resource Utilization

Technological Change

Companies are spending billions of dollars each year to research and develop new products. Technological expansion has vital economic, sociological and political implications.

The economic impact of technology is so great that some industries derive most of their current business from products that did not exist 20 years ago. A study of 11 industries indicated that somewhere from 46 to 100 percent of anticipated short-term corporate growth could be attributed to new products.[1] It is now common for major companies to derive 50 percent or more of current sales from products developed and introduced in the past 10 years.

The impact of technical developments such as lasers, jet aircraft, atomic energy and communication devices, to name a few, has been significant. In the future are such developments as new rapid transit systems, mechanical devices to efficiently replace human organs, undersea farming and mining, economically useful desalinization of sea-water, new synthetic materials for ultra-light construction, automatic language translators, and reliable weather forecasts. Other major technological breakthroughs are not so remote as to preclude planning for the future integration of these developments. In some environments, managers must be alert and plan to compensate for change; in other situations, a prime managerial function is to instigate technological change. In either case, the manager must be aware of the technological impact and be sensitive to the need for more precise planning for the future. The development of technological forecasting has been a response to this need.

Technological forecasting, as distinct from general forecasting activity, has been described as, "the probabilistic assessment, on a relatively high confidence level, of future technological transfer."[2] Technological forecasts are not a picture of what the future will bring; they are predictions, based on confidence, that certain technical developments can occur within a specified time period with a given level of resource allocation. Considering the high rate of technological change in the business environment and the importance of the impact of this changing environment on business operations and on strategic planning, it seems appropriate to examine technological forecasting in more detail.

The time span of technological forecasting will vary from company to company, industry to industry. In the dress trade, a forecast of six months may be too long. In the chemical industry, ten years may be too short. No precise time span can be given; each company or industry must calculate what seems most relevant to it. On the average, three to ten years seems to be desirable for most industrial companies.

It is important to recognize the two fundamental types of technological forecasts, namely, exploratory and normative.[3] The exploratory technological forecast starts from the existing base of knowledge and proceeds to the future on the assumption of logical technological progress. Exploratory technological forecasting is passive and primarily an analysis and reporting of anticipations. It would seem that most industrial firms could effectively use exploratory forecasting. Reasonable identification of emerging technology and analysis of technological implications could provide clues for the firm as to competition, possible expansion of existing product lines, related product lines which the firm could ease into, and new product areas where a foothold could provide a competitive edge. In short, a look into the future would enable better planning, more effective use of resources and considerable avoidance of human and capital obsolescence.

Normative forecasting represents a different approach; it is mission - or goal-oriented. As distinct from exploratory forecasting, normative forecasting is an active or action-directed process. In the normative method, future objectives are identified exclusive of the fact that technological gaps may currently exist, that might act as constraints to the attainment of these technological objectives. Normative technological forecasting can provide incentives to technological progress by focusing on the problems to be surmounted and solved.

In normative forecasting situations, the analyst works backward from the planned mission operational date and determines the technical obstacles. Normative forecasting could act as a directional force to channel effort and resources. Since resources are limited, normative forecasting can be used in deciding priorities, and decisions can be made in conjunction with cost effectiveness studies to determine whether a) the mission requirements are as critical as presented, b) are possible within the stipulated time and c) if the ultimate accomplishment of the mission is worth the resource expenditure.

Normative forecasting has been used primarily by the military services, but industrial organizations can also use it. With the normative approach, the firm could examine the market potential, explore the technical feasibility, look at its expertise in the area, estimate the cost to accomplish product development and then decide whether the project should be undertaken.

In general, technologies tend to decline in importance before their performance limit is reached. For example, propeller-driven aircraft converted to jet-aircraft, military weapons systems, etc. Technology also tends to rise and decline in a reasonably smooth progression. It is often possible, therefore, to forecast the comparative decline of a technology and the approximate time when a new technology will take over from it.[4]

ADVANTAGES AND APPLICATION OF TECHNOLOGICAL FORECASTING

The incorporation of technological forecasting into the process of management is an extension of existing methodology. In the past it would appear that management has often intuitively drifted in this direction. To be useful, technological forecasting does not have to be precise. If an innovation can be identified, and if the innovation can be translated into constructive action within a reasonable and discernible time frame, it can substantially contribute to the decision-making process.

Generally, technological forecasting can assist management in several ways. It can present an organized approach to a selective search for information. It can provoke thought by expanding horizons. It can help provide perspective and facilitate interdisciplinary communication. It can encourage operational sensitivity. It can assist management in determining the magnitude of anticipated change and provide a basis for estimating costs and requirements for people, facilities, equipment, etc. It can aid in giving direction to product development and market penetration. It can assist in recognizing competition and other possible restraints, such as natural resources or technological limitations. It can also be used to help determine sociological and economic trends.

LIMITATIONS OF TECHNOLOGICAL FORECASTING

Information may be the greatest limitation to contributive technological forecasting. The information problem is extensive. For instance: what information is needed? How much information is required? Is the information accurate? Have related and unrelated disciplines been explored for possible information transfer?

Information interpretation is a vital ingredient in technological forecasting. No relevant mechanical process presently exists that will evaluate the information in terms of available technical solutions, cost and value, product applicability and market potential. Human judgment is a factor in interpreting information and interpretation can be colored by optimism or pessimism and courage or conservatism. Information analysis can also differ due to the competence of the analyst and his functional orientation. Augmenting the difficulties cited is the fact that often pertinent information may not be available because of security restrictions and trade secrets.

The facts that limitations exist in technological forecasting, just as there are limitations in other techniques, should not discourage management; awareness should lead to more critical and productive application.

In summarizing our discussion of technological change, we can say that:

1. We live in a dynamic environment in which technological innovation occurs almost continuously.

2. The impact of technological innovation and change upon business firms is tremendous and it has wide-ranging implications for continued profitability and survival.
3. Technological forecasting, especially exploratory technological forecasting, helps firms to anticipate technological innovations and thereby allows firms to include such anticipations in their strategic planning alternatives and make more efficient use of its scarce resources.

CHANGE IN MARKET STRUCTURE AND DISTRIBUTION METHODS

As was the case with technological change, the ability of management to anticipate future changes in market structure and distribution methods, allows management to incorporate the consequences of these changes and the firm's desired response, into their strategic plans. The markets and distribution methods for many firms are in a continual state of flux for many reasons. Some of the major reasons are as follows:

1. Changing Technology in Product Development
2. Recent global restructuring of the market place
3. Changing techniques and channels of distribution

Changing Technology in Product Development

As new products are developed, the firm must change or expand its marketing horizons. If a particular firm is not the innovator of new products, it may be pushed out of its former markets and will have to search for new markets or change its product line. Although products, like consumers, have life cycles that can provide useful information for planning purposes, these product life cycles are often suddenly distorted by competitive breakthroughs which through the introduction of new technology suddenly eliminate a preceding product and send it into an accelerated decline.[5] Therefore, there is an increasing need for companies to spend greater amounts of effort in forecasting and planning for new product development and the resulting effect on markets, as well as planning on the basis of hypothesized product life-cycle analysis.

A New Product Development Department or committee helps to assure that new ideas for products are carefully evaluated and good ones profitably marketed. A well-organized development procedure might enable a firm to copy others' attractive innovations quickly and profitably. This possibility should not be overlooked. No one company can hope to be first always, with the best products.

Recent Global Restructuring of the Market-Place

A global restructuring of the market-place refers to the invasion of domestic markets by foreign manufacturers, as well as the opening up of foreign markets to domestic firms. This is a market phenomenon that has been gaining substantial momentum in recent years, as witnessed by the vast number of foreign-made goods being offered for sale in the American market.

Between 1949 and 1959, for example, the rate of U.S. investment abroad grew approximately 175 percent. The growth rate of foreign investment in the U.S. during the same period was approximately 500%, although the absolute value of foreign investment in the U.S. was much lower than the absolute value of U.S. investment abroad. Thus, we can see the magnitude of this global restructuring of the market-place. Now, let us look at the impact of this restructuring on individual firms.

The firm may face much stiffer competition in its domestic markets from the new foreign competitors. The degree of competitiveness of the foreign products depends to some extent on the government policy with regard to restrictive tariffs that are sometimes imposed to protect some domestic industries.

Thus, we can see the importance of firms being able to anticipate changing world markets, and the importance of firms increasing their adaptability by planning ahead of time what they will do if certain foreign markets are opened or closed to them.

Changing Techniques and Channels of Distribution

New and more efficient methods of transporting or shipping goods from the producer to retail outlets and ultimate consumers have wide-ranging effects for firms in the transportation business, firms with their own transportation systems, as well as for firms who have to ship their goods to distant market locations. Examples of recent new distribution techniques would include refrigerated ships and rail cars, containerized shipping, and jumbo-sized ocean tankers. Obviously, the firms involved in transportation would be at an advantage if they could anticipate these changes and plan for action, if and when such innovations occur. Other firms not directly involved in transportation themselves (but who depend upon other firms to take their goods to market), would also be better off if they could anticipate these changes and make contracts with the most innovative transportation firms.

With regard to changing channels of distribution, firms should be aware of current trends and hopefully anticipating future trends in the most efficient channels of distribution. In the past, the most common channel strategy for producing firms has been to ship goods to regional wholesalers, who in turn distribute the goods to appropriate retail outlets. This of course varies with the type of product being produced and who the users of the product are. For example, a producer-owned sales outlet may be the most effective marketing agent for industrial goods.

An example of a currently changing distribution channel for consumer goods are department stores and supermarkets. Here, the development of large-scale retail chains capable of bearing the costs of holding large inventories has led to the elimination of many wholesaling firms. The large retail outlets receive shipments directly from producers and by doing away with the costs of the wholesaling middle-man, can offer the products for sale at a lower price than was possible before.

Situations such as this obviously have implications for the wholesaling firm, but there are also implications for producing firms who are currently still distributing their goods to regional wholesalers. For the wholesaling firms, they should re-evaluate their situation and either increase their effectiveness or leave the industry altogether. For the producing firms still using wholesalers, they should re-evaluate their channel strategy or they will find that their now higher-priced products are not selling to consumers.

If the majority of firms in an industry find a cheaper method of physical distribution or find ways of eliminating distribution channel members, without decreasing efficiency, a firm that is not able to anticipate these changes and adapt quickly will be at a competitive disadvantage and may even have to leave the industry.

Changes in Resource Utilization

The third and final area of innovative developments to be examined is the innovative developments in the use of resource inputs or raw materials. This topic will be discussed under two major headings:

1. Expanding Uses for Currently Exploited Resources
2. Discovery of New Uses for By-Products

Expanding Uses for Currently Exploited Resources

Many resources, primarily natural resources and raw materials, are discovered and found useful for producing particular goods. They are used for years as inputs to the production process of the particular finished good. Then later, it is discovered either by accident or through extensive research and development activities, that these same resources could be used profitably to produce a previously undiscovered product.

The example that comes to mind, is the use for many years of crude oil to produce fuel for lamps and internal combustion engines, as well as the many other products that can be produced from crude oil. The later discovery, made in the 1930's, that polymer products or plastics could also be produced from this resource resulted in a whole new industry being established. The advantages of plastics, such as its lightness, ease of manufacture, and corrosion and wear resistance led to large scale development of a plastics industry producing a wide variety of products.

Such a discovery has implications for the petro-chemical industry as well as for producers of products which must compete with plastics in the market-place. This example shows the benefit to companies of committing some of their resources to research and development activities. It should also be obvious, that those firms who are able to anticipate such radical developments or have contingency plans available in case such developments occur, would be in a better position to adapt to these changing environmental conditions and continue existence in a profitable manner.

Discovery of New Uses for By-Products

Often, when producing a good from raw materials, by-products are produced. Some by-products are of a limited selling value, while others are simply treated as waste and discarded. If, however, these by-products can be further refined or used as inputs for another economically viable product, then the firm could likely increase its profits. This is especially true if the firm is currently discarding by-products as waste, because then the acquisition cost of the raw materials for the new product will be negligible.

An example of a by-product that was refined into new products is the sawdust and woodchips left over after trees have been cut into lumber. These woodchips and sawdust had historically either been discarded or used as fuel to heat the lumber camps and mills. It was later discovered, that these by-products could be used as inputs in the production of press or particle board sheeting. Particle boards could be manufactured and offered for sale at a relatively low cost. In recent years, the market for such products has expanded dramatically as they are being used for low-cost sheeting or floor underlay by construction trades and individual consumers.

Again we see the advantages to firms of committing some of their current resources to research and development projects. The innovative development of such products is relevant to companies in the industry where the new products are developed, as well as being relevant to companies in an industry that has competing products. Smaller companies may find exploratory forecasting techniques valuable in this area, in that reasonable identification of emerging technological trends could provide the firm with clues as to future competition and profitable expansion of existing product lines. For larger firms, normative forecasting techniques could be useful, in that future goals and opportunities could be identified and more resources allocated to research in promising areas.

In summarizing this section on the effect and prediction of innovative developments in an industry, we can note that changes in technology, market structure and distribution methods, and resource utilization can have profound effects on the environment in which firms operate. Such changes can make current products obsolete, cause a complete shift in a firm's competitive emphasis and result in the utilization of previously discarded materials. The most salient facts to be emphasized from this section of our analysis is that by using forecasting techniques firms can anticipate innovative developments in their environments and consequently include such possibilities in their strategic planning alternatives. Also important is the fact that by using normative forecasting techniques, firms can identify areas of profitable development and pursue research in those areas; thereby influencing their environments in profitable directions, consistent with their objectives and present capabilities.

PREDICTION AND EFFECT OF INTERVENING CONTINGENCIES

In the context of this discussion, the term "intervening contingencies" refers to changes in a firm's environment, resulting from changes in the attitudes and expectations of consumers, general public and governments, both national and international in scope. Another potential intervening contingency lies in the area of resource availability, including both natural shortages and man-made shortages of resources required for the operation of the firm. This section will concentrate on the effect and prediction of intervening contingencies in the following three areas of the business environment.

1. Political and Legal Intervening Contingencies
2. Sociological Intervening Contingencies
3. Economic and Resource Availability Intervening Contingencies

Political and Legal Intervening Contingencies

Business enterprises, like individuals, are subject to the laws of the land in which they carry on operations. Therefore, since governments have the right to impose any legislation they believe to be in the best interest of the public, the political and legal sphere of its external environment is critically important to any business entity. With regard to the political and legal environment in which firms operate, two major factors warrant closer examination:

1. Ideology of Major Political Parties
2. Laws affecting Business Operations

Ideology of Major Political Parties

The ideology of groups such as political parties refers to their fundamental beliefs on such questions as: What is our reason for existence? What do we hope to accomplish? How do we hope to accomplish our objectives?

Since political parties can wield strong influences on the business environment of all firms, it is important that these firms understand the ideology of major political platforms. The need for such an understanding arises, because it is a prerequisite to anticipating future actions of the parties, as well as being a prerequisite to successfully influencing the stand that various political parties will take on an issue of interest to the business community in general or to particular firms.

Anticipation of future government action can be accomplished through the use of common forecasting techniques discussed earlier in this analysis. The expert opinion of political scientists or others close to the major government decision-makers provides one source of forecast information in this area.

Another potentially useful forecasting technique would be the extrapolation of past and current attitudes and trends of government towards business or industries in particular. This could provide useful insights into what future legislation may bring to the business community.

The business community may also be able to influence the decisions made by governments. Influencing government decisions is most often successfully accomplished if many firms or even industries provide a temporary or permanent lobbying force near the seat of government. In this way, the government is able to get a clear presentation of the views of industry and what courses of action industry will be forced to take if any particular legislation is passed.

By understanding the ideology of political parties and by forecasting changes that are expected in the governing parties or the policies of existing governments, firms can have viable alternative plans available, so that if an important change in the political environment does take place, the firm will be able to respond quickly. One alternative, for example, might be to move operations to a different state if an official with an unfavorable attitude towards a certain business is elected to power in the present location.

Laws Affecting Business Operations

As was stated above, a business organization must abide by the laws of the country, state, county, and municipality in which it carries on operations. Thus the laws and the judicial system are important factors in the external environment of all firms. Laws which have substantial impact on the operating freedom of companies in the United States include:

Patents, Trademarks and Copyright Acts

Patent Laws protect the rights of inventors to be the sole producers of their invention for a legally specified period of time.

Trademark Laws protect the brand names of a company's product, by preventing producers of similar goods from using the same trademarks or tradenames in selling their products. This is to allow producers to help consumers distinguish their product from those of competitors.

Copyright Laws protect the writings of an author from being copied and published by people other than the author, who do not have the author's permission. Such protection usually lasts for a legally specified period.

Anti-Trust Laws

The purpose of these laws is to maintain competition and achieve economic efficiency and maximum output, and so, ultimately and ideally, a maximization of the standard of living with the given level of available scarce resources. To accomplish this task, a range of restrictive trade practices are illegal. The relevant laws include: Sherman Act, Clayton Act, Federal Trade Commission Act and the Robinson-Patman Act. These acts prohibit such activities as, monopolies, price discrimination, predatory pricing and misleading advertising.

Thus, we can see that any planned actions that a company may take could possibly bring them into conflict with the law and the judicial system. It is therefore imperative, that companies understand the laws of the country in which they operate and that they understand how these laws would affect any actions that they have contemplated and planned for the future. However, even if companies do understand the laws of the land and how they would limit company actions, it is useful for firms to try and anticipate changes in the laws and even legal structure of the country. The best forecasting technique in this situation could be to attain the judgments of experts. Consultation with law professors, practicing attorneys or government officials could possibly provide indications of future legal trends.

We have seen that an understanding of the ideology of political parties and of the laws of the country, are necessary for business organizations in their planning and day to day operations. We have also seen, that if firms attempt to forecast future trends in political thought and laws, they can often be more successful in planning for the future. It is through examining potential future developments in politics and laws, that firms can plan accordingly and thereby prevent the extreme disruption to operations that would occur if they were caught unaware by political and legal intervening contingencies.

Sociological Intervening Contingencies

By sociological intervening contingencies we are referring to the changes in attitudes and expectations of the general public or specific groups toward issues, such as, ecology or environmental protection and consumer's rights. Since changes in attitudes and expectations of the public with regard to these issues, could lead to substantial changes in the external environment of many firms, it is important that these firms determine the effect of such probable changes and try to anticipate these changes before they occur. These topics will be discussed under the following headings:

1. Consumerism
2. Environmental Protection

Consumerism

The issue of consumer rights has been prevalent in recent years. Though the issues that come under the encompassing title "consumerism" (i.e. misleading advertising, high prices, confusing packages, labels and weights) have been discussed and argued over for many years by such groups as the Better Business Bureaus, it is only in recent years that large segments of the general public have become quite vocal and active in the "fight" for consumer rights. This great interest on the part of the public has, in part, led to important federal and state government legislation concerning consumer rights and protection.

Environmental Protection

In the United States, the land area and resources were so large that until recently they seemed almost unlimited. This led business organizations in general, to extract resources and eliminate waste (through air or water) in the cheapest, most efficient manner, with little concern for what they were doing to the environment. In recent years, the polluted air and rivers and the scarred countryside have resulted in an increasing concern by the general public and government for some form of environmental protection. This concern has been manifested in the formation of numerous environmental protection or anti-pollution groups among the concerned public and also in recent environmental protection legislation.

The two cases discussed above have been chosen as being representative of changes in attitudes and expectations of the public that can have dramatic effects on the efficient operation of business organizations. These cases are not the only important ones, but they do serve as examples.

Essentially, the changing attitudes of the public can affect business organization in either or both of two ways. They can be the instigating force behind restrictive legislation or they can simply refuse to buy the products of what they consider to be an offending or irresponsible firm. We have seen throughout this analysis that companies should be aware of changes within their external environments. The same holds true for attitude changes of the general public. The ability to anticipate these changing attitudes and plan accordingly, is an important first step for any company to insure that its policies and products will be in line with changing attitudes and thus hopefully receive the respect and the patronage of the general public.

Economic and Resource Availability Intervening Contingencies

Two factors, which are of vital importance to the profitable and efficient operation of any firm are:

1. Availability of Resource Inputs
2. Impact of a Change in Economic Conditions

Intervening contingencies, that disrupt either or both of the above two factors essential to profitable operations of firms, will cause dramatic changes in the external environment of all firms within the business community. Although these two factors are somewhate related, they will be discussed separately in this analysis.

Availability of Resource Inputs

Most firms, especially those concerned with the manufacturing of tangible goods, are dependent upon an adequate supply of resource materials. Resources, as the term is used here, refer primarily to raw materials, although the meaning of the term could be expanded to include other resources such as skilled labor, financial capacity and plant and facilities.

The most recent and perhaps the most dramatic example of how intervening contingencies in the area of resource availability can disrupt the efficient operations of many firms within an economic system, was the shortage of oil and its derived products that struck most of the Western, European and Asian World recently. The oil shortage resulted from the decision of the oil-exporting Arab nations to cut production and apply oil embargos as a political lever to swing world opinion away from supporting the Israeli cause to support the Arab cause in the Middle-East. The effects of the oil shortage in North America and especially in the United States, were dramatic and wide-ranging. The following list contains some of the most important effects on industry:

1. General slowdown of industrial activity as energy stockpiles depleted.
2. In the automobile industry, high gas-consumption cars did not sell as they did before, because people feared increasing gasoline shortages.
3. Airlines had a number of their flights stopped or reduced by government order.
4. Consumers were no longer willing to drive many miles to shop at their preferred shops, because of the shortage of gasoline. Therefore sales in many stores plummeted.

We can see from the above incomplete list of effects of the oil shortage on various industries that the impact was indeed great. Although, the Arab oil embargo has been used as an example of resource shortages, natural resources depletions would likely have a similar impact. In fact, perhaps the most positive result of the oil crisis was that industry, government and the general public were made aware that presently known reserves of oil will be depleted within a predictable period of time if current rates of consumption continue.

What are the implications of shortages in resource supply for strategic planning? First, the firm must realize the criticality of its various resources to its productive process. Second, the firm must attempt to anticipate intervening contingencies in the supply of resources. Extrapolation techniques can usually be utilized to forecast natural depletion of resources. However, within the realm of artificial or man-imposed shortages the forecasting becomes more difficult. This does not mean however that it is impossible. In the example of the Arab oil embargo, the increasing hostility between Israel and the Arab States should have indicated a high probability of a new war and given the outbreak of war, one possible action of the Arab States should have been seen to be an oil embargo. Granted, the probability assigned to the occurrence of both these events would likely have been relatively small, but nonetheless if a firm did this forecasting and outlined a plan of action to be taken if the event occurred, it would be far ahead of the firm without any plan for such occurrences.

Impact of a Change in Economic Conditions

The statement that economic recession or the development of galloping inflation in an economy will have dramatic and profound effects on the profitable operation of most business firms would likely not evoke much argument from any critics. The extent of the effect of such developments on firms depends, of course, upon the type of industry the firm is in and the degree of recession or inflation.

Since the impact of such developments is potentially great for most firms, it is essential that firms attempt to forecast and anticipate such developments and have alternative plans into which they can move if such developments do occur. The failure to react quickly to changing economic conditions, such as general slowdowns or recessions and inflationary cost spirals could spell disaster for even the currently most profitable firms. The most useful forecasting techniques in the area of economic change would appear to be:

1. Extrapolation of past and current economic cycles and trends
2. Seeking the advice of economists and other experts
3. Observing developing trends in the economies of other similar countries in the world.

Although no plan is likely to increase or even maintain profitability at current levels under conditions of recession or inflation, some alternatives such as utilizing cheaper raw materials or closing down marginally-efficient plants, may at least insure survival of the enterprise until conditions become more favorable.

Assessment of the Impact Upon the Firm of the Predicted Innovative Developments and Intervening Contingencies

As has been mentioned briefly throughout this Chapter, it is just as important for a firm to assess the impact of innovative developments and intervening contingencies upon the firm, as it is to make the initial forecasts. Initially the firm must forecast possible intervening contingencies and innovative developments. Once these forecasts have been made, the firm must then determine to the best of its ability, what the impact of the changes in its environment will be or in other words, what will these changes mean for continuing or improving efficient operations.

In the area of innovative developments, for example, the firm will have to examine the questions: What will be the impact on operations if we come up with a new innovative development? What will the impact be if our competition comes up with a new innovative development? It is through thinking about and answering questions such as these, that the firm will be able to determine the most efficient course of action and plan to permit the feasibility of such a course of action.

The assessment of the impact on a firm of changes in its environment can be accomplished by a variety of assessment techniques. One of the more effective and popular assessment techniques is model building and computer simulation.

Model Building and Computer Simulation

A model is, essentially, a representation of part of all of the characteristics of a larger system. In a strategic and profit planning context, it is usually a series of mathematical equations from which, through manipulation, it is possible to infer real life situations.

The object of constructing models is to clarify and formalize ideas about the system as well as to make it possible to predict (from the behavior of the model) how the system will behave, and where possible, how it can be influenced.[7]

The more complex the structure of the model, the more likely it will be to give erroneous results. A complex model will also take longer to build. It might be better to have several reasonably small models which need no complex event interaction built into them. Models should be capable of adaptation and extension where necessary and should be designed with this in mind. A time allowance for testing, adaptation and refinement should be considered when the model is projected and built.

Questions to be examined when building a model of the firm should include: What data is required for the model and how accurate must it be? Can the required data be obtained at all? In addition, the cost of building models should be compared with the results which are likely to be produced.

Once the forecasts of potential environmental changes have been made and the model of the firm constructed, the management of the firm can separately incorporate each change into the equations of the model, while holding all other variables constant. Thereby the impact of each change on the firm's operations can be determined. The impact of more than one change in the firm's environment can also be estimated by incorporating the various changes into the model. This simulation of changes in the firm's environment can be greatly facilitated by using a computer to do the calculations, especially if the number of forecasts is large or the model relatively complex.

Some Advantages of Modeling and Simulations

1. Models give the company the ability to experiment with ideas and alternatives without unduly affecting or taking up the time of top management. Normal company operations are not disrupted.
2. The probable results of applying alternatives can be seen without incurring great expense.
3. The act of gathering information for the model often helps to

motivate management into re-thinking their data requirements for decision-making purpose. Thus data requirements are made more completely explicit.
4. The act of model-making should help to integrate interdepartmental activities.
5. The use of computer simulations allows management to get vast amounts of informational data in relatively short time periods.

Some Disadvantages of Modeling and Simulations

1. Models may not be able to respond fast enough to mirror real life situations.
2. Models rely upon data and operate under constraints which are often difficult to obtain and may not be very accurate when obtained. Also, some data essential for a models' success may not be considered so by the model-makers and, therefore, be left out completely.
3. The use of computers for simulation can be expensive.

Thus the use of models and simulations can be applied to determine the impact on the firm's operations, of various environmental changes that have been predicted. Once the impacts of the forecasts have been assessed, the firm should be in a position to outline alternative strategic plans that will capitalize on profitable impacts and avoid negative impacts of the changes, should they occur as predicted.

ASSESSMENT ANALYSIS

Up to this point, we have examined various forecasting techniques, the resulting predictions of future environmental change and the impact of these changes on the firm's operations. There seems to be general agreement that such techniques and practices are vey useful and helpful to firms in their strategic planning activities. However, eventually each firm must ask itself: should we devote more or fewer resources to forecasting activities? What is the optimum resource allocation to forecasting activities for our firm as a whole? How should forecasting activities be divided among the various areas of technological forecasting, market and demand forecasting, and political and sociological change forecasting?

The decision criteria for allocating the firm's scarce resources to forecasting future environmental change (whether change in innovative developments or intervening contingencies), are wide and diverse and will vary from firm to firm. Generally, however, the following three criteria would appear to be relevant to most firms and to most areas of forecasting:

1. Degree of Environmental Stability
2. Degree to Which the Firm's Operations are Vulnerable and Responsive to Environmental Change
3. Costs and Benefits Associated with Forecasting

Degree of Environmental Stability

If the environment in which a firm operates is relatively stable and unchanging and has a history of stability, then the need for comprehensive forecasting is likely not too critical for insuring survival of the firm, for example, the Swiss watch industry. If, however, the firm's environment is highly unstable and has seen dramatic changes during the past, then the need for devoting significant resources to forecasting activities is likely quite strong, for example, the aero-space industry.

Before making its decision with regard to how much forecasting is optimum for the firm, management must examine the stability of all areas of its environment. For example, the firm may discover that its political and social external environment is quite stable and all indications are that this stability will continue. The same firm may discover, however, that the technical and economic environment in which it operates has been in the past and is currently very unstable. This would indicate that resources could most profitably be directed towards forecasting of innovative developments in its environment. Even for the firm that finds most aspects of its environment to be relatively stable, the potential benefits of devoting resources to normative forecasting should be examined, because if the firm itself can become the industry innovator, the potential rewards can be substantial.

Degree of Vulnerability and Responsiveness of Firm to Environment Changes

The more vulnerable and responsive a firm's operations are to changing conditions in its environment, the more important it is for the firm to engage in forecasting activities. The more responsive such a firm is to environmental change, the more resources it should devote to forecasting in an attempt to anticipate such changes before they occur, so that the firm can plan accordingly. On the other hand, if environmental change has in the past had little effect on a firm's operations, then perhaps the need for forecasting would diminish, with corresponding re-allocation of scarce resources to uses more profitable than forecasting.

Costs and Benefits Associated with Forecasting

The benefits of forecasting activities to a firm who is then able to anticipate environmental changes and plan accordingly have been discussed at length in this analysis.

The costs of forecasting activities are essentially the opportunity costs of the scarce resources which must be allocated to the forecasting activities. In other words, the materials and skilled manpower employed in forecasting activities that could also be potentially employed in other perhaps more productive areas of operations.

Because of the costs associated with forecasting, a firm must decide to what extent it wants to allocate its scarce resources to this activity. No matter how interesting or useful a forecast might be, the profit-maximizing firm will not support it if its costs exceed its benefits. A cost-utility imbalance can also occur if the forecast is relatively inexpensive, but is of little or no use to the company. Each firm must determine at what point the costs of forecasting outweigh the benefits received and the efficient firm will not increase resource allocation to forecasting activities beyond this point.

SUMMARY

The assessment process is not complete without determining which potential innovative developments or intervening contingencies could have an impact upon the future operations of the firm. The ability to react quickly to changes in its environment is crucial to the long-run survival and profitability of any firm. The firm which can successfully anticipate future organization or environmental change, will be in a good position to develop strategic alternatives which can cope with the changed situation.

The firm which utilizes forecasting techniques may be in a position to not only anticipate future environmental change, but also be in a position to identify areas of opportunity which have potential competitive advantage for the firm which can exploit them. Thus, the forecast information can be used through the planning process to alter a firm's present capabilities and to take advantage of predicted future situations.

In today's rapidly changing world of business, no firm of any consequent size can afford to ignore the potential benefits of detailed strategic planning. Strategic planning to be of use, must be based upon an assessment of the present and future capabilities of the firm and the present and forecasted future environment in which the firm operates. Only after this rigorous and systematic assessment process has been completed can the next stage of strategic planning, that of the generation of strategic alternatives, logically begin.

ENDNOTES

1. *Management of New Products,* 4th ed., Booz, Allen and Hamilton, Inc., New York, 1969, p. 6.
2. Jantsch, E.; *Technological Forecasting in Perspective,* Organization for Economic Cooperation and Development, Paris, 1967, p. 15.
3. Bonge, John A. and Coleman, Bruce P.; *Concepts for Corporate Strategy,* MacMillan, New York, 1972, p. 241.
4. Walley, B.H.; *How to Apply Strategy in Profit Planning,* London: Business Books Ltd., 1971, p. 83.
5. Ansoff, H.I.; *Business Strategy,* Penguin, Middlesex, 1969, p. 24.
6. Ibid., p. 111.
7. Walley, B.H.; op. cit., p. 64.

CASE

WALL DRUG

Ted and Bill Hustead, primary owners and managers of Wall Drug, in Wall, South Dakota, faced a serious decision in the winter of 1973. Should they invest heavily in stock for the tourist season of 1974 anticipating an increase in business, or should they buy conservatively? Should they continue to expand Wall Drug in the future or should they seek some other alternative? Although the Hustead's Wall Drug had experienced unprecedented growth for the last 27 years and had been written up in newspapers and magazines for several years, times seem to be more precarious now. Rising gasoline prices, periodic shortages and gasoline stations closing, trouble with American Indian Movement (AIM) at Wounded Knee, the highway beautification laws threatening more of Wall Drug's famous roadside signs seemed to threaten tourist travel, and Wall Drug in particular.

The History of the Wall Drug — Free Ice Water[1]

In June of 1969 *America Illustrated,* the United States Information Agency publication in the Soviet Union and Poland, featured a story entitled "The Lure and Fascination of Seven Fabulous Stores," by Mal Oettinger. The seven stores were Macy's, Wall Drug Store, Rich's, L.L. Bean, Inc., Neiman-Marcus, Gump's and Brentano's.

In the late summer of 1973, the *Wall Street Journal* carried a story about Wall Drug. These are but two of the many feature articles about Wall Drug that have appeared in newspapers and magazines all over North America. The *Wall Street Journal* article is typical of those appearing over the years and accurately describes much of the history and operations of this famous establishment that has become an institution of South Dakota.

---

[1]   Dana Close Jennings, *Free Ice Water, The Story of Wall Drug.*

This case was prepared by Professors James D. Taylor, Robert L. Johnson, and Gene B. Iverson of the University of South Dakota, as the basis of class discussion rather than to illustrate either effective or ineffective handling of an administrative situation.

Presented at a Case Workshop and distributed by the Intercollegiate Case Clearing House, Soldiers Field, Boston, Mass. 02163. All rights reserved to the contributors. Printed in the U.S.A. Used with permission.

Ted Hustead is a pharmacist and graduated from the University of Nebraska, class of 1929, at the age of 27. He and his wife Dorothy, a Colman, South Dakota girl, bought the drugstore in Wall in December, 1931. Dorothy and Ted, and their four year old son Bill, lived in the back twenty feet of the store. (See map in Figure 1.)

Wall in 1931 is ably described by Dana Close Jennings in his book about the Wall Drug entitled *Free Ice Water.*[2]

> Wall, then: a huddle of poor wooden buildings, many unpainted, housing some 300 desperate souls; a 19th century depot and wooden water tank; dirt (or mud) streets; few trees; a stop on the railroad, it wasn't even that on the highway. US 16 and 14 went right on by, as did the tourists speeding between the Badlands and the Black Hills. There was nothing in Wall to stop for.

The drugstore, and the town of Wall did not prosper until Dorothy Hustead conceived the idea of placing an advertising sign on the highway to advertise free ice water. Ted put the sign up and cars were turning off at Wall to go to the drugstore before he got back to the store. This turning point in the history of Wall Drug took place on a blazing hot Sunday afternoon in the summer of 1936.

Ted recognized the value of the signs and began putting them up all along the highways leading to Wall. In an article in *Good Housekeeping* 1951, the Hustead's signs were called "the most ingenious and irresistible system of signs ever devised."[3]

During World War II, Wall Drug signs began to be put up by servicemen from South Dakota who were familiar with the sign advertising in South Dakota. Later some servicemen wrote back requesting signs. During World War II one appeared in Paris: "Wall Drug Store 4,278 miles (6,951 kilometers)." They later appeared in many places including the 38th parallel in Korea, the north and south pole areas, and Vietnam jungle trails. These signs led to news stories and publicity which further increased the notoriety of the store.

The sales and size of Wall Drug have grown spectacularly since the 1940's. From 1931 until 1941 the building was rented and was on the west side of Main Street. In 1941 an old lodge hall, which acted as the gymnasium in Wasta (15 miles west of Wall), was bought and moved to become the new Wall Drug. It was placed on the east side of Main across the street from the original store.

When World War II ended tourist travel greatly increased and the Wall Drug signs brought so many people into Wall Drug that the Husteads claim they were embarrassed because the facilities were not large enough. There were no modern restrooms even. Sales in the 1940's after the war were from $150,000 to $200,000 per year.

In 1951 Bill Hustead, the son of Ted and Dorothy, now a pharmacy graduate of South Dakota State College at Brookings joined his father in the store.

In 1953 Wall Drug was expanded into a former store room to the south. This became the Western Clothing Room. In 1954 they built an outside store on the south of the Western Clothing Room. This was accompanied by a 30% increase in business. In 1956 a self-service cafe was added on the north side of the store. In the early 1950's sales were in the $300,000 per year range and by the early 1960's had climbed to $500,000.

---

[2] Dana Close Jennings, *Free Ice Water,* p. 26.
[3] *Ibid.,* p. 42.

FIGURE 1

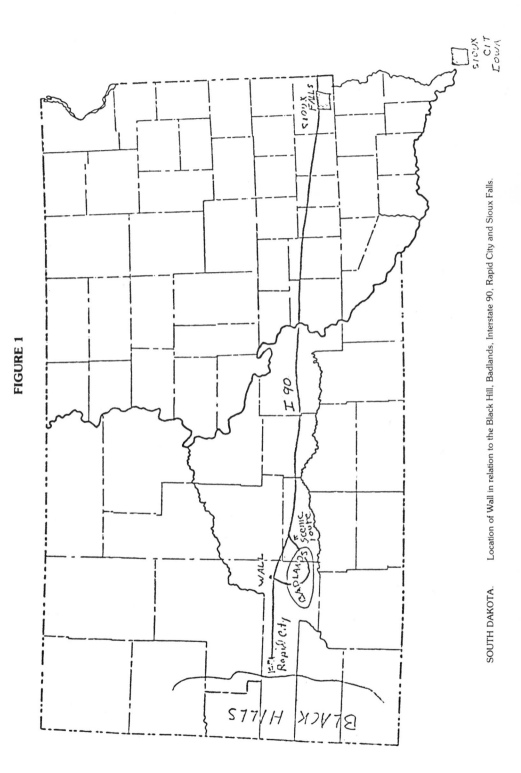

SOUTH DAKOTA.   Location of Wall in relation to the Black Hill, Badlands, Interstate 90, Rapid City and Sioux Falls.

In the early 1960's, Ted and his son Bill began seriously thinking of moving Wall Drug to the highway. The original Highway 16 ran by the north-side of Wall, about two blocks from the store. It was later moved to run by the south side of Wall, about two blocks also from the drugstore. In the late 1950's and early 1960's a new highway was built running by the south side of Wall paralleling the other highway. Ted and Bill Hustead were considering building an all new Wall Drug along with a gasoline filling station alongside the new highway just where the interchange by Wall was located.

They decided to build the gasoline station first, and did so. It is called Wall Auto Livery. When the station was finished they decided to hold up on the new store and then decided to continue expanding the old store in downtown Wall. This was a fortunate decision, since soon after that the new interstate highway replaced the former new highway and the new interchange ran through the site of the proposed new Wall Drug.

Thus, since they decided to stay in their present site in 1963 a new fireproof construction coffee shop was added where the present soda fountain is on the front just north of the main store.

In 1964 a new kitchen, again of fireproof construction, was added just in back of the cafe and main store. In 1964 and 1965 offices and the new phar-macy were opened on the second floor over the kitchen.

IN 1968 the back dining room and backyard across the alley were added. This was followed in 1971 with the Art Gallery Dining Room.

By the late 1960's and early 1970's annual sales volume went to $1,000,000.

In 1971 the Husteads bought the theater that bordered their store on the south. They ran it as a theater through 1972. In early 1973 they began con-struction of a new addition to the old theater location. This is called the "Mall." By the summer of 1973 the north part of the Mall was open for business. The south side was not ready yet. That year the Wall Drug grossed $1,600,000 which was an increase of about 20% over 1972. Bill believes the increase was due to their new Mall addition.

THE MALL

The development of the Mall represents a distinct change in the develop-ment of Wall Drug. All previous development had been financed out of retain-ed earnings or short-term loans. In effect each addition was paid for as it was built or added.

The owners of Wall Drug broke with their previous method of expansion when they built the Mall by borrowing approximately $250,000 for 10 years to finance the Mall and part of 20 large new signs which stand 660 feet from the interstate highway.

During the last half of the 1960's and early 1970's Bill Hustead had thought about and planned the concept of the Mall. The Mall was designed as a town within a large room. The main strolling mall was designed as a main street with each store or shop designed as a two story frontier Western building. The Mall is thus like a re-created Western town. Inside the stores various woods are used in building and paneling. Such woods as pine from Custer, South Dakota, American black walnut, gumwood, hackberry, cedar, maple, and oak are among the various woods used. The store fronts are re-creations of building fronts found in old photos of Western towns in the 1880's. Many photos, paintings, and prints line the walls. These shops stock products that are more expensive than the souvenir merchandise found in most other parts of the store. The shops are more like Western boutiques.

The northern part of the Mall was open for business shortly after July 10, 1973. In the fall of 1973, Bill was uncertain as to whether or not to open the south side.

THE STORE OPERATION

By the end of 1973 the Husteads were operating Wall Drug and Wall Auto Livery as two separate corporations. Financial statements for 1972 and 1973 may be found in the Appendix. Within these two corporations are trailer rental and interest income. The theater was operated only until the Mall was built on the theater site. Sales for their corporations were at an all time high in 1973.

The two corporations are mainly dependent on tourist travel. Wall is a small town of 786 people as of 1970. The economic base of the town is primarily built around the Wall Drug and is dependent on tourist business also.

Wall is situated right on the edge of the Badlands and 52 miles east of Rapid City. For miles in either direction, people in autos have been teased and tantalized by Wall Drug signs. Many have heard of the place through stories in the press, or have heard their parents speak of the Wall Drug. In the summer of 1963, in a traffic count made on the highway going by Wall, 46% were found to be eastbound and 54% were westbound. Of the eastbound traffic, 43% turned off at Wall. Of the westbound traffic, 44% turned off at Wall.

When people arrive at Wall, (those westbound usually after driving 40 miles or more through the Badlands) they are greeted by the large Wall Drug sign on the interchange and an 80 foot high, 50 ton statue of a dinosaur. The business district of Wall is one block long and is about three blocks from the interchange. The town has eleven motels and a number of gasoline filling stations.

Cars from many states line the street in front of and several blocks on either side of the drugstore. Tabulation of state licenses from autos and campers parked in front of Wall Drug, and in the camper and trailer park one block from Wall Drug on Wednesday, June 4, 8 a.m. and 10 a.m. resulted in the following:

Neighboring States and South Dakota (Non Local) 37%
South Dakota, Local County 32
Balance of States and Canada 31

The store occupies 31,217 square feet with 11,918 square feet of storage space and 960 square feet of office.

Wall Drug is more than a store. It is a place of amusement, family entertainment, a gallery of the West, a gallery of South Dakota history, and a place that reflects the heritage of the West. Nostalgia addicts have a "field day" in the Wall Drug. Children are delighted with animated life-size cowboys singing, tableau of an Indian camp, a stuffed bucking horse, six foot rabbit, a stuffed buffalo, old slot machines that pay out a souvenir coin for 10¢, statues of cowboys, a coin operated quick-draw game, and souvenirs by the roomful which make up some of the attractions.

The food is inexpensive and good, and although as many as 10,000 people might stream through on a good day, the place is air conditioned and comfortable. The dining rooms are decorated with beautiful wood paneling, paintings of Western art are displayed, and Western music plays. One can dine on buffalo burgers, roast beef or steak, 5¢ coffee or select wine, beer or a "Jack Daniels" from the rustic, but beautiful, American walnut bar.

Wall Drug does most of their business during the summer months. Sales for June, 1973 were $258,000; July, $423,000; and August, $414,500. April ran about $30,000 and May, $100,000. September and October are fair months when late tourists and hunters travel through.

About one-fourth of the sales in Wall Drug is food, plus about 5% to 10% for beverages and the soda fountain. (This varies with the weather.) About 10% to 15% is jewelry, 15% clothing and hats, 35% to 40% souvenirs, and 5% to 10% for drugs, drug sundries and prescriptions.

The store is manned by a crew of about 150 people, 45 of which are college girls and 15 to 20 are college boys who work there in the summer. Student help is housed in homes that have been bought and made into dormitory apartments for these young people. There is a modern swimming pool for their use, also. The clerks are trained to be courteous, informed and pleasant.

MERCHANDISE ORDERING

The inventory in Wall Drug varies from around $300,000 in the summer peak to a low of around $80,000 at the end of the year. Orders for the following summer season begin being placed in the preceding fall. Orders begin arriving in December, but most arrive in January, February, March and April. Many large souvenir companies post-date their invoices until July and August. Each year brings new offerings from souvenir companies and other suppliers. Much of the purchasing is done by Bill and/or Ted, who admit they rely on trusted salesmen of these houses to advise them on purchasing. Many of these companies have supplied Wall Drug for 20 years or so.

Wall Drug generally buys directly from the producers or importers in most cases. This is true of their photo supplies and clothing, also.

Years ago, much of what Wall Drug bought and sold was imported or made in the East. In recent years much of the merchandise is United States made, and much more is made locally and regionally. The Indian reservations now have small production firms and individuals who make much handicraft which is sold through Wall Drug. Examples of such firms are Sioux Pottery, Badlands Pottery, Sioux Moccasin, and Milk Camp Industries.

Bill Hustead relies a great deal on his department managers for buying help. The manager of the jewelry, for instance, will determine on the basis of last year's orders and her experience with customer reaction and demand how much to order for the next season. All ordering is centered through Bill and Ted.

PROMOTION

Over the years Wall Drug has relied greatly on many roadside signs to bring people to the store. By 1968 there were about 3,000 signs displayed along highways and roads in all 50 states. Two men and a truck service signs in South Dakota and adjoining states, however, many signs are put up by volunteers. The store gives away about 14,000 6" × 8" signs and 3,000 8" × 22" signs a year to people who request them and these people place them all over the world. These are plastic signs and will stand the weather. Many people will send a photo back showing the Wall Drug sign displayed in some unusual place. These photos are then posted in the store.

In time Wall Drug became noted enough to be considered news worthy and articles abouth Ted Hustead and Wall Drug began appearing. In the late 1950's *Redbook Magazine* carried a story which was later picked up and condensed in *Reader's Digest.* Since then the number of newspapers and magazines carrying feature stories or referring to Wall Drug has increased greatly. Examples are:

National Enquirer, November 11, 1973
Grit, October 28, 1973
Las Vegas Review - Journal, September 22, 1973
Senior Scholastic Magazine, October 4, 1973, p. 11
Congressional Record, September 11, 1973, S16269
Wall Street Journal, September 5, 1973
Omaha World-Herald, May 15, 1972

Elsevier, (Dutch magazine) February 12, 1972
Rapid City Journal, April 12, 1970
A Cleveland daily paper, May 16, 1971
The New York Times, Sunday, January 31, 1971
Oshkosh, Wisconsin, *Daily Northwestern,* August 2, 1969
Sunday Picture Magazine, Minneapolis Tribune, September 21, 1969
America Illustrated, USIA in Poland and Russia
Ojai Valley News and Oaks Gazette, August 14, 1968
Chicago Tribune, Norman Vincent Peale's syndicated column, "Confident Living," October 8, 1966
Norman Vincent Peale's book, *You Can If You Think You Can,* p. 34
San Francisco Examiner, February 12, 1966
Women's Wear Daily, September 16, 1966
Coronet Magazine, April, 1964
Cleveland, Ohio, *The Plain Dealer,* date not known

In the mid 1960's during President Lyndon Johnson's administration, Congress passed the Highway Beautification Act reducing the number of roadside signs. South Dakota businesses that depend on tourists use outdoor advertising extensively, and Wall Drug was a well known user of signs. The Husteads were concerned with the threatened loss of signs.

To compensate for the threatened loss of signs, Bill and Ted believed the news stories helped, as would their sign give-away referred to earlier.

Bill and Ted also decided that they must gain as much visibility and notoriety as possible, and to help achieve this they began using unusual advertising means. They began taking small ads in *The Village Voice,* in New York City's Greenwich Village, advertising 5ᶜ coffee and 49ᶜ breakfast at Wall Drug and animal health remedies. This brought a telephone call and some letter inquiries. It also brought an article in the *Voice* and perhaps attracted other media. The article in the *New York Times* and other notoriety led to Bill's appearance on Garry Moore's television program "To Tell the Truth."

For awhile the Wall Drug was advertised in the London Underground (subway). As a result, the BBC called and taped a twenty minute interview on the telephone with Ted Hustead. Also, many English newspapers carried stories about Wall Drug because of the signs in the London Underground trains.

Wall Drug is also advertised in the Paris Metro (subway) in the English language, and on the dock in Amsterdam where people board sight seeing canal boats.

The Husteads have been preparing for the time when all signs would have to come down along highways in the United States. In the meantime, they have invested in new signs to be seen the required 660 feet back from the highway. There is concern that these will be knocked out by new federal legislation at anytime.

Another strategy has been devised by Ted and Bill to gain the attention of motorists driving through South Dakota. This is a reciprocal favor with motels and campgrounds. Wall Drug has two brochures printed which are: (1) *Motel Guide for South Dakota,* and (2) *South Dakota Campground Directory of Privately Owned and Operated Campgrounds and Trailer Parks.* Over 200,000 of these guides are given away to Wall Drug patrons each summer. The plan is that the Husteads believe each of these motels and campgrounds will reciprocate by displaying a sign on their premises for Wall Drug, if asked. This plan is in its infancy at present.

Bill and Ted also plan to put up signs to be seen when people turn off the interstate at many of the exits east and west of Wall.

FINANCE

Until December, 1973, all expansion was financed with internally generated funds supplemented with short-term borrowing. The first long-term debt was a 10 year, $250,000 loan in the form of a real estate mortgage taken on December 3, 1973 to fund the construction of the Mall. Payments on this loan, including 8% interest, will be about $34,000 in 1974 and $37,000 annually from 1975 through 1983.

In the Winter of 1973, Bill must place orders for the tourist season of 1974. Should he buy light or buy heavy? What should he do with the Mall? Part of it remains unfinished.

Supplies have been purchased, but to finish, means using more of the borrowed money and stocking these new stores.

Decisions to purchase inventory must be made several months before each tourist season. Seasonal billings on purchases provide much of the financing needed for the temporary inventory expansion. Obviously a cash problem could occur if a large inventory was left unsold at the end of any tourist season. This potential problem is aggravated by the fixed payments due on the long-term loan.

In view of the new sign legislation, the high price and possible future shortage of gasoline and the effects this may have on auto tourist traffic should the Husteads be considering other long-run alternatives for investment? Should Wall Drug expansion continue, or should funds be diverted elsewhere?

EXHIBIT 1
WALL DRUG STORE, INC.
BALANCE SHEETS

ASSETS

	December 31, 1973	1972
Current Assets		
Cash on hand	$ 1,037	$ 946
Cash in bank	2,450	138
Investment in commercial paper, at cost	70,000	-
Accounts receivable-trade	12,121	7,183
Accounts receivable-officers and employees	4,300	3,323
Accounts receivable-income tax refund		
Inventories	144,013	86,890
Accrued interest receivable	463	-
Prepaid insurance	9,455	9,068
Total current assets	243,839	127,372
Investment and Other Assets		
Bonds, at cost	1,675	1,675
Organization cost, at cost	972	972
Total investments and other assets	2,647	2,647
Property, Plant and Equipment, at cost		
Land	70,454	50,079
Buildings, building improvements and parking lot improvements	692,488	527,456
Equipment, furniture and fixtures	366,651	303,108
	1,129,593	880,643
Less accumulated depreciation	427,866	369,743
Depreciated cost of fixed assets	701,727	510,900
Goodwill, at cost	31,386	31,386
	$ 979,599	$672,305

The accompanying notes are an integral part of these financial statements.

LIABILITIES AND STOCKHOLDERS' EQUITY

Current Liabilities		
Notes payable-Wall Auto Livery, Inc.	$ 20,000	$ 50,000
Notes payable-bank	-	20,000
Current maturities of long-term debt	20,058	-
Accounts payable-trade	22,709	30,979
Income taxes payable	11,161	-
Accrued taxes payable	25,880	18,457
Profit-sharing contribution payable	30,542	18,231
Accrued payroll and bonuses	40,073	28,559
Accrued interest payable	2,573	- 255
Total current liabilities	172,996	166,481
Long-Term Debt		
Real estate mortgage payable	232,742	-
Contract for deed payable	11,200	-
Total long-term debt	243,942	-
Stockholders' Equity		
Preferred stock, $100 par value, 4%, cumulative, non-voting, 1,000 shares authorized, 300 shares outstanding	30,000	30,000
Common stock, $100 par value, Class A, 500 shares authorized, 480 shares outstanding	48,000	48,000
Common stock, $100 par value, Class B, non-voting, 4,500 shares authorized, 400 shares outstanding	40,000	40,000
Retained earnings	444,661	387,824
Total stockholders' equity	562,661	505,824
	$979,599	$672,305

EXHIBIT 2
WALL DRUG STORE, INC.
STATEMENTS OF INCOME AND RETAINED EARNINGS

	Years ended December 31, 1973	1972
Net sales	$1,606,648	$1,335,932
Cost of goods sold	805,827	687,613
Gross profit	800,821	648,319
General and administrative expenses	690,461	577,767
	110,360	70,552
Interest income	2,946	188
Rental income	3,647	4,248
Trailer park income	6,020	4,600
Theatre income	-	5,197
Gain on sale of assets	176	4,286
Other income	747	902
	123,896	89,973
Other deductions		
Interest	19,735	4,072
Theatre expense	-	2,689
Trailer park expense	4,223	3,433
Loss on sale of assets	-	1,674
Loss on demolition of theatre building	-	13,860
	23,958	25,728
Income before income taxes	99,938	64,245
Provision for income tax-current year	40,701	20,176
Net income	59,237	44,069
Retained earnings		
Beginning	387,824	343,755
Dividends paid	2,400	-
Ending	$ 444,661	387,824
Earnings per share	$ 65.95	$ 48.71

The accompanying notes are an integral part of
these financial statements.

EXHIBIT 3
WALL DRUG STORE, INC.
STATEMENTS OF CHANGES IN FINANCIAL POSITION

	Years ended December 31,	
	1973	1972
Financial resources were provided by		
Net income	$ 59,237	$ 44,069
Add income charges not affecting working capital in the period-		
Depreciation	58,723	43,862
Demolition loss on theatre building	-	13,860
	117,960	101,791
Proceeds from borrowings	264,000	-
Basis of property and equipment sold	625	2,750
Total resources provided	382,585	104,541
Financial resources were used for		
Acquisition of land	21,000	5,799
Acquisiton of building	165,031	149,924
Acquisition of equipment and signs	64,144	50,636
Reduction in long term debt	20,058	-
Dividends paid	2,400	-
Total resources used	272,633	206,359
Increase (decrease) in working capital	109,952	(101,818)
Working capital		
Beginning	(39,109)	62,709
Ending	$ 70,843	$ (39,109)
Increase (decrease) in components of working capital		
Current assets		
Cash	$ 2,403	$ (1,850)
Investment in commercial paper	70,000	-
Marketable securities	-	(59,375)
Accounts receivable-trade and other	(13,909)	684
Inventories	57,123	7,204
Other current assets-net	850	(3,650)
	116,467	(56,987)
Current liabilities		
Note payable-Banks and others	(50,000)	70,000
Current maturities of long-term debt	20,058	-
Accounts payable-trade	(8,270)	12,891
Income tax payable	11,161	(32,272)
Other current and accrued liabilities-net	33,566	(5,788)
	6,515	44,831
Increase (decrease) in working capital	$109,952	(101,818)

The accompanying notes are an integral part of
these financial statements.

EXHIBIT 4
WALL DRUG STORE, INC.
NOTES TO FINANCIAL STATEMENTS

NOTE 1-SUMMARY OF ACCOUNTING POLICIES

Accounting Method-The corporation uses the accrual method of accounting for income tax and financial statement purposes.

Inventories-Inventories are generally valued at the lower of cost or market on a first-in, first-out basis computed under retail method.

Fixed Assets-Fixed assets are stated at cost. Depreciation is calculated under the straight-line method, 150% declining balance method and 200% declining balance method. The same depreciation methods are used for financial and tax purposes. The useful lives selected for the assets are as follows: Buildings and building improvements, 15 to 40 years; parking lot, 8 years; and furniture, fixtures and equipment, 5 to 10 years. The provision for depreciation for 1973 of $58,723 and 1972 of $43,862 was charged to operations.

Repairs and maintenance costs are generally charged to expense at the time the expenditure is incurred. When an asset is sold or retired, its cost and related depreciation are removed from the accounts and a gain or loss is recognized on the difference between the proceeds of disposition and the undepreciated costs as the case may be. When an asset is traded in a like exchange, the cost and related depreciation are removed from the accounts and the undepreciated cost is capitalized as a part of the cost of the asset acquired.

Income Taxes-The provision for income taxes is based on the elements of income and expense, as reported in the statement of income. Investment tax credits are accounted for on the "flow-through" method, which recognizes the benefits in the year in which the assets which give rise to the credit are placed in service.

NOTE 2-LONG-TERM DEBT

The real estate mortgage is an 8% mortgage dated December 3, 1973 and due October 1, 1983. The mortgage is to be paid in annual installments of principal and interest as follows:

10-1-74	$34,035.28
10-1-75 and thereafter	$37,257.50

The Drug Store in downtown Wall is pledged as security on this real estate mortgage.

The contract for deed payable is a 7% contract for deed, dated January 16, 1973 and is due January 16, 1978. The contract is to be paid in annual installments of $2,800 plus interest. This contract is for the purchase of approximately 202 acres of land which is the security for the contract for deed.

NOTE 3-PROFIT-SHARING PLAN

The company has a profit-sharing plan for all full time employees who meet the qualification requirements. The company contributed $30,542 in 1973 and $18,231 in 1972 to the profit-sharing trust.

EXHIBIT 5
WALL AUTO LIVERY, INC.
BALANCE SHEETS

ASSETS

	December 31, 1973	1972
Current Assets		
Cash on hand	$ 100	$ 100
Cash in bank	14,590	19,916
Marketable securities, at cost	58,715	-
Notes receivable-Wall Drug Store, Inc.	20,000	50,000
Accounts receivable-trade	1,967	8,205
Credit cards	2,010	-
Miscellaneous receivables	-	75
Inventory, at lower of cost (FIFO) or market	8,462	9,261
Prepaid insurance	1,557	1,469
Accrued interest receivable	729	247
Total current assets	108,130	89,274
Property and Equipment		
Land	7,367	7,367
Buildings	103,133	103,133
Equipment	26,297	26,076
	136,797	136,576
Less-accumulated depreciation	57,685	52,549
Depreciation cost of fixed assets	79,112	84,027
	$187,242	$173,301

LIABILITIES AND STOCKHOLDERS' EQUITY

	1973	1972
Current liabilities		
Current maturity of long-term debt	$ 5,000	$ 5,000
Accounts payable-trade	754	5,696
Income taxes payable	7,286	2,774
Accrued profit-sharing contribution	2,666	2,446
Accrued payroll and sales taxes	840	756
Accrued interest payable	125	250
Total current liabilities	16,671	16,922
Long-Term Debt		
Note payable non-interest bearing contract payable to F.M. Cheny maturing March 1, 1979	5,000	5,000
Note payable-6% to Perpetual National Life Insurance Company maturing in annual installments of $5,000 plus interest	-	5,000
Total long-term debt	5,000	5,000
Stockholders' Equity		
Common stock, $100 par value, 2,000 shares authorized, 444 shares outstanding	44,400	44,400
Retained earnings	121,171	101,979
Total stockholders' equity	165,571	146,379
	$187,242	$173,301

The accompanying notes are an integral part
of these financial statements.

EXHIBIT 6
WALL AUTO LIVERY, INC.
STATEMENTS OF INCOME AND RETAINED EARNINGS

	Years ended December 31, 1973	1972
Net sales	$191,969	$172,195
Inventories-beginning of year	9,261	9,467
Purchases	132,698	124,399
Freight	35	-
	141,994	13,866
Inventories-end of year	8,462	9,261
Cost of goods sold	133,532	124,605
Gross profit	58,437	47,590
General and administrative expense	44,568	41,443
Income from operations	13,851	6,147
Interest income	5,441	2,436
Rental income	17,917	15,440
Miscellaneous income	-	1,434
	37,209	25,457
Income before federal income tax	33,694	21,554
Provision for income taxes	14,502	7,574
Net income	19,192	13,980
Retained earnings		
Begining	101,979	87,999
Ending	$121,171	$101,979
Earnings per share	$ 43.23	$ 31.49

The accompanying notes are an integral part
of these financial statements.

EXHIBIT 7
WALL AUTO LIVERY, INC.
STATEMENTS OF CHANGES IN FINANCIAL POSITION

	Years ended December 31, 1973	1972
Financial resources were provided by		
Net income	$ 19,192	$ 13,980
Add income charges not affecting working capital in the period-		
Depreciation	5,137	5,390
Working capital provided by operations	24,329	19,370
Financial resources were used for		
Acquisition of equipment	221	3,310
Reduction of long-term debt	5,000	5,000
Total resources used	5,221	8,310
Increase in working capital	19,108	11,060
Working capital		
Beginning of year	72,352	61,292
End of year	$91,460	$ 72,352
Increase (decrease) in components of working capital		
Current assets		
Cash	$ (5,326)	$ 15,394
Marketable securities	58,715	(58,087)
Notes receivable	(30,000)	50,000
Accounts receivable	(6,238)	3,371
Credit cards	2,010	-
Miscellaneous receivables	(75)	(57)
Inventory	(799)	(206)
Prepaid insurance	88	73
Accrued interest receivable	482	40
	18,857	10,528
Current liabilities		
Accounts payable-trade	(4,942)	1,064
Income taxes payable	4,512	(1,925)
Other current and accrued liabilities	179	329
	(251)	(532)
Increase in working capital	$19,108	$11,060

The accompanying notes are an integral part of
these financial statements.

EVALUATION OF THE
WALL DRUG CASE

SUMMARY

This case involves essentially future strategy and planning. It deals with a drug store in a town of 300 in Western South Dakota that was started in the 1930's. Over the years, it grew to become one of the most famous retail enterprises in the United States because of the owner's unique promotion, showmanship, merchandising, and financial management. As a result of recent events that may threaten tourist-oriented businesses and road sign legislation, the owner-managers are now faced with a re-consideration of their future strategy and plans.

KEY ISSUES

1. Should Wall Drug continue its expansion at its present site, or should funds be diverted elsewhere for diversification?
2. Should Wall Drug invest heavily in stock (inventory), anticipating an increase in tourism, or should Wall Drug buy conservatively?
3. What will be the effects of the elimination of roadside signs, and will the other promotional methods compensate?
4. What effect will the oil crisis have on tourism in general, and in South Dakota in particular?
5. What should be done with the Mall?

DISCUSSION

Basically, Wall Drug needs to analyze its strategic planning. In other words, the Husteads need to delineate their business objectives and methods of accomplishment; they should then study those factors and determine if they are valid in light of the environment in which Wall Drug operates. In the discussion of key issues given below, the scopes of the problems facing Wall Drug are presented in an attempt at providing a clarity of understanding, leading to effective strategic planning through the presentation of relevant alternative solutions to those problems.

Wall Drug has been very successful in the past in its expansion at the present site. Tourism has increased every year, justifying all of the expansion with increasing sales. However, Wall Drug is dependent on the base, namely, tourism, and if something happened to upset that base, the Husteads could be in for troubled times. The emergence of the oil crisis and the troubles with the Indians have, indeed, threatened to upset that base. The effects of these factors are unpredictable, making the future very uncertain. Therefore, to continue to expand the present site may be an unwise decision, at least until the manifestations of the oil and Indian problems are determined. If the Husteads diversified in the future, their dependence on one base could be alleviated, lessening the business implications of a tourist slowdown.

Historically, each year has seen an increase in tourism, but, as pointed out above, the coming year could be different. If the Husteads buy heavily as usual, they could be left with a large unsold inventory at the end of the year. This could create a cash problem, which would be aggravated by the fixed payments due on the long-term loan taken out for the Mall. Still, if they choose to buy light, they could lose a lot of sales.

The elimination of the roadside signs will undoubtedly hurt Wall Drug, although to what degree is uncertain. It could be that the signs may never be eliminated; they may just be regulated as to size, numbers, and distance from roads. Even so, with such regulation some of the Wall Drug signs will probably have to come down given the great numbers of them. The other promotional strategies developed by the Husteads are good, and will probably effectively compensate for any lost signs if fully utilized.

It is difficult to say what exactly the effects of the gasoline shortages will be on tourism. Nevertheless, the mere uncertainty that is present in this regard would mitigate against going too far out on a limb as far as expansion, buying, and the Mall are concerned.

In considering what to do about the Mall, it must be pointed out that the supplies have already been purchased for its completion, so it could easily be finished before the new tourist season. This would incur the further costs of construction labor, and, of course, the Mall would have to be stocked, entailing the use of more of the borrowed funds. If the tourist season is slow, then these costs would be unjustified if sales cannot cover them. On the other hand, if the season is good, the Husteads will have lost a prime opportunity by not finishing the Mall.

All of these considerations are focused on the factor of tourism. In the short-run (next year's season), the tourist traffic is too unpredictable to go ahead with any major plans. In the long-run, the dependence on the sole base of tourism seems to indicate some strategic reorientation toward diversification, or at least a slowdown in the expansion of Wall Drug until specific and fairly accurate projections can be made concerning the future success of the company.

ALTERNATIVE CONSIDERATIONS

The following include several alternatives which should be considered by Wall Drug in addressing present and future problems. Additional factors will undoubtedly also influence long-range strategy and planning as more information becomes available and its relevancy can be determined.

1. Finish Mall.

   Advantages: Supplies already purchased; funds available from long-term loan; be ready for next tourist season; no loss of sales.
   Disadvantages: Upcoming tourist season may be slow; and there might not be enough business to cover the costs of finishing the Mall.

2. Leave Mall unfinished.

   Advantages: Save on funds; can always finish later; cost-benefit prudence.
   Disadvantages: Might lose sales; tourist season may be great; supplies for finishing already purchased; idle facilities.

3. Invest heavily in inventory for upcoming season.

   Advantages: Be ready for normal tourist traffic, should it occur; no lost sales.
   Disadvantages: Uses up a lot of money for inventory; season could be slow, putting Wall Drug in a cash bind.

4. Buy conservatively.

   Advantages: Wall Drug will not be out on a limb; avoid using funds until upcoming season is certain.

Disadvantages: Could lose sales if tourism does not fall off; could alienate customers.

5. Alternative long-term investments.

Advantages: Diversify to avoid strict dependence on tourist base; would add more stability; possible greater profit potential.

Disadvantages: Could involve further use of borrowed funds; may get into areas not fully-understood by Wall Drug.

6. Continue expansion of present site.

Advantages: Has been successful in past; Husteads understand the business.

Disadvantages: Future tourist situation is uncertain; dependence on one base; may result in over-expansion of present site, or return on investment may not justify the expansion.

7. Conduct a tourist study; contact state and federal agencies, oil companies, tourist agencies to determine their forecasts.

Advantages: Could allow for more accurate planning; costs are minimal.

Disadvantages: Might not provide any useful information.

8. Continue present promotional efforts; emphasis on roadside signs.

Advantages: Signs may never be outlawed; proven worth; signs can be of great benefit until outlawed.

Disadvantages: Signs will probably be restricted, if not outlawed, so investing in them may be wasteful to a degree.

9. Direct more emphasis toward alternative promotional strategies.

Advantages: Preparation for the future; get other methods implemented and well-established before signs are regulated or outlawed; more well-rounded marketing.

Disadvantages: Signs will probably be restricted, if not outlawed, so investing in them may be wasteful.

10. Franchise or lease Mall shops to local handicraft producers for upcoming season or longer; complete Mall to implement this.

Advantages: Help cover costs of finishing Mall; will not have to invest in inventory for new Mall shops; no idle facilities; minimize risk.

Disadvantages: Could be making those sales for Wall Drug; helping competition.

Any decisions by Wall Drug must incorporate short-term and long-term strategy considerations. A possible plan could take a form similar to the one suggested below.

1. Perform the tourist study proposed in the alternative solutions section. The costs are minimal, and any information gained will probably be of some use in planning.

2. Since the supplies for completion are already on hand, the Mall should be finished, but franchised or leased to local firms to avoid

the inventory costs. In this manner the current plans for expansion can be accomplished and the risk minimized.

3. Wall Drug should buy conservatively for the upcoming summer season. They certainly do not want to lose sales, but they cannot know for sure what will happen, so it is best to play it safe and not risk a potential cash shortage. If tourist traffic does not fall off, they can use this experience in subsequent seasons. If tourism does, indeed, fall off, they will be ready for that possibility. In addition, in their dealings with the firms that supply Wall Drug, the Husteads could investigate the possibility of obtaining goods on consignment. Since Wall Drug will be buying light, these firms might be quite receptive to such a plan of action.

4. The owners should begin looking into other investment alternatives beyond the expansion of Wall Drug. Possibly, the areas of real estate and business in bigger cities nearby could offer some opportunities. Another possibility that would complement the Wall Drug operation is the production and/or wholesaling of souvenir items, either within South Dakota or outside of the state. They could also develop the Wall Auto Livery into a truck stop operation in addition to its gas station and rental functions. Such alternatives would relieve the dependence on the single "cash-crop" of tourism and possibly provide greater profit potential. The main advantage to be gained is risk minimization.

5. Wall Drug should put more effort (time and money) into promotional methods that could compensate for a loss of some or all of the signs. Certainly, the signs are successful, and there is no reason for the Husteads to not continue to use them, but they are limiting themselves to a dependence on a single base, just as they rely on tourism. The promotion of news stories and magazine articles is a good strategy and can be expanded. The reciprocal favor plan should be implemented on a wide basis throughout South Dakota and beyond; the costs of this plan are not substantial, but the benefits to be derived are.

This plan advocates a cautioned approach. The company is in good shape financially at the present time, and could get into trouble given the reliance on tourism and the uncertain future of that base. Both the threatened loss of the signs and the oil crisis have caused that uncertainty. The signs can be compensated for, but the oil situation is not so easily dealt with. There is very little that Wall Drug and its owners can do in the short-run to deal with the possible tourist problem except to be conservative in their purchasing so as to minimize the risk. In the long-run, however, diversification would provide a more well-rounded base to the company's business operations and opportunities.

7

Strategic Analysis

STRATEGIC SEARCH

As discussed in Chapter 2, if a gap does exist, we are looking for an area of growth either internally or externally. Ansoff[1] has proposed a method of explaining the growth dimension by means of the product-market scope concept.

Product-Market Scope

The *product-market scope* specifies the particular areas or industries for which a firm has defined its product-market position. By determining what these areas are by means of past performance data and economic forecasts in the industries, common threads can be determined or potential areas of growth can be identified. Ansoff further indicates the *direction* towards which the firm is moving with respect to its product-market posture by means of a growth vector. An analysis of this nature establishes the *rate* at which entry into specific areas has taken place and indicates whether growth has been accelerating or decelerating. Four measures of growth are identified (Figure 1):

1. *Market Pentration:* indicates the rate of growth in the *current* product market posture. A measure of this is market share.
2. *Market Development:* is the rate of entry into *new markets.*
3. *Product Development:* indicates new products produced to replace old ones.
4. *Diversification:* indicates growth into *new products* and *new markets.*

By identifying the areas in which a firm has developed, and the rate and direction of growth into these areas, the firm's competitive advantage can be determined. To get a more thorough understanding of the underlying factors which are responsible for this advantage, Ansoff further suggests the use of competence profiles and synergy to distinguish a firm's "distinctive competence" from that of its competitors.

Competence Profile

A competence profile* is an assessment device whereby a firm's strengths and weaknesses can be identified. The method employed to determine a firm's capabilities is the grid technique which matches a particular pat-

*See also Chapter 5

FIGURE 1

PRODUCTS / MARKETS		PRESENT	NEW
PRESENT		MARKET PENETRATION	PRODUCT DEVELOPMENT
NEW		MARKET DEVELOPMENT	DIVERSIFICATION

tern of skills to specific functional areas. The skills are the columns in the matrix (facilities and equipment, personnel, raw materials, organization capabilities) and the functional areas are the rows in the matrix (research and development, marketing, general management, operations). Each cell entry can have a vector of components which describe the match between one component in the row and another in the column.

An example is shown in Figure 2 for the cell entry consisting of the row "research and development" and the column "facilities and equipment." This cell includes such items as special lab equipment, general lab equipment and test facilities.

A study of this type allows the firm to determine broad capabilities such as marketing expertise but it also gives the *underlying specific reasons* for the success. This information can be extracted from the detailed cell entries. It is important to note here that the input data required for an analysis of this nature is provided by the micro-analysis discussed under "gap analysis" in Chapter 2.

INTERNAL ALTERNATIVE ANALYSIS

As mentioned previously under "gap analysis," the gap may be filled solely by internal expansion or a combination of both external and internal expansion. To determine the extent to which a firm can fill the gap internally, the method of synergy is employed.

1. Synergy

Synergy is a measure of joint effects. Joint effects are measured between two product-markets. To be more specific, if a firm is considering internal expansion, some method has to be adopted to determine how it can utilize its present resources in order to shift from the *current forecast* line in *gap analysis* to the *revised forecast* line. Synergy is a useful device whereby a firm can compare its competence profile with other firms in the *same* industry to determine if its performance is comparable to the industry as a whole. By examining other firm's profiles, discrepancies can be identified and a firm can obtain direction as to *how* it might be able to better employ its resources and thus reach the revised forecast line.

FIGURE 2

ONE CELL

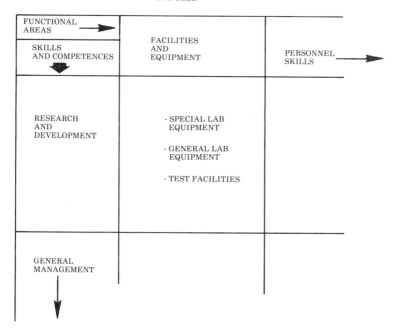

There are varying degrees of synergy. High positive synergy between two firms indicates that their characteristics are very similar, whereas negative synergy suggests that firms or industries are dissimilar in some respects. There are also different types of synergy:

1. sales synergy,
2. operating,
3. investment,
4. management synergy. (Similar skills and management backgrounds may be transferred to new areas.)

The point is, that synergy allows management to identify strengths and weaknesses in order to exploit existing capabilities and at the same time it helps to identify new entries (products, markets or both) which may be investigated.

The competence profile tells the firm its current properties of the individual product-markets and which ones will give the firm a strong competitive advantage, while the synergy is a measure of the firm's ability to enter new product-markets.

An analysis of this nature may unfold some of the following internal weaknesses[2]:

1. Organization structure may not facilitate communication, coordination, delegation of authority, etc;
2. the absence of an effective accounting system;
3. a marketing program which does not explore future markets;
4. absence of an efficient research and development team; and
5. inefficiency in present operations.

It may also identify *current strengths* such as:

1. key management personnel;
2. efficient use of equipment and facilities; and
3. strong organizational structure.

Alternative solutions to this type of an internal investigation may range from[3]

1. improvements in the organizational structure;
2. better utilization of key management personnel;
3. increased market penetration;
4. the development of new products; and
5. the development of new markets.

The last three categories indicate expansionary policies. Any one of these alternatives or a combination thereof may be available to the firm. If internal expansion is required, it may result in increasing, reducing or maintaining the existing business. It depends upon the particular organization. If objectives cannot be met by expansion alone, such factors as product obsolescence, drop in demand, competitive pressures, the product life nearly expired, and a declining rate of return on investment, can be justification for looking beyond the confines of the present firm.

EXTERNAL ALTERNATIVE ANALYSIS

Again referring to "gap analysis," often the gap cannot be filled entirely by internal policies. It may require either internal or external expansion, or both. If external expansion is required, an examination of growth into new products and new markets is necessary. From Figure 1, the diversification alternatives fit this criterion.

The procedure required for an external search is similar to the internal search. The competence profile shows the existing firm's strengths and weaknesses. This profile is compared to the industry profiles *outside* the *product-market* that the firm is presently involved in. Whether a particular industry should be further considered depends on the following: Does the opportunity

1. meet objectives?
2. fit in with the firm's existing strategies?
3. can it be assessed accurately enough to determine the effects on the present firm?
4. does it affect the present product-market position?
5. affect the projects currently underway?
6. affect the potential future products which may be developed?

The use of synergy is helpful in an analysis of this type. There are other factors which determine whether an industry will be considered for further screening, such as, the nature of the firm itself.

1. Nature of the Firm

There are several components of the firm itself reflected in its internal environment which indicate the characteristics of the firm. For example, *where* the firm is in its life cycle indicates the type of diversification which might be considered. A well-established firm may consider diversification even if synergy is low provided retained cash earnings are high. However, a younger firm may not be in a position to take a high risk proposition and may tend to select an industry with higher synergy and lower risk. Other factors such as the size, managerial characteristics and organizational structure can influence alternative choices.

The firm cannot neglect the external environment either. Such considerations as government policies, growth of economic activity, anti-trust acts, legislation and social responsiveness must all affect the strategic search. In addition to these considerations, the cost of entry, start-up costs, timing and the availability to éntry (competition) must also be considered.

Given the characteristics of the firm, its external and internal environment, its past and present performance and most important its objectives, there are different types of diversification it may consider.

TYPES OF DIVERSIFICATION

Vertical diversification takes place when a firm decides to branch out into production of components, parts and materials for the present product line. This may extend from supplying the firm with raw material to the distribution of the final product. This requires a new customer, namely the firm itself, and the use of potentially unrelated technology.

Horizontal diversification can be described as the introduction of new products which cater to customers of a similar type for which the firm has know-how and experience in technology, finance and marketing. The new product does not add to the present product line. The technology required by the new product may be related or unrelated to the existing technology.

Lateral diversification requires the firm to move beyond the confines of the industry to which it belongs. This type of diversification can be segmented into two classes:

1. *Concentric diversification* exists when either the technology or the marketing or both are related.
2. *Conglomerate diversification:* this is the extreme case where neither present technology or marketing are related.[5]

Both horizontal and vertical diversification have a high degree of synergy, while concentric and conglomerate differ in the degree of synergy. Concentric diversification has positive synergy related to either technology or marketing. Conglomerate diversification tends to have a very low degree of synergy.

Diversification can take place in several ways: By merger or acquisition; joint venture; or internally, by the firm itself. In the case of merger or acquisition, the resources of the firm that will be incorporated are acquired. Generally, this expanded resource base will permit the firm to expand the scope of its activities. A further consideration with respect to merger or acquisition is the source of funds. If additional equity must be obtained to purchase the firm, it is done at the expense of expanding the control base of the organization. Merger or diversification may be used to improve the risk position of the organization. If the parent company operates within a high risk environment, merger could be sought to lower the overall company risk. Similarly, the low risk parent organization may be in a position to improve its overall rate of return by acquiring a higher risk company.[6]

The joint venture involves the co-operation of two or more firms on a specific project, usually for a limited time period. No one company may be in a position to undertake the project by itself because of a lack of resources or the high risk nature of the project. The joint venture permits the participants to undertake the project and upon completion, the companies disassociate.

In the case where the firm diversifies from within itself, there is no dilution of control. This type of company would tend to be highly liquid and possess high retained cash earnings.

All types and methods of diversifying must be considered by a firm in the strategic search for external expansion. Andrews[7] stresses one important aspect of the strategic search which is often overlooked. Before a decision is made, the effects of organization structure on synergy must be examined. Synergy and structure are not mutually exclusive, but are dependent. Ratings in regards to cost of entry, synergy criteria and competition are not sufficient to give an overall evaluation of an alternative. When strong synergy exists at all levels, a tightly integrated organization structure would be used. The acquisition would be absorbed into the respective functional departments of the firm and responsibility would be centralized (functional departmentation). When synergy is strong in general management, but not in functional areas, a decentralized organization is indicated. The acquisition would be set up as a division and assigned profit and loss responsibility. If synergy is weak throughout the organization, a holding company structure is more appropriate.

It is apparent that the strategic search for alternatives, both internally and externally, is a very complex process. One last remaining alternative is liquidation. This decision may be considered if the strategic search, both internally and externally, offers no acceptable alternative solutions.

At this point, the firm may have several groups of alternatives (portfolios), each of which could be undertaken by the firm within its present resources to fill in the gap. The next step is to evaluate these portfolios and select the appropriate alternative. Any given portfolio may consist of a combination of both internal and external expansion policies.

SELECTION OF ALTERNATIVES

The purpose of this section is to evaluate the portfolio or set of portfolios obtained from the strategic search and select that which best fills in the total gap or meets the organization's objectives.[8] Each portfolio in a set may be comprised of either internal or external alternatives or some combination of both. It may consist of possible plans of actions, some of which may never be activated. This often is the case, however, the point is that the alternative courses *exist* in the event that they need to be called upon. They are backup or reserve courses of action.

In order to evaluate the set of portfolios, it is necessary to compare each portfolio's projected performance with the target line obtained from the stated objectives. This approach was used in the strategic search but at a broad general level. Since the objectives have been translated into quantitative targets, we need to go back one step further and examine the external and internal environmental factors responsible for the determination of the desired targets. Only by conducting an in depth analysis at this level will a comprehensive assessment of each portfolio be possible.

It should be recalled that the main objective of a firm is to make a profit and profit expressed as return on investment can be represented by the following objective function:

ROI (Profit) = f (Sales, Market share, Risk, Competition, Social cost,......)

Where each of the independent variables become objectives in themselves and the aggregation contributes to the overall objective. To evaluate the set of portfolios each alternative is compared on the basis of each entry in the profit function. A rating is established for each component and a total evaluation for the portfolio is obtained. This quantitative value is indicative of the rate of return that could be expected if this portfolio is selected.

This sounds like a very simple process but indeed it is not. For example, a quantitative value for projected sales volume may not be easily obtained. It may be necessary to examine the environmental factors which would affect sales volume before a value for expected sales could be arrived at. Therefore to conduct an assessment requiring this much detail, techniques such as Bayesian decision theory, weighting measures, and statistical probability may be used in conjunction with forecasting methods.

It is not our purpose here to conduct a search at this level. Instead, some questions will be raised as a guideline for an investigation of their nature. Some questions are directly related to the diversification alternative, while others could be used for both internal and external analysis.

EVALUATION VARIABLES

Economic: Will the joint organization place the firm in a favorable competitive position? Will the joint entry permit the company to enter new areas, "joint opportunities", which allow for growth outside the union? Does the alternative fully exploit both domestic and international opportunities? These questions are mainly concerned with competitive forces in that the alternative selected must have a "distinctive competence" which gives the organization a definite competitive advantage.

Social: Are there possible social costs associated with the alternative which may interfere with future success? This question addresses itself to the social responsibilities of the firm. If a plan proves to be socially irresponsible, serious repercussions could be brought to bear on a company.

Legal: What are the legal restrictions relating to the activity under consideration? Legislation such as antitrust laws must be considered.

Technological: Is the technology expertise adequate in both present and future situations? Technological change can produce equipment obsolescence but it can also result in improved technology which facilitates product growth.

Ecological: Are adequate natural resources available at a reasonable cost? If not, product-market expansion may not be possible.

All of the above external environmental factors must be considered when evaluating a portfolio. Another important question which may be raised here is: Does the firm have the knowledge and expertise to access the external environment required as a result of the joint (new) organization? This question concerns itself with the internal control mechanisms necessary for a firm to monitor and adjust its operations to changed environmental conditions.

The next set of questions are more related to the internal environment.

Can the plan be expressed in both qualitative and quantitative terms in order to measure its long term and short term performance in conjunction with existing plans? If the alternative cannot be expressed at least qualitatively, the firm is unable to evaluate whether it is a viable alternative. Therefore one criterion for portfolio selection is that alternatives must be measurable.

If the answer to the above is affirmative, then the firm must know: How compatible are the short run operating policies with the long run plan? Are they consistent or are there possible areas of conflict? Another way of stating this: Do the short run policies add up to the overall long run plan? There are a whole host of factors to consider when answering these questions. Such as

1. *the size* of facilities, start up costs, and availability;
2. *operational ability* which is concerned with technology and marketing skills;
3. *potential contribution* of the acquired firm to the parent company; and
4. *availability* of future business, are all considered in synergy analysis.

It is important to note that all of these factors influence the product-market plan and that they are not mutually exclusive but rather dependent. Figure 3 shows the interaction amongst all of the individual major plans. Each major plan consists of several components with both short and long range plans. For example, the operating plan includes sub-plans for manufacturing, purchasing, distribution, and marketing, all of which could be illustrated as a separate network. The final selection must be assessed in terms of compatibility and consistency in both the short and long run. Potential conflicts can be identified by a close examination of the interactions between all the functions.

FIGURE 3

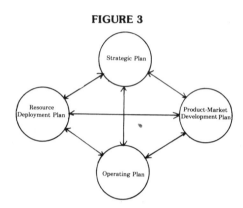

Network of interaction between all functions at all levels

By conducting this type of analysis, the firm can evaluate how flexible the alternative is. This question concerns the responsiveness of the plan to both the internal and external environment. It should answer the following: Does the firm have procedures to cope with unexpected events if the portfolio is accepted? This analysis should also determine whether the plan threatens the firm's existing strengths in the long run.

There are other important factors to consider in evaluating an alternative with respect to the internal environment. Such as : Does the strategy complement the personal values and aspirations of key management? Does it provide for their personal growth? These are important factors to consider because maintaining top management loyalty can often be a competitive advantage in itself since consistency and stability are vital for optimal performance.

Another factor to be considered when evaluating a portfolio is the risk component of the objective function. For example, is the risk level of the alternative in keeping with present and future management capabilities? To answer this requires an investigation into management's attitudes towards risk. Ansoff describes three classes of management,[9] the *reactor* who pays no attention to risk, the *planner* who is a risk avoider and plans in a defensive manner in order to remedy weaknesses, and the *entrepreneur* who is a risk taker, operating in an aggressive manner to take advantage of opportunities. The portfolio risk to be tolerated depends to a large extent on the type of management a firm has. For example, if vertical or horizontal integration (differentiation) is decided upon rather than concentric or conglomerate, it *may* indicate a defensive strategy as in the case of the risk avoider. Other viable alternatives may be rejected because of this factor alone. Often vertical and horizontal integration offer limited potential for achieving objectives. Only if the present economic status is healthy, will these alternatives offer opportunities for future growth.

Another manifestation of management's attitude toward risk is the organization design. The planner may make changes in structure only where necessary, whereas the entrepreneur sees structure change as the most effective means at his disposal to implement new ideas and plans.[10]

It can be seen that there are a multiplicity of factors to consider when selecting a portfolio. These include external environmental factors, the internal organization environment and management's attitude toward risk. The final selection of the portfolio of alternatives will include those alternatives which *best match the objectives* of the organization as discussed in a previous section. The alternatives selected will hopefully permit the firm to attain its targets and thus fill in the gap. Included in the portfolio will be methods of internal expansion or external expansion or a combination of both. The presence of a particular alternative within the portfolio does not mean that it will necessarily be implemented. Recalling that certain strategic aspects are activated only under specified conditions of environmental change, it may be that a particular strategy is never activated. However, should the requisite conditions develop, the alternative is available.

SUMMARY

Strategic search may be seen as taking place in three steps. The size of the gap serves to determine the magnitude of the task facing the firm. If the gap is small, then the task is relatively small and the search need not consider a wide range of alternatives. On the other hand, if the gap is large, many alternatives will have to be examined. From this point of view, the gap analysis is the first step of the strategic search. The second step of the strategic search involves consideration of internal alternatives. If a range of internal alternatives can be defined to close the gap, then the search can be terminated. However, if the search must be continued, the third step is taken, involving an examination of external alternatives. The task will have been made smaller through the contribution of the internal analysis of the previous step and only those alternatives which would fill this smaller gap need be examined.

Once a list of alternatives, both internal and external, has been determined, the process continues with a choice of alternative. This portfolio of alternatives is chosen on the basis of compatibility with the firm's environment. Several alternatives are selected to allow for the uncertainty which exists in the organizational environment. This, then, permits the firm to adjust to changes which can be expected to occur during the time horizons which have been defined for the strategic planning process.

ENDNOTES

1. H. I. Ansoff, *Corporate Strategy* (New York: McGraw-Hill, 1965), pp. 108-110.
2. K. Andrews, *The Concept of Corporate Strategy* (Chicago: Dow-Jones-Irwin, 1971), pp. 75-103.
3. John Argenti, *Corporate Planning* (London: Allen & Unwin, 1968), pp. 137-140.
4. Ansoff, *op. cit.,* pp. 213-4.
5. R.A. Howell, "Plan to Integrate Your Acquisitions." Harvard Business Review, XLVIII (November-December, 1970).
6. D.W. Ewing, (ed.), *Long Range Planning for Management* (New York: Harper and Row 1975), pp. 127-8.
7. Andrews, *op. cit.,* pp. 185-7.
8. K. J. Cohen and R. M. Cyert, "Strategy: Formulation Implementation and Monitoring". *The Journal of Business,* XLVI (July, 1973), p. 360-1.
9. Ansoff, *op. cit.,* p. 208.
10. R. L. Ackoff, *A Concept of Corporate Planning* (New York: Wiley Interscience, 1970), pp. 5-15.

CASE

INTERNATIONAL BUSINESS MACHINES, INC.
CORPORATE STRATEGY

THE INDUSTRY TRENDS

IBM is a producer of information handling and processing equipment and currently is the largest manufacturer in the industry worldwide. It has been said that as IBM moves so moves the industry. The industry is defined by the U.S. Bureau of Domestic Commerce to encompass the following product classifications: Typewriter, Electronic Computing Equipment, Calculators, Accounting Machines, and other Office Machines.[1] This industry with numerous manufacturers, both domestic and foreign, appears to be becoming increasingly competitive. To meet this competition many nations are encouraging smaller companies to combine into a national corporation backed by the government assistance.

Exports of IBM computer-related products, primarily to the Federal Republic of Germany, France, United Kingdom, and Japan increased in 1972 approximately by 11%. Buoyed by expansion anticipated in the electronic computing industry, business machine industry shipments are expected to grow 10 percent annually and approach $20 billion by 1980.

The most significant trend in the industry is the further utilization of advanced electronics to improve productivity and reliability in industrial products. Although the U.S. computer industry holds over 90 percent of the world market, pending suits in the U.S. Federal courts may adversely affect this share of the market.

The potential of the Eastern Europe market for computing equipment is estimated by industry observers at from $400 million to $880 million annually throughout the seventies.[2] The U.S.S.R. has shown strong interest in large computers, minicomputers, and peripherals, as displayed at the American Computer Exhibit in Moscow in 1972. The French, British, German, and Japanese computer producers are currently gaining a foothold in the East European market. A comparison of installed computers in the U.S. with Soviet

This case was prepared by Assistant Professors William Tomlinson and M. Reza Vaghefi of the University of North Florida's College of Business Administration. The case is intended for discussion purposes and does not reflect good or bad administration of the firm.

Distributed by the Intercollegiate Case Clearing House, Soldiers Field, Boston, Mass. 02163. All rights reserved to the contributors. Printed in the U.S.A. Used with permission.

computer installations indicates the possibilities of growth in this market. The U.S.S.R. has approximately 5,500 computers with other communist nations having approximately 1,500 computers. The U.S. on the other hand has more than 85,000.[3]

To meet domestic demands the Communist Bloc of nations now have a joint venture aimed at producing third-generation computers.[4]

CORPORATE HISTORY

In 1914, Thomas J. Watson joined the Computing-Tabulating-Recording Company as its general manager after having been previously employed as an executive with the National Cash Register Company. The C.T.R. Company has evolved into the present IBM Corporation which enjoys annual sales of approximately $10 billion. Mr. Watson is credited with developing primarily the institutional goals, beliefs and philosophy of the present corporation. He began by borrowing $40,000 for development when research and development requirements were not even budgeted. About $25,000 of this amount was expended in research on tabulating machines. Also, he was a marketing-oriented executive who stated that nothing happens in the plant until something is sold. Another policy which he brought from National Cash was the company's emphasis on developing a work force of secure and company-oriented employees. He emphasized the constant need for education by establishing the first class of tabulating machine employees in 1916. His concern for corporate image as well as self improvement was already apparent. The company spread from Endicott, N.Y., and in 1924, it acquired a sales office on Fifth Avenue. Its opening launched the new name of International Business Machines. In 1933 IBM acquired Electramatic Typewriters, Inc. of Rochester, N.Y., and after an investment of over a million dollars the new electric typewriter was first sold in 1935.

The Great Depression did not depress IBM's growth and optimistic spirit. IBM built an impressive display for the Century of Progress Exposition at the Chicago World's Fair in 1933. This optimistic outlook continued when IBM machines, like those exhibited at the World's Fair, were selected by the Social Security Administration in 1935 to handle what was called "the biggest accounting operation of all times". Tom Watson's determination to succeed sometimes made IBM appear more important and larger than they really were. Their public image was again promoted successfully by their displays at the 1939 World's Fair in New York.

During WWII, IBM offered its entire facilities to the government. The plant in Poughkeepsie produced guns and airplane parts. It was significant that the [employee] absenteeism was one half the national rate. It was in the 1940's that IBM built the giant one-of-a-kind electro-mechanical computing machines, starting with the 50-foot-long Mark I. It was not until the 701 was announced that IBM was catapulted into manufacturing and marketing the large-scale electronic computer in 1952.

As the complexity of marketing electronic data processing systems increased, the size of the business and the stiffening competition made demands on the organizational structure. A reorganization was needed. According to T. J. Watson Jr., the organizational chart was comprised of about 30 lines going from Tom Sr. The result was a basic decentralization effort in 1956. At that time the corporation was organized into eight operating groups and two independently operated subsidiaries, providing a flexible framework for future growth as T.J. Watson Jr. was assuming the leadership role.

A major technological innovation allowed IBM to announce their faster and cheaper second-generation, solid-state computer technology in 1959. The 1401 systems, IBM's second-generation line, are still in use in almost every city in the United States. In 1960, the company multiplied the usefulness of the computer with the introduction of the IBM Tele-Processing equipment. This was the beginning of the current international system of reservations used both for hotel accommodations and transportation.[5] Other major systems and technological advances have maintained the continued industry leadership by IBM. These advances include great strides in price performance, reliability, servicability and in software developments. The Information Handling Industry is currently undergoing a dramatic change from the third-generation to the fourth-generation equipment and software.

From a company of 1200 employees, in 1914, IBM has grown to 274,108 members in 1973; it has led in innovations and managed its resources to provide dividends to stockholders each and every year.[6]

ORGANIZATIONAL CHANGE

Thomas Watson Jr., attributes the success of the company, in part, to its ability to anticipate the need for change in all aspects, including reorganization, as was done in 1956. By 1970 the organization had split into 12 divisions. Another readjustment occurred in 1972, leaving the current organizational structure with only two subsidiaries. The twelve divisions are:

System Manufacturing Division—manufactures systems 360, and 370 data-processing systems and associated equipment.

Information Records Division—develops, manufactures, and markets data-processing cards, magnetic tape and cards, business forms and other consumable products used in information-handling systems.

System Development Division—develops, through a multinational effort, IBM's mid-range and large information-handling systems and associated peripheral equipment, including system-related programming support.

Real Estate and Construction Division—manages the selection and acquisition of sites, the design and construction of buildings and the purchase or lease of facilities.

Federal Systems Division—concentrates on advanced technology and systems for the ground-based, airborne and spaceborne information-handling and control needs of the U.S. Government.

Advanced Systems Development Division—identifies and establishes the potential value of innovative concepts that can lead IBM into new business areas for the future, and develops advanced systems, new technologies, product and application prototypes.

Date Processing Division—markets IBM's full line of information-handling systems, equipment, program products, systems engineering, education, custom contracts and other related services through offices across the United States.

General Systems Division—develops and manufactures low-cost information-handling systems support.

Field Engineering Division—provides maintenance and related services for the company's domestic information-handling systems, equipment and programming systems.

Office Products Division—develops, manufactures, markets and services electric typewriters, magnetic media typewriters, dictation equipment, direct-impression composing products, copying equipment, and related supplies.

General Products Division—worldwide development and United States manufacturing responsibility for computer tape units, disk files, and printers.

Subsidiaries:

    IBM World Trade Corporation—conducts IBM's business outside the United States directly or through subsidiaries.

    Science Research Associates, Inc.—develops and produces textbooks, educational kits, learning systems, guidance products, and wide range of testing materials and services for elementary and secondary schools, colleges and industry.[7]

Still further change is taking place within the structure. In 1973 the Federal Systems Division was reduced in its activities. A vertical integration of the functions of the General Systems Division, Data Processing Division, and the Field Engineering Division is being contemplated currently. The new structure would remain the same but the total responsibility for the basic systems products including the small computer products would be given to the General Systems Division. It would retain responsibility for manufacturing, marketing, installing, and maintaining these products. This change has not been clearly made but the News section of *Datamation* believes it is to occur shortly. They claim that IBM feels this will increase the profitability of the System/3 which has sold more computers than any other IBM machine but the profitability is not as high as other products in the Data Processing Division line.[9]

IBM has remained steadfast to the practice of vertical alignment from corporate management levels through design, manufacture, distribution, and ultimate user direct marketing. This type of approach is in keeping with the basic principles of marketing.

MARKETING PRACTICES

The marketing practices of IBM are developed by a special corporate level staff and then are directly reviewed by the president and the board of directors. This procedure resulted from the external pressures placed on the corporation in 1969 by the United States Department of Justice. If these practices are violated anywhere in the company, the responsible employee is subject to immediate dismissal.

Since IBM is a marketing organization, directed by marketing oriented executives, it strives to maintain the best customer service and expects each employee to strive for perfection in every area of endeavor. In research and development areas scientists are encouraged to remain constantly aware of possible applications of new technology to existing and new products. This includes constantly searching for better performance in the regions of reduced cost to program, to maintain, to provide greater reliability, and in developing new applications for industry needs.

The channels of feedback lie with the salesman himself. Special requirements by certain customers are being submitted on a daily basis to the design and manufacturing divisions to see if similar needs have been submitted by others. The strength of this channel is that there are literally thousands of standard "Requests Per Quotation" already available upon request by customers. It is therefore a daily matter for the salesman to submit the new hardware and software needs for approval. Once a quotation is given, IBM will build and maintain the RPQ as any other of its products.[10]

Marketing management at the corporate level has staff personnel that evaluate the RPQ's and are constantly weighing the changing marketplace by their trends. Many new products and systems have stemmed from this source.

Still other channels of feedback come from the industry marketing representatives who are specialists in the specific industry. They are closely tuned to the needs of their marketplace and usually coordinate the emerging applications being achieved by systems engineers and often make program products of specific applications. Still another echelon of feedback comes from the degree of goal achievement of the goals designated by the individual salesman, branch office, district, region, division, and the corporation itself. The first sign of a missed target prompts management of that level to review the reason for the missed goal and determine if it is attributable to product offering or for other reasons. The changes and constant expansion and contraction of demand requirements with IBM's organizational structure accentuates the organization's dynamic nature.

According to Mr. Vincent Learson, president of IBM in 1970, "A major factor in our past accomplishments has been the ability to react and, in fact, anticipate the need for change."[11] Thomas Watson feels that the future challenge lies in management's ability to manage change.

CORPORATE STRATEGY

The corporate strategy is developed around IBM's Basic Beliefs and Corporate Principles. Others have called the Beliefs, goals.

IBM'S BASIC BELIEFS

Respect For The Individual

(In 1963 Thomas Watson felt this was the most important belief in his opinion.)

To Give The Best Customer Service Of Any Company In The World.

Pursue All Tasks With The Idea That They Can Be Accomplished In A Superior Fashion.[12]

IBM, in addition to the Basic Beliefs, has some guiding principles that also dictate the long range and daily operational decision making processes but are considered extensions of the beliefs. Mr. Watson has stated that where conflict occurs between the beliefs and principles the beliefs will take precedence.

The Corporate Principles follow:

- **Adequate Return To The Stockholder**
- **Intelligent, Aggressive Management At All Levels**
- **Maximum Employee Satisfaction**
- **Continually Improve Products**
- **Effective Customer Service**
- **Play a Constructive Role in Community**
- **Good Citizen of Nation and World**

The principles are incorporated into every action that IBM endeavors to accomplish. They form a significant portion of the manager's training schools.[13]

The strategic decisions at all levels within IBM are based on the above basic beliefs. Fairness in all personnel matters is of prime concern to management. This is traceable to the institutional philosophy of Thomas Watson Sr. in the early days. The original idea came about because when Mr. Watson came to C-T-R, in 1914, the work force was totally demoralized. Despite the questionable condition of the company at that time, no one was fired. There was no management shake-up. Instead he began to challenge, buff, and polish the people who were already there and made a success of what he had been given. Notably, the decision in 1914 led to the current IBM policy on job security which has served as a basic strength for the corporation's structure.

IBM goes to great length to develop its people, to retrain them when job requirements change and to give them another chance if management finds them experiencing difficulty in their current assignment. It has been IBM's ability to avoid lay-offs that has led to the employee loyalty and diligence on the job. Today frequent attitude surveys show that the importance attached to job security is one of the primary reasons why people like to work for IBM. People occupy more IBM management time than that of the products. "Our early emphasis on human relations was not motivated by altruism but by the simple belief that if we respected our people and helped them to respect themselves the company would make greater profits."[14] This statement by Thomas Watson Jr. is still true today. The institution of the Open-Door Policy whereby an employee can discuss his problems with his management from the immediate supervisor to the president of IBM has provided for many levels of appeal and some major reforms in management's personnel practices. In fact, the writer believes this is the reason that IBM has been able to avoid the wholesale invasion by labor unions into their labor force.

Job enlargement occupies a prime level, especially in plant jobs of a repetitive nature. IBM has fought this problem of lack of self-accomplishment attainment in all areas. Personnel are trained in multiple operations including the set-up of their own machine, producing unit assemblies, and job rotation. These practices are directed at helping a person to keep his sense of dignity, accomplishment and *involvement.* On a corporate-wide basis it has been found that as much as 25 percent of the total IBM force has been in training at once. In this changing environment education plays an important role in service and employee retention.[15]

"IBM Means Service" was the theme of an ad a number of years before they entered the computer business. It is a succinct expression of the second belief. IBM wants to give the best customer service of any company in the world. It is the responsibility of the service forces within the corporation to maintain their reputation for excellent service. They have long ago established high standards for the selection and training of salesmen and customer engineers.[16]

To attract top-quality salesmen, IBM used sales commissions, advances, quotas, and guaranteed territories; at a time when most of those practices were considered innovations in industry. Incentive plans and awards, cash and other special benefits, are given to all employees that have any involvement with customers. These incentives are based on contribution to the business and the nature of service to the customer. In customer engineering, there now exists a mechanism for staging resources to equipment problem resolution. This conserves resources and insures better service to the customer at the same time. *Two* of the points under the service issue plan are staged inventories. All frequently used parts are at the district warehouses. If the severity of a problem is too great with a piece of equipment it might be replaced with another machine. The red alert system is used to call in additional forces as soon as greater levels of training are needed. It is possible to have a design engineer who initially designed a piece of equipment to be working on it by telephone or flown in within eight hours after failure, if no progress has been made by field maintenance personnel.

Service begins with a reliable design both in software and in the hardware. Before either a hardware or software product can be released for rent or sale the design is tested to rigid criteria and no internal pressures can cause a poor design to be produced. A system of formal product testing, within IBM, responds directly to corporate headquarters, and if the design does not meet the specified standards no lower level of management can release it for announcement or for production. This process of review, free from internal pressure to let a product go, has provided the customer with the consistent caliber of product in every area of the business.

Internal education, both technical and professional, has assisted IBM in providing the best service to the customer. "We don't sell equipment, we sell solutions to problems." This phrase permeates the sales-training programs of IBM. It is therefore necessary for IBM sales personnel to understand the customer's business and problems in depth. They have formal classes in the different industry applications to solve these problems and are kept current by continued seminars.

In 1963 the statistics showed that one out of every twenty-five technicians interviewed were selected to work for IBM.[17] The caliber of equipment and personnel motivated to customer service is the simple answer to IBM's market position. And each person is encouraged to continue to provide the best possible service to his customer.

The third belief is really the force that makes the other two effective. IBM believes that an organization should pursue all tasks with the idea that they can be accomplished in a superior fashion. IBM expects and demands superior performance from its people in whatever they do. Thomas Watson Jr. admits that an environment that calls for perfection is not likely to be easy: but aiming for it is always a goal to progress. Stated a little differently: maintains that believing in success can help attain it. Part of this belief or approach is continued optimism.

Guarding against complacency in management and in every endeavor is requisite to success, and it is for this reason that benefit can come from issuing new challenges to people and insuring that opportunity to meet new and different problems is essential within IBM.[19]

WHAT GROWTH AND CHANGE HAS TAUGHT IBM

Review of the long-range plans of the divisions and the subsidiaries are conducted, and major decisions are the responsibility of the group executives, the board chairman, and the president. IBM decentralized to divide the business into more manageable units and make sure decisions would be made when and where they should. IBM is not the kind of business the textbooks say can be decentralized sensibly. IBM is not, as many large companies are, a grouping of unrelated or merely partly related businesses. Its corporate philosophy does provide the cohesive agent to make its brand of decentralization work in an environment of growth and change.

In a speech Mr. Thomas Watson stated: "We are one business and, for the most part, a business with a single mission. Our job, and that of each division of IBM, is to help customers solve their problems through the use of data processing systems and other information-handling equipment. While many of our higher executives have incentives besides their salary; these plans are based on the overall IBM performance. I can attest *to the value* of the following five lessons for us.

1. There is simply no substitute for good human relations and for the high morale they bring. It takes good people to do the jobs necessary to reach your profit goals. But good people alone are not enough. No matter how good your people may be, if they don't real-

ly like the business, if they don't feel totally involved in it, or if they don't think they're being treated fairly it's awfully hard to get a business off the ground. Good human relations are easy to talk about. The real lesson, I think, is that you must work at them all the time and make sure your managers are working with you.

2. There are two things an organization must increase far out of proportion to its growth rate if that organization is to overcome the problems of change. The first of these is communication, upward and downward. The second is education and retraining.

3. Complacency is the most natural and insidious disease of large corporations. It can be overcome if management will set the right time and pace and if its lines of communications are in working order.

4. Everyone—particularly in a company such as IBM—must place company interest above that of a division or department. In an interdependent organization, a community of effort is imperative. Cooperation must outrank self-interest, and an understanding of the company's particular approach to things is more important than technical ability.

5. And the final and most important lesson: Beliefs must always come before policies, practices, and goals. The latter must always be altered if they are seen to violate fundamental beliefs. The only sacred cow in an organization should be its basic philosophy of doing business.

The British economist Walter Bagehot once wrote: "Strong beliefs win strong men and then make them stronger." To this I would add, "And as men become stronger, so do the organizations to which they belong."[20]

DOMESTIC ENVIRONMENT

The prime issue in the domestic environment has become the anti-trust issue. The Federal Government has become increasingly concerned with IBM's increasing leadership position in the computer industry.

In January 1969, the Department of Justice filed a civil antitrust complaint against IBM under Section 2 of the Sherman Antitrust Act, charging the company with monopolizing commerce in "general purpose digital computers" in the United States. The government requested that IBM be required to stop certain practices which it claims lead to a monopoly, and asks the court to give such other relief by way of divorcement, divestiture and reorganization as it may deem necessary to dissipate the effects of the practices charged.[21]

In January 1972 and March 1972, The Telex Corporation instituted two lawsuits against IBM alleging violations of the Federal antitrust laws. These complaints, which have been consolidated, seek injunctive relief and damages to be fixed by the court. In April 1970, Xerox Corporation filed a suit against IBM charging patent infringement and misuse of confidential information in connection with the IBM Copier.

All of the foregoing cases were brought against IBM to the Federal district courts. IBM denied the charges in all of these cases and is engaged in preparing its defenses against them.[22]

In July 1972, the trial of the Greyhound Computer Corporation suit against IBM in the Federal district court resulted in a directed verdict in favor of IBM. The plaintiff sought damages and injunctive relief for alleged violations of the Federal antitrust laws and in connection with IBM's 1969 announcement changing the way it charges for the supports of its data processing equipment. The Greyhound Computer Corporation has appealed this decision to the Federal Circuit Court of Appeals. IBM continues to deny the charges in this case and is engaged in contesting the appeal.

In January 1973, the litigation between Control Data Corporation and IBM in the Federal district court was dismissed pursuant to an out-of-court settlement which included mutual releases of all pending claims between parties. The principal terms of the settlement provide that IBM: sell The Service Bureau Corporation (SBC) to Control Data Corporation (CDC) for approximately $16,000,000 (SBC operations for 1972 are included in the consolidated financial statements and amounted to approximately $1,500,000 of net earnings on gross revenues of $63,000,000); not engage in the data services business in the United States for six years; contract for data-processing services for SBC for approximately $5,000,000 per year for five years; contract for research and development work by CDC in the amount of $6,000,000 per year for five years with rights to products developed there and available to both parties; provide for reimbursement to SBC for retirement and other fringe benefits of current SBC employees of approximately $2,600,000 for ten years; and reimburse CDC for expenses, including legal fees, in the amount of $15,000,000. CDC and IBM also extended their agreement for worldwide patent crosslicensing until 1978. Appropriate provision was made in 1972 for costs of the settlement.[23]

DOMESTIC AND THE INTERNATIONAL INTERFACE

Professor Henry C. Wallich, wrote an article in the *Newsweek* issue of October 1, 1973 entitled "Trust-Busting the U.S.A." One of its sections described his version of "Our Best Corporation."

"IBM is probably this country's best corporation. It is the envy-and the dream-of other countries. The Japanese are making their computer companies merge in order to make them more like IBM. Instead of the present six, the plan of MITI, the powerful Ministry of International Trade and Industry, is for three or even two. In Europe, Siemens (Germany), Phillips (Holland) and CII (France) ar forming Unidata for the same purpose. All these countries believe that one big company is better in the computer field than a bevy of small ones. Only the U.S. believes that it can improve itself by breaking up its big successful company.

The Japanese, who until very recently were keeping out American computers, are expected to start marketing theirs in the U.S. in 1975 or 1976. Who is to defend the interest of American industry and of the American worker in the battle that looms ahead? Telex? Or is it the computer divisions of other American companies that, before their number had shrunk to five or six, used to be referred to as IBM and the seven dwarfs? If it can be done at all, IBM will do it—provided the Justice Department will let it."[24]

Mr. Thomas Watson Jr., stated as late as the 1972 annual report that he was confident that IBM could rise to the future challenges if they were allowed to compete freely and on the same basis as other foreign corporations.[25] He felt that it would prove beneficial to both the domestic as well as the foreign marketplace. Although Mr. Watson is currently playing less of a role in the decision-making process; his ideals and those of his father are still adhered to by the new management. (These ideals have been inculcated in the current management by their predecesors.)

In September 1973, Mr. Paul Rizzo, IBM chief financial officer, acknowledged that the currency "float" makes life more complicated for IBM but he foresees bright prospects for continued growth abroad. "... it helps to think of inflation as an economic disease and currency fluctuation as a symptom of it."

Mr. Rizzo feels that the recent attention to devaluation has had no major impact on IBM's business. "Although we are in a very different financial climate than a few years ago, far the greatest part of our assets overseas are invested long term in plants, labs, production machinery, and data-processing rental equipment. Since these fixed assets are valued in dollars at the time they were acquired they are unaffected by sudden shifts in exchange rates between various currencies. The only immediate area of concern is the working capital. This includes cash, receivables, payables, and inventories. To combat the effect on working capital it is kept at a minimum. There are other hedges that can be taken by capitalizing on the currency exchange traffic ourselves. The measure of performance of foreign operations is accomplished in both dollars and in their local currency. The dollar is used to measure in the consolidated statements to the stockholders."[26]

Rizzo's final statement reflects the attitude of the corporation about fluctuations in the currency exchange as follows:

"We can't afford to become preoccupied with the temporary ups and downs of different currencies. Certainly they affect us.

But they are generally short-term charges. What we try to do is look several years out in the economic life of a particular country. We ask, "Is the growth of that country healthy? How does its growth compare with that of other overseas markets and what of the U.S.?"

We have a small staff of economists who, incidently, use some quite sophisticated computer techniques, as well as published data, to help us do this. We plan for growth abroad and in the U.S. based upon the fundamental demands of the marketplace.

While currency fluctuations can affect the way we finance our operations and report our financial results, the bright prospects for growth of our business are still apparent in the marketplace."[27]

Stated more succinctly IBM corporate management feels that with careful financial management they not only can meet the challenge of the changing levels but can probably capitalize upon them to the advantage of domestic stockholders.

INTERNATIONAL OPERATIONS

Since CTR opened an office in France in 1914, IBM's influence in world commerce has passed through three phases:

1. sales outlets in Europe began on a general scale in 1924;
2. the effort to make its overseas businesses autonomous got underway with manufacturing facilities, in 1924; finally,
3. drawing upon the creative genius of other lands led to the building of development and research laboratories abroad. Much of the current product line offered in the United States was jointly developed in foreign laboratories. The promotion of international technological interchange had proved to work extremely well for IBM even before the rest of the world was actively using it.

The World Trade Corporation is a wholly owned subsidiary of IBM Corporation and makes relatively independent operating decisions from its U.S.

parent. The president of the World Trade Corporation is from France, Jacques G. Maisonrouge.

In 1968, World Trade Corporation's gross income increased to over $2 billion dollars, $2.9 billion in 1970, $3.4 billion in 1971 and $4.1 billion in 1972. This rate of growth is much faster than that in domestic operations.

At this point it is necessary to address the challenge of worldwide competition. Many countries are nationalizing the data-processing equipment and services industry by combining internal companies. The effect of economic nationalism creates some major concern for IBM management. IBM feels that the best way to meet this challenge both at home and abroad is to provide the marketplace with superior products and services consistent with the needs and priorities of the countries in which they operate.[29]

There has evolved some sentiment toward protectionism in this country but IBM opposes it. Documentation indicates multinational companies like IBM contribute substantially to the U.S. balance of payments and support thousands of jobs in the U.S. IBM estimates that one of every eight jobs in the U.S. plants is supported by their export trade.

IBM business continues to grow in 112 nations. Although the head of the World Trade Corporation is from France, the board of directors are mostly from the United States. The nature of IBM's business in these 112 countries is generally the same, and the needs of the marketplaces are similar to a large extent. The challenges in Europe are felt to be similar to the rest of the world.[30]

The key to the World Trade Corporation's success is in its coordinated management. "The human resources you use to represent your company to the customers is the vital factor"; this statement of Mr. Maisonrouge again reflects the essence of IBM's Basic Beliefs. He stresses IBM's good fortune to find nationals in most of the 112 countries who can meet the challenge, who can go out and hire and train a marketing force to deliver the same excellence of service all over the world. "I think, too, that it has been extremely helpful to have common policies in all the countries where we operate."[31]

In 1970, for the first time, the World Trade Corporation produced more than half of IBM's net revenue. There is a feeling that two potentially lucrative areas have been virtually untapped to date. They are the U.S.S.R. and Red China. Until most recently, the Chinese marketplace has been completely closed to U.S. businesses. In October, 1971 IBM had an exhibit at the Leningrad Fair. The net result was that every single piece of equipment was immediately snapped up by the Russians. In addition, the Russians were extremely eager to negotiate continuing sales in items such as the IBM composer and the Selectric Typewriter.[32]

IBM's current policy with the Communist Bloc nations has been one of cash only in dollars and no rentals. This business was about $30 million annually. The state of the art in World Trade is on a par with that in the U.S.[33]

Mr. Gilbert Jones, WTC board member, states that: "When I look at IBM World Trade, I envision a continuance of the growth pattern we've had in the last ten years. I think the potential is not only in extending geography, not only in extended applications, but in the vast potential of new technology."[34]

Can IBM retain its present reputation as America's "best corporation" with its present strategies in the dynamic internal and external environments in which it operates? What should be the support responsibility, if any, of the Federal Government in assisting U.S. corporations making a substantial contribution to a favorable U.S. balance of payments? What strategy changes, if any, should IBM consider in developing a market position in the U.S.S.R., the People's Republic of China, and the Communist Bloc countries? Are its Basic Beliefs and Principles equally valid in developing the Communist market?

REFERENCES

1. Stephen L. Schilling, *U.S. Industrial Outlook - 1973* Washington D.C.: Published by U.S. Dept. of Commerce, 1972 Government Publishing Clearinghouse, p.320.
2. Ibid., p. 324.
3. Richard A. Szuprowicz, "Monopoly Is Not A Game," *Datamation Magazine*, Vol. 19, No. 9 (September, 1972), p. 86.
4. "IBM World Trade Corporation: An Assessment, "*THINK Magazine*, Vol. 38. No. 1, (Jan/Feb., 1972), pp. 37.
5. Thomas Watson, Jr., "A Business and Its Beliefs," *IBM NEWS*, Vol. 1, No. 9, (May 10, 1964), pp. 8-16.
6. *IBM Annual Reports 1971 and 1973*. Armonk, New York, IBM Corporate Headquarters, 1972 and 1974, p. 2.
7. *IBM Annual Report 1972*. Armonk, New York, IBM Corporate Headquarters, 1973, p. 25.
8. "System/3 Marketing Shift Considered," *Datamation Magazine*, Vol. 18, No. 9 (May 10, 1964), p. 7.
9. Jerome McCarthy, *Basic Marketing*, Homewood, Illimois: Richard D. Irwin, Inc., 1971.
10. Pearce Wright, "It's Deeper Than It Looks," *Datamation Magazine*, Vol. 18, No. 8 (August, 1972), p. 74.
11. *IBM Annual Report 1970*. Armonk, New York, IBM Corporate Headquarters, 1971, p. 2.
12. Thomas Watson, Jr., "A Business and Its Beliefs," *IBM NEWS*, Vol. 1, No. 9, (May 10, 1964), p. 8.
13. Thomas Watson, Jr. "A Business and Its Beliefs,;; *IBM NEWS*, Vol, 1, No. 9, (May 10, 1964), p. 14.
14. Thomas Watson, Jr. "A Business and Its Beliefs," *IBM NEWS*, Vol. 1, No. 9 (May 10, 1964), p. 12.
15. *IBM Annual Report 1969*. Armonk, New York, IBM Corporate Headquarters, 1970 p. 4.
16. Thomas Watson, Jr., "A Business and Its Beliefs," *IBM NEWS*, Vol 1, No. 9, (May 10, 1964), p. 14.
17. Thomas Watson, Jr. "A Business and Its Beliefs," *IBM NEWS*, Vol. 1, No. 9, (May 10, 1964), p. 13.
18. Thomas Watson, Jr., "A Business and Its Beliefs," *IBM NEWS*, Vol. 1, No. 9, (May 10, 1964), p. 16.
19. Ibid. p. 16.
20. Thomas Watson, Jr. "A Business and Its Beliefs," *IBM NEWS*, Vol. 1, No. 9, (May 10, 1964), p. 16.
21. *IBM Annual Report 1971*. Armonk, New York, IBM Corporate Headquarters, 1972, p. 9.
22. *IBM Annual Report 1972*. Armonk, New York, IBM Corporate Headquarters, 1973, p. 13.
23. *IBM Annual Report 1972*. Armonk, New York, IBM Corpoate Headquarters, 1973, p. 13.
24. Henry C. Wallich, "Trust Busting the USA," *Newsweek Magazine*, October 1, 1973.
25. *IBM Annual Report 1972*. Armonk, New York, IBM Corporate Headquarters, 1973, p. 2.
26. James D. Kelly, "How the International Monetary System Works," *THINK Magazine*, Vol. 39, No. 7, (September, 1973), pp. 28-29.
28. *IBM Annual Report 1972*. Armonk, New York, IBM Corporate Headquarters, 1968, pp. 4-5.
29. "IBM World Trade Corporation: An Assessment," *THINK Magazine*, Vol. 38, No. 1, (Jan/Feb., 1972), p. 38.
30. "IBM World of Manufacturing," *THINK Magazine*, Vol. 39, No. 10, (November, 1973), p. 14.
31. "IBM World Trade Corporation: An Assessment", *THINK Magazine*, Vol. 38, No. 1 (Jan/Feb, 1972), p. 37.
32. Angeline Pantages, "IBM Abroad," *Datamation Magazine*, Vol. 18, No. 12, (December, 1972), p. 54.
33. Stephen L. Schilling, *U.S. Industrial Outlook-1973*. Washington D.C.: Published by U.S. Dept. of Commerce, 1972. Government Publishing Clearinghouse.
34. "IBM World Trade Corporation: An Assessment", *THINK Magazine*, Vol. 38, No. 1, (Jan/Feb, 1972), p. 36.

APPENDIX

EXHIBITS:

1. COMPARATIVE CONSOLIDATED FINANCIAL STATEMENTS
2. PLANT LOCATIONS
3. MEASURES OF SIZE
4. IBM PRODUCT AND SERVICE OFFERINGS
5. INDUSTRY TRENDS AND PROJECTED GROWTH
6. CUSTOMER ASSESSMENT OF IBM

EXHIBIT 1
COMPARATIVE CONSOLIDATED STATEMENT OF OPERATIONS

	1972	1971	1970	1969	1968	1967	1966	1965	1964	1963
Gross income from sales, services and rentals	$9,532,592,642	$8,273,603,369	$7,503,959,600	$7,197,295,441	$6,888,549,209	$5,345,290,993	$4,247,706,091	$3,572,824,719	$3,239,359,581	$2,862,732,727
Earnings before income taxes	$2,425,267,555	$2,055,846,907	$2,011,521,072	$1,978,873,194	$1,864,497,991	$1,297,449,558	$1,054,130,192	$959,902,490	$897,159,766	$777,828,404
U.S. Federal and foreign income taxes	$1,146,000,000	$977,000,000	$994,000,000	$1,045,000,000	$993,000,000	$646,000,000	$528,000,000	$483,000,000	$466,000,000	$413,573,426
Net earnings	$1,279,267,555	$1,078,846,907	$1,017,521,072	$933,873,194	$871,497,991	$651,499,558	$526,130,192	$476,902,490	$431,159,766	$364,254,978
Per share (see note)	$11.03	$9.38	$8.92	$8.21	$7.71	$5.81	$4.71	$4.40	$4.00	$3.39
Cash dividends	$626,156,605	$598,207,496	$547,604,277	$407,825,977	$292,646,157	$243,172,836	$230,671,168	$210,767,482	$165,964,452	$118,039,971
Per share (see note)	$5.04	$5.20	$4.80	$3.60	$2.60	$2.17	$2.10	$1.95	$1.54	$1.11
Stock dividend and splits*:										
Percent	--	--	--	--	*100%	2½%	*50%	--	*25%	--
Shares issued	--	--	--	--	56,230,420	1,363,723	17,645,985	--	6,990,140	--
Shares sold	865,002	947,027	868,898	749,699	623,670	302,356	1,577,301	176,655	136,297	114,212
Number of shares outstanding	116,393,995	115,533,993	114,586,966	113,718,068	112,968,369	561,114,279	54,558,200	35,224,914	35,048,259	27,921,822
Net investment in plant, rental machines and other property	$5,271,025,074	$5,162,744,738	$4,470,047,108	$3,863,461,372	$3,415,039,187	$3,496,207,204	$3,098,618,614	$2,303,509,000	$1,747,924,457	$1,585,581,367
Long-term debt	$772,932,774	$676,146,705	$572,899,761	$554,821,353	$545,090,514	$521,459,702	$458,871,518	$398,849,604	$370,429,536	$549,590,394
Working capital	$2,562,468,943	$1,860,702,787	$1,511,950,760	$1,814,119,609	$1,770,069,996	$916,382,993	$723,096,414	$698,652,848	$899,933,243	$805,435,060
Number of stockholders	558,332	580,621	586,786	549,463	501,390	359,495	328,427	275,650	266,086	233,761

NOTE: Adjusted for stock dividend and splits.

239

EXHIBIT 2
PLANT LOCATIONS AND SIZE
(1968)

United States	Purpose	Square Feet
Chicago, Illinois	Adm. & Mktg.	1,830,000
† East Fishkill, New York	Mfg. & Dev.	640,000
Boca Raton, Florida	Mfg. & Dev.	636,000
White Plains, New York	Adm.	627,000
* Austin, Texas	Mfg.	462,000
† San Jose, California	Mfg.	346,000
*† Burlington, Vermont	Mfg. & Dev.	300,000
† Gaithersburg, Maryland	Dev. & Adm. *	266,000
*† Boulder, Colorado	Mfg. & Dev.	261,000
† Rochester, Minnesota	Mfg. & Dev.	184,000
*† Harrison, New York	Adm.	150,000
† Owego, New York	Mfg.	100,000
.† Poughkeepsie, New York	Mfg.	100,000
† Huntsville, Alabama	Dev.	52,000
*† Sherman, Texas	Mfg.	34,000

Other Countries	Purpose	Square Feet
Stuttgart, West Germany	Adm.	488,000
† Toronto, Canada	Mfg.	250,000
* Madrid, Spain	Adm. & Mktg.	178,000
† Sindelfingen, West Germany	Mfg.	146,000
† Boeblingen, West Germany	Dev.	140,000
† La Gaude, France	Dev.	137,000
Havant, England	Mfg.	117,000
† Mainz, West Germany	Mktg.	107,000
Hannover, West Germany	Mktg.	100,000
* Manila, Philippines	Adm. & Mktg.	88,000
Bogota, Colombia	Adm. & Mktg.	87,000
*† Boeblingen, West Germany	Mfg.	84,000
Havant, England	Adm.	62,000
† Montpellier, France	Mfg.	54,000
Lidingo, Sweden	Mktg.	53,000
* Amagi, Japan	Mktg.	37,000
Osaka, Japan	Mfg.	28,000
† Uithoorn, Netherlands	Dev.	20,000

* *Completed in 1968.*
† *Expansion of existing facilities.*

EXHIBIT 2A
IBM PLANT LOCATIONS
(1973)

Major Plants	Primary Product Areas			
	Data Processing Components and Equipment	Office Products	Information Records	Federal Systems Division Products
NORTH AMERICA				
Austin		•		
Boca Raton	•			
Boulder	•	•	•	
Bromont	•			
Brooklyn	•			
Burlington	•			
Campbell			•	
Dayton			•	
East Fishkill	•			
Endicott	•			
Greencastle			•	
Huntsville				•
Kingston	•			
Lexington		•		
Manassas	•			•
Mexico City		•		
Owego				•
Poughkeepsie	•			
Raleigh	•			
Rochester	•			
San Jose	•			
Sherman			•	
Toronto	•	•	•	
Washington, D.C.			•	
SOUTH AMERICA				
Bogota		•	•	
Buenos Aires	•		•	
Sumare	•	•		
ASIA				
Bombay	•			
Fujisawa	•			
Yasu	•			
EUROPE				
Amsterdam		•	•	
Berlin		•	•	
Bolgny		•	•	
Bordeaux	•			
Essonnes	•			
Greenock	•			
Hannover	•			
Havant	•			
Jarfana	•		•	
Mainz	•			
Montpellier	•			
Sindelfingen	•			
Vimercate	•			

EXHIBIT 3
MEASURES OF SIZE
1972

Total Assets-	$10,792,402,032
Net Investment in Plant and Rental Machines-	$ 5,271,025,074
Long-term Debt-	$ 772,932,774
Working Capital-	$ 2,562,468,943
Number of Employees-	262,152
Number of Stockholders	558,332
Number of Shares of Stock	116,398,995
Market Value ' $300/Share	$ 3,491,698,500

EXHIBIT 4
IBM PRODUCTS AND SERVICES OFFERED

- Electronic data-processing systems for business, education, government, and science.
- Electric typewriters, magnetic-card and tape typewriters, dictation equipment, direct-impression composition equipment, office copier equipment and related supplies.
- Small visual display terminals that enable many people at many remote locations to share time and the power of a large centralized information system.
- Special-purpose and advanced computer systems for commercial, military, and space use.
- Low-cost punched card accounting equipment and electronic typing calculators.
- Magnetic character sensing equipment and optical character sensing readers.
- Control systems for use in such industries as petroleum, paper, utilities, and primary metals.
- Components, including relays, reed switches, programmable logic cards, and industrial-grade integrated circuits.
- Products used in data processing equipment, including: magnetic tapes, cards, paper, and typewriter ribbons.
- Portable data recorders that can be adapted, on site, to collect a broad range of information for direct entry to computer.
- Program products, related to application of an IBM system to user tasks, are offered for a charge under licence agreements.
- systems engineering services are provided for a charge, to assist customers in the installation, application, and enhancement of IBM systems.
- Custom contract services are provided for a charge by IBM in systems design and analysis, application and program development, and systems installation and evaluation.
- Professional education courses are offered for a charge, to teach programming, systems planning and other data processing skills.

EXHIBIT 5
INDUSTRY TRENDS AND PROJECTED GROWTH

Business Machines: Projections 1972-80[1]
(Value of shipments in millions of dollars except as noted)

SIC code	Industry	1972	Percent increase 1971-72	1973	Percent increase 1972-73	1980	Percent increase 1972-80[2]
3572	Typewriters	720	6	756	5	1,192	6.5
3573	Electronic computing equipment	5,965	12	6,740	13	13,746	11.0
3574	Calculator and accounting machines	588	11	647	10	1,189	9.2
3579	Office machines (not elsewhere classified)	634	5	666	5	937	5.0

[1]Estimated by Bureau of Domestic Commerce.   [2]Compound annual rate of growth.

EXHIBIT 6
CUSTOMER ASSESSMENT OF IBM

LIVE UP TO CLAIMS				AFTER SALES SERVICE			
Rank	"Best" Votes	"Worst" Votes	Ratio	Rank	"Best" Votes	"Worst" Votes	Ratio
IBM	127	49	2.6	IBM	173	21	8.2
DEC	9	4	2.25	Univac	11	17	.64
Burroughs	17	11	1.5	NCR	10	16	.62
Univac	15	11	1.36	Burroughs	9	15	.6
CDC	11	9	1.2	CDC	7	22	.58
HIS	15	15	1	HIS	12	22	.54
NCR	13	22	.6	DEC	5	10	.5
RCA	5	16	.3	RCA	5	11	.45

SUPPORT				PRODUCT PERFORMANCE PER DOLLAR			
Rank	"Most Complete" Votes	"Worst" Votes	Ratio	Rank	"Best" Votes	"Worst" Votes	Ratio
IBM	192	15	12.8	DEC	18	1	18
CDC	15	4	3.75	Burroughs	28	3	9.3
HIS	16	15	1.06	CDC	15	4	3.75
DEC	4	7	.57	Univac	21	6	3.5
Burroughs	6	13	.46	RCA	8	6	1.3
Univac	8	18	.44	HIS	20	16	1.25
NCR	8	22	.363	NCR	21	17	1.23
RCA	4	11	.363	IBM	64	73	.87

Source: Survey taken by DATAMATION, results presented in September, 1973 issue. Used with permission.

EVALUATION OF THE INTERNATIONAL BUSINESS MACHINES, INC. CASE

SUMMARY

In 1914 Thomas Watson joined the Computing-Tabulating-Recording Company as general manager and through extensive investment in development, a marketing oriented policy, and a strong emphasis on employee morale, built C.T.R. into the present IBM corporation which enjoys annual sales of approximately $10 billion annually. Being the largest manufacturer of information handling and processing equipment in the world, IBM is considered the industry leader. The expected growth rate is 10% annually and is anticipated to reach $20 billion by 1980.

As the organization grows in size and complexity, reorganizations are made to suit the company's needs. Having resulted in the current decentralized structure based on product departmentation, management feels this design is justified because of the company's unique nature. The company's basic beliefs (goals) are:

1. respect for the individual,
2. to give the best customer service of any company in the world, and
3. to pursue all tasks with the idea that they can be accomplished in a superior fashion.

It is felt that these goals can be reached by following defined company guidelines. Neither the goals nor the guidelines are expressed in quantified terms.

Because of its success in the industry, IBM has grown to a size that may be questionable under Section 2 of the Sherman Antitrust Act. If growth is not controlled, the company may be forced into divestiture of some of its holdings. On the other hand, to compete successfully in the international market, size is a crucial competitive factor. IBM is also aware of the inflation and currency fluctuation problems that arise when dealing with external markets. The extent of IBM's market share abroad is such that is influences the U.S. balances of payments.

KEY ISSUES

1. Are company goals adequately stated?
2. Is the organizational structure and design optimum in aiding this company to attain its goals?
3. How should IBM view the antitrust situation?
4. How can IBM best handle problems involving international inflation and currency fluctuations?
5. How should IBM optimally compete on the international level?

DISCUSSION

1. Company Goals

As defined, the company goals are idealistic, and difficult to assess because one never knows if they have been attained. Granted that IBM got to be where it is by using them, but IBM cannot be sure of exactly where it is except in relation to other companies' goals - profits. The statement made by Mr. Watson in IBM NEWS, May 10, 1964. "It is better to aim at perfection and miss than it is to aim at imperfection and hit it" is difficult to place into a strategic planning frame, since it is quite possible to miss perfection and end up even farther from it than by attaining the attainable goal. This may be supported by the fact that IBM seems to be slowly losing its share of the domestic market using this strategy.

2. Organizational Structure

IBM decentralized to divide the company into more manageable units and to assure that decisions were made at the appropriate level. It is not the type of company that lends itself easily to this type of organization design. However, IBM is not, as many large companies are, a grouping of unrelated or partly related businesses. Its corporate philosophy provides the cohesive agent to make its type of decentralization work in a dynamic environment.

3. Antitrust Issue

The Justice Department is concerned because IBM holds such a large share of the market. This issue requires much energy and resources to avoid legal problems. One could question the strategic priorities and implications of risking divorcement and divestiture with resultant loss in profits as well as repercussions in the international market where size is directly related to success.

4. Economic International Interface

Any company that deals with and in foreign countries must be sensitive to their economic situation. Inflation and fluctuations in currency exchange rates can seriously affect corporate profits. Currently, IBM has a policy of investing mainly in long term assets overseas and of keeping working capital at a minimum in order to minimize this problem.

5. The International Market

There are several issues involved in the international area:

1. A large percentage of company profits (gross) come from this market. If it is lost or reduced it will have substantial impact on the rest of the company.
2. This share of the market is substantial and its contribution to the U.S. balance of payments has been considered significant; hence there would seem to be more to it than one company's profits.
3. It is not clear whether the "philosophy" that has heretofore been so successful domestically will also be so abroad. It is probable that new strategies will have to be developed and tailored to foreign customers and markets.

ALTERNATIVE CONSIDERATIONS

Following are several alternatives that should be considered in evaluating the strategy of this organization. These are not intended to be all inclusive but rather to provide examples of the alternative analysis process.

1. Company Goals

a. Status Quo

This would involve little expense from an accounting standpoint but economically, the company may be paying the price of benefits given up. If the goals remain as vague as currently stated, the organization will continue to measure itself in terms of other companies' goals.

b. Restate philosophy as quantifiable goals and objectives.

Quantifying its objectives in terms of such variables as ROI, sales, production, etc., would enable IBM to continue its current philosophy, and also allow it to see how well it is doing by its own standards. Attainment of goals is a motivational factor which should reinforce the basic philosophy. The disadvantage to this is the effort required to define and quantify the objectives.

2. Organizational structure

The current organizational design seems to be meeting the needs of the company at this time and appears flexible enough to change with the company's needs. Whether it will accommodate rapid expansion and growth remains to be seen.

3. Antitrust issue

At the current rate of growth, IBM can continue to expect proportional profits and relatively little concern as to competitors. If strategy is developed carefully, problems relating to monopoly may not arise. If the company plans to compete more in the international market, size and growth becomes even more crucial.

However, the possibility of changes in existing anti-trust laws is always present. Strategic analysis must incorporate probabilities that may affect current size and market share. Any significant changes may seriously affect the company's position in the domestic as well as the international markets.

4. Economic International Interface

Currently, IBM is relatively insensitive to economic fluctuations. Fixed assets purchased as long term investments are valued in dollars at the time they were acquired and are relatively unaffected by economic shifts. Working capital kept to a minimum reduces the chances of loss but this also reduces the working potential of that capital - the purpose for which that asset is intended.

It is difficult to argue with success. Strategic analysis for a company like IBM would of necessity have to be primarily a type of alternative analysis. Essentially, what is required is a set of alternative strategic plans that recognize different probabilities relating to expansion, growth, markets (domestic/international) and products. Environmental factors would, therefore, be crucial in assessing probabilities and priorities under different environmental conditions and changes.

PART IV

The Implementation of Strategy and Planning

THE PRACTICAL
APPLICATION OF
ALTERNATIVE ANALYSIS

INTERPRETIVE PLANNING PROCESS DESIGN

The main objective of this chapter is to determine where alternative generation fits into the total corporate strategy. Figure 1, is a pictorial representation of our interpretation of the place for alternative generation. The areas identified for analysis are:

1. Objectives
2. Constraints
3. Alternative Generation
4. Choice
5. Tactics

1. Objectives

   The objectives of a firm are basically an answer to the question, "Where are we aiming and when do we want to get there?" It is our conclusion that the objective of any firm is to make a profit.[1] It is generally accepted that this is a perfectly moral objective if it is achieved through moral means.[2] Thus, to stay within the moral means, and to assure the viability and permanence of the firm, the firm must employ certain objective-setting tactics, in this stage, pertaining to:

   a) timing
   b) concentration
   c) innovation

      a) Timing
         Objectives must be tied into the dynamics of the environment in which the firm is operating. Proper assessment of this variable, and a coordination of timing into objective setting, allows the firm an opportunity to prepare for future trends.

Figure 1: Planning Process

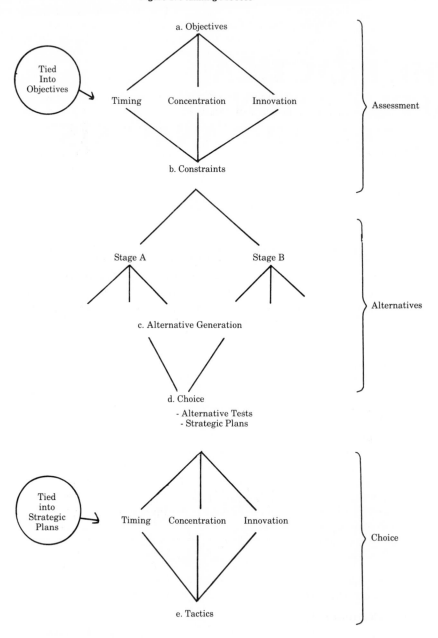

b) Concentration

If a firm is to achieve its objective of profit it must assess the market in terms of the advantages and disadvantages of concentrating in that market or markets. The ability to choose the correct course and set further objectives according to this choice is integral to total operating strength.

c) Innovation

Innovation usually results from a concerted effort on the part of the firm to explore new areas. As such, the firm's objectives should reflect the innovative stance.

Thus, the objectives of a firm (i.e., profit and the many sub-objectives) determine the moral stance of the firm in the marketplace.

2. Constraints

Constraints differ from objectives as they determine what the firm *will not or cannot do,* on moral grounds, regardless of the consequences on profit.[3] Constraints place limitations on alternative generation, and because of this, keep alternatives consistent with the firm's objectives. Constraints deal with such issues as the law, misleading practices, discrimination, quality of goods, espionage, safety, and other issues. In formulating constraints, the firm establishes the groundwork for its relationships with employees, customers, suppliers, competitors and government.

The importance of constraints in alternative generation is that they determine whether possible courses of action are feasible. In this way constraints tend to limit the total set of alternatives. Thus, we have examined basically the "do's" and "don'ts" and the relationship of these variables to both the objectives of the firm and to alternative generation. It is important that these do's and don'ts be identified and agreed upon early in the planning process.

The importance of objectives and constraints on alternative generation cannot be overstressed. These variables ultimately determine the long-run course of action of a firm and thus its success or failure. As such, objectives and constraints cannot be formulated in a vacuum. Their formulation must include an assessment of available resources, competitors' characteristics, industry dynamics and market opportunity. Stated another way, the variables of timing, innovation and concentration must be thoroughly analyzed before the alternative generation process may begin.

3. Alternative Generation

This is one of the most difficult and complex parts of the corporate planning process and the place where a systematic approach is vital. Basically, alternative generation involves preparing a list of actions that the company might take in order to achieve their objectives, keeping in mind the limitations imposed by the constraints. Argenti[4] refers to alternatives as possible actions most likely to close the profit gap. The profit gap is defined as the difference between actual and target profits. The importance of this approach is that no action is taken unless it will improve profits, therefore keeping the analysis in line with the major profit objectives.

The significant point of this phase of the planning process is that assessment of the environment, in terms of objective setting and determining constraints, has been completed. In other words, before the alternatives involving capital expenditures, new commitments, expansion, diversification and others are voiced, the assessment process must have reached its logical conclusion. Upon completion of the assessment process, the means by which the goals of the firm are to be achieved are generated. It is this specific phase, alternative generation, which has been examined from a theoretical point of view and will, in subsequent sections be examined through a practical approach.

4. Choice (alternative testing)

This aspect of the planning process concerns itself with examining the merits of each possible course of action which is generated in the previous section of the planning process. The alternative plans, or courses of action, are ultimately tested in terms of their contribution to defined objectives and ranked accordingly. If profit is the objective, that particular alternative which most reduces the total profit gap is adopted as the strategic plan.

The strategic plan can be segmented into four subplans:
a) organization plans
b) product and market development plan
c) resource development
d) operations plan

These strategic plans are further analyzed in terms of the strategic variables of timing, concentration and innovation which were discussed earlier. These variables act much in the same way as when they were applied to objectives. In other words, they are determinants of the direction the strategic plans will take.

More than one alternative may be adopted and broken down into a strategic plan framework, ready for immediate application to the firm's operations. Those alternatives not adopted should also be broken down into strategic plans. In such a way, minor environmental changes can be quickly met by these alternative plans as long as they remain consistent with the objectives and constraints of the firm.

5. Tactics

Tactics are the detailed operating plans, for each department, for each strategic plan area, and for each alternative course of action. Tactics are usually short term and are translated directly into cost and profit benefits. Thus, tactics are generally part of the budget system of the firm and concerned with its day to day operation.

PLANNING MODELS

Business strategy is a set of management guidelines which provides a unifying theme for all the firm's activities.[5] Each firm tends to employ its individual pattern of strategy. The process of strategy formulation may or may not be recorded in company documents, however, consistency is a major determinant in the relative success or failure of planning. Because explicit and formal strategy formulation is needed, models have been developed to ease the transition from informal to formal planning. One such model is Argenti's Five Step Planning Process, shown in Figure 2.

This model relies heavily on the single objective of profit and the fact that all alternatives must reduce the profit gap. Thus, those alternatives which have no effect on reducing the profit gap are not considered. The environment is reviewed in an overall sense, however, the final analysis always utilizes profit as the major criterion. From this profit basis a theoretical structure, or process, is developed. These structures have evolved as an extension of the micro-economic theory of the firm, since this theory failed to explain behavior in firms and, therefore, could not be used in decision making.[6] Thus, from the simplistic micro-economic theory have emerged the strategic process models, one of which we are currently examining. By introducing objectives and constraints, alternatives, tactics and, in general, strategy, these models can explain behavior in the firm, and can be an integral part of the decision making process. The final product of these models is a set of detailed operating plans and/or tactics, and only the method of achieving this end is different.

The Argenti Model could be classified as a single step away from the micro-economic theory concept. The reliance upon profit is evident, however, the addition of other objectives and constraints helps to better define profit maximization; a term which has a questionable connotation to most students of business. In other words, Argenti's analysis breaks away from the purely economic variables which measure inputs and outputs, and begins to deal with the behavioral and informational variables. Thus, people and their relationships within the firm as well as the state of knowledge with the firm, are introduced as variables worthy of consideration during the planning process.

FIGURE 2: ARGENTI'S FIVE STEP PLANNING PROCESS

Step 1

Determine the objective
Determine the owners
Set the target

Step 2

Stage 1   Analyse revenue, volume, costs
Stage 2   The projections
Stage 3   The factors affecting profits
Stage 4   The forecasts
Determine errors

Step 3

Calculate the gap
Decide the task

Step 4

Determine the constraints
Decide the means:

Alternative
Generation
Stage A   Review seven possible means
Stage B   Review the three business areas
Stage C   Test the means in existing
business area
Stage D   Test the means in new business
areas
Stage E   Consider liquidation
Stage F   Draw up policy statements

Step 5

Draw up Detailed Plans
Monitor and revise continuously

A graphic interpretation of his concept as discussed in: J. Argenti, *Systematic Corporate Planning*, London: T. Nelson & Sons, 1974. Used with permission.

The remainder of discussion will address itself to a further discussion of the Argenti model in terms of alternative generation and the theoretical framework presented earlier. The Argenti model is utilized for this analysis because:

1. it represents a unique approach to strategic planning, and it lends itself well to analysis, under a heuristic model of alternative generation.
2. the Argenti model has been extended by other authors in terms of a network analysis. We shall be examining some of these extensions.

Figure 2 indicates the idea identified as the alternative generation section of the Argenti process. This section has been extended in Figure 3.

FIGURE 3: THE ALTERNATIVE GENERATION SECTOR OF ARGENTI'S PLANNING PROCESS

Step 4

Determine the constraints
Decide the means:

    Stage A Review seven possible means
           1. Invest capital
           2. Overcome obstacles
           3. Exploit opportunities
           4. Use of strengths
           5. Overcome weaknesses
           6. Institute profit improvement plan
           7. Use of management techniques
    Stage B Review the three business areas
           1. Existing business to be
             a.   reduced
             b.   maintained
             c.   increased
             d.   forced
           2. New business
             a.   integration forward
             b.   integration backward
             c.   diversify
           3. Liquidation

ALTERNATIVE GENERATION

The Argenti Model essentially breaks alternative generation into two distinct stages. Those in Stage A refer to what types of action a firm might take to improve profit. Stage B deals with the areas of business activity where these activities might be effective. Since no method of generating these alternatives is discussed, it will be our task to discuss various theoretical alternative generation models, and the applicability of these to selected sections of the Argenti Model.

The remainder of this analysis will follow a structure similar to the format presented in Figure 3. This should help clarify the applicability of the various alternative generation methods as they are utilized in the analysis.

a) Determine the Constraints

Essentially our starting point for this analysis is Step 4 (see Figure 2), and thus our initial topic is determining the constraints. As noted previously, constraints differ from objectives in that they determine the "don'ts," or the action the firm should not take. When combined with the firm's objectives, (i.e. the do's), constraints tend to limit the set of feasible alternatives. Thus, any given alternative may be immediately deleted if it is inconsistent with the firm's objectives and/or constraints.

b) Alternative Generation in Stage A

The initial step in alternative generation under Stage A is for the corporate planner to make a list of all those actions by which companies in general, and his own company, in particular, might be able to generate profits. For the purpose of further analysis, these actions are classified into seven categories.

1. Investment of Capital

Before alternative investment plans can be formulated, there are many aspects of the firm, the corporate planner must consider. He must know the extent to which the firm relies upon capital expenditure, how much capital is available, the status of current cash flow and reserves, and the extent of current financing. Other factors such as debt capacity, required rate of return and desired rate of return must also be known. From these facts the planner is able to begin his analysis of capital investment alternatives.

It was our previous conclusion that a heuristic model could be utilized in alternative generation. In the area of investment, this approach has been utilized more than in any other. G.P.E. Clarkson[7] has formulated a heuristic model which is directly applied to choosing an investment portfolio, given the objectives and constraints of the investor. Alternatives are generated on the basis of acceptance or rejection given the objections and constraints of the investor and the characteristics of the particular stock in question (see Figure 4). This model consists of a series of binary decisions on the performance and expectations of those attributes deemed important.[8] It should be noted, that since the importance of specific attributes depends upon the objectives and constraints of the investor, the alternatives generated will vary with each individual investor.

The Clarkson Model generates two acceptable solutions, or alternatives, as shown in Figure 4. The model successfully considers the objectives and constraints of the investor and suggest two alternative solutions. Although acceptance in both cases brings the same result, the investor must decide whether conditions T12 and T13 are important, and if so, he will consider acceptance at T11 insufficient. Further, the choice to continue the analysis, or reject the proposal, can be made at any stage. Reaching acceptance at T13 may represent an optimal level, however, this once again depends upon the rationale of the investor.

For purposes of our analysis, we have assumed that the major objective of any firm is to make a profit. A possible means of achieving this profit is through investing capital and the Clarkson Model was introduced as a possible method to generate investment alternatives. The investment of capital is not, however, the only means by which the profit objective can be reached.

2. Overcome Obstacles

Obstacles usually arise from the assessment of the external and internal environments in which the firm operates. This assessment should result in some form of trend analysis. These trends will reflect certain expectations or events that may alter or weaken the firm's current market position if they occur. To deal with such developments, the firm should adopt contingency plans. In other words, given a possible environmental change, the entire planning process should be reworked according to this change.

Contingency planning should also be undertaken for totally unforeseen events. For example, the behavior of competitors and the

Figure 4: Example of Clarkson's
Investment Portfolio Model

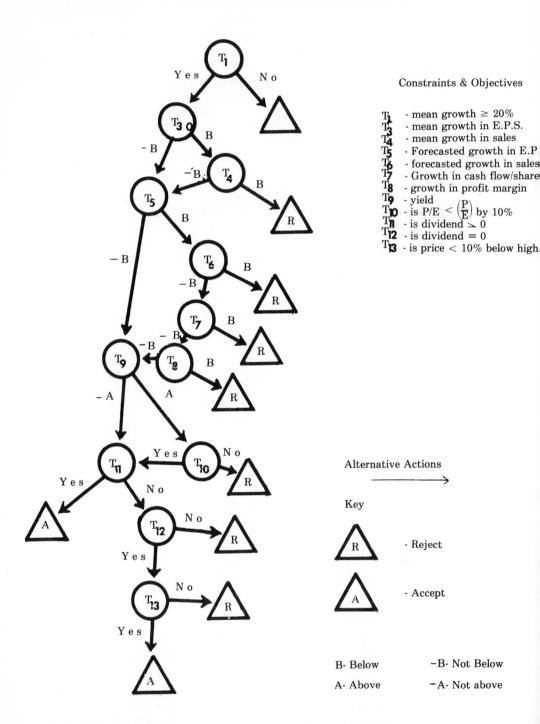

Constraints & Objectives

T_1 - mean growth ≥ 20%
T_3 - mean growth in E.P.S.
T_4 - mean growth in sales
T_5 - Forecasted growth in E.P
T_6 - forecasted growth in sales
T_7 - Growth in cash flow/share
T_8 - growth in profit margin
T_9 - yield
T_{10} - is P/E $< \left(\frac{P}{E}\right)$ by 10%
T_{11} - is dividend ≥ 0
T_{12} - is dividend = 0
T_{13} - is price < 10% below high

Alternative Actions

Key

R - Reject

A - Accept

B- Below   −B- Not Below

A- Above   −A- Not above

SOURCE: G.P.E. Clarkson, A Model of Trust Investment Behavior, in Cyert & March, A Behaviorial Theory of the Firm (Prentice-Hall, 1963) p. 263. Used with permission.

dynamics of the industry are important considerations, plus those internal factors such as strikes, union entrance, unforeseen equipment obsolescence and other events. It is clear that alternatives must be generated to cover each of these contingencies or any combination of events. This takes us back to the importance of a forecasting model in assessing the impact of these changes on company performance.

The network concept is applicable in this instance in that it offers an easy reference to possible courses of action given the event. By utilizing the network concept, the firm can easily cope with unforeseen contingencies. This, of course, is dependent upon a total commitment by the firm to the strategic planning process, and a thorough assessment of possible contingencies.

3. Exploit Opportunities

The subject here is the degree to which the firm is capable of exploiting events which might represent an opportunity for the company. It is important to note that planning does not take the form of searching for opportunities at this juncture; the planner is merely creating alternatives which will be applicable should the opportunities present themselves.

On a more practical level, the various alternatives concerned with diversification are applicable here. For example, if a company is facing difficult times ahead it should be aware that its competitors will probably also be facing difficult times. The possibility that one of these competitors will become suitable for merger should be included in the alternatives. The formulation of specific diversification objectives depends upon examining the firm's capability for adapting to a changing environment. It should be kept in mind that merger is only one method of diversification and therefore a spectrum of possible diversification alternatives can be formulated.

The network process is applicable in this instance also. Given that a firm practices well founded strategic planning and is therefore aware of its environment, the opportunity to exploit diversification possibilities has probably been recognized. In generating the appropriate alternatives, the firm should first list those areas of diversification that the constraints of the firm will allow. These constraints would include such areas as financial resources, resource utilization advantages, holding company criteria choices and other areas. Once this list of alternative diversification possibilities is complete, all possible effects of the "difficult times" should be applied to these alternatives. In this way the firm can react to environmental changes and their effect on diversification. By defining both desirable and undesirable actions, in response to environmental change, the possibility of an improper choice of diversification alternatives is minimized. Thus, opportunities may be exploited as they arise, given a proper alternative generation process.

4. Exploit Strengths; Overcome Weaknesses

Strengths and weaknesses differ from obstacles and opportunities in that they are internal to the firm itself. They arise from the quality of staff, the method of recording financial data or other factors. One method of enhancing strengths and/or reducing weaknesses in the firm is to examine various organizational design alternatives as part of the total planning process.

Organization design alternatives can be examined in many ways. The usual method would be to analyze the advantages and disadvantages of the various design strategies; for example, functional, clientele, geographic, or product design alternatives. The importance lies in examining the homogeneity of activities that affect the firm's strengths and weaknesses, and applying the optimum design alternative. Three such areas of activity will be examined; take-over bids, research and marketing.

In the previous section, which discussed diversification alternatives, we stated that diversification is basically undertaken to obtain better use of resources and to increase the capability of a firm to adapt to its environment. Stated differently, diversification, or takeover bids, help to enhance strengths and reduce weaknesses.

The addition of a company through merger, however, can create special problems for the expanded firm. Lines of communication, authority, and responsibility may become helplessly confused and could eventually reduce any possible benefit. The corporate planner, in order to avoid such problems, must consider structural adjustments to negate these problems. Again the network concept may be applied. By listing all possible foreseeable problem areas and then analyzing the problem negating qualities of each design alternative, a solution is possible. For example, a merger with a company which markets a similar product, but to a different market area, may suggest that a clientele (customer-based) structure be adopted. The important fact here is that the impact of diversification on organization design must be recognized before the expansion, with clear and complete alternative courses of action formulated, also in advance. In this way the firm can exploit a strength rather than create a weakness.

More firms each year are recognizing that one of their inherent weaknesses is a lack of research. Corporate research allows the entire innovative strength of a firm to be channelled through a specially designed and equipped area. Deciding to engage in research, however, cannot be done haphazardly. The design of the organization must be adjusted to enable all its innovative strength to be properly channelled. The various design alternatives may once again be considered in terms of their effect on the research effort. A functional design-structure may be more suitable to comprehensive research, as one example. Deciding to undertake research in itself does not ensure strength exploitation; design alternatives must be formulated as part of the planning process in this area.

The importance of design alternatives to the marketing function, and the subsequent exploiting of strengths, is perhaps most obvious. An organizational design based on product departmentation may be most advantageous to a firm which relies heavily on its marketing function. However, consideration during planning must also be given to other design alternatives as the particular environment and circumstance of any firm may indicate that other designs are more desirable.

In order to properly assess and exploit strengths or overcome weaknesses, the firm must engage in the planning process we have outlined in order to help clarify these variables. Once this has been completed, the design alternatives may be generated and applied in a systematic logical manner.

5. Institute Profit Improvement Plan

The institution of a profit improvement plan encompasses the entire area of cost accounting alternative methods. Basically what is required is to break down virtually every activity into detail. Targets are then set for improvement in each cost area. An important factor here is goal congruence, that is, the cost accounting system must reflect the objectives and constraints of the firm to be meaningful. In other words, when responsibilities are set for each executive he must have his attention focused on the goals of the company as well as the efficiency generated by the new accounting system.

Alternative courses of action when implementing, or considering the implementation of a profit improvement plan are many and varied. These alternatives should all be considered in terms of the firm's desired cost and profit relationship and further, as an integral part of company profit objectives. The cost accountant and the corporate planner must work closely together to generate those alternatives which coincide with the overall planning strategy of the firm, and thus improve those areas where weaknesses are currently evident.

Alternative generation is related to the various cost accounting alternative methods available to be used. For example, there are two ways of accounting for inventories, either the perpetual inventory method or the periodic inventory method. Cash flows can be discounted by time adjusted rate of return or net present value methods. Overhead variance rates can be calculated using either expected activity or practical capacity as the denominator base. Inventories may be costed according to the contribution or traditional approaches. Without expanding upon any of these alternatives it is sufficient to say that implementing a profit improvement plan can generate many alternative courses of action. It is the responsibility of the corporate planner and the cost accountant to strive for and achieve goal congruence when such a plan is considered.

6. Management Techniques

This last section of the analysis of alternative generation is most closely related to our theoretical discussion of alternative generation using the heuristic model. Management techniques are tools utilized to help solve problems. The applicability of specific techniques to each management problem must be the subject of careful consideration. The heuristic model is a technique which can be used by the corporate planner to identify important problem areas or help differentiate between alternative courses of action. Four pertinent comments can be made about the use of management techniques.

First, management techniques are highly specific and their application by the corporate planner is usually restricted to one or a few areas. For example, we have seen the applicability of the heuristic model for alternative generation, however, its use in product development may be limited. The problem at hand usually determines which technique can be used.

Second, because the problems of one company may not be those of another, two companies may not have the same need for any one technique or set of techniques.

Third, most complex firms require that a variety of management techniques be utilized in the planning process. In other words, to properly complete the planning process and arrive at a viable set of strategic plans, many management tools, from highly specialized to general knowledge types, must be applied.

Finally, the use of systematic and detailed management techniques has an effect on almost all areas of the organization. By systematically analyzing functions and operations, and making decisions as a result of this systematic analysis, improvements in efficiency, as well as profits, should result.

c) Alternative Generation in Stage B

The Argenti Model presents the company with three alternative courses of action when engaging in its planning process. These alternatives are, first, continue operations with the existing business, second, create a new business through diversification, and finally, liquidation. This analysis shall approach each of these alternatives separately on the assumption that the "firm" has elected this course of action. The various subalternatives which must be generated and analyzed under each major alternative will then be discussed.

1. The Existing Business

A decision to continue operations with the existing business results when the planners feel that, given the objectives and constraints, the firm can close its profit gap with its own resources. There are basically four alternative methods of reducing this gap.

First, the existing business may be reduced. This may take the form of; reducing the size of top management, if the firm is top heavy; reducing middle management, if communication is thwarted by a dense middle management belt; instituting short-cut methods to reduce costs, and other alternatives. It can be seen that many alternatives must be generated at each level of this process. By doing this, consistency with objectives and constraints is assured.

Second, the firm may decide to merely maintain its current position. This is a "status quo" approach usually followed by the less dynamic firms. This alternative requires more effort than a "do nothing" approach. Status Quo requires planning to maintain the firm's current position. "Do nothing" obviously requires no planning at all.

Third, the existing business may be expanded. Given that there is an under-utilization of resources, the firm may plan for better utilization thus adopting an expansionary policy. Finally the existing business can be "forced to act." This usually results from a poor assessment of the environment and subsequently, inaccurate objectives and constraints. For example, if the profit gap is overstated, the effort to reduce this gap might expand resources which need not have been committed.

A decision to continue operations with the existing business creates a situation where a large number of alternative courses of action are possible. We have indicated that proper assessment and objective setting are necessary to limit this infinite number of alternatives. It is also apparent, however, that some systematic approach to formulating these alternatives is necessary. The network concept is a method of generating these alternatives.

2. New Business

Assuming that the firm's planning process has been carefully completed, and that a decision to search for new business has been made, many alternatives are available. We must assume that certain obstacles lie in the path of the firm which tries to continue functioning with its present business, therefore, the decision to find a new business has been made. The decision to diversify can be influenced from other sources as well.

When considering alternative diversification actions, the corporate planner, at this alternative generation stage, cannot recommend one unequivocal course of action. Some of the less desirable actions are eliminated because of the objectives and constraints of the firm and/or because these alternatives merely reflect the obstacles which initially brought about the decision to diversify. The remaining alternatives should be subjected to a systematic analysis, as each acceptable major diversification alternative carries with it may subalternatives. The following include alternative diversification actions that should help clarify this concept.

First, the firm may analyze the alternative of forward integration. If the firm's current product requires further processing after leaving the plant, merger or purchase of such a processing plant may be considered. Depending on the complexity of the product and the channels of distribution, the various forward integration alternatives may be many or few.

Second, the firm may analyze the possibility of backward integration. Alternatives here include purchase or merger with raw materials suppliers, transport companies, initial raw material processors or any combination of the three.

Third, the firm may diversify by selling a new product in the same market, or four, by selling a new product in a new market. Alternative courses of action are many and varied in this section. A final alternative course of action may be to diversify by finding new markets for the old product. Once again, the possible alternatives are many and varied, such as buying-out competitors, wholesalers, agent distributors and others.

In conclusion, when the various alternatives concerned with diversification are analyzed two important facts must be of prime concern to the corporate planner. First, diversification often brings on substantial extra costs and financial risks. Thus diversification opportunities, or alternatives, must be carefully reviewed. Second, diversification should not be used as a substitute for exploiting other possible opportunities in the present product area.[9] Diversification can change the make-up of the firm but it may not alter the objectives of the firm.

3. Liquidation

The alternative of voluntary liquidation is considered after the analysis of all other courses of action indicate that the firm has no chance of achieving a profit that is sufficient to give the shareholders a satisfactory return. A company should consider the various alternatives associated with liquidation, even if only the remotest chance of such an alternative course of action being implemented exists. Liquidation is considered here as a single alternative to demonstrate its finality and second, its reflection of poor planning by the firm.

The purpose of this section was to analyze alternative generation and to indicate where network analysis could be utilized. This having been accomplished, we can now see the relationship between systematic network analysis and alternative generation in the planning process. It has been indicated that many techniques can be utilized to generate and assess alternatives; however, in view of the theoretical analysis results presented earlier, network analysis appears to be an efficient and effective technique.

SUMMARY

This chapter has dealt with the discussion of practical planning models available to the corporate planner. One must consider the definition of a model in order to realize its significance. A model is an analogy used to visualize, usually in simplified form, the processes of the real world. It serves to guide the corporate planner through the maze of details that would otherwise be overwhelming. Thus, the model serves as a useful tool for the corporate planner in organizing and processing the maze of details into a number of feasible alternatives or proposed solutions.

ENDNOTES

1. J. Argenti, *Systematic Corporate Planning,* (London: T. Nelson, 1974) p. 41.
2. Ibid., p. 42.
3. Ibid., p. 130.
4. Ibid., p. 137.
5. H.I. Ansoff, *Business Strategy* (Middlesex: Penguin, 1969), p. 7.
6. Ibid., p. 12.
7. R. Cyert & J. March, *A Behavioral Theory of the Firm,* (Englewood Cliffs: Prentice-Hall, 1963) p. 253-267.
8. Ibid., p. 263
9. H.I. Ansoff, p. 295.

CASE

TRIANGLE CONSTRUCTION COMPANY, INC.

Alf Jacobson, the President of Triangle Construction Company, was born in Sweden in 1924. He was educated in Sweden and received a degree comparable to a Bachelor of Science in Civil Engineering in 1945 from the Stockholm Institute of Technology. His major was structural design, and after graduation he worked for five years as a consulting engineer in Stockholm. The main part of his work there was in construction of large industrial plants.

Alf came to America in 1950 and stayed in Chicago for two years, working for one of the major building contractors as a chief engineer. His basic duty was surveying layout areas. In 1952 he returned to Sweden to his position as consulting engineer.

In 1953, Alf came back to the United States and went to California. He obtained a job with Fredickson and Watson Construction Company, a large engineering and grading contractor. It was in California that he started working on highway construction. His work consisted of estimating and bidding jobs, managing work, and acting as superintendent of some of Fredickson and Watson's largest construction jobs.

In 1962, Alf left Fredickson and Watson and, together with two partners, formed the Triangle Construction Company, with the base of his operations in Tucson, Arizona. "We started on a fairly small scale with capitalization of approximately $30,000. We had pretty good fortune. We kept going, and we increased our gross each year and also were able to purchase small amounts of machinery," Alf commented.

In 1965, Alf bought out his two partners and thus obtained a majority of the stock. At that time he brought in a new partner that was only interested in the company from a financial point of view, and Alf became president of the Triangle Construction Company. The population of Tucson in 1968 was estimated to be near 250,000. Phoenix was about 500,000, while Pima and Maricopa Counties' combined population was estimated to be near 1.2 million.

Copyright 1974 by Brigham Young University. This case was prepared by Mr. Bryan A. Lowe and Professor Melvin J. Stanford as a basis for class discussion. This case is disguised. Used by permission. All rights reserved.

The private work consisted of subdivisions and parking lots: basically the earth-moving portions, the concrete block work, curb and gutters, drainage structures, drainage pipes, and asphalt pavings. In public works, Triangle constructed bridges and larger concrete structures. In 1968 Triangle was not doing any large structural work but normally sublet this type of work out to specialty contractors.

Triangle had also diversified into Construction Equipment rentals and ran this subsidiary as a separate entity. The earnings and other financial data were consolidated into the Triangle Construction Company's financial statements (see Exhibits 1 through 4). Triangle had increased in volume from a modest half-million dollars in 1962 to approximately two million dollars a year, which was gross for 1967-1968. (Exhibit 3). The joint venture business was not included in those figures (Exhibit 4).

The largest contract that Triangle had been involved in was the joint-venture contract for Interstate road construction, near Flagstaff, Arizona. The joint-venture partners were Babel Sand and Gravel Company, Triangle Construction Company, and Barton Construction Company. Triangle had the engineering and administrative responsibilities, and Babel was supplying the bonding capacity and equipment (rented to the joint venture). Barton was participating with Triangle in administrative duties. Because of relative size and financial position, Babel had 50 percent interest in the contract, while Triangle and Barton shared equally the other 50 percent.

The number of contracts for construction work had increased tremendously during the 1960's in Arizona. All surveys appeared to indicate a continued growth, even though not necessarily at a uniform rate. A heavy program of construction was expected to continue into the 1970's and even the 1980's. For the engineering contractor, the prospects for work looked very good volumewise.

Arizona was expected to have a continued influx of residents. More homes, schools, churches, and business establishments would have to be built. Road construction would be less affected by such influx, however. The growth of road construction tended to be cyclical in nature, even though there was an overall upward trend. During the late 1960's the road-building industry had experienced a substantial decline in Arizona. The years of the early 1960's were probably the best in the area, with the peak coming in 1965.

Subdivision developers were finding it difficult to meet the current and future demands for construction. The sharp rise in expenditures for the war in Vietnam and the international monetary problems had made the money market extremely tight. Consequently, the cost of capital was going up and reached a point in 1968 where there was often no money available at any reasonable price. This caused subdividers to postpone their plans for expansion. The number of subdivisions in the city of Tucson and county of Pima during 1967 dropped off 50 percent from previous years.

This downward trend in construction had made it very hard for individual engineering firms. It caused price cutting and nearcost competitive bidding.

Management of labor and equipment was difficult, for if a contractor geared himself for a peak demand he would have a hard time trying to utilize the skilled manpower and equipment when the work slackened. Reduction of manpower, machinery sitting idle, and postponed purchases of new equipment, made it hard to maintain orderly scheduling of work. A small contractor with a limited number of pieces of equipment and a limited number of men had an easier management task than the larger contractors when demand fluctuated sharply. The flexibility was generally greater for the smaller firm; but because of limited amounts of equity capital, such declines can be fatal to a highly leveraged firm.

There had been a trend for smaller construction companies to be absorbed into larger firms. One of the main difficulties of the smaller company was the lack of availability of raw materials for construction projects. The deposits that were suitable for production of crushed-rock bases, asphalt, and concrete were pretty well known and had been under lease or ownership of larger companies that quite often combined their raw material production with contracting in their own names. The construction company that did not have its own aggregate sources would, in the future, have a hard time remaining competitive. The purchasing of raw materials involved a profit by the manufacturer. The construction company that had to buy these materials from the manufacturer would place another profit on them. The raw material producer, therefore, could contract a job on a more competitive basis because he would often be satisfied with just one increment of profit in order to get the work.

The major partner in the joint-venture Babel-Triangle-Barton was Babel Sand and Rock Company, with headquarters in Prescott, Arizona. The president of Babel was Mike Hebert, a personal friend of Alf Jacobson. They had met several years previously and had business connections together during Alf's employment with Fredickson and Watson Construction Company. During the latter part of 1967, Mr. Hebert called on Alf and said he was contemplating bidding on a large project near Phoenix, Arizona, and wondered if Alf would like to go over the high points of the job with him. During their conversation, the idea of combining their two companies and bidding on the job as a joint venture came up and was discussed.

The history of Babel went back a number of years to its original founder who operated a small sand and rock business in Prescott. A Mr. Fred Roberson took over sometime in the 1940's and built up the company and apparently had a very successful business venture. However, he died in 1964 and was succeeded as President by his oldest son, Tom Roberson. Apparently Tom wasn't particularly interested in remaining head of the corporation and was succeeded by Mr. Mike Hebert, who was married to Fred Roberson's oldest daughter and, through marriage, had an interest in the business.

Mr. Hebert was by profession a certified public accountant and had a large public accounting office in Prescott, Arizona. In addition, he had a half a dozen other business enterprises in the geographical area surrounding Prescott. He admittedly was not an expert in construction, though he possessed a fair knowledge of the business itself.

Babel Sand and Rock Company was incorporated under the laws of the State of Arizona on June 1, 1965, as successor to the business originally founded in the 1940's. The Company's principal activities were as follows: (1)the processing and sale of basic construction materials, i.e., rock mix (a portion of the basic materials processed was used in the company's own construction projects); (2)the performance of public and private construction contracts covering highways, street and bridges, on-site and off-site subdivision improvements, and water, sewer, and drainage projects; and (3) the rental of its construction equipment to other contractors.

Babel's products were sold throughout the Prescott area of Yauapai County, Arizona. Construction contract work was generally limited to the same locality. That area, in terms of construction activity, represented about 25 percent of the total of such activity in the entire county of Yauapai.

Babel's general offices, maintenance facilities, and equipment storage yard were located in Prescott. The Prescott ready-mix concrete plant was also at this location.

Other permanent Babel facilities were as follows:

Ash Fork   -   Aggregate (rock and sand) plant, asphalt plant, and ready mix concrete plant.

Prescott   -   Aggregate plant, asphalt plant, and ready mix concrete plant (see above).

Cottonwood- Aggregate plant and asphalt plant.

Each of these locations had its own source of raw materials at the plant site. All plant sites and raw material deposits were owned by Babel or its shareholders.

The Prescott area, having experienced sustained population growth since the early 1950's, was by 1968 one of the key centers of construction activity in Yauapai and Coconino counties, as can be seen in a breakdown of building permit valuatons:

	Permit $ Valuation	Percent To Total
Flagstaff	$22,077,340	28
Prescott	19,337,570	24
All Other Areas	37,842,700	48
	$79,257,610	100

The major centers of population in the area were as follows:

1.	Prescott	15,000
2.	Williams	3,500
3.	Flagstaff	33,000

The city of Flagstaff had long been noted as one of the nation's popular and growing resort areas. During the 1967-1968 season, direct airline flights were begun to the city from major areas of Arizona.

It should be noted, however, that growth in the Prescott area had generally been greater than that of Flagstaff itself. These communities had increased in size by 78 percent between 1960 and 1966.

In the decade 1950 to 1960, the cities of Prescott and Cottonwood recorded Yavapai County's highest and third highest percentage gains in population for the ten-year period. They increased by 84 percent and 76 percent, respectively.

In the short term, there were indications that the desert area was on the threshold of a period of greatly-increased construction activity. Building permits in 1968 in the Prescott area have increased about 40 percent over the 1967 level. There was impending a substantial, well-rounded program for the construction of industrial, commercial, and residential units, together with street improvements and additional freeway construction. Some indication of these developments is shown by the following:

Description of Job	Budgeted Amount
Highway 89 to Ash Fork	$33,026,000
Highway 89A Cottonwood	986,000
Interstate 17 near Flagstaff	11,000,000
	$45,012,000

The above projects, all of which called for very substantial amounts of basic construction materials, were due to be bid by the middle of 1969.

Since Babel's inception, it had achieved and maintained a dominant position in the market in its particular fields. This was especially true with regard to the supply of basic construction materials. It was estimated that Babel provided approximately 75 percent of all of such materials used in its marketing area. Such materials were either put in place by Babel itself or were sold for placement by others.

Competition in contracting operations had been keen, especially in recent years. There was only one other contractor actually based in the area, however, who could be considered equal to Babel in ownership of equipment, bonding capacity, and construction experience.

As of 1968, the following were the officers and key personnel of Babel Sand and Rock Company:

President - Mike Hebert
Secretary - Thomas Roberson
Treasurer - Daniel Roberson

The following were additional key personnel:

Name	Title	Age	Years with Babel
Howard Watson	Chief Engineer	49	14
Jack Gibson	Construction Superintendent	47	22
Marvin Glenn	Maintenance Superintendent	51	21
Harold Babcock	Plant Production Superintendent	44	21
John Adams	Chief Accountant	37	9

The ownership of Babel at July 31, 1967 was:

Capital stock ($100 par value)
  Authorized -- 15,000 shares
  Issued and outstanding—

Thomas Roberson	2,976 shares
Daniel Roberson	2,976 shares
Mike and Janet Hebert	5,952 shares
	11,904 shares

Due to personal federal income tax considerations, no dividends had ever been paid on the capital stock.

Year-end consolidated balance sheets at July 31, 1966, 1967, and 1968, are found in Exhibit 5. A summary of Federal income tax returns covering the years 1947 through 1968 is given in Exhibit 6. Such statements had been prepared either directly from Babel's Federal income tax returns or from the Company's audited financial statements. Babel's tax returns had been audited and closed by the Internal Revenue Service through 1963.

In the years since Babel's inception, it had seen fit to conduct various phases of its business through subsidiary companies. Babel Investment Company controlled these subsidiaries, and its statements were consolidated with Babel Sand and Rock Company. All financial data contained in Exhibits 5 and 6 were consolidated in order to reflect the operations of Babel as one economic entity.

The invitation to some sort of a joint venture between Babel and Triangle was born out of the fact that Alf Jacobsen had an extensive background in the engineering and construction field, and Mike Hebert felt that Alf could supplement Mr. Hebert's own limited knowledge of construction. The first project that they discussed in Phoenix was a large undertaking, and they felt that bidding it was premature. Subsequent to that project they discussed several other contracts and bid on one or two projects without being the successful bidder. Also, they bid on the current job in Flagstaff, in which they were low bidders: they got this contract in February of 1968.

The idea of a closer tie between the two companies had come up for discussion and at September 1, 1968 was developing toward a possible merger of the two firms, Triangle Construction Company and Babel Sand and Rock Company. Alf Jacobsen felt that it would be advantageous for Triangle Construction Company to enter into a merger for the following reasons:

1. The natural resources of sand and rock and asphalt plants that Babel has would provide a suitable competitive backgound to get work in the Prescott and Flagstaff areas.
2. The competition in the general area of Prescott was pretty well limited to one other company with similar raw materials, resources, men and equipment to enter a bid and enter into contract of any size in that area.
3. The Babel Sand and Rock Company had considerable assets in equipment and also in capital that would help to provide a basis to tackle larger jobs. In that respect, the greater economic resources would allow bonding on a larger project that would otherwise be prohibitive for a smaller construction company.
4. The specialized financial knowledge that Mr. Mike Hebert possessed would help the combined company and would prove to be very helpful in any business decision they make in the future.

Alf felt that there were obviously some disadvantages in going ahead with a merger. The area of the main business of Babel Sand and Rock Company was isolated from major population centers. Prescott is surrounded by some small towns, but the construction activities were not great in any one of them.

Babel's market area for sand, rock and asphalt was basically concentrated in the Prescott-Flagstaff area. Along with these factors, Alf Jacobsen was concerned about the loss of control of his own business. In preparation for further merger discussions with Mike Hebert, he began a thorough review of the financial and other data to get a better idea for himself just what the relative positions of the parties might be in a merged company.

EXHIBIT 1
TRIANGLE CONSTRUCTION COMPANY, INC.
CONSOLIDATED STATEMENT OF FINANCIAL POSITION
JUNE 30, 1968

ASSETS

Current Assets:

Cash on hand & in banks		$ 22,463.13	
Accounts receivable	$188,545.75		
Less: Allowance for doubtful accounts	6,976.53	181,569.22	
Notes receivable		775.59	
Due from Babel-Triangle-Barton Joint			
Venture (Note 1)		25,000.00	
Cost of jobs in progress		4,855.54	
Prepaid expenses		5,884.00	
Total current assets			$240,547.48

Fixed Assets:

Cost		220,553.50	
Accumulated depreciation		137,395.45	
Net book value			83,158.05

Other Assets:

Real estate—pledged		17,884.30	
Due from Triangle-Barton Joint Venture		336.31	
Due from shareholder		8,100.00	
Deposits		2,484.90	
Organization expenses—net		59.76	
Total other assets			28,865.27
Total assets			$352,570.80

Reference is made to the accompanying letter and note to financial statements (Exhibit 4).

LIABILITIES AND CAPITAL

Current Liabilities:

Accounts payable		$121,765.21	
Note payable—due shareholder		15,000.00	
contracts payable	$ 27,425.75		
Less: Long-term portion	4,059.23	23,366.50	
Mortgage payable—due shareholders	12,065.73		
Less: Long-term portion	10,349.73	1,716.00	
Payroll taxes withheld and accrued		4,738.84	
Accrued federal income tax		4,474.04	
Accrued expenses		14,073.96	
Total current liabilities			$185,133.55

Long-term Liabilities:

Contracts payable		$ 4,059.23	
Mortgage payable		10,349.73	
Total long-term liabilities			14,408.96

Capital:

Capital stock		$ 33,391.00	
Retained earnings		119,637.29	
Total capital			153,028.29
Total liabilities and capital			$352,570.80

EXHIBIT 2
TRIANGLE CONSTRUCTION COMPANY, INC.
CONSOLIDATED STATEMENT OF RETAINED EARNINGS
JUNE 30, 1968

	Triangle Construction	Triangle Equipment	Total
Balances—June 1, 1968	$96,172.75	$49,198.25	$145,371.00
Adjustment of over accural of federal income taxes—year ended June 30, 1967	2,816.09	939.00	3,755.09
Refund due from Internal Revenue resulting from current year's loss carryback	2,008.99		2,008.99
Net income (loss)—year ended June 30, 1968 (Exhibit 4)	(47,648.17)	21,623.69	(26,024.48)
Net loss Alpha Division—year ended June 30, 1967	(999.27)		(999.27)
Provision for federal income taxes—year ended June 30, 1968		(4,474.04)	(4,474.04)
Balances—June 30, 1968	$52,350.39	$67,286.90	$119,637.29

Reference is made to the accompanying letter and note to financial statements.

EXHIBIT 3
TRIANGLE CONSTRUCTION COMPANY, INC.
CONSOLIDATED STATEMENT OF NET INCOME
JUNE 30, 1968

	Amount		%
Sales		$1,660,163.47	100.00
Cost of Sales		1,594,755.58	96.06
Gross profit		65,397.89	3.94
Sales Expenses			
Sales salaries	$ 1,950.00		.12
Travel and entertainment	3,070.87		.18
Auto lease	5,322.69		.32
Plans and specs	677.23		.04
Advertising	141.00		.01
Total sales expenses		11,166.79	.76
		$ 54,231.10	3.27
Administrative Expenses			
Clerical salaries	$17,907.08		1.08
Officers salaries	25,925.00		1.56
Office supplies	2,256.56		.14
Postage	225.99		.01
Rent	1,800.00		.11
Dues and subscriptions	2,329.42		.14
Legal and accounting	2,877.20		.17
Telephone	6,019.79		.36
Office maintenance	747.75		.05
Bad debts	2,643.61		.16
Group insurance	808.44		.05
Equipment rental	1,870.00		.11
Taxes and licenses	7,311.47		.44
Insurance—general	494.33		.03
Amortization of organization expense	59.69		.00
Utilities	988.72		.06
Depreciation—office equipment	260.67		.02
Commissions and bonus	1,103.76		.07
Total administrative expenses		75,629.48	4.56
		($ 21,398.38)	(1.29)
Other Expenses—Net			
Purchase discounts	($ 675.61)		(.04)
Interest income	(1,168.51)		(.07)
Miscellaneous	(240,57)		(.01)
Gain on sale of equipment	(428.53)		(.03)
Interest expense	7,139.32		.43
Other expenses—net		$ 4,628.10	.28
Net loss—(To Exhibit 3)		($ 26,024.48)	(1.57)

Reference is made to the accompany letter and note to financial statements (Exhibit 4).

EXHIBIT 4

TRIANGLE CONSTRUCTION COMPANY, INC.
NOTE TO FINANCIAL STATMENTS

Note   1:

In February, 1968, the company entered into a joint venture with two other construction companies to construct a section of Arizona freeway. The original bid price of the venture was $3,888,047.50. Triangle Construction's share of the venture will be 25% of the profit or loss.

The joint venture keeps its own books and records which were not available for our inspection and we were informed at this time that they have not been audited by independent accountants. Our examination, therefore, was restricted to confirmation of a $25,000.00 loan made to the venture and physical verification of the construction equipment rented to the joint venture.

Completion date of the joint venture is March, 1969, at which time collection of the loan is intended. We were informed that the joint venture was 37% complete at June 30, 1968, which is approximately seven percent ahead of schedule.

EXHIBIT 5
TRIANGLE CONSTRUCTION COMPANY, INC.
BABEL SAND AND ROCK CO. AND
BABEL INVESTMENT CO.
BALANCE SHEETS

ASSETS	June 30, 1966	June 30, 1967	June 30, 1968
CURRENT ASSETS			
CASH	$ 48,639.47	$ 33,520.56	$ 87,478.67
NOTES AND ACCOUNTS RECEIVABLE (NET)	1,636,078.87	1,117,801.91	851,623.61
INVENTORIES	62,495.71	171,434.15	196,737.96
OTHER CURRENT ASSETS	31,505.15	17,058.34	58,842.86
TOTAL CURRENT ASSETS	$1,778,719.20	$1,339,814.98	$1,194,683.10
LESS: CURRENT LIABILITIES	826,167.58	749,573.29	438,199.56
NET WORKING CAPITAL	$ 952,551.62	$ 590,241.69	$ 756,483.54
FIXED ASSETS (LESS RESERVES FOR DEPRECIATION)	998,297.46	995,878.03	914,664.50
OTHER ASSETS	109,700.78	103,694.68	100,676.24
TOTAL ASSETS (NET)	$2,060,549.86	$1,689,814.40	$1,771,824.28
LIABILITIES AND CAPITAL			
LONG TERM LIABILITIES	$ 301,228.59	$ 237,191.42	$ 263,024.98
CAPITAL AND SURPLUS	1,759,321.27	1,452,622.98	1,508,799.30
TOTAL LONG TERM LIABILITIES AND CAPITAL	$2,060,549.86	$1,689,814.40	$1,771,824.28

EXHIBIT 6
TRIANGLE CONSTRUCTION COMPANY, INC.
BABEL SAND AND ROCK CO. AND BABEL INVESTMENT CO.
SUMMARY OF FEDERAL INCOME TAX RETURNS
COVERING THE YEARS 1949 THROUGH 1968
YEAR ENDING JUNE 30

	Total Income	Operating Expenses	*Operating Profit	Depreciation	Net Profit
1949	$ 459,123.92	$ 361,828.96	$ 97,840.96	$ 42,938.40	$ 54,902.56
1950	546,053.67	433,796.57	112,257.10	52,052.89	60,204.21
1951	504,506.71	400,484.00	104,002.71	62,423.41	41,500.30
1952	481,244.83	363,383.84	117,860.99	58,991.51	58,869.48
1953	574,517.92	464,600.65	109,917.27	47,941.75	61,975.52
1954	602,949.76	487,678.27	115,271.49	52,972.57	62,298.92
1955	672,105.37	558,265.98	112,839.39	50,713.65	63,125.74
1956	794,259.24	664,381.14	129,878.10	71,879.79	57,998.31
1957	1,330,409.03	1,052,406.68	278,002.35	110,882.30	167,120.05
1958	1,936,064.27	1,526,219.22	409,845.05	118,503.31	291,341.74
1959	2,594,071.57	2,163,658.35	430,413.22	191,297.34	239,115.88
1960	4,093,417.54	3,370,244.48	723,173.06	297,376.34	425,796.34
1961	5,125,484.23	4,513,647.03	611,837.20	447,123.86	164,713.34
1962	4,133,843.37	3,618,847.02	514,986.35	442,697.60	72,288.75
1963	4,533,233.12	3,934,653.62	598,579.51	459,232.89	139,346.62
1964	5,474,852.70	4,966,560.14	508,292.56	426,026.74	82,265.82
1965	6,661,680.62	6,236,720.22	424,960.40	430,968.91	(6,008.51)
1966	4,600,140.61	4,267,845.60	332,295.01	266,193.22	66,101.79
1967	4,911,590.58	4,502,514.33	409,076.25	289,307.19	119,796.06
1968	6,981,321.27	6,581,418.84	399,902.43	301,203.99	89,698.44
TOTAL	$57,010,870.34	$50,468,618.94	$6,542,251.40	$4,229,728.04	$2,312,523.36

NOTE:
(1)   The above totals are for the twenty year period.
(2)   *Operating profit excludes depreciation.
(3)   Net profit as indicated above is before percentage depletion allowance and Federal income tax.

EVALUATION OF THE
TRIANGLE CONSTRUCTION COMPANY CASE

SUMMARY

The Triangle Construction Company, Inc. case involves the potential merger of Triangle Construction Company with Babel Sand and Rock Company. Triangle Construction was formed in 1962, with its base of operations in Tucson, Arizona, by three partners and subsequently controlled by Alf Jacobson in a partner stock interest buy-out in 1965. At this time an additional partner was obtained, but the only involvement of the partner was a financial one. Alf became president of the Triangle Construction Company, Inc.

Historically, Triangle Construction Company's contracts had been 60-70 percent private work, and the remaining 30-40 percent had been public work. Both kinds of contracts, private and public, proved to be equally profitable. The largest portion of the contracts was acquired through competitive bidding, with a very small portion being negotiated. Triangle had shown growth from a contract volume of one-half million in 1962 to approximately two million gross in 1967-68. Industry trends in the highly cyclical construction industry caused the decision to expand his capital base and thereby increase the competitive position of Triangle relative to other larger construction companies. There had been a trend for smaller companies to be absorbed into larger firms. Construction in Arizona, such as housing, was experiencing a very cyclical but continued growth and was anticipated to continue into the 1970's and even into the 1980's. During 1967 there was a substantial decline in new road construction, which tended to be cyclical in nature even though there was an overall upward trend.

Babel Sand and Rock Company is a closely-held single family owned business pre-dating the 1940's. All 11,904 of its $100 par outstanding shares are owned by four family members. Mr. Fred Roberson took control in the mid-forties and expanded the business substantially up to his death in 1964. Tom Roberson, his oldest son, succeeded as president. However, due to lack of interest in remaining as corporate head, Tom Roberson passed control to Mike Herbert, who was married to Fred Roberson's oldest daughter, and through marriage, had an interest in the business. Mr. Hebert was a Certified Public Accountant with an office in Prescott, Arizona. He also maintained interest in half a dozen other business enterprises in the geographical area surrounding Prescott. He was not an expert in construction but did possess a fair knowledge of the business itself. Babel's products are: (1) the processing and sale of basic construction materials, i.e., rock mix; (2) the performance of public and private construction contracts covering highways, street and bridges, on-site and off-site subdivision improvement, and water, sewer, and drainage projects; and (3) the rental of its construction equipment to other contractors. Discussion relative to combining the expertise of Hebert and Jacobson in joint venture bidding on contracts occurred in early 1968 and resulted in successful low bids on a contract in February 1968. Continued discussion in this direction has occurred up to the present time.

KEY ISSUES

1. Is the proposed expansion necessary?
2. Is the proposed organization structure conducive to efficient managerial autonomy?
3. Are the proposed individual goals and objectives congruent with the overall organization goals?
4. What is the potential for smooth operations concerning the additional business interest held by both parties?
5. Have strategic plans for the proposed organization been made?

DISCUSSION

1. Expansion

Triangle Construction Company is presently showing a loss at the rate of 1.57 percent of its sales. Since the highly competitive bidding procedures of the construction industry, especially during a slack period of building, generate very small gross profits (3.94 percent) because of the high cost of sales (96.06 percent); this added to the fixed administrative, miscellaneous, and variable selling expenses totalling 5.49 percent of sales, leaves the company in a deteriorating position unless its cost of sales percentage can be reduced. The Triangle Equipment division is providing a source of cash capital which presently is being absorbed by the losses of the construction company (consolidated revenue).

In a recent joint venture with Babel, Triangle, and Barton Construction Company, additional financial bonding capacity was 50 percent of total interest, with Triangle and Barton having 25 percent each. Presently, of the public works contracts held by Triangle, for bridge and larger concrete structures, they are not doing any large part of the structural work and normally sublet this type of work out to specialty contractors. The downward trend of construction made it difficult for individual firms because of the price cutting and near cost bidding. One of the main difficulties of the smaller company was the lack of availability of raw materials for construction projects. Larger construction firms usually owned their own aggregate sources which enables their competitive bid to not include a typical profit for the aggregate producer which the independent small contractor would have to include. This single increment of profit allowed for a lower bid by the large company and increased the number of contracts which could be secured to produce revenue. Industry trends seemed to indicate that the construction company that did not have its own raw material aggregate sources would, in the future, have a hard time remaining competitive.

Babel's current financial statement shows a cash position with a debt-equity ratio of .17. The net working capital is 43 percent of the total assets thereby providing a good position for bonding capacity, however, these capital assets are showing potential idleness in the years 1961 through 1968. Increased operating expenses, depreciation and a deterioration of net profits implies inefficient utilization of these assets. This, however, may not be completely accurate since all the Babel Investment Company controlled subsidiaries operations are consolidated into the Babel Sand and Rock Company entity financial report. Therefore, a more complete analysis of the exact position would require a breakout of these separate entities.

2. Organization Structure

The potential merger is seen by Hebert as being advantageous since the extensive background in the engineering and construction field held by Alf Jacobson would greatly supplement Hebert's own limited knowledge of construction. Additionally, Hebert's specialized financial knowledge would help the combined companies in future business decisions. The geographic location of Babel's raw material plants poses some degree of dysfunction to the Triangle bidding potential since they are situated somewhat separated from major population centers. The substantial assets of Babel relative to Triangle, could undermine Jacobson's autonomy within his company since Hebert will probably not wish to relinquish control of family assets in connection with construction. The expertise to be provided by Alf to the Babel organization potentially would not increase the overall expertise or abilities of its existing engineers and construction personnel.

3. Goals

A company geared for peak demand will tend to incur idle capacity of fixed assets during slack periods of construction. This can cause problems with scheduling of work, possibly lost profits. Flexibility is generally greater for smaller firms during slack periods since there is a smaller amount of fixed equipment and manpower to be utilized but because of limited amounts of equity capital, declines could cause difficulties. Babel construction contract work represented about 25 percent of the total of such activity for Yavapai County, Arizona. Its facilities were located in Prescott and two smaller towns. Prescott: General Office, ready-mix concrete plant and asphalt plant; Ash Fork: Aggregate plant, asphalt plant and ready-mix concrete plant; Cottonwood: Aggregate plant and asphalt plant. Since Babel's inception, it had achieved and maintained a dominant position in the market in its particular fields. This was especially true with regard to the supply of basic construction materials. It was estimated that Babel provided approximately 75 percent of all of such materials used in its marketing area which were either put in place by Babel itself or sold for placement by others. There was only one other contractor actually based in the area who could be considered equal to Babel in ownership of equipment, bonding capacity, and construction experience.

4. Additional Business Interests

The Babel Investment Company's interest will have to be dealt with closely in any merger agreement. The construction functions and equipment rental functions of both Babel and Triangle can more easily be evaluated relative to the new organizational strategies. A separation of power will probably have to occur such as Jacobson heading the construction and bidding phases and Hebert advising and directing financial matters and administering investment functions to increase the merged organization's assets. Possible difficulties could arise between Jacobson and the existing construction personnel of Babel; the additional interest of Babel might require separation from Jacobson's interest in a proposed merger.

5. Strategic Planning

The proposed organization has not specifically determined the strategies by which goals and objectives can be established. Strong emphasis must be placed in the area of peak maximization of the existing equipment of both companies to increase efficiency in the bidding and acquisition of project contracts of all sizes. Additionally, planning should include the supplying of idle capacity of the companies to other contractors. Responsibility accounting should be implemented with financial accounting procedures established to insure organizational goal congruency. Growth projections, goals and objectives must be identified by each separate entity and analyzed to determine inconsistencies. These results can then be integrated into an overall strategy.

ALTERNATIVE CONSIDERATIONS

The following include some of the factors that should be considered by the planning analyst in evaluating the alternatives available in this case.

1. The companies can continue to exist as separate entities.

   Advantages: Both companies can maintain their own autonomy. Risks as encountered at present will continue. Minimal internal organizational shake-up.

   Disadvantages: Potential lost profits to both companies since contract bidding of materials for projects cannot be optimized. Combination of expertise in construction and financial areas will not be fully realized. Probable increased costs to both companies due to inefficiency of operations and asset utilization. Inflexible organization structures. Inefficiency in long-range planning and strategy. Lack of feedback and expertise interrelation required to handle larger project contracts.

2. The companies can develop a joint venture of contracts.

   Advantages: Increased profits to both companies due to expertise and assets utilization efficiencies. Dissolution of association can be quickly implemented merely by dissolving the joint venture. Larger projects can be more easily handled by combining assets. Increase in market share in the geographic area. Allows for an analysis period through which evaluation of cooperation can be determined without the commitments of a more permanent association. Provides a period for analysis of strategy plans relating to merger possibilities and proposed organization structure.

Disadvantages: Additional accounting procedures will have to be implemented to control the joint venture operations. Organizational responsibility will have to be established relative to the various aspects and relationships of the joint venture. Profit distribution criteria will have to be established. Long-term association and industry reputation as a single entity of operation and capacity cannot be attained. Outside financing may be more difficult. Autonomy of individuals within the Babel company might be disrupted because of responsibility changes.

3. Triangle Construction Company Inc. and Babel Sand and Rock Company can merge.

Advantages: Combination of expertise and assets to increase profits and market share in geographic area. Capitalization potential available through stock issue. Larger projects possible due to asset/expertise merger. The merger would make them competitive to the one other firm in the Prescott/Flagstaff area with comparable resources to enter into contracts of any size in that area. Modified accounting procedures can monitor performance of the entity relative to organization goals.

Disadvantages: Babel's market area for sand, rock and asphalt was basically concentrated in the Prescott/Flagstaff area. Loss of control, potentially, of Alf Jacobson of his company due to asset disproportionality. Family-owned Babel may not like the entrance of an outsider into its upper circle. Potential necessity to separate other Babel holdings from the new organization. Organization restructure to include the Triangle organization. Personnel in the Babel organization involved with construction might resent the aspect of working for Jacobson or Jacobson personnel with the Babel organization.

A PROPOSED APPROACH

The following represents a possible approach to arriving at a solution to the present case. This proposal is not intended, however, to represent the optimum or right solution but is simply illustrative of one way of approaching this type of strategic problem. The steps are shown in terms of a short-range and long-range sequence.

Short-range:

1. Implement a joint venture of contracts in the areas of contract bidding, constuction, and equipment rental operations.

2. Begin analysis of contribution for each of the business interests held by both organizations to determine relevancy, profitability and asset contribution.

3. Set up performance evaluation criteria by which the contribution of personnel and operations procedures can be determined. This program can be useful in the determination of cooperation and work/project efficiency of each of the organization bodies.

4. Provide separate accounting controls for the joint venture from those of the two companies.

5. Provide an analysis which can evaluate the potential asset proportion on which further planning can be based. Outline a proposed merged organizational structure considering present upper management levels.

6. Establish a strategic plan which sets specific goals and objectives for the proposed merged organizations and guidelines for their implementation.

7. Based on the analysis results obtained from the above six criteria, implement the merger of the two companies if the analysis shows positive reaction to each of the established strategic guidelines. A time limit should also be established by which the merger decision must be made. This will not only call for action to be taken in a positive direction but will not tie the two companies up in an open-ended situation.

Long-range:

1. Initiate procedures to merge Triangle Construction Company, Triangle Equipment Company, and Babel Sand and Rock Company.

2. Begin an analysis to determine the feasibility of a holding company absorbing the assets of the above companies as well as the additional business interest associated with Babel.

3. Develop financial and cost accounting controls for the new organization based on goals and objectives as established in the organization strategic plans.

4. Investigate areas in which further cost of sales percentages can be reduced.

5. Develop a marketing strategy for the services and materials available from the combined organization.

The resulting organizational strategy should incorporate planning guidelines which allow for calculated growth, minimizing potential risks and maximizing asset utilization for goal congruency. These guidelines are the standards to measure performance against the goals and objectives of the organization.

Strategy Implementation and Control

STRATEGY IMPLEMENTATION

In previous chapters we have discussed how the organization selects a portfolio of alternatives from the list of alternatives which are available to the firm and how the plan(s) is developed. The final step in the process is the implementation of the strategic plan. This is necessary so that an appraisal may be made of the strategic planning process.

The development of the strategic plan is a meaningless exercise if it is not eventually implemented by the organization. We have seen how the plan has progressed through the various steps which included an examination of the environment, the determination of organizational goals, the gap analysis and the selection of a group of alternatives. In each of these steps, the focal point has been at the corporate management level. Now the process must be reversed and the strategic plan implemented in the lower levels of the organization. Implementation of the strategic plan could therefore be viewed as a reversal of the micro-process which was discussed under "gap analysis." Corporate management must now communicate to the lower levels the results of the planning process. From this point of view, implementation begins at the topmost corporate level.

Strategic Plan
(overall corporate level)

↓

Specific plans relating
to markets, finance, personnel, etc.
(Divisional or product-market level)

↓

Task - Job description

This somewhat simplified diagram shows the influence upon the organization of the strategic plan. The point of departure is the overall view at the corporate level. At the divisional or product-market level, specific plans are developed relating to the division's markets, financing, personnel requirements and other aspects which are relevant at that level. The final result is the individual task or job description. In this manner, the strategic plan exerts its influence at all organizational levels.

CORPORATE MANAGEMENT

Corporate management is involved in the implementation process in a selective manner. At this level, management decides what is to be done and determines a schedule for implementation. Within the defined framework, the actual implementation is the responsibility of the manager of each individual sub-unit. If the implementation of a specific aspect of the strategic plan involves two or more sub-units of the organization, the task must be divided among the individual units with the appropriate skills. The efforts of the sub-units must be coordinated and reintegrated at the corporate level.

If expansion or diversification is a part of the strategic plan, an examination of the organizational structure will be required. In order to adapt to new projects or skills, it may be that the structure will have to be altered in order to permit the free flow of communication from one administrative jurisdiction to another. This is an aspect which is often overlooked. Tasks must be defined within the context of the firm's current strategy and not in terms of what may have been appropriate in the past.

THE STRATEGIC BUDGET

Central to the implementation of the strategic plan is the development of the strategic budget. We have seen that the strategic plan is defined as "the key document which gives guidance and allocates resources among the activities of the firm."[1] The plan is translated into a strategic budget which is a time-phased schedule for the implementation of decisions. The definition of the strategic budget does not include only the financial budget. There is a danger in expressing the strategic plan in terms of only a financial budget because qualitative aspects of the firm's strategy may be lost. The strategic budget consists of the following:

1. The performance budget - a schedule of actions to be taken and milestones to be achieved.
2. The resource budget - a time schedule of resource commitments.
3. A forecast of results to be achieved - expressed in terms of a profit/loss forecast.[2]

The development of the strategic budget can, therefore, be linked directly to the implementation of the strategic plan. The performance budget indicates what must be done and when. Goals are provided which serve as a measure of performance. The allocation of scarce resources may be seen as the essential activity of the business enterprise. The resource budget determines where resources are employed and when they are committed. A forecast of results to be achieved provides an estimated measure of performance in terms of impact upon the profit picture of the organization.

CONSIDERATIONS IN IMPLEMENTATION

Once the strategy is selected, the first step is to identify the tasks which must be performed. After these are identified, responsibility must be assigned at the appropriate level for the completion of the task. In this manner, implementation may be viewed as an exercise in decision flow analysis. The sub-units of the organization do not pursue their activities in a vacuum. One sub-unit or division influences the activities of other sub-units and also the overall corporate performance. The "sub-strategies" developed by the sub-units within the context of the strategic plan are highly interrelated.

Decision flow analysis permits an examination of the complex interrelationships and helps to define a hierarchy of tasks. The analysis will indicate that certain tasks are of central importance for the organization. Within these areas, it is crucial that attention be directed to ensure the successful completion of the tasks. Success in implementation will therefore require open lines of communication. Communication is necessary to ensure tasks are well defined and the different activities within the organization are coordinated. Information flow may be defined as the essence of communication. The information system is an important aspect in the coordination of the "sub-strategies" of the organizational sub-units.

We have seen that the implementation of the strategic plan requires more than a definition of tasks, it also requires that the tasks be arranged in a time sequence to define a program of action or a schedule of targets. It is, therefore, necessary that provision be made to monitor the actual performance under the plan. Comparison (both quantitatively and qualitatively) of observed performance with the budgeted performance (in the wide sense of the word) is an ongoing process. In this way, problems which may develop are identified and remedial action can be taken.

Deployment of personnel resources involves a wide range of considerations. Management skills must be matched to appropriate tasks. Once the tasks are assigned, the design of incentive programs should be considered. Incentive programs are defined as rewards, not only in terms of various forms of compensation, but also in the sense of personal satisfaction obtained. Incentives should be designed in such a way that the performance of the various sub-units insures optimal performance of the overall organization.[3] Such incentives should operate to maintain harmony between the various activities within the organization, minimizing rivalries which are detrimental to the overall effectiveness.

Merger or acquisition increases the personnel resource availability. There appears to be a tendency to neglect the capabilities acquired under such circumstances in favor of those present in the parent company. This is especially true in respect to managerial personnel. It is often the case that the skills which are available in the acquired company may be redeployed to improve the operation of the combined organization. In cases of merger or acquisition outside the parent organization's product-market, retention of managerial personnel of the acquired firm may be the only way in which the merger or acquisition can be successfully integrated into the overall corporation.

STRATEGY AND STRUCTURE

Implementation of the strategic plan cannot be carried out without first considering the organizational structure. The firm's structure will undergo change as the firm expands in size. Expansion may include geographical dispersion, product complexity or sales volume. Types of appropriate organizational design may include: 1) a structure based upon the function performed (manufacturing, sales, etc.) which is a functional departmentation; 2) a divisional or product departmentation incorporating different activities with a common purpose or product grouping; 3) a place departmentation which groups activities according to geographic location. The size of the company will determine to a large extent the appropriate type of structure and the degree of centralization or decentralization which is required. If the firm is small, a functional, centralized structure is often appropriate. The larger company with diversification, may choose a less centralized structure delineated by its major product lines. With the multi-product, multi-national, large organization, the structure is frequently decentralized and the choice of an organizational design may be that of a place or clientele departmentation.[4]

The choice of strategy is one which involves the very nature of the organization. The organization structure which was appropriate in the past may now be inappropriate once the choice of strategy has been made. It is therefore, in this respect, that "structure follows strategy,"[5] The development of the new strategic position requires that the organization be evaluated to determine if the administrative details can be carried out by the present organization design. Questions which may be asked in this evaluation may include the following: Can the activities (both new and old) be coordinated through the present organization? Do adequate lines of communication exist between the different sub-units and with corporate management? Is the structure consistent, easily understood and conducive to the grouping of activities? If the answer is no to any of these questions, then the organizational structure must be redesigned in order that the requirements listed above may be met.

Merger or acquisition poses a different problem with respect to organization structure. Two or more firms are combined to become one business entity. In the past the participants led independent existences. They must now combine their efforts in order to act in a manner which is in the interest of the overall good of the new organization. When the product-market is identical or very similar, there may be a duplication of personnel resources. Under these circumstances, the new structure should place management personnel in the capacities for whch they are best suited taking advantage of the management synergy component. This however, will pose a problem with respect to individual managers because not all may need to be retained by the new organization. Resolution of this conflict is a difficult one for corporate management. Merger or acquisition outside the parent firm's product market is perhaps a lesser problem. Normally, the appropriate structure defines the new product-market in terms of a divisional sub-unit. The interests of the overall organization are best served in this case by maintaining the independence of the sub-unit except for broad policy level coordination.

The above discussion outlines the steps in the implementation of the strategic plan. The next step is to evaluate the planning process. This is the "acid test" of strategic planning -- how well has the task been performed? This question will be answered by monitoring the control system to obtain feedback on how well the organization is attaining its goals.

FEEDBACK AND CONTROL OF THE STRATEGIC PLANNING PROCESS

After the strategic plan has been selected, the planning process is not complete. As discussed in the previous section, the plan must be implemented and this involved breaking it down into manageable parts and parcelling them out to particular units in the organization. However, this does not complete the process either. Strategic planning is a dynamic process requiring continual observation and processing to adjust to a changing environment.

This requires a method whereby an organization can set up an efficient information gathering and communicating system to enable it to keep a close watch on important trends and take action when necessary. This controlling mechanism permits the firm to check for discrepancies between expected and actual performance and monitor the system after the reason for the variation has been determined and corrected.

Five main steps to feedback and control are outlined below.

1. Predicting outcomes of decisions in the form of performance measures.
2. Determining actual performance.
3. *Appraisal.* Comparing actual performance to predicted performance.
4. Determining the cause of the discrepancy.
5. Adjustment and control.

The above steps are not mutually exclusive and independent. However, for convenience each will be discussed separately.

PREDICTING OUTCOMES

This involves the following: Assessing the environment, determination of the firm's objectives, and quantifying the objectives in conjunction with the environmental factors to determine the goals or targets used in the gap analysis. The goals are the *expected* or *predicted* outcomes of the strategic plan selected. These stages were discussed in detail in the previous chapters.

DETERMINING ACTUAL PERFORMANCE

In order to obtain some measure of actual performance, an information retrieval system *(feedback system)* is required. The best device to achieve this end is the organization structure itself. The effectiveness of the organization structure as a communication device can be assessed in terms of the following:

1. How well are organizational goals and results communicated to individual members?
2. Can relevant information be gathered and processed within a reasonable time period?

The first question is important with respect to relevant data. If goals and results are not communicated clearly, then data obtained may be nonsensical in view of its use. The second question addresses itself to the time lag between information requested and actual receipt of data.

This second point is extremely important in strategic planning. The greater the time lag between actual occurrence and notification of an event, the less it is likely that corrective action can be taken.[6] Just as it is important not to make a decision too late, it is equally important not to be too early. Action taken too soon can often commit resources unnecessarily and be wasteful. Decisions made too soon without the necessary reliable information may have serious repercussions. Therefore, it is important to arrive at an appropriate lead time. The lead time is the time necessary for the action to have the desired effect.

The effectiveness of an organization structure as a feedback device can be determined by the extent to which it performs the above functions well. The content of the information transmitted by means of the communication channels gives some measure of actual performance. To extract this information all the important underlying assumptions pertaining to the target in terms of both the external and internal environment have to be monitored *relative* to *actual performance* rather than expected performance. Measurement can only take place if information concerning the progress towards the target is available. It is necessary to continually collect and evaluate information concerning progress. The assumptions behind the target (inflation, rate of taxation, etc.), the factors affecting profits (market share, selling price, fixed cost, government behavior, competition, technological change), the expected effect of the plan (profit expected, new products, extensions to factories, etc.) will be recorded as each becomes known. The data collected may be in the following forms: The company's costing system, reports from field salesmen, or the project manager, or research and development, etc. These data must then be translated by means of some criteria or bench marks into the same format as the target measurements (market share, expected sales, etc.). The firm is then in a position to appraise its performance.

APPRAISAL

The method employed to appraise a company's performance is a comparison between actual and predicted performance. As mentioned previously, the overall corporate strategy is broken down into several substrategies related to particular divisions within the organization structure. Each substrategy has its own targets and procedures which are embedded in the overall corporate strategy. In order to evaluate the performance of the strategic plan it is necessary to perform an appraisal of each substrategy, then sum across all substrategies to arrive at a corporate appraisal.

An in-depth analysis of this type can be segmented into two parts, an internal appraisal and an external appraisal. An internal appraisal involves an investigation at the micro level whereby each division or sub-unit's performance is compared with its expected performance. If a deviation exists, a further examination is conducted to determine whether the variance is caused by some internal malfunctioning of the organization itself. If the discrepancy cannot be explained internally, then an external appraisal is activated whereby the firm's performance is compared to other related and unrelated industries. Both internal and external appraisal permit the company to identify the source of deviation.

These two types of appraisal are discussed separately to enlarge upon the individual processes.

1. Internal Appraisal

The internal appraisal examines sub-unit's performance. Each sub-unit consists of several components. For example: the marketing division may be composed of a marketing research team, an advertising and promotion group, and a sales division. Each one of the components contribute to the overall performance of the marketing sub-unit. Using Figure 1 for clarification of this process, sub-unit i (2), represents a particular division in the organization as in the case of the marketing division above. Each component j's (i.e., advertising and promotion) actual performance is compared with the expected performance (3). If a discrepancy exists, further investigation is required and the individual activities of the members of component j, are assessed (4) to determine if any one member or group of individuals may be responsible for the variance. If the deviation is explained within the component itself this course is noted (6). However, if it is not, then this may require an examination of the following (7) a) other components in sub-unit i, b) other sub-units within the organization, or c) an external source. Whichever reason is discovered, it is noted (6) and will be examined later.

Referring to assignment block (8), component j's performance is added to the total subunit performance regardless of whether expectations were met. The procedure is repeated until all components of the sub-unit have been evaluated (9). At this point the total sub-unit performance is obtained and is then added to the total corporate performance (10). In a similar fashion the remaining subunits of the organization are examined (11) until the overall corporate performance has been determined.

Figure 1
INTERNAL APPRAISAL

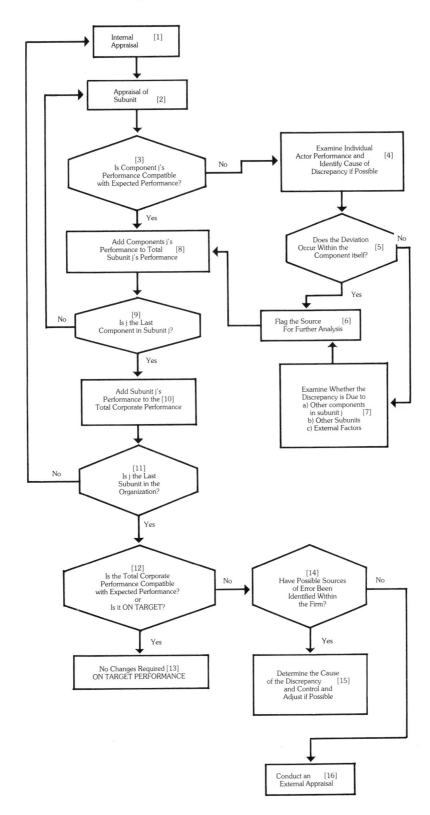

The next question asked (12) is: How does the total performance compare with expected performance for the organization? If no deviation exists (13), then no changes are required and an on target performance indicates that strategic planning has been effective. However, if total performance does not meet expectations, sources of variation which have been previously identified, are examined (14). These may be internal or external. If they have been identified internally, then the cause of the deviation must be determined and the necessary adjustment made *within* the organization (15). If the sources are external (16), then an examination of the external environment must be conducted.

It is reasonable to expect that some deviations will be noted within components of subunits. However there is a danger in focusing solely upon these variations. If overall corporate performance is on target then minor variations may be deemphasized. Too much attention on particulars may cloud the overall picture.

2. External Appraisal

If the discrepancy cannot be identified within the firm's internal environment, an external appraisal is conducted. To pursue an investigation of this nature, the company compares its performance to other firms with a similar product-market. The competence profiles discussed in a previous chapter can be used for this purpose. This grid technique matches a particular pattern of skills to specific functional areas. Using the concept of synergy, company profiles can be superimposed for the purpose of identifying discrepancies between firm performance. If the variance cannot be explained by comparing similar organizations, then this may indicate a symptom related to a particular industry. If this is the case, in order to identify the nature of the discrepancy, a synergy analysis with industries having dissimilar product-markets may be required.

Thus, the investigation can be conducted at three levels if necessary:

1. an internal appraisal;
2. an external appraisal within the industry; and
3. an external appraisal outside the industry.

The degree of appraisal that is required could be some indication of how effectively the strategic planning has been carried out. It should also be noted that each successive level of appraisal requires a more comprehensive analysis of the environment. However this does not imply that an examination of the environment takes place only at two stages: objective formulation and appraisal. The firm must continually address itself to a changing environment.

There is one other point that should be mentioned here which is related to deviations obtained by comparing actual to expected performance. A deviation by itself does not necessarily indicate that the firm has problems or that performance was below expectations. The opposite case may occur where the performance exceeds the company's projected target line. It is important that a firm identify both the source and cause of the difference and control and adjust the system accordingly.

The data generated from an appraisal evaluation may indicate the following:[7]

APPRAISAL INFORMATION

1. Continued growth of sales in keeping with the industry.
2. Maintenance of present market share (no growth).
3. Increase in relative market share.

4. Expansion of customer market (market penetration).
5. Growth in earnings per share to attract new capital.
6. Growth in earnings to provide resources for reinvestment.
7. Absence of excessive seasonal or cyclical fluctuations in sales and earnings.
8. Continued addition of new products and product lines.
9. Efficient utilization of the firm's resources (measured in terms of turnover, advancement, return on sales, working capital, net worth, inventory, debt equity, etc.).
10. Efficient utilization of key management, skilled personnel and research and development talent.

This type of information could be the result of either an external or internal appraisal, or both. These data may be used by the firm to assess its present performance and compare it with expected results.

DETERMINING THE CAUSE OF THE DISCREPANCY

After the degree of variation has been established, the next question is: *Why* did it occur? This could be restated in terms of symptoms and causes. The appraisal procedure identifies areas where a discrepancy exists *(symptoms)*. *Causes* explain the reason for the occurrence. It is important that a firm determines *why* the discrepancy takes place, rather than merely adjusting the system to attempt to correct for it. Changing the plan does not necessarily get to the source of the problem. Thus, if periodically reviewed, a sound long-range plan can serve as a control check for the day-to-day operations of the company.

Tilles,[8] outlines several criteria for evaluating strategy. Some of these can be used to give some insight as to possible *causes* for discrepancies:

1. *Internal Consistency:* Do individual (sub-unit) policies conflict with the overall corporate goals? If this is the case then disunity, inconsistency and poor integration could result.
2. *Consistency with the Environment:* Do the policies make sense with respect to the external environment? How do government fiscal policies, foreign investment and labor relations affect the firm and do the existing plans make provisions for these external constraints?
3. Is the strategy appropriate in view of *available resources?* This question asks: does the plan maximize strength and minimize weaknesses? Resources refer to personnel skills, financial resources, raw materials and physical facilities.

The answer to questions like these may tell the firm the reason or *cause* of the discrepancy. Once the source has been identified the firm is then in a position to take action.

CONTROL AND ADJUSTMENT

The last step of the total feedback and control process involves the actual adjustment to be made to the system. The degree of discrepancy determines the amount of adjustment required. Thus, a serious variation may indicate that the firm or the plan must undergo major changes. This might require going back to the beginning, re-evaluating the environment and adjusting the target line upwards or downwards. Figure 2 points out the interrelationships among all the stages in the strategic planning process. An upwards shift of the target line may indicate that the firm's actual performance exceeded the expected by a wide margin. This may indicate that there are more opportunities available to the company or that the original goal was too "easy", and a new target line should be developed. On the other hand, if the performance was well below the expected, this indicates that the original environmental analysis was not performed adequately and perhaps the target line should be lowered. In either case, a discrepancy of this magnitude (see block 15, Figure 2) may require a total re-evaluation of the entire strategic planning process and returning to the first stage (block (1)).

If the discrepancy was not serious then minor adjustments within the organization itself are required (see block (16)). An adjustment of this type may require a modification of a particular substrategy. This may be accomplished by a change at the implementation level (block (10)). Steps 11 to 16 describe the feedback and control mechanism of the strategic planning process. The location of this mechanism within the context of the overall system is indicated by means of the simplified flowchart diagram.

SUMMARY

In this chapter we have discussed the implementation of strategic planning. This phase follows that of strategic development. Strategy is translated into action. The plan which has been defined in broad terms up to this point is now put into effect. Activities are determined at the sub-unit level of the organization as a part of a time-scheduled program. If external expansion is to take place, the necessary arrangements are made, again within the context of the scheduled program. This expansion must also be integrated within the context of the overall organization.

The final phase of strategic planning deals with both the effectiveness of the planning process and the effectiveness of the implementation phase. The question asked is: Does the plan accomplish what is expected of it? The answer may be found by assessing the data which is provided by the organizational information system. If performance measures up to criteria established by the goal setting process, the planning and its implementation have been successful. If, on the other hand, performance is not at an acceptable level, then a re-examination of the strategy is called for. In any case, the information concerning performance becomes an input into the firm's strategy and the plan is refined. The strategic process assumes its continuous on-going nature in this manner.

Strategic planning is an involved, time consuming process. It is, however, necessary in order to relate the business organization to the dynamic, ever-changing environment which characterizes the present day business world.

ENDNOTES

1. H.I. Ansoff, *Corporate Strategy*, (New York: McGraw-Hill, 1965) p. 22$
2. *Ibid.*, p. 218.
3. R.L. Ackoff, *A Concept of Corporate Planning*, (New York: Wiley Interscience, 1970) p. 105
4. Rolf E. Rogers, *Organizational Theory* (Boston: Allyn & Bacon, 1975), pp. 62-73.
5. Alfred D. Chandler, Jr., *Strategy and Structure* (Cambridge: M.I.T. Press, 1962), p. 14.
6. J. Argenti, *Corporate Planning*, (London: T. Nelson & Sons, 1974), pp. 195.
7. Ansoff, *op. cit.*, p. 50.
8. S. Tilles, "How to Evaluate Corporate Strategy." *Harvard Business Review*, XLI (July-August, 1963), 111-21.

Figure 2: Decision Sequence for Strategic Planning

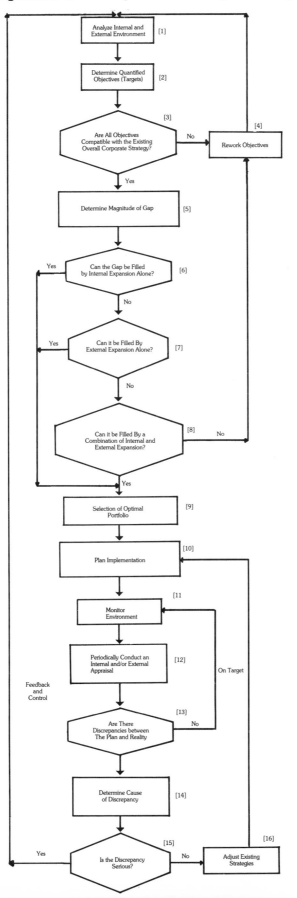

CASE

INDEPENDENCE FEDERAL SAVINGS AND LOAN ASSOCIATION

In the Spring of 1973 Independence Federal Savings and Loan Association was making preparations to celebrate its fortieth anniversary. With assets of $52,000,000, the Association had come a long way in 39 years, and the question now facing management was in what direction should the Association move to continue its recent history of outstanding growth.

FIGURE 1
DISTRIBUTION OF SAVINGS ASSOCIATIONS, BY ASSET SIZE
DECEMBER 31, 1972

Asset Size (Millions)	Number of Associations	Percentage of Total	Assets (Millions)	Percentage of Total
Under $1	660	12.1%	$ 272	0.1%
$ 1 and under $ 5	766	14.1	2,030	0.8
$ 5 and under $ 10	769	14.1	5,781	2.4
$ 10 and under $ 25	1,383	25.4	24,876	10.2
$ 25 and under $ 50	857	15.7	32,599	13.4
$ 50 and under $100	515	9.5	38,483	15.8
$100 and under $150	205	3.8	26,961	11.1
$150 and under $200	89	1.6	15,127	6.2
$200 and under $300	82	1.5	20,136	8.3
$300 and over	122	2.2	77,305	31.7
TOTAL	5,448	100.0%	$243,570	100.0%

Sources: Federal Home Loan Bank Board, United States Savings and Loan League

Independence traced its roots to the First Federal of South Philadelphia, a mutual savings and loan association, founded in 1934. Originally founded to serve the ethnic populations of South Philadelphia, the Association found its base of depositors moving out of the old neighborhoods and into the suburbs. By 1965 this shift was so pronounced that it became necessary for the Association to move from its home in South Philadelphia.

Prepared by Karl Price, School of Business Administration, Temple University as a basis for class discussion. Copyright @ 1974 by Karl Price.

Presented at the Southern Case Research Association Workshop and distributed by the Intercollegiate Case Clearing House, Soldiers Field, Boston, Mass. 02163. All rights reserved to the contributors. Printed in the U.S.A. Used with permission.

Since the depositors had moved to a number of different suburban locations, it was not possible to simply follow the depositors to the suburbs. As a result, the management of the Association decided to remain in the city, and make the best of it. It was decided that the Association would attempt to develop the image of a metropolitan financial center serving the entire Philadelphia metropolitan area.

After an exhaustive search, the decision was made to move the Association to its current location in the heart of the most historic section of Philadelphia. The location chosen was diagonally across the street from Independence Hall, and the name of the Association was changed to represent this significant move. First Federal of South Philadelphia became Independence Federal Savings and Loan Association and redefined its base as the Philadelphia metropolitan area.

The selection of this location really started Independence on its path of rapid growth. Assets which were $22,000,000 at the time of the move grew to $52,000,000 in six years. Savings activity and loan volume also grew, and the potential for future growth seemed excellent. Not only had Independence moved into the heart of the historic section of Philadelphia, it was also located in the middle of the Market Street East Redevelopment Area. Old stores and small buildings were being demolished to make room for significant new construction. Within two blocks of the new office, new federal construction of major proportion was planned. In 1973 a new U.S. mint had been constructed and construction was under way on the new U.S. court house and the new home of the Federal Reserve Bank of Philadelphia. New commercial and office buildings were also springing up in the area.

The growth from $22,000,000 to $52,000,000 in slightly over six years had not been easy. Independence had launched aggressive campaigns to attract and retain savings deposits. These campaigns included a variety of premiums to new accounts, the highest legal interest rates (usually ¼% higher than commercial banks could legally pay), introducing savings by mail with telephone withdrawals, and a variety of savings certificates available to all customers. Cumulatively, these actions increased the Association's savings customers from 8500 in 1968 to 13,800 at the end of 1972. Deposits grew at even a faster rate from $25,440,000 at the end of 1968 to $44,600,000 at the end of 1972. This was accomplished with only one location, with mail transactions taking the place of branches.

FIGURE 2
SAVINGS ACTIVITY

Year	Total Savings	% Passbook	% Certificates	Number of Accounts
1968	$25,440,000	73%	27%	8,490
1969	27,356,000	56	44	10,074
1970	30,699,000	47	53	11,100
1971	39,369,000	41	59	13,136
1972	44,598,000	39	61	13,784

The mix of deposits also changed as depositors shifted funds out of savings accounts and into longer term, higher yielding, savings certificates. Since the Association traditionally "borrowed" funds on a short-term basis (savings deposits) and lent on a long-term basis (mortgages) this shift to longer maturities on deposited funds was seen as adding stability. Since the withdrawal of a certificate before it matured resulted in the loss of ninety days interest, it was felt that certificates would reduce the flow of "hot" (interest sensitive) money, and thereby creating a stable deposits base.

As aggressive as Independence was in attracting funds, it was even more aggressive in putting those funds to work. Closely regulated by the federal government through the Federal Home Loan Bank Board, federally chartered savings and loan associations are limited to lending with real estate as collateral. This limits the S & L's to lending to builders (construction loans) and building owners (mortgages), with the amount of assets in the different loan categories clearly defined by law. Traditionally, the savings and loan associations had limited their lending to home mortgages, leaving the bigger construction loans and mortgages on commercial property to the banks. This policy spread the associations' money over a number of loans, reducing the risks to the associations, but the money was tied up for periods of from 20 to 30 years at fixed interest rates. In times of low inflation and stable interest rates this is not a real problem, but the War in Vietnam and its aftermath had changed all of that. Interest rates were climbing and the cost of obtaining money was also climbing. To offset those climbing costs and to increase the Association's return on assets, a policy of more aggressive investing was instituted. In 1970 the Association shifted its lending policy away from single-family home mortgages and into multi-family building mortgages and construction loans. The interest rates on these loans were usually at least 2% higher than that allowed on single family home mortgages. As a result, while loan volume increased, the number of loans decreased.

FIGURE 3
LOAN ACTIVITY

Year	Loan Volume	Number Single Family	Average Size	Total Number	% of Assets
1968	$5,536,000	317	$ 16,100	344	83.6%
1969	5,742,000	328	16,600	345	87.1
1970	5,487,000	138	19,100	287	85.6
1971	7,579,000	38	70,800	107	76.4
1972	9,070,000	2	312,800	29	76.2

Management was aware that this strategy involved a different degree of risk, but felt that the additional time that could be spent researching the bigger loan proposals would allow them to satisfy themselves about the quality of the loans.

In an attempt to diversify and increase the return on their depositors' funds, Independence bought the Bourse Building located next door to their current office. Even though this purchase reduced the amount of money available for lending in the short run (and reduced profits), projections indicated that after renovations, the rate of return on the building would be significantly higher than for alternative investments available to the Association. The building, facing out onto Independence Mall, was once the home of a variety of commercial exchanges. Over the years, the owners of the building allowed it to run down and most of the prime tenants moved out to new buildings. Independence acquired the 77-year-old building with 250,000 square feet of usable space on 8 floors in 1972 at a price which would allow the needed rehabilitation at a profit. Management felt that in addition, the Bourse Building would provide the Association with:

> "...sufficient space for present operational needs.
> ...control of necessary space to provide for future planned expansion.

         . . .an investment alternative to mortgage loans and governmen-
tal securities with two important differences:
1. Possible higher rate of return.
2. An inflation hedge."

    Face-lifting and modernization began in early 1973 and Independence intended to move into its new office in the Bourse Building in April 1974.

    An aggressive policy of attracting funds and an equally aggressive lending and investment policy had built Independence to $52,000,000 in assets, the question facing management now is: where do we go from here?

PLANNING FOR THE FUTURE

    The first step in the planning process was to develop reasonable goals. After a number of consultations, the management of the Association developed the following set of goals and underlying assumptions:

"GENERAL GOALS
1. Survival of the organization
2. Maintenance of control by current management
3. Increased profitability

SPECIFIC GOALS
1. Improve management team
2. Develop image as metropolitan financial center
    Sophisticated
    Aggressive
    Innovative
    Successful
3. Growth in Assets
    $200,000,000 in ten years
4. Satisfaction of staff
5. Develop service corporation (Indebourse)
    Provide diversification
    Provide services that a S & L cannot provide for itself

ASSUMPTIONS WHICH UNDERLIE GOALS
1. Savings
    Develop plans to attract money
    Develop program to reduce "hot money" on deposit
2. Loans
    Shift to higher rate loans
    Shift to shorter term loans (construction)
    Participation with builders
3. Borrowed funds
    Use of borrowed funds to gain leverage
4. Diversification
    Indebourse and other spinoffs
    Complete service to builders
    Investment advisory portfolio service
    Joint ventures
    Bourse building
5. Investing
    Non-mortgage investments to obtain higher rate of return
6. Growth
    $200,000,000 in assets a reasonable growth goal without merger

7. Image
Metropolitan image will attract the customer mix required to sustain growth
Downtown gives better image than mall or neighborhood''

The question of how to achieve the goals came next. To management the key seemed to be growth. Through growth the Association could achieve economies of scale, increase the strength of the institution, open new and more challenging jobs to employees and develop its soughtafter image as a major metropolitan financial center. Everything seemed to revolve around continuing the pattern of growth that had been developed in the past. Four approaches to growth seemed to be open to management: (1) continue to grow as a one-office operation, attracting deposits and lending and investing wisely, (2) open branches to attract deposits, (3) merge with one or more other S & L's, or (4) some combination of the first three.

Growth as a One Office Institution: Taking into consideration various sets of assumptions concerning growth, projections were made to see if the Association could grow to $200,000,000 as a one-office operation. With the most conservative projections it appeared reasonable that the growth goal could be reached. The advantage of this strategy would be the insured maintenance of control of the Association by the current management along with the gradual rate of growth that would allow orderly organizational growth. The major disadvantages would be that the advantages of economies of scale would come slowly, and this approach would not generate sufficient funds (increases in Reserves and Undivided Profit)* in the short run to support complete renovation of the Bourse Building. At present the Bourse is a low-earning asset, with major expenses needed for renovation.

Branching: Another approach to growth would have the Association open branch offices in areas which would attract new customers to the Association. The Association was large enough to support branches but in the past had decided to pass up that approach. Clearly, the major advantage of branches would be to make saving more convenient to customers and hopefully increase the total savings deposits of the Association. If branches are well placed they should generate increases in savings which would more than offset the added costs of branch operations. The major disadvantage of branch operations would be the short-run costs of setting up the branches and subsidizing the operations until they could become profitable.

FIGURE 4
SAVINGS AND LOAN ASSOCIATION BRANCH OFFICES

Year End	Assns. With Branches	% of All Assns.	Number of Branches
1960	826	13.1%	1,611
1961	928	14.9	1,851
1962	1,027	16.3	2,179
1963	1,142	18.3	2,469
1964	1,240	19.9	2,769
1965	1,321	21.4	2,994
1966	1,367	22.4	3,206'
1967	1,395	23.1	3,357
1968	1,500	25.2	3,938
1969	1,579	26.8	3,938
1970	n.a.	n.a.	4,318
1971	n.a.	n.a.	4,961
1972	n.a.	n.a.	5,793

*Under the regulations concerning the ownership of property, the FHLBB required that Reserves and Undivided Profits had to equal or exceed the value of owned property. It was estimated that the completely renovated property would have a value of about three times the current Reserves and Undivided Profits of the Association.

FIGURE 5
AVERAGE ASSETS AND POPULATION PER ASSOCIATION OFFICE

Year End	Assets (Millions)		Population	
	Per Assn.	Per Office	Per Assn.	Per Office
1960	$11.3	$ 9.0	28,440	22,663
1961	13.2	10.1	29,201	22,526
1962	14.9	11.1	29,461	21,880
1963	17.2	12.3	30,080	21,560
1964	19.2	13.2	30,619	21,189
1965	21.0	14.1	31,145	20,986
1966	21.9	14.4	31,799	21,030
1967	23.8	15.3	32,531	20,905
1968	25.7	15.9	33,342	20,625
1969	27.8	16.6	34,356	20,512
1970	31.1	17.6	35,827	20,337
1971	37.2	19.6	37,065	19,561
1972	44.7	21.7	38,052	18,442

Sources: Federal Home Loan Bank Board, Bureau of the Census, United States Savings and Loan League.

Merging: A third major growth strategy open to the Association would be to consummate one or more mergers with other savings and loan associations. The advantage to this strategy would be the immediate infusion of Reserves and Undivided Profits to help cover the FHLBB requirement concerning owned property. This would allow the Association to continue its plans for turning the Bourse Building into an earning asset. Another advantage would be that the Association would add competent people from the merged institution. There would also be the advantages of economies of scale and the fact that the new offices added from the merged operation would present operating branches without the need for absorbing high start-up costs. The major disadvantage of this strategy is that the associations in the Philadelphia area are mutual associations, owned by the depositors, not stockholders. Merger is not the simple process of buying out the other owners' stock, or a simple stock swap. In a mutual association the depositors of the two associations would have to vote for a merger, and probably would not if the management of the two associations didn't recommend the merger. In any merger, there would be a surviving institution and a non-survivor, and unless the management of the non-survivor could be convinced that it was to their benefit to merge, no merger could be possible. This would require making board positions available to members of the management of the non-survivor association, thereby risking loss of control.

FIGURE 6
MERGERS OF FHLB MEMBER ASSOCIATIONS

Year	State Chartered	Federally Chartered	Total
1960	13	10	23
1961	14	9	2
1962	24	7	31
1963	14	9	23
1964	14	18	32
1965	18	14	32
1966	30	12	42
1967	42	22	64
1968	36	11	47
1969	72	24	96
1970	87	38	125
1971	73	67	140
1972	38	64	102

Source: Federal Home Loan Bank Board

This is where the Association found itself in June 1973, trying to determine the best growth strategy. But events were changing even faster. Under the pressure of inflation, interest rates were rising. There was also pressure on the money supply as the federal government attempted to use monetary policies to control the inflationary trend. In late June, the Federal Reserve Board and then the Federal Home Loan Bank Board passed regulations to allow banks and savings and loan associations to increase the rates of interest paid on all types of savings accounts and savings certificates. At the same time alternative investment opportunities were offering higher interest rates and returns to attract money away from thrift institutions. This put real pressure on the savings and loan associations, particularly since the maximum rate of interest they could charge on home mortgages was fixed by state law, and there was pressure on the legislature not to change that rate. Independence found itself in the position, as did most S & L's, of having its return fixed while it was forced to pay higher rates to attract and keep savings deposits (See Exhibit 1). Since the banks got the jump on the savings and loan associations in offering the new rates, there was an outflow of funds from savings and loan associations all over the country. And even when the S & L's did react, there was strong pressure from government securities which were paying higher rates than the savings and loan associations could legally pay. During the two months following the new regulations, Independence saw savings deposits fall almost $4,000,000. It was obviously a new ball game.

INDEPENDENCE FEDERAL SAVINGS AND LOAN ASSOCIATION OF PHILADELPHIA

July 13, 1973

IMPORTANT NOTICE OF NEW INTEREST RATES

As you know, regulations governing interest rates on savings accounts have been liberalized for all financial institutions. As with all new programs, there exists a certain amount of confusion and misunderstanding concerning these new rates and their provisions.

We think it important to communicate with you at this time with complete information on these new types of accounts and with our suggestions on how to maximize their benefits for your best interest.

You should know that for every type of account for which a limit has been set by regulation, we will offer the maximum rate allowed.

May we suggest you read the following material carefully. We believe we have included everything necessary for you to make an intelligent decision on your continued financial security.

Please remember, we are anxious to help you in any way we can. We will be glad to discuss any additional questions with you in person or on the phone.

Sincerely,

David Shapiro
President

I. PASSBOOK AND NO PASSBOOK REGULAR SAVINGS ACCOUNTS

Effective July 1, 1973, these accounts will earn at the rate of 5.25%. Daily compounding means an effective rate of 5.47%. This higher rate will be paid on both existing and new accounts. If you have this type of account you need do nothing. Your next quarterly statement will reflect the higher rate.

II. 5 1/4% 90 DAY NOTICE ACCOUNTS

Each of these accounts is hereby converted to regular passbook or no passbook accounts as shown above. They will continue to earn 5.25% (effective 5.47%), but in addition, they will require no notice or penalty for withdrawal.

Of course, you may transfer all or any part to one or more of our higher interest savings certificates.

III. NEW SAVINGS CERTIFICATE RATES

TERM	MINIMUM DEPOSIT	RATE	COMPOUNDED DAILY (EFFECTIVE RATE)
90 Days	$ 250	5.75%	6.00%
1 Year, less than 2½ Years	$ 250	6.50%	6.81%
2½ Years to 10 Years	$ 250	6.75%	7.08%
4 Years, less than 10 Years Subject to availability	$ 1000	7.50%	7.90%
10 Years Subject to availability	$ 1000	8.00%	8.45%

While these new rates are substantially higher than before, the new penalty provision should be thoroughly understood. All new certificates MUST contain the following penalty clause or its equivalent.

"In the event of withdrawal before maturity of all or part of this certificate account, the amount withdrawn shall earn at the rate for regular passbook savings accounts for the period held less ninety (90) days. In the event the funds are on deposit for less than ninety (90) days no interest shall have been earned."

FOR EXAMPLE - A 4 year certificate is to be redeemed at the end of the 39th month, it will have earned 36 months interest at 5.25%.

If interest has been credited and accumulated, only the amount earned will be paid. If interest has been paid, the difference between the amount paid and the amount earned will be deducted from principal.

In addition, there are no borrowing privileges available with the new certificates.

IMPORTANT NEW FEATURE

We will accept additional deposits to certificate accounts <u>IN ANY DOLLAR AMOUNT</u>. The entire certificate will then mature at the date calculated by adding the original term to the date of the last deposit.

EXAMPLE:

2 year certificate opened	9/2/73 . . . . maturity	9/1/75
additional deposit	11/2/73 . . . . new maturity	11/1/75
additional deposit	9/2/74 . . . . new maturity	9/1/76

Note: We reserve the right to limit or refuse any additional certificate deposits at our option.

INTEREST ON <u>ALL</u> CERTIFICATE ACCOUNTS AND NO PASSBOOK REGULAR ACCOUNTS MAY BE PAID MONTHLY, QUARTERLY, SEMI-ANNUALLY OR ANNUALLY AT YOUR OPTION.

IV. EXISTING CERTIFICATES

Because the rates, terms, and the penalties of the new certificates differ so substantially from existing certificates <u>THERE CAN BE NO AUTOMATIC CONVERSION.</u>

No existing certificate may be converted without cashing subject to the current penalty provision for early withdrawal. This penalty is ninety (90) days interest, or all interest from issue or renewal date if the certificate is less than ninety (90) days old.*

If you currently own one or more certificates it may not be wise to cash them immediately because of this penalty clause.

For your convenience, we have calculated approximate <u>conversion break-even</u> points. If an existing certificate has a remaining term to maturity less than that indicated in the chart below, we believe it to your advantage to wait to convert until maturity. There is, however, the risk that at a later date the new higher rate certificate may not be available.

NEW CERTIFICATE RATES

	5.75%	6.50%	6.75%	7.50%	8.00%
If current rate is 5.75%	hold to maturity	hold if 23 mos. or less	hold if 17 mos. or less	hold if 9 mos. or less	hold if 7 mos. or less
If current rate is 6%	hold to maturity	hold if 36 mos. or less	hold if 24 mos. or less	hold if 12 mos. or less	hold if 9 mos. or less

*IMPORTANT NOTE: If the penalty provision governing existing certificates is withdrawn, and if you have paid that penalty to convert to one of our new higher rate certificates, we will refund the amount collected <u>PLUS</u> interest at the new certificate rate.

TO HELP YOU DECIDE !

To provide you with sufficient time to properly consider the rather large number of choices available to you without loss of earnings, we announce the following:

FOR NEW CERTIFICATES AT 5.75% to 6.75%

Any conversion by redemption of an existing certificate to one or more of these new certificates will be effective on conversion date. HOWEVER, certificates converted on or before September 13, 1973 will earn interest at their new rate from July 16, 1973.

FOR NEW CERTIFICATES AT 7.50% or 8.00%

Any conversion by redemption of an existing certificate to one or more of these maximum rate certificates will be effective on conversion date. These maximum rate certificates are available only while they last.

EXISTING CERTIFICATES

This announcement is required notice that each existing certificate shall terminate at its maturity date or next renewal date and will thereafter earn at the rate designated for regular savings accounts.

The ultimate decision is yours. You may choose to retain your existing certificates and convert at a later date; you may choose to convert now, and of course you may choose to invest additional funds into our higher rate certificates.

Whatever your decision, the entire transaction may be completed by mail. The enclosed CONVERSION FORM has been designed for your convenience. When canceling an existing certificate it will be necessary to surrender the old certificate or to sign a lost certificate affadavit.

We are also enclosing a NEW ACCOUNT FORM should you want to put some idle funds to work earning this new higher interest.

Please read both of these forms carefully and fill in completely. For your added convenience, we are also sending along a postpaid envelope to return completed forms to us.

We hope you now have a better idea of the different types of accounts available. We are certain you will choose wisely.

Please feel free to contact one of our Customer Representatives with any additional questions you may have.

WA 5-7667

EXHIBIT 2

STATEMENT OF CONDITION

December 31, 1972

ASSETS

First Mortgage Loans	$38,704,138.54
All Other Loans	427,785.75
Loans and Contracts made to Facilitate Sale of Real Estate . .	494,324.49
Office Building — Less Depreciation	1,871,935.44
Investments and Securities	9,413,906.63
Cash on Hand and in Banks	342,280.16
Fixed Assets Less Depreciation	91,157.60
Deferred Charges and Other Assets	672,149.54
Total Assets	$52,017,678.15

LIABILITIES AND NET WORTH

Savings Accounts		$44,598,392.55
Advances from Federal Home Loan Bank		2,525,000.00
Loans in Process		117,839.93
Other Liabilities . . . . :		1,546,246.44
Deferred Income		118,279.69
Specific Reserves . . . . :		500.00
General Reserves	1,795,556.56	
Surplus	1,315,862.98	$ 3,111,419.54
Total Liabilities and Net Worth		$52,017,678.15

Independence federal savings and loan association of Philadelphia

NORTHEAST CORNER 5th AND CHESTNUT STREETS ● PHILADELPHIA, PENNA. 19106

Organized March 8, 1934, Charter #178
Accounts Insured October 31, 1934
Certificate of Insurance No. 104
Chartered and Supervised by U. S. Government

EXHIBIT 3
CONDENSED STATEMENT OF CONDITION OF ALL SAVINGS AND LOAN
ASSOCIATIONS AS OF DECEMBER 31, 1972

Item	Amount (Millions)	Percentage of Total
ASSETS:		
Mortgage Loans Outstanding	$206,367	84.7%
Passbook and Other Non-Mortgage Loans	3,921	1 .6
Federal Home Loan Bank Stock	1,675	.7
Cash on Hand and in Banks	2,673	1.1
Liquid Investments	17,106	7.0
Other Investments	4,723	1.9
Building and Equipment	3,300	1.4
Real Estate Owned	600	.2
Other Assets	3,205	1.3
Total Assets	$243,570	100.0%
LIABILITIES AND RESERVES:		
Savings Deposits		
Earning Regular Rate or Below	$104,847	43.0%
Earning Above Regular Rate	102,443	42.1
Federal Home Loan Bank Advances	7,974	3.3
Other Borrowed Money	1,873	3.3
Loans in Process	6,215	2.6
Other Liabilities	5,459	2.2
General and Unallocated Reserves	14,759	6.1
Total Liabilities and Reserves	$243,570	100.0%

Sources: Federal Home Loan Bank Board, United States Savings and Loan League

EXHIBIT 4

INDEPENDENCE FEDERAL SAVINGS AND LOAN ASSOCIATION

FIVE-YEAR STATEMENT OF CONDITION

	1968	1969	1970	1971	1972
ASSETS:					
Mortgage Loans Outstanding	$24,418,207	$27,286,565	$30,337,568	$34,311,839	$38,704,139
All Other Loans	274,895	230,070	313,495	325,236	427,786
Loans to Facilitate Sale of Foreclosed Real Estate	2,054	0	0	0	494,324
Stock in FHLB	300,000	300,000	300,000	300,000	318,100
Cash on Hand and in Banks	162,456	230,888	234,494	165,262	342,280
Liquid Assets (except cash)	2,499,869	1,449,050	2,909,500	8,753,204	5,650,833
Other Investment Securities	1,300,264	1,423,026	849,050	349,050	3,763,073
Fixed Assets (Net of Depreciation)	57,133	96,947	94,599	96,573	1,963,093
Other Assets	210,159	321,953	398,412	618,100	354,049
Total Assets	$29,225,038	$31,338,499	$35,437,118	$44,919,264	$52,017,678
LIABILITIES:					
Withdrawable Savings:					
Earning regular rate or below	$18,477,217	$15,427,908	$14,481,976	$16,163,462	$17,451,416
Earning in excess of regular rate	6,963,176	11,928,082	16,216,594	23,205,205	27,146,976
Federal Home Loan Bank Advances	0	0	543,200	138,000	2,525,000
Other Borrowed Money	0	0	0	0	0
Loans in Process	0	0	0	929,202	117,840
Other liabilities	1,146,830	1,263,135	1,459,305	1,627,688	1,664,526
Specific Reserves	28,743	500	500	500	500
Total Liabilities	$26,615,966	$28,619,625	$32,701,575	$42,064,057	$48,906,258
NET WORTH:					
Reserves	$ 1,820,521	$ 1,840,019	$ 1,795,824	$ 1,795,742	$ 1,795,557
Earned Surpluses	788,550	878,856	939,717	1,059,465	1,315,863
Total Net Worth	$ 2,609,071	$ 2,718,875	$ 2,735,541	$ 2,855,207	$ 3,111,420

EXHIBIT 5
TOTAL ASSETS OF SAVINGS AND LOAN ASSOCIATIONS
(MILLIONS OF DOLLARS)

Year End	Mortgage Loans	Investment Securities	Cash and Deposits	Real Estate Owned	FHLB Stock	Other Assets	Total Assets
1960	$ 60,070	$ 5,208	$2,680	$ 153	$ 978	$ 2,382	$ 71,476
1961	68,834	5,874	3,315	291	1,097	2,724	82,135
1962	78,770	6,249	3,926	404	1,114	3,142	93,605
1963	90,944	7,244	3,979	571	1,149	3,672	107,559
1964	101,333	7,755	4,015	802	1,195	4,255	119,355
1965	110,306	8,223	3,900	1,065	1,236	4,850	129,580
1966	114,427	8,683	3,366	1,271	1,313	4,873	133,933
1967	121,805	10,499	3,442	1,353	1,327	5,108	143,534
1968	130,802	11,116	2,962	1,026	1,328	5,656	152,890
1969	140,232	10,873	2,438	822	1,424	6,360	162,149
1970	150,331	13,020	3,506	800	1,539	6,987	176,183
1971	174,385	18,293	2,783	700	1,550	8,592	206,303
1972	206,367	21,839	2,673	600	1,675	10,416	243,570

Sources: Federal Home Loan Bank Board, United States Savings and Loan League

EXHIBIT 6
TOTAL LIABILITIES OF SAVINGS AND LOAN ASSOCIATIONS
(MILLIONS OF DOLLARS)

Year End	Savings Balances	FHLB Advances	Reserves and Undivided Profits	Loans in Process	Other Liabilities	Total Liabilities
1960	$ 62,142	$ 2,197	$ 4,983	1,186	968	$ 71,476
1961	70,885	2,856	5,708	1,550	1,136	82,135
1962	80,236	3,629	6,520	1,999	1,221	93,605
1963	91,308	5,015	7,209	2,528	1,499	107,559
1964	101,887	5,601	7,800	2,239	1,729	119,355
1965	110,385	6,444	8,704	2,198	1,849	129,580
1966	113,969	7,462	9,096	1,270	2,136	133,933
1967	124,493	4,775	9,546	2,257	2,463	143,534
1968	131,618	5,705	10,315	2,449	2,803	152,890
1969	135,538	9,728	11,228	2,455	3,200	162,149
1970	146,404	10,911	11,991	3,078	3,799	176,183
1971	174,472	9,048	13,187	5,072	4,528	206,303
1972	207,290	9,847	14,759	6,215	5,459	243,570

Sources: Federal Home Loan Bank Board, United States Savings and Loan League

EVALUATION OF THE INDEPENDENCE
FEDERAL SAVINGS AND LOAN ASSOCIATION CASE

SUMMARY

The First Federal of South Philadelphia, a mutual savings and loan association, formed in 1934, was founded to serve the ethnic populations of South Philadelphia. Over the years this base of depositors gradually moved out of the old neighborhoods and into the suburbs. By 1965, this trend had become so pronounced that the organization felt the need to move its location. It was impossible for First Federal to follow these depositors, since they had dispersed throughout several areas, so management decided to develop the image of a metropolitan financial center serving the entire Philadelphia area. To facilitate this plan, the company moved to its present location in the heart of historic Philadelphia. The name was changed to Independence Federal Savings and Loan Association.

This move started Independence on a path of rapid growth: in 6 years assets grew from $22,000,000 to $52,000,000, and the potential for future growth appeared excellent. Aggressive campaigns to attract and retain savings deposits were used to accomplish this growth. Also, the mix of deposits changed over these years as depositors shifted from savings accounts to longer-term, higher-yielding savings certificates, which was seen as adding stability by reducing the flow of "hot" (interest sensitive) money.

Savings and Loans are closely regulated by the federal government through the Federal Home Loan Bank Board (FHLBB), being limited to lending with real estate as collateral. Savings and Loans can lend to builders (construction loans) and building owners (mortgages), with the amount of assets in the loan categories defined by law. Usually, Savings and Loans limited themselves to mortgage loans in order to spread their money over a wide base and minimize risk, although this policy tended to tie up money for 20 to 30 years at a fixed interest rate. The Vietnam War and its aftermath sent interest rates up along with the costs of obtaining money. Independence sought to offset these factors in 1970 by shifting from single family home mortgages to multi-family building mortgages and construction loans. The interest rates on these loans were usually 2% higher, but there was also a higher risk.

In 1972, Independence purchased the Bourse Building, a 77-year-old 8-floor structure located next door. This was an attempt at diversification designed to increase the return on depositors' funds. The acquisition reduced the firm's short-run money supply and profits, but the projected rate of return on the building was much greater than for alternative investments available to Independence. The benefits to be derived from the Bourse Building are as follows:

1. space for present operations
2. control of necessary space for future expansion
3. investment alternative to mortgage loans and government securities (higher return, inflation hedge)

In planning for the future, the management of Independence developed a set of goals and underlying assumptions, designed as reasonable guidelines for the firm (see Exhibit I). As for the achievement of these goals, management determined the key to be the continuation of the pattern of growth that had been developed in the past.

It appeared reasonable to management that growth to $200,000,000 in assets could be accomplished as a one-office operation. This would ensure the maintenance of control by the current management, but economies of scale would not come quickly, and sufficient funds for the renovation of the Bourse Building would not be generated in the short-run.

The Association could open branches, making savings more convenient to customers and hopefully increasing the total savings deposits of Independence. Such branches should be able to offset the added costs of branching in the long-run, but short-run costs would be a disadvantage.

The strategy of merger could be used to gain immediate funds for the completion of the Bourse Building plans. Competent people would be gained, advantages of economies of scale would arise quickly, and operating branches would be provided. However, this could result in the loss of some control by the current management because of the provision of board positions for members of the management of the merged association.

In June of 1973, Independence was in the midst of deciding which growth technique to employ, as inflation and interest rates climbed, and the federal government used monetary policy measures in response. In June, the maximum rates of interest paid on all types of savings were increased by the Federal Home Loan Bank Board. This, and the higher rates of return offered by alternative investment opportunities put pressure on all Savings and Loans, whose rate of interest charged on home mortgages was fixed by state law. Banks got the jump on the Savings and Loans with the new rates, and Savings and Loans associations across the nation suffered an exodus of deposits. In July and August, Independence lost almost $4,000,000 in savings deposits.

KEY ISSUES

1. Is the strategic planning of Independence relevant to its situation? Should it be altered in any way?
2. What is the best long-run method of achieving the goals set up by the management of Independence?
3. What should be done regarding Independence's short-run problem of a shortage of funds?

DISCUSSION

The strategic planning of Independence is a well-developed system designed by management to provide future direction and identity for the firm. The goals and assumptions of this planning are, for the most part, reasonable and in line with the company's environment. However, the aspects of "hot" money and growth require close analysis.

The reduction of "hot" money is a major assumption underlying the stated goals. The question is whether such deposits can be reduced to the point where Independence will not be significantly affected by changes in the interest allowed by law. It is questionable whether this is possible. In analyzing the firm's financial statements it is evident that over the past 6 years the ratio of "hot" to stable investments has shifted substantially toward the latter, yet the company has recently suffered a $4,000,000 drop in deposits because of a change in the interest rate payable. The only way that this could be avoided would be to avoid so many potentially "hot" accounts that the organization would lose a sizable portion of its business. Therefore, this factor should have been taken into account when management decided on a move such as the purchase of the Bourse Building. At the present time Independence needs funds to complete the Bourse renovations and convert it into a high-earning asset, and it has just experienced the afore-mentioned loss of deposits.

Management has determined that growth is the key to the achievement of its stated goals. They have set a growth goal of $200,000,000 in assets in 10 years. Is this a reasonable goal in light of the factor of "hot" money? This factor presents an unpredictable element that adds uncertainty to the future and to the ability of Independence to actually attain the growth goal.

Furthermore, is growth really the key to the achievement of the stated goals? The outlined general and specific goals (Exhibit I) do not necessitate growth. The only goal that does so is the $200,000,000 target itself, but this is not required for any of the others. Perhaps, the image as a metropolitan financial center could be enhanced by such growth, but that image could be cultivated quite well on the basis of the company's present status. After all, Independence has already grown to the position of being in the top 18% of all savings and loans associations. Diversification, may require some growth, but, here again, this could be carried out on the basis of present operations. Of course, the degree of diversification desired is relevant in this consideration. The goal of developing a service corporation will probably require growth in order for Independence to have the funds to implement this. Such a service corporation would be advantageous, so this is quite likely the only goal justifying growth, but it is a long-term goal, so it need not be a factor in attempting to solve the company's short-term problem of a shortage of funds.

The shortage of funds has arisen from a recent increase in demand by Independence and decrease in supply as a result of the "hot" money outflow. Independence purchased the Bourse Building as a long-term investment, planning to renovate it and convert it into a revenue earning asset, so in addition to reducing its own ready supply of funds the association demanded more for the face-lift of the structure. Shortly after this, the loss of the $4,000,000 in deposits occurred, putting Independence in a bad spot. It would appear that the long-term strategy of the company is sound, promising to increase profitability and provide a basis for growth, but if the short-term funds problem is not overcome, the company may experience a severe setback by having to liquidate some of its assets. It is apparent that management, after 6 years of uninterrupted and significant growth, assumed that the growth trend would continue as before; however, this placed the organization into a weakened condition at the very time when the set interest rates were changed. Indications of this change must have been present in some form prior to the actual changing of regulations; at least, the mounting pressure should have been noted and considered for its implications on strategy.

ALTERNATIVE CONSIDERATIONS

The following represent alternatives which could be used to evaluate possible strategic options available to this organization. They are not intended to be all inclusive or to necessarily represent the only considerations available.

SHORT-TERM CONSIDERATIONS:

1. FHLBB advance

Advantages: Immediate infusion of funds; projected ability to cover this in the long-run.

Disadvantages: Increased dependence on FHLBB. FHLBB has to be convinced.

2. Borrow funds

Advantages: Immediate infusion of funds; projected ability to cover this in the long-run.
Disadvantages: Interest expense; fixed loan payments; increased dependence on borrowed funds.

3. Merger

Advantages: Infusion of funds; operating branches; competent management infusion.
Disadvantages: May take too long to arrange, given the fact that all of the Philadelphia savings and loans are mutuals; loss of some control by current management.

4. Increased aggressiveness in attracting and retaining deposits

Advantages: Help prevent loss of and compensate for loss of "hot" money.
Disadvantages: Have already lost $4,000,000 in deposits.

5. Liquidate some assets
Advantages: Substantial amounts of money invested in liquid assets; immediate infusion of funds; no dependence on loan or FHLBB advances.
Disadvantages: A step backward, which is probably not necessary.

LONG-TERM CONSIDERATIONS:

1. No further growth or expansion

Advantages: Maintenance of current management's control; allows concentration on other goals, which do not require growth; less risk.
Disadvantages: Limits degree of diversification and development of service corporation; may cause company to stagnate; management wants growth to help with other goals of the company.

2. Growth

Advantages: Could help facilitate other company goals; growth is possible; economies of scale.
Disadvantages: Increased risk; need for increased funds; not absolutely necessary for other goals of firm.

GROWTH

1. Merger

Advantages: Infusion of funds: infusion of competent managers; operating branches.
Disadvantages: Could cause a loss of some control by current management; may take a long time to work out.

2. Branching

Advantages: Independence is large enough to support branches;

increase in total deposits; branches should be able to offset costs of branching; maintenance of control by current management.

Disadvantages: Initial costs are high; substantial time involved before branches become profitable; may change the company image.

3. Growth as a one-office operation

Advantages: Space available in Bourse Building; growth is possible as a one-office operation; maintenance of control by current management; orderly growth.

Disadvantages: Growth would be gradual, so advantages of economies of scale would come slowly.

DISCUSSION OF ALTERNATIVE CONSIDERATIONS

The first decision that must be made is how to overcome the short-term difficulty of the fund shortage. Once this decision is reached and an alternative is implemented, the association can direct itself toward a long-term decision. This progression of the decision-making process is vital, because of the implications of the success or failure of the short-term operations.

To obtain the funds needed on an immediate as possible basis, the FHLBB could be approached for an advance in addition to the seeking of a loan from other soures. Aggressive campaigns to attract and retain deposits should also be carried out, but the company already practices this to a degree, so it will take time to regain and exceed the $4,000,000 drop. Therefore, the advance and loan ideas come into the picture as means of a more quickly-realized procurement. If these methods do not work, Independence will probably have to liquidate some assets, however, the probability of this occurring is considered low, because Independence should be successful in getting funds on the basis of its record, its size, and its promising future.

Given the successful effort to overcome the short-run problem, Independence should make a decision concerning growth. The growth alternative is reasonable, because management appears capable of handling it properly and growth can help in the accomplishment of some of the major goals set forth. To achieve growth, an orderly, controlled approach is called for, given the susceptibility of a savings and loan association to interest-responsible depositors. Also, an orderly expansion will be much more easily controlled and will not be as likely to negate some of the goals that were set down earlier, such as maintenance of control by current management. Therefore, at first, growth should be accomplished as a one-office operation, and at a later date branches could be started. The image desired by management will not necessarily suffer by branching if a proper marketing strategy is used.

To give the strategic planning of the company a decisive aspect, priorities should be assigned to the various goals envisioned by management. This would not involve a major expenditure of time or money, but it could provide much more clarity and insight into what management is really interested in. A situation could arise where two goals are in conflict; the satisfying of one may negate the other. Priorities would do much to help make a decision in such a situation.

What is advocated in this program is a rather careful approach to the future. This carefulness seems justified because of the direct affects of the total economic situation on savings and loans and by the flow of "hot" money.

The organization has problems at the present time, but not so significant that they cannot recover and move on. The fact that these problems have occurred, should temper management's desire for growth and more growth. Independence has just gone through 6 years of spectacular growth, but that does not imply that such growth will always be possible, or even desirable.

EXHIBIT I

General goals
1. Survival of the organization
2. Maintenance of control by current management
3. Increased profitability

Specific goals
1. Improve management team
2. Develop image as metropolitan financial center
3. Growth in assets; $200,000,000 in 10 years
4. Satisfaction of staff
5. Develop service corporation (Indebourse); provide services that a S & L cannot provide for itself and diversification

Assumptions that underlie goals
1. Savings; develop plans to attract money; develop program to reduce "hot" money on deposit
2. Loans; shift to higher rate loans; shift to shorter term loans; participation with builders; packaging and selling to builders
3. Borrowed funds; use of borrowed funds to gain leverage
4. Diversification; Indebourse and other spinoffs, joint ventures; Bourse Building; complete service to builders
5. Investing; non-mortgage investments to obtain higher rate of return
6. Growth; $200,000,000 in assets without merger; branching possible but not priority item
7. Image; metropolitan image to attract customer mix required to sustain growth; downtown better image than mall or neighborhood.

APPENDIX

THE THEORETICAL ANALYSIS OF ALTERNATIVE STRATEGIES

This appendix has been added to present some theoretical discussion of corporate strategy that deals with alternative generation. Alternatives may be initally defined as different courses of action that must be discovered, designed or synthesized and utilized in goal or objective satisfaction.

In our discussion of alternative generation, two significant facts will become apparent. First, the number of potential alternatives is practically unlimited. In other words, without the use of some theoretical approach to alternative generation, the number of potential alternatives would become too numerous to be of any value to the strategist. Second, the generation of alternatives is a time consuming, costly exercise. The need for a theoretical framework is again evident.

It is our aim to not only discuss a theoretical framework for alternative generation but also to include an in-depth application of such a method to a corporate planning process. Such an analytical approach will enable the reader to focus on the place of alternatives in business strategy as well as the importance of concise alternative generation under varied planning processes.

A THEORETICAL FRAMEWORK OF ALTERNATIVE GENERATION IN THE PLANNING PROCESS

Any discussion of a theoretical framework for strategic planning must consider two important ideas; one is the type of decision being made and the other is the structure of the problem being considered. With reference to Figure 1, the table of classification of management decisions, it is evident that the type of decision that we are concerned with here is the unprogrammed and non-automated decision.

In the programmed decision, the traditional decision making technique is described by intuition, experience, creativity, search, trial and error. If the breadth of these words are taken into consideration it becomes apparent that indeed this involves an extensive process of thought and logic in order to generate a set of alternatives. This type of decision-making technique lies below that of the technique of direct communication between man and man and rather implies a nebulous idea which involves an innate characteristic of man that cannot be readily expressed. When using the modern decision-making technique, as in the traditional techniques, there seems to be a fine line drawn again between the innate abilities of man and the expressed methodology.

Moving to the far right of the table, the structure of the problem is considered. Again the difference between the second and third types of decisions is not clearly labelled, but it is evident that the structure of the problem at the very least is not explicitly clear. C.E. Lindblom has written an article[1] on the idea of the structure of the problem and, although he confines his discussion to public administration, the article points out some very important considerations in the generation of alternatives. The part of the analysis that we are concerned with here is Section 4a (see Figure 2). When comparing the Root and

FIGURE 1
CLASSIFICATION OF MANAGEMENT DECISIONS FROM THE POINT OF VIEW OF AUTOMATION.

Types of Decisions	Decision making Techniques		Structure of the Problem
	Traditional	Modern	
1. Programmed decisions. Can be automated without heuristic programming.	Full defined rules and clear instructions.	Mathematical analysis, linear programming, information modeling.	Good structure, clear mathematical formulation of the problem is possible.
2. Programmed decisions (automated decisions)	intuition, experience, creativity, search, trial and error.	Heuristic programming on the basis of modeling processes.	Bad structure, clear formulation of the problem not possible.
3. Unprogrammed and non-automated decisions.	Direct communication between man and man is necessary. Decisions are based upon social experience.	The quality of the decisions taken can be improved by research into the psychology and sociology of management.	This type of decision cannot be given to machines.

Source; H.A. Simon, *New Science of Management Decision*, Prentice Hall, 1977, p. 48. Modified adaptation, used by permission.

Branch approaches, it is apparent that they lie at different ends of a spectrum; one of which is all inclusive and the other which concerns itself with only important possible alternatives.

FIGURE 2
STRUCTURE OF THE PROBLEM

Rational-Comprehensive (Root)	Successive Limited Comparisons (Branch)
1a Clarification of values or objectives distinct from and usually prerequisite to empirical analysis of alternative policies.	1b Selection of value goals and empirical analysis of the needed action are not distinct from one another but are closely entertwined.
2a Policy formulation is therefore approached through means-ends analysis. First the ends are isolated, then the means to achieve them are sought.	2b Since means and ends are not distinct, means-ends analysis is often inappropriate or limited.
3a The test of a "good" policy is that it can be shown to be the most appropriate means to desired ends.	3b The test of a "good" policy is typically that various analysts find themselves directly agreeing on a policy (without their agreeing which is the most appropriate means to an agreed objective).
4a Analysis is comprehensive: every important relevant factor is taken into account.	4b Analysis is distincly limited: (i) important possible out-comes are neglected; (ii) important alternative potential policies are neglected; (iii) important affected values are neglected.
5a Theory is often heavily relied upon.	5b a succession of comparison greatly reduces or eliminates reliance on theory.

Source: C.F. Lindblom, "The Science of Mudling Through," *Public Administration Review,* American Society for Public Administration, Washington, D.C., Vol. 19, Spring 1959, pp. 79-88. Used with permission.

Lindblom's argument for the Branch method lies in the following quote: "Limits on human intellectual capacities and in available information set definite limits to man's capacity to be comprehensive." This tends to suggest two ways of simplifying the investigation:

1. To only consider the marginal differences between alternatives therefore limiting the amount of investigation that has to be done in each policy (policy refers in his paper to a branch; later in our discussion, a policy would be equated to a branch of a network analysis).
2. To ignore some of the important possible consequences of the different policies and to neglect values that might be attached to the consequences. Values would be considered in his article to describe possible beliefs that society, the corporation, or the individual has.

It should be realized, that indeed the generation of alternatives needs some limiting factor or constraint and this is where the theoretical framework, to be discussed later, will differ from Lindblom's idea about the Branch method.

The rationale for applying a theoretical framework to the generation of alternatives is twofold. First, it provides a method that can be described by the limits generated by the number of alternatives. Second, because of the lack of a clear formulation of the problem, such a framework will enable us to apply a definite system of logical analysis that will help in the generation of alternatives. By using heuristic programming as the theoretical framework one should be able to approach more clearly the third type of decision-making process (unprogrammed and non-automated decisions). Also, by expanding upon some of the ideas that writers such as Newell, Shaw, and Simon have proposed about the differences between programmed and unprogrammed decisions, it should become evident that some of these innate characteristics of man can indeed be conceptualized to some extent.

HEURISTIC PROGRAMMING

Perhaps at this point, by defining the term heuristic programming, an idea of the type of process that is involved will become evident. Heuristic programming is an approach "serving to guide, discover or reveal, valuable for stimulating or conducting empirical research but unproved or incapable of proof...use of arguments, methods or constructs that assume or constructs that assume or postulate what remains to be proven or that lead a person to find out for himself."[2] The important point here is that this approach does use a logical process in trying to attain a set of alternatives.

1. Definition of a problem

It is usual to think of a problem as a series of routes or paths some of which lead to a desired goal. The idea of solving the problem then is to choose a route or path that does lead to a desired goal. Complexity is evident when uncertainty is added to the paths or when the paths are not clearly distinguishable from each other. Also, where the desired goal is not known or where there are several different goals, which may be in conflict with each other, or mutually exclusive, this complexity is again evident. The graphical display which usually represents a problem is a maze or a decision tree (see Figure 3). An idea of the size of a maze could be obtained by consulting the mathematical formulas for permutations or combinations. For example, referring to the maze diagram and using a simple example of permutations for the three element set illustrated, there are thirty different permutations. Therefore a complex problem could contain an extremely large number of alternatives.

2. Alternative generation

A distinction has been made between alternative generation and alternative testing by numerous authors. Alternative generation involves discovering, designing or synthesing proposed solutions. This is somewhat like the basic idea of mathematical permutations or combinations, and although the type of alternative generation for nonautomated or unprogrammed decisions is highly complex, the method still relies on some constraints, as do combinations, in limiting the number of subsets generated. Alternative testing involves testing how satisfactory a proposed alternative is, either to the goals or to the type of values that are implicitly included in the proposed alternative.

The principal idea behind alternative generation is that this process should determine the order in which the paths are to be explored. The paths that are to be explored represent possible solutions rather than the actual solutions. The distinction is that an actual solution requires that the alternative, or proposed solution, be verified as satisfying the goals or objectives.

The idea that must be understood is that only a small proportion of all possible solutions are actual solutions. This may seem like a very simple statement but it implies that alternative generation is only concerned with the generation of alternatives that are going to be, or could be, possible solutions. These possible solutions could then be verified by the alternative testing technique.

It should also be noted, that the type of problem involved directly influences the generation of alternatives, for, in a complex problem, whole branches of a network may constitute possible alternatives. Thus the type of strategy used in the generation of alternatives is very important as it may limit the numbers of alternatives considered and the depth (number of elements) to which the alternatives are considered. The depth to which alternatives are to be considered greatly increases the complexity of alternative generation, for, as the network grows in length, there are more minor branches that must be explored. Thus, there is a decrease in the distinctions between the proposed solutions and hence the effectiveness of alternative generation is lost.

Figure 3: A Typical Maze Diagram

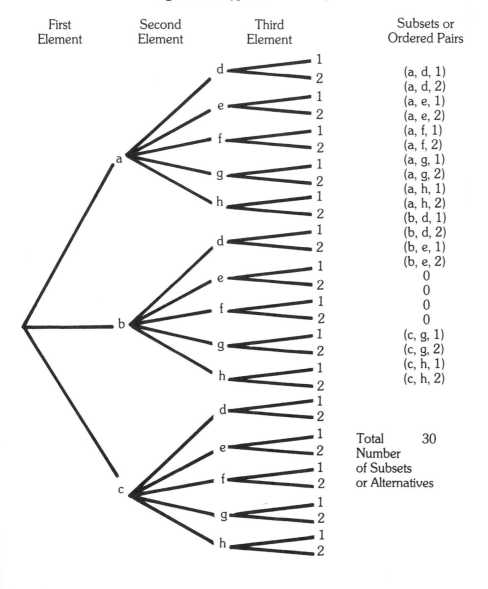

318

There is a distinct disadvantage in proceeding too far into the network analysis as the proper coverage of all possible solutions is lost and alternative generation becomes very narrow in scope. There is a trade-off present between the depth and the breadth of the network to which alternative generation can be applied. This is one of the most important points often neglected in the idea of alternative generation. This is also the fundamental difference between strategic and tactical alternative generation, for tactical alternative generation proceeds after a strategic alternative has been verified as a solution. The more depth a branch of a network analysis is subjected to, the finer are the distinctions made and the closer one comes to the basic tactical alternatives (see Figure 4).

We are concerned with alternative generation in relation to strategic planning. Thus, the network analysis that is being considered is one which involves a limitation in depth and a maximum coverage taking into consideration the firm's resources and the time available.

Figure 4

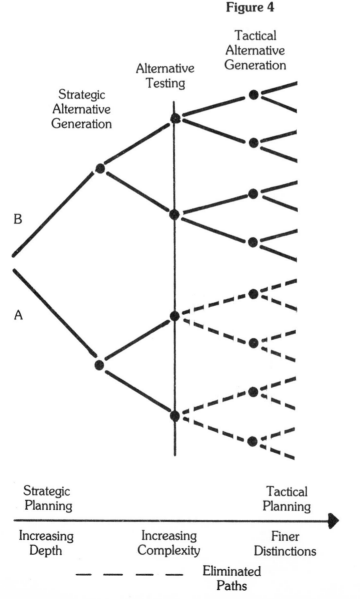

Tactical
Alternative
Generation

Alternative
Testing

Strategic
Alternative
Generation

B

A

A and B are both synthesized from the same goals but with Alternative Testing, considering both goals and value judgments, B is satisfactory and A is eliminated.

Strategic
Planning

Tactical
Planning

Increasing
Depth

Increasing
Complexity

Finer
Distinctions

— — — — Eliminated
Paths

3. Efficient generators

The idea of efficient generators is related to the idea by Lindblom, namely, that of limiting the scope of the analysis. The efficient generator includes constraints which should avoid those parts of the problem maze which are highly improbable, or beyond the firm's resources. The type of generator to be chosen depends upon 1) the constraints which are the most difficult to satisfy and 2) on the relative cost of generation. An example which examines the types of constraints used in a generator follows:

a) Three constraints exist that must be taken into account in alternative generation. The three constraints are mutually exclusive;
b) Which constraints should be considered in the alternative generation process; remember the high cost of generation in terms of time and money in trying to satisfy all three constraints;
c) The probability of satisfying the constraints are for:
   A = .75
   B = .60
   C = .30
d) Since C has the lowest probability of being satisfied, C should be considered first as C will limit the number of possibilities in A and B. If time and money warrant continuance, the next lowest probability should be considered; otherwise just consider the alternatives generated with C, as the combined probability of satisfying both A and B constraints together is .45;
e) B should be considered next, using only those alternatives generated by constraints C. Note that the cost is directly proportional to the number of alternatives available, therefore this step will cost less than the previous step. If time and money warrant continuance, the next lowest probability should be considered; otherwise just consider the alternatives generated by constraints C and B, as the probability of satisfying constraint A is now .75;
f) A should be considered next, if time and money warrant the continuance. Remember the cost should be less for this step as the number of alternatives available is limited by C and B. Now all three constraints are included; therefore the alternatives that are left will satisy all of them.

The example points out that probabilities are useful in deciding what constraints should be used in a generator. Complexities arise in the use of constraints in a generator when some constraints are not mutually exclusive but are highly interdependent upon each other, while others still may be mutually exclusive. Still the general rule applies; use the constraint with the lowest probability. The two important factors which limit the use of generators are:

1. The constraints may be in conflict with each other and trade-offs may have to be made;
2. Certain constraints may not be known until actual alternative generation begins.

USE OF HEURISTICS

The selection of the proper constraints for an alternative generator have been discussed earlier but the question remains; how is this generator used? When solving a complex problem the alternative generator, which is characterized by the constraints within it, will be applied to the problem or problem maze. The constraints within the generator should immediately limit the number of paths that will have to be explored or considered. Newell, Shaw and Simon have an example of the magnitude of this saving:

> "to see the worth of this procedure, consider a maze having alternatives at each branch end length k. If there were a single correct path to the goal, finding that path by random search would require, in the average $\frac{1}{2}$ m^k trials. If a heuristic test (efficient generator) were available that could immediately weed out half of the alternatives at each branch point as unprofitable, then a random search with this heuristic would require only $\frac{1}{2}$ $(\frac{1}{2}m)^k$ trials on the average. This is a reduction in search by a ratio of 2^k, which, if the maze were only seven steps in length, would amount to a factor of 128, and if the maze were ten steps in length, a factor of just over a thousand."[3]

This sample points out that great economies of effort can be gained by proper use of an efficient generator (see Figure 5).

The efficient generator reduces the size of the problem maze; however, definite strategies are needed to pick out branches of the maze (alternatives) that are feasible or that are directly related to the goal. The alternatives that are left will then be subject to the process of alternative testing. There are basically four different types of network analysis that can be used in formulating alternatives:

1. working backward from the solution or goals;
2. selection heuristics;
3. functional or means-end analysis;
4. planning.

Although all four of these types of analyses will be discussed in this chapter, only some will be directly related to the type of decision with which we are dealing here, namely, non-programmed and non-automated decisions.

1. Working backward from the solution of goals

This procedure can be described as organic and has been called the process of working forward mechanical. Although basically there is little difference in the outcome of the two, the backward procedure is generally considered to be more efficient but to work backwards, one needs to know the solution or a single point. Otherwise exploring several paths at the dividing line between strategic and tactical analysis is very inefficient. Note: a generator is not useful unless there is one starting or beginning point, otherwise the paths may contain different arguments, methods, or constraints, and this may lead to serious difficulty in trying to develop initial constraints for a generator. The procedure of working backwards cannot be easily used on the type of decision being made here, because a complex problem usually does not have one specified goal or objective, that is, in terms which can be used in the network analysis. Also arguments, methods or the constraints can seriously alter the method of analysis by relying upon previous choices of routes or alternatives.

2. Selection Heuristics

Returning again to the idea of arguments, methods or the constraints being used in the different branches of the network, it can be seen that clues may only become available as the generation of alternatives continues.

There are two different ways of describing any point in a maze. One is specification by state description. This entails a simple statement of where it

Figure 5:   Identical Problem Mazes

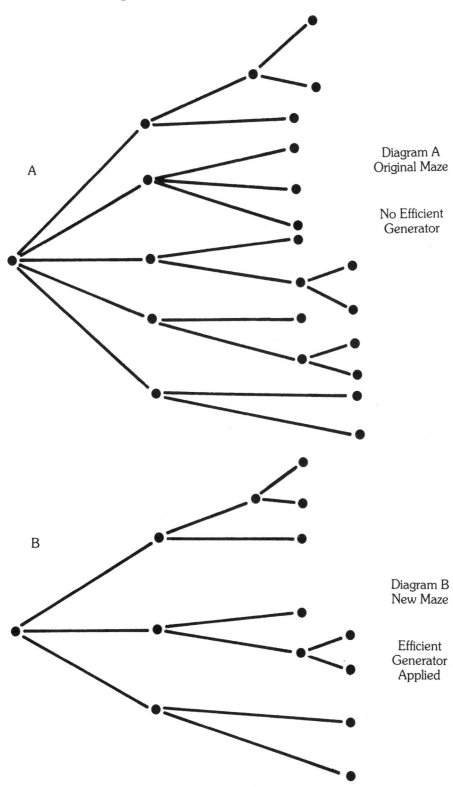

Diagram A
Original Maze

No Efficient
Generator

Diagram B
New Maze

Efficient
Generator
Applied

lies in the maze (i.e., third element of B). The other is specification by process description which uses the idea of how the point developed (i.e., left branch of B, right branch of D and then middle branch). Often a partial state description of the solution or a description of one or more of the starting points or an idea of the allowable process is known even in complex problem solving. The idea behind this procedure is to use clues as guides to try to find a sequence of processes that will produce the final state.

This is referred to as the "strategies of search" for each time a process is applied to a new state, a different description results. This in turn is compared to the idea of the final state. Also the problem solver may have some idea of the distance to the final state and therefore this also provides information as to whether the proper branch was taken. As each new comparison is made, the difference between the two states should become smaller and smaller.

3. Functional Analysis

A functional or means-end approach utilizes expression and the difference between expressions, operators, goals, subgoals and methods. Each goal or subgoal is associated with methods (procedures) which will help attain the next higher level goal. As subgoals are attained, a new procedure is used (procedure would include expression and operators) until the final goal is reached.

It should be noted, that this approach emphasizes the use of subgoals in the network analysis and assumes that these subgoals, or even the goal, is known in operational terms in advance. They must be in operationalized terms if one is to use a procedure for finding a higher level goal. Also both the expressions and operators used must be in concrete terms. Otherwise the procedure will not help in the attainment of the higher level goal.

Functional analysis does not really use logic and merely by changing or redefining the expression or the difference in the operators, the analysis can be used to solve different problems. This type of heuristic analysis is limited to the programmed decision as both the goals and expressions, operators or differences in operators must be known in advance. Therefore, its use is restricted to problems that can be quantified and is only included in our discussion as evidence of a different approach to heuristic problem-solving.

4. Planning

This class of heuristic planning uses the idea of subtasks as a means of generating feasible alternatives. Subtasks are part of the complete task of generation. Each subtask contains a cue that will direct the analysis into the next subtask and so on. These cues occur at every second or third branch and thus they serve to limit the number of trails that are needed.[4]

This type of analysis differs from the selection analysis in that the planning analysis has cues that divide the problem maze into subtasks. But the planning analysis does not rely on expressions or operators, etc., as functional analysis does. It is possible that a complex process will have cues along the maze network which will lead the search processes to the generation of feasible alternatives.

It appears that selection heuristics is one of the better devices to describe the processes of generation of alternatives. To some extent the ideas contained in the planning analysis may prove very beneficial in reducing or subdividing the generation of alternatives into more manageable tasks.

INNATE CHARACTERISTICS OF MAN

Where does heuristic programming differ from the process of thought used by individuals in strategic planning? What we are referring to is the innate characteristics of man that seem to differentiate the programmed decisions from the non-programmed decisions. The definition of the difference between the type of decisions shown in Figure 1 differs from Newell, Shaw and Simons' definition of the difference. It seems that to some extent the latter exploration of the innate characteristics of man is more inclusive and uses a general framework for the discussion of such characteristics as creativity. This is where Figure 1 is less elaborate. The table includes the term creativity in programmed decisions. This would suggest that a more simplified view has been used rather than a philosophical interpretation.

This dichotomy points to some serious considerations in the general use of heuristics to an unprogrammed or non-automated decsion.

Unconventionality and Creativity

What is learning? Newell, Shaw and Simon[5] distinguish between short-run or temporary changes and longer-run or permanent changes. They classify short-term change as changes in a set and long-term changes as learning. Since the human problem solver is a serial rather than a parallel instrument (substantiated by the use of heuristics), only a small part of the human problem solver's repertoire is available to a particular problem at any one point in time. Therefore, change is a mobilization of the heuristics that are guiding the search and learning is a change in the repertoire or heuristics that are available to the human problem solver.

Heuristics which have been effective in the solving or generation of alternatives in the past for a particular set of problems, may be out of context when used in new problems. This type of behavior is commonly called stereotyping and is used to describe a subject's persistence in using a system of heuristics which is out of context.

How often it is heard that the alternatives should be unconventional in order to out-wit competitors. Does unconventionality simply reject the heuristics that restrict a search to a limited portion of the problem? This cannot be so, for then one is back to the trial and error method of trying to generate alternatives which is bound to be highly ineffective. This argument for unconventionality stems from the fact that at times the alternatives generated just do not seem to satisfy (or are disjointed from) the objectives or goals and values that we have used to test the solution. The problem cannot be solved by trying to be as unconventional as possible but by the replacement or change of the inappropriate efficient generator with one which will allow the size of problem space to be reduced to a more appropriate subset.

SUMMARY

This appendix has examined alternative generation from two focal points. In our discussion of a theoretical framework we expounded upon the developmental aspects of the heuristic framework. The major idea behind the presentation of a theoretical framework was to try to reveal one of the approaches to organizing a logical analysis of strategic or complex problems. This involved shedding some light about the structure of logical thought processes as it relates to alternative generation. We noted, that the theoretical framework cannot be directly applied to the generation of alternatives in strategic planning or complex problem solving. Rather it is used as a basis for the development of the practical model. The framework provides the essential ingredients to the model, that is, the network analysis in heuristics.

ENDNOTES

1. Lindblom, C.E., "The Science of Modling Through," *Public Administration Review,* Vol. 19, Spring 1959, pp. 79-88.
2. Websters, *Third New International Dictionary,* 1964.
3. Newell, A., Shaw, A., Simon, H.A., *The Process of Creative Thinking,* in Grueber, H.E., Terrel G. and M. Wertheimer (eds.) *Contemporary Approaches to Creative Thinking* (New York, Atherton, 1962), p. 80.
4. Ibid., p. 91.
5. Ibid., p. 104.

PART V

SELECTED INTEGRATED CASES IN CORPORATE STRATEGY AND PLANNING

Table of Contents

Cases

1. Fredonia State Bank
2. Quality Supermarket, Inc.
3. United Products, Inc.
4. Carter Distribution Corp. (A)
5. Carter Distribution Corp. (B)
6. Carter Distribution Corp. (C)
7. Hartz Mills (A)
8. Hartz Mills (B)
9. Hartz Mills (C)
10. Carson/Burger/Weekly, Inc.

CASE 1

FREDONIA STATE BANK

The Fredonia State Bank was chartered in September, 1963, to serve the University community. The bank opened for business on April 1, 1964 in the former College Coffee Shop directly across from the northwest corner of the Stephen F. Austin State University campus in Nacogdoches, Texas. The bank leased the building, which contained about 4,000 square feet of floor space. The decision to lease the building was prompted by a desire to curtail the expense of occupancy in the early stages of the bank's operation until a new permanent facility could be constructed.

The decision to locate in close proximity to the university was made primarily by M.M. Stripling, first president of the bank. Stripling believed that the college area would be the focal point of new growth in the community. Rowland Vannoy, executive vice president, was the chief operating officer since Mr. Stripling was actually inactive in the bank's operations. Including Mr. Stripling and Mr. Vannoy, there were fourteen members on the original board of directors. Initially, ownership of bank stock was distributed among approximately 60 stockholders living in the community.

Besides the president and executive vice president, other original bank employees were a cashier, assistant cashier, secretary, and a teller-bookkeeper.

When the Fredonia State Bank opened, it became the third bank in the city. The other two banks, the Commercial National Bank and the Stone Fort National Bank, were founded in 1901 and 1903 respectively. Both of these banks were and still are located in the downtown area approximately two miles south of the university campus. First-year deposits of Fredonia were $1.7 million compared with $12.4 million and $13.6 million for the other banks. The deposits of the three banks since 1963 are shown in Table 1.

NEW LOCATION

Ground was broken on October 13, 1969, for a new building about two blocks north of the previous site. The main reason for the move was that the old location had become inadequate to handle the bank's growing volume of business. The old location had one drive-in window and four tellers' windows in the lobby.

This case was made possible by the cooperation of the Fredonia State Bank, Nacogdoches, Texas and by a grant from the Tenneco Foundation. It was prepared by Robert McGlashan, Associate Professor of Management, University of Houston at Clear Lake City, and Ed Roach, Associate Professor of Management, Stephen F. Austin State University. It was prepared as a basis for class discussion rather than to illustrate either effective or ineffective handling of an administrative situation. Copyright Robert McGlashan and Ed Roach, 1974. Distributed by the Intercollegiate Case Clearing House, Soldiers Field, Boston, Massachusetts 02163. All rights reserved to the contributors. Printed in the U.S.A. Presented at a Case Workshop. Used with permission.

The new bank building was opened for business on June 22, 1970. The total investment in the bank premises and furnishings was approximately $450,000. The building is owned outright by the bank. The new building contains 10,000 square feet of space on the first floor and an additional 5,400 square feet on a second floor which can be accessed by moving a portion of the first floor ceiling if the need for this space should arise because of future growth. There is parking space for 40 customers' cars in the front and on one side of the bank. Behind the bank there is parking space for 18 employees' cars. The new bank building is modern and attractive. There is a large lighted sign in front of the bank. The sign is used constantly to display various types of messages. In the new building there are eight teller's windows. In addition, there is one drive-in window apparently intended for commercial customers and three adjacent drive-in lanes each connected to the drive-in window by a pneumatic tube system. The bank management feels that this system is fast, secure, and flexible. At all four lanes the customer can see and talk with the teller at the drive-in window.

TABLE 1
DEPOSITS OF NACOGDOCHES BANKS (IN THOUSANDS)

Year	Stone Fort National Bank	Commercial National Bank	Fredonia State Bank
1963	13,622	12,406	
1964	13,474	11,648	1,764
1965	14,811	12,100	2,492
1966	16,465	12,670	2,948
1967	21,248	16,599	3,487
1968	24,323	17,405	4,431
1969	24,526	19,176	6,486
1970	30,223	21,200	6,588
1971	32,385	23,463	11,849
1972	37,139	26,092	14,407
1973	42,789	26,944	17,247

CITY OF NACOGDOCHES

The city of Nacogdoches is located in deep East Texas about 140 miles north of Houston and 160 miles southeast of Dallas. It is reputed to be the oldest town in Texas. It is the county seat of Nacogdoches County. The major types of business activity in the city include poultry processing plants, brass-valve manufacturing, furniture manufacturing, business forms, candy, clothing, wood products, and fertilizers.

The population of the county has increased from 28,046 in 1960 to 36,362 in 1970. During the same period the city's population has increased from 12,674 to 22,544.

The city is the site of Stephen F. Austin State University, a state-supported institution located on North Street. North Street is also U.S. Highway 59, the main thoroughfare through the city. The university has had rapid growth recently as indicated in Table 2.

The city is served by one daily newspaper, the *Daily Sentinel,* and three radio stations. Television service is provided by means of cable.

ORGANIZATION AND PERSONNEL

The present organization chart is shown in Exhibit 1. At the present time there are ten officers of the bank. Their names, positions, ages and years of experience in banking are shown in Table 3.

TABLE 2
STEPHEN F. AUSTIN STATE UNIVERSITY GROWTH DATA

Year	Student Enrollment [a]	Faculty and Staff Employment [b]	Faculty and Staff Payroll (thousands) [c]
1963-74	3335	NA	2,173
1964-65	4290	NA	2,490
1965-66	5784	NA	3,390
1966-67	6862	701	3,852
1967-68	8102	797	5,873
1968-69	8717	1014	7,101
1969-70	8740	1109	8,159
1970-71	9814	1164	8,661
1971-72	9976	1198	9,663
1972-73	10227	1212	10,189
1973-74	9962	1270	11,087
1974-75	10884	1280	12,016

a -Fall Semester
b -Full-time equivalent positions reported on legislative budget request.
c -Budgeted salaries (12 month basis).

There are presently fifteen members on the board, none of whom were directors when the bank opened in 1964. The directors are elected by the stockholders and according to the president, "Generally speaking, they are selected because of their various areas of influence in the community and their business backgrounds and the fact that they are successful business people." Vocations represented on the board include physicians, attorneys, newspaper publishers, and administrators in the field of real estate, construction, investments, and feed and fertilizer.

Rowland Vanney was elevated to the presidency of the bank in 1971. He graduated from business college in Waco, Texas in 1935 and later attended graduate schools of banking at Rutgers and Southern Methodist University. He is the chief operating officer of the bank and is one of six officers who receive loan applications and approve loans. The others who may give loan approval are the executive vice president, senior vice president, the two vice presidents and the assistant vice president.

> The ownership of the stock in our bank is very widely spread throughout the community and we feel that this has helped us in building the bank. No one stockholder owns more than 10% of the total outstanding shares.

Mr. Godfrey also shared this belief concerning the diverse stockownership and its effect on bank growth:

> We have a wide range of stockholders, some of whom own very few shares, and they work hard for us. This is their bank and I work for them because they are stockholders and they want to see the bank grow. They have seen the value of their stock increase over the years. They have made money in the bank and want to keep making it.

The other officers also felt that it was vitally important that bank customers be given personalized service and that they feel they can see any bank officer at any time concerning any problem. Bank management stated this type of relationship was necessary because the Fredonia State Bank basically had no different services to sell that the other two city banks did not also have.

EXHIBIT 1. FREDONIA STATE BANK ORGANIZATION CHART

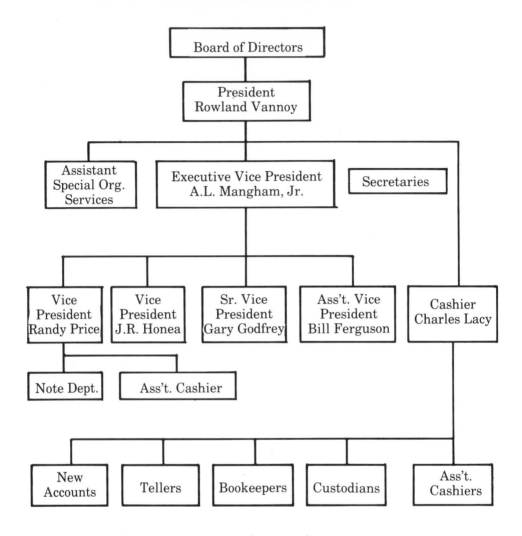

Source: As described by management personnel to case writer.

TABLE 3

FREDONIA STATE BANK MANAGEMENT

NAME	POSITION	AGE	BANKING EXPERIENCE
Rowland Vannoy	President	58	38 years
A.L. Mangham, Jr.	Executive Vice President	52	7 years
Gary C. Godfrey	Sr. Vice President	33	10 years
J.R. Honea	Vice President	36	13 years
Randy C. Price	Vice President	29	3 years
Bill Ferguson	Asst. Vice President	33	1 year
Charles R. Lacy	Cashier	46	7 years
Billie Blakey	Ass't. Cashier	46	5 years
Louise Stanfield	Ass't. Cashier	39	7 years
Beverly Eubank	Ass't. Cashier	28	8 years

The bank management is involved in many different community activities. In addition to Mr. Mangham's position as mayor, other officers are involved in such activities a the Nacogdoches Chapter of the Future Farmers of America, Optimists Club, Cancer Society, Kiwanis Club and United Fund. Mr. Vannoy stated that he felt it was vital that the bank management be involved in activities such as these.

In general, the Fredonia State Bank prides itself in being "the bank that cares," a phrase which was used by management to put across its philosophy at the time the bank opened for business at its new and present location.

BANK SERVICES

Mr. Vannoy stated the the services provided by the bank were basically the same as those offered by any commercial bank. These include checking accounts, savings accounts, safety deposit boxes, drive-in facilities, bank-by-mail, travelers checks, 24 hour depository and loan services.

Mr. Vannoy further stated that:

One of the primary responsibilities of the bank is to handle the loan needs of individuals and businesses in our trade territory (county). There are many legal limitations and requirements which we must comply with. We believe that all loans should have a good sound reason for being made and that we should avoid anything that is speculative or of high risk. We feel a responsibility to protect the borrower's interest as well as that of the bank.

Unsecured loans of $10,000 and above and secured loans of $25,000 and above must be approved by the loan committee which is composed of all officers except the cashier and assistant cashiers. The loan committee meets at least once a month and at other times when requested to do so by a loan officer. A breakdown of the total loans outstanding is shown in Table 4. About 5% of the loan total is accounted for by student loans.

TABLE 4
FREDONIA STATE BANK LOANS OUTSTANDING

Type of Loan		Percentage
Automobile		20
Personal single payment		17
Mobile homes, travel trailers		6
Personal installment		5
Other retail and consumer goods		5
Farm equipment and livestock		3
Commercial and industrial		24
Other secured (speculative real estate)		9
Other miscellaneous		11
	Total	100

Mr. Vannoy said that although the set of services offered by the bank is quite standard, "we do try to introduce innovations and, occasionally give special emphasis to some service. An example of this is the SOS program which we have recently inaugurated." The SOS (Special Organizational Services) program was added in February, 1974. It is designed to help survivors in time of need in regard to such matters as the proper authorities to notify, immediate practical measures to be taken, and gathering basic information for claims in such areas as social security benefits, life insurance, etc. Comprehensive check lists are used to give a methodical review of all possible benefits. This courtesy service is available to anyone regardless of present banking connections.

The bank management is anxious to provide all possible service to customers; however, they are aware that competition is becoming more fierce even to the extent of giving free services, such as SOS, in order to attract and hold customers. They expressed concern over the bank's ability to continue to provide free or low-cost services in view of the tight money market and high interest rates prevailing in mid 1974 and future uncertainty in these areas.

MARKETING AND PUBLIC RELATIONS

Several members of management acknowledged that there is no formal marketing or public relations program as such. Speaking about the growth of the bank, Mr. Godfrey stated:

> The economy was right when this bank was founded, the town was ready for a third bank, and the town grew during this time. We've had a lot of business come our way just because we're here and not because of any super-marketing strategy. We are at a point now where this is coming to a halt, not because of anything we've done wrong, but because we've got all the available loose business that we could. Now our growth is going to be directly related to how we get out and work to get new accounts. We are going to have to convince people they ought to do business with Fredonia Bank.

Mr. Godfrey went on to relate the difficulties that were encountered in soliciting new business:

> We get wrapped up in administrative duties and account solicitation is not number one on our minds. We call on a customer when we're through doing everything else. It should be the opposite. Bill Ferguson is going to be helpful in this respect. With his chamber of commerce orientation and fund raising experience he is going to be helpful in urging all of us to do account solicitation work. But my main job is to make sure I don't have any past dues and to make good bond investments. Performance in that area is directly related to me, but if we don't grow that's everyone's fault.

Mr. Honea shared Mr. Godfrey's concern about the source of future growth for the bank. His opinion was that the bank's growth had occurred because of newcomers to Nacogdoches and that future growth would come from new businesses and the university. He felt it was difficult to obtain the business of people who had been in the city for any length of time and who did not now bank at Fredonia.

Mr. Vannoy had these comments concerning the bank's advertising program:

> Advertising is a very difficult thing for a bank to handle, inasmuch as service is the only thing we can sell. We have tried to stay with a very simple approach and have, of necessity, used most of the same media that other banks use, that is, newspaper, radio, a little TV, give-aways, and donations to various worthwhile organizations. The cost of advertising to the bank is very high and we realize that sometimes it is difficult to get our dollars' worth spent on it. All along we have tried to use it to express our gratitude to the people in our community for the business they entrust to us.

OPERATIONS

The bank has membership in the FDIC and in most of the trade associations including the American Bankers Association, Texas Bankers Association, Bank Administration Institute, TBA Trust Section, and all local organizations.

The primary correspondents for the bank are Continental Bank of Texas in Houston, First City National Bank in Houston, First Bank in Lufkin, Lufkin National Bank, First National Bank in Dallas, and Chase Manhattan Bank in New York.

Mr. Lacy stated that although no specific data was available, he thought that the bank had about 60 to 70% of the university student accounts and that these amounted to approximately 5% of the bank's deposits. The largest depositors are the university, hospital, and various business organizations.

Mr. Honea expressed concern over the profit margins available in some transactions. Many transactions are small in dollar value. He felt it was going to be increasingly difficult to make a profit in these small transactions and even in some larger ones. For example, he said, it is difficult for an East Texas farmer to understand why he should have to pay the interest rate the bank must charge to show a profit.

The bank's report of financial condition for the past ten years is shown in Exhibit 2.

THE FUTURE

Bank management is hopeful that growth will continue to occur although there are no objectives which have been established. The president feels that there are too many uncontrollable factors in the banking business to make growth projections feasible. In anticipation of future growth, management has purchased some property adjoining the present bank property at the rear. Because of increased patronage on Mondays, Fridays, and the first day of each month, some thought is being given to opening the space available over the current lobby. Management is unsure, however, what services should be placed on the new second floor, when it should be done, and how to finance the expansion. The present bank building was financed by the sale of additional stock.

Management follows a general policy, according to Mr. Vannoy, of trying to anticipate areas where problems might develop and working on these areas so that no major problems arise. Some areas which he and other officers believe might produce problems include overextension of personal debt, overdrafts, forgeries, and possible increase in loan delinquencies.

In parting the president said:

> We do not consider that we have any major weaknesses but naturally we do have some problems which arise from a somewhat rather rapid rate of growth. In our day-to-day activities, of course, there are many things which arise and which some people would consider to be problems where we consider them to be routine matters of business.
>
> I guess it should be remembered that bankers are very much like psychiatrists, ministers, and doctors, in that we spend a lot of our time listening to other peoples' problems.

EXHIBIT 2
FREDONIA STATE BANK
CONSOLIDATED REPORT OF CONDITION (IN THOUSANDS)

	Years Ending December 31									
	1964	1965	1966	1967	1968	1969	1970	1971	1972	1973
Assets										
Cash and due from banks	386	287	351	521	411	567	879	1,243	1,309	2,911
U.S. Treasury Securities	808	1,147	1,312	1,476	2,262	3,563	1,551	2,283	2,085	2,757
Obligations of other U.S. government agencies and corporations								2,591	3,284	3,294
Obligations of states and other political subdivisions			25			189	842	1,350	1,822	1,921
Other securities	10	10	10	10	10	10	10	10	10	10
Federal funds sold and securities purchased under agreements to resell other loans	891	1,399	1,616	1,837	2,038	2,915	3,729	5,082	7,108	8,453
Bank premises, furniture and fixtures	28	46	43	41	43	37	469	431	438	421
Real estate owned other than bank premises				8	107	81				42
Other assets	21		1			48	6	164	235	383
Total Assets	2,144	2,889	3,358	3,893	4,871	7,410	7,486	13,154	16,291	20,192
Liabilities										
Demand deposits of individuals, partnerships, and corporations	803	853	1,117	1,239	1,452	2,053	2,326	3,246	4,402	5,473
Time and savings deposits of individuals, partnerships, and corporations	245	389	374	462	945	2,030	2,329	3,117	4,097	5,473
Deposits of United States Government	57	68	72	70	140	213	148	64	150	478
Deposits of states and political subdivisions	536	1,069	1,212	1,508	1,809	2,108	1,634	5,333	5,591	5,788
Deposits of commercial banks	105	96	167	174	39	10	10	30	25	51
Certified and officers' checks etc.	18	17	6	34	46	72	141	59	142	116
Total deposits	1,764	2,492	2,948	3,487	4,431	6,486	6,588	11,849	14,407	17,247
Total demand deposits	1,277	1,155	1,445	1,740	1,863	2,534	3,116	3,939	5,326	6,581
Federal funds purchased and securities sold under agreements to repurchase								300	700	1,000
Other liabilities										389
Total Liabilities	1,764	2,492	2,948	3,487	4,431	6,486	6,588	12,149	15,107	18,636
Reserves and Capital Accounts										
Reserve for bad debt losses on loans						40	47	72	106	132
Common stock - total par value	150	150	150	150	300	330		330	330	475
Surplus	80	97	110	106	132	276	188	273	310	362
Reserve for contingencies and other capital reserves					8	8	3		108	112
Total Capital Accounts	380	397	410	406	440	884	851	1,005	1,184	1,424
Total Liabilities, Reserves, and Capital Accounts	2,144	2,889	3,358	3,893	4,871	7,410	7,486	13,154	16,291	20,192

CASE 2

QUALITY SUPERMARKET, INCORPORATED

In 1974, Jack Williams, Owner of Quality Supermarket, Incorporated, located in St. Cloud, Minnesota, would be 50 years old. He was at the stage in his career when he was starting to enjoy some of the fruits of his labor. The store was running well. He felt that he had excellent department heads. Jack felt no reluctance in taking his wife, Dora, on a five-week trip to Europe in 1973. Each year for the past five years, as a matter of fact, Jack and Dora had been able to take a two-to three-week vacation trip as well as participate in short trips usually sponsored by the cooperative. Jack's Quality Supermarket has been a perennial winner in the various contests sponsored by the voluntary cooperative since joining the co-op in 1968. In his annual physical examination in 1971, the doctor noted a heart murmur. Although the condition was not serious, the doctor had prescribed some diet parameters and advised Jack to pace himself in his work. Jack had followed the doctor's suggestions fairly well and no change had been noted in successive physical examinations, although Jack had continued concern regarding the effect that his heart condition might have on his ability to operate his business in the future.

ST. CLOUD ENVIRONMENT

Quality Supermarket was located in St. Cloud, Minnesota, a midwestern town surrounded by farms and small communities. St. Cloud was located about sixty miles northwest of the Twin Cities of Minneapolis and St. Paul, Minnesota. This placed St. Cloud close to the geographic center of Minnesota.

The transportation net in Minnesota favored St. Cloud. St. Cloud is located on main north-south, east-west roads. North-south and east-west railroads also pass through St. Cloud. Included in the above are an interstate highway and major railroad from Chicago to the west coast.

This case was prepared by Dr. Alfred A. Pabst and Dr. Darrell F. Wentworth, as a basis for classroom discussion rather than to illustrate either effective or ineffective handling of an administrative situation. Presented at a Case Workshop and distributed by the Intercollegiate Case Clearing House, Soldiers Field, Boston, Mass. 02163. All rights reserved to the contributors. Printed in the U.S.A. Used with permission.

In 1974, St. Cloud had become one of Minnesota's most rapidly growing industrial centers. Since, 1955, the year St. Cloud Opportunities Inc., a community development agency, was organized, a 182-acre, fully serviced, industrial park had been nearly filled with eight new or expanded industries including Fingerhut Manufacturing Company, Inc., Electric Machinery Manufacturing (now Turbodyne Corp.), Franklin Manufacturing, Vision-Ease (a subsidiary of Buckbee-Meers, Inc.) six major optical lens manufacturers and two bottling companies. The vigorous program conducted by the St. Cloud Opportunities organization contributed in a major way to the steady growth of the St. Cloud Business community.

St. Cloud citizens had a history of active cooperation with the industries that have located within the city. The impressive history was coupled with aggressive civic action to improve the city and make it an attractive center for persons to live, shop and work. Numerous civic improvements were completed through the years, and, as a result, many industries discovered the community to be an excellent base for their manufacturing operations. The market area was also influenced a great deal by the three fine institutions of higher learning in the greater St. Cloud area: St. John's University, St. Benedict's College (combined enrollment of 3500) and St. Cloud State College (enrollment of 9,000) along with two very excellent trade schools — St. Cloud Area Vocational-Technical Institute and the St. Cloud Business College.

The primary trade area included the counties of: Benton, Sherburne, Stearns, Mille Lacs, Morrison and Wright with a total population of 216,170. The population of St. Cloud was 46,000 in 1974 with an estimated buying income of $129,366,000. The trend in population growth can be seen in the following figures:

St. Cloud Population

Year	
1940	24,173
1950	28,410
1960	33,815
1970	39,691
1971	42,223
1974	48,000 (estimated)
1980	55,000 (projected)

The major retail shipping areas include: East Side, Downtown, Westgate, Centennial Plaza, Crossroads and Millers which are all located within a five mile radius serving the six county primary trade area. (See map at Exhibit 1)

The retail sales distribution for 1973 was as follows:*

Type	Amount
Food	$ 22,084,000
General Merchandise	85,684,000
Furniture, Household & Appliances	3,667,000
Automotive	17,388,000
Drug	4,459,000
Total	$167,878,000
Percent of U.S.	.0428

*St. Cloud Chamber of Commerce, 1973

EXHIBIT 1

ST. CLOUD MARKET AREA *

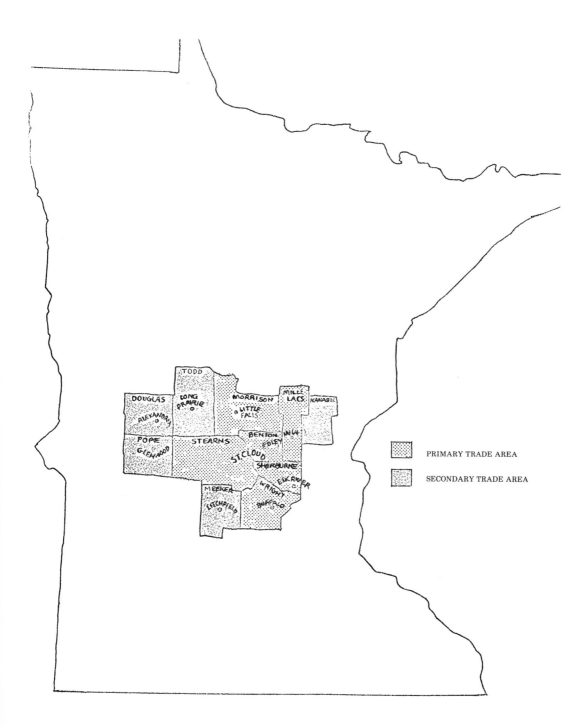

PRIMARY TRADE AREA

SECONDARY TRADE AREA

*Source: St. Cloud Chamber of Commerce

The figures comparing St. Cloud Super Market's share of retail sales within the state of Minnesota can be analyzed from the following table:

Retail Sales* (000's)

Food	1961	1967	1972	1973
Total	11,807	20,577	47,391	57,007
Super Markets	no	13,618	38,985	46,789

*Dollars in the year of sales. Source: St. Cloud Chamber of Commerce

Supermarkets in the St. Cloud area include Red Owl and National Foods in the Crossroads Shopping Center, Coborns in the Centennial Shopping Center, Super-Valu at Shop-Ko Center, Coborns and Sanitary Market in Downtown, Coborns in Sauk Rapids, Carl Supermarket in East St. Cloud.

QUALITY SUPERMARKET

One morning in the spring of 1974 Jack Williams, owner of the Quality Supermarket, reflected on the past as he looked over his modern 15,000 square foot plant which was the leading single market in the city of St. Cloud. It hadn't always been this way. There had been many ups and downs — many critical decisions which had marked the course of development of Jack's operation.

Jack Williams was born in the small town of Waseca, Minnesota and, literally, grew up in a grocery store. Jack's father owned and operated a small grocery store and Jack worked in the store during his boyhood years. After high school, Jack went into the Army and served until the end of World War II. Jack graduated from St. Johns University as a Liberal Arts major and then went to business college. Jack's ambition was to own a grocery store. To gain experience, he took a job as produce manager for a National T chain grocery store. He made a list of things that he considered important in the selection of the store he would purchase: The store had to have good growth potential; the price had to be right; the town had to be a pleasant place to raise his children; and the town had to have a parochial school.

Jack located a store in St. Cloud that met his criteria and purchased it in October 1953. The store was not in good shape when Jack took it over. It, as well as most all of the major stores in St. Cloud, operated on a "credit-home-delivery' basis. The store was doing $6,500 sales per week. Jack immediately closed the store in order to reorganize it. When Jack opened the store fifteen days later, he initiated a "cash-and-carry" operation, with substantially lower prices on all items. Jack's "cash-and-carry" policy met with considerable resistance from competing grocers whose higher prices had to be maintained to carry the costs of doing business on credit. Of course, the customers had been accustomed to credit grocery shopping, and, found it difficult to adapt to Jack's new policy. As a result, sales dropped from $6,500 under the old management to $1,000 per week under the new management. Jack lost $10,000 during the period from October 1953 to January 1954. To make matters worse, in January 1954, Jack contracted a serious illness and was bedridden for a period of three months. His doctors recommended that he sell the business. Two of Jack's employees pledged their support and efforts to keeping the store running if Jack decided on that course of action. Jack's store, somehow, survived this crisis, and, at the end of three months, Jack began slowly (one day a week, at first) to take an active role in running the store. Jack fully recovered from his illness but only after five years had elapsed.

Jack looked at his competition's use of credit as their method to increase sales—a method employed by many retailers today. In turning from the policy of "credit-home-delivery" to "cash and carry" Jack Williams implemented a strategy of increasing sales through lower prices and promotional incentives. One of the first of these promotional incentive programs was "Bonus Bucks." Based on the amount of the purchase, the customer received a certain number of "Bonus Bucks" which were "money-like" pieces of paper. These "Bonus Bucks" were redeemable for premiums — mainly household items such as appliances — which were prominently displayed on the walls of Williams' store. This was the first such promotion in St. Cloud and was evaluated by Jack Williams as "highly successful."

It took over five years for Jack William's store to reestablish the volume of $6,500 per week that the store had when Jack purchased it. Jack's store in St. Cloud had 2100 square feet of usable space. It was located in the center of town near a bank, telephone office and funeral parlor. As the business developed, floor space and parking became serious limitations to continued growth.

In 1958, Jack Williams decided that the time was ripe for expansion. He tried to buy a city park which was located next to his store, but met with insurmountable resistance. He had no money to finance the sizable capital outlay required in an expansion. As an independent grocer, Jack had no access to free service in areas such as store development, market research or financing which were available to many who were affiliated with chains, and voluntary cooperative groups.

At a social gathering, in 1958, Jack Williams happened to overhear two of his friends discussing the loan programs of a church-sponsored insurance association. Jack Williams was a religious man who had been active in the local church. Armed with this information Jack requested and secured an $85,000 loan from the church sponsored insurance association for the construction of a building. The only suitable store location available in the downtown area of St. Cloud was across the railroad track from the main shopping area. Jack purchased the land which included an old house which had to be demolished. This was purchased for $25,000 and was secured by a 20,000 mortgage 20 year mortgage at 6½% interest. The $85,000 loan was at 7% over a term of 20 years. Jack invested an additional $20,000 in fixtures. Jack personally designed and contracted for his new store. It had 72,000 square feet of usable floor space and a large parking lot in front and back. At that time, the store was the largest grocery store in St. Cloud and with the new departments took on the character of a supermarket. Jack's rationale for selecting his new location was as follows: "I looked around town and had the choice of a number of locations, I decided that the downtown location across the railroad tracks was the right spot. Sure, it was somewhat of a gamble; we were the first ones to move over here. I was confident that it was the right move. The majority of the local businessmen told me that I had made a mistake. One even went as far as to say that I had 'lost my marbles.' My landlord, in the old location, said, 'You'll be back.' However, I was confident that it was the right move!"

Jack Williams' strategy to get people to cross the tracks to shop at his new store included continuation of the "cash and carry" policy, which was now being adopted by other merchants in St. Cloud; adoption of a regular trading stamp plan (first grocery store to give trading stamps in St. Cloud); self-service meat counter (first in St. Cloud); and use of a series of crowd-attracting promotions. One original and very successful promotion consisted of loading an inexpensive used car with groceries, parking the car in the parking lot for a period of time while tickets were give to customers purchasing groceries, and raffling off the car at a specified time. The winner had to be present at the drawing. As Jack put it, "There was a remarkable interest in these raffles. We had people packed into all the aisles of the store and the surrounding parking lot." Other crowd drawing promotions included the Jay Gould Circus and an annual milking contest. The new Quality Supermaket was an instant success. Jack's Quality Supermarket had an annual real growth rate of about 15% in sales for the period 1958 to 1968.

By 1968, the Quality Supermaket was by far the leading market in St. Cloud. Its success showed that Jack was right and the businessmen, who had doubted Jack's choice of location, were wrong. In 1968, Jack Williams joined a large voluntary cooperative group as an independent store owner. This move enabled Jack to take advantages of many services of the cooperative. Since the size of the store was a constraint to further growth, Jack sought counsel from the cooperative's market research, store development and store expansion experts. An expansion was undertaken which included the following: the property on which the Quality Supermarket was located was enlarged through the purchase of an adjoining house and lot (cost: $25,000 purchased for cash); a little used one block street was petitioned closed and acquired (cost: $10,000 acquired for cash); the direction of the store was turned 180 degrees to provide better access to the enlarged parking facility; the usable floor-space was increased to 15,000 square feet on which 9,000 square feet was selling area; and a bakery was added within the store. This expansion of Quality Supermarket involved the removal of walls, relocation of merchandise, and lowering the ceiling. Despite this major renovation, Quality Supermarket closed for only one day. The expansion allowed Quality Supermarket to grow in size and number of items carried in line with trends evident in the grocery industry. Sales profile is shown in Exhibit 2.

EXHIBIT 2

Sales Profile of Quality Supermarket

Grocery	45%
Meat	22%
Dairy	10%
Haba/Gen. Merchandise	10%
Produce	7%
Bakery	6%

After the expansion, in 1968, sales of Quality Supermarket continued to grow at a rapid rate. Quality Supermarket acquired its own trailers for use in hauling groceries from distribution centers. Sales at the new location in 1958 were $10,000 per week. Quality Supermarket was open 24 hours per day seven days a week. By 1974, these sales had climbed to $100,000 per week. Profits were generally in the range of national averages for similar-sized stores. Quality Supermarket was one of the major supermarkets in the St. Cloud area. With 75 employees, Quality Supermarket was a major employer in the city. Quality Supermarket was noted for its good variety of high quality merchandise, excellent selection of brands and sizes, low prices, periodic promotions and trading stamps. The organization of Quality Supermarket is shown in Exhibit 3.

EXHIBIT 3

ORGANIZATION CHART
QUALITY SUPERMARKET, INCORPORATED

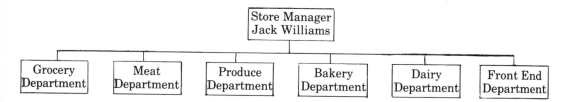

Total of 75 employees

Jack felt an organization should be run with very little emphasis on any formal chain of command. He thought that everyone would accept responsibility much more willingly and that problems would be reduced because of little prescribed - designated lines of authority. Jack's department managers were competent and experienced. The most experienced manager had been with him for five years, while the average length of service with Quality Supermarket among department managers was three years. There was a high turnover among courtesy boys (boys who bagged groceries) who were, in the main, local high school students. There was also a considerable turnover of cashiers. Courtesy boys and cashiers were under the "front-end" manager. Jack Williams, as the owner/manager constantly sought new means of cutting costs and improving service. He was the first supermarket in the mid-west to install a power cleaver in his meat department. This device enabled his butchers to cut up certain parts of beef and pork four times as quickly as could be done by hand. Jack also installed plastic bag inflating devices to speed up the bagging of poultry and vegetables. This eased the worker's job and saved 50% in labor connected with bagging.

Jack Williams was a community leader. He had been member and officer of a number of civic/business organizations. Jack was known to be an efficient, pleasant hard-working man. In 1974, Jack's two children had finished college and were married. Jack had hoped that his boy would be interested in the grocery business, but he chose another profession. Jack's assistant was his grocery manager. All department managers reported directly to Jack. The department managers were held accountable for the performance of their respective departments. Jack reviewed the performance figures for each department with its manager on a regular basis. Quality Supermarket, Incorporated, was a private corporation owned jointly by Jack and Dora Williams. The primary assets of the corporation were the building and fixtures which housed the supermarket, a five and one-half acre parcel of ground on which the supermarket was located, one 1970 Ford pick up truck and two Fruehauf trailers, used to carry groceries from the cooperative distribution point. The Profit/Loss statement for 1973 is at Exhibit 4. The balance sheet for December 1973 is at Exhibit 5. The buildings and land had a market value of $210,000.

Quality Supermarket, Inc., had grown considerably from its modest beginning to the year 1974. The pattern of that growth is shown in Exhibit 6.

Jack had located a piece of property on the outskirts of the city which could be purchased for about $1.00 per square foot. It was located on the second most desirable of three highway arteries which bisected the city. There were no supermarkets or shopping centers on the fringe of the city. Jack had the option to develop this land as a free-standing supermarket or share it as a shopping center complex. The size of the land parcel was 14 acres. Construction costs were estimated at from $20 to $30/per square foot depending primarily on the nature of the finishing materials and luxury appointments involved. Taxes were estimated at $1.00 per square foot and insurance $.75 per square foot of building area. Fixtures cost from $20-$37 per square foot depending on the quality, appointments and major departments included. For example, a low-budget supermarket with a bakery and delicatessen could be fixtured from $26 per square foot. Break-even point was estimated at weekly sales of $3 per square foot of selling space.

Jack was considering a 32,000-square-foot store. In this store he would have the same departments that were included in the old store plus a delicatessen. The new store would have 22,000 square feet of selling space and would be equipped with the most modern fixtures and equipment. Jack estimated that he could begin operations in the new store in 6 months and was confident that he could start with his present store sales volume. He felt that he would get "his share" of new business brought about by increases in general business in the St. Cloud area. Jack felt that operational costs in the new store would be proportionately similar to the present store.

For a shopping center, a nucleus could be made up of Quality Supermarket, a bank, a hardware store, a drug store, a beauty parlor, a barber shop, and a restaurant.

Money was tight. Quality Supermarkets, Inc. could expect to pay 14% for a 20-year loan of funds required. Jack felt that he could get any needed amount at this rate. The businessmen in the city questioned whether a shopping center would be a success on the fringe of a city the size of St. Cloud.

An alternative to building a new store was to expand the present store again. Exterior expansion was not possible, but the present facility could be used more intensively. Different meat and produce cases could triple the amount of products displayed with no increase in area used. Similar improvements in display cases could increase display area by 20%. Use of super cash registers could enable Quality Supermarkets to handle twice as many customers when the system was fully operational in eight months. The parking lot at the present location was adequate for twice the present number of customers at any one time. The cost of making these major alterations to the present store were about $10 per square foot of selling area. These alterations would permit an estimated 30% increase in sales volume.

ANNEX 1
BACKGROUND MATERIAL ON THE GROCERY INDUSTRY*

In the early 1900's "grocery shopping" consisted of many stops. There was the meat market, the bakery, the fruit stand, and the grocery store. In those days, many people had their food delivered.

Into this simple, relatively static, situation came the chain store. Since the chains purchased directly from the manufacturer, they could sell at lower prices, and people flocked to these stores. Chain stores grew rapidly during the 1910's and broke into full bloom in the 1920's.

To stay in business, the small grocery stores and their wholesalers had to change their method of operations. Some banded together and started the "supermarket" concept. (This will be discussed later). The customers waited

*Primary source of data and material contained in this note are publications of *Progressive Grocer* and the *Super Market Institute*.

EXHIBIT 4
PROFIT AND LOSS STATEMENT

Grocery Sales		$2,065,635.48
Dairy Sales		459,348.62
Meat Sales		928,696.53
Haba/Gen Merchandise		444,346.11
Produce Sales		303,333.47
Bakery		397,944.00
TOTAL SALES.		4,599,304.21
Grocery Gross Profit		378,152.61
Dairy Gross Profit		82,072.41
Meat Gross Profit		147,313.12
Haba/Gen Merchandise		79,753.17
Produce Gross Profit		54,348.29
Bakery Gross Profit		71,674.46
TOTAL GROSS PROFIT		813,314.06
Controllable Expenses		
Advertising		42,674.07
Bad Debts		295.17
Delivery Expense		5,437.16
Donations		732.07
Dues/Subscriptions		8,420.50
Freight		1,625.14
Cleaning Service		1,200.00
Fuel/Heating		10,230.76
Garbage Disposal		560.20
Laundry		1,100.00
Electricity/Water		11,847.48
Parking Lot Expense		150.00
Repairs		2,645.37
Salaries Front End	110,153.40	
Grocery	95,017.04	
Security	8,000.00	
Meat	75,465.32	
Bakery	60,534.68	
Manager	20,000.00	
TOTAL (Including Taxes)		369,170.44
Pension Fund		45,000.00
Supplies		2,237.46
Sundry		1,247.75
Telephone		1,242.62
Travel Expense		2,540.76
Trading Stamps		91,811.13
TOTAL CONTROLLABLE EXPENSES		600,168.08
Non-Controllable Expenses		
Accounting		1,245.37
Welfare Insurance		2,457.75
Depreciation Expense		4,250.00
Insurance Expense		2,473.50
Service Fees on Merchandise		38,557.60
Taxes and License (Except on Income)		23,470.76
TOTAL NON-CONTROLLABLE EXPENSE		76,029.98
TOTAL EXPENSES		676,198.06
OPERATING PROFIT		137,116.00
Other Expenses and Income		
Salary Officers		(24,000.00)
Income (other)		2,140.00
Sale of Fixed Assets		363.97
TOTAL OTHER EXPENSES AND INCOME		(21,496.03)
NET PROFIT BEFORE TAX		$115,619.97
NET PROFIT AFTER TAX		57,809.98

on themselves in an "assembly line" manner in large barnlike buildings on a strictly cash and carry basis. This enabled the "Independents" and their wholesalers to compete with the chains. They started competing in the 1930's and continue to compete today.

INDEPENDENTS

An independent grocery store may be defined as a single store, individually owned, with a purchasing arrangement with a wholesaler.'

Before the advent of the chain store, the independent store was the dominant form of grocery outlet. Some independents offered the services of credit and delivery. Wholesalers would send salesmen to call on each independent periodically (usually weekly) to take orders. The respective grocery order would be delivered and the store owner would generally have 30 days to pay for his order. Thus, the wholesaler provided short term financing for the independent. Obviously, these costs had to be passed on to the independent, making his costs higher than those in the chain operation.

EXHIBIT 5

BALANCE SHEET FOR DECEMBER 1973

Current Assets		
Cash on Hand		$ 1,574.45
Cash in Bank		25,637.45
Accounts Receivable		357.30
Returned Checks		45.00
Inventory:Grocery		93,242.73
Dairy		2,543.64
Meat		8,584.05
Haba/Gen Merchandise		13,640.44
Produce		3,558.93
Bakery		2,800.00
Prepaid Trading Stamps		6,453.53
Coupons		1,143.74
Prepaid Insurance		1,245.65
TOTAL CURRENT ASSETS		170,827.54
Fixed Assets		
Store Equipment and Fixtures		75,453.43
Depreciation Reserve for Store and Eqpt		45.374.64
Delivery Equipment		9,473.43
Depreciation Reserve for Del Eqpt		8,474.46
TOTAL FIXED ASSETS		138,775.96
TOTAL ASSETS		309,603.50
Current Liabilities		
Accounts Payable (Voluntary Cooperative)		80,463.43
Accounts Payable (Other)		2,540.73
Accrued Interest		301.10
Accrued Taxes and Licenses		2,100.04
TOTAL CURRENT LIABILITIES		85,405.30
Deferred Liabilities		
Notes Payable Long Term (Mortgage/Loan)		55,480.50
TOTAL DEFERRED LIABILITIES		55,480.50
TOTAL LIABILITIES		140,885.80
Net Worth		
Common Stock	36,000.00	
Paid-in Surplus	80,000.00	
Net Earnings	57,809.98	
NET WORTH AS OF 12/31/73		$173,809.98

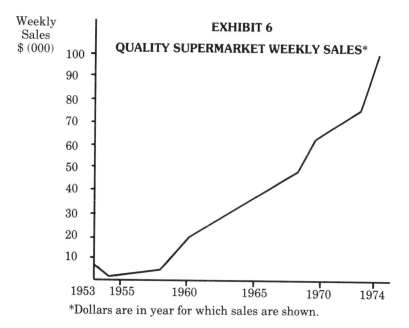

Weekly
Sales
$ (000)

EXHIBIT 6

QUALITY SUPERMARKET WEEKLY SALES*

*Dollars are in year for which sales are shown.

To meet the competition of the chains, the independents and their wholesalers either had to develop an arrangement which would cut costs or go out of business. They developed two new concepts: "retailer-owned wholesalers" and "voluntary wholesalers", which will be discussed in the next section.

VOLUNTARY WHOLESALERS

As the name implies the individual retailer would "voluntarily" affiliate with a wholesaler in return for services rendered. The services which the wholesaler performed in return for grocery orders consisted of managerial assistance, merchandising help, and the use of the wholesaler's name. Other services offered included: engineers to help with construction and layout of new buildings, accountants to help keep records, and in some cases financing of a new store. IGA, Red and White, Super Valu, and Jack Spratt are examples of the voluntary wholesaler concept which are operating today.

The key to success for the voluntary wholesalers, as with the retail-owned wholesaler, is to minimize costs. Mail-ordering of merchandise eliminates wholesalers' salesmen. The orders are filled from huge one-story merchanized warehouses on an assembly-line basis with delivery to the affiliates on a pre-arranged schedule.

SALES AND MARGINS
INDEPENDENTS

The independents showed healthy growth in 1971 by posting a 6% increase in sales. The Independent group consists of three categories: Supermarkets, Superettes, and Small Stores. Independent supermarkets showed the largest increase of the group, with a 9.7% increase in sales (vs. 7.8% for chain stores). While accounting for only 11% of the stores, supermarkets posted 61% of the sales of independents for the year. (Small stores are not within the scope of this report and therefore will not be discussed at length).

Independents tend to earn a slightly higher net profit than do chains because of their ownership and flexibility of operation. As a result of their "smaller operation" they are better able to adapt to changing conditions than corporate chains.

The Independents posted a 18.9% gross margin, unchanged from 1970. Wage expenses increased .4% from 1970 (8.1% - 7.7%); however, other expenses showed a decrease of .5% (8.7% - 8.2%). These factors combined to give the Independents a .1% increase in net profit (before Taxes), from 2.5% to 2.6% for the year.

INDEPENDENT FOOD RETAILING (1971)

	Number of Stores	Percentage of Stores	Sales	Percentage of Sales
Supermarkets	18,200	11%	29.965B	61%
Superettes	25,200	15%	9.790B	20%
Small Stores	126,000	74%	9.355B	19%
Total	169,400	100%	49.110B	100%

The following categories are used for analysis:

Supermarket: Any store, chain or independent doing $500,000 or more in sales per year.

Superette: Any store doing $150,000 to $500,000 in sales per year.

Small Store: Any store doing less than $150,000 in sales per year.

Source: *Progressive Grocer:* April 1972

SALES AND MARGINS

Mixed results is the best description of food chains from 1971. Sales increased but margins, as a percent of sales, decreased. The chains posted a 7.8% increase in sales, which proved to be the best retail performance of the recession year. Net profits, on the other hand, dipped to a record low, to .86% (as a percent of sales). In 1970, the chains showed .92% net profit. The causes of the decline in net profit in 1970 and 1971 were increased expenses, and the inability to increase prices while remaining competitive. Another factor contributing to the depression of the industry as a whole were the losses of the nation's number one and three chains (A & P and Kroger).

In the last few years, supermarkets have altered their merchandising approach in an effort to build their sales volume. The outcome has been the practice known as "discounting". To appeal to the specific customers' need value, the supermarkets have increasingly changed to discount operations. Basically, the practice of discounting entails reducing product margins about 3% in return for increased sales, generally about 20%. In effect, the supermarkets are trading product margin for increased product turnover. The discounting is largely on grocery items, originally on national brands; but trends show supermarkets leaning toward discounting both national and private labels. Some retailers, whose sales volume have not been sufficient to compensate for the discounts, have resorted to higher margins on perishables. However, costs are rising on these items (for example, produce and meats); and they are also price-sensitive to a certain extent. As a result, the supermarkets are turning to general merchandise and areas such as delicatessen, hot foods, and bakery goods for increased margins where price is not so apparent.

NEW SUPERMARKETS[3]

STORE AREA

The total area and selling space of stores increased in size in 1970. However, the ratio of selling space to total remained relatively constant at 70%. The largest stores in terms of selling area were located in regional shopping centers. Stores of this type had an average of 17,800 square feet of customer selling area. Stores in neighborhood shopping centers, on the other hand, had 12,934 square feet of customer selling area.

OWNERSHIP

The majority of new supermarkets were leased. The next largest category was ownership by operator, followed by build-sell-lease-back.

	Ownership of New Supermarkets		
	Independent landlord	Build-sell-lease-back	Owned by Operator
1969	66%	19%	15%
1970	76%	7%	17%
1971	76%	8%	16%

The smaller companies were more likely to own stores outright than were the larger companies. In addition, free-standing supermarkets were least likely to be rented from a landlord; 69% of this type were rented from a landlord compared to 90% of the stores located in shopping centers.

CHARACTERISTICS OF LEASED STORES[4]

Ninety percent of new supermarkets rented from a landlord were leased from an independent landlord; the remaining had a build-sell-lease-back arrangement.

Twenty-one percent of new free-standing supermarkets had build-sell-lease-back arrangements. Eighty-nine percent of supermarkets in shopping centers operated under this type of arrangement.

An average of 14% of new supermarkets were build-sell-lease-back in the Midwest.

The length of leases under build-sell-lease-back tended to be longer than those from independent landlords.

RENT COST AS A PERCENT OF SALES

On the average the cost of rent was 1.7% of sales. Stores in regional shopping centers averaged 1.7% while free-standing supermarkets paid 1.5%. Rent as a percent of sales was highest in New England.

MINIMUM RENT

Of new supermarkets paying rent, 72% had a minimum annual rent obligation. The minimum rent on this average was $2.10 per square foot of the store's total area. Minimum rents in the Midwest tended to be above the na-

[3]*Facts about New Supermarkets;* Supermarket Institute; 1971.

[4]*Facts About New Supermarkets*

tional average. Additionally, minimum rents tended to be higher for stores in regional shopping centers, than for stores located in other areas. Regional stores paid an average of $2.72 vs. $1.70 per square foot for free-standing stores.

BUILDING COSTS

In 1971, two thirds of the capital expenditure for a new supermarket went for the building itself. The average expenditure for a new supermarket building was $360,000. That figure is 12.5% above 1970 for only 850 more square feet. The cost per square foot increased with the size of the store.

	Size	Cost per square foot
Small	less than 12,000 square feet	$11.42
Medium	12,000 - 17,999	$15,000
Large	greater than 18,000	$16.36

The average cost per square foot, for all sizes of stores, increase one dollar per square foot over 1970 figures. Costs of buildings were highest in the Midwest ($23.89). The lowest costs per square foot were reported in the Southwest region. Costs of buildings were most expensive in regional shopping centers. Supermarkets located in neighborhood shopping centers were least expensive while costs of free-standing supermarkets were in between.

Supermarkets are expanding the types of merchandise they carry in both food and non-food areas. Frozen foods are playing an increasing role in new supermarkets. Specialty departments also are adding to the new look of the seventies. Restaurants, delicatessen, bakeries, and other specialty departments are becoming more frequent sights in the new supermarket. In 1971, the supermarket with a high proportion of non-food items and services represented a larger share of the new supermarkets than ever before.

There has been an evolutionary development of various services in the supermarket. In the early sixties, when discount department stores became prominent, grocery stores were usually located nearby. The grocery stores helped to bring people to the discount stores and vice versa. As the discount stores developed, they became larger and offered more services. The supermarket of the seventies could very well include: grocery, bakery, delicatessen, pharmacy, liquor store, plus the non-food items of the discount store.

CASE 3

UNITED PRODUCTS, INC.

Having just returned from lunch, Mr. George Brown, president of United Products, Inc., was sitting in his office thinking about his upcoming winter vacation where he and his family would be spending three weeks skiing on Europe's finest slopes. His daydreaming was interrupted by a telephone call from Mr. Hank Stevens, UPI's General Manager. Mr. Stevens wanted to know if their two o'clock meeting was still on. The meeting had been scheduled to review actions UPI could take in light of the currently depressed national economy. In addition, Mr. Brown was concerned about his accountant's report detailing results for the company's recently completed fiscal year. Although it hadn't been a bad year, results were not as good as expected and this in conjunction with economic situation was forcing Mr. Brown to re-evaluate alternative actions being considered for the future.

COMPANY HISTORY

United Products, Inc. established in 1941, is engaged in the sales and service of basic supply items for shipping and receiving, production and packaging, research and development, and office and warehouse departments. Mr. Brown's father, the founder of the company, recognized the tax advantages in establishing separate businesses rather than trying to operate the business through one large organization. Accordingly, over the years companies were created as business warranted and in some cases companies were either closed or sold off. By the mid 1960's, he had succeeded in structuring a chain of four related companies covering the geographic area from Chicago eastward.

In 1967, feeling it was time to step aside and turn over active control of the business to his sons, the elder Mr. Brown recapitalized the company and merged or sold off the separate companies. When the restructuring process was completed, he had set up two major companies. United Products, Inc., was to be run by his youngest son, George Brown, with its headquarters in Massachusetts, while his other son, Richard Brown, was to operate United Products Southeast, Inc. headquartered in Florida.

Although the Brown brothers occasionally work together and are on each other's Board of Directors, the two companies operate on their own.

This case was prepared by Assistant Professor Jeffrey C. Shuman of Babson College as the basis for class discussion rather than to illustrate appropriate or inappropriate handling of administrative situations.

Copyright ©, Babson College, Babson, Park, Massachusetts.

Distributed by the Intercollegiate Case Clearing House, Soldiers Field, boston, Mass. 02163. All rights reserved to the contributors, Printed in the U.S.A. Used with permission.

As Mr. George Brown explained, "Since we are brothers we often get together and discuss business, but the two are separate companies and each files its own tax return." This case only considers United Products, Inc. and the activities of Mr. George Brown.

During 1972, United Products moved into its new offices in Woburn, Massachusetts. From this location, it is believed, the company is able to effectively serve its entire New England market area. "Our abilities and our desires to expand and improve our overall operation will be enhanced in the new specially designed structure containing our offices, repair facilities and warehouse," is the way in which George Brown spoke about the new facilities. Concurrent with the recent move, the company segmented its over 3,500 different items carried into eight major product categores:

1. *Stapling Machines* including Wire Stitchers, Carton Stitchers, Nailers, Hammers, Tackers, Manual - Foot - Air - Electric.

2. *Staples* to fit almost all make of equipment — all sizes - types - steel, bronze, monel, stainless steel, aluminum, brass, etc.

3. *Stenciling Equipment* and supplies, featuring Marsh Hand and Electric Machines, Stencil Brushes, Boards, Inks.

4. *Gummed Tape Machines,* Hand and Electric, featuring Marsh, Derby, Counterboy equipment.

5. *Industrial Tapes* by 3M, Mystik, Behr Manning, Dymo— specializing in strapping, masking, cellophane, electrical, cloth, nylon, waterproof tapes.

6. *Gluing Machines* — hand and electric.

7. *Work Gloves* — cotton, leather, neoprene, nylon, rubber, asbestos, etc.

8. *Marking and Labeling Equipment.*

In a flyer mailed at the time of the move to United Products' 6,000 accounts, the company talked about its growth in this fashion:

Here we grow again—thanks to you—our many longtime valued customers...

Time and Circumstances have decreed another United Products transPLANT—this time, to an unpolluted garden-type industrial area, ideally located for an ever-increasing list of our customers.

Now, in the new 28,000-sq.-ft. plant with enlarged offices and warehouse, we at UNITED PRODUCTS reach the peak of efficiency in offering our customers the combined benefits of maximum inventories, accelerated deliveries, and better repair services.

By 1974, the company had grown to a point where sales were $3.5 million (double that of four years earlier) and employed 34 people. Results for 1973 compared to 1972 showed a sales increase of twenty-two percent and a 40 percent increase in profits. Exhibit 1 contains selected financial figures for 1971, 1972, and 1973 in addition to the fiscal 1973 balance sheet.

COMPETITION

Mr. George Brown believes that UPI does not have clearly defined competition for its business. It is felt that since UPI carries over 3500 different items they have competition on parts of their business, but no one competes against their whole business:

> It is hard to get figures on competition since we compete with no one company directly. Different companies compete with various product lines but there is no one who competes across our full range of products.

On a regular basis, Mr. Brown receives *Dun & Bradstreet* Business Information Reports on specific firms with which he competes. Mr. Brown feels that since the competing firms are, like his own firm, privately held the financial figures reported are easily manipulated and, therefore are not sound enough to base plans on. Exhibit 2 contains comparative financial figures for two competing companies, and Exhibit 3 contains D & B's description of their operations along with two other firms operating in UPI's prime New England Market area.

EXHIBIT 1
UNITED PRODUCTS, INC.
SELECTED FINANCIAL FIGURES

	11-30-1971	11-30-1972	11-30-1973
Curr. Assets	$862,783	$689,024	$ 937,793
Curr. Liablities	381,465	223,004	342,939
Other Assets	204,566	774,571	750,646
Worth	685,884	750,446	873,954
Sales			3,450,000

Following statement dated Nov. 30, 1973

Cash	$ 46,961	Accts Pay	$ 320,795
Accts Rec	535,714	Notes Pay	20,993
Mdse	352,136		
Ppd Ins., Int., Taxes	2,980		
Current	937,793	Current	342,939
Fixt & Equip	42,891	RE	471,655
Motor Vehicles	49,037	CAPITAL STOCK	519,800
Real Estate	658,768	Surplus	354,154
Total Assets	$1,688,486	Total	$1,688,486

MANAGEMENT PHILOSOPHY

When Mr. Brown took over UPI in 1967 at the age 24, he set a personal goal of becoming financially secure and developing a highly profitable business. With the rapid growth of the company, he soon realized his goal of financial independence and in so doing began to lose interest in the company. "I became a rich person at age 28 and had few friends with equal wealth that were my age. The business no longer presented a challenge and I was unhappy with the way things were going."

EXHIBIT 2
UNITED PRODUCTS, INC.
COMPETITIVE INFORMATION

East Coast Supply Co., Inc. - Sales $1m.

	Fiscal Dec. 31, 1971	Fiscal Dec. 31, 1972	Fiscal Dec. 31, 1973
Curr Assets	88,555	132,354	166,426
Curr Liabilities	44,543	47,606	77,055
Other Assets	16,082	18,045	27,422
Worth	63,165	102,793	116,793

Statement dated Dec. 31, 1973

Cash	$ 42,948	Accts Pay	$ 41,668
Accts Rec	86,123	Notes Pay	27,588
Mdse	34,882	Taxes	7,799
Prepaid	2,473		
Current	166,426	Current	77,055
Fixt & Equip	15,211	CAPITAL STOCK	10,000
Deposits	12,211	RETAINED EARNINGS	106,793
Total Assets	193,848	Total	193,848

Atlantic Paper Products, Inc. - Sales $6m.

	June 30, 1970	June 30, 1971	June 30, 1972
Curr Assets	$101,241	$1,243,259	$1,484,450
Curr Liabilities	574,855	502,572	1,120,036
Other Assts	93,755	101,974	107,001
Worth	403,646	439,677	471,415
Long Term Dept		402,094	

After taking a ten-month "mental vacation" from the business, George Brown felt he was ready to return to work. He had concluded that one way to proving himself to himself and satisfying his ego would be to make the company as profitable as possible. However, the amount of growth that UPI is able to realize is limited by the level of energy exerted by Mr. Brown. "The company can only grow at approximately 20 percent per year, since this is the amount of energy I am willing to commit to the business."

Although Mr. Brown is only 31, he feels that his philosophical outlook is very conservative and he tends to operate the same as his 65-year-old father would. He has established several operating policies consistent with his philosophy that are constraining on the business.

I am very concerned about making UPI a nice place to work. I have to enjoy what I'm doing and have fun at it at the same time. I cannot make any more money since I'm putting away as much money as I can. The government won't allow me to make more money since I already take the maximum amount.

I like to feel comfortable, and if we grew too quickly it could get out of hand. I realize the business doesn't grow to its potential but why should I put more into it, I have all the money I need. The company could grow, but why grow? Why is progress good? You have to pay for everything in life and I'm not willing to work harder since I don't need the money.

EXHIBIT 3
UNITED PRODUCTS, INC.
DESCRIPTIONS OF COMPETITION

EAST COAST SUPPLY CO. INC.

Manufactures and distributes pressure sensitive tapes to industrial users throughout New England area on 1/10 net 30 day terms. Thirty-four employed including the officers, thirty-three here. LOCATION: Rents 15,000 square feet on first floor of two-story brick building in good repair. Premises are orderly. Non-seasonal business. Branches are located at 80 Olife Street, New Haven, Connecticut and 86 Weybosset Street, Providence, Rhode Island.

ATLANTIC PAPER PRODUCTS, INC.

Wholesales paper products, pressure sensitive tapes, paper specialties, twines and other merchandise of this type. Sales to industrial accounts and commercial users on 1/10 net 30 day terms. There are about 1,000 accounts in Eastern Massachusetts and sales are fairly steady throughout the year. Employs 60 including officers. LOCATION: Rents 130,000 sq. ft. of floor space in a six-story brick mill type building in a commercial area on a principal street. Premises orderly.

THE JOHNSON SALES CO.

Wholesales shipping room supplies including staplings and packing devices, markets and stencil equipment. Sells to industrial and commercial accounts throughout the New England area. Seasons are steady. Terms are 1/10 net 30 days. Number of accounts not learned, 15 are employed including the owner. LOCATION: Rents the first floor of a two-story yellow brick building in good condition. Housekeeping is good.

BIG CITY STAPLE CORP.

Wholesales industrial staples, with sales to 2000 industrial and commercial firms, sold on 1/10 net 30 day terms. Territory mainly New Jersey. Employs 10 including officers. Seasons steady and competition active. LOCATION: Rents 5,000 square feet in one-story cinder block and brick structure in good condition, premises in neat order. Located on well-traveled street in a commercial area.

> Another thing, I am a scrupulously honest businessman and it is very hard to grow large if you're honest. There are many deals that I could get into that would make UPI a lot of money but I'm too moral of a person to get involved and besides I don't need the money.

> To me, happiness is being satisfied with what you have. I've got my wife, children and health; why risk these for something I don't need. I don't have the desire to make money because I didn't come from a poor family, I'm not hungry.

> Another thing, I have never liked the feeling of owing anything to anyone. If you can't afford to buy something, then don't. I don't like to borrow any money and I don't like the company to borrow any. All of our bills are paid within 15 days. I suppose I've constrained the business as a result of this feeling, but it's my business. The company can only afford to pay for a 20 percent growth rate so that's all we'll grow.

ORGANIZATIONAL STRUCTURE

Upon his return to the company George Brown realigned UPI's organizational structure as shown in Exhibit 4 (company does not have an organizational chart; this one is drawn from the researcher's notes).

> We have to have it on a functional basis now. We are also trying something new for us by moving to the general manager concept. In the past when I was away, there was no one with complete authority; now my general manager is in charge in my absence.

In discussing the new structuring of the organization, Mr. Brown was quick to point out that the company has not established formalized job descriptions. "Job descriptions are not worth anything. My people wear too many hats, and, besides, we're too small to put it in writing." At present the company employs 34 people including Mr. Brown.

Mr. Brown is quick to point out that he has never had a personnel problem. "All my people enjoy working here." He believes that "nobody should work for nothing" and has, therefore, established a personal goal of seeing to it that no one employed by UPI makes less than $10,000 per year. Mr. Brown commented on his attitude toward his employees:

> The men might complain about the amount of responsibility placed on them but I think it's good for them. It helps them develop to their potential. I'm a nice guy who is interested in all of my people. I feel a strong social obligation to my employees and have developed very close relationships with all of them. My door is always open to them no matter what the problem may be.

> I make it a policy never to yell at anyone in public, it's not good for morale. Maybe it's part of my conservative philosophy but I want everyone to call me Mr. Brown, not George. I think it's good for people to have a Mr. Brown. Although I want to run a nice friendly business, I have learned that it's hard to be real friends with an employee. You can only go so far. Employers and employees cannot mix socially, it just doesn't work out over the long run.

> This is not your normal business. I am very approachable, I don't demand much and I allow an easy open dialogue with my employees. Seldom do I take any punitive action. I'm just not a hard-driving tough guy...I'm an easy-going guy.

> It would take much of the enjoyment out of the business for me to come in here and run this place like a machine. [Researchers note: When the researcher arrived at the plant one afternoon he observed Mr. Brown running around the office deeply involved in a water fight with one of his office girls. By the way, he lost.]

> I find it hard to motivate the company's salesmen. Since we have so much trouble finding good capable men, I'm not likely to fire any that I have. This situation makes it hard for me to put pressure on them to produce.

> The bonus system, if you want to call it that, is I guess what you'd call very arbitrary. I have not set up specific sales quotas, or targeted goals for my inside people, so as a result, I base my bonus decisions on my assessment of how well I feel an employee performed during the past year.

> Recently, I've given some thought to selling the company. I could probably get around $3 to $4 million for it. If I did that, I'm not sure what I would do with my time. Besides my family and UPI there is not much that I am interested in. A couple of years ago when I took my extended vacation I got bored and couldn't wait to get back to the company.

UPI'S PLANNING PROCESS

George Brown claims to be a firm believer in planning. "I find myself spending more and more time planning for the company. Currently, I'm averaging about 50 percent of my time and I see this increasing." As he

EXHIBIT 4

UNITED-PRODUCTS, INC.

Organization Chart - December, 1974

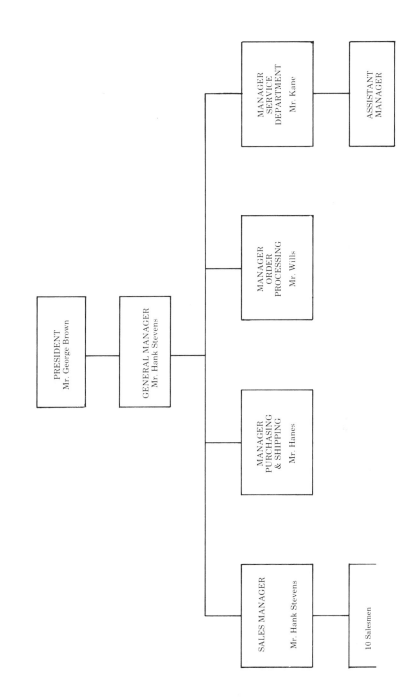

described it, the planning process at United Products is really a very loose system. "We have no planned way as to how we do the planning."

> Basically, the process is directed at ways of increasing the profitability of the company. I look at the salesmen's performance on a weekly and monthly basis, and use this information in the development of the plans.
>
> Since we have a very informal planning process we only forecast out one year at most. The company's plans are reevaluated each month and if necessary new plans are set. Only on rare occasions have we ever planned beyond one year.
>
> However, I think the current economic and political situation may force us into developing plans that cover a two-year period.

Although goals are not formally developed and written down, Mr. Brown had identified objectives in three areas: sales, profits and organizational climate.

Specifically they are:

1. Increase sales volume of business by 20% per year,
2. Increase gross profit margin ½ to 1 percent per year, and
3. Make UPI a friendly place to work.

Mr. Brown feels that the company has been able to grow at about 20 percent a year in the past and, therefore, should have no problem realizing that level in the future. In addition he believes that sales growth is a necessary evil. "Those companies that don't grow are swallowed up by the competition, and besides given the level of energy I'm willing to exert, I think 20 percent is a reasonable level of growth."

In the area of profits, the company actually sets no specific targeted figures other than saying they simply want an increase in the percentage of profits. Mr. Brown commented that:

> We do not set a goal because we would not have a way of measuring it. I have no way of knowing how much money I am making until the end of the year without considerable time and effort.

With respect to the third goal, Mr. Brown is concerned about the workplace environment and wants UPI to be a big happy family and wants everyone employed to be happy.

In describing the planning process used at UPI, Mr. Brown emphasized the unstructured informal nature of the process.

> I am familiar with commonly accepted theory about planning systems but I do not feel it is necessary for UPI to institute, in a formal manner, any of those I've read about. We perform many of the activities advocated in the planning models, but we do them in a relaxed, casual fashion. For example, I am a member of many organizations connected with my business and receive industry newsletters on a regular basis. In addition, I receive input from friends and business. Since we do not have a formal process, planning tends to be a continuous process at UPI.

When asked about UPI's strengths and weaknesses Mr. Brown indicated that the company has four areas of strength and one major weakness:

Strengths
1. The number of different products carried
2. The quality of its employees, particularly salesmen
3. No debt, and
4. Purchasing capabilities

Weaknesses
1. An inability to get and train new personnel—primarily in the sales function of the business.

The salesmen are not assigned a sales quota for the year but rather are evaluated based on Mr. Brown's assessment of the particular salesman's territory and initiative. He feels his salesmen make more than competitive salesmen. Several of the ten salesmen have earned as much as $40,000 in a single year. All salesmen are compensated on a straight commission basis, as shown below:

8% for first $180,000 sales
7% for next $60,000
6% for next $60,000
5% for everything over $300,000.

Mr. Brown is pleased with the sales success of his company and feels that United Products' greatest strength is its ability to "sell anything to anybody." However, the problem for UPI has been in finding good salesmen. "There just aren't any good salesmen around and this is a problem because the salesmen are the lifeblood of our business."

INTERPERSONAL RELATIONSHIPS

Since Mr. Brown is concerned about the climate in the company, he has paid particular attention to the nature of the relationship within UPI. At the time of the company's reorganization, Mr. Hank Stevens was brought into the organizaton as general manager and assistant to the president. Over the past several years, Mr. Stevens' areas of responsibility have grown to the extent that they now comprise approximately 80 percent of the activities that were formally done by Mr. Brown. As a result of this, George Brown sometimes finds himself with little to do and often times works only five hours per day. As he describes it:

Hank's management discretionary power has increased steadily since he has been here; partly as a result of the extent of responsibility I've placed on him and partly due to his aggressiveness. As it now stands, he makes almost all of the daily operating decisions for the company, leaving me with only the top management decisions. Let's be realistic, there just aren't that many top-management decisions that have to be made here in the course of a day. A lot of the time, I walk around the plant checking on what other people are doing and, I guess, acting as a morale booster.

When asked about the management capabilities of Hank Stevens, Mr. Brown responded by saying, "Hank probably feels that he is working at a very fast pace, but when you evaluate the effectiveness of his actions, he is actually moving forward at what I would consider to be a very slow pace. However, everything else considered, Hank is the best of what is around. I guess if I would find a really good sales manager, I would add him to the company and relieve Hank of that area of responsibility."

MR. HANK STEVENS

Mr. Hank Stevens, 32, joined UPI at the time of the reorganization in 1970 after having graduated from a local university with a B.S. in Economics. As general manager, Mr. Stevens' responsibilities include planning, purchasing, sales management as well as involvement in other decisions that affect UPI policy. Mr. Stevens feels that he has been fortunate in that "Ever since I came to UPI, I've reported to the president and in essence have had everyone else reporting to me."

When asked about the goals of UPI, Mr. Stevens responded that, "As I see it, we have goals in three major areas: profitability, sales level, and personal relationships." In discussing his own personal goals Hank explained that he hoped that the organization would grow and as a result he would be able to grow along with it.

Since Mr. Stevens works so closely with Mr. Brown he has given considerable thought to his boss's business philosophy:

> I feel that George's business philosophy is unique. I guess the best way to describe it is to say that above all he is a businessman. Also, he has very high moral values and as a result of that he is extremely honest and would never cheat anybody. Actually, the company would probably look better financially if it was run by someone who didn't operate with the same values as George.

When asked about the salesforce at UPI, Mr. Stevens commented that "when a new salesman starts with the company, he does so with full salary. After a period of about two years we change him over to a commission basis." As has always been the case, UPI concentrates its sales efforts on large customers. Mr. Stevens noted that "on the average the company processes approximately 105 orders per day, with an average dollar value per order of roughly $132. It's not that we won't write small orders, we just don't solicit business from small accounts. It just makes more sense to concentrate on the larger accounts."

MR. JIM HANES

Jim Hanes, age 24 has been with UPI for over six years and during that time has worked his way up from assistant service manager to his current position as the number-three man in the company functioning as the Manager of Purchasing and Shipping. Jim is responsible for the front office, repair work and the warehouse. He feels that his reporting responsibility is approximately 60 percent to Mr. Stevens and 40 percent to Mr. Brown. "Since I have responsibility for all merchandise entering and leaving the company I get involved with both Hank and George, and, therefore, I guess I report to both of them."

In talking about where he would go from his present position he explained that:

> I guess the next step is for me to become a salesman so that I can broaden my background and move up in the company. However, I am a little worried; I don't think the salesmen in our company are given the right sales training. As the system works a new man is assigned to work with an experienced salesman for about six weeks after which time he is given his own territory. Perhaps if our sales manager had more experience as a salesman he would handle the training differently.

In commenting on his understanding of Mr. Brown's philosophy, Jim summed up his position by noting that, "George is a very open person. I think he is too honest for a businessman. He certainly gives his people responsibility. He gives you the ball and lets you run with it. I don't think enough planning is done at UPI. At most it appears that we look ahead one year and even then what plans are developed are kept very flexible."

UPI STRATEGY

When asked about the current strategy at UPI, Mr. Brown responded that "the company is presently a distributor in the industrial packaging equipment, shipping supplies, and heavy duty stapling equipment business. In the past when we've wanted to grow, we have done one or both of the following, either add new lines of merchandise or additional salesmen. For example, this past year I got the idea of what I call a contract sales department. It is a simple concept, I took one man, put him in an office with a telephone and a listing of the *Fortune* top 1000 companies and told him to call and get new business. You would be surprised at how easy it was to pick up new accounts."

Mr. Stevens looks at UPI as being in the distribution and shipping of packaging supplies business. "In order for UPI to reach the goals that have been set we have to sell more products. That is, we can grow by doing the following:

1. Adding new salesmen
2. Adding additional product lines
3. Purchasing more effectively, and
4. Undertaking more aggressive sales promotions."

Mr. Brown believes that UPI should try to maximize the profit on every item sold. To do this the company tries to set its prices at a level which is approximately ten percent above the competition. Mr. Brown explained his pricing philosophy:

> I don't understand why people are afraid to raise prices. If you increase the price you will pick up more business and make more money. That allows you to keep the volume low and still make more money. In addition, although the customer may pay more, he gets more. The higher price allows me to provide top notch service to all my customers.

Mr. Brown feels that UPI is an innovative company. "Until very recently we were always innovating with new products and new applications. Now I think it's again time that we started to look for additional new and exciting products."

As a reult of the stated strategy of UPI and Mr. Brown's conservative philosophy, it is widely recognized that the organization is larger than it has to be given the level of business. Mr. Brown explained the reasoning behind this condition, "I know the organization is bigger than it has to be. We could probably handle three times the present volume of business with our present staff and facility. I think it's because of my conservative attitude; I've always wanted the organization to stay a step ahead of what is really needed. I feel comfortable with a built-in backup system and, therefore, I am willing to pay for it."

In December, 1973, Mr. Brown had talked optimistically about the future. He felt that sales should reach the $6-7 million range by 1978. "Looked at in another way, we should be able to grow at 20-25 percent per year without any particular effort."

> I want to grow and, therefore, I am making a concerted effort. I am constantly looking for possible merger avenues or expansion possibilities. I do not want to expand geographically. I would rather control that market area we are now in.

I recently sent a letter to all competitors in New England offering to buy them out. Believe it or not, no one responded.

I do not see any problems in the future. The history has been good, therefore, why won't it continue to happen?

Growth is easy. All I have to do is pick up a new line and I've automatically increased sales and profits. Basically we are distributors, and we operate as middlemen between the manufacturers and users, as shown:

In light of what has been happening in the environment, I feel that supply and demand will continue to be a problem. Therefore, I am giving serious thought to integrating vertically, i.e., become a manufacturer. This will guarantee our supply.*

Actually, I don't want to do the manufacturing. I think it would be better if I bought the manufacturing equipment and then had someone else use it to make my products.

THE FUTURE

After reviewing with his accountant the results for the just completed fiscal year, Mr. Brown was concerned about the nature of changes that should be made with respect to the actions taken by UPI in the future. "I know changes have to be made for next year as a result of this year, but I'm not sure what they should be." Mr. Brown continued:

I think next year is going to be a real bad year. Prices will probably fall like a rock from the levels they reached during 1974 and as a result those items that would have been profitable for the company aren't going to be, and we have much too large of an inventory as it is. It isn't easy to take away customers from the competition. As a result of this I feel we have to step up our efforts to get new lines and new accounts. Recently, I've given some thought to laying off one or two people for economic reasons but I'm not sure. I will probably give raises to all employees even though it's not a good business decision, but it's an ingrained part of my business philosophy.

When asked if he had informed his employees of his concern about the future, Mr. Brown referred to the minutes of a sales meeting that had been held in November 1974:

...Mr. Brown then presided at the meeting, and announced that Al King had won the coveted award of "Salesman of the Month." This was a "first" for our Al, and well deserved for his outstanding sales results in October. Congratulations and applause were extended him by all present. The balance of the meeting was then spent in a lengthy, detailed discussion, led by Mr. George Brown of the general, overall picture of what the future portends in the sales areas as a result of the current inflationary, recessionary and complex competitive conditions prevailing in the economy.

*Refer to the Appendix which contains minutes of a United Products sales meeting held at the end of 1973.

The gist of the entire discussion can be best summarized as follows:

1. Everyone present must recognize the very real difficulties that lie ahead in these precarious economic times.

2. The only steps available to the salesmen and to the company for survival during the rough period ahead are as follows:

   a) Minimize the contacts with existing accounts

   b) Spend the *majority* of time *developing new accounts* on the less competitive products; and *selling new products to established accounts.*

3. *Concentrate on and promote our new items.*

4. Mr. Brown and inside management are making and will continue to make every concentrated effort to find new products and new lines for the coming year.

In preparation for his meeting with Hank Stevens, Mr. Brown had prepared a list of activities to which Hank should address himself while running UPI during George's upcoming vacation. Mr. Brown believed that upon his return from Europe his activities at UPI would be increasing as a result of the problems caused by the uncertain economic conditions. The first item on the list was a possible redefinition of UPI marketing strategy. Mr. Brown now believed that UPI would have to be much more liberal with respect to new products considered for sale. "I'm not saying we are going to get into the consumer goods business, but I think he will give consideration to the inclusion of consumerable products requiring no service and at the same time capable of being sold with a high-profit-margin factor for the company."

As he sat at his desk thinking about possible changes which he could make in UPI's planning process, Mr. Brown was convinced that if he hadn't done some planning in the past, the situation would be more drastic than it was. Yet at the same time, he wasn't sure that if he had a more structured and formalized planning process, UPI might be in a better position with which to face the troubled times that lay ahead.

APPENDIX
UNITED PRODUCTS, INC.

SALES MEETINGS
December 5, 1973

Mr. Brown presided at the meeting. His opening remarks highlighted the extraordinary times our country and our company are going through as far as the general economy and the energy crisis are concerned, and the extraordinary effects of these unusual crises on people and businesses, including our company and our sources of supply.

He thanked all present for the many thoughtful, considered and excellent suggestions which they had offered in writing as to how best the salesmen and their company might handle the gasoline crisis without incurring an undue loss of sales and profits, and still maintaining the high standards of service to which UNITED PRODUCTS' thousands of satisfied customers are accustomed.

The whole situation, according to Mr. Brown, boils down to a question of supply and prices. Mr. Brown reported that on his recent trip to the Orient, there were very few companies who wanted to sell their merchandise to us--rather, THEY WANTED TO BUY FROM US MANY OF THE ITEMS WE NORMALLY BUY FROM FOREIGN COMPANIES, i.e., carton-closing staples, tape, gloves, et cetera . . . and at inflated prices!!! The Tokyo, Japan market is so great that they are using up everything they can produce--and the steel companies would rather make flat steel than the steel rods which are used for making staples. A very serious problem exists, as a result, in the carton-closing staple field not only in Japan, but also in Europe and America.

Mr. Brown advised that every year the company's costs of operating increase just as each individual's cost of living goes up and up yearly. Additional personnel, increased group and auto insurance premiums, increased Social Security payments, new office equipment and supplies, new catalogues, "Beeper system" for more salesmen--and all of these costs accumulate and result in large expenditures of money. Manufacturers cover their increased operating costs by pricing their products higher--but to date, UNITED PRODUCTS has never put into their prices the increased costs resulting from increased operating expenses. Last year, the 3% increase which the company needed then was put into effect by many of you. HOWEVER, in order for the company to realize that additional profit, this 3% price increase had to be put into effect ACROSS THE BOARD . . . all customers . . . all items!

THAT DID NOT HAPPEN!!!

Mr. Brown advised that UNITED PRODUCTS got LAMBASTED when all of the sources of supply started to increase their prices. When SPOT-NAILS, for example, went up to 10%, the salesmen only increased their prices 7%, et cetera. We did *not get the 3% price increase ABOVE the manufacturers' price increase*--and we needed it then and need it even more NOW.

Eliminating the possibility of cutting commissions, there are three possible solutions for the problem of how to get this much needed and ABSOLUTELY IMPERATIVE additional 3% PRICE INCREASE ACROSS THE BOARD to cover the constantly growing operating costs for running a successful, progressive-minded and growing business whose high standards of service and performance are highly regarded by customers and sources of supply alike, namely:

1. A 3% increase on all items to all customers across the board.
2. A surcharge on all invoices or decrease in discounts allowed off LIST.
3. A G.C.I. charge (Government Cost Increase) on all invoices.

Considerable discussion regarding these three possibilities resulted in the following conclusions concerning the best method for obtaining this special 3% ACROSS THE BOARD PRICE INCREASE, as follows:

1. A new PRICE BOOK should be issued with all new prices to reflect not only the manufacturers' new increased prices, but in addition the 3% UNITED PRODUCTS PRICE INCREASE. All of the salesmen agreed that it would be easier to effect the additional 3% price increase if the 3% was "Built in" on their price book sheets.
2. This new PRICE BOOK will be set up in such a way that prices will be stipulated according to quantity of item purchased . . . with no variances allowed. WITH NO EXCEPTIONS, the Price of any item will depend on the quantity a customer buys.

3. Some items will continue to be handled on a discount basis--but lower discounts in order to ascertain that UNITED-PRODUCTS is getting its 3% price increase.
4. Until these new PRICE BOOKS are issued, all salesmen were instructed to proceed IMMEDIATELY to effect these 3% price increases.

TEN NEW ACCOUNTS CONTEST

Seven of our ten salesmen won a calculator as a result of opening up 10 new accounts each . . . a total of 70 NEW ACCOUNTS for our company!!! However, both Mr. Brown and Mr. Stevens confessed that the dollar volume amount stipulated in the contest had been set ridiculously low, as a "feeler" to determine the success and effectiveness of such a contest. All the salesmen voiced their approval of all of the contests offered to them--and agreed that they had enjoyed many excellent opportunities of increasing their personal ex-checquers.

NEW CUSTOMER LETTERS

Mr. Brown again reminded all present that we have an excellent printed letter, which is available for sending to every new customer--and urged all to take advantage of this service by the office personnel by clearly indicating on their sales and order slips "NEW CUSTOMER." This procedure is but another step towards our goal of becoming more and more professional in our approach with our customers.

CASE 4

CARTER DISTRIBUTION CORPORATION (A)

The Carter Distribution Corporation was created to support the marketing effort of its potential customers in all facets of physical distribution. It was formed as a major project of Carfam, Ltd., a family limited partnership initiated by Dr. and Mrs. Jeff Carter to finance such projects. The CDC, located in Little Rock, Arkansas, was developed as a Total Distribution Center (TDC). The systems concept upon which a TDC is based was described by Dr. Carter in his *Managerial Logistics*. This book was one of the early leaders among the textbooks written in the newly-evolving field of physical distribution. His concept of logistics requires examination of all the separate logistics activities (transportation, warehousing, inventory management, location of production and distribution points, order processing, materials handling, packaging, distribution, market forecasting, customer service, etc.) as interdependent parts of a whole logistics system. This system is subsequently viewed as one of several interdependent parts of the whole system of the firm. As Dr. Carter saw it, these components of logistics were not ends in themselves, but were the means to an end—the support of the marketing effort and ultimately the over-all effectiveness of the organization.

Traditionally, most traffic management thinking has focused on the reduction of transportation costs through rate negotiation and selection of carriers. A less widely used concept, the "total cost approach", recognized that the transportation rate is only one element of the total logistics cost. Other costs included in this approach were interest, spoilage, and pilferage costs; cost of inventory; opportunity cost of money invested in inventory (both in warehouses and in transit); differential packaging costs of various transportation modes; and warehousing costs. In Dr. Carter's opinion, both of these methods were insufficient and reflected the failure of the transportation and warehouse industries to properly recognize their functions and their relationships to their

This case was made possible through the cooperation of a firm which prefers to remain anonymous. It was prepared by Professor Roger M. Atherton and Dennis M. Crites of the University of Oklahoma for educational purposes only and is not intended to convey effective or ineffective administrative procedure. Since all data are disguised, this case should not be used as source material for research purposes. Distributed by the Intercollegiate Case Clearing House, Soldiers Field, Boston, Mass. 02163. All rights reserved to the contributors. Printed in the U.S.A. Presented at a Case Workshop. Reprinted with permission.

customers. He believes that most of the firms in these industries do not understand or do not care to practice the approach he believes is needed—a combination of a systems viewpoint and customer orientation, frequently described as the "marketing concept."

Dr. Carter's approach was to go beyond the "total cost approach" to cost management and profit maximization concepts. This method involves examining all the additional costs and benefits which might result from activities such as: (1) relocation of aspects of the production process; (2) faster or slower delivery times; and (3) shipping in bulk to different geographic locations, breaking bulk, and then performing additional activities, such as packaging, labeling, storing, assembling components, or whatever would decrease the total costs of producing and distributing the goods. The goal is to generate maximum profit by performing services which can be done less expensively after, or during, distribution. Other possibilities include the provision of meeting rooms; sales and display rooms; office space; quality control facilities; repair facilities; and anything else that would make the total distribution system more efficient, productive, and profitable. The key to this approach is the Total Distribution Center. Such a center would perform all these kinds of services, rate investigations, and comparative economic studies to help determine the most profitable combination of distribution activities and modes.

A second, but equally important, key idea in this concept is a different rate structure than used in the ordinary warehouse. The standard contract provides for half-monthly or monthly rates depending upon when the goods are received. Dr. Carter had developed a rate structure of daily charges per pallet (container). According to Dr. Carter, this has a distinct competitive advantage in that current rate structures have built up over the years and, for individual shipments, frequently have very little relationship to the economics of the industry. He also contends that most shippers and warehousemen have no idea as to their actual costs by specific items, weight, volume, or any other criteria. As a result, there is a considerable economic opportunity for those willing and able to see the overall transportation-marketing-organization system, provide an integrating service, and charge in relation to the actual costs. Dr. Carter is convinced that there are many opportunities going unexploited. This presented an opportunity for him to put together an organization of people who, believing as he does, could achieve both financial and personal rewards.

THE TRANSPORTATION ENVIRONMENT*

Carriers. Some companies acquire their own vehicles and provide their own transportation. These operations are referred to as private carriers. Most companies prefer to retain the services of common carriers, who provide transportation as for-hire carriers. The Interstate Commerce Commission (I.C.C.) recognizes a number of types of common carriers by the type of commodity: general commodities, bulk commodities, frozen food, and a dozen or so more. Common carriers must have approval of a regulatory body to operate, publish their rates, offer certain types and qualities of service, and so on. Railroads, airlines, and bus companies are examples of common carriers of both people and goods. Contract carriers offer a very specialized service and limit themselves to serving relatively few customers. They too must have authority to operate and can not discriminate unduly among customers. Some automobile haulers and some freight airlines are examples of contract carriers. Freight forwarders are also a specialized type of carrier. Their main function is to consolidate shipments from many shippers and to forward them. They may use their own trucks or they may buy transportation from other common carriers. They too must have authority to operate. Exempt carriers are those which are exempt from econo-

---

* This section has been largely derived from Logistics Management and Operations (Chapter 17), in *Marketing Strategy and Management* by J. A. Constantin, R. E. Evans, and M. L. Morris, (to be published by Business Publications, Inc., Dallas, Texas in 1976). Used with permission.

mic regulation, although they are subject to safety regulation. Exempt carriers haul only commodities exempt from regulation, mainly certain kinds of agricultural products such as grain, cattle, eggs, and fish. There are also express companies and small parcel delivery companies. These carriers are limited to shipments which meet size and weight requirements and for which a premium is paid for quick delivery. Depending upon the company, the goods to be shipped, and the speed required, a company may use any or all of of these types of carriers and forms of transportation. The mix will depend on the service available, costs, and the objectives and strategies of the firm.

Rate Structure. Most items transported on common carriers move on a class rate determined for an individual shipment by a two-step process. The first step is to find the class into which a commodity has been placed. Classes are found in a book called a classification. The second step is to find the applicable tariff, a price list. The charges levied for a shipment for given distances are shown in the tariff for each of the major classes of goods. These class rates are uniform throughout the nation. Cost factors which affect the price are the density, the possibility of damage (for which the carriers may be liable), the loading characteristics, and other related considerations such as direction of travel, frequency of shipments, and regularity of shipments. A second type of rate is the exception rate*. It involves a modification of the classification governing the movement of the commodity between certain points. The exception means that those particular goods can be shipped at reduced cost, wherever the rate applies. The third type of rate is the commodity rate. Unlike class and exception rates, these rates are quoted directly in a tariff instead of through a classification. They apply to specified goods such as major commodity and raw materials. Both shippers and the I.C.C. have agreed these deserve special considerations and reduced rates. These rates are lower than the corresponding class and exception rates for goods of similar physical characteristics. A proportional rate is a part of a through rate. It is used in transit privileges, a service made available so that a shipper may stop his goods off at some point and later resume the shipment without losing the benefits of a through rate. There are many kinds of transit privileges. Grain may be stored in transit; metal may be fabricated in transit; cattle may be fed in transit; etc. There are many services available and carriers are generally responsive to requests for additional services if they can be done profitably. In order to prevent discrimination among persons, places, and commodities, special services must be published in a tariff and made available to everyone on the same terms.

THE WAREHOUSE ENVIRONMENT**

Warehouses. A private warehouse, like a private carrier, is for the use of its owner and is not open to the public. A general merchandise public warehouse handles almost anything that does not need special facilities or special care. Specialized warehouses are equipped for special purposes: grain elevators, bulk vegetable oil tanks, household goods, frozen foods, etc. There are two basic functions performed, the first is storage and the second is warehousing. Stor-

---

* Rates are set by the carriers, but approval of the I.C.C. (or state regulatory commission) is necessary. Carriers and shippers are constantly negotiating with one another for rate changes. Every year the I.C.C. approves thousands of rate changes. Sometimes approval is granted without a hearing when there are no protests. The rates on which practically all goods move are far from being uniform. There are many unusual and seemingly inconsistent rates which have resulted from the interaction of supply and demand in different geographic areas. As a result, generalizations regarding the rate structure are virtually impossible.

**This section has been largely derived from Logistics Management and Operations (Chapter 17), in *Marketing Strategy and Management* by J.A. Constantin, R.E. Evans, and M.L. Morris, (to be published by Business Publications, Inc., Dallas, Texas in 1976). Used with permission.

age is providing space for goods to be placed until there is a need for them. Warehousing involves the actual movement of the goods. It includes breaking bulk shipments, mixing them, and forwarding them to other members of the distribution channel. Another set of functions involve serving as a sort of field office, order taker, disbursing agent, and inventory reporter. Some warehousemen have rooms for desk space for customer's salesmen as well as rooms in which customers can set up displays of merchandise.

Rate Structure. Typically warehouses charge for their services in several categories: (1) so many cents per square foot for storage; (2) charges for handling in, handling out, and clerical tasks such as processing reports and freight bills; and (3) miscellaneous charges for such services as stencilling packages, repairing broken crates, and breaking bulk shipments into smaller shipments. Storage charges are frequently based on a two-week or monthly basis, and customers pay for the entire period even if their goods are in storage only for a fraction of the base period.

THE OPPORTUNITIES

In the past 10-15 years, manufacturers, wholesalers, and retailers have begun to give a great deal of attention to physical distribution. This is partly due to the large amount of working capital that is tied up in inventory, which some studies report is about 30 percent of working capital for the average firm. The increased attention is also due to the large costs represented by physical distribution, which some studies have shown to be about 20 percent of sales, on the average. One marketing objective of almost every sales organization is to have goods available where and when the customer wants them. Different degrees of customer service will have different costs and different impacts of sales as well as profits. Through the impacts on other departments such as purchasing, production control, production, and finance, the logistics function can have substantial effects on both managerial efficiency and organizational effectiveness. The achievement of both customer service and cost management objectives, according to Dr. Carter, is the responsibility of the transportation and warehousing industries.

A study at a major mid-western university found that users of public warehouses had a generally low opinion of the typical public warehouseman. The users reported that the typical warehouseman: (1) is interested in selling space to his customers rather than in providing a distribution service, (2) does not understand how he can complement the user's distribution system. (3) is not creative in discovering innovative ways to reduce distribution costs, and (4) is not sufficiently concerned with the user's needs and wants. The reasons for these dissatisfactions are many. The major cause, however, is probably that the costs and efficiency of the warehouse operation is the typical warehouseman's primary objective. He only becomes concerned with his customer's goods when they arrive at his warehouse and loses interest when they leave it. He is operating the warehouse as a separate, or discrete, step in the distribution process. He may well be performing his specific task efficiently, but the opportunities for overall (total system) integration, synergy, and profit are being ignored.

CDC PROGRAM AND SERVICE*

CDC is a market-oriented company which has a broad view of its role in distribution. The firm has coined and adopted a term that describes its function: a marketing support system. Rather than viewing themselves in the

---

* This section has been largely derived from private correspondence between Dr. Carter and the authors. Used with permission.

business of providing warehousing, breaking bulk, and delivery service, CDC people see themselves in business to support the marketing effort of business firms through the provision of warehousing, breaking bulk, and delivery service. The company believes there is a subtle but profound difference between the two approaches. In the first method, attention of management is directed inward, focusing on the operation of the warehouse. In the second method, the attention of management is directed toward the customer, operating the warehouse is only one of several means to satisfying and serving the customer's needs.

The CDC systems viewpoint and philosophy are: to help their customers fulfill profit and service objectives through finding the optimum combination of transportation, warehousing, and related costs and services. The achievement of an optimum combination might involve the following:

1. Reduced transportation costs through:
   a. Finding a more economical type of carrier;
   b. Recommending changes in processing or packing methods so that the customer's goods either:
      (1) Weigh less or are less bulky for shipping purposes, or,
      (2) Qualify for a lower rate classification;
   c. Recommending changes in *location* of certain processing operations so that the customer may benefit from a more favorable combination of production costs and processing-in-transit through-type freight rates;
   d. Consolidating the customer's goods with those of other customers to obtain benefit of larger-volume rates;
   e. Negotiating with carriers for a lower classification, type, or level of rate, sometimes on the basis of certain loading or other services the distribution center could perform, but that are less feasible for the customer or a regular public warehouse;
   f. Handling or facilitating the making of damage claims or the auditing of carrier's bills (to avoid overcharges).

2. Reduced warehousing and related handling costs by:
   a. Introducing a price system with a charge for storage for only the actual days stored (rather than the traditional monthly storage charge minimum);
   b. Suggesting changes in storage module sizes, packaging, packing, palletizing, containerizing, or other handling or storing features.

3. Improved or increased service and sales to their customers' customers by:
   a. Quicker delivery to their clients' customers;
   b. A lower market price and perhaps resultant sales their client could not otherwise obtain;
   c. Lower total inventories both for their client and for their client's customers;
   d. Provision of market information that might identify market opportunities for their clients;

4. Imaginative and continuing efforts to implement the two key CDC "philosophies" of *customer-orientation* and a *marketing support systems viewpoint* by:
   a. Recommending to customers or prospects the use of another city (or storage system) if CDC analysis indicated that other alternatives might be more favorable to the client; or,
   b. Investigating establishment of a CDC in another city if a present customer indicated a significant need for such services.

Outwardly, CDC might appear to be a public warehouse. The following examples of CDC accomplishments illustrate the integration and support activities which distinguish CDC from a traditional warehouse. It must, of course, be remembered that CDC is just starting up operations and that the opportunities to do all the things planned are limited.

#CDC is having bulk shipments of some commodities such as canned peas, delivered to its warehouse. It breaks the bulk, labels some of the cans with the private label of the supermarket and some with the customers label, and ships directly to the various locations as requested. Alternatively, the customer can ship to CDC and await specific orders, have CDC do the labeling, and have the goods delivered in far less time than a direct factory shipment at a much lower overall cost.

#Certain items can be shipped much less expensively in a disassembled condition. CDC has made proposals to do the actual assembling for those customers who want to purchase the completed product. Items such as ball bearings, bicycles, swing sets, and furniture are examples.

#CDC discovered that if orders of one customer were routed through a different warehouse in another city, they could be delivered 3 days sooner at a substantial saving. The customer accepted the proposal which meant an initial loss in sales to CDC, but since then the customer has been promoting CDC and has routed other business to CDC.

#CDC recommended changes in inventory levels of several items. This cut down stock-outs on some items and reduced inventory levels on others. The effect was improved service on some and lower cost on others.

#By working with a customer's order department a change in procedures of giving shipping orders was installed. Emergency deliveries were cut from 2 or 3 a week to 1 or 2 a month. These emergency deliveries cost the customer 3 or 4 times the cost of a normal delivery.

#CDC negotiated rates with a carrier in behalf of a customer which made it possible for the customer to improve the efficiency of its distribution system.

#CDC advised the customer of one of their customers on several matters which improved his receiving system and reduced stock-outs.

#CDC has completed a study for one company which shows the effect of their innovations in pricing. It shows a 60 percent reduction in storage costs as a result of the daily pricing system. The tentative savings: $152,000 per year.

RESOURCES

In addition to its unique approach to providing customers with a marketing support system, CDC has acquired a number of human, physical, and financial resources.

Human. Dr. Carter serves as Chairman of the Board. He has been at Templeton University since 1953, and has advanced to the rank of Professor of Marketing and Transportation. Templeton is approximately 400 miles from Little Rock, so that Dr. Carter usually restricts his visits to weekends, school vacations, and summers. Dr. Carter is one of the most knowledgeable experts in the field of logistics management. He is also considered an expert in planning.

Richard Kirk was hired as President in March, 1973. He had previously been a manager of physical distribution with a large national manufacturer of light machinery. He was a former student of Dr. Carter's. They had developed a close friendship over the years, both on an intellectual and common interest level as well as a personal and social level. Kirk had recently given up his job with the large company as too confining and no longer challenging to open up a bar near his home town, when Dr. Carter asked him to join CDC. His initial responsibilities were in planning, arranging equipment and space for the firm's warehousing needs and office, and in making a number of sales calls.

In mid-fall 1973, Kirk was joined by Mark Kallister, Dr. Carter's son-in-law, who was designated as Vice-President of CDC. Kallister, a regular army officer for seven years, had some army logistics experience and several recent BBA and MBA courses in physical distribution. It was while attending Templeton that Kallister met and married Dr. Carter's daughter. It was through both the courses he took and family discussions that he learned about Dr. Carter's concepts and ideas about logistics management. At his earliest opportunity, he resigned from the Army to join CDC to help implement these ideas.

Arrangements had been made to obtain additional help, as required, from temporary-manpower employment services. In addition, Dr. Carter was considering the immediate employment of one other former student and the eventual employment of another son-in-law, as business developed. With access to both temporary help and managerial talent established, the personnel needs for the foreseeable future were deemed more than adequate.

Physical. For a warehouse and office, CDC was renting two bays (about 25,000 square feet) in a newly constructed, well-located, and well-equipped eight-bay warehouse building. They also held options to rent up to four of the remaining bays as needed. An adequate supply of racks, pallets, office materials, and other supplies had been purchased. A fork-lift truck had been leased. As the facilities actually rented were well above usage requirements, the facilities were considered quite satisfactory for the foreseeable future.

Financial. Since most of the equipment and facilities were leased or rented, there was little need for long-term capital. There were, however, a lot of expenses for salaries, rents, leases, publicity, entertaining, and other operating expenses which were not yet covered by sales revenues. Initial calculations were that they would need about $62,000 for equipment and start-up wages. At least one of the executives took a reduction in salary, and the difference was provided in stock. They estimated they would need $870,000 revenue per year, a rate which they believed could be attained in about two years. The seed money for these purposes was obtained from family members and the executives employed. There were neither bank debts nor outside stockholders.

PERFORMANCE

In early spring 1974, they were still negotiating with several firms. Each of these could provide CDC with revenues of thousands of dollars a year. It was even conceivable that if their proposals were completely accepted, revenue well above $100,000 annually could be provided. Actual revenues were fluctuating between one-or-two hundred dollars a month. Only two small-volume customers were really using CDC services on a regularly established basis. Dr. Carter and his CDC associates had expected that it would take time for their sales efforts to pay off. Their prospective customers would often have to do a lot of checking and internal coordinating among departments before buying CDC's services. It was often difficult to determine whether to call upon the traffic manager, the purchasing manager, or the marketing manager. The CDC approach was substantially different from the past practices and traditions which have built up among traffic managers, shippers, warehousemen, and others involved in the distribution process. In many respects CDC was attempting to sell receiving, handling, storage, and related services of the same sort offered by most public warehouses. By selling these services as a marketing support system, CDC and its management team were offering a set of ideas and a way of doing business that they believed were uniquely valuable to their prospective customers.

CASE 5

CARTER DISTRIBUTION CORPORATION (B)

Dr. Jeff Carter, Chairman of the Board of the Carter Distribution Corporation, was understandably concerned. Earlier, he had carefully developed statements about his organization's purpose, mission, and objectives. Recognizing that these objectives were somewhat philosophical and were primarily reflections of his personal objectives for the organization, he decided to try to make them more operational. He requested his two key managers—and two other men who were to be considered for managerial positions—to provide with their personal objectives, what they wanted to accomplish for themselves, along with some suggested operational statements to implement both the corporate and their personal objectives. He had asked for responses in a few weeks. Six months later he had received only one reply and that was from one of the "candidates." Both of his key people were extremely busy helping to start up this new company. Resources were scarce; the break-even point had not yet been approached; and, although interest was extremely high, only a few customers had made actual commitments. Dr. Carter was undecided whether to make a second request for the submission of these reports, with the more immediate and greater need for survival. He was aware of the crucial importance of executive morale to his fledgling company, yet he also saw the possible negative impact on his relationships with his managers if he did nothing. He also knew the importance of concentrating the company's limited resources, both financial and managerial, on a restricted set of agreed-upon objectives. He also believed that unless the company's objectives were made more operational, it would be difficult to determine how effectively the organization was accomplishing its mission. Furthermore, unless the top managers felt involved in the determination of objectives and were committed to their accomplishment, the company would have little chance for success.

The Carter Distribution Corporation—designed "to support the marketing effort" of its potential customers "in all facets of physical distribution"—began

This case was made possible through the cooperation of a firm which prefers to remain anonymous. It was prepared by Professors Roger M. Atherton and Dennis M. Crites of the University of Oklahoma for educational purposes only and is not intended to convey effective or ineffective administrative procedure. Since all data are disguised, this case should not be used as source material for research purposes.

Presented at a Case Workshop and distributed by the Intercollegiate Case Clearing House, Soldiers Field, Boston, Mass. 02163. All rights reserved to the contributors. Printed in the U.S.A. Reprinted with permission.

its business development operations in the summer of 1973. Formed as a major project of Carfam, Ltd.—a family limited partnership initiated by Dr. and Mrs. Jeff Carter to finance such projects—the CDC, located in Little Rock, Arkansas, was to be developed as a Total Distribution Center (TDC).

BACKGROUND

Dr. Jeff Carter has been at Templeton University since 1953, and has progressed to the rank of Professor of Marketing and Transportation. Almost from the time he arrived, he spoke with various professional, transportation, and industrial development groups of the need for a new concept in distribution centers. By the early 1960's, the systems concept upon which a Total Distribution Center is based was described by Dr. Carter in his *Managerial Logistics*. This book was one of the early leaders among the textbooks written in the newly-evolving field of physical distribution. The logistics concept he was recommending involved looking at all the separate logistics activities (transportation, warehousing, inventory management, location decisions, order processing, materials handling, packaging, distribution, customer service, etc.) as interdependent parts of a whole logistics system, which is only one of several interdependent parts of the whole system of the firm. As he saw it, these components of logistics were not ends in themselves, but were means to an end—the support of the marketing effort of the firm.

Previously, most traffic management thinking had focused on the reduction of transportation costs through rate negotiation and routing of freight. An interim concept, the "total cost approach," recognized that the transportation rate is only one element of the total logistics cost. Others include interest, spoilage, and pilferage costs; cost of inventory; opportunity cost of money invested in inventory (both in warehouses and in transit); differential packaging costs of various transportation modes; and warehousing costs. In Dr. Carter's opinion, the transportation and warehouse industries have not recognized their role; their relationships to their customers; and either do not understand, or do not care to practice, the marketing concept.

TOTAL DISTRIBUTION CENTER

Dr. Carter's approach was to go beyond the "total cost approach" to cost management and profit maximization concepts. This involves examining all the additional costs and benefits (increased sales and profits) which might result from relocation of aspects of the production process; changes in sales which might result from faster or slower delivery times; and shipping in bulk to different geographic locations, breaking bulk, and then performing additional activities, such as packaging, labeling, storing, assembling components, or whatever would decrease the total costs of producing and distributing the goods. The goal is to generate maximum profit by performing services which can be done less expensively after, or during, distribution. Other possibilities include the provision of meeting rooms; sales and display rooms; office space; quality control facilities; repair facilities; and anything else that would make the total transportation more efficient, productive, and profitable. The key to this approach is the Total Distribution Center. Such a center would perform all these kinds of services, rate investigations, and comparative economic studies to help determine the most profitable combination of activities and distribution modes.

A second, but equally important, key idea in this concept is a different rate structure than used in the ordinary warehouse. The standard contract provides for half-monthly or monthly rates depending upon whether the goods are received before or after the fifteenth. Dr. Carter had developed a rate structure of daily charges per pallet (container). According to Dr. Carter, this has a distinct competitive advantage in that current rate structures have built up over the years and, for individual shipments, frequently have very little relationship to the economics of the industry. He also contends that most shippers and warehousemen have no idea as to their actual costs for specific items or by weight, volume, or any other criteria. As a result, there is a considerable economic opportunity for those willing and able to see the overall transportation-marketing-organization system, provide an integrating service, and charge in relation to the actual costs. Dr. Carter was convinced that there were many opportunities going unexploited. He knew this presented an opportunity for him to put together an organization of people who, believing as he does, could achieve both financial and personal rewards.

LITTLE ROCK, ARKANSAS LOCATION

During the 1965-1970 period, Dr. Carter and different associates worked on several studies, papers, and proposals concerned with transportation and economic development in the Arkansas River Basin, including the area around Little Rock, Arkansas. A number of executives and officials in Little Rock became especially interested in some of the concepts and findings involved. Some of these executives indicated to Dr. Carter that anyone who would organize a distribution center in Little Rock could be assured of very favorable support. The assurances included financing, physical facilities, and assistance in developing customers and patronage. A general study was made and Little Rock was found to be least-cost location for an area extending from Chicago to New Orleans and Houston, and from Atlanta to Dallas. It is also a seaport in the nation's midsection (via the Mississippi River and the McClellan-Kerr Arkansas River Navigation System). The Port of Little Rock Foreign Trade Zone is new and is capable of meeting a rapidly growing international market and of becoming a prime port and center for serving U.S. markets across the country. The Free Port Law of Arkansas provides a strong incentive to base inventory and distribution as well as manufacturing activities in Arkansas.

FROM THEORY TO PRACTICE

In late 1972 and early 1973, enthusiastic interest was being expressed by three or four former students, who held physical distribution or related positions, in joining Dr. Carter in initiating a Total Distribution Center in Little Rock. These were persons who both as students and in their careers had displayed superior insight and potential. In particular, they had shared with Dr. Carter, both socially and at professional meetings, many hours in discussion of the concepts, philosophies, and values necessary for optimum implementation of a Total Distribution System or Center.

One of these men, Richard Kirk, had previously been in physical distribution management with a large company. Dr. Carter and Mr. Kirk started to work out capital needs. They concluded that they would need about $62,000 for equipment and start-up wages. They estimated they would need $870,000 revenue per year, a rate which they believed could be attained in about 2 years. If results were as predicted, they would make an attractive profit as well as respectable salaries for their executives. In March, 1973, Dr. Carter asked Kirk to take charge of setting up the Little Rock operations. The company's Little Rock activities for the summer of 1973 were essentially a one-man operation. As president, Kirk spent most of his time planning, arranging equipment and space for the firm's warehousing needs and office, and in making a number of sales calls. A policy had been adopted that CDC would try mainly to bring into Little Rock "new" distribution activities, e.g., by firms not previously distributing in that area. In other words, CDC was not trying to take business from Little Rock's currently-operating warehouses, carriers, and related firms. To this end, Kirk made some sales trips to Chicago where he had a number of professional and business contacts in the physical distribution field.

In mid-fall, 1973, Kirk was joined by Mark Kallister, Dr. Carter's son-in-law, who was designated as Vice-President of CDC. Kallister, a regular army officer for seven years, had some army logistics experience and several recent BBA and MBA courses in physical distribution. Early planning, in which Kallister had participated, was that Kirk, with his lengthier time in industrial physical distribution, could "train" Kallister and help prepare him not only for his initial CDC-Little Rock responsibilities but also for starting up the next CDC-TDC venture, tentatively planned for Nashville, Tennessee. Kallister's work at first was to share in, and to learn from Kirk more about the work and to handle some of the pick-up, delivery, and related tasks for the first customers the firm acquired. He accompanied Kirk on some of the sales calls to Chicago and by the spring of 1974 was making sales calls on his own in Little Rock and Chicago. Kallister was becoming active with civic groups and individuals involved in developing the new Port of Little Rock.

The company's policy on bringing new distribution activities to Little Rock, combined with the major impact of broad-scale physical distribution changes on the decision-making processes of potential clients, was leading to a long lag before sales development calls "paid off." By summer of 1974, however, CDC was facing an odd situation. In terms of physical materials and revenue actually being handled in Little Rock, it was still a very small operation. The vice-president was literally driving a delivery truck on the same day that he would make an evening presentation to some of the state's leading bankers regarding economic development of the Little Rock area. The firm's proposed purpose, objectives, and resources had, however, stimulated such interest that the firm was going to have to decide within a very few weeks which commitments to undertake from among several very promising projects being negotiated. In anticipation of further expansion, Dr. Carter was considering the immediate employment of a former student, Shawn Costello, who was employed as a sales manager at a major railroad. He would be asked to help obtain additional clients, negotiate with rail and other carriers, and work with the others in preparation for assuming responsibility for one of the developing projects. Another member of the Carter family, Bob Bentley, was also being considered, although nothing specific had been decided about the timing.

MANAGERIAL VALUES

The managerial values of J.A. Carter were expressed in a memorandum prepared for CDC internal use and dated June, 1973, as follows:

"While the mission of the organization and its objectives are stated in terms of the organization itself, they are directed toward the ultimate purpose: satisfaction to me. In this context, satisfaction has many dimensions, and my personal motives and objectives are hard to sort out. Even so, they are important because they determine the direction the organization will take. Among the forces underlying my personal objectives are:

(1) To create a family organization to satisfy a parental need;
(2) The desire to introduce some innovative concepts to satisfy a professional need; and,
(3) The desire to build, to satisfy an entrepreneurial urge.

"The fact that neither profit nor creation of wealth is mentioned does not imply that they are ignored. If we are successful in operating the business to satisfy my wants, profit and capital accumulation will be the result. In fact the amount of profit and the rate of capital accumulation will be partial measures of success in each of the three areas mentioned."

To Satisfy a Parental Need

"By means of a family organization, several parental needs will be met. First, security for each of our children especially our daughters, is one of our significant objectives. To this end future investments for them will be made in their family oriented objectives is to provide our sons, daughters, and their spouses with the opportunity for employment in a family enterprise and to allow them to earn further ownership via stock options, bonus, profit sharing, and the like. The ownership thus earned will be for performance as managers and thus ownership will be vested in the manager."

"The foremost among the possible dangers is associated with sibling primacy—who runs what. Another recognized danger centers on potential problems related to productivity and compensation. Externally, a potential problem arises from the effect of family participation on executives, employees, and investors. While there are very real dangers, I think the organization plan will minimize them."

To Satisfy a Professional Need

"There are many 'gaps' in the field of physical distribution because others have not seen them or have not had the interest to seek to close them. Our organization will seek to close those gaps where analysis discloses potential profits consonant with risk. This 'need' establishes an innovative direction for the organization. As a result, managers will be expected to search out new opportunities for development within the framework of our mission statement which gives direction to the firm."

"Despite the importance I place on the mission statement as a device to keep us from going every which way, I do not consider it to be inviolate. As strongly as I feel about the firm as a vehicle to bring me satisfaction, I must also allow others (executives, family and non-family colleagues) the same privilege. Accordingly, while we will not lightly go beyond it, it may be modified to embrace some area particularly appealing to key members of the organization. To do so is entirely consonant with my philosophy of seeking out opportunities and problems."

To Satisfy an Entrepreneurial Urge

"I am interested in building an effective and efficient enterprise for its own sake. It will be a source of personal enjoyment and satisfaction to participate in the development of an organization dedicated to searching out opportunities and exploiting them. Again, I mention the framework established by the mission statement, and repeat that it is the unifying force which gives direction. It is subject to reevaluation and possible re-writing from time to time. In fact, periodically, key people directing the firm will be asked to consider its continued suitability."

PURPOSE AND MISSION

A ten-page description explaining several other aspects of "CDC thinking" was prepared in July, 1973. Although prepared primarily for internal guidance this description was also intended for selected use in the company's selling and promotional efforts and began with the following paragraphs:

Purpose: To support the marketing effort of our customers everywhere especially those customers serving the more critical areas of public need—through innovative strategic, managerial, and operational leadership and communication in all facets of physical distribution. By so doing, we will seek to improve the effectiveness of the distribution system and the efficiency of the several distribution processes.

Mission: To be in all facets of physical distribution necessary to fulfill our purpose and meet market requirements.

Implications: Our purpose establishes the character of our organization; our mission establishes its direction; together they have several implications. First, with a commitment to support the marketing efforts of our customers, our function transcends that of a public warehouse, a distribution warehouse, a distributor, or what have you. It means that our concern is not only with the processes of physical distribution—warehousing, transportation, and the like—but also with the function of the distribution system in facilitating the marketing effort. It further means that we do not concern ourselves with the efficiency of operation of any one element of the system, but we are concerned with the effectiveness of the system first and the efficiency of the parts second. It further means that we are as concerned with conceptual matters to at least the extent of our concern with operational matters.

Second, when we refer to our customers everywhere, we identify our areas of operation: local and regional; regional and national; national and international. By that reference we imply that our area of operation is not to be confined to Little Rock, Arkansas. Not implied, but certainly meant is that our choice of future locations will be powerfully influenced by the needs of our customers in a given location.

Third, our special reference to customers serving the more critical areas of public need establishes a direction for our initial marketing effort. This is, of course, only one of several criteria which include opportunity and profitability. Also, of course, the critical areas of public need may change from time to time. The immediate needs which offer opportunity for service to the public and profit, and, in general, entrepreneurial opportunity, are the food industry, hospitals in cooperative effort including food, linens, supplies, the petroleum industry (energy), and the housing industry. Accordingly, our first efforts will be directed to anything within reason which will come along and will yield us revenue to help us stay alive. When we are able to pick and choose, our efforts will go toward canned foods; building materials and household items; oils and greases; and hospital supplies.

Fourth, our commitment to innovative leadership in strategic, managerial, and operational matters has several implications. For our organization, it implies that we must have a complete dedication to developing and/or applying better ways of doing things. It implies that we must be prepared to seek out key managers and employees who have a particular managerial philosophy. It further means that our organizational structure, our systems of rewards, and our methods of control must be "different."

Further, as we emphasize strategic, managerial, and operational leadership, we commit ourselves to a certain relationship to our customers and to our industry. For one thing, we may—and will—help our customers devise strategies to help them attain their objectives which may cause us a loss in revenue. Or we may devise managerial and operational approaches for them which have the same result. The short-term effect may be a loss in revenue for us, but we will make it up in the long run either by receiving more business or in the satisfaction of having done our job well.

Fifth, we commit ourselves to the improvement of the effectiveness of the distribution system as a whole and the efficiency of its several parts. While not stated, this implies to us that we are concerned with the total logistics environment as it affects our customers directly and as it affects the economic development of the regions we are a part of. Thus, we accept as a challenge and a commitment the role of helping improve the total logistics environment to the end of making an area a more attractive place for job creation. (And, at the same time creating a greater demand for our services).

Sixth, our mission statement establishes our direction and thus indicates the general areas we will be searching to discover opportunities to exploit and problems to solve. It is not a confining statement, only a guiding one. First, our purposes and missions are subject to study and restatement periodically; so they are not ever to be considered final. Second, while we will not actively seek opportunities outside our field, as we run across them or as they are brought to us, we will ask ourselves if it is time to reevaluate our mission. Then, if appropriate, we will evaluate the opportunity.

The ten-page description continued with a listing and explanation of the company's fifteen major objectives, from which the following were selected for heaviest emphasis in its promotional literature*:

OBJECTIVES

The major objectives and their implications are as follows*:

1. *Objective*
   To create and retain satisfied and profitable customers.
   Implications
   This requires continuing analyses to determine customer wants and needs, to develop new concepts of service, and to increase our productivity.
2. *Objective*
   To be an agent of effective change in our own spheres of operation.
   Implications
   This objective will necessarily shape our philosophy of operation, have an impact upon our organizational structure, and influence our relationships with our employees and customers.
3. *Objective*
   To provide leadership in improving the effectiveness and efficiency of the international flow of goods, services and ideas.
   Implications
   Our activities and expertise will be directed equally to the support of international and domestic marketing efforts of our customers. Our own marketing efforts will be directed toward foreign customers as well

as domestic; so our firm must improve its understanding of cultural and economic practices of the major trading nations.

4. *Objective*

To be a marketing support system and consider ourselves as extensions of our customers' managerial group.

Implications

We will be in effect an extension of our customer's distribution system. This also implies that so far as possible, our goals and strategies should mesh with those of our customers.

In September, 1973, Dr. Carter decided that the objectives needed to be made somewhat more specific and operational. He also wanted to modify them to include the personal objectives of the present and anticipated members of the management team. On several previous occasions the opinions and contributions of these prospective managers had also been solicited in anticipation of their joining as soon as the expansion was warranted. See Exhibit 1 for a condensed copy of the letter Dr. Carter sent asking them for help.

EXHIBIT 1

MEMO

To: Richard, Mark, Shawn, Bob   Date: 9-14-74
From: Jeff   Subject: Objectives

All of you have copies of our objectives. Clearly, they are mostly identifying the general direction—even tho' much more specifically than the Purpose and Mission statements. As such, they are mostly philosophical statements. Eventually, I will get around to writing them in an operational way.

  •••Will you give them some study and suggest operational statements?•••

By and large, those objectives, purpose and mission, reflect ME, my philosophies, aspirations, etc. I know that generally we all adhere to the same general notions. Nevertheless, if we are to accomplish what we say we are going to accomplish in those statements, we need more than ME, my notions and aspirations. We NEED yours.

Specifically we comment on our managers and things being "different." So far as I can tell, most of the managers we educate in our Colleges of Business are not the type that modern business needs. Certainly, they are not the type that we need. Strike that—they are not the type that we are going to have. Our people will be as "at home" in "staff" work of planning as they are in the "line" work of managing—at least the line managers will. There will be none of this horse manure that "I've got to run my department and haven't got time for planning." I do not have time for that type of person. Line managers MUST work for the organization first and help determine organization objectives, plans, and policies as well as the strategic aspects of departmental policies. A system cannot function effectively otherwise.

There will be none of the "stuff" such as we heard from one of our potential customers. Richard told the guy that he was using off-size pallets which created a problem. His response in effect was that he knew it, that the decision on pallets was the manufacturing department, and that might as well be another company.

The other side: While our line managers MUST engage in these things for the organization as a whole, the reverse does not necessarily hold true. Our staff people need not be line people. All of this implies certain types of people with certain types of personal objectives.

  •••Over the course of the next several weeks, will each of you give some thought to your own objectives, what you want to accomplish for YOU, write them up and send them to me?•••

One of these days, we will all talk about these things and modify our overall objectives to see that they somehow or other reflect your aspirations. Since our objectives reflect ME, they are in my opinion incomplete. Mine must be modified somewhat to reflect US, not ME. I consider this to be one of the most important things we will do. Each of us has different "satisfactions" to attain, and all of those satisfactions must be CONSIDERED. If we were not generally in agreement, we would not have the association that we have; but we have to consider all of us.

(The rest of the letter went on to describe progress with several different prospective customers and the fact that at this point "We don't have a customer yet.")

In October, Costello forwarded his response after "sitting on it for a month." The other managers had not responded as of early spring, 1974. Both of the managers already employed had been working long hours. Even their social contacts were directed at potential customers, and they were constantly in touch with one another by telephone at all hours of the day and night. The company's scarce resources needed constant monitoring and careful attention. The break-even point had not been reached, but progress toward it was encouraging. New prospects and new opportunities were continuously coming to the attention of management. Although few organizations had made actual commitments, the reason appeared to be that it took time to convince typical traffic managers of the advantages. There was always a potential for increased customer service; there usually, but not always, was a potential for increased profit. It subsequently took even more time for the traffic managers to convince their own organization's higher management of the potential gain of taking the systems view of logistics management. There were some disappointments along the way, but enough companies appeared to recognize the potential benefits to make the TDC in Little Rock economically feasible. It also appeared that the same idea might work in other locations and management earnestly began to explore additional opportunities.

However, Dr. Carter knew that one basis for selection of projects would be how well they suited the company's objectives. Since these objectives were incomplete, it would be more difficult to analyze alternatives. He also realized that the way he reacted to this dilemma would have a lot of influence on his relationships with his top managers. If he forced them to respond, he might detract their efforts from promotion, customer service, or other urgent operating matters. He might also reduce their feelings of independence, entrepreneurship, flexibility, or innovation. Morale of these key executives was an important consideration, and to require them to do this might lessen their involvement and commitment. However, without operational targets, it would be difficult for Dr. Carter to determine the progress the company was making, particularly since financial results were secondary to personal objectives. Dr. Carter was also concerned because open communications among the management team are essential to his philosophy of doing business, yet in this important area, the communications appeared to be mostly one way. Due to the impending need for major project decisions, he would have to do something soon to obtain their personal objectives and operational statements in time for use in making these key decisions.

APPENDIX 1

OBJECTIVES OF THE CARTER DISTRIBUTION CORPORATION

Rather than develop a "free standing" creed for our company, we state our beliefs about several things and then identify our objectives in light of those beliefs. Naturally, our creed, purpose, and mission are interdependent. It is probably immaterial whether our beliefs shaped our purpose—but they probably did—or whether our purpose shaped our beliefs—as they probably did.

1. *Belief*

Effective and efficient support of our customers' marketing effort depends upon our determining and satisfying their needs and our making a profit in the process.

Objective

To create and retain satisfied and profitable customers.

Implications

This requires that key managers be equally concerned with (1) analyses leading to the development of objectives, plans, strategies and policies for the effectiveness of our organization as a whole, and (2) the rationalization process of using modern methods to improve the efficiency of our operations. Specifically, it includes market analyses to determine what our customers want and need or should want and need. Also, it includes keeping an eye on the future to discover opportunities and problems. In addition, it means the development of new concepts of service and methods of operation to increase our productivity.

Further, it means we must know our costs if we are to know which customers are unprofitable, develop ways of making them profitable, or barring that, drop them. Too, it means that we recognize that an unprofitable customer places a burden on our ability to satisfy others.

Overall, it means that we are a marketing-oriented company dedicated to serving our customers well and making a profit.

2. *Belief*

We believe that change is the only constant in the economic environment.

Objective

To be an agent of effective change in our spheres of operation.

Implications

This objective will necessarily shape our philosophy of operation, have an impact upon our organizational structure, and affect our relationships with our employees and customers.

3. *Belief*

We believe that we can and should actively design our own future rather than passively adapt to change to the extent that we make happen those things we want to have happen—for ourselves and our customers.

Objective

Determine to the best of our ability what (1) is likely to happen in the future, and (2) what we want to have happen and design a program to accommodate our conclusions.

Implications

This means that we keep the past in perspective for the lessons it taught, recognize that the present is only a transitory path to the future, and know that our future is what we make—and that it will soon be our past. All of which implies that we must devote a great deal of attention to planning.

4. *Belief*

In the future our country must be more involved in international intercourse than at any time in the past, and that it is now in, or approaching, the resource posture such great trading nations as the Netherlands, Great Britain, and more recently Japan have had for decades.

Objective

To provide leadership in improving the effectiveness and efficiency of the international flow of goods, services and ideas.

Implications

Our activities and expertise will be directed equally to the support of the international and domestic marketing efforts of our customers. This implies that our expansion program will include opening distribution centers in foreign countries, probably starting in Canada and Latin America.

5. *Belief*

Effective international intercourse demands that our nation buy abroad as well as sell abroad.

Objective

To support the marketing effort of foreign firms marketing here with the same diligence we apply to domestic firms marketing abroad.

Implication

The nationality of our customers is important in only one broad way: we must improve our understanding of the cultural and economic practices of foreign people in order to better serve their needs here and American needs abroad.

6. *Belief*

Our greatest potential for service to the public at large is in those areas of basic human needs: food, health, shelter, and energy.

Objective

Direct our efforts primarily to the canned food industries serving housing, hospitals, and petroleum items.

Implications

These industries provide a direction for our first marketing efforts. It may become necessary to broaden the normally viewed functions of distribution to include canning and packaging of such items as oil, detergents, and the like which are received in bulk.

7. *Belief*

There are dislocations and dysfunctions in the logistics environments which militate against both the economic flow of goods and the economic development of regions, and thus restrict markets.

Objective

To improve the logistics environment in the geographic areas in which we are located.

Implications

We will have to become involved in restructuring rates and practices of carriers and warehousemen and improving service to small towns. This is in our interest as well as in the interest of our community and region.

8. *Belief*

The economic development of the regions where we are located is enhanced by bringing new firms to the region.

Objective

To attract as customers those firms not now using Little Rock or any other city we locate in as a distribution point.

Implications

Our efforts will not be directed toward attracting customers away from public warehouses in our area. It (1) makes no net contribution to the area, and (2) it is probably more difficult than attracting new customers.

9. *Belief*

The economic development of our area benefits us.

Objective

Work with other agencies and companies in a leadership position to further economic development.

Implications

We support these efforts now with our expertise. As we become capable of doing so, we provide financial support. We will join with carriers, other warehousemen, bankers, civic groups in joint efforts. Specifically, in Little Rock we will participate in furthering the development of the Foreign Trade Zone and the port.

10. *Belief*

A total distribution complex is necessary to provide a complete support system for international and domestic marketing efforts.

Objective

To create a distribution complex consisting of a distribution center, intermodal transfer facilities, consolidated terminal operations, satellite terminal facilities in small towns, and other facilities and services.

Implications

The distribution center is only one facet of a total complex. Its strategies must be directed toward its ultimate role as nucleus of the complex.

11. *Belief*

Transportation and warehousing companies as a group have not been as diligent in supporting the marketing effort of their customers as we think is desirable and profitable.

Objective

To innovate in conceptual, managerial, and operating areas to improve the effectiveness of the physical distribution system, the efficiency of the parts of the system, and thus reduce cost and/or improve service to users.

Implications

The discovery process has been largely ignored by distribution people. We have adopted as one of our major functions the discovery of problems and opportunities of today and of the future in order to (1) identify what we want to have happen, and (2) to develop plans to make happen what we want to have happen.

13. *Belief*

Increases in productivity should be shared with employees and customers.

Objective

To pass along to our employees and customers a portion of improvements in productivity through higher wages, better service, lower prices, etc.

Implications

Our marketing orientation recognizes that our employees in concert with our customers, those performing tasks for them, and our managers developing concepts of service all convert the hollow words "customers service" into a real-life working concept. One of the ingredients of customer service is "good service at low cost." As our productivity increases our employees and customers are "partners" in our program of advancement of the industry. We will become leaders in the industry in all matters including price. Some will refer to us as price cutters, we will be productivity leaders.

14. *Belief*

Small towns have notoriously bad service from transportation and distribution companies despite their vitality and growth rates.

Objective

To bring good distribution service to the small towns of the areas where we are located.

Implications

Many are unaware of the growth rates of small towns and of the opportunities they present for distribution companies. We see opportunities for service and profit—just as clearly as we see the problems involved.

15. *Belief*

We have a very strong belief in the competitive system, the profit motive, and the many dimensions of satisfaction for entrepreneurs and managers.

Objective

To manage our business in such a way that we advance the industry through our innovative activities, make a substantial profit from our efforts, and reap the many personal intangible rewards from our activities.

Implications

We will not meet competition, we will make it. We seek our rewards from profits and from the professional satisfaction of doing a job well. Our allusions to public service have not been solely from an altruistic posture. We merely believe that if we operate from the bases discussed we will have built a better mousetrap and will catch more mice. Perhaps our major altruism stems from our patriotic thought that if we render better service to our customers and our community we will be privileged to pay more income taxes in the highest corporate bracket in progressively high personal brackets!

CASE 6

CARTER DISTRIBUTION CORPORATION (C)

Dr. Carter's Questions

In midspring 1974, Dr. Jeff Carter, Chairman of the Board for the Carter Distribution Corporation (CDC), and a Professor of Marketing and Transportation at Templeton University, was musing with mixed emotions over a letter from Shawn Costello, one of his former students. Shawn had been an outstanding student in several of Dr. Carter's classes five years earlier.

In class and in several lively social conversations both then and during Shawn's successful business career since, Dr. Carter and Shawn had discussed the rich opportunities for major improvements in physical distribution programs. Indeed, the fledgling one year old CDC—a "different" Total Distribution Center* —was partly an outgrowth of many similar discussions Dr. Carter had enjoyed during his professional career. The letter now in his hands included several of Shawn's usual stimulating ideas; more importantly, however, it reiterated another topic Shawn and Dr. Carter had discussed two or three times during the last several months—Shawn's abilities and interest in joining CDC when the time was appropriate. Shawn's abilities and interest were a welcome part of the careful planning Dr. Carter had done in preparing for and initiating CDC. But he wondered, had the appropriate time arrived? Might it possibly never arrive?

The fledgling CDC effort had been greeted with enthusiastic interest by many of its prospective customers—and new interest and opportunities were appearing almost daily. Over eight months of sales development efforts, however, had produced very, very meager sales revenue. Dr. Carter and his CDC associates had expected that it would take time for their sales efforts to pay off. Their prospective customers would often have to do a lot of checking

---

*The nature of a Total Distribution Center (TDC) and of CDC activities is developed in sections following this introduction.

This case was made possible through the cooperation of a firm which prefers to remain anonymous. It was prepared by Professor Roger M. Atherton and Dennis M. Crites of the University of Oklahoma for educational purposes only and is not intended to convey effective or ineffective administrative procedure. Since all data are disguised, this case should not be used as source material for research purposes.

Distributed by the Intercollegiate Case Clearing House, Soldiers Field, Boston, Mass. 02163. All rights reserved to the contributors. Printed in the U.S.A. Presented at a Case Workshop. Reprinted with permission.

and coordinating before buying CDC's services. Were the CDC ideas and services, however, really harder to sell (and to "buy") than they had believed? Or had there been some weaknesses in the CDC selling efforts? Did Shawn have some strengths and experience that might be just what CDC needed at this time? These were among the questions that Dr. Carter knew he would have to answer in his own mind and discuss frankly with Shawn—before inviting Shawn to share CDC's odd situation: a rapidly growing "crop" but some doubts about "harvesting" methods and results.

The Background

The Carter Distribution Corporation—designed "to support the marketing effort" of its potential customers "in all facets of physical distribution" began its business development operations in the summer of 1973. Formed as a major project of Carfam, Ltd—a family corporation initiated by Dr. and Mrs. Jeff A. Carter to finance such projects—the CDC, located in Little Rock, Arkansas, was to be developed as a "different" Total Distribution Center (TDC).

The development of a TDC was an indirect culmination of a body of concepts developed by Dr. Carter through more than twenty years of professional study and research. His principal teaching and writing work was in the area of physical distribution and logistics. This expertise—combined with a strong background in the field of industries and resources—led industrial development agencies in several states, including Arkansas, to retain him for studies and consultation. A recurring theme, not only in courses being taught but in speeches he gave and in many of his studies, was the need for a Total Distribution Center viewpoint. Some of the Arkansas industrial development people with whom Dr. Carter worked had on two or three occasions during the late '60's and early '70's broached the subject of Dr. Carter's setting up a TDC in Arkansas, an area several hundred miles from Dr. Carter's home and work at Templeton.

In late 1972 and early 1973, another set of circumstances led Dr. Carter to analyze more carefully the initiation of a Total Distribution Center in Little Rock. Enthusiastic interest was being expressed by three or four former students, now holding physical distribution or related positions, in joining Dr. Carter in such a venture. These were persons who both as students and in their careers had displayed superior insight and potential. In particular, they had all shared with Dr. Carter socially and at professional meetings many hours in discussion of the concepts, philosophies, and values necessary to optimum implementation of a Total Distribution System or Center. The sale of some stocks and other investments also provided Dr. Carter and Carfam, Ltd., with the funds which would be needed. Consequently, detailed planning and analysis which had begun in late 1972 resulted near the end of March, 1973 in a decision to start operation of a Little Rock TDC that summer. (See Appendix A for fuller details.)

Initial Operations

The CDC's Little Rock activities for the summer of 1973 were essentially a one-man operation. The president, Richard Kirk, previously in physical distribution management with a national manufacturer of machinery and a former student of Dr. Carter's—spent most of his time in planning, arranging equipment and space for the firm's warehousing needs and office, and in the making of a number of sales calls. A policy had been adopted that CDC would try mainly to bring into Little Rock "new" distribution activities, e.g., by firms not previously distributing in that area. In other words, CDC was not trying to take business from Little Rock's currently operating warehouses, carriers, and related firms. To this end, Richard made some sales trips to Chicago where he had a number of professional and business contacts in the physical distribution field.

In mid-fall, 1973, Richard was joined by Mark Kallister, Dr. Carter's son-in-law and also a former student, who was designated as Vice-President of CDC. Mark, a regular army officer for seven years had some army logistics experience and several recent BBA and MBA courses in physical distribution. Carfam planning, in which Mark had participated, was that Richard, with his lengthier time in industrial physical distribution, could "train" Mark and help prepare him not only for his initial CDC-Little Rock responsibilities but for starting up the next CDC-TDC venture, tentatively planned for Nashville, Tennessee. Mark's work at first was partly to share in and to learn from Richard the work Richard was doing and partly to handle some of the pick-up, delivery and related tasks for the first customers the firm acquired. He accompanied Richard on some of the sales calls to Chicago and by the Spring of 1974, was making sales calls on his own in Little Rock and Chicago. Mark also was becoming active with civic groups and individuals involved in developing the new part of Little Rock, part of the Arkansas River Navigation project.

For their warehouse and office, CDC was renting two bays (about 25,000 square feet, well above their usage at that time) in a newly constructed, well-located and equipped eight-bay warehouse building. They also held options to rent up to four of the remaining bays as needed. An adequate supply of racks, pallets, office materials, and the like had been purchased and a fork-lift truck leased. Arrangements had been made to obtain additional help, as required, from temporary-manpower employment services; these arrangements, with plans to add permanent employees as business developed, were deemed adequate for foreseeable office and warehouse operating personnel needs.

By early 1974, it was becoming clear that the sales development efforts of CDC were taking—again, somewhat as expected—a long time to "pay off." In many respects CDC was attempting to sell receiving, handling, storage, delivery and related services of the same sort offered by most public warehouses. By selling these services as a TDC, however—operated by a firm with a carefully developed marketing concept viewpoint and related philosophies—CDC was offering a set of ideas that they believed were uniquely valuable to their prospective customers.

The CDC Viewpoint

One part of the CDC planning effort developed "an Outline of the CDC View of its Role in the Distribution System." In this outline, a "distribution system" was defined, in effect, as a means of facilitating the several different "distribution processes" of transportation, warehousing and so forth." The CDC outline described its own role as a "distribution system" thusly:

"In supporting the customers' marketing effort(s), we 'operate' or integrate the several processes."

Based on Dr. Carter's years of working with shippers, carriers, and warehousemen—and on the experience of others in the company—the CDC executives believed the vast majority of companies achieved relatively minimal integration among these different distribution processes and the marketing efforts of the sellers involved. Basically, this was because of the complexity of the activities, the division of labor into highly specialized tasks and agencies, and a still great shortage of persons with the knowledge, experience, breadth of viewpoint, attitudes, and related skills needed to work effectively towards broad-scale integration of effort. For example, the agricultural chemicals decision for a major oil company might have several hundred potential dealers in the Midwest and South Central states. Selecting the type, number, and location of wholesale distribution points—or middlemen—in those areas would be a formidable and critical marketing task in itself. Supporting, guiding, and supervising their subsequent promotion efforts, sales forecasts, inventory levels, and customer service activities would be equally challenging and important marketing responsibilities. Help would be needed from specialists in transportation and warehousing. Information and guidance would be necessary in deciding both the initial locations and the continuing operation of these physical distribution services.

In deciding upon the locations, for example, the company's physical distribution manager might have to turn to a number of sources of information, such as carriers, warehouse companies, or consultants in deciding whether to ship by rail or motor carrier and in comparing the total cost efforts of the different rates to different sites. He possibly might even query the different common carriers on negotiating a lower type of rate—especially if the sales forecast showed sufficient volume for a given area. Very probably, too, he might ask a public warehousing company for a general quotation on their charges—and receive something like the following:

Warehouse space
    By Month $.18/sq. ft.; includes utilities, security system, etc.
    By Year $.15/sq. ft. by month; $1.70/sq. ft. by year; tenant pays security charges and special utilities; construct walls, fences, etc.

Small office
    (Air-conditioned) $3.50/sq. ft./yr.

Warehouse labor
    Normal customer $9.00/hr.
    Contract-(40 hr. min.)—$7.00/hr.

    (and so forth, for rates through probably five to ten major headings and ten to twenty sub-heading quotations)

Alternatively or in further explanation, the following sort of response might be received to the query:

In general, our handling rates are based on $1.50 to transport one load into or out of stock one way. Modifications depend upon picking requirements, palletizing involved, or any manual labor needed. Palletizing of product per case would vary from $.03 per case to $.25 per case depending upon the weight and number of people required to palletize. Order picking would vary from $.04 to $.10 per case depending upon method of picking, size of orders, and weight of product. Storage is based on square foot and cubic foot utilization as we discussed. The specific question you asked regarding palletized charges per 36 inch height pallets 40 x 48 inches in storage rack would be $1.20 per pallet per month storage. Storage of these same pallets with a stacking limit of two high would be $2.00 per pallet per month. Clerical charges are normally added into either storage or handling and are based on estimates from operation of similar accounts and customer descriptions of requirements. If the customer desires it can be a separate document (bill of lading, warehouse receiver, OS&D etc.) charge.

Before using such a "quotation" to arrive at a final cost or rate for his warehousing requirements, the physical distribution manager would obviously have to acquire and calculate considerable data such as sales distribution forecasts; the physical dimensions, packing and shipping characteristics of his products; and the likely inventory turnover or average storage period. Coordinating these informational tasks with marketing, production, finance, shipping and other departments in his own company, with different carriers, and with other possible storage facilities may further complicate and delay a decision. The additional communication and negotiation will usually wind up—probably after several days and perhaps weeks—with a warehousing cost figure—e.g. an "average" of $.07 1/2 cents per case sold—that can be "plugged in" to the company's total cost calculations and profit approximations.

Fundamentally, public warehousing charges are mainly of two types: (1) the handling in and handling out or related activity costs, usually at a given price per carton or unit, and (2) the storage costs, quoted as a given charge per month. CDC officials are fairly certain that most warehouse firms (and also most carriers) have insufficient data on relationships between their actual costs of performing their various activities (for different types of goods stored) and the charges they levy for such services. CDC gave special attention to developing such data on their own costs and to relating the prices they charge to such costs. The result (shown subsequently in Exhibit 2) was a pricing structure and method that provided significant advantages both to CDC and to their customers.

In further explaining differences between their own distribution center concept and the usual public warehousing operation, CDC included in their "Outline" (of their view of their role) the following excerpted portions:

II (A) Comparison of Public Warehousing and (the) Distribution Center Concept

    A. Customer and warehousing
        1. Function: Public warehousing
        2. Activities: Receive handle in, store, handle out, documentation
    B. Customer and distribution center
        1. Function: Support marketing effort
        2. Activities: Relate processes (of transporting, warehousing, etc.) to each other and to the distribution system.

And,

    VI. Public Warehousemen—CDC
      A.Warehousemen
        1. Mechanistic approach
        2. Assumes "rightness of each process or step" in the distribution system.
        3. Assumes each process to be discrete step
      B.CDC
        1. Environmental approach
        2. Assumes each process or step to be a variable subject to adjustment to meet customers' objectives
        3. Assumes the processes to be a continuum in the system; arranges for flow of goods through the process; integrates activities with customers' needs

CDC's "Three Facets" and Selling Approach

In essence, CDC recognized that almost all the services they were offering were—when viewed as separate activities—the same as those offered in varying degrees by the already-existing public warehouse firms. They were firmly convinced, however, that three facets of their operation made them capable of vastly greater potential service—in an overall sense—for every one of their prospective customers. The three facets were:

1. The "marketing support systems" viewpoint they had adopted;
2. The carefully stated and integrated list of objectives developed by CDC—particularly as these identified CDC responsibilities to its customers, and,
3. The pricing structure and system established by CDC upon the basis of its cost analyses.

The first two facets were interwoven into essentially a single theme which ran throughout a ten-page description of the company's purpose, mission, principal beliefs, objectives, and the implications of these for the company's operations. This description was prepared for the firm's "in-house" guidance and used on some occasions in selling interviews with prospective customers. Based upon it a promotional brochure was prepared (see Exhibit 1). In the fall of 1973 a mailing of this brochure went to approximately 300 members of the American Association of Physical Distribution Managers (AAPDM). The brochure was also used in sales calls upon physical distribution managers in the Chicago area and in two or three other midwestern cities.

The third of the facets which distinguished CDC—its pricing systems—gave CDC the ability to reply almost immediately to customer queries on the price for obtaining warehousing services on given customer needs and an ability to price on a "daily" basis. One prospective customer, in a telephone call, described his requirements for storing and wound up with the question, "Can you prepare a quotation on this and get it to me before the end of next week?" The Vice-President, Mark Kallister, responded: "I can give it to you right over the phone now if you wish." The caller's expression of pleasant surprise was typical of reactions to this aspect of CDC operations. The "daily" pricing for storage charges—described more fully below—contrasted significantly with usual public warehouse charges for a month or half-month at a time. It was of special import to customers with high turn-over of their inventory.

In addition to speed and ease in quoting prices, the pricing system gave CDC reasonably high confidence that their prices for different services were based as closely as feasible upon their costs. This implied both that they could be competitive in pricing (assuming they achieved the operational efficiency to which they were dedicated) and that they would avoid accepting unprofitable business. Exhibit 2 shows the price groups and cost modules used to determine the CDC price structure.

The Results

The mailing of the introductory brochure (Exhibit 1) was designed mainly to "introduce" the company. Some addressees were persons upon whom 'phone calls were planned to obtain appointments for a sales interview. Others were ones who might seek further information from CDC and incorporate it into their future physical distribution decisions and plans. Two or three recipients telephoned CDC as soon as they received the brochure and expressed enthusiastic approval of the CDC concepts. One or two very complimentary letters were also received within a few days, from other recipients. All of these expressed or implied that their present physical distribution arrangements were well set but that CDC appeared to be a firm of the type with which they would like to do business whenever they had a need to change. No other queries or responses were directly traceable to the mailing. Apparently the brochure did "pave the way" for several of the sales interviews obtained by the president and vice-president on sales trips they made during the late fall and early winter.

Both the president and vice-president had a very good grasp of general physical distribution concepts and of the CDC viewpoint. Neither, however, had very much in the way of professional sales training or experience. On their sales trips, they first used an AAPDM membership roster and later the yellow pages to obtain names of physical distribution managers upon whom to call. They selected mainly larger, more progressive, and well-known companies of a size that were apt to have distribution in the Little Rock Area. Telephone calls were then made in an attempt to obtain an appointment for a sales interview. About twenty-five or thirty telephone calls were required in order to schedule the five or six interviews per day they tried to arrange.

Described later by the vice-president as largely PR (or public relations) interviews, there was typically no attempt to "close a sale" or obtain a commitment for some use of CDC services. Normally, the interviews began with a verbal description by Richard Kirk of the CDC firm's background and particularly the ideas underlying its operations. Usually a part of this included a discussion of why CDC had selected Little Rock as the first of its planned locations.[1] Typically, the vice-president would then question the prospect about the nature of his company's physical distribution operations and which aspects might be presenting problems. In almost all interviews, the prospects expressed an active interest in the CDC ideas and operations; they also tended to discuss freely their own activities and problems. At the end of the interview, the brochure in Exhibit 1 would be left with the prospects. On only two interviews was the reception inhospitable—but in those instances it was markedly so!

From the forty presentations made in the late fall and early winter trips, about six or seven companies provided enough information and in turn asked the CDC representatives for further information such that Richard and Mark believed they had some "really ripe apples to chew on." Prospects at the other companies tended to indicate that if and when they had needs for CDC services they would get in touch with CDC at that time. Upon returning to Little Rock, Richard and Mark usually divided the work of following up the leads they had acquired.

For example, one major food products company had indicated that they were studying the process of disposing of a number of company-owned warehouses—in order to free the capital invested—and using public warehouse facilities. They asked for CDC charges on storage and related services for a projected amount of specified goods. Utilizing this information, the food company made initial computer analyses in their Chicago divisional office of the effects on their total costs and profits. When these analyses indicated very favorable results for the use of CDC, the divisional office asked for further information from CDC and made an operations research type of analysis involving 24 computer runs. This analysis compared total costs of using public warehouses in Dallas, St. Louis, and other selected cities in the midwest. All of these analyses also showed results favorable to the use of CDC.

The food company's Chicago division next made a recommendation which went to corporate headquarters in New York. By early spring of 1974, both the physical distribution and marketing offices at the corporate level had concurred with the Chicago recommendation and forwarded it to the corporate finance office. In mid-spring, the finance office recommendation on the matter was part of a series of related recommendations being considered by the corporate policy committee.

---

[1] This discussion usually referred to the progressive attitude of people in Little Rock, the city's physical resources (especially the international distribution potential of the Port of Little Rock), and CDC's "concept of location." This concept is to avoid major distribution cities such as Dallas, St. Louis, and New Orleans, but to seek points where "the economic hinterlands" of these major cities overlap and where their distribution services are therefore competitively more vulnerable.

Although their experience with the food company was somewhat more drawn out than with the others, it was indicative of CDC's experience with all the "ripe apple" prospects obtained on their selling trips. Two of the firms had to alter their planning because of shortages of raw materials; one was enjoined by the Federal Energy Administration from carrying out distribution channel changes and allocations that would have been involved in moving to the use of CDC; the others required further study and price comparisons before committing themselves.

The CDC Anomaly

Thus, in early spring 1974, CDC was in an anomalous position. They were still, after a number of months, negotiating with several firms, each of whose business could provide CDC with revenues of thousands of dollars a year. Indeed any one of three of the firms would provide revenue well above $100,000 annually. In addition, other firms in the Little Rock area which had contacted or been contacted by CDC in recent weeks, had expressed interest of the same sort as the "ripe apples" contacted on the Chicago and other selling trips. The company's actual revenues, however, were varying between one or two hundred dollars a month and three or four hundred. Only two small-volume customers were really utilizing CDC services on a regularly established basis; a limited number of special or ad hoc jobs had been undertaken and even a couple of these had turned "sour".

Meanwhile, interest and pressure were coming up "ahead of schedule" on the long-range objectives and plans of the company—to establish a number of TDC's in "economic hinterland areas" similar to Little Rock and to move eventually into international distribution activities. For example, one firm is offering to finance, on any of two or three very attractive bases, the construction as soon as feasible of a TDC to be operated by CDC near El Paso, another port-of-entry. The same firm had also arranged prospective customers for the new TDC; many of these potential customers, because of very poor distribution services and facilities they currently were using, appeared so interested that CDC executives believed signed contracts for use of CDC services could be obtained almost immediately. In addition, some individuals that Mark Kallister (the CDC V.P.) had met through civic organizations or social contacts were trying to get some local groups interested in more dynamic development of the Port of Little Rock. They were tapping Mark for expert help in these efforts; mention had even been made of having CDC take over management of a TDC in the Port complex and perhaps manage the Port and its FTZ (free trade zone) itself.

Thus, physically, CDC in early spring 1974 was still essentially a two-man operation with an absentee chairman of the board, a small amount of rented warehouse and office space, a pick-up truck, and a leased fork-lift. The president and the vice-president, often times disagreeing on the best sales strategy,[2] were alternating as time permitted between major managerial tasks, selling activities, and warehouse or delivery labor efforts. The vice-president, for example, was literally driving a delivery truck on the same day that he would make an evening presentation to some of the state's leading bankers regarding economic development of the Little Rock area and its Port.

Dr. Carter's Role

Dr. Carter, as chairman of the board for CDC, had steered a middle course through the several months of CDC efforts at sales development. He was deter-

---

[2] These disagreements involved such matters as "which department or manager would be best to call on at the Ajax Widget Company?" . . ."spending all that time and money wining, dining, and socializing with prospects is wrong!". . . "Why didn't you fill me in more on those calls that came from the Ardly-Bend people while I was out yesterday?"

mined to leave the presidential and related responsibilities to the two executives hired for those duties. At the same time, his own deep interest and financial involvement in the firm were coupled with frequent occasions when either the president or the vice-president called him for guidance of a decision on a major policy point. Long distance phone calls or fairly lengthy letters were in almost daily flow between Dr. Carter and his two men in Little Rock. Many of the exchanges were in regard to specific major tasks; for example, preparing for Dr. Carter to visit the investor firm and some of the potential customers at El Paso. A large proportion of the exchanges involved, directly or implicitly, the tasks of "operationalizing", re-examining, and—almost always—reaffirming the basic ideas upon which the firm had been originated.

For example, one very large manufacturer and assembler of industrial components contacted the CDC people in Little Rock to see if they might obtain more favorable rates and services than they were presently receiving elsewhere. A quickly prepared analysis indicated clearly that CDC could provide the manufacturer decidedly more advantageous rates and services than they currently received. The business would provide CDC with five to six thousand dollars in revenue per month and probable entry into the manufacturer's sizeable international distribution (these operations were to be extended to the Port of Little Rock in the near future). The same analysis that showed CDC a better alternative than that presently used also indicated rather clearly that the manufacturer would benefit even more by finding a suitable distribution center in the eastern part of the United States.

The CDC president and vice-president decided to handle the contract in accordance with the following excerpt from the CDC guidelines:

> "... we commit ourselves to a certain relationship to our customers ... For one thing, we may—and will—help our customers devise strategies (and approaches) to help them attain their objectives which may cause us a loss in revenue ... "

When notified of and asked to confirm this decision—to recommend to the manufacturer to seek an eastern distribution center—Dr. Carter immediately gave his approval.

Another series of exchanges among Dr. Carter and the Little Rock executives resulted from a "lead" mentioned casually to Mark one day by a truck carrier salesman visiting the CDC office. Mark followed up and obtained an appointment with the plant traffic manager for a leading national manufacturer's facility located some thirty miles north of Little Rock. The interview quickly disclosed (and secured agreement upon) an opportunity for the firm to obtain major advantages in both rates and service by changing their present methods of routing and shipping a significant proportion of their shipments. As part of this opportunity, CDC approached the common carrier truck line being used by the manufacturer and requested a change from the class-type rate on the re-routed shipments. They cited to the carrier that the changes would result in larger size shipments, that CDC would expedite handling, stacking, and loading of the shipments to allow fuller use by the carrier of his trucks, and that the overall changes would permit lower costs and greater total revenue for the carriers. The proposed commodity rate was greeted with approval by the carrier's management personnel first contacted by CDC; subsequently, however, other executives in the carrier's organization rejected the idea. In the exchanges that evolved, Richard, Mark, and Dr. Carter mutually explored over a period of four or five months several alternatives on how best to serve the manufacturer. The exploration involved, at various times, other carriers, the manufacturer's local plant traffic manager, his divisional marketing and traffic managers in Memphis, and corporate level marketing and physical distribution executives in New York.

Another category of exchanges among CDC executives concerned the need to refine the company's pricing structure. A key advantage of CDC pricing to many customers was its system of charging only for the actual number of days goods were stored. Standard warehouse terms provide that with certain exceptions, "a month's storage charge shall apply to goods stored for any fraction of a month." The exceptions involve mainly a possible agreement between the warehouseman and storer that only one-half month's storage will be charged on goods received between the 16th and the last day of a calendar month. Dr. Carter pointed out that CDC's daily pricing system—for many, perhaps most customers—"really turns them on." Mark Kallister also noted that the ability to quote prices quickly was impressive to many prospects and "flashy" but that practically every customer, before making a commitment to use CDC, required a "hard copy" quotation. It was in the reaction to these quotations that the need for refinement of the pricing structure was becoming apparent. For example, Dr. Carter admitted, "We may have lost a lot of people (prospects) that way; it puzzles me, but one prospect looked at our quotation and said 'your storage charge (component) is too high'; he wouldn't use us despite the fact that *his total costs* for using us would be lower. He was having about three months' average and six months maximum storage on his goods, was paying $1.50 per case for the first month and 30¢ for each additional month; our rates were $1.20 for the first month and 35¢ for each added month; but he wouldn't use us because of that 5¢ a month!"

The general consensus in CDC was that: (1) prices and services competitive with other public warehouses were essential before most customers would become very interested in the additional advantages that CDC might provide; (2) the estimated costs utilized in initial construction of the cost modules were probably too conservative and actual costs were somewhat lower; and, (3) the allocation of costs to the storing modules, although conceptually sound, made that component somewhat higher than storing charges quoted by competitors, especially on low density items where large-cube boxes or material were quite light in weight (e.g., cases of facial tissues).

CDC's anomalous situation and a variety of exchanges such as those above were the background against which Dr. Carter was considering the letter from Shawn Costello. Shawn was presently serving very successfully as a midwestern sales representative for one of the country's leading railroads. Dr. Carter had discussed several times with Richard and Mark the possibility that Shawn would be one of the leading "candidates" for the next opening whenever CDC might have need to add to its managerial ranks. In the letter Dr. Carter had just received, Shawn indicated that he had encountered in sales calls near his home base in St. Louis several firms who appeared to be excellent prospects for use of CDC. And he reiterated his enthusiastic interest in joining CDC as soon as feasible.

Dr. Carter started thinking more carefully through the probable answers to the questions on which he had started musing earlier.

APPENDIX A
CDC EMPHASIS ON TRADE-OFF IMPLICATIONS AS A BASIS FOR THEIR TDC

The CDC viewpoint, borne out by experience with a variety of firms, industries, and research, was that their operation as a marketing support system for their customer provided a unique service. Their systems viewpoint and philosophy were: to help their customer fulfill his respective profit and other objectives through finding the optimum combination of transportation, warehousing, and related costs and services. Among the several different actions that could be pursued to an optimum combination might be the following.

1. Reduced transportation costs per unit through such means as:
   a. Finding a more economical type of carrier;
   b. Recommending changes in processing or packing methods so that the customer's goods either: (1) Weigh less for shipping purposes, or, (2) Qualify for a lower rate classification;
   c. Recommending changes in *location* of certain processing operations so that the customer may benefit from a more favorable combination of production costs and processing-in-transit through-type freight rates;
   d. Consolidating the customer's goods with those of other customers to obtain benefit of larger-volume low rates;
   e. Negotiating with carriers for a lower classification or type or level of rate, sometimes on the basis of certain loading or other services the distribution center could perform but that are less feasible for the customer or a regular public warehouse;
   f. Handling or facilitating the making of damage claims or the auditing of carrier's bills (to avoid overcharges).

2. Reducing warehousing and related handling costs by:
   a. Introducing a price system with a charge for storage for only the actual days stored (rather than the traditional monthly storage charge minimum; see the case text for further details);
   b. Seeking storage module sizes, packaging and other handling or storing features so that a lower rate could be charged;
   c. Suggesting forms of packing, palletizing or "containerizing" that might lower handling costs not only in the CDC-TDC but in the customer's plant and storage and/or at other points in the distribution process.

3. Improving or extending service to their customers' customers so that their customers attain a stronger market position; for example, the distribution center might by reason of its location or operating efforts facilitate:
   a. Quicker delivery to their clients' costomers;
   b. A lower market price and perhaps resultant sales to customers their client could not otherwise serve;
   c. Lower total inventories both for their client and for their clients' customers;
   d. Provision of market information that might identify market opportunities for their clients;

4. Imaginative and continuing efforts to implement the two key CDC "philosophies" of *customer-orientation* and a *marketing support systems viewpoint;* for example, CDC might:
   a. Recommend to customers or prospects the use of another city (or storage system) if CDC analysis indicated that other alternative might be more favorable to the client; or,
   b. Investigate establishment of a CDC-TDC in another city if a present customer indicated a significant need for such services in the other city for his own distribution there.

EXHIBIT 1
WHO WE ARE

Here are some of the things we do at the MANAGERIAL and OPERATIONAL levels:

Assure precise and correct shipments of goods.

Provide dependable on-time shipments to meet the goals of our customers.

Maintain consistent high quality service performance.

Communicate!

WE ARE A MARKETING SUPPORT SYSTEM: on behalf of our customers we examine all aspects of the physical distribution environment; we assume each step along the channel whether it is transportation, warehousing, or other, to be a variable which is subject to adjustment to meet our customers' objectives; we assume each of the processes to be parts of a continuous system of distribution which exists to attain the objectives of users.

WHY LITTLE ROCK!

The concept of physical distribution starts and ends with the geographic market, customer demand and marketing effort. For the past decade, markets in this country have been served primarily from five strategic distribution points, Northern New Jersey, Chicago, Atlanta, Dallas and Los Angeles. These locations "skims the cream," however, markets are demanding much more than these distribution points can provide. there are several potential prime distribution locations that can meet today's market demand for improved physical distribution activity and scope—Little Rock is one such place and it is ready to go.

Little Rock is a 360 degree distribution center-cost and service allows deep penetration into existing distribution areas. Congestion in the larger cities will allow us to take an even greater share of the once impregnable service areas of the "Big 5" locations.

Little Rock is a seaport in the Nation's midsection. The Foreign Trade Zone here is less than one year old and is capable of meeting a rapidly growing international market and serve as a prime port and center for serving U.S. markets across the country. The The Free Port Law of Arkansas provides a strong incentive to base inventory and distribution as well as manufacturing activities in Arkansas.

Little Rock—it is National and International; Regional and National; and Local and Regional—THAT IS WHY WE ARE HERE.

(Note: For mailing, this "WHO WE ARE" column was the back of a folded-letter-size mailer and the "Presenting..." column the cover. Under "WHO WE ARE" was a brief paragraph describing each of the principal officers of the firm, Carter, Kirk and Kallister. The descriptions stressed both the academic and "real world" backgrounds and such points as "...he has long recognized the need to improve physical distribution through stronger marketing implication in distribution systems...", "..." ... and A strong believer in total customer service...")

Presenting . . .

THE CARTER DISTRIBUTION CORPORATION

MARKETING SUPPORT SYSTEMS

PURPOSE AND MISSION

PURPOSE:

To support the marketing effort of our customers everywhere through innovative strategic, managerial, and operational leadership and communication in all facets of physical distribution; to improve the effectiveness of the distribution system and the efficiency of several distribution processes.

MISSION:

To be in all facets of physical distribution necessary to fulfill our purpose and meet market requirements.

IMPLICATIONS:

Our purpose establishes the character of our company; our mission establishes its direction; together they have several implications.

First, with a commitment to support the marketing efforts of our customers, our function transcends that of a public warehouse, distribution warehouse, or what have you. It means that our concern is not only with the processes of distribution—transportation, warehousing, etc.—but also with the function of the distribution system in facilitating the marketing effort.

Second, by reference to our customers everywhere we identify our areas of operation as national and international; regional and national; and local and regional.

Third, our commitment to innovative leadership implies our complete dedication to developing and/or applying better ways of doing things. Also, it identifies our own orientation to our customers in helping them devise distribution strategies to meet their objectives.

OBJECTIVES

Rather than develop a "free-standing" creed or statements of beliefs, we have stated our beliefs about several things and identified objectives to sustain those beliefs. Among our stated objectives are the following:

1. **BELIEF:**
   Effective and efficient support of our customers' marketing effort depends upon our determining and satisfying their needs and our making a profit in the process.

OBJECTIVE:
To create and retain satisfied and profitable customers.

IMPLICATIONS:
This requires continuing analyses to determine customer wants and needs, to develop new concepts of service, and to increase our productivity.

2. **BELIEF:**
   Change is the only constant in the economic environment.

OBJECTIVE:
To be an agent of effective change in our own spheres of operation.

IMPLICATIONS:
This objective will necessarily shape our philosophy of operation, have an impact upon our organizational structure, and influence our relationships with our employees and customers.

3. **BELIEF:**
   Our country in the future must be more involved in international intercourse than at any time in the past.

OBJECTIVE:
To provide leadership in improving the effectiveness and efficiency of the international flow of goods, services, and ideas.

IMPLICATIONS:
Our activities and expertise will be directed equally to the support of international and domestic marketing efforts of our customers. Our own marketing efforts will be directed toward foreign customers as well as domestic; so our firm must improve its understanding of cultural and economic practices of the peoples of the major trading nations.

4. **BELIEF:**
   Transportation and warehousing companies have not been as diligent in supporting the marketing effort of their customers as we think is desirable and profitable.

OBJECTIVE:
To be a marketing support system and consider ourselves as extensions of our customers' managerial group.

IMPLICATIONS:
We will be in effect an extension of our customers' distribution systems. This also implies that so far as possible, our goals and strategies should mesh with those of our customers.

Note: Our full statement of purpose, mission, and objectives is available upon request.

OUR PERSPECTIVE OF THE DISTRIBUTION SYSTEM

An anecdote will help explain our role in distribution. An observer asked one worker what his job was. "I'm mixing mortar" was the answer. A second responded that he was installing glass. The third, obviously a bricklayer, said, "I'm building a cathedral."

Many view transportation, warehousing, management of inventory, and other elements of the distribution system as the first two workers viewed their jobs. CDC has a broader view both of the system and of its role in the system. More so than even the bricklayer! As we see it, the role of physical distribution is to support the marketing effort of a company. So, we say that we are a Marketing Support System, working at the strategic and managerial and operational levels of management to help our customers attain their objectives effectively and efficiently.

Here are some of the things we do at the STRATEGIC level:

Here our customers attain THEIR international and domestic marketing objectives via physical distribution.

In effect become a part of our customers managerial staff: recommend means of carrying out customers' policies; provide our customers with distribution information.

Help our customers identify effective channels of distribution and develop means for going through that channel.

EXHIBIT 2

A. Price Groups*

Number	Received	Shipped
1	Unpalleted	Case
2	Unpalleted	Pallet
3	Palleted	Case
4	Palleted	Pallet
5	Unpalleted	Broken cases
6	Palleted	Broken cases
7	Other	Other

B. Price and Cost Module Calculations

The price for each of the six cost groups above was arrived at through a build-up of costs projected for the first year of operations for the entire range of salaries, wages, equipment costs, rental, taxes, and so forth. These costs were grouped into the six cost modules shown below. Fixed and related costs were allocated on bases judged most appropriate by management for the nature of the specific cost item and module. These were figured both in total and per slot projected. Variable costs reflect wage and equipment costs to perform the tasks concerned. Different "mixes" of resources are required to perform different tasks. Principal tasks were calculated as to minutes required; total costs for these tasks per operation, per slot, and for the entire year were projected.

Module Nature and Content

"Fixed Costs"
    Module 1-Salaries, supplies equipment
    Module 2-Storage area rent, racks, and pallets

       Total "fixed costs"

"Variable Costs"
    Module 3-Handling in
    Module 4-Handling out
    Module 5-Supplies
    Module 6-Clerical time and costs

Exhibit 2 —continued

C. Costs and prices per slot for different price groups*

Line	Source Module	*For Group Number 1	2	3	4	5	6
1 Variable Costs							
2 Receiving	3	$2.90	$2.90	$1.17	$1.17	$2.90	$1.17
3 Shipping	4	1.76	.82	1.76	.82	2.64	2.64
4 Supplies	5	.40	.40	.40	.40	.40	.40
5 Sub-total (2,3,4)	3,4,5	5.06	4.12	3.33	2.39	5.94	4.21
6 Clerks	6	.44	.44	.44	.44	.44	.44
7 Total Variable	3,4,5,6	5.50	4.56	3.77	2.83	6.38	4.65
8 Fixed Costs							
9 Salaries, etc.	1	.80	.80	.80	.80	.80	.80
10 Lines 7 & 9	1,3,4,5,6	6.30	5.32	4.57	3.63	7.18	5.45
11 Storage	2	1.60	1.60	1.60	1.60	1.60	1.60
12 Total Cost		$7.90	$6.02	$6.17	$4.93	$8.78	$7.05
13 Line 12 Index (Group 1=100.0)		100.00	87.60	78.10	62.40	111.10	89.20
*14 Price as (Line 12 x 125%), per slot		$9.88	$8.65	$7.71	$6.61	$10.98	$8.81
15 Price as (Line 14 Minus 12, Group 1)		1.98					
*16 Price as (Line 12 plus $1.98),		$9.88	$8.90	$8.15	$6.91	$10.76	$9.03

*The charges shown are for handling in and out for one month's storage. Additional CDC data permitted rapid conversion to arrive at the appropriate charges for any specific number of days. A "slot" is the space required for one pallet or load of given dimensions.

CASE 7

HARTZ MILLS, INC. (A)

In July of 1972 Oscar Allmann, President of Hartz Mills, met with Perry Singer, the general manager of his dyeing division, Carolina Industries. A sudden increase in the demand on those facilities had come to Allmann's attention. Singer had suggested either acquiring more equipment or refusing additional orders, but Mr. Allmann was unhappy with either of these alternatives.

BACKGROUND

Hartz Mills, Inc. produced a line of popular-priced women's sweaters and sportswear. It operated three divisions: Queen of Hartz sweaters, Lady Hartz sportswear, and Carolina Industries. A family concern, Hartz Mills had grown from the sales organization built by Harry Hartz, father-in-law of Mr. Allmann. In 1971 Mr. Hartz served as Chairman of the Board of the firm. Consolidated statements appear as Exhibit 1.

Manufacturing operations began in 1956 when Mr. Allmann moved from New York to Deeville, North Carolina to organize and manage the first mill. Although dyeing facilities had not originally been planned, it quickly became apparent that they would be necessary. Mr. Allmann explained the problem:

> "In 1956 the nearest paddle dyer to Deeville was in Brooklyn. Our first load of samples took six weeks round trip. This is a fashion industry! Six weeks is a season! Few people enter paddle dyeing because of its limited uses; not many firms are sure of a steady flow of synthetic knits to keep the tubs full. We had no choice.

> Yarn-dyeing plants were available, but we couldn't afford either the higher price or quality of that process. No paddle dyeing, no sweaters. We had to create Carolina and just hope we would supply enough business to keep it going."

Despite Mr. Allmann's initial apprehension, not only did Carolina keep operating, but a steady stream of outside business made it the most profitable

This case material has been prepared as a oasis for class discussion and is not designed to present illustrations of either effective or ineffective handling of administrative situations.

This case was prepared by Richard I. Levin and Richard Osborne under support provided by the Business Foundation of North Carolina. Richard I. Levin is Professor of Business Administration, University of North Carolina, Chapel Hill.

Distributed by the Intercollegiate Case Clearing House, Soldiers Field, Boston, Mass. 02163. All rights reserved to the contributors. Printed in the U.S.A. Used with permission.

part of Hartz for the first three years of operations. Both Allmann and Hartz attributed a large part of the ensuing success of the company to this complete vertical integration. Mr. Hartz recounted the initial plan.

> "We always had trouble when we had work contracted out. We wanted to take the yarn, knit it, cut it, sew it, and sell it directly to the retailer. Every step would be under our control and supervision. Though we hadn't planned to dye it ourselves, I think we further strengthened our quality and cost control and our overall competitive position with the addition of Carolina."

Hartz and all its divisions enjoyed steady growth since 1956. Although Carolina continued growing, it gradually became a relatively smaller part of the firm as a whole.

OPERATIONS

Carolina Industries occupied a 76,000-square foot building directly across the street from the main Hartz plant. The dye tubs had a combined capacity of 3900 pounds, and were serviced by three extractors and twenty-eight tumble dryers. This equipment dyed synthetic, single-knit cloth, such as that used in sweaters. A 100-pound washer processed yarn-dyed mohair cloth. A heat-setting frame and dry-cleaning equipment were installed when Hartz introduced a line of double-knit, polyester sportswear.

The present plant could accommodate up to six additional 400-pound dye tubs. These would require no further dryers or extractors. Each sold for about $6200 in 1971, though used machines could sometimes be had at a substantial discount. Since 1967 major equipment purchases had been made through Channel Leasing Company, an equipment leasing firm owned by Allmann, Harry Hartz and Mr. Michael Hartz (Harry Hartz' son). Channel Leasing rented equipment to all divisions of Hartz Mills.

Carolina ran two, eight-hour shifts on dyeing and only first shift on double-knit finishing. Operating statements for the Carolina Division appear as Exhibit 2.

PERSONNEL

Perry Singer had started as a worker at Carolina in 1957 and had become general manager six years later. He had been taught enough practical chemistry by his predecessors to prepare the required chemical compounds. He had also developed the acute color sensitivity necessary for finely matching color samples submitted by customers. Allmann jokingly referred to him as "my very competent prima donna."

Singer had over the years selected his two shift foreman who, though apparently capable, were delegated very little authority in their jobs. The workers performed very strenuous, physical labor. The turnover tended to be high; one foreman attributed this turnover to the seemingly arbitrary wage structure administered by Singer.

Singer knew nothing of the heat-setting process, and Allmann had hired Charlie Band to supervise that operation. Band had started actively seeking out-of-house business when the Lady Hartz requirements no longer filled the capacity of the frame. His efforts were hampered by the lack of facilities to dye polyester double-knits at Carolina.

Hartz was forced to buy only yarn-dyed polyester for its sportswear line, as Singer had balked when Allmann suggested buying the Turlington pressure dryers required for piece dyeing polyester cloth. Mr. Allmann discussed this situation.

"Initially I'd wanted to jump right in and buy a pair of Turlingtons. I realized that they were quite an investment at $40,000 each, so when Perry bucked about going through the training program offered by the manufacturer, I threw in the towel. Our volume of sportswear just didn't warrant that much investment at that time unless we could really use them well. Dyed polyester yarn costs us about 50% more than natural yarn, and someday we'll make the switch."

Carolina had no sales personnel and, therefore, no organized sales effort. A salesman had once been retained, but Singer had found him too inflexible and persuaded Allmann to release him. The fairly substantial outside work was generated solely by word-of-mouth (trade talk). Four or five local firms provided the bulk of outside business. Initial contact came generally through Allmann, but thereafter Singer handled all dyeing accounts.

The dyeing process in the Queen of Hartz production schedule immediately followed knitting. Every morning the knitting from the previous day was trucked across the street to the dyehouse where it was weighed and then scheduled for various dye tubs by Singer. On the reverse leg of these morning trips, the finished cloth was taken to the separating department. Carolina owned three, 2½-ton trucks and a van which it regularly used for this purpose. For the remainder of the day, these vehicles operated out of the Hartz shipping department.

Mr. Jim Ruth, manager of Scheduling and Inventory Control, estimated that an average of three or four days elapsed from the time he scheduled a lot for knitting until its arrival at the dyehouse. When he had offered to post Singer daily on his scheduling, Singer replied that it was unnecessary; "Queen of Hartz always gets priority. That's where the bread is buttered. Anyway, we hardly ever have a real pinch, and if we did, three or four days' notice wouldn't help."

The central office came under the sweater division and provided staff services common to all the Hartz divisions. These included payroll processing, computer services and the procurement of office supplies. Carolina itself had four secretaries, a lab assistant and a shipping supervisor.

CURRENT PROBLEMS

Ekoprem Brothers, a national textile firm, met the demand for inexpensive, double-knit garments with single-knit material bonded on a thin, woven material. This process offered some qualities of a real double-knit cloth at a much lower cost. As that particular Ekoprem division was headquartered in nearby Essburg, they knew of Carolina and, in early 1971, began shipping several thousand pounds weekly for processing. By August these shipments had grown to over 19,000 pounds weekly, and Ekoprem was actively pressing Carolina to take another 13,000 pounds a week.

Singer opposed increasing the capacity of Carolina to accommodate Ekoprem.

"They're here today and gone tomorrow! We'll get all geared up to handle their goods and then find ourselves stuck in a lurch when they build their own paddle dyehouse or when this fad dies down. If anything though, we should add another machine or two rather than adding another shift. If Ekoprem disappears and we've got another couple of tubs, we can always keep them running some, but another shift would be hard to keep busy. Besides, folks working on the third shift are a pretty worthless lot, and we have enough lazy freeloaders on the payroll here as it is."

That was the gist of Singer's advice at his meeting with Allmann. Allmann replied that he realized the inherent danger in relying too heavily on a single customer for a single service; he suggested however, that considering the premium price paid by Ekoprem, nearly 30% more than other outside customers, and accepting that Ekoprem accounted for a relatively small part of the whole Hartz picture, an exception might be in order.

When Singer left his office, Allmann began jotting down some thoughts on the dyehouse. He felt that Perry had overlooked the potential gains in dealing with Ekoprem. At that moment, however, the knitting engineer and the sample designer entered arguing over a piece of cloth. A call from the New York office came through, and the General Office Manager stood at the door with the computer supervisor waiting to discuss a procedural problem.

EXHIBIT 1
HARTZ MILLS, INC.
QUEEN OF HARTZ, LADY HARTZ & CAROLINA INDUSTRIES
COMBINED STATEMENT OF
PROFIT AND LOSS

	Six Months Ending		Year Ending	
	6/30/71	6/30/70	12/31/70	12/31/69
Sales (net)	$4,434,880	$3,869,904	$9,094,051	$6,673,834
Cost of Goods Sold	3,577,789	3,068,400	7,381,461	5,466,498
Gross Profit	857,091	801,504	1,712,590	1,207,336
Selling & General Exp.:				
Executive Salaries	113,600	97,600	227,200	195,200
Sales Commissions	285,064	253,787	590,442	447,693
Advertising Promo.	23,989	19,994	34,412	37,659
Other selling	36,699	43,934	80,331	82,725
N.Y. Office expenses	73,666	63,358	139,909	93,595
Factoring	119,259	159,125	303,709	252,364
Contributions	8,773	1,810	8,819	11,952
	661,050	639,558	1,384,795	1,121,188
Net Profit-Operations	196,041	161,946	327,795	86,148
Other Income:				
Gross Profit, dyeing	188,003	16,043	37,616	(19,544)
Sale of fixed assets	2,034	17,213	21,931	1,718
Interest	3,830	3,776	7,574	6,208
Net Profit-Pre-tax	398,908	198,978	394,916	74,530
Provision for Taxes	179,200	96,848	188,021	37,158
Profit After Taxes	$ 210,708	$ 102,130	$ 206,895	$ 37,372

EXHIBIT 1
(CONTINUED)
HARTZ MILLS, INC.
QUEEN OF HARTZ, LADY HARTZ & CAROLINA INDUSTRIES
COMBINED BALANCE SHEET
6/30/71

Assets

Cash	$ 41,060
Receivables	98,637
Merchandise Inventories	2,637,440
Prepaid Expenses	43,742
Total Current Assets	$2,820,879
Deposits and Advances to Channel Leasing	$ 161,725
Fixed Assets (pledged)	2,058,334
Less: Accumulated Depreciation	1,058,026
Net Fixed Assets	1,000,308
Deposits, Investments, etc.	12,066
Total Assets	$3,994,978

Liabilities

Accounts Payable	$1,903,734
Notes Payable	166,062
Accrued Liabilities	517,075
Provision for Income Taxes	190,578
Total Current Liabilities	2,777,449
Notes Payable (Due after 1 year)	11,139
Total Liabilities	$2,788,588
Capital Stock	$ 100,000
Retained Earnings	1,106,390
Total Capital	$1,206,390
Total Liabilities	3,994,978

EXHIBIT 2
HARTZ MILLS, INC.
CAROLINA INDUSTRIES DIVISION
SCHEDULE OF GROSS PROFIT

| | Six Months Ended | | | |
| | 6/30/71 | | 6/30/70 | |
	Amount	per lb.	Amount	per lb.
Income:				
Dyeing Charges				
Queen of Hartz	$112,538	$.280	$ 51,974	$.260
Others	368,654	.345	126,616	.277
Washing, etc.				
Queen of Hartz	6,717	.100	8,992	.100
Others	—	—	1,080	.110
Finishing				
Lady Hartz	124,811	.300	64,837	.297
Others	142,939	.195	149,114	.182
Total Income	755,659	.281	402,613	.225
Cost of Operations:				
Dyes & Chemicals	121,357	.045	50,645	.028
Direct Labor	197,205	.073	130,509	.073
Indirect Labor	47,848	.018	42,571	.024
Heat, Light & Water	59,949	.022	47,123	.026
Plant Supplies	10,050	.004	2,398	.001
Maintenance	23,242	.009	17,173	.010
Rent	23,520	.009	23,520	.013
Depreciation	11,936	.004	13,376	.007
Shipping & Freight	14,757	.005	8,627	.005
Autos & Trucks	8,541	.003	6,213	.003
Factoring Expense	9,541	.002	7,056	.002
Commissions*	25,579	.011	13,840	.008
Equipment Rental	47,578	.018	36,795	.008
Outside Processing	—	—	(2,141)	(.001)
Allowances	1,032	—	—	—
Total Expenses	602,335	.229	397,705	.223
Inventory at Beginning	10,789	.004	12.944	.007
	613,117		410,649	
Inventory at End	19,680	.007	10,240	.006
Cost of Operations	539,437	.221	400,409	.224
Gross Profit	$162,222	$.060	2,204	.001

*The New York Sales Office of Hartz Mills receives a flat 5% commission on all outside revenues. This stems from the time when that sales force existed separately as a partnership, H. Hartz & Associates.

EXHIBIT 2
(CONTINUED)
HARTZ MILLS, INC.
CAROLINA INDUSTRIES DIVISION
POUNDS PROCESSED

| | Six Months Ended | |
	6/30/71	6/30/70
Dyed		
Queen of Hartz	401,920	199,899
Others	1,069,323	457,290
Washed		
Queen of Hartz	67,166	89,925
Others	—	9,798
Finished		
Lady Hartz	415,955	218,150
Other	734,170	818,194
Total	2,688,534	1,793,256

CASE 8

HARTZ MILLS, INC. (B)

Hartz Mills, Inc. a manufacturer of popular-priced women's sweaters, had its best year to date in 1968. Sales had risen 15.2% from the previous year, profits 52.7%, and the firm had returned 32% on its equity base. With this year of success still fresh in their minds, the owners of Hartz had scheduled a meeting in mid-January 1969 to discuss several proposed changes for the upcoming fall season.

BACKGROUND

Hartz Mills was a family concern that had developed from the sales organization of H. Hartz & Associates. In 1956 Oscar Allmann, son-in-law of Harry Hartz, moved to Deeville, North Carolina to organize the first manufacturing efforts. Several years later Mr. Michael Hartz, youngest in the family, joined the firm in the sales office.

Hartz manufactured its own garments. Synthetic yarn and some dyed mohair yarns were knitted in the main Hartz plant and then processed and dyed in the wholly owned dyehouse across the street. Separating took place in the main plant, while the final and longest steps of cutting and sewing were performed both in the main plant and in a smaller rented building, plant 2. A national organization of salesmen, co-ordinated from the New York showroom, sold directly to small specialty stores and independent and chain department stores. Sweaters were sold under the house label, "Queen of Hartz" neutral labels and the retail labels of the purchasers.

Hartz garments had an industry reputation for reliable quality, relatively good delivery and generally conservative styling. Stores selling Hartz sweaters catered primarily to the Misses trade (women in their late twenties and older). Hartz sold three groups of sweaters each year; in order of importance, these were the Fall Line, the Holiday (Christmas) Line and the Spring Line. The basic core of sweaters in each line remained unchanged from year to year, but colors and accessories might vary greatly. Various fashion garments were also included in each group. The basic garments did, as expected, a

This case material has been prepared as a basis for class discussion and is not designed to present illustrations of either effective or ineffective handling of administrative situations.

This case was prepared by Richard I. Levin and Richard Osborne under support provided by the Business Foundation of North Carolina. Richard I. Levin is Professor of Business Administration, University of North Carolina, Chapel Hill.

Distributed by the Intercollegiate Case Clearing House, Soldiers Field, Boston, Mass. 02163. All rights reserved to the contributors. Printed in the U.S.A. Used with permission.

generally steady trade, while fashion entries fluctuated wildly in their success. Basics provided about 75% of the dollar volume.

Mr. Allmann, Vice President and General Manager, directed all manufacturing. Harry Hartz, President and Chairman of the Board, headed the merchandising effort, and his son Michael served as Sales Manager. Hartz employed about 440 people, exclusive of sales personnel.

Mr. Hartz considered the steady success of the business due to "reasonable quality at a reasonable price," which Hartz achieved through the complete vertical integration of production. "We've built a strong base of small shops and main floor departments in large stores that support us year after year. If we hit a really hot fashion number, like the 'poor boy' a few years ago, we have a really big season. Otherwise, we just sell a little more each year. You'll never go broke that way!"

DIVERSIFICATION CONSIDERED

By the end of 1968, however, the three owners of Hartz had sensed what they thought was a change in the market. "In October," Mr. Allmann recalled, "we saw the first imported sweater that not only beat our price but also clearly held the edge in quality. It was a full-fashion Orlon cardigan that a large West Coast chain had ordered from Japan. At that moment, I knew the smooth sailing was over."

Hartz had been approached in August 1968 by Joe Kim, Ltd., a South Korean syndicate interested in an arrangement with an established American sweater house. They required technical and styling expertise and a means of distribution. Hartz offered both. As the agreement would have compelled Allmann to travel frequently to Korea, he had initially brushed aside the proposal. In November, however, Hartz re-established contact, and, shortly thereafter, Allmann made a trip to Korea.

Allmann returned from the Orient on December 1, his fears about imports confirmed. Meeting briefly in New York with his two associates, he assured them, "we cannot possibly compete with their incredibly cheap labor. They can import American fiber, spin it, knit it, produce a finished garment, ship it across the Pacific and still undercut us by 15%. A brief outline for the proposed venture appears as Exhibit 1.

Another possible tact first discussed at this time was to enter the booming market for double-knit polyester sportswear. Double-knit polyester cloth, developed several years earlier, revolutionized women's clothing; it required neither dry cleaning nor ironing. Although several more expensive houses had already entered the market, production for main floor sales had only begun very recently.

Allmann in particular felt that the company could easily grab a piece of this expanding market. "This is the trend of the future," he urged, "and we should get aboard. Our salesmen could sell a moderately priced Misses line along with 'Queen of Hartz'." Allmann planned to study the feasibility of manufacturing a line of polyester sportswear, and a final decision was postponed until January.

THE JANUARY MEETING

The principals of Hartz met every January in Deeville to review the final financial statements for the preceding year, Exhibit 2. The meeting quickly moved to a report on the feasibility of producing polyester sportswear.

"We could do it, and, for the most part, we could do it with our girls and our machines. The only new equipment we would need are knitting machines; double-knit machines are hard to get right now, but I think we could pick up five basic ones at about $20,000 each. We could run the sportswear in Plant 2. A minor problem would be dying; we lack the machinery to dye polyester cloth, so we'd have to knit dyed-yarn, even for the solids. We'd also have to contract out the heat setting.

Our main problem would be quality. Sportswear requires much more rigid tailoring than sweaters. With sweaters there is always a little room for error in both design and execution, but not in sportswear. If it isn't styled just right, it looks like hell, and the same if the cutting or sewing is sloppy. We'd need a very good man to design and watch quality for us. I won't say this doesn't worry me, because it does."

Michael Hartz then brought up the Korean proposition and suggested that the domestic sportswear boom might dissolve in the same flood of imports threatening the sweater business. His father replied that sportswear is too fashion oriented for imports. "The only way they keep their price advantage is bulk shipping by sea; that requires an enormous lead time. That lead time is impossible in the sportswear business."

Finally Allmann broke into the conversation. "I've seen their plant and their workers, and we've all seen their product. Eventually the imports will take the moderate-and cheap-sweater markets, lock, stock and barrel. If we join them, get in with these Koreans, we could be a part of it. Now that would require me to make frequent trips to Korea for a period of years. Deeville is as far into the 'provinces' as I care to go. I am just very uncertain about any long term commitments with the Koreans for that reason, and that reason alone."

"Well," Mr. Hartz began, sensing Allmann's concern, "we could just sit tight and pull in this year. If things really nosedive, we can re-evaluate our position. After all, we're not really overextended; this year we couldn't even handle all the orders we had."

EXHIBIT 1

OUTLINE OF TENTATIVE TERMS
FOR PROPOSED KOREAN VENTURE

1. Hartz Mills and Joe Kim, Ltd. will for a period of five years work in the agreed upon fashion. This arrangement may be cancelled by either party at the end of the first year with 30 days notice; thereafter the contract is binding through the end of the fifth year unless it is mutually terminated.
2. Joe Kim, Ltd. will produce only finished knitted outerwear and only for distribution and sale by Hartz Mills. Joe Kim, Ltd. must produce and Hartz accept a minimum volume of $3,000,000 for the first year, $6,000,000 the second year and $8,000,000 annually thereafter. The garments will be priced at cost plus 10%.
3. Hartz is responsible for providing full technical assistance to Joe Kim, Ltd. including advice on equipment, operations and scheduling. Styling will be completely at the discretion of Hartz. The two firms will bear equally the travelling and lodging expenses incurred by corporate personnel in implementing this agreement.
4. At the conclusion of the fifth year, the principals of Hartz or that firm itself or any designated third firm controlled by them will have the option of buying 3000 of the 10,000 shares of Joe Kim, Ltd. at a price of 3 times the average annual net earnings of Joe Kim, Ltd. during the last three years of the contract.

EXHIBIT 2
HARTZ MILLS, INC.
COMBINED STATEMENT OF PROFIT & LOSS

	Twelve Months Ended:	
	12/31/68	12/31/67
Net Sales	$6,572,680	$5,939,752
Cost of Goods Sold	5,438,044	4,924,763
Gross Profit	1,314,636	1,014,989
Selling & General Costs:		
Executive Salaries	195,200	195,200
Sales salaries, commissions	394,262	304,848
Advertising, promotion	27,136	22,730
Other selling	63,986	55,898
New York Office Expenses	80,102	72,842
Factoring	199,806	185,509
Contributions	5,278	14,090
Bad Debts	—	1,534
Total Expenses-Operations	965,770	852,651
Net Profit-Operations	348,866	162,338
Other Income:		
Gross Profit-Dying	171,074	143,858
Gain on Sale of Assets	25,358	362
Total Other Income	196,432	144,858
Net Profit Before Tax	545,298	306,558
Provision for Taxes	285,090	136,206
Net Profit After Tax	$ 260,208	$ 170,352

EXHIBIT 2

(CONTINUED)
HARTZ MILLS, INC.
COMBINED BALANCE SHEET
12/31/68

Assets

Cash	$ 101,448
Receivables	202,563
Merchandise Inventory	989,563
Prepaid Expenses	21,914
Total Current Assets	1,314,951
Due from Channel Leasing Co.*	57,600
Net Fixed Assets (partially pledged)	936,878
Deposits, investments, etc. (at cost)	25,469
Total Assets	$2,334,898

Liabilities and Equity

Accounts Payable	$ 990,968
Notes Payable (secured)	57,742
Accrued Liabilities	180,581
Provision for Income Tax	262,527
Mortgage Payment (secured)	29,574
Total Liabilities	1,521,392
Capital Stock	100,000
Surplus	713,506
Total Liabilities and Equity	$2,334,898

*Channel Leasing Co., another family entity, purchased heavy equipment for Hartz Mills and leased it to that firm.

CASE 9

HARTZ MILLS, INC. (C)

In January 1973 the three owner-managers of Hartz Mills, Inc. met to review the preceding year. Although the overall profit and volume of the firm had increased, this growth had not developed as had been originally expected.

BACKGROUND

Hartz Mills was a family-owned concern with three operating divisions, Queen of Hartz sweaters, Lady Hartz sportswear and Carolina Industries synthetic, piece dying. The first two divisions sold finished ladies' garments directly to retail outlets, while the dying division did work for both Hartz and other garment manufacturers. The sweater and dying divisions dated from 1956, while the sportswear line had only been added in 1969.

Harry Hartz, 73, served as Chairman of the Board. His son-in-law, Oscar Allmann, 50, was President and General Manager of Manufacturing, and his son, Michael Hartz, 41, was Vice-President-Merchandising. Although the elder Hartz ceased direct supervision of sales and merchandising in 1970 when he stepped down as President, he remained in close contact with the business as an active advisor.

MARKET TRENDS

Hartz had entered the polyester sportswear field as a precaution against what the principals had seen as a rapidly declining market for popular-priced domestic sweaters. The anticipated wave of imports, however, had undermined Hartz' sweater sales much less than they had expected. Several factors, especially the uncertainty of delivery for East Coast and Mid-western stores, saved the domestic sweater industry from complete oblivion. Pressure from the imports did drive out many northern sweater houses with high production costs.

The market for polyester sportswear, on the other hand, had boomed as expected in 1969 and 1970 but was suddenly oversaturated in the fall of 1971.

This case material has been prepared as a basis for class discussion and is not designed to present illustrations of either effective or ineffective handling of administrative situations.

This case was prepared by Richard I. Levin and Richard Osborne under support provided by the Business Foundation of North Carolina. Richard I. Levin is Professor of Business Administration, University of North Carolina, Chapel Hill.

Distributed by the Intercollegiate Case Clearing House, Soldiers Field, Boston, Mass. 02163. All rights reserved to the contributors. Printed in the U.S.A. Used with permission.

This oversaturation led to higher quality requirements and downward price pressure. At this critical time, late 1971, Peter Cardino, the designer and manager of Lady Hartz, had gone into business for himself; he acted with no prior warning and in clear violation of his contract. He took Huey Blake, Hartz Knitting Engineer, with him. Allmann recounted the seriousness of this occurrence.

"I have never been so shocked in all my life. Huey had been with us 14 years, and neither he nor Peter even talked with us about any problems they had. Huey we could replace, but Peter was a real talented guy. Our people were not at ease with the rigid requirements of the sportswear business.

We were in a real jam. We had thought the sweater business would fall so badly that we would just switch production facilities from sweaters into sportswear. As it was, we had to add plant and machinery. We had opened another plant in nearby Deeville and produced our Lady Hartz there and in Plant 2. We were also at our absolute limit for knitting space in the main plant. Before total finished-goods output could grow any further, more knitting capacity would be needed."

Following is a summary of the trend in Hartz operations from 1968 through 1972. Dying income comprises the major portion of "Other Income."

| | (All dollar figures in thousands) Twelve Months Ended: | | | | |
	12/31/68	12/31/69	12/31/70	12/31/71	12/31/72
Net Sales	6,573	6,674	9,094	10,466	10,685
Queen of Hartz	6,573	5,212	4,816	5,660	7,313
Lady Hartz	—	1,462	4,278	4,806	3,373
Net Profit-Operations	349	86	326	229	129
Other Income	196	(12)	q67	206	327
Net Profit-After Tax	260	37	205	281	322
% Sweaters	100.0%	78.1%	53.0%	54.1%	68.4%
% Sportswear	—	21.9%	47.0%	45.9%	31.6%

THE MEETING

The January meeting immediately focused on the problems of Lady Hartz. Allmann began. "The guy we hired to replace Peter is only second rate. We'll have to let him go and try again. I think we should hire a couple of technicians as sub-managers and put the cutting and sewing of Lady Hartz under Les MacAdoo, just like the Queen of Hartz production. That way we won't have to worry about a guy like Peter putting it to us again."

"But can MacAdoo handle Lady Hartz?" Mr. Hartz asked.

"With technical assistance, yes. We'll also need a full-time sportswear designer, but that shouldn't be a problem."

"I think Oscar's right," said Michael Hartz. "Let's integrate the Lady Hartz operation with Queen of Hartz, so we're not so vulnerable to the pressure of one employee."

"Exactly," replied Allmann. "We're in a very volatile industry, and we've got to protect ourselves and hedge our bets whenever we can."

CASE 10

CARSON/BURGER/WEEKLY, INCORPORATED

"Carson/Burger/Weekly, Inc. is a young, rapidly growing corporation dedicated to designing and building automation equipment. Our standard products include general purpose, light duty conveyors and stacking systems for plastic injection molded lids and containers. We also custom design and build specialized automatic equipment for nearly any purpose. We believe that we offer several hard-to-find qualities that will make you enjoy doing business with us."

Production Promotion Catalogue
Carson/Burger/Weekly, Inc.
April, 1973

C/B/W had all the earmarks of a thriving, vibrant money-making firm: a dynamic unconventional set of owners who zealously defended their peculiarly idyllic corporate "goals"; a respectable set of financial balance sheets, evidencing an optimistic future for this fledgling, two-year-old company; an impressive plant facility under construction, to be entirely financed by the government; professional promotion and support services which one would expect to see attached to a more sophisticated and established business than C/B/W; and a creative logo which captured the very essence of this fast-paced, constantly-expanding enterprise. While one could not help but be impressed by these promising indicia of success, such fantastic development raised an ominous suspicion. The corporation had almost grown too fast, expanded too hastily, and had managed its affairs too naively. The company which had witnessed profits sky-rocket some 400% in 1972 over its first year's performance of 1971 would also bear witness to the incessant threat of bankruptcy in early September, 1973. Perhaps it had all been too much, too soon.

This case was written by W. Terrance Schreier, a graduate student pursuing the Juris Doctor and Master in Business Administration degrees concurrently at the University of Kansas, Lawrence, and under the supervision of Professor Charles B. Saunders. It is designed as a basis for class discussion rather than to illustrate either effective or ineffective handling of an administrative situation.

Distributed by the Intercollegiate Case Clearing House, Soldiers Field, Boston, Mass. 02163. All rights reserved to the contributors. Printed in the U.S.A. Used with permission.

HISTORY AND FORMATION OF THE COMPANY

David Carson and Phil Burger were engineering students at the University of Kansas, Lawrence, in December, 1969. Well into the senior year of their collegiate studies, both became somewhat concerned about their postgraduate future, since no employment prospect loomed brightly for either of them. They were "good" students. Burger wished to pursue a career in the engineering field, while Carson was more interested in the business aspects of the engineering profession.

During the 1969 summer, Carson and Burger had worked on an engineering project for Packer Plastics, Inc.—a Lawrence manufacturer of plastic injection molded containers (e.g., butter and dessert tubs). Encouraged by Gene Burnett, owner of a local precision instrument company, the two engineering students designed and constructed an automated handling system which transferred newly produced containers from the molding machines, conveyed them to an "orienter" which mechanically turned these containers top-side up in preparation for the final collection, stacking and bagging. The device used to orient these molded products was a conveyor equipped with a series of tiny air jets which collectively forced a sufficient amount of air up through the floor of the machine so as to gently flip or toss the containers into a desired position for eventual packing and shipment. See Figure 2. This orienting principle was a real innovation in the plastics industry. Months later, Carson and Burger obtained a patent for this air jet idea.

Packer was quite pleased with this summer work and requested that the two students complete other projects during the 1969-70 academic year. Thus, the summer vacation "hobby" began to assume certain characteristics of a small business venture. Faced with unattractive employment options, encouraged by the Packer success, and enthusiastically pushed on by Burnett, Carson and Burger decided to form a partnership bearing their names, armed with but a single patent and a storehouse of energy and desire.

The partners were immediately confronted with the problem of locating a place of business; basements and small garages had been utilized from September, 1969 through April, 1970—the partner's final year of college. Needing a more permanent location, the two owners discovered a fairly large garage located in the home of John Weekly, a Lawrence builder, who rented this space to the young businessmen in May, 1970, the real beginning of this business as a full-time enterprise.

Packer continued to order the design and construction of additional conveyors and orienting systems from the partnership. However, increasing sales necessitated more production equipment which the partnership could not afford, financially, due to an almost total lack of capital resources. Packer's President, Jim Schwartzburg personally loaned the required capital, approximately $25,000, to the partners to keep the young business on its feet. When Schwartzburg's note came due a few months later, Carson and Burger had inadequate capital resources necessary to repay the loan. Rather than force the concern into involuntary bankruptcy, Schwartzburg agreed to accept a portion of the new business' ownership, in the form of corporate stock, in place of the cash payment. In order to stay financially afloat and satisfy the Schwartzburg obligation, Carson and Burger fully incorporated in July, 1970, as a limited partnership, at which time the capital stock was issued, 10% of which went to Schwartzburg, with the remaining 90% evenly split between Carson and Burger.

In the 1970 summer, with the construction business beset by generally unfavorable economic conditions, John Weekly's home-building enterprise was dissolved on account of his construction company's failure. Coincidentally, Carson and Burger realized the need for hiring an individual with some actual machine and production experience. It was one thing to build a plastics-handling device in one summer and quite another to construct such devices on a regular production basis, each machine differing from previous models. John Weekly had this requisite experience. The partnership hired him in October, 1970, to fulfill its needs.

The enterprise remained in Weekly's garage until the increasing volume of business forced yet another move in early 1971. While few financial records were kept reflecting the monetary health of the firm for 1970, Phil Burger succinctly summarized what these records would have demonstrated: "Business was going so well that we soon found ourselves assembling conveyors in the midst of snowfalls and rainstorms—we never dreamed that things would move as fast they did, especially towards the end of 1970 and into 1971." The company took over a vacated mechanic's garage during March, 1971, after moving out of Weekly's garage.

While sales were brisk in the early 1971 months, an anticipated pool of cash resources had not developed, out of which Weekly's salary could be drawn. The cash flow shortage became increasingly more critical as the incorporated partnership strained to expand with the pace of its business. Consequently, late in 1971, the retention of Weekly's employ with little, if any, compensation became a particularly vexatious concern. Rather than lose Weekly and his valued experience, the partners decided to equally divide its corporate ownership among the three principals of Carson, Burger and Weekly and then re-incorporated under the C/B/W herald. This was accomplished in August, 1971. By November, C/B/W, Inc. was again forced to move to larger quarters due to the ever-expanding business it had experienced. The firm located in the basement of the Lawrence Paper Company. The company remained at this location until October, 1973, when it moved to its newly completed plant facility in the northeastern industrial corridor of Lawrence.

C/B/W'S PRODUCT LINE AND MARKET

By September of 1973, the company's automated system products had been rapidly expanded from the original Packer Plastics automatic lid stacker to a comprehensive line of various conveyor and orienting components. C/B/W described its product line in terms of "systems," rather than as individual items. According to David Carson, Secretary-Treasurer and coordinator of the firm's sales effort:

> The majority of our customers are manufacturers of plastic injection molded lids and containers. While the manufacturer is concerned with the actual production of these butter cups or dip containers from raw materials, our job is to offer machinery which transfers the completed products from the injection molding machine, unscrambles and orients these lids and tubs, and finally counts and stacks these products in preparation for packaging and eventual shipment. Consequently, we believe that our customers are usually not interested in automating a particular facet of this manufacturing process, but are more concerned with the entire processes or systems. When a customer wants to do away with human operators, performing jobs which machines do more efficiently and at faster rates, obviously such a manufacturer doesn't want to automate his production process on a piecemeal basis. In terms of efficiency and financial economics, such a component-replacement approach would ordinarily be unwise. C/B/W recognizes this and seizes such an opportunity to push a custom-adapted "system" on the manufacturer. And we've been pretty successful in the past using this approach in our sales efforts.

In C/B/W's standard line the orienters and the conveyors have traditionally formed the backbone of the automated systems offerings. By their very nature, the adaptability of each group to the other has always been well suited to the "systems" approach the company had taken in its sales promotion.

The orienters are conceptually built around the particular market demand for automatic unscrambling, orienting, and stacking (either vertical or horizontal) of round injection-molded lids and containers. The conveyors were particularly designed so as to adapt to the various orienting needs of the customer. While some conveyor units had been sold separately, the "systems" approach had been heavily emphasized in the sales of the standard conveyor models as coupled with one or several orienting devices. Custom-adapted conveyors systems could be specially ordered when a buyer had no specific need for orienting equipment. C/B/W had sold a large number of custom-designed conveyors to companies dealing in assembly line production of such items as automobiles and small appliances.

TABLE I:
PRODUCT MODELS SOLD BY C/B/W—STANDARD LINE
(GROUPED AS ORIENTERS AND CONVEYORS)

Model Type	Price*	Units Sold		
		1971	1972	1973 (6 mos.)
Model A—Automatic Lid Orienter	$ 4,100	5	8	3
Model C—Automatic Lid Stacker	5,000	5	18	20
Automatic Container Stacker	6,300	7	17	5
Lid Inventory System	4,250	0	2	4
CB III Container Bagger**	11,800	n/a	n/a	0
Roller Stacker	900	1	2	2
Spin Bar Staker	600	0	5	0
Inclined Conveyor	600	1	7	0
Carry Out Conveyor	650	5	31	0
Carry To Conveyor	600	0	3	5
Vacuum Unscrambling Conveyor	1,750	0	0	6

*Prices as of September 1, 1973.
**Not prepared for sales until November 1, 1973.

Nineteen hundred seventy-two was an outstanding year for this corporation in terms of unit sales in both the orienting and conveyor areas. Table 1 indicates that the Model C and the Automatic Container Stacker sold very well, in addition to the Carry-Out Conveyor model. However, as not only Table 1 points out, but as is also dramatically seen in Tables II and III, sales in the standard line fell sharply, leaving a $49,623 loss for the firm during the first half of 1973. While the Model C sales continued to climb, the revenues from the Automatic Container Stacker slipped, as did those of the Inclined Conveyor and particularly the Carry-Out Conveyor.

No marketing studies had ever been undertaken by C/B/W to determine the vital characteristics and parameters of the customers or the markets which the firm sought to penetrate. No engineering programs had been initiated as a step to cope with the increasing product obsolescence rate of the C/B/W standard line. In only a very rough, sketchy manner did the company even know of its direct competition in the plastics-handling field or of its particular market share of this specialized segment of the plastics production equipment business.

Moreover, plastics-handling industry data was virtually nonexistent. Because of the highly specialized nature of the clientele which C/B/W served, market studies were likewise very difficult to find. The U.S. Department of Commerce had virtually no information concerning either the size of the plastic injection molded container industry or the constituent corporations which served it. *Dun's Review* did not develop a separate classification for this servicing industry, except by the general, catchall category of "miscellaneous manufacturing machinery companies." C/B/W was, indeed, involved in a highly specialized, but ambiguous, business.

However, C/B/W was well aware of its competition. Its primary concern was with the Husky Company of Canada. Not only did Husky manufacture container orienters and conveyors, it also constructed the molding machines, designed and built plants to house these machines and their ancillary handling devices, and trained foremen and technicians to manage and operate these plants. As John Weekly, C/B/W's production chief, exclaimed, "Husky is like the IBM of the plastics industry; they've got us beat on every corner of the market but one—systems handling, *our* specialty. In this particular area, it appears that Husky and C/B/W share a similar competitive market."

C/B/W had, in fact, appeared on the plastics-handling scene almost too late. David Carson estimated that ". . . between 1965 and 1972, some 600 container handling machines had been sold in the plastics industry. Husky had probably sold the the first 400 units before we competitively entered the market in 1971. Thereafter, C/B/W sold approximately 160 of the remaining 200 handling devices, with Husky selling the remaining 40 units. Thus, we feel that C/B/W can more than compete with Husky in this conveyor and orientor line of the plastics business. Actually, since 1971, we have reason to believe that our company dominated this facet of the industry."

Two other companies, although much smaller, peripherally compete in this business, Automated Systems, Inc. of Nassuha, New York and the William H. Ledderer Company of Canada. "Both firms offer little real competitive concern to C/B/W," continued Carson. "Those two companies may not even survive another 1 to 2 years," he speculated.

In August, 1973, C/B/W purchased some $120,000 worth of sheet-metal fabricating machinery for installation in the firm's new plant. Management believed that this would give C/B/W the additional capability of forming and shaping heavy steel and metal for both internal use (for building the conveyor and orienter bench assemblies) and external use (for fabrication of outside corporations' bench work on the basis of price/job quotations). This in-house capability afforded the company the use of transfer pricing in its standard line manufacturing costs. Additionally, C/B/W could more easily modify its conventional products to suit particular customers' desires in specialty jobs. C/B/W's "external" market for this service was largely regionalized in an area between Topeka, Kansas and Kansas City, Missouri. However, C/B/W's sheet metal machinery could work with unusually thick metal, a rather unique shop capacity for the mid-western U.S.

The company was also engaged in a significant amount of custom or specialty-prototype work, whereby customers would request that C/B/W custom-design and/or construct equipment for a given fee, determined under a closed bid procedure used in the government contract-letting areas. Among the recently completed prototype jobs were a foundry core-plate cleaner for the North American-Rockwell Corp., a card-stock, sheet-feeder apparatus diagramed and built for Hallmark cards, and a petri-dish stacker, orienter and assembler completed for the Bio-Quist Corp, a division of Falcon Plastics, Inc. It should be noted that due to the competitive, closed bid arrangement, C/B/W experienced significant financial project losses due to the lack of any company-devised costing criteria (accept/reject) and pricing-budgetary constraints. In fact, because of the absence of adequate records,* only a very rough estimation could be made regarding the ongoing cost status of individual prototype projects. Phil Burger, engineering head, once commented, "We always seem to lose our asses on these projects simply because we under-quote our competition purposely to get these jobs and then can't realistically estimate our true costs in such work. But we feel that we really cannot afford to turn down any custom job which comes along."

FINANCIAL STATUS

While Tables II and III summarize the financial specifics of C/B/W, some discussion is necessary to fill out the data therein presented. The critical situation, previously touched upon concerning declining sales for 1973, was the ominous loss of $49,623 shown for the first half of that year. This loss assumed a particularly sobering import when compared with the 1972 net profit of $72,186. Cash shortages were also frequent concerns of the company. As a result, heavy short-term financing was constantly being arranged by the firm so as to satisfy current obligations.

Direct labor unexpectedly increased from its 1971 and 1972 percentage levels for the first six months of 1973. Indirect labor (administrative and support personnel) similarly rose during the same period, in terms of actual expenditures. Operating supplies experienced a slight increase; sales salaries, expenses, and commissions alarmingly soared, while sales slumped, in spite of Carson's hiring of a company sales manager in January, 1973. Materials expenses also climbed relative to its 1971 and 1972 amounts. Additionally, C/B/W's debt/equity financial ratio for the first half of 1973 skyrocketed (as a result of an increase by 67% in the firm's internal debt financing) from a 1.80 ratio in 1972, which is itself quite high, to a phenomenal 3.41 for the period ending June 30, 1973. These figures underscore the excessive amount of debt extension which C/B/W undertook throughout that year.

Of alarming concern to the company was the sudden decrease in sales volume. Carson was quite anxious to rationalize the decline in these revenue figures; "The market has obviously dried up—we've got to start diversifying. I just can't believe that this decrease is the fault of the sales department entirely." Burger was not as willing to jump to such conclusions. He declared, "I think we're too fat; we're carrying way too many people for the business we're presently doing." John Weekly believed that C/B/W was not too fat: "It's Carson's sales department which is laying down. That sales dude he hired has done nothing for the company but help us spend money"!

The firm had enjoyed certain "personnel luxuries" in both the production and support services areas when compared with other firms of comparable sophistication and size. In the machine shop, there were 4 machinists where there was an economic need for only 2. Similarly, in the assembly room, 3 men were employed where just 1 was required. Two sheet metal workers had been carried on the payroll since January, 1973, even before C/B/W had fully installed its new sheet metal machine capacity. Weekly responded, "Well, what do you expect me to do, fire all of these guys and then try and re-hire extras when business picks up again"?

In the engineering department, salaries paid to staff workers greatly exceeded the amount of wages which the company's principals drew themselves. And, with production declining, the justification for these salaries and the positions themselves became increasingly difficult to justify. In sales, the high expenditures incurred in developing a national sales manager proved fruitless

---

*C/B/W's records consisted of a primary set of (oftentimes unbalanced) financial data, such as a periodic balance sheet and an income statement. In addition, "shop-time" job records were kept, but only on an infrequent basis.

as well, direct sales expenses tripled during 1973 over the prior year with no "real" growth in sales.

C/B/W paid approximately $3,400 in excess production wages each month of 1973 and some $3,500 in wasteful monthly overhead costs (such as advertising, clerical assistance, sales expenses and wasted professional staff time) for support of these production activities. Sales prices for each product were never adjusted in response to these excesses. Consequently, C/B/W's standard line sales yielded fluctuating returns, ranging from 16% unit losses on one conveyor to 36% individual profit excesses on a particular handling machine, based upon a cost allocation study prepared for the company in late 1973.

Not only were costs on the increase, but actual sales volume in terms of units, was on a decline from the 1973 projections and fell beneath the recorded 1972 sales levels. In fact, the increasing sales rate of 1972 had begun to level off late in that year as a signal of what was to come in 1973. All of these excesses only worsened the resounding loss figure exhibited on June 30, 1973.

Furthermore, the company carried some $58,000 worth of accounts payable about which many of its creditors were becoming increasingly more unhappy. All of the company's major suppliers had placed C/B/W on a strict C.O.D. basis which exerted heavy financial pressure on the firm's precious little cash flow. The strain became so intolerable that in October of 1973, some of the company's larger creditors threatened certain legal actions, the culmination of which foreseeably could have led to the circulation of involuntary bankruptcy petitions if past due accounts were not immediately balanced.

This pressure, in turn, forced C/B/W to find ready cash; one obvious source was the company's primary financial backer, a Lawrence bank. C/B/W had already borrowed, on a short-term basis, its yearly limit of $90,000 and had pledged all of its accounts receivable to date to this bank. The bank, realizing the financial shortage under which C/B/W was currently operating, regarded the company as an increasingly more risky venture and thus seemed reluctant to extend further credit above this debt ceiling. The monetary situation looked bleak.

Possible avenues of remedy were suggested to the company. A sales-leaseback arrangement of the new plant facility, the value of which had been appraised at near $310,000, had not yet been pursued. Venture capital firms had not been contacted. The idea of offering public ownership in the corporation via a stock issue could be investigated. And even the disposition of the corporate assets to a larger firm could be checked, although an admittedly bitter alternative. But the ominous cloud of financial instability seemed to smother these unexplored, cash-generating ideas.

In November, 1973, Dun and Bradstreet assigned a "risky" financial notation to the C/B/W enterprise as a consequence of the company's lopsided balance sheet and monetary conditions. The report noted the young company's early 1973 sales decline and financial loss, all of which tightened the credit market for the firm. Third-quarter indicators appeared to portend even greater losses for C/B/W; sales dwindled to a mere trickle.

And finally, the energy crisis loomed forebodingly on the economic horizon late in 1973, threatening to squeeze the life out of the whole plastic industry. Already C/B/W's customers were reconsidering previously given orders; the volume of molding-machine sales was down considerably as of September 30, 1973, a depressing index of the plastic-handling appetites of the lid and container manufacturers for 1974.

C/B/W had experienced additional problems with respect to sales collections and delinquent account receivables — a total of $33,000 in 1973's first half. The problem was further complicated because the company had not taken a legal security interest (a formal agreement specifying that in case of a

TABLE II
BALANCE SHEET ANALYSIS
FOR CARSON/BURGER/WEEKLY, INC.

ASSETS	1971	1972	1973 (6 Mos.)
Current Assets:			
Petty Cash	10.00	10.00	10.00
Cash in Bank	18,439.87	637.00	15,168.23
Accounts Receivable	3,240.53	25,733.36	61,652.96
Employee Advances	427.41	-0-	-0-
Merchandise Inventory	4,202.83	22,857.17	35,617.66
Work-in-Process	5,731.37	19,048.04	25,108.41
Compeleted Machines	19,835.77	28,280.00	-0-
Total Current Assets	51,887.78	96,565.57	137,557.26
Long-Lived Assets:			
Equipment	9,289.59	23,617.25	38,643.32
Less: Accum. Depr. Equip.	781.54 (cr)	2,730.26 (cr)	7,028.69 (cr)
Net Equipment	8,508.05	20,876.99	31,513.63
Automobile	-0-	3,200.00	5,502.00
Less: Accum. Depr. Auto	-0-	500.00 (cr)	1,033.33 (cr)
Net Automobile	-0-	2,700.00	4,468.67
Patent	1,015.00	1,015.00	1,015.00
Less: Accum. Depr. Pat.	59.75 (cr)	119.47 (cr)	149.33 (cr)
Net Patent	955.25	895.53	865.67
Small Tools	-0-	2,232.99	-0-
Less: Accum. Depr.	-0-	1,000.00	-0-
Net Small Tools	-0-	1,232.99	-0-
Office Equipment	-0-	-0-	864.65
Less: Accum. Deprec.	-0-	-0-	212.50 (cr)
Net Office Equipment	-0-	-0-	652,15
Total Long-Lived Assets	9,463.30	25,715.51	37,601.12
Other Assets:			
Incorporation Costs	365.78	385.00	385.00
Less: Accum. Depr.	57.78 (cr)	154.00 (cr)	192.50 (cr)
Net Incorporation costs	308.00	231.00	192.50
Goodwill	4,716.92	4,716.92	4,716.92
Utilities Deposits	50.00	50.00	50.00
Constr.-in-progress(temp)	-0-	-0-	2,811.25
Total Other Assets	5,074.92	4,997.92	7,770.67
TOTAL ASSETS	66,426.00	127,279.00	182,929.05

	1971	1972	1973 (6 Mos.)
LIABILITIES			
Current Liabilities:			
Accounts Payable	15,029	15,528.25	35,725.73
Sales Tax Payable	53.86	1,151.67	599.76
Income Tax Payable	4,643.60	1,516.46	1,241.93
Unemployment Payable	524.61	598.62	1,416.20
Kansas Withholding Pay.	255.77	311.80	600.03
Customer Advances	29,147.00	8,350.00	8,216.08
Note Pay. Coast to Coast	14.50	-0-	-0-
Note Payable-Bank	8,355.00	24,296.30	71,282.60
Total Current Liabilities	58,023.44	61,573.10	119,082.33
Long-Term Liabilities:			
Stockholder Loan; Berger	4,800.00	-0-	-0-
Stockholder Loan; Carson	6,400.00	-0-	-0-
Stockholder Loan; Weekly	4,600	-0-	-0-
L.T. Note Pay	2,500.00	-0-	-0-
Income Taxes Payable	-0-	-0-	33,000.00
Note Payable C/B/W	595.75	1,333.31	38,281.62
Equipment Loan	-0-	-0-	4,830.00
Note Payable-Bldg. Loan	-0-	18,859.75	1,333.31	4,830.00

	1971	1972	1973 (6 Mos.)
Owners Equity:			
Common Stock Issued	1,200.00	1,200.00	1,200.00
Capital Surplus pd-in	8,078.08	10,578.08	10,578.08
Retained Earnings	-0-	(19,771.27)	20,420.44
Net Income (loss)	(19,771.27)	72,185.78	(49,263.42)
Total Owners Equity	(10,493.19)	64,192.59	(17,064.90)
TOTAL LIABILITIES &	66,426.00	127,279.00	182,929.05
OWNERSHIP			

TABLE III

COMPARATIVE INCOME STATEMENT ANALYSIS

Description	1971		1972		1973	
Merchandise Sales	69,476.00	98.0%	320,937.79	99.23%	133,031.04	98.1%
Salary Reimbursement	992.00	1.5	1,088.00	.34	-0-	0.
Miscellaneous Income	303.64	.5	1,387.05	.43	1,504.70	1.5
Gross Income	70,774.43	100.00%	323,412.84	100.00%	134,535.74	100.00%
Merchandise	23,771.30	33.59	95,040.44	29.39	49,108.94	26.%
Direct Labor	14,963.65	21.14	45,643.53	14.11	46,008.72	25.
Direct Labor (Overtime)	-0-	0.	-0-	0.	728.16	.7
Overhead Expense	6,812.79	9.63	-0-	0.	-0-	0.
Freight-in	1,251.54	1.77	2,369.40	.73	2,080.70	1.3
Inventory Adjustment	-0-	0.	(31,418.07)	(11.88)	(18,820.86)	(10.2)
Total Cost of Sales	46,799.28	66.12%	104,635.30	32.35	79,105.66	43.0%
Balance on Total Costings	23,975.15	33.88%	218,777.54	67.65%	55,430.08	41.0%
Contract Labor	2,498.77	3.52	617.08	.19	-0-	0.
Operating Supplies	3,421.31	4.82	7,197.44	2.23	8,438.63	4.45
Repairs and Maintainance	66.03	.09	3,296.37	1.02	264.65	.01
Building Rental	2,212.30	3.13	4,737.00	1.46	3,372.00	1.8
Utilities	610.80	.86	1,065.43	.33	734.93	.04
Insurance	527.10	.74	3,501.44	1.08	2,782.93	1.51
Equipment Rental	68.88	.10	334.86	.10	64.16	.003
Depreciation, Equipment	826.84	1.17	1,948.72	.60	1,076.61	.58
Patent Amortization	59.75	.08	59.72	.02	29.86	.001
Incorporation Costs Amort.	77.00	.11	77.00	.02	38.50	.001
Laundry and Cleaning	35.65	.05	315.69	.10	168.98	.009
Overhead Applied	(10,399.43)	(14.69)	-0-	0.	-0-	0.
Indirect Labor	-0-	0.	40,212.72	12.43	24,109.97	13.11
Indirect Labor (Overtime)	-0-	0.	-0-	0.	100.84	.005
Automobile Depreciation	-0-	0.	500.00	.15	500.00	.49
Small Tools Depreciation	-0-	0.	1,000.00	.31	1,000.00	.81
Research and Development	-0-	0.	1,850.00	.57	1,251.82	.68
Small Tools	-0-	0.	-0-	0.	329.29	.017
Total Operating Expenses		14.69%	66,714.17	20.63%	44,263.17	23.54%
Balance on Operations	23,975.15		152,083.37	47.02%	11,116.91	8.6%

TABLE III (continued)

Description	1971		1972		1973	
Advertising	3,174.73	4.49%	3,524.00	1.09%	2,159.48	1.17
Car and Delivery/Auto	597.81	.84	834.74	.26	777.87	.42
Equipment Moving	185.00	.26	-0-	-0-	0.	0.
Entertainment	234.17	.33	784.54	.24	159.70	.08
Crating and Packaging	-0-	0.	257.58	.08	144.04	.07
Travel, Food and Lodging	-0-	0.	7,585.13	2.35	11,905.45	6.57
Sales Salary	-0-	0.	-0-	0.	9,444.98	5.13
Sales Commissions	-0-	0.	-0-	0.	302.97	.16
Total Selling Expenses	4,191.71	5.92%	12,985.99	4.02%	24,894.49	13.54%
Balance on Selling Expenses	19,783.44	27.95%	139,077.38	43.00%	13,727.58	10.31%
Officers Salaries	27,028.00	38.19%	43,556.08	13.47%	16,055.00	8.73
Clerical Supplies	2,373.13	3.35	-0-	0.	-0-	0.
Office Supplies	1,127.87	1.59	1,468.61	.45	3,295.96	1.79
Telephone	1,228.99	1.74	3,899.38	1.21	2,619.52	1.42
Legal and Accounting	1,546.00	2.18	4,028.04	1.25	3,379.50	1.83
Payroll Taxes	3,519.21	4.97	8,604.24	2.66	1,416.20	.77
Taxes, Other	413.61	.58	800.70	.25	5,032.81	2.73
Dues and Publications	98.25	.14	191.35	.06	583.26	.39
Banking Fees	54.25	.08	79.89	.02	49.65	.02
Travel	1,679.15	2.37	-0-	-0-	0.	0.
Employee Benefits	228.21	.32	751.86	.23	511.37	.27
Cash; long-short	178.45	.25	(107.24)	(.03)	-0-	0.
Interest Expense	18.35	.03	1,425.35	.44	746.56	.40
Penalties	61.24	.09	232.18	.07	5.00	0.
Group Insurance	-0-	0.	1,901.16	.59	436.68	.23
Contributions	-0-	0.	60.00	.02	12.50	0.
Miscellaneous Expenses	-0-	0.	-0-	0.	1,391.83	.75
Total Admin. Expenses	39,554.71	55.89%	66,891.60	20.68%	35,535.66	19.33%
Total Expenses	100,766.38	-loss-	251,334.30	45.30%	183,798.98	-loss-
NET PROFITS (LOSS)	(19,771.27)	27.94%	72,185.78	22.32%	(49,263.42)	37.0 %

buyer's default concerning payment of an item's purchase price, the seller has the legal right to repossess that item sold as collateral for satisfaction of the unpaid obligation) in the products it has sold. C/B/W could neither collect from these defaulting customers to which it had sold the machinery (many of whom were insolvent or had filed for bankruptcy) nor could the firm legally take back the products which it had sold to these delinquent buyers. Thus, the company was left virtually empty-handed.

The balance sheet and income statement complexion was somewhat improved when C/B/W realized that it could capitalize its research and development expenditures for both accounting and tax purposes. See Tables IV and V. While the underlying financial weaknesses were still present on September 30, 1973, the outward indicia of the firm's "health" seemed greatly enhanced by this capitalization move. When confronted with the obvious question of why these research and development costs had not been capitalized before, Carson replied, "I just didn't know you could do that in business. After all, I'm just a re-converted business-engineer, not a tax accountant or a finance wizard."

CORPORATE ORGANIZATION

In terms of administration, organization, and ownership of C/B/W, the three principals comprise the company's leadership triad. Management decisions required unanimous consent by all three owners. Since there was no formal Board of Directors, the three principals decided *all* policy and business issues. The unanimity requirement had frequently created costly delays and bottlenecks which adversely affected the corporation. No one in the organizational hierarchy had any business expertise or experience from which to draw in the management decision process. None of the principals really could comprehend a balance sheet or an organizational flow chart. Of the few points upon which the three agreed was the corporate goal, "...to get rich from the success of the business and eventually sell out as individual millionaires to some big outfit."

Phil Burger, the current President (this office was a floating position, alternating among the three owners bi-annually) was head of the engineering and design section. His supervision included the areas of standard product engineering and modification, prototype design work, adaptation of prototype work into the standard product line, and engineering responsibility for the C/B/W research and development department. Regarding the standard line and prototype work, Burger led a team of two engineers; Burger devoted about 75% of his professional engineering time in assisting his staff. Various responsibilities were assigned by Burger among his staff.

The research and development department was a three man operation headed up by Larry Zeigler, a metal-working craftsman. Although he was assisted by two staff engineers, Zeigler's primary concern was with the prototype/custome work construction of the firm. While this department was overseen by Burger, Zeigler was given "a pretty fair amount of freedom in custom designing and building of the prototype projects." The only real control over this department, which incurred some $67,000 in expenditures for the first six months of 1973, was in the form of time records kept on each custom job. Burger was also responsible for price quotations on custom engineering and design work on all prototype projects.

Burger, age 28, was the most spontaneous of the three owners. His collegiate friendship with Carson had evolved into a less personal and more professional relationship. Weekly, however, occasionally accused these two younger owners of conspiring to cut him out of the company and of withholding valuable business information from him. Burger jealously guard-

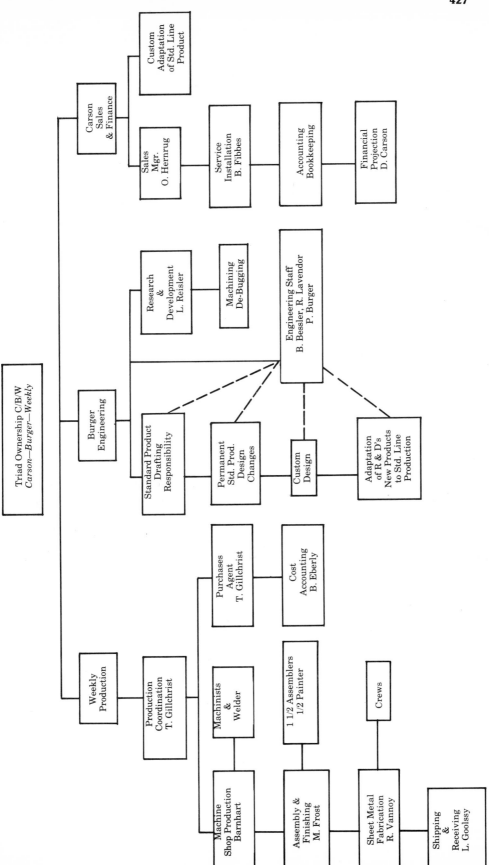

TABLE IV
CARSON/BURGER/WEEKLY, INC.
BALANCE SHEET
SEPTEMBER 30, 1973

ASSETS

Current Assets:

Petty Cash	$ 100,00	
Cash In Bank	1,137.07	
Payroll Deposit Account	118.98	
Accounts Receivable	84,500.74	
Materials Inventory	40,515.55	
Work in Process Inventory	24,84$.23	
Completed Machines Inventory	29,890.00	$181,103.57

Fixed Assets:

Machinery and Equipment	43,678.69		
Less Accumulated Depreciation	7,843.60	35,835.09	
Automobiles	5,502.00		
Less Accumulated Depreciation	1,283.33	4,218.67	
Office Equipment	864.65		
Less Accumulated Depreciation	389.68	474.97	
New Building Under Construction	82,583.72	123,112.45	

Other Assets:

Patent	1,147.00		
Less Accumulated Amortization	164.26	982.74	
Incorporation Costs	385.00		
Less Accumulated Amortization	210.00	175.00	
Research & Development Investment	66,733.22		
Less Accumulated Amortization	5,004.99	61,728.23	
Goodwill	4,716.92		
Utilities Deposits	50.00	67,652.89	
Total Assets		$371,868.91	

LIABILITIES

Current Liabilities:

Customer Advances	10,824.65	
Notes Payable - Bank	83,598.83	
Notes Payable - Carson/Burger/Weekly	33,000.00	
Accounts Payable	45,370.73	
Sales Tax Payable	2,348.08	
FICA & Federal WH Tax Payable	13,554.06	
Kansas Withholding Tax Payable	(115.39)	
Income Tax Payable	1.83	188,582.79

Long-term Debt:

Equipment Loan	56,180.66	
Building Loan	85,897.36	188,582.79

Capital:

Common Stock Issued	1,200.00		
Paid In Surplus	10,578.08		
Retained Earnings 12/31/72	18,813.14		
Add Net Income to 9/30/73	10,616.38	29,429.52	41,207.60
Total Liabilities and Capital			$371,868.91

TABLE V
CARSON/BURGER/WEEKLY, INC.
INCOME STATEMENT
YEAR TO DATE THRU SEPTEMBER 30, 1973

Sales	$226,428.64	
Salary Reimbursement	3,765.00	
Miscellaneous Income	1,046.25	
Capitalization of Investment in Research and Development of New Machines	66,733.22	
Total Gross Income		$297,973.11

Cost of Goods Sold:

Completed Machines on Hand 1-1-73	none	
Cost of Goods Manufactured	177,762.41	
(See attached statement)		
	177,762.41	
Less - Completed Machines on Hand 9-30-73	29,890.00	
Total Cost of Goods Sold		147,872.41
Gross Profit on Sales		150,100.70

Operating Expenses:
Selling Expenses:

Crating and Packing	422.53	
Advertising	2,352.67	
Automobile	1,779.08	
Entertainment	159.70	
Travel, Food, Lodging	15,115.04	
Sales Salaries	14,119.87	
Total Selling Expense		33,948.99

Administration Expenses:

Indirect Labor	38,130.93	
Indirect Labor Overtime	258.04	
Officers Salaries	23,230.00	
Office Supplies	6,614.03	
Telephone	4,812.95	
Professional Fees	6,602.90	
Taxes - Payroll	11,658.24	
Taxes - Other	1,361.03	
Dues & Subscriptions	611.43	
Bank Fees	11.50	
Depreciation Office Equipment	177.18	
Amortization Research & Development	5,004.99	
Group Insurance	617.92	
Employee Benefits	544.84	
Contributions	12.50	
Miscellaneous Expense	654.75	
Interest Expense	5,166.67	
Penalties	65.43	
Total Administration Expense		105,535.33
Total Operating Expenses		139,484.32
Net Profit		$10,616.38

ed his position as President (even though little power attached to his office in reality), as well as his engineering department. When news of the first half 1973 loss reached him, Burger's initial response was, "We'll just have to slice Weekly's production staff in half and begin to save that money we've been throwing away on unskilled labor."

John Weekly was the John Wayne of the owners. Charisma was his long suit. He was intuitively brilliant, but yet impulsive;Weekly was the archetype of the truly non-professional businessman. Some 24 years senior to both Carson and Burger, Weekly had been formally educated through the eighth grade, although he frequently claimed, "My school of hard knocks has taken me farther than any damned college sheepskin will ever take most people." Physically a rough-hewed individual, he put in the longest hours of the three; Carson and especially Burger believed in working the ideal Galbraithian 40-hour work week, with no infringement upon their personal lives by business-related matters *whatsoever*.

Weekly was traditional; a hard worker. There was a genuine generation (if not ideological) gap between Weekly and the younger principals. Such chasms ultimately blocked the effective operation and organization of the company. It was more of a mutual suspicion or distrust.

Weekly was suspicious of the youthful ideals of Carson and Burger; at the same time, Weekly continually talked down to these owners which never set well. In their periodic meetings, John harangued and Carson and Burger would silently sit through the sessions until they could stomach no more. The result: a verbal explosion during which nothing was accomplished except for the widening of the chasm.

This division among the owners was particularly aggravated because of Weekly's position as head of the production arm of C/B/W, the company's largest department. Weekly's responsibility was simply to see that the right product was built at the right time. He supervised the entire production process, the sheet metal department, all of the component shops and was in charge of the construction work on C/B/W's new plant. He was just the man for this job.

Weekly's right-hand assistant was a sharp, 25 year-old graduate chemist, Tom Gilchrist. As production coordinator, Gilchrist did much of the organizing and completion of machines through the various sub-component manufacturing processes as machining, assembly, finishing and shipping.

The machine shop was well outfitted and tightly run. The section chief was a cooperative and eager fellow, who evidenced the shop's efficiecy. The assembly crew was "notoriously negligent, slow-working and grossly inefficient." In Phil Burger's mind, "the assembly shop traditionally caused our delays in the production schedule. In fact, C/B/W lost customers over these delays, customers who simply got fed up with waiting for delayed machinery shipments. I could readily sympathize with these buyers; I got fed up, too"! Weekly's justification for employing an unusually large group there was that the government's veteran retraining program was subsidizing about 50% of each assembler's wage. Still, that rationalization did little to eradicate the troublesome inefficiency and the increasingly large direct-labor expenditures.

With the supervision of the new sheet metal department came the further responsibility of the competitive bidding for sheet metal jobs, for which Weekly had absolutely no previous experience. However, the sheet metal business began to come to life soon after C/B/W had moved into its new facility. Additional laborers were employed to supplement the original skeletal crew as a result of increasing outside job orders. By November, 1973, C/B/W's sheet metal department had received contracts for the manufacture of large, one hundred feet long, conveyor systems utilized in the manufacturing of wiring harnesses for automobiles. As Weekly exclaimed, "We've struck a gold mine; in one month we've gotten business totaling over $110,000 and it's still coming in strong.

Weekly also supervised the shipping and receiving operations of the corporation. However, he turned the full responsibility of the parts and inventory purchases over to his production coordinator, Gilchrist, who also oversaw the installation of a very elementary cost accounting system in the production department in December, 1973.

David Carson was the Secretary-Treasurer and business manager of the company. He had no academic training in business and any knowledge he did possess in this field was acquired while occupying his position. Carson never really wanted to be an engineer; during those summer months when he and Burger worked together, Carson did the bookwork and some construction, but never any of the actual engineering or drafting.

Carson was often on the defensive. However, given the abrupt losses C/B/W had sustained and the pressure which Weekly and Burger exerted upon him as a result, there was little wonder why Carson assumed such an attitude. He had developed C/B/W's first accounts and had watched the company's revenues grow to their 1973 level. He was a dreamer. On a wall behind his desk hung a four-foot-square graph which tracked the upward progression of sales since the firm's formation. It included a forecasted volume of sales which climbed, after 1978, completely off the graph and onto the wall itself. That was the kind of dreamer he was.

Carson himself set prices, drew up company estimates and forecasts, and chartered the firm's financial pathways. He was a curiously introverted individual whose positions concerning financial matters were not always spelled out in the greatest degree of clarity. He was a hedger, never willing to totally commit himself on an issue.

He oversaw a staff of four individuals. Although Carson initially did most of the sales work, he hired a sales manager, Dick Hornug, in January of 1973, in order to be allowed more time for concentration upon the firm's financial woes. It was anticipated that a handsome salary and a liberal expense account would draw a responsible and devoted salesman to C/B/W, the ultimate effect of which was hoped to generate an even greater amount of sales revenues. But the company was severely disappointed when it learned of the unusually depressed sales figures for 1973, which totaled less than 62% of the period's forecasted amount.

Carson supervised a bookkeeper, a genuine asset regarding the accounting and records-keeping functions in the company. Carson's responsibility also included the installation and servicing of C/B/W's standard products. This was largely handled by Bill Fiddis, one of the most respected employees in the entire firm. Carson assumed the role of planning, budgeting and financial control, tasks for which he had little business competence. An illustrative example of this is easily recalled.

Late one October afternoon in 1973, a truck driver came into the office to see Carson. Confronting him, the driver presented Carson with a bill of lading, C.O.D., for one of the new sheet-metal machines the company had recently ordered. The bill was for some $8,000. Carson looked up and reluctantly declared, "We've only got $21.16 in the bank; I can't pay you." The driver, thinking this was some kind of joke, immediately broke out laughing. After his humor had subsided somewhat, the driver glanced down at Carson's blank face and said, "You really aren't kidding me, are you?" Carson silently shook his head. Fortunately, a healthy order arrived in the mail the following day which covered the machine's cost.

PLANNING, BUDGETING AND CONTROL

Planning was an after-thought for C/B/W. Because there was such an absence of financial business expertise, justifications for decisions already implemented were the essentials of the corporate planning process for the firm.

The decision to construct the company's new $300,000 plant was determined largely by the principals "...as a gut-level, seat-of-the-pants vote." Similarly, the financing decisions supporting such a capital expenditure were made in a procedure of almost *ex post facto* acquiescence.

Economic and financial plans were completed by David Carson. No management tools or techniques were utilized; Carson's game theory was primarily that of historical-prospective planning, i.e., focusing upon past performance and thereby speculating on the future. The fundamental weakness in such schematics was the assumption of the past as a reliable indicator of the future.

Table VI illustrates this type of planning fallacy. This table compares the projected sales volume in units for each product in C/B/W's standard line (made by Carson) for the first half of 1973 with the actual data for the same accounting period. These projections were based upon the historic sales data of 1971 and 1972. Note that some of the products' sales volumes greatly exceeded or fell beneath these 1973 estimates; no estimates were made with regard to the firm's conveyor machinery. Additional evidence of this C/B/W financial scheming process is presented in Tables VII and VIII, where actual data is compared with estimates of financial balance sheet and income statement amounts.

C/B/W had virtually no budgeting procedures; in fact, the company had never prepared a budget for operational purposes. As a result, the corporation did not know of its approximate operating guidelines simply because there were none in existence. Further, the company had no future intention of initiating any budgeting processes. As in the planning area, the three principals literally "guessed" whenever a financial decision of any magnitude was made.

One of the most serious problems the firm faces was a complete absence of any type of control over the financial operation of the corporation. The accounting records generally were inaccurate and seldom in balance. Income statement data was never collected. No company time records or cost accounting tactics were employed in monitoring the standard products or any of the custom prototype projects.

TABLE VI:
COMPARISON OF ACTUAL AND PROJECTED
C/B/W SALES DATA

Model Type	Actual 1973 (6 mos.)	Projected 1973 (6 mos.)	Projected 1974	Projected 1975
Model A	3	2	3	5
Model C	20	8	7	7
Container Stacker	5	4	0	0
CB III Bagger	0	3	15	19
Lid Inventory System	4	2	4	4
Roller Stacker	2	1	3	7
Inclined Conveyor	0	n/a*	n/a	n/a*
Carry-Out Conveyor	0	n/a	n/a*	n/a*
Carry-To Conveyor	5	6	15	30
Vacuum Conveyor	6	5	30	30

*no estimates made by C/B/W for 1973 and beyond.

TABLE VII: COMPARISON OF ACTUAL AND ESTIMATED
BALANCE SHEET ACCOUNTS
(DATA IN $000'S)

Account	Actual 1973 (6 mos.)	Estimated 1973 (6 mos.)	1974
Current Assets:			
Cash	15	5	10
Accounts Receivable	62	46	150
Merchandise Inventory	36	15	50
Work-in-Process	25	14	45
Completed machines	0	0	0
Total Current Assets	136	80	255
Long-lived Assets:	38	49	110
Other Assets:	5	2	5
Total Assets	183	131	370
Current Liabilities:			
Notes Payable	104	93	212
Accounts Payable	36	7	28
Customer Advances	8	6	25
Total Current Liabilities	119	106	266
Owners' Equity:			
Common Stock	1	1	1
Paid-in Surplus	11	11	11
Retained Earnings	20	13	36
Total Liabilities & Equity	183	131	370

TABLE VIII: COMPARISON OF ACTUAL AND ESTIMATED
INCOME STATEMENT EXPENDITURES
(DATA IN $000'S)

Expenditure	Actual 1973 (6 mos.)	Estimated 1973 (6 mos.)	1974
Sales	135	213	800
Cost of Sales:			
Inventory Adjustment	(19)	(3)	(14)
Materials	49	64	238
Direct Labor	46	32	123
Total Cost of Sales	79	93	347
*Gross Profit	55	120	453
Operating Expenses:			
Equipment	10	21	45
Indirect Labor	24	32	100
Other Expenses	11	6	20
Total Operating Expenses	45	59	165
Total Selling Expenses	13	12	50
General & Admin. Expenses	36	21	50
*Operating Profit (Loss)	(49)	26	188
Interest Expense	0	7	10
Profit before bonus	(49)	19	178
Bonus	0	17	80
Profit before taxes	(49)	12	98
Taxes	0	3	42
*Net Profit (Loss)	(49)	9	56

C/B/W had no records-keeping capability. This precluded the development of a budget or of any cost control mechanisms. No financial activity thermometers were established or even tested. Since there were no budgetary guidelines, periodic performance checks were unknown to management, except for the quarterly financial statements (which were finally balanced a quarter after their initial compilation). No subsequent performance regulators could be maintained on the firm's various activities, apart from the customary *ex post* procedure.

Price setting and quotations on the standard and custom products were accomplished independently and individually by the three principals: Carson, for the standard product line; Burger, for the prototype work; and Weekly, for the sheet metal projects.

Thus, in the classical sense, there was no management control. With no marketing studies, no accounting controls, no activity measures, and no budgetary constraints, C/B/W's managers had practically lost touch with the financial indices of the plastics industry in general and its own corporation in particular.

Furthermore, the company did not have a functioning Board of Directors; actually, no directors had ever been elected by the corporation's shareholders. Phil Burger reasoned, "Why should we install a board when the three owners make all of the really important decisions?" It would appear that without a functioning board, the company was, perhaps, ignoring certain vital statutory prerequisites which, if not fulfilled, could legally operate in removing the corporate "veil," thereby subjecting the owners to personal liability on behalf of the corporation's acts and deeds.

C/B/W had not pursued the patent infringements made by other companies against this corporation. A small Kansas City, Missouri firm had literally copied the air-jet idea, already patented by C/B/W, and had manufactured several machines containing such a copied air-jet attachment and sold these products, nationally. C/B/W had not attempted to patent certain unique devices, such as the vacuum bed of the Carry-Out Conveyor and the CB III Bagger's automatic air-jets, for which legal protection was a virtual necessity since other companies were closely following the design of these orienter and conveyor machines as well.

Finally, the firm's management-ownership decision processes lacked total logic and procedure. Communication, the requisite forerunner of control, was effectively non-existent. General meetings accomplished very little. The mere mention of "control" signaled the start of a verbal fireworks display in which personal accusations and finger-pointings were the typical bill of fare. This lack of control among these owners necessarily precluded control within this corporate enterprise.

FUTURE DIRECTIONS

Although the corporate existence of C/B/W did appear in doubt somewhat, 1974 presented challenges and demanded resolutions of certain directional issues.

Standard Products

The standard product line was clearly in trouble. Sales had dangerously fallen off, and a petroleum shortage threatened to ruin the entire plastics industry.

The company could become involved with a German manufacturer who held the key to a possible arrangement whereby C/B/W gained access to the production and sale of an entire line of plastic injection molding machines in

North America. While newly developed prototype products, such as the Bagger, the Stuffer, and the Petri-Dish Handler, were on the verge of exposure to the market, the regular machinery line became increasingly obsolescent. Updating of these inadequate models meant incurring heavy engineering and support costs, at a time when real company losses were staggering. And what if such revampings were successful? What kinds of markets would be left in the wake of an international energy crisis?

Sheet Metal Impact

The monetary potential of the added sheet-metal department was a virtual unknown. While early indicators seemed to foretell of an unexpected and substantial stream of cash flows, the depth of this financial well was simply unknown. Although outside work was encouraged, C/B/W had not yet determined the proper mixture of in-house *and* external work which could be tolerated without shifting the firm's internal sheet metal needs from this new department.

Utility Building Opportunity

C/B/W had been approached by a particular manufacturer's representative inquiring into the possibility of forming a second corporation, earmarked to design, fabricate and construct small, metal utility or plantshop buildings. It was speculated that C/B/W's sheet metal department could be expanded and then re-tooled for such an enterprising mission. It had been suggested that companies such as Butler Manufacturing and Star Buildings, Inc. did not compete directly in this medium-sized, 30-by-50-foot metal frame building market.

Conveyor Line Expansion

The expansion and beefing-up of the company's conveyor line products, capable of transferring margarine containers or wiring harnesses for compact automobiles, presented an additional dimension of potential for C/B/W in 1974. Having given this entire area a relatively low business profit in previous years, could the company economically afford further diversification into fiercer competitive circles and unfamiliar markets?

Financial and Organizational Dilemmas

How was the corporation to regain its financial stamina? While venture capitalists stood ready to negotiate a sale-leaseback of the new C/B/W plant, business consultants alternatively urged a stock issue. Consideration also would be given to merger possibilities, or even a complete "buy-out" of C/B/W's assets via a larger organization's acquisition.

And of organization, confusion had been the synonym for C/B/W's concept of "control." The firm had grown so dynamically that time did not permit consideration of the word; in a sense, it was almost academic to speak of establishing that ability in this corporation. Until the doomsday knock of threatened bankruptcy, C/B/W had boomed in terms of profit, sales and production, would the management trio now heed its import before the knock becomes a reality?

Index

Ackoff, R. L., 7, 14, 40, 118, 225, 288
Advertising, 77
Alternative Analysis, 313
Alternative Generation, 254, 313, 316
Alternative Strategies, 150, 151
Alternatives
  Analysis, 249
  Selection, 222
  Variables, 223
Analysis of Competition, 70
Andrews, K., 5, 14, 225
Ansoff, H. I., 5, 8, 14, 40, 196, 225, 262, 288
Anti-Trust, 189
Appraisal, 284
Argenti, J., 31, 40, 225, 262, 288
Assessment
  External Environment, 143
  Internal Environment, 145
Atherton, R. M., 367, 375, 387

Bain, J. S., 76, 82
Barnes Lumber Case, 119
Blankenship, Bill, 119
Bowers, D., 104, 118
Buying
  Internationally, 115
  Locally, 115
  Materials, 115

Capital, 96
Carson, Burger, Weekly Case, 415
Carter Distribution Case, 367, 375, 387
Chandler, A. D., 288
Change, 192, 195
Chaotic Competition, 71, 72
Chen, G. K. C., 83
Claunch, S. J., 83
Cohen, K., 12, 14, 225
Coleman, B. P., 41
Collusion
  effective, 71
  limited, 71
  perfect, 71

Competency Profile, 147, 149, 217
Competition
  Analysis of, 70
  Behavior, 70
  Chaotic, 71, 72
  For Capital, 96
  For Manpower, 103
  For Materials, 1110
  Nature of, 66
  Strategy, 78
  Structure, 72
  Tactics, 68
Competitive Behavior, 70
Competitive Tactics, 68
Consequences of Competition, 74
Copyrights, 189
Corporate Debt, 100, 101, 102
Corporate Developement, 139, 142
Corporate Objectives, 138
Cottage Gardens Case, 41
Crites, D. M., 367, 375, 387
Cyert, R. H., 12, 14, 225, 262

Debentures, 99
Debt Financing, 98
Denning, B. W., 153
Distribution Channels, 186
Diversification, 221
Dobler, D., 114, 118
Donaldson, G., 95, 118

ECONOMIC FORECASTING, 13
Effective Collusion, 71
ENVIRONMENT
  EXTERNAL, 10
  INTERNAL, 11
  Objectives, 30
Environmental Protection, 190
Equity Financing, 97
External Alternative Analysis, 220
External Environment, 10
External Gap Analysis, 39
Extrapolation, 180, 181

Ewing, D. W., 225

Feedback, 282
Finance, 146
Finances, 96, 97, 98
Financial Models, 96
FORECASTING, 12, 33, 180, 195
Fredonia State Bank Case, 329
Functional Analysis, 321
Functional Objectives, 29

Gap Analysis, 35
   Internal, 37
   External, 39
Goals, 33

Hartz Mills Case, 403, 409, 413
Heinritz, S., 112, 118
Hevristic Programming, 316, 319, 320
Howell, R. A., 225

Income Bonds, 100
Independence Federal Savings and Loan
   Association Case, 291
Innovation, 182
Internal Alternative Analysis, 218
Internal Environment, 11
Internal Gap Analysis, 37
International Business Machines Case, 227
Inverson, G. B., 197

Jantsch, E., 196
Johnson, R. 197

Kalachek, E. D., 76, 82
Knutzen, J. V., 15

Lee, L., 114, 118
Levin, R. I., 403, 409, 413
Likert, R., 104, 118
Limited Collusion, 71
Lindblom, C. E., 323

Manpower
   Competition for, 103
   External Sources of, 107
   Internal Sources of, 106
March, J., 262
Market
   segmentation, 77
   slave of, 76, 80
   structure, 185
Marketing, 66, 146
Marketing strategies, 77
Materials
   Buying, 115
   Competition for, 110
   Demand, 111
   Planning, 111
   Sources, 114
   Strategy, 111, 112
McGlashan, R., 329
Mockler, R. J., 153
Models, 193, 252
Mortgage Bonds, 99
Mount Carmel Mercy Hospital Case, 155

Naumes, W., 79, 82
Nature of Competition, 66
Nelson, R. R., 76, 82
Newell, A., 323

Objectives
   Classification, 32
   Determination, 31, 32
   Environmental, 30
   Fuctional, 29
   Organizational, 29
   Stylistic, 29
Organizational Objectives, 29
Osborne, R., 403, 409, 413

Pabst, A. A., 337
Paine, F., 79, 82
Patents, 189
Peck, M. J., 76, 82
Perfect Collusion, 71
Personnel Planning, 105
PLANNING HIERARCHY, 7
Political Ideology, 188
Price Coordination, 71
Price Leadership, 71, 73
Price, K., 291
Public Debt Financing, 99

Quality Supermarket Case, 337
Quinn, J. B., 78, 82

Rakish, J. S., 155
Raw Material, 147
Resource Audit, 145
Rich, S. U., 119
Roach, E., 329
Rogers, Rolf E., 282, 288
RUES, L.W., 6, 14

Saunders, C. B., 415
Schreier, W. T., 415
Shaw, A., 323
Shuman, J. C., 351
Smithson Plastics Case, 83
Simon, H. A., 323
Simulation, 193
Situation Audit, 143
Southeastern Shipyards Case, 15
Stanford, M. J., 263
Steiner, G. A., 8, 13, 14
Strategic Budget, 280
STRATEGIC DEVELOPMENT, 5
STRATEGIC PLANNING, 6, 7, 8
Strategic Search, 217
Strategy of Competition, 78
Strategy Implemenation, 279
Strategy Policy Formation, 79
Structure of Competition, 72
Stylistic Objectives, 29
Synergy, 218

TACTICAL PLANNING, 7
TARGETS, 33
Taylor, J. D., 197
Technological change, 183
Technological Forecasting, 184
Thain, D. H., 139, 153

Tilles, S., 288
Tomlinson, W. H., 15, 227
Trademarks, 189
Triangle Construction Company Case, 263

United Products Case, 351

Vaghefi, M. R., 15, 227

Wall Drug Case, 197
Walley, B. H., 150, 153, 196
Wentworth, D. F., 337
Weston, F., 98, 118
White, K., 100, 118